Professional Genealogy

A MANUAL FOR
RESEARCHERS
WRITERS
EDITORS
LECTURERS
AND
LIBRARIANS

Professional Genealogy

A MANUAL FOR RESEARCHERS • WRITERS • EDITORS • LECTURERS • AND LIBRARIANS

EDITOR

Elizabeth Shown Mills, CG, CGL, FASG

EDITORIAL BOARD

Donn Devine, J.D., CG, CGI
ASSOCIATE EDITOR FOR LEGAL CHAPTERS

James L. Hansen, FASG
Helen F. M. Leary, CG, CGL, FASG

2001
GENEALOGICAL PUBLISHING COMPANY
Baltimore, Maryland

Library of Congress Cataloging-in-Publication Data

Professional genealogy : a manual for researchers, writers, editors, lecturers, and
librarians / editor, Elizabeth Shown Mills ; editorial board, Donn Devine, James L.
Hansen, Helen F.M. Leary.
    p. cm.
  Includes bibliographical references and index.
  ISBN 0-8063-1648-9 (pbk.)
   1. Genealogy--Methodology. I. Mills, Elizabeth S.

CS9 .P76 2001
929'.1--dc21

                                                            00-067225

PUBLISHED BY

Genealogical Publishing Company, Inc.
1001 N. Calvert St., Baltimore, MD 21202

Made in the United States of America

To the authors, whose expertise made this volume possible and whose understanding eased my own tasks.

— esm

Contents

Contents

Figures

Figures

Appendixes

Acknowledgments

The presentation of a manual for any profession is a particular challenge. To be truly representative it should stretch far beyond the knowledge and skill of any one person—reflecting not just the habits or preferences of an individual but the practices and standards held in common by the best people the field has to offer. The chapter authors bylined in *Professional Genealogy: A Manual for Researchers, Writers, Editors, Lecturers, and Librarians* surely meet that criteria, but they and your editor owe much to many dozens of others for the concepts and the content represented here.

We are especially grateful to past and present trustees of the Board for Certification of Genealogists (BCG), who offered a platform from which the project could be launched, and to the Association of Professional Genealogists (APG) and the American Society of Genealogists who also proffered financial support, should it be needed. Two members of *ProGen*'s editorial board, Helen F. M. Leary and James L. Hansen, came onto the board as representatives of BCG and APG, respectively.

Nearly a hundred genealogists from the United States and Canada, Europe, the British Isles, Australia, and New Zealand have enriched this project with their suggestions, their peer review of manuscripts, and their technical assistance. Individually and collectively, they have epitomized the age-old saw: the difference between ordinary and extraordinary is that little *extra*. For all the ways in which they have challenged, stretched, and strengthened us, we thank Cameron Allen, J.D., FASG, California; Alexandra Graves Baird, CG, Alabama; Gale Williams Bamman, CG, CGL, Tennessee; Lloyd D. Bockstruck, FNGS, Texas; Curtis Brasfield, CGRS, Illinois; Barbara J. Brown, CGRS, CLS, Colorado; Annette K. Burgert, FASG, Pennsylvania; Carole C. Callard, Michigan; Sharon DeBartolo Carmack, CG, Colorado; Peter E. Carr, California; Joseph Carvalho III, Massachusetts; Ann Theopold Chaplin, CG, New Hampshire; Duncan Dunbar Chaplin III, CLS, New Hampshire; Sandra McLean Clunies, CG, Maryland; Dr. John Philip Colletta, Washington, D.C.; Christine Cutler, Utah; Karen L. Daniel, CG, New Mexico; Robert de Berardinis, Texas; Dr. Alice Eichholz, CG, Vermont; Nancy J. Emmert, CG, Wisconsin; the late Mary Smith Fay, CG, FASG, Texas; Connie Siverly Ferguson, CGRS, Ohio; Kay Haviland Freilich, CG, Pennsylvania; Jake Gehring, Utah; Myra Vanderpool Gormley, CG, Washington; Dr. David L. Greene, CG, FASG, Georgia; Jeffrey L. Haines, CG, North Carolina; George B. Handran, J.D., CG, Massachusetts; Helen L. Harriss, CG, Pennsylvania; the late Ruth Land Hatten, CGRS, Mississippi; Blaine Hedberg, Wisconsin; Russell L. Henderson, Virginia; James Hennessy, AG, Utah; Marty Hiatt, CGRS, Virginia; Jane S. Hill, North Carolina; Dr. Ronald A. Hill, CG, Idaho; Dr. Helen Hinchliff, CG, British Columbia, Canada; Kathleen W. Hinckley, CGRS, Colorado; Henry B. Hoff, J.D., CG, FASG, Washington, D.C.; Marian Hoffman, Genealogical Publishing Co.; Dr. John Forster Holt, Australia; Dean Hunter, AG, CGRS, Utah; Kay Germain Ingalls, CGRS, California; Dr. Thomas W. Jones, CG, CGL, Virginia; Roger D. Joslyn, CG, FASG, New York; Linda Pazics Kleback, Florida; Ann Smith Lainhart, Massachusetts; Donna Rachal Mills Lennon, CGRS, Alabama; Connie Lenzen, CGRS, Oregon; Edward Hapgood Little, CLS, Connecticut; Karen Livsey, New York; Anita Anderson Lustenberger, CG, New York; Harry Macy Jr., FASG, New York; Rudena Kramer Mallory, CGRS, Missouri; Linda Caldwell McCleary, Arizona; Lynn C. McMillion, CLS, Virginia; Suzanne McVetty, CG, New York; Marie Varrelman Melchiori, CGRS, CGL, Virginia; Kory L. Meyerink, AG, Utah; Paul Milner, Illinois; Dr.

The difference between ordinary and extraordinary is that little *extra*.

—*from The Immortal Whoever Said It First*

Acknowledgments

Joan Kirchman Mitchell, Alabama; Gary Mokotoff, New Jersey; Michael John Neill, Illinois; Eileen O Dúill, CGRS, Ireland; Alycon Pierce, CG, Virginia; Eileen Polakoff, New York; Ettie Pullman, DipFHS, Australia; Donald Pusch, Texas; Gordon L. Remington, FASG, Utah; David E. Rencher, AG, Utah; Philip W. Rhodes, CG, Virginia; Marsha Hoffman Rising, CG, CGL, FASG, Missouri; Donna Valley Russell, CG, FASG, Maryland; George Ely Russell, CG, FASG, Maryland; George R. Ryskamp, J.D., AG, Utah; Melinde Lutz Sanborn, FASG, New Hampshire; Cornelia Schrader-Müggenthaler, Italy; Henning Schröeder, Germany; Craig Roberts Scott, CGRS, Maryland; Dawne Slater-Putt, CG, North Carolina; the late Mary Speakman, CG, Texas; Kip Sperry, AG, CG, CGI, FASG, Utah; Beth Stahr, CGRS, Louisiana; Jackie Wesson Stewart, Alabama; John Hale Stutesman, California; Kenneth Thomas Jr., Georgia; William Thorndale, Utah; Nick Vine Hall, DipFHS (Hons.), Australia; James W. Warren, Minnesota; Paula Stuart Warren, CGRS, Minnesota; Jackie Stewart Wesson, Alabama; Shirley Langdon Wilcox, CG, Virginia; Curt B. Witcher, Indiana; Jan Worthington, DipFHS, Australia; and John Vincent Wylie, Texas.

Other colleagues generously provided information on programs they administer or otherwise assisted chapter authors: Robert Charles Anderson, FASG, New Hampshire; Marthe Arends, Bellevue Community College, Washington; Dr. Richard C. F. Baker, Institute of Heraldic and Genealogical Studies, England; Carlene Brown, University of Washington; Mary Lou Delahunt, Genealogical Institute of Mid-America, Illinois; Dr. Patricia Dice, University of Alabama; David Dobson, St. Andrews, Scotland; Yves du Passage, Chambre Syndicale des Généalogistes et Héraldistes de France; Albert Frank, Moravian Archives, Pennsylvania; Cynthia Hightower, U.S. National Archives; Edith James, U.S. National Archives; Gordon W. Miller, James Madison University Library; Marilyn Miller Morton, Alabama; Vernon Nelson, Moravian Archives, Pennsylvania; Margaret O'Sullivan, Genealogical Research Institute of New Zealand; Constance Potter, U.S. National Archives; Dr. David H. Pratt, AG, Brigham Young University, Utah; Dr. Allen B. Robertson, CG(C), Genealogical Institute of the Maritimes; Marie-Antoinette Rohan, Brittany, France; Jane Schwerdtfeger, New England Historic Genealogical Society; Margery Stirling, University of Stirling, Scotland; Elisabeth Thorsell, Federation of Swedish Genealogical Societies; Jean Thomason, Institute of Genealogy and Historical Research, Samford University, Alabama; and Constantine Tsatso, Smithsonian Associates, Washington, D.C.

A wise man once said, "The ladder to success is like an extension ladder. Just when you think you have reached the top, you *can* extend yourself and go a little higher." The authors of the twenty-nine chapters that follow and all the colleagues who assisted us all behind the scenes, well prove those words. All have reached or neared the top of the ladder in their areas of expertise, but their combined knowledge is a humbling reminder of just how much there is for the professional genealogist to learn above and beyond our fundamental expertise in the use and interpretation of records. Together, on the pages that follow, all offer an irresistible challenge to extend ourselves at least a little higher.

The ladder to success is like an extension ladder. Just when you think you have reached the top, you *can* extend yourself and go a little higher.

—*David Miner**

*David Miner, quoted in *The Quill Pen Pal* [newsletter of the Quill Corporation] 5 (May 1990): 1.

Chapter Authors

Mary McCampbell Bell, CLS, CGL

Chapters 16: Transcripts and Abstracts, 24: Lineage Papers

A longtime lecturer at major genealogical conferences and institutes and a former supervisor of the Lineage Research Committee Office of the National Society, Daughters of the American Revolution, Mary McCampbell Bell specializes in colonial Virginia and land platting. She is currently a trustee of the Board for Certification of Genealogists, president of the National Capital Area Chapter of the Association of Professional Genealogists, and a governor-at-large of the Virginia Genealogical Society.

Claire Mire Bettag, CGRS

Chapters 2: Educational Preparation, 3: Certification and Accreditation

A professional genealogist based in Washington, D.C., Claire Mire Bettag has made a lifelong commitment to education. Holding an M.A. in French, she was a Woodrow Wilson Scholar at Columbia University; studied in France as a Fulbright Fellow; conducted further studies in Mexico, Canada, and Spain; and received certificates from several of the major educational programs in genealogy. She lectures at the National Institute on Genealogical Research and serves as vice-president of the National Genealogical Society.

Bettie Cummings Cook, CG

Chapter 22: Record Compilations

A specialist in early Kentucky research, Bettie Cummings Cook is the compiler and publisher of the Kentucky Record Series, a set of abstracted early county court records. A Certified Genealogist since 1974, she has served four terms as a trustee of the Board for Certification of Genealogists.

Joan Ferris Curran, CG

Chapter 27: Preparing Books for Press

As a Certified Genealogist, Joan Ferris Curran's professional specialty is writing family histories for publication; and reviewers cite her work as models. She is a trustee and former vice-president of the Board for Certification of Genealogists and has been a longtime trustee and officer of the New England Historic Genealogical Society.

Donn Devine, J.D., CG, CGI

ProGen editorial board; author of chapters 1: Defining Professionalism, 17: Evidence Analysis

A lawyer and professional genealogist from Wilmington, Delaware, Donn Devine is a director of the National Genealogical Society, a trustee of the Board for Certification of Genealogists, and a regular columnist for *Ancestry* magazine. He was the first Certified Genealogical Instructor and played a leading role in the Board's decision to drop the use of the term *preponderance of the evidence.*

Regina Hines Ellison, CGRS

Chapter 19: Genealogy Columns

Regina Hines Ellison came to genealogy from journalism. Indeed, her long-running genealogy column treating the Gulf South was launched amid a full-time career as a newspaper reporter. In addition to professional research as a Certified Genealogical Records Specialist, Regina is a founding member and former president of the Council of Genealogy Columnists (now known as the International Society of Family History Writers and Editors).

Chapter Authors

Linda Woodward Geiger, CGRS, CGL
Chapter 15: Research Procedures

An accomplished genealogist and author, Linda Woodward Geiger is active in genealogical and historical societies at all levels. She teaches research principles at national-level conferences and the National Archives–based National Institute on Genealogical Research; is the owner and editor of *Woodwards WeSearch,* a quarterly surname newsletter; and currently serves as secretary of the Genealogical Speakers Guild.

Val D. Greenwood, J.D., AG
Chapter 7: Copyright and Fair Use

Few people succeed in authoring "the classic work" in their field. Val D. Greenwood is one of those few. For a quarter century his *Researcher's Guide to American Genealogy*— now in its third edition—has remained unchallenged and unmatched. As one of the first Accredited Genealogists and a member of the Utah Bar, he has recently retired from the Temple Department of The Church of Jesus Christ of Latter-day Saints, where he was a specialist in LDS Church policies relating to genealogy and temple work.

James L. Hansen, FASG
ProGen editorial board; author of Foreword

A reference librarian and genealogical specialist at the State Historical Society of Wisconsin, James L. Hansen specializes in frontier genealogy and has published genealogical studies treating several frontier areas. He is a former president of the Association of Professional Genealogists, serves on the editorial board of the *National Genealogical Society Quarterly,* a recipient of the National Genealogical Society's Award of Merit, and one of the best-known lecturers in American genealogy.

Patricia Gilliam Hastings, J.D.
Chapter 6: Executing Contracts

An attorney, an avocational genealogist, and a local historian, Patricia Gilliam Hastings is a past president of the Middle Tennessee Genealogical Society and an editor and transcriber of early Tennessee records for publication.

Patricia Law Hatcher, CG, FASG
Chapter 13: Time Management

A professional genealogist who juggles research, writing, editing, lecturing, teaching, and typesetting assignments, Patricia Law Hatcher still finds time for volunteer service and continuing education. She specializes in genealogical problem resolution, has published in more than a dozen periodicals, frequently lectures at national conferences, wrote the groundbreaking manual *Producing a Quality Family History,* and serves as a trustee of the Association of Professional Genealogists.

Birdie Monk Holsclaw
Chapter 26: Proofreading and Indexing

A genealogical consultant, editor, lecturer, and writer, Birdie Monk Holsclaw has served as copyeditor for the *Association of Professional Genealogists Quarterly* since 1989 and was indexer of the *National Genealogical Society Quarterly*, 1989–96. Her lectures emphasize the appropriate blending of technology with her research specialties—land records, neighborhood reconstruction, and research on the deaf and blind and the states of Colorado and Pennsylvania. She is a fellow of the Utah Genealogical Association.

Chapter Authors

Melinda Shackleford Kashuba, Ph.D.

Chapter 9: Structuring a Business

Holding a doctorate in Geography from UCLA, Melinda Shackleford Kashuba has pursued genealogy professionally for nearly two decades. Her lectures and her writings—which include the column "Small Business Squibs" in the *Association of Professional Genealogists Quarterly*—attest her conviction that success as a self-employed professional requires business acumen as well as research skills.

Elizabeth Kelley Kerstens, CGRS

Chapters 8: Alternative Careers, 11: Marketing Strategies

A specialist in federal records at the National Archives, Elizabeth Kelley Kerstens has worn many career hats since she began genealogical research in 1982. She currently edits *Genealogical Computing* and *OnBoard* and previously edited the *Association of Professional Genealogists Quarterly*. She is codirector of the National Genealogical Society's Research Trips to Dublin, Ireland; co–North American representative for the Irish Genealogical Congress; and creator of the software program Clooz®, the electronic filing cabinet for genealogical records.

Helen F. M. Leary, CG, CGL, FASG

ProGen editorial board; author of chapters 12: Business Record Keeping, 14: Problem Analyses and Research Plans, 29: Lecturing

Helen F. M. Leary virtually epitomizes the genealogical entrepreneur—the full-time professional who juggles business concerns with lecturing, writing, and superior success in problem resolution for her research clients. She is the developer and course coordinator of the Professional Genealogy track of the Samford University Institute of Genealogy and Historical Research, the editor and principal author of both editions of the highly acclaimed *North Carolina Research*, and a fellow of both the National Genealogical Society and the American Society of Genealogists.

Sandra Hargreaves Luebking

Chapters 10: Setting Realistic Fees, 28: Classroom Teaching

A course coordinator and lecturer at two nationally known genealogy institutes, Sandra Hargreaves Luebking authored the Instructional Materials chapter of Ancestry's *Printed Sources*. She has been the longtime editor of the Federation of Genealogical Society's *Forum* and has coedited two major reference works, including the award-winning *The Source: A Guidebook to American Genealogy*. Her international clientele has included the Smithsonian Institution and numerous publishers and attorneys. She is a fellow of the Utah Genealogical Association.

Elizabeth Shown Mills, CG, CGL, FASG

ProGen editor; author of chapters 3: Certification and Accreditation, 18: Research Reports, 20: Proof Arguments and Case Studies, 21: Book and Media Reviews, 25: Editing Periodicals

A specialist in the resolution of thorny research problems, Elizabeth Shown Mills has edited the *National Genealogical Society Quarterly* since 1987 and has authored or compiled eight books and more than 300 articles published by professional, academic, and commercial presses—including *Evidence! Citation & Analysis for the Family Historian*. She is current president (and fellow) of the American Society of Genealogists, former president of the Board for Certification of Genealogists, a lecturer and course-developer at the Samford University Institute of Genealogy and Historical Research, and a fellow of the National Genealogical Society and the Utah Genealogical Association.

Chapter Authors

Jimmy B. Parker, AG
Chapter 3: Certification and Accreditation

A former manager of the Family History Library in Salt Lake City, Jimmy B. Parker has administered numerous other programs and organizations critical to the genealogical field. An Accredited Genealogist, he has served as president of both the Association of Professional Genealogists and the Utah Genealogical Association, was an early trustee of the Board for Certification of Genealogists as a representative of the library community, and has played a major role in the development of an accreditation program to replace the one previously conducted by the Family History Library.

Joy Reisinger, CG
Chapter 4: The Essential Library

For more than three decades as a researcher and publisher, Joy Reisinger has lived two hours away from a reference library and even farther from her specialty area, Quebec. To fill the void, she has built a very large and carefully selected library of her own. She is current vice-president of the Board for Certification of Genealogists and a former vice-president of the Association of Professional Genealogists. She has published in the *National Genealogical Society Quarterly, The American Genealogist,* and elsewhere; but will always be remembered for her creation and editorship of the original *Lost in Canada.*

Christine Rose, CG, CGL, FASG
Chapter 23: Family Histories

A genealogist of forty years experience, Christine Rose's professional specialty is nationwide on-site research and military records. A columnist and popular lecturer at the Samford University Institute of Genealogy and Historical Research and elsewhere, Christine is a former vice-president of the Association of Professional Genealogists, a coauthor of the bestselling *Complete Idiot's Guide to Genealogy,* a fellow of the American Society of Genealogists, and founder of the Rose Family Association. Her two genealogies on unrelated Rose families won the prestigious Donald Lines Jacobus Award in 1987.

Elisabeth Whitman Schmidt, CLS
Chapter 24: Lineage Papers

Recently retired as Ethnic and Minority Genealogist for the National Society, Daughters of the American Revolution, Elisabeth Whitman Schmidt is a former treasurer of the Association of Professional Genealogists and a former officer and trustee of the Board for Certification of Genealogists. She remains an active member of several lineage societies at the local, state, and national level.

Paul F. Smart, AG
Chapter 3: Certification and Accreditation

Currently the Outreach Coordinator of the Family History Department, Church of Jesus Christ of Latter-day Saints, Paul F. Smart previously oversaw the Department's accreditation, training, and library publications areas and supervised the British area of the Family History Library. He has participated in many seminars around the world and led a number of research tours to Great Britain. He is a former president of the International Society for British Genealogy and Family History and a fellow of the Society of Genealogists (London).

Chapter Authors

Neil D. Thompson, LL.B., Ph.D., CG, FASG

Chapter 5: Ethical Standards

A native of Calexico, California, Neil D. Thompson received his Ph.D. from Columbia University and his LL.B. from Harvard Law School in the same year. Now a retired attorney, he is a professional genealogist, author, editor, and lecturer, whose particular interests are the colonial United States, sixteenth-to-eighteenth-century Britain, and medieval Europe. He is a former president and fellow of the American Society of Genealogists, a former president of the Board for Certification of Genealogists, and a fellow of both the Society of Genealogists (London) and the Utah Genealogical Association.

Foreword

by James L. Hansen, FASG

Of the making of genealogies there may indeed be no end, and much the same is true of genealogical guides. Since Gilbert Doane's day, each generation has had its standard introductions to the special pleasures and perils of genealogical research. But there was always more to be covered than a beginner's manual could reasonably include. In more recent years the needs of the intermediate and advanced researcher have begun to be met by texts like *The Source* and a plethora of more specialized works. But what about the professional genealogist? There simply hasn't been a full-scale manual, textbook, or resource book for the researcher who is actually trying to make a living at "doing genealogy." Until now. Now there's *Professional Genealogy: A Manual for Researchers, Writers, Editors, Lecturers, and Librarians.*

ProGen (as it is already known in the genealogical community) is the distillation of years of professional experience and wisdom on the part of the authors and the many other researchers they have encountered, worked with, discussed ideas with, and shared knowledge and experiences with. Editor Elizabeth Shown Mills and her capable corps of authors have provided a comprehensive and timely vade mecum for the many aspects of the field of genealogy that should be familiar to a professional or a prospective one.

But *ProGen* is not just for the professional genealogist. It's for all genealogists who want to understand—and produce—quality work. Many of the chapters, particularly those in the sections Professional Research Skills, Writing and Compiling, and Editing and Publishing, are state-of-the-art discussions of topics that have been little covered by other genealogical texts.

Professional Genealogy is a landmark in the development of genealogy as a professional discipline. Is it even possible to imagine compiling and publishing such a guide ten or twenty years ago? As the consumer base of practicing researchers grows, so does the need for more mentors. While much of any genealogist's knowledge base (whether personal or professional) will be intensely specific, many of the basic tenets of research and the dissemination of its results will be the same (or very similar) for all. That's why guides are so useful—and even necessary. Like the computers we use, our professional skills are always in need of an upgrade. There are always new (or newly available) resources to comprehend. There are ways to work more efficiently and effectively that we haven't yet discovered. And there are topics we haven't explored because there weren't manuals available—like many of the issues covered here.

ProGen is as much a reference book as it is a text. Read right away the chapters that speak directly to your present situation. Read later those that will have particular resonance then. This is a resource to come back to again and again as your needs change. Of course, the field will be changing too. Textbooks need to be revised, and—as much as their editors and authors may cringe at the thought—even standard reference works need periodic revision. This one can be no exception. But much of the knowledge and wisdom included here will undoubtedly survive many future editions.

—November 2000, State Historical Society of Wisconsin

ProGen is not just for the professional genealogist. It's for all genealogists who want to understand—and produce—quality work.

Preface

by Elizabeth Shown Mills, CG, CGL, FASG

Professional Genealogy has been a long time aborning. So has professional genealogy. Never mind that recitals of begats date to the earliest bards and griots, or that men of greatness or ambition have long paid others to immortalize their pedigrees on paper. It is hard to find in history the modern concepts of genealogy or professionalism. When Pierre Durye, former archivist of France, wrote his introduction to European genealogy several decades ago, he pointed out the "proverbial saying" *to lie like a genealogist.* Then he backed up his barb with a quote from *Mercure Galant,* 1685: "Farewell! I go to look for a genealogist who for a few *louis* . . . will make me, on the spot, come from wherever I wish."[1]

The study of ancient and medieval lineages also has a long history in academia, where it cloaks itself in a robe called *prosopography.* However, the scholarly discipline of genealogy dates only from the early twentieth century, when George Andrews Moriarty, a classics professor, and Donald Lines Jacobus, a professional genealogist, began to lay down disciplinary rules.[2] Not until 1979 would the international Association of Professional Genealogists (APG) be chartered in Salt Lake City. Yet even then, genealogy as a *real* profession to which one might seriously aspire would still spend years adrift.

In 1983, a young Colorado resident named Kathleen Westberg Hinckley approached me at the third annual conference of the National Genealogical Society. She had been a "family researcher" for several years and wanted to be a professional. *Full* time, not part time. A *real* professional—not a hobbyist who took odd jobs on the side to "support her habit." Yet outside Salt Lake City, the mecca of the family-history world, she saw little hope for realizing her aspirations. Because I was a "full-time professional" from Alabama, a site one might expect to be genealogy's polar opposite of Salt Lake City, she approached me with a question: *how did I make it happen?*

Finding little to guide her in genealogy's published literature, Kathleen said, she had already turned to manuals on general entrepreneurship and gleaned the basics. She had set for herself a five-year plan for education, networking, and professional development. Hence, her attendance at the conference and her initiative in approaching speakers to ask for their advice. Although none of us had a structure or a system to offer her, she listened to our random thoughts and then culled, adapted, and built upon them. By the end of the five-year program she charted for herself, Kathleen had become a Certified Genealogical Record Searcher[3] and held a seat on the board of the Association of Professional Genealogists.

Initiative breeds success in entrepreneurship. But aspiring professionals in genealogy should not have to reinvent for themselves the wheels—indeed the whole vehicle—they need to venture into this field. Kathleen did not know it at the time, but she had planted the seed for *ProGen.* Our field clearly needed a manual. Coincidentally, a new publishing company in Salt Lake City soon approached me for ideas: *genealogy was to be its specialty; what were our needs?* A professional manual? One that would tap the collective wisdom of the best and brightest in our field? *Well, perhaps, but*

> Initiative breeds success in entrepreneurship. But aspiring professionals in genealogy should not have to reinvent the wheels— indeed the whole vehicle— they need to venture into this field.

where was the market? Their message was clear: a manual for professionals was a rather esoteric idea.

Meanwhile, the American Society of Genealogists (ASG) had established a niche unique at the time. This scholastic honor society, founded by followers of the Jacobus school of genealogical scholarship, had tried to fill some of our discipline's need for guidance. Through its two-volume *Genealogical Research: Methods and Sources,* its provision of seed money for a new scholarly journal (*The Genealogist*), and its launch of the respected Jacobus Award for superior quality in compiled genealogy, it had encouraged scholarship among researchers ignored by the educational world. ASG, whose membership was an eclectic mix of academics and professionals in a variety of fields, seemed to be a natural sponsor for a professional manual—and I was a new member with enough cheek to propose it. But ASG presidents were more prudent. Yes, there was a need, they acknowledged, but *would there be adequate sales to make the venture practical?*

In 1989, the profession celebrated a milestone. The new Association of Professional Genealogists was ten years old, though its membership barely numbered two hundred. The older Board for Certification of Genealogists (BCG), which ASG members had founded in 1964, boasted a more substantial number of associates; but few of them dared try a full-time living from the practice of genealogy. Meanwhile, a new program took root in Alabama, at the Samford University Institute of Genealogy and Historical Research, where Sandra Luebking (the author of chapters 10 and 28) and I had taught for several years. Samford's administration had already gambled on one program expansion, allowing me to add an Advanced Methodology track in 1986. Attendance boomed. But the students that class drew from across the country gave us a higher bar to meet: *What now?* they asked. *Where can we go from here, education-wise?* Samford responded with another track: Professional Genealogy, with Helen F. M. Leary as its course leader.

Predictably, Samford's new forum heard questions and issues from practicing genealogists for which answers did not exist in print. And so, as BCG president and vice-president respectively, Helen and I took the *ProGen* concept to the certifying board and found support at last. Not only did BCG's trustees agree to underwrite publication in the event no commercial publisher materialized, but trustee Roger D. Joslyn proposed that *ProGen* be jointly sponsored by the Association of Professional Genealogists, which he then headed. The endorsement of the American Society of Genealogists was added shortly thereafter. Ironically, the editor of the BCG newsletter which announced the forthcoming manual to the world in November 1992 was a new BCG trustee, Kathleen Westberg Hinckley.

Still, *ProGen* has been some time aborning. The 1990s was an incredibly dynamic decade for genealogy. From its image as a whimsical hobby, genealogy exploded into a symbol of the millennium: a universal quest for identity. As the Internet linked the globe into a web of "people helping people"—long the motto of genealogists—websites promising answers to the question *Who am I?* numbered among the World Wide Web's most popular hits. Outside of cyberspace, membership societies welcomed the throngs with new codes of conduct and standards for research that would have offended hobbyists just a generation earlier.

Samford's new forum heard questions and issues from practicing genealogists for which answers did not exist in print.

The changes were commercial as well as scholastic. Professional genealogists in the eighties had pleaded with software developers for programs that permitted documentation of research findings. They were dismissed with a brusque "only a few professionals like you are interested in *that*." From that staging point, nothing could attest the professionalization of genealogy in the nineties better than the adoption of source-citation features by virtually every software firm courting the genealogical market. Hugh Wilding, a family researcher in England with highly professional standards, recently spotlighted the radical change of attitude when he matter-of-factly commented: "In the early days (the mid-1990s), I used [*program XYZ*]. It impressed me not only with its ease of use but also because it had a source field for each fact recorded."[4]

The software Hugh cited is the field's most popular program—one whose marketing targets new hobbyists. In just ten short years, "professional standards" had become *the* standard for the masses.

Genealogy's explosive growth created a similar surge in professional ranks and immense changes in many of its practices. APG's twentieth-anniversary directory cites an international membership more than six times that of its ten-year benchmark.[5] Its advertising pages offer products that did not exist a decade ago—from electronically searchable census images (at a fraction of the cost of the computerized indexes that were "revolutionary" in the 1980s) to electronic filing cabinets for the storage of documents, photos, and maps. In the meanwhile, countries that once sent floods of immigrants across the world not only lifted their iron curtains but also the bars that kept researchers from their records. Mega corporations and commercial presses discovered the genealogical market and found it ripe. And so, a lofty but impractical idea became a commercially realistic one by the time *Professional Genealogy* was ready for the marketplace.

The manual you now hold in your hand is also radically different from the one first envisioned in 1984. In fact, it greatly differs from the concepts that the officers of BCG, APG, and ASG drafted in 1992. The explosive growth in technology, record access, and professional activity has changed much of the focus and content. In some cases, it changed that content several times over, as innovations continued to replace traditional resources and approaches. We send these pages to press now with a very acute sense of the old saw that printed matter is out of date before its ink can dry.

In this new century, we fully expect *change, growth, standards,* and *education* to be the keywords of professionalism in our field. That change will continue to make obsolete many of the points our present authors treat. *Professional Genealogy*, like professional genealogy itself, should continue to be a work-in-progress as our ranks swell, technology advances, and academic opportunities continue to expand.

In the meanwhile, *ProGen* is a milestone. Practitioners of other fields, who have discovered genealogy as a hobby and contemplate a career change, can find here—for the first time—the realistic financial and technical advice such a move demands. Students who discover genealogy through a classroom project or the Internet and think they see career potential can find—at last—the kind of guidance that career centers routinely offer for other vocations. Family researchers who have no thought of "going professional" but want their work to live up to quality standards can find here a wealth

Trained professionals in other fields, who have discovered genealogy as a hobby and contemplate a career change, can find here—for the first time— the realistic financial and technical advice such a move demands.

ProGen is a guidebook for all genealogists who want quality and success to be both their signature and their legacy.

of explicit discussions and examples available nowhere else in print. In short, *ProGen* can be a guidebook for all genealogists who want *quality* to be both their signature and their legacy.

Users accustomed to traditional genealogical guidebooks should be forewarned on one point. *ProGen* is a manual, not a directory. Readers will find discussions of many resources, agencies, and websites worldwide. But ours is a world in which addresses, phone numbers, and URLs continually change—and ours is an age in which one should turn to the Internet, not the printed word, for the most up-to-date contact and access information.

Genealogy today is a global pursuit in every respect. Few of us can trace ancestors without crossing national lines, and all of us are bound together by organizational and digital networks. From Auckland to Oslo, from Tel Aviv to Toronto, we share many resources, techniques, and concerns. *ProGen* tries to reflect that. Its roots are American, but genealogists across the globe have contributed to its chapters and our authors have focused upon countless issues common to all. Although no work can be truly universal, we hope this one can fill many of the needs that are shared by family historians worldwide and that it will be a launchpad for similar works internationally.

—esm
Tuscaloosa, Alabama
November 2000

1. Pierre Durye, *Genealogy: An Introduction to Continental Concepts,* 4th edition, Wilson Ober Clough, trans. (New Orleans: Polyanthos, 1977), viii, 13–14.

2. For an overview of the growth of genealogical standards in the twentieth century, see Elizabeth Shown Mills, "Working with Historical Evidence: Genealogical Principles and Standards," *Evidence: A Special Issue of the National Genealogical Society Quarterly* 87 (September 1999): 165–84; for Moriarty and Jacobus, see especially 167–68.

3. In 1989, the Certified Genealogical Record Searcher credential was changed to Certified Genealogical Records Specialist to better reflect the expertise and standards required of its holders.

4. Hugh Wilding <hstjw@lineone.net> to Mills, 7 January 2000.

5. *Directory of Professional Genealogists: 20th Anniversary Edition, 1999–2000,* Kathleen W. Hinckley, cgrs, comp. and ed. (Denver, Colorado: Association of Professional Genealogists, 1999).

Professional Preparation

1

DEFINING
PROFESSIONALISM

**DEFINING
PROFESSIONALISM**

Keynotes

Defining Professionalism

by Donn Devine, J.D., CG, CGI

Professionalism has many facets. Dictionary definitions cite high standards, skill, and experience; services provided for personal profit or public good; and even the pursuit of sport as a livelihood. Genealogists reflect all these as they daily engage in a broad spectrum of activities—archival administration and preservation, book selling, broadcasting, editing, lecturing, librarianship, publishing, software development, and teaching, as well as the commonly recognized research and writing and the oft-touted "fun." Working on commission, on salary, and pro bono, they assist both the public and other professions such as genetics, history, and law.

At its core—in genealogy as elsewhere—professionalism calls for the mastery of a body of theoretical knowledge. That body of knowledge and its continued growth constitute a scholarly discipline. A profession arises out of an intellectual discipline when practitioners apply their learning to the solution of real-life problems—and when they accept personal responsibility for both expertise and ethics in their dealings with clients, patrons, students, scholarship, and the field. Modern genealogy belies the old saw that the only difference between a professional and an amateur is that the professional gets paid for what the amateur does for love. Countless avocational and volunteer genealogists are totally professional in terms of discipline, knowledge, problem resolution, and responsibility.

In a broad sense, professionalism is three-dimensional—reflecting public perception, peer perception, and self-perception. These are the elements this chapter and this book develop.

> A profession arises out of an intellectual discipline when practitioners apply their learning to the solution of real-life problems —and when they accept personal responsibility.

Public Perception

How can others recognize us as professionals? In practice, our expertise is reflected in the quality of our output over time. Yet most potential clients lack adequate technical knowledge to distinguish us from those with fewer skills or a less developed sense of responsibility. The public, therefore, looks to surrogate measures of professionalism and finds them in four areas.

- *Certification or licensing*—as well as guild membership. All professions provide, as part of their collective responsibility to the public, some means of assuring consumers that their practitioners perform at a minimum level of competence and ethics.

- *Service in the public interest*—often on a pro-bono basis. This concept originated in the traditional medieval professions of arms, law, medicine, and religion.

- *Conformity to basic conventions*—at least the ones widely known as the accepted ways of doing things.

- *Comparison to other learned professions*—in dress, ethics, manners, and speech. These expectations vary widely by place, time, and circumstances. Yet they are often the initial basis on which professionalism is judged.

DEFINING

PROFESSIONALISM

Genealogy is a scholarly discipline. It comprises an extensive body of knowledge that must be acquired by anyone who aspires to professionalism.

Peer Perception

Genealogy professionals judge a colleague's work product and scholarly output by these same factors (although sometimes from a different slant) and by others more technical. Peer evaluation will commonly consider our mastery of knowledge, our experience, our communication skills, our observance of conventions, our achievement of credentials, and our conformity with professional codes and standards—not necessarily in that order.

Mastery of knowledge

Genealogy is a scholarly discipline. It comprises an extensive body of knowledge that must be acquired by anyone who aspires to professionalism in the field. Its principles, facts, methods, and cautions are well defined; but they are applied in many different settings globally. Individual locales have their own culture, history, language, and traditions that must also be mastered before the core knowledge can be used. Major concepts and basic methodology are found within a relatively small number of books and journals that specifically treat genealogy as an intellectual discipline. However, perspective is acquired from fields as diverse as anthropology, archaeology, demography, economics, geography, history, law, linguistics, paleography, religion, sociology, and the physical and biological sciences.

Many professional genealogists have educated themselves. Building upon the foundation of formal schooling in other fields, they identify gaps in their learning and the resources that can fill these needs. In years past, there was virtually no other method. Today there is a large and expanding array of formal opportunities for aspiring and practicing professionals. Some offer a structured approach to learning that minimizes the major risk of self-instruction—a failure to identify some vital area that still needs to be mastered. Regardless of where we live or what our personal schedule may be, we can find rich and reasonably priced occasions to expand our technical knowledge—a point chapter 2 discusses at length.

Experience

Education provides a certain level of technical knowledge. Experience develops that into true expertise. A survey by the U.S.-based Board for Certification of Genealogists, which polled its associates and others with applications in progress, dramatically emphasizes this point. Certified associates averaged twenty-three years of personal experience and twelve of professional experience. For preliminary applicants, the figure was fifteen years personal and three years professional. In short, in both groups professional genealogists logged about a dozen years of personal research experience before they considered themselves proficient enough to enter the field professionally. For those who were certified as lecturers, the experience level rose even higher.[1]

Communication skills

We need not be gifted orators or great writers to be professional genealogists, but we should be able to express ourselves in a clear and orderly manner. Our stock-in-trade is abstract knowledge; if we cannot communicate effectively, we cannot trade in it. Both our written work and our speech—formal or informal—are compared to those expected of professionals in other fields. Thus, we strive to stay close to standard forms of our language, avoiding colloquialisms and dialects that may not be generally accepted. In both written and oral communications, we avoid specialized jargon (which less experienced genealogists may not understand) and excessive erudition (which is sure to befuddle the very things we try to explain).

Conventions

Like all fields, genealogy has its accepted ways of doing things; and we depart from them only at our peril. The conventional way is seldom the only possible way. In a few cases it may not be even the most rational, understandable, or useful way. Still, the value of conventions lies in their familiarity. When we use them, we don't trip up our readers with mental stumbling blocks or, worse, raise warning flags. We are certainly free, in appropriate forums, to advance the merits of alternative forms; but it is self-defeating to foist them—even with an explanation—upon readers of our research reports, self-published books, or manuscripts to be submitted to journals.

Conventions also vary across national boundaries. If we are globally active gene-alogists, we are expected to know, and conform to, the standards and practices of all regions in which we work. While it is a fact that standards of genealogical scholarship are stricter in some areas than others, as competent professionals we exhibit the highest of standards in a manner that is still respectful of regional habits.[2]

The bedrock convention in genealogy is proper source citation. Beyond that, the three most common conventions center upon data arrangement, date and calendar usage, and numbering genealogies and pedigrees. Each of these is briefly addressed below.

SOURCE CITATION

The hallmarks of a credible genealogist are thoroughness and quality in citing evidence. Reliable researchers never report a genealogical fact—or any information that is not public knowledge—without identifying the source from which that information came. They follow this standard regardless of the format in which they record their findings—be it an ancestor chart, a database, a family group sheet, a compiled genealogy, or a research report. They cite those sources *fully,* which means that they understand the essential elements of a citation for each type of material they use. They cite those sources *individually,* which means that they clearly link each fact to the specific source that yielded the information. They understand the difference between reference notes and bibliographies and do not proffer a generic list of materials in vague and haphazard support of a mass of details within a composite sketch.

They follow this convention because they realize one fact: it is impossible to analyze evidence or weigh its reliability without knowing the precise origin of the information. To help themselves and their readers reach sound conclusions about the validity of

The hallmarks of a credible genealogist are thoroughness and quality in citing evidence.

each piece of genealogical data, they also include (at least in their personal research notes) an appraisal of the source they are citing—noting any strengths or weaknesses that source may have. Many published style manuals explain the principles of sound citations, including one manual specifically designed for genealogists.[3]

DATA ARRANGEMENT

The sequence of data in an original record frequently conveys information in addition to what the individual entries explicitly state. Examples are the order in which homes were visited to count people or assess taxes and the arrangement of gravestones in a cemetery. In each case, nearby entries imply physical proximity, which may point to relationships among the people listed. If the extracts or transcriptions are rearranged in alphabetical order, to "help" researchers, an important element of information is lost: who was located near whom. Therefore, the genealogical convention is to copy information in its original order, so that no locational detail or implication is obscured. Users of the data can then be further (and better) helped by providing a separate alphabetical index.

DATE AND CALENDAR USAGE

One of the most basic conventions observed at large in the U.S. and Canada puts North America at odds with much of the world—that is, the writing of dates in month/day/year format. Thus, American genealogists (like the American military) follow the European custom of citing by day/month/year—with the latter expressed in all four digits: 1 January 2001 (no commas). Careful genealogists also avoid the ambiguous all-numeral expressions used as common shortcuts—that is, 10/1/1990, which would mean 1 October 1990 in North America or 10 January 1990 elsewhere.

Another dating convention traces to the Western world's transition from the Julian to the Gregorian calendar. While most Catholic areas of Europe made the switch between 1582 and 1587, the Protestant dominions did not convert until the 1700s; two major Eastern Orthodox countries did not until the twentieth century; and other cultures still use other calendars. North American genealogists who work the British-American colonies (but not the adjacent French and Spanish ones) follow a special convention for the years between 1582 and 1752, when Britain finally converted to the Gregorian system, dropping eleven days from the calendar.[4] Because the start of the civil year was simultaneously changed in some countries and regularized in others, from 25 March to 1 January, we double-date years for the months of January, February, and March during that 1582–1752 period. To illustrate: 1 February 1688 is written 1 February 1688/9, showing that the year would have been 1689, had it started on 1 January.

NUMBERING GENEALOGIES AND PEDIGREES

Few things in genealogy cast a shadow on our image of professionalism more quickly than a failure to follow the conventional systems of numbering genealogies and pedigrees. All researchers in this field agree that the perfect system has not been invented. Most concede that a perfect system probably never will be devised. Experimentation is so rampant that most "new" systems proclaimed by enthusiasts

Few things cast a shadow on our image of professionalism more quickly than a failure to use conventional systems of numbering genealogies and pedigrees.

are mere reinventions of wheels that already litter library shelves, to the frustration of all who waste valuable research time trying to decipher the "unique" arrangements of other writers.

Centuries of trial and error have winnowed the number of truly workable systems to a meager but flexible few. For pedigrees, the almost universal convention is the Sosa-Stradonitz (aka Ahnentafel) system, named for the Spanish genealogist Jerome de Sosa, who first used it in 1676, and for Stephan Kekule von Stradonitz, who popularized it in his 1896 "ahnentafel atlas" (ancestor table). Most genealogists recognize it from commercially available blank-form charts and genealogical database software. For descending genealogies, in the United States the conventional systems (which genealogy software also incorporates) are the slightly varying *NGS Quarterly* System, named for the National Genealogical Society's scholarly journal, and the *Register* System, named for the quarterly of the New England Historic Genealogical Society. Detailed descriptions of each of these are widely available.[5] Most British genealogists use outline-style arrangements of letters and numbers, grouping families in order of descendant lines, not by generations as in the U.S. systems. Researchers in other countries variously use all of these schemes.

> Centuries of trial and error have winnowed the number of truly workable systems to a meager but flexible few.

Credentials

Many professions today are regulated by local, state, provincial, or national law. Genealogy has no formal entrance requirements—except in a few jurisdictions that require private-investigator examination and licensing as a prerequisite to charging for services. Historically, our field has resisted government regulation, for several valid reasons. In lieu of official oversight, genealogical professionals in several countries have developed programs of voluntary evaluation. Practitioners who demonstrate high levels of professional performance, either through examinations (the North American standard) or a course of instruction (the more common practice internationally), are awarded credentials. With these come the right to use certain postnomials by which the public can recognize our demonstrated qualifications. Chapter 3 discusses these programs in some detail.

Professional memberships and codes

In all professional fields, practitioners are inevitably judged by the extent to which they contribute to and participate in recognized professional organizations. These groups establish standards, promote (even provide) education, and monitor legal situations that may affect the conduct of the field. Genealogy is no exception. The lack of government regulation for professional researchers places considerable responsibility upon our professional bodies to regulate the practice in a manner that protects consumers. The fact that genealogy does not enjoy parity with other subjects in educational institutions increases our dependence upon genealogical agencies for ongoing training. And the utter dependence of all genealogists upon the preservation of open records makes it imperative that every professional actively support the records preservation and open access campaigns of the major organizations within

DEFINING
PROFESSIONALISM

True professionals give
back to the field in mea-
sures at least equal to the
benefits they take from it.

---

our field. In all these areas, "support" means not only membership dues but also contributions of labor and talent. True professionals give back to the field in measures at least equal to the benefits they take from it.

Codes of conduct are formal statements adopted by professional organizations to express their minimum expectations in the ethical arena. In the United States the standard codes are those of the Board for Certification of Genealogists and the Association of Professional Genealogists (APG); and both are followed by many associates abroad. Additionally, the APG in 1995 adopted a set of guidelines for the ethical use of postnomials which is also helpful to both professionals and the public. Internationally, several standard-setting bodies follow somewhat similar codes. (See appendix B.) All emphasize personal integrity in one's individual conduct and in the professional relationship with clients, colleagues, and recordkeepers. Both of the American organizations offer a dispute-resolution service to which the public can bring complaints against an affiliated genealogist for a violation of that body's code.

Standards

After a century of declining respect, genealogy reemerged as a scholarly discipline in the 1920s and 1930s. Its intellectual rebirth traces to a quiet revolution led by Donald Lines Jacobus (1887–1970), the father of modern genealogical scholarship. The first issue of the publication Jacobus launched in 1922—the *New Haven Genealogical Magazine,* which became *The American Genealogist* ten years later—states his credo: "We will print neither bunk nor junk, nor warmed over material filched from the pages of other quarterlies."

Most standards applied by responsible genealogists today were first enunciated by Jacobus and the colleagues who joined him to form the American Society of Genealogists.[6] Those principles spread from Jacobus's magazine to the other journals that are today considered standard-bearers of the field,[7] and they are emulated by every publication that aspires to credibility. Many precepts of the "Jacobus School" were later incorporated into books that have become genealogical classics.[8]

JACOBUS STANDARDS

Fundamental to the Jacobus movement were careful documentation and analysis of all genealogical research. No modern genealogist can earn respect without exhibiting four traits:

- thorough understanding of the nature of the records used.

- considerable skill at analyzing the credibility of data from individual records.

- meticulous care in providing a reliable source for each and every assertion of fact.

- well-reasoned explanations of every assumption or conclusion.

Excellent guides to these bedrock principles have been widely available over the past two decades.[9]

NGS STANDARDS

Aside from documentation and evidence analysis, no attempt was made until recently to abstract, classify, and list the genealogical standards that have come into general use. Since 1997 the National Genealogical Society has filled this void with four models, each a succinct statement of the norms of modern genealogy. To encourage wide distribution, the society's copyright notice includes a license to reproduce or republish each in its entirety. (See appendix B.) The major emphases of these four sets of guidelines are as follows:

Sharing Information with others
Considering the extent to which research depends upon the sharing of information, the society addresses nine ways in which genealogists can (and should) respect others' legal rights to intellectual property and privacy and their moral rights to credit for their labors and respect for their sensitivities and sensibilities.

Sound genealogical research
Recognizing genealogy as a quest for truth, this model defines minimal requirements for acceptable research. It covers such concepts as the use of original records or reproduced images whenever possible, proper citation of evidence, integrity in reporting facts, the distinguishing of hypotheses from solid conclusions, and openness to criticism and new evidence. Of particular importance to professionals should be item 7, which cautions genealogists to "avoid misleading other researchers by either intentionally or carelessly distributing or publishing inaccurate information." In at least this one regard, standards for professional genealogical researchers are higher than that set for scientific research by the federal government—where misrepresentation must be deliberate to be considered faulty conduct.[10]

> The personal responsibility each of us has for our work product transcends any and all reliance upon databases, networks, or software.

Use of technology in genealogical research
Computers and digital technology have made an indelible impact on the practice of genealogy, with both positive and negative results. NGS's standards emphasize the personal responsibility each of us has for our work product—an obligation that transcends all reliance upon databases, networks, or software. Particularly stressed are the need to distinguish derivative or compiled data from actual images; to keep complete source identification associated with electronic data; and to personally verify, or describe as unverified, information passed to others in any electronic form.

Use of record repositories and libraries
Addressing basic issues, this set of guidelines is intended primarily for newcomers to genealogy, who often lack documentary research experience—especially in original records. As advanced genealogists, we already apply these standards, but the society's summation provides a useful and authoritative guide we can share with our patrons and students.

BCG STANDARDS
The most significant discussion of genealogical standards—applicable to all historical and family researchers whether they follow genealogy as an avocation, a profession,

> Once we deem ourselves
> qualified to undertake work
> for others, we are judged
> as professionals. Whether
> we earn a significant part
> of our living through this
> enterprise is irrelevant.

or an adjunct to another intellectual discipline—is *The BCG Genealogical Standards Manual*. Issued at the millennium to codify the standards of acceptability within genealogy, this work offers copious examples upon which researchers can pattern their work and evaluate the offerings of others.[11]

Self-Perception

In an unregulated profession, self-perception is crucially important because it is the most common test for entrance into the field. As aspiring professionals we decide when our knowledge and skill level is sufficient for us to adequately meet our responsibilities to clients, to genealogy as an intellectual discipline and a profession, and to the public at large. Should we be uncertain about self-evaluation, we can seek an impartial outside assessment through any of the credentialing programs.

Once we deem ourselves qualified to undertake work for others, we are judged as professionals. Whether we earn a significant part of our living through this enterprise is irrelevant. The work of an unpaid volunteer can be—and should be—totally professional. How we are judged will depend on how well we have prepared ourselves before we enter the field and how well we stay current with developments in both scholarship and resources.

Entry into the professional community also requires a major adjustment in self-perception. Both the skilled avocational genealogist and the professional who serves the public are expected to demonstrate high levels of ethics and knowledge, but a significant difference exists in the particulars of their work. The avocational genealogist enjoys the luxury of working at a self-defined pace. The professional must carry out a specific assignment within the time and financial limits set by the client or employer. It is not enough for the research, analysis, and writing to be performed *well*. It must also be performed with the greatest degree of *efficiency* possible in both time and cost. And it must adhere to the dictates of the person or agency who funds the project—while still meeting the field's own standards of acceptability.

Summary Concepts

For success, the professional genealogist is expected to exhibit the characteristics of any professional. In sum: a mastery of a body of knowledge, expertise in applying it, a reasonable degree of business acumen, a commitment to intellectual growth, conformity to accepted conventions, observance of peer-enforced standards of work and conduct, membership in professional organizations, and pursuit of the professional credentials that represent the field.

NOTES

1. Elizabeth Shown Mills, CG, CGL, FASG, "Professionalism and Fees: BCG Survey Results," *OnBoard* 3 (January 1997): 1–4. *OnBoard* is the educational newsletter of the Board for Certification of Genealogists. For complete results of this survey, see also Mills, "Client

Assignments—Quality and Quantity: BCG Survey Results," *OnBoard* 3 (September 1997): 17–20; and Mills, "Equipping Ourselves for Quality Service: Physical Plant and Continuing Education—BCG Survey Results," *OnBoard* 3 (May 1997): 9–10, 14.

2. The most explicit and up-to-date description of these standards can be found in *The BCG Genealogical Standards Manual* (Orem, Utah: Ancestry Publishing and The Board for Certification of Genealogists, 2000).

3. Elizabeth Shown Mills, *Evidence! Citation & Analysis for the Family Historian* (Baltimore: Genealogical Publishing Co., 1997).

4. For more on this complex subject, see A. F. Pollard, "New Year's Day and Leap Year in English History," *English Historical Review* 55 (1940): 177–93; C. R. Cheney, *Handbook of Dates for Students of English History* (London: Royal Historical Society, 1978); William Thorndale, AG, CG, "The Julian Calendar: New Year's Day and the Julian Calendar," *Teaching Genealogy* 4 (November 1988): 1–8; and William Dollarhide, "It's about Time: Calendars and Genealogical Dates," *Genealogy Bulletin* 15 (March/April 1999): 1, 6–13.

5. The de facto standard for guidance with all major numbering systems is Joan Ferris Curran, CG; Madilyn Coen Crane; and John H. Wray, Ph.D., CG, *Numbering Your Genealogy: Basic Systems, Complex Families, and International Kin,* National Genealogical Society Special Publication no. 64 (Arlington: NGS, 2000), which is an expanded edition of Curran's bestselling *Numbering Your Genealogy: Sound and Simple Systems* (Arlington: NGS, 1992).

Useful specifically for the *Register* System is Margaret F. Costello and Jane Fletcher Fiske, FASG, *Guidelines for Genealogical Writing: Style Guide for The New England Historical and Genealogical Register with Suggestions for Genealogical Books* (Boston: New England Historic Genealogical Society, 1990). Also see Thomas Kozachek, *Guidelines for Authors of Compiled Genealogies* (Boston: Newbury Street Press, 1998); and Donn Devine, J.D., CG, CGI, "Numbering People in Pedigrees and Genealogies," *Ancestry Newsletter* 4 (January–February 1986): 1–4.

6. The American Society of Genealogists (ASG) is not a membership organization. Created by Jacobus and colleagues who adhered to his high standards, it is the field's honorary association of genealogical scholars, tapped for the quality and breadth of their published works. Its roll of fellows, who are elected for life, is at all times limited to a maximum of fifty active genealogists worldwide.

7. Most notably these are, in alphabetical order, *The Genealogist* (published by ASG), the *National Genealogical Society [NGS] Quarterly,* the *New England Historical and Genealogical Register,* the *New York Genealogical and Biographical Record,* and the *Virginia Genealogist.*

8. Particularly see Donald Lines Jacobus, FASG, *Genealogy as Pastime and Profession* (1930; 2d rev. edition, Baltimore: Genealogical Publishing Co., 1968); Milton Rubincam, CG, FASG, ed., *Genealogical Research: Methods and Sources,* vol. 1 (1960; rev. edition, Washington: American Society of Genealogists, 1980); Kenn Stryker-Rodda, Ph.D., FASG, ed., *Genealogical Research: Methods and Sources,* vol. 2 (1971; rev. edition, Washington: American Society of Genealogists, 1983); and Rubincam, *Pitfalls in Genealogical Research* (Salt Lake City: Ancestry, 1987).

9. In addition to the more recent *Evidence!* by Mills and her sequel, "Working with Historical Evidence: Genealogical Principles and Standards," *NGS Quarterly* 87 (September 1999): 165–84, several classic volumes explore these themes. Val D. Greenwood, AG, *The Researcher's Guide to American Genealogy,* 3d edition (Baltimore: Genealogical Publishing Co., 2000), has been kept up-to-date by its author; and Noel C. Stevenson, J.D., FASG, *Genealogical Evidence: A Guide to the Standards of Proof Relating to Pedigrees, Ancestry, Heirship and Family History,* rev. edition (Laguna Hills, Calif.: Aegean Park Press, 1989) is still current. Long the standard guide to documentation but now considerably out-of-date, is Richard S. Lackey, CG, FASG, *Cite Your Sources: A Manual for Documenting Family Histories and Genealogical Records* (1980; reprint, Jackson, Mississippi: University Press of Mississippi, n.d.). For evidence in general and Canada specifically, see also Brenda Dougall Merriman, CGRS, CGL, *About Genealogical Standards of Evidence: A Guide for Genealogists* (Toronto: Ontario Genealogical Society, 1997).

10. "Imanishi-Kari Cleared, HHS Panel Rejects Misconduct Charges," *Chemistry and Engineering News* 74 (6 July 1996): 6. As reported in this journal of the American Chemical Society, a U.S. Department of Health and Human Services adjudication panel cleared Dr. Thereza Imanishi-Kari of charges that her published misrepresentation of research results

A genealogist should not be opinionated, but should always keep an open mind and be ready to admit, on occasion, that his first conclusion was a mistaken one. Those who fear that an admission of error will damage their professional reputations are usually those whose reputations as genealogists will not suffer much from any admission. Adherence to truth is more important than professional pride.

—Donald Lines Jacobus, FASG[12]

DEFINING

PROFESSIONALISM

constituted misconduct. Rather, the panel held that no intent to deceive had been proved and that errors in the paper were due to "sloppiness in recording and maintaining data" and to "carelessness in writing and editing the paper" by all participants in the publication—including coauthors, journal reviewers, and editors.

11. Board for Certification of Genealogists, *BCG Genealogical Standards Manual*, previously cited.

12. Jacobus, *Genealogy as Pastime and Profession,* 44.

13. Sir Winston Churchill (1874–1965), British statesman and writer, quoted in Ted Goodman, ed., *The Forbes Book of Business Quotations: 14,173 Thoughts on the Business of Life* (New York: Black Dog & Leventhall Publishers, 1997), 720.

The price of greatness is responsibility.

—*Winston Churchill[13]*

FURTHER STUDY

Barzun, Jacques, and Henry F. Graff. *The Modern Researcher.* 5th edition. Fort Worth, Texas: Harcourt, Brace Jovanovich College Publishers, 1992. (A text and reference on methodology for historians, advocating research standards almost as rigorous as those of genealogy.)

Devine, Donn. "Are Earnings the Mark of the Professional?" *Association of Professional Genealogists [APG] Quarterly* 8 (December 1993): 91–92.

Durye, Pierre. *Genealogy: An Introduction to Continental Concepts.* 4th edition. Translated from the French by Wilson Ober Clough. New Orleans: Polyanthos, 1977.

Mills, Elizabeth Shown. "Making a Living at Genealogy: Analyzing Our Problems and Our Options." *APG Quarterly* 7 (December 92): 87–92. Offers a self-analysis that spotlights numerous aspects of professionalism.

———, and Ingalls, Kay Germain, CGRS. "Have Checkbook—Am a Professional." *OnBoard* 2 (September 1996): 17–18.

Rising, Marsha Hoffman, CG, CGL, FASG. "Is There Such a Thing as a Professional Hobby?" *APG Quarterly* 8 (March 1993): 3–6.

———. "Genealogists: Professional vs. Hobbyist?" *APG Quarterly* 10 (December 1995): 23–24.

Wyett, Marcia K., CGRS. "From Hobbyist to Professional." *APG Quarterly* 10 (December 1995): 121–22; and 11 (March 1996): 18–19.

2

**EDUCATIONAL
PREPARATION**

EDUCATIONAL
PREPARATION

Keynotes

Keynotes (cont.)

Educational Preparation

by Claire Mire Bettag, CGRS

"The professional genealogist should possess certain natural aptitudes, sharpened by experience. He should be painstaking, thorough, and accurate. He should be able to weigh evidence; to assemble in logical order a host of details; to construct hypotheses and test them. He needs the detective instinct, and experience must have taught him which of several clues is most likely to lead him to his object. He needs imagination, toned down by long training, and directed by sound reasoning. Especially he needs an excellent memory. Granted this natural equipment, *much study and special knowledge are essential.*"[1]

The words are those of the late and eminent genealogist Donald Lines Jacobus, FASG. The emphasis is added. Jacobus points to the importance of strong natural talents. But equally essential are *long training, much study,* and *special knowledge*—that is, education. It is our foundation in genealogy. As we gain experience, it deepens and strengthens our grasp of concepts and techniques. Indeed, rapidly changing technology and increasing competition make continuing education imperative. Whatever form it takes—formal instruction or independent study—ongoing education is basic to our effective conduct of professional genealogical research.

Leaders of the genealogical community have emphasized this theme for decades. Since 1940, the American Society of Genealogists has promoted education as a way to secure recognition for genealogy "as a serious scientific subject of research in the historical and social fields of learning."[2] The Board for Certification of Genealogists expects significant educational accomplishment of successful applicants, even though it prescribes no specific educational prerequisite. Internationally, genealogical credentials are commonly linked to educational coursework—a subject addressed in both this chapter and the next.

The seriousness with which we view and pursue educational opportunities is a hallmark of our profession. It will never be possible to know everything; but, as professionals, we owe it to ourselves and our prospective clients to continually study new methodologies, interpretations, resources, and technologies.

> The seriousness with which we view and pursue educational opportunities is a hallmark of our profession.

Setting Objectives

Genealogists enter the profession through many doors. Those who planned from the start to become researchers, who earned a degree in family history or genealogy, and who went on to become professionals are rare. Typically, by the time we decide to make a career in the field, we have had years of research experience; have participated in society activities at various levels; and have attended lectures, read widely, and otherwise taught ourselves. Because there is no standard approach, no uniform training, and no minimum requirement for professionals in family history, each person joins with a unique set of qualifications—and a unique set of gaps in education and experience. The decision to "go pro" marks a good time to take stock of both strengths and weaknesses—and to fashion a personal education plan with specific objectives. One approach is to

- begin with a frank assessment of our "professional preparedness."
- hammer out explicit goals, then identify gaps and weak points that might stand in the way of reaching those goals.
- define specific objectives—perhaps to hone certain research skills, to learn more about federal records, to study more extensively the historical background of our special area, to improve our report writing, or to sharpen our analytical abilities.
- develop a plan or methodology for accomplishing each objective—for example, taking courses; attending conferences, institutes, or seminars; reading professional and scholarly literature; or participating with colleagues in a variety of activities.
- set a timetable for completion of various phases of the plan—a certain number of months or even years.
- devise and schedule periodic evaluation procedures.

None of these steps needs to be complicated, but they should be specific. It helps to write them down.

Ideally, the elements of a sound professional-education plan should balance courses of formal instruction against a variety of self-education options. Regardless of format, our plan should encourage us to examine genealogical research techniques; probe the nature, use, and interpretation of records; and explore major repositories. Related studies can ground us in geographic and ethnic specialties; political, social, and family history; and other areas.

Evaluating Opportunities

Finding the best means to accomplish our objectives can present a challenge amid today's proliferation of opportunities. An abundance of educational options does not mean that all are equally worthwhile. One principle underlies all else: let *quality* drive the search.

Several key elements contribute to the total quality of a given program: qualifications of the instructors and authors, standards imposed by organizers, instructional methods used, admission prerequisites, and completion requirements, for example. A careful search can identify sound programs with high standards. Those that have stood the test of time are excellent choices, but new programs that meet recognized standards can be enriching experiences also. The following considerations are basic to evaluating our available options.

Presenters

Whether educational options are in the form of books, classes, distance-learning or online programs, lectures, tapes, or workshops, presenters should be qualified.

An abundance of educational options does not mean that all are equally worthwhile. One principle underlies all else: let *quality* drive the search.

> At the least, authors and teachers should have relevant credentials and experience *in the field of genealogy* and, often, in more specialized areas as well.

At the least, authors and teachers should have relevant credentials and experience *in the field of genealogy* and, often, in more specialized areas as well. Formal educational degrees and other types of earned recognition help demonstrate professional commitment; but experience is important. It distinguishes established genealogists from newcomers. It reflects the extent to which presenters have dealt with technical issues—both general and specialized. Consumers have a right to expect from teachers and authors a mastery of the subject, careful preparation, organized presentation, and a commitment to deliver what is promised.

Questions to ask: What are the presenters' credentials? Are they professional genealogists? Have they earned certification? If so, in what categories or areas? What academic degrees have they earned? Do their credentials relate to their offerings? How experienced are they? What general and specialized research have they done? What are their professional affiliations? Have they published? If so, what and where? How relevant are those publications to the present course of instruction—and how much scholarship do those publications demonstrate? Do their publishers require peer review prior to publication? Do those firms specialize in genealogy or are they general publishers that may not know the standards of our field? How much teaching have the presenters done? Are their presentations well prepared, organized, and clear? Are detailed handouts distributed? Do they deliver what they advertise?

Programs

Program descriptions need to be scrutinized. Unless promotional materials provide adequate information, we cannot be certain whether the program is right for us. Those with national or regional reputations usually advertise offerings in sufficient detail to allow an informed decision. If the outlines of the offerings are not sufficiently clear, it is best to investigate before registering.

Questions to ask: What specific topics will the program address? Does it meet my current interests or needs? Is it at the right level for me? Will I be in a large or small group setting? What is the instructional method—a lecture course, hands-on exercises, or practical problem-solving? Does it allow for interaction with the instructor? Is it an intensive course, or can I work at my own pace? Is it an on-site or independent-study option? Are there completion requirements? Will it present new material—or will it delve more deeply into familiar matters? Will it introduce innovative ways to consider information? If it does not address my area of interest directly, can I make use of the information or adapt it to my specialty? Is the program appropriately priced? Is the physical setting conducive to learning?

Program sponsors

The sponsor of an educational program may be a commercial enterprise, a genealogical or historical organization, a library or archive, a public institution, or even an individual. We should be sure the sponsor is a reliable and solvent entity. When a large establishment is involved, this is not usually an issue. More caution is in order when smaller or independent organizations, companies, or self-employed individuals offer courses or products.

Questions to ask: Is this a reliable institution? Will it deliver the product it is advertising? Has it established a reputation for sponsoring quality programs? How does it handle complaints? What is its policy regarding unsatisfactory products? If it is an academic forum, is it accredited by one of the regional accrediting agencies (Middle States, New England, North Central, Northwest, Southern, or Western Association of Colleges and Schools)?

Overall concerns

Before our moment of decision, we should do some energetic comparison shopping. Talking to organizers, teachers, and colleagues who have participated in various programs helps us compare reputations. We should weigh advantages and disadvantages *to us* of programs that are local versus regional or national, long versus short, general versus specialized, theoretical versus practical. Our best guide is clearsightedness about our own need, bearing in mind that there is no match for a high-quality program with both an academic and a professional orientation and a solid reputation. In the long term, it may be the wisest financial investment.

> There is no match for a high-quality program with both an academic and a professional orientation and a solid reputation.

U.S. Programs

No list can be exhaustive. Even if space allowed, programs sprout up and disappear too often to make a comprehensive list possible. For enduring value, this review focuses upon the most accessible, recognized, and stable programs with high-quality educational content. Within this framework, opportunities are divided into six broad categories: academic degree programs, academic credit programs, structured noncredit or certificate programs (not to be confused with actual certification), major conferences, other forums, and self-instruction. Contact information for each of the programs discussed below is readily available online.

Academic degree programs

Relatively few institutions offer academic credit in genealogy—thus, few people enter the profession through an academic route. At this writing, Brigham Young University in Provo, Utah, is the only institution awarding a full, regular degree in genealogy. Some schools allow students to tailor degree programs that emphasize genealogy or family history: Norwich University's Vermont College and the University of Alabama's External Degree Program are examples discussed below. Other programs exist that are similarly structured and express a willingness to work with students interested in obtaining a genealogy degree. If they do not report having awarded such a degree or have only an isolated case to offer, however, the effectiveness of their program in this field cannot be evaluated.

Genealogists who choose the self-structured degree programs may face special challenges belied by the seeming ease of the degree. Because the ultimate goal of

EDUCATIONAL
PREPARATION

BYU is unique in its commitment to genealogical education. Its curriculum in the field is the most comprehensive of all higher educational institututions in the United States.

every degree program is to provide a quality education in that field—not a sterile diploma—the success of any effort will depend heavily upon each student's own initiative. Few such programs have qualified genealogical instructors on their faculties. Those that choose instructors for genealogical students may have little or no familiarity with the standards that constitute sound genealogical teaching. Some invite students to select their own advisors via their contacts in the field, but students are often handicapped by the limits of their personal networks. In other cases, students fail to recognize that quality education requires study under many stringent teachers with widely varying fields of expertise. Consequently, they may limit their "independent" course work to only one or two mentors who grant them "free rein." Some programs have very minimal standards, routinely granting course credits and high grades for virtually anything students submit. Genealogists may obtain diplomas in this fashion; but if they do not choose a program well respected in the education field, they may find that their degree does not provide them the breadth and depth they need to live up to their potential or to public expectations.

Brigham Young University: Provo, Utah
BYU is unique in its commitment to genealogical education. Its curriculum in the field is the most comprehensive of all higher-education institutions in the U.S.—possibly worldwide—and it is the only American institution offering a four-year bachelor's degree in family history and genealogy. Its courses prepare students for professions in this field or for advanced study of archival administration and preservation, education, history, or library science. Requirements include classes in geography, history, paleography, research methodology, technological tools for genealogy, and writing family history. The comprehensive nature of the program makes it a desirable option for anyone wanting a traditional academic approach. Responding to alternative needs, BYU offers various other programs, including an on-site or home-study certificate program, described on pages 24–25.

Norwich University: Montpelier, Vermont
An innovative approach to earning an undergraduate or graduate degree in liberal studies, with a genealogy focus, is offered by NU's Vermont College. Through its Adult Degree Program, students collaborate with faculty mentors to tailor individual courses of study. A genealogy degree typically incorporates such cross-disciplinary studies as geography, genealogical sources and research methods, sociology, and writing—examining family origins within a broad historical and social context. The program's flexible and brief residency feature allows students to work closely with mentors through personal, electronic, and written contact, while completing academic requirements and independent projects off-site. Independent projects could include genealogical and historical study and research.

University of Alabama: Tuscaloosa, Alabama
As one of the nation's oldest research universities, UA also offers a flexible academic degree program designed to meet the needs of adult students. This alternative,

nonresidential approach, which the University's External Degree Program has conducted for more than a quarter century, allows students to pursue an inter-disciplinary degree with a special focus of their choice. Instead of a major, students complete thirty-two semester hours in an academic area of concentration—or "depth study"—and a senior project or thesis of twelve academic hours. (By way of example, genealogists might pursue a social-studies curriculum that embraces history, geography, economics, and women's studies, integrating these subjects with family history for learning contracts and senior projects.) One adult-learning seminar is the only residential requisite. The balance of the 128 semester hours needed for a B.A. or B.S. can be satisfied through transfer credits from other accredited institutions, independent study, on-campus attendance, out-of-class learning contracts, or prior-learning portfolios.

Academic credit programs

Still other schools offer academic credit but not degrees. Programs in this group assure us that they have met the standards of a fully accredited university. However, the inclusion of genealogical programs among their academic offerings is often the result of a particular faculty member's interest in the subject. There can be no assurance that a given program would continue should the teacher leave the school.

Gallaudet University: Washington, D.C.

A long-running, three-credit genealogy course at Gallaudet falls within the school's traditional academic program. Offered every two years, exclusively to students in the Honors Program, it is an introduction to methodology and sources of gene-alogical research. It emphasizes use of original source materials and documentation of family relationships. Team-taught by two education-department professors—both experienced genealogists and one of them certified—the course combines classroom discussion of techniques with hands-on assignments. Students are evaluated primarily on portfolios assembled for the course (including research reports, a three-generation family history, and a nine-generation chart) and a final examination. Because Gallaudet's student body is mostly from the deaf community, the curriculum includes the application of genetics and genealogical data in tracing such family characteristics as deafness, health problems, and physical traits. The course is taught in sign language.

James Madison University: Harrisonburg, Virginia

In the mid-1990s, a three-credit-hour academic course in genealogy evolved from a noncredit workshop that has been offered several times yearly since the 1980s. The program includes thirty-six hours of classroom study, plus written as-signments and hands-on research at a library and a Family History Center of The Church of Jesus Christ of Latter-day Saints. In addition to basic genealogical research, the course emphasizes holdings of regional repositories and resources on the Internet.

Still other schools offer academic credit but not degrees. Programs in this group assure us that each has met the standards of a fully accredited university.

University of Alabama: Tuscaloosa, Alabama
Family History and Biographical Research is a traditional, academic credit course for seniors and graduate students in UA's history department. Taught by a history professor who coedits a scholarly journal in genealogy, the course provides a firm grounding in principles of genealogical research and introduces students to the major record types. Particular emphasis is placed upon holdings of the National Archives and means of accessing them from a distance. Assignments include research conducted on site at courthouse record offices, university and public libraries, and LDS Family History Centers.

Structured noncredit or certificate programs

Most genealogical education comes not from traditional academia but from forums created by the professional community—conferences, home-study courses, institutes, seminars, and workshops—combined with independent study. Some are found in academic settings; others are available online or via teleconferencing. Most feature lectures or workshops. Some assign research projects and set completion requirements. Whether national or local, long or short, basic or advanced, on site or home study, each type has something to offer. Collectively, they emphasize fundamental genealogical concepts, advanced methodology, and professional issues. Without exception in the United States, institutions that grant certificates emphasize one point: the completion of a certificate program does not constitute professional certification. All recognize that a considerable distinction exists between classroom attendance and public assurance that a genealogist's actual work product exhibits a high level of competence.[3]

HOME-STUDY OPTIONS

Two well-known institutions offer the opportunity to earn a certificate through distance learning: Brigham Young University and the National Genealogical Society. While the first is billed as a less rigorous alternative to a degree program and the second is self-described as "basic," both merit consideration as training for the professional. Both present a structured and comprehensive approach to resources and methods that self-taught genealogists often lack. Additionally, they require students to investigate previously unexplored territory, broadening the educational experience. Both are built upon the framework of graded assignments.

Brigham Young University: Provo and Salt Lake City, Utah
As an alternative to its more rigorous academic degree track described on page 22, BYU offers a certificate program that can be completed through home study or at one of the university's two campuses. It targets fundamental genealogical training, with emphasis in a particular geographic area. To earn a certificate, students must complete eighteen semester hours of course effort—including such subject matter as family and law in American society, the history of specific geographic areas, paleography, and special genealogical topics. The curriculum is rigorous and demands substantial work. Throughout the program, students submit

Without exception in the United States, the completion of a certificate program does *not* constitute certification.

assignments for evaluation by instructors, and they arrange for proctored final examinations. The course is considered good preparation toward professional activity although its certificate of completion does not confer any credential.

National Genealogical Society: Arlington, Virginia

Since 1981, NGS has offered American Genealogy: A Basic Course—a highly acclaimed and accredited home-study program in sound genealogical research. One hallmark of the course is its mix of concept and practice. Step by step, it presents in considerable depth the fundamental principles of genealogical investigation; a practical assignment at each step requires students to put the principles to work. Sixteen progressive lessons teach students to find and interpret records; abstract documents; write proper citations; compile, analyze, and evaluate evidence; and maintain family records. Students work at their own pace—completing the readings, field research, written assignments, and tests one lesson at a time. Instructors evaluate student work, grade assignments, and offer written advice.

For a certificate of completion, students have eighteen months to finish all assignments and pass a self-administered final examination. (Extensions are granted for good cause.) The mix of theory, written reports, and "hands-on" research conducted in archives, courthouses, libraries, and elsewhere has proved to be particularly effective. Concurrently, an online Resource Center at the NGS website includes links to other sites that may help students complete the assignments.

The quality and reputation of the NGS course have earned it widespread endorsement. The Board for Certification of Genealogists lists it among educational opportunities that help prepare for the certification exam. Samford University's Institute of Genealogy and Historical Research also accepts completion of this course as a fulfillment of the prerequisite for enrollment in its advanced methodology track. Both NGS and its course are formally accredited by the Accrediting Commission of the Distance Education and Training Council, a nationally recognized agency. NGS also offers an online course, described on page 31 of this chapter.

> The quality and reputation of the NGS course have earned it widespread endorsement. Both NGS and its course are formally accredited.

INSTITUTES

Four programs are priority choices for those who consider genealogy as a profession. Two are long-established national forums that have distinguished themselves for decades—intensive, full-week courses whose teachers rank among the nation's best-known authorities. Two are institutes under the auspices of major societies, with established track records and well-known presenters. Other institutes are offered, intermittently, by private individuals or local societies. While this chapter focuses upon those with the longest and most consistent offerings, we certainly should consider all that seem feasible, applying the guidelines covered on pages 19–20.

National Institute on Genealogical Research
National Archives, Washington, D.C.

Since 1950, NIGR has led the movement to encourage high research standards through professional education. Its intensive program focuses on material in federal repositories. Held at the National Archives for a full week each July, the institute

EDUCATIONAL
PREPARATION

NIGR has long enjoyed distinction for its comprehensive curriculum, in-depth treatment of subjects, and excellent faculty.

draws participants nationwide, some for the second or third time. Unlike other programs, it is designed exclusively for experienced archivists, genealogists, historians, and librarians who are already well schooled in research techniques. Limited enrollment (about forty participants) gives attendees unusual access to leading genealogical authorities and National Archives staff members who teach the courses. NIGR has long enjoyed distinction for its comprehensive curriculum, in-depth treatment of subjects, and excellent faculty. Its governing board consists of the American Society of Genealogists, the Association of Professional Genealogists, the Board for Certification of Genealogists, the Federation of Genealogical Societies, the National Genealogical Society, and the NIGR Alumni Association—with strong support from the Archives itself.

Focusing upon record content rather than research methodology, the classes offer thorough treatment of census, land, military, and passenger arrival records. More specialized sessions examine less frequently used resources—captured German and Confederate documents, cartographic archives, Freedman's Savings and Trust Company records, French spoilation cases, pre-federal materials, seamen's protection certificates, State Department files, and wartime-damage claims, for example—with varying subject matter in different years. While other courses can teach about record holdings and research at the Archives, this institute is unique in that the records are literally down the hall from the lectures. The ability to access records immediately after they are discussed greatly enhances the learning experience—although assignments are not part of the course. A special tour also gives participants a glimpse of the behind-the-scenes workings of the archives. Limited financial assistance is available.

Institute of Genealogy and Historical Research
Samford University, Birmingham, Alabama

Since 1964, Samford University has offered an intensive, week-long, multilevel instructional program at its main campus in Birmingham, Alabama—one that now includes study abroad. Also since its inception, the institute has been cosponsored by the Board for Certification of Genealogists. Each year in the month of June, IGHR's nationally recognized lecturers (including several fellows of the American Society of Genealogists) teach a full range of genealogical and historical research skills and methods. Small classes ensure maximum student participation and allow for consultation between instructors and students. Some courses feature hands-on workshops and student assignments. Some—but not all—carry academic credit, and all offer continuing-education units for teachers who attend. Seven basic tracks—with eighteen to twenty-one sessions each—move students from introductory to advanced to professional levels, with several specialty options.

- *Techniques and Technology*—an introduction to research principles and online resources, with hands-on, directed courthouse and library research.

- *Library and Archival Resources*—a lecture course of intense instruction on the location and nature of church, court, immigration, military, naturalization, and similar records.

- *Southern Genealogy*—a course that rotates annually between two curricula: the older (eastern) Southern states and the newer (more western) Southern states. Emphasis is upon resources and repositories.

- *Advanced Methodology*—a combination lecture-workshop course that concentrates on problem-solving techniques; the in-depth analysis, correlation, and interpretation of evidence; and the use of law and government-document libraries. A concise but intense examination of the underpinnings of the American legal system and an extended workshop devoted to the critical analysis of evidence constitute two of the more exigent sessions on the agenda. Enrollment prerequisites exist.

- *Professional Genealogy*—a track that alternates annually between two subject areas. One examines practical and specialized issues relating to careers in genealogy—for example, managing clients; conducting forensic, genetic, and other specialized types of research; and documenting work for tax purposes. The second focuses intensely upon genealogical writing of all types. Instructors include several authors of chapters within this book.

- *Specialty Research*—a program that examines a different ethnic or resource area each year—for example, military records, Native American or German research, U.S. migration, or forensic genealogy.

- *British Research*—a campus course that prepares students for participation in the site-based British Institute described below. Students are instructed in the location and nature of records and methodology for using them, as well as the type of Stateside research that must precede a successful trip abroad. Individual problem-solving consultations are also scheduled.

The IGHR British Institute, a special feature since 1986, offers three weeks of on-site study in Great Britain. Each year, the course treats a different part of the Isles. The advance-preparation track takes place during the regular IGHR—a full year prior to the tour, so that students may better prepare themselves for effective research abroad by identifying and closing gaps in their American study. (While the on-campus instruction is not required, it is strongly recommended.) The three-week study tour is based at Samford University's London Center. The first two weeks offer combined lectures and guided research; the third week is devoted to independent investigations, complemented by one-on-one consultations.

As a long-standing role model, the IGHR is often called the dean of American genealogical institutes. Students in the beginning course commonly return for the more advanced studies, completing in several years a comprehensive and systematic genealogical training program. Registrants may choose to live on campus or in nearby hotels. Limited financial assistance may be available.

The IGHR is often called the dean of American genealogical institutes.

Genealogical Institute of Mid-America
Springfield, Illinois
Since 1994, GIMA has sponsored an intensive, four-day program of instruction by experienced teachers. Sponsored jointly by the Illinois State Genealogical Society and the University of Illinois at Springfield, the institute combines classroom

**EDUCATIONAL
PREPARATION**

GIMA's beginning track is
virtually unique among today's institute offerings.

lectures with hands-on assignments and field trips. Each year's core offering is
divided into two sections: one for students with no formal training in genealogy,
and another for those who have mastered basic genealogical record-keeping skills
and terminology. (GIMA's beginning track is virtually unique among today's
institute offerings.) Other courses have included military records, Eastern U.S.
sources, and research in the British Isles. Evening sessions and optional general
assemblies focus on such special-interest topics as copyright law and genealogy on
the Internet. Small classes allow participants to interact with well known faculty.

Salt Lake Institute of Genealogy
Salt Lake City, Utah
Launched in 1996 by the Utah Genealogical Association, SLIG is scheduled each
January. The week-long program features instruction by recognized genealogical
educators, hands-on research exercises by students, feedback to help attendees
assess their progress, and convenient access to Salt Lake City's Family History
Library. Limited registration permits student-teacher interaction, and efforts are
made to ensure similar student levels in each class. Students apply to attend one
of eight or so courses each year, in which enrollment is limited to thirty students
per class. The curriculum varies somewhat from year to year but generally covers
the following:

- *Intermediate U.S. Research*—with a focus on records relating to the colonial
  and early-federal periods.
- *U.S. Regional Research*—such as Southern or New England states—with
  emphasis on resources, ethnic groups, migration patterns, and special research
  techniques.
- *European Research*—such as Germanic, Scandinavian, or Eastern European.
- *British Research*—English, Irish, Scottish, or Welsh.
- *Special Topics*—such as use of immigration resources, advanced research
  methodology, or technological tools for family-history research.
- *Professional Topics*—such as genealogical librarianship, professional research,
  teaching, or writing.

Most classes are aimed at the intermediate-level student. Optional sessions include
orientation to the Family History Library and use of the library's catalog.

LONG-TERM PROGRAMS

Brigham Young University–Family History Certificate Program
Provo and Salt Lake City, Utah
See HOME-STUDY OPTIONS, page 24.

University of Washington–Educational Outreach Program
Seattle, Washington
Since 1991, the University of Washington has offered the comprehensive three-

course, nine-month Certificate Program in Genealogy and Family History that, the sponsors caution, should not be confused with certification. Designed by an advisory board of scholars, archivists, and active genealogists, the program is approved by the University of Washington–Seattle's History Department and the Graduate School of Library and Information Science. It is team-taught by a well-known professional genealogist and a social historian. Classes meet weekly for three terms of ten sessions each—the principal teaching modes being assignments, discussions, field trips, and lectures. Emphasis is on the use of genealogical technique and research to place the family in a broader social context.

To be admitted, applicants must have two years of college or comparable educational training that demonstrates ability to perform college-level academic work. They must also submit written evidence of interest in genealogy and a commitment to complete a family-history project. Participants must complete each course to proceed to the next term. Students finishing the course receive a certificate and nine continuing-education units. The program does not award either academic credit or certification. Graduates may join an advanced genealogy course each fall that focuses on library-research skills, problem solving, and selected readings in social history.

University of Wisconsin–Educational Teleconference Network
Madison, Wisconsin

Since 1976, the extension program of the University of Wisconsin has offered a beginning and an advanced noncredit, noncertificate lecture course in genealogy, taught by a nationally known genealogist. Teleconferencing technology brings this quality course into remote areas of the state where other programs are not available. Courses originate on the Madison campus, where students can attend the lectures on site. Through the Educational Teleconference Network (ETN), the courses are connected by phone technology to one location in every county in the state, where registrants assemble to listen to the lecture, ask questions, and participate in discussion. Offered every third semester in a five-part series, each course meets weekly. The introductory course focuses on basic research in American sources, especially those in the eastern United States and Wisconsin. The advanced course covers access to records, more sophisticated research techniques, problem solving, and other skills.

> Teleconferencing technology brings this quality course into remote areas of the state where other programs are not available.

ONLINE COURSES

"Televersities" or "virtual universities" of varying quality, format, and endurance are mushrooming on the World Wide Web. A few of these instructional programs are formally structured—with assignments, lesson outlines, and prescribed reading material posted online. Communication between students and instructors is generally asynchronous, with assignments turned in and evaluations received via e-mail. These courses are usually fee-based and may be sponsored by an established organization or school. Other online options exist in the form of tutorials, lesson plans, how-to tips for beginners, and a variety of other instructional approaches.

EDUCATIONAL
PREPARATION

Assuming that quality, standards, and commitment to long-term service are not compromised, Web-based classes can be a valuable innovation.

Some are free of charge—mostly sponsored by commercial entities, institutions, and individuals.

Assuming that quality, standards, and commitment to long-term service are not compromised, Web-based classes can be a valuable innovation (particularly for those living in relatively remote areas). Before investing in this type of program, we would want to appraise them closely—using the same criteria that apply to other coursework—as well as the reputation of the program within academia in general. Addressing the latter subject as part of an examination of the problems and prospects of distance education, a leading American educator writes in the Winter 1999 *National Forum*:

> Virtual universities may also have a difficult time overcoming the perception that their undergraduate degrees are not as good as those from traditional institutions, especially since regional accrediting agencies are not rushing to certify them. We know there is a "value hierarchy" for degrees, and the annual ratings of institutions by news magazines keep this hierarchy in the public eye. Although it is possible to get a good education—or a poor one—at any institution, the perception of value largely drives the demand.[4]

We would particularly want to consider the *genealogical* credentials and experience of the instructor—indeed, we should attempt to confirm those credentials, given that online education is still an unregulated one. (A survey of online educational "opportunities" at the time of this writing reveals distinct problems of inflated credentials and claimed or implied genealogical certification/accreditation that the instructor does not actually possess.) We should also expect a detailed course description and syllabus—and then examine the kind of teaching method used (whether it requires work to be submitted and offers interaction with, and/or evaluation by, an instructor). Also important is whether the course is only a tutorial with online prompts or whether students have some modicum of access to a teacher who provides criticisms, evaluations, and suggestions. We might also watch for reviews of these courses in recognized publications.

Two leaders in online courses are Bellevue Community College and the National Genealogical Society.

Bellevue Community College
Bellevue, Washington

This college's program may well be genealogy's longest-running online program with a U.S.-based academic affiliation. At this writing, it offers three eight-week courses—an introduction to online genealogy for beginners (which teaches some mechanics of organizing data, software options, online sources of genealogical data), an intermediate course (in which lessons focus on the use of charts, maps, genealogical software, and graphics, along with some National Archives material), and U.S. genealogy (which explores seven common types of records in greater depth). Assignments include up to four hours of homework and reading each week. The college's website offers a week-by-week syllabus and information about the course's instructor, assignments, discussion forums, and general procedures.

All classes use beginner- and/or intermediate-level textbooks, as well as web-page links, e-mail, and asynchronous conferences with the instructor. Given that not one of the course descriptions or outlines mentions instruction in source citation or evidence analysis, the content may be too basic for individuals at the point of considering a professional career in genealogy; but the program's history suggests that its offerings may continue to expand.

National Genealogical Society—Education Department
Arlington, Virginia

NGS's six-lesson, online course is also a very basic introduction—much more so than the society's classic correspondence course. The focus is on sources (particularly those for birth, death, and marriage information) and fundamental methodology (which does include proper recording of genealogical information and citation of sources). Lessons include links to relevant websites. Quizzes are graded electronically, but students have e-mail access to an instructor for consultation. Those who complete the course receive a discount coupon for the more comprehensive NGS home-study course, described on page 25.

Major conferences

Attendees at the annual national conferences find a smorgasbord of educational opportunities that commonly includes 100 to 200 hour-length presentations. Lectures by nationally known speakers, as well as regional experts, are presented in thematic tracks. In contrast to the institute model, attendees do not have to enroll in a single track but can, each hour, pick from among all options. While the full-course structure of the institutes best ensures that gaps will be closed in our body of knowledge, the free-choice structure of the conferences allows us to tailor our education to our own preferences. Some formal lectures present advanced-level instruction, and audiences are frequently quite large. In other sessions, smaller attendance or looser structure allows lively interaction between attendees and presenters. Exhibit halls offer dozens to hundreds of vendor booths, providing an opportunity to examine books, maps, software, and other products. Major software producers also conduct classes, with hands-on instruction in the use of their products. Local repositories usually host special research opportunities.

Conferences truly provide *continuing* education because of two adjunct offerings: syllabi and audiotapes. Sponsors typically provide a bound publication to which lecturers submit up to four pages of essential data relating to their presentations. Distribution is designed for actual registrants, but nonattendees can order photo-copies of selected pages from libraries that collect syllabi for patron use.[5] Planners also arrange for the services of a professional audiotaping firm, and most lecturers permit recording. The reasonably priced tapes are a boon for conference-goers who wish they could attend multiple sessions in the same time slot—and they are a major source of education for genealogists who cannot attend but realize their need for advanced-level instruction. (See AUDIOTAPES, page 34.)

While the full-course structure of the institutes best ensures that gaps will be closed in our body of knowledge, the free-choice structure of the conferences allows us to tailor our education to our own preferences.

EDUCATIONAL
PREPARATION

The Board for Certification
of Genealogists, at every
major conference, conducts
a workshop that is excellent
training, whether or not one
foresees certification.

National conferences also reach out to professionals. Specially planned pre-conference programs for genealogical librarians and professional researchers are scheduled in conjunction with some conferences. The Association of Professional Genealogists regularly hosts roundtables and mini-conferences that focus on matters of business and ethics. The Board for Certification of Genealogists, at every major conference, conducts a certification workshop that is excellent training whether or not one foresees certification. Both groups—as do the Genealogical Speakers Guild and the International Society of Family History Writers and Editors—sponsor lectures. Not least among the many benefits of the national-conference experience are collegiality, the chance to renew and expand professional contacts, and the general opportunity to keep abreast of developments in the field. The major conference offerings include the four programs discussed below.

Brigham Young University: Provo, Utah
In the first full week of every August, BYU sponsors a genealogy and family history conference on its main campus. Courses at both beginning and advanced levels are offered to several hundred attendees. Topics cover a broad range and include research methodology, research in U.S. and international regions, writing family history, using technological tools, reading early handwriting, and many others. The BYU conference, unlike the others discussed in this section, does not tape its sessions for public distribution.

Federation of Genealogical Societies
In late summer or early fall for the past quarter-century, in one or another major American city, the FGS conference attracts some 1,500–2,000 attendees with a well-rounded, four-day program of national scope, offering more than one hundred sessions. Given its nature as an umbrella organization for local or specialized societies, FGS devotes its first day to society-management workshops. Aside from this distinctive feature, its topics and presenters display the same scope and quality as those of the larger NGS conference, described below.

GENTECH
As a national, educational, all-volunteer, and nonprofit group, GENTECH promotes effective, responsible use of technology in family-history research. Its annual conferences, held since 1992, feature presenters who combine genealogical and technological skills—along with laboratory sessions, software exhibitors, online-services demonstrations, user-group meetings, and similar activities. The continuing growth of technological resources serving the genealogical community has enhanced the popularity and value of this conference, which also rotates its site annually.

National Genealogical Society
Highly recommended for professional genealogists, NGS's annual conference has, for two decades, brought quality genealogical education to all parts of the United States. Offering 175–200 sessions over four days each spring, the conference

attracts some 2,000 participants. True to its nature as an individual membership organization, NGS offers instruction on many ethnic groups and such wide-ranging topics as genetics, land studies, migration patterns, religious resources, research methodology, and technological tools. Each NGS national conference includes regional studies of the area where the conference is held, and the society's supplemental program of regional mini-conferences brings national topics and speakers to local areas.

Other forums

Wide-ranging but less publicized opportunities exist throughout the United States. Lecture series, seminars, workshops, or other programs sponsored by cultural or educational institutions, ethnic groups, genealogical and historical societies, LDS Family History Centers, local or regional archives, libraries, and other community organizations provide a wealth of resources. As professional genealogists, we view these localized and specialized programs as opportunities to participate as planners, lecturers, and teachers—not just as attendees or students. Many genealogists have started professional work by teaching basic courses locally. It's a good way to broaden our scope, refine our thought processes, and build name recognition. A select number of larger programs in this group are discussed below.

Brigham Young University, Campus Education Week
Provo, Utah
Each August, BYU sponsors a week of concentrated adult-education programs at its main campus. More than a thousand noncredit classes are offered in many fields—including a number of genealogy sessions. Such topics as research methods, technological tools for genealogy, and writing family history are mainstays.

National Archives and Records Administration Workshops
Washington, D.C., and regional sites
Through its capital-area and regional facilities, the National Archives system sponsors many genealogy workshops annually. Some programs provide a basic introduction to family history. Others are specialized classes for experienced researchers who are beginning to work with federal records. Offerings in the D.C. area (held at the Pennsylvania Avenue building) are commonly two- to three-hour sessions presented by staff archivists or professional genealogists from the District or its surroundings. Those in the regions are independently sponsored, often in collaboration with genealogical groups, and are frequently full-day programs. For specifics about the National Archives offerings closest to us, we should contact whichever facility serves our area.

New England Historic Genealogical Society
Boston and other sites
The Boston-based NEHGS, the oldest genealogical society in the United States,

> As professional genealogists, we view the localized and specialized programs as opportunities to participate as planners, lecturers, and teachers.

offers richly varied instruction through conferences, courses, seminars, and tours. Genealogy 101 at 101 Newbury Street, an intensive, four-week course held twice a year, trains beginners in research techniques and organization. A summer conference is held annually in the New England region. A two-day program typically includes lectures about immigration and settlement, regional repositories and records, and research techniques. Additional one- and two-day conferences, including one annually on the West Coast, are held throughout the year. Special one-week programs—intensive seminars, annual research tours, and heritage tours (including excursions to England and Canada)—all feature lectures and consultations.

Smithsonian Institution's "Campus on the Mall"
Washington, D.C.

The D.C.-based Smithsonian Resident Associates' Campus on the Mall program sponsors occasional genealogy courses for capital-area residents. In a series of six to eight weekly sessions, generally presented collaboratively with other genealogical groups, professional genealogists teach basic techniques and methods or otherwise address a broad range of genealogical topics. Course content, focus, and instructors change for each series.

Self-instruction

As in all professions, excellence requires a constant effort to learn from what our colleagues are writing and saying—more generally, to keep abreast of rapid substantive and technical developments in the field. Listening to educational audiotapes, reading current literature, networking with other professionals, and volunteering for society initiatives are all important ways to advance our growth.

AUDIOTAPES

A rich source of informal education is the body of audiotaped lectures generated by major genealogical conferences since the mid-1980s. A number of libraries in the United States maintain large but selective collections. A far more complete set, numbering in the thousands, is available from the longtime conference taper, Repeat Performance of Hobart, Indiana. At modest costs, RP's catalog offers not only its own products but also those of its predecessor on the conference scene, Triad (although many lecturers taped by Triad in the mid- to late 1980s do not authorize distribution of their now-outdated presentations).

Of particular instructional value is the Skillbuilding Series, with learning packets sponsored by the Board for Certification of Genealogists at two major conferences in 1996 and 1999. Each integrated series, composed of twenty or so lecture tapes by prominent certified professionals, represents essentially a course of advanced training in genealogical methodology. Each presentation, accompanied by the lecturer's handout materials and key visual aids, is available from Repeat Performance.

As in all professions, excellence requires a constant effort to learn from what our colleagues are writing and saying.

PEER REVIEW

An extremely valuable mechanism in the self-teaching process is the submission of written materials for professional evaluation and detailed feedback. Too few of us voluntarily submit our work to a critiquing process when it is not prescribed, but a growing number of those who apply for certification cite the opportunity for peer review as their motive. Some major journals, such as the *National Genealogical Society Quarterly,* provide professional critiques of all incoming manuscripts that show publication potential—and some more specialized journals of quality reputation, such as the *New York Genealogical and Biographical Record* and the *Virginia Genealogist,* do so on occasion. Anticipation of the imposed critique usually sharpens our research and writing efforts. The ensuing feedback enhances the text and contributes to our educational development.

PRINTED MATERIALS

Journals, particularly those with high editorial standards, are invaluable resources. Reading essays, case studies, family histories, research reports, and other articles in such scholarly periodicals as the *National Genealogical Society Quarterly;* the *New England Historical and Genealogical Register; The American Genealogist (TAG);* and the once-private *The Genealogist (TG),* which was assumed in 1997 by the American Society of Genealogists, exposes us to quality work and new insights. Reading back issues of these journals, whose material virtually never goes out of date, is equally educational. Other publications, such as *Ancestry* magazine, the *Forum* (news magazine of the Federation of Genealogical Societies), the *NGS Newsmagazine,* the New England Historic Genealogical's Society's *New England Ancestors,* and *OnBoard* (newsletter of the Board for Certification of Genealogists), keep us informed about what is going on in the genealogical arena. Subscriptions to at least some of these should be a part of every professional's educational budget.

An immense quantity of published monographs is accessible. Like periodicals, they vary widely in quality. Chapter 4 offers sound guidance for building our home library or pursuing our education at other libraries.

PROFESSIONAL ASSOCIATIONS

Ours is a field in which many practitioners keenly feel a sense of isolation—we may even be the only professional genealogist in our community. Opportunities to meet with other practitioners and discuss issues of concern are much too limited. Two professional organizations offering excellent forums through which we can learn from colleagues and stay abreast of developments in the genealogical world are those commonly known by their acronyms, APG and GSG.

Association of Professional Genealogists

An international membership body formed in 1979, APG offers a quarterly periodical that treats a wide variety of professional concerns and invites dialogue. Indeed, it is without counterpart in the field of genealogy. The association cosponsors many programs of educational value, and its local chapters conduct practical and educational activities and discussions. Its membership is international.

Reading essays, case studies, family histories, research reports, and other articles in scholarly journals exposes us to quality work and new insights.

**EDUCATIONAL
PREPARATION**

Many disciplines contribute to genealogical excellence. We can find considerable satisfaction in developing complementary skills from them.

Genealogical Speakers Guild
Organized in 1991, the guild focuses specifically upon the concerns of genealogical lecturing. Through its quarterly newsletter, *Speak!,* through the sessions that it sponsors at major conferences, and through its online list-serve, guild members help each other hone delivery skills, draft successful proposals for slots on conference programs, execute appropriate contracts with societies that sponsor our presentations, prepare quality audiovisuals, and otherwise develop our potential for profitably and effectively sharing what we have learned.

RELATED INSTRUCTION
Many other disciplines contribute to genealogical excellence. Cartography, genetics, geography, heraldry, languages, law, paleography, writing, and of course history—social, political, and economic—are among the most common. Adequate training in all these related fields will not normally be found in the genealogical educational programs reviewed in this chapter. To develop the skills needed to probe other specialties, we may be able to find convenient academic courses or we may have to put together a bibliography and undertake a self-tutoring program.

We might consider here just one problem common to many genealogists: reading old records, particularly those in languages not native to us. The first solution that comes to mind might be to hire someone with the expertise to transcribe and translate the documents. But we can find considerable satisfaction in developing complementary skills of this type, through the study of languages and paleography. For some areas, formal programs of instruction exist. For others, we must rely upon self-directed study. Five examples illustrate the range of options:

English paleography
No formal course is conveniently available internationally, but two excellent guides exist for the motivated:

- Dawson and Kennedy-Skipton's manual, *Elizabethan Handwriting: 1500–1650,* introduces various forms of early English handwriting through fifty documents taken from the archives of the Folger Shakespeare Library, Washington, D.C. Each specimen is accompanied by a transcript and brief notes that discuss the nuances and styles adopted by each writer. The antiquated forms that genealogists confront in dealing with English texts from this period are well illustrated.[6]

- A 1993 article in *Genealogical Journal,* "Interpreting the Symbols and Abbreviations in 16th and 17th-Century English Documents," is an excellent guide to the most crucial points. Author Ronald A. Hill, an American academic who specializes in English genealogical research, provides examples reproduced from English probate and chancery-court proceedings. Hill illustrates the plethora of contractions, abbreviations, and medieval symbols used by scribes to save time and space. Included are examples of the interchange of *i* and *j, u* and *v,* the Old English runic thorn, the medieval symbols used for *pro* and *per* or *par,* and the multiplicity of superscript contractions encountered in most documents of genealogical interest in this time period.[7]

French paleography

A three-volume, self-teaching course titled *Lire les écritures anciennes: Comment s'etrainer* (Reading Old Handwriting: A Self-study Method) has been designed by Silvain Bertoldi, an archivist, paleographer, and curator of the Archives of the City of Angers. An exceptionally good introductory section gives writing samples of letterforms and numbers at various time periods, plus additional discussion of the peculiarities of old, written forms of the language. A step-by-step methodology for training ourselves to decipher old documents is presented in the first volume. Following this are texts that progress in age and difficulty, accompanied by transcriptions. While the course offers no interaction with a teacher, it is excellent if we can already read the printed language and wish to develop skill in deciphering old documents.[8]

> A step-by-step methodology for training ourselves to decipher old documents is presented in the first volume.

German paleography

Since 1971, the Moravian Archives at Bethlehem, Pennsylvania, has offered the two-week German Script Seminar, which appears to be the only one of its kind in the United States. Taught each June by archivists and intended for archivists, curators, independent researchers, and others working on an advanced level with German- script documents, it emphasizes the ability to read mostly eighteenth- and nineteenth-century materials from Germany and America. A reading knowledge of German—probably the equivalent of two years of college German—is a prerequisite. Instruction is in English, and no aspect of German language per se (grammar, pronunciation, vocabulary, etc.) is taught. The program puts students through a series of in-class and homework exercises, teaching them to read and write progressively older and more difficult scripts. Directly related subjects, such as abbreviations and the history of German script, are included in the lectures. There are no formal examinations.

Latin paleography and translations

Genealogists working in many European (and some American) records must develop a proficiency in Latin—not only its penmanship but also its etymological changes across centuries and national bounds. Among the most useful self-study guides are the following three:

- Latham's *Revised Medieval Latin Word-List from British and Irish Sources* offers a handbook of Latin words coined in England and Ireland through the medieval period. Not only does it contain entries not found in dictionaries of classical Latin, but it also presents numerous variations on words as they occur in documents.[9]

- Gooder's *Latin for Local History* is a text intended to help researchers interpret Latin used in historical records. Its focus is not classical language, but the Latin developed by medieval (and later) clerks and lawyers for administrative and practical purposes. The first half of the text reviews the rules of Latin grammar. The remainder of the book presents a wide variety of local documents (charters, deeds, estate accounts, etc.), together with the author's English translations. It is an excellent collection of models from which we can draw to interpret similar documents. There is also a section on Latin paleography, a list of Christian names, and a word list.[10]

- Martin's *Record Interpreter: A Collection of Abbreviations, Latin Words, and Names Used in English Historical Manuscripts and Records* presents selected abbreviated forms of Latin and French words used in English records and manuscripts, along with their meanings. It also includes a glossary of Latin words (nonclassical), place names, Latin names of bishoprics, Latin forms of English surnames, and Latin Christian names with their English equivalents.[11]

Spanish paleography
Valuable instruction in reading Spanish handwriting from 1116 to 1637 can be found in Conrado Morterero y Simón's *Apuntes de iniciación a la paleografía española.* The first eighty-two pages trace the development of Spanish script during these five centuries; the remainder of the book (nearly a hundred pages) presents single-page sample documents, clearly reproduced with full transcriptions that allow us to practice reading the types of documents that genealogists use.[12]

International Programs

Genealogical quality, standards, and professional integrity are similar around the world; but the international education front is still highly varied. Several countries have at least one major educational program. In many, aspiring professionals find virtually no readily available training opportunities. They must teach themselves through reading and participating in the activities of local or regional societies. All express the hope that, as respected professional communities emerge within more countries, the importance of genealogical education will be stressed. Meanwhile, a growing number of international professionals attend American conferences and institutes or avail themselves of Brigham Young University's distance-education program, which offers concentration in international areas. (See pages 24–25.)

Considering the quite mixed international scene, it is beyond the practical scope of this chapter to comprehensively cover the status of genealogical education in every country. Rather, this chapter briefly treats the most visible programs.

Australia

The principal sources of genealogical education in Australia are society journals and lectures, continuing-education classes (termed College of Advanced Education classes), and presentations at regional genealogical congresses. Australia is also the home base of the International Genealogical Congress, which began in 1988 and was held in the United States in 1992. Since 1974, the Society of Australian Genealogists, located in Sydney, has offered the Diploma in Family Historical Studies—Australia's only professional credential in genealogy. For specifics, see chapter 3, Certification and Accreditation.

Genealogical quality, standards, and professional integrity are similar around the world; but the international education front is still highly varied.

British Isles

England, Ireland, and Scotland offer at least one significant program each. Together, they represent a quite varied menu in a relatively concentrated area.

Institute of Heraldic and Genealogical Studies: Canterbury, England
Founded in 1961, this charitable educational trust promotes the study of the history and structure of the family. It trains genealogists wishing to acquire recognized professional skills. The institute's educational program consists of full-time, part-time, evening, residential, and correspondence courses taught by qualified instructors on several levels. A progressive scheme of instruction and study, combined with a series of assessments and certificates, allows IHGS graduates to acquire professional credentials. (See chapter 3.)

The institute's comprehensive correspondence course is accredited by the English Open and Distance Learning Quality Council and the Training Authority of the British government. Twenty-four home-study lectures provide in-depth study of both sources and research techniques. These are supplemented by additional readings, hands-on research projects, seminars, tutorials, and weekend courses. Students work with assigned tutors who provide evaluation and feedback throughout the course. Examinations are taken at the midway point and at the end. In addition to its residential and home-study courses, the institute offers classes around the country—in a variety of forms—for both beginners and more advanced researchers.

Irish Genealogical Congress
Ireland's major forum is held every three years, at various sites, and features lectures by well-known, highly qualified genealogists and other experts. Some lectures are designed for beginners, others for more advanced researchers. Typically they cover a wide range of topics related to Irish family history—in addition to discussions of censuses, church archives, civil collections, land records, and military files; research in specific geographic areas and historical periods; Internet resources; and research abroad. Handouts, with bibliographies for further study, are distributed to participants; and audiotapes of each presentation are available through the American firm Repeat Performance. Commercial sales, exhibitions, and video presentations fill out the week's schedule.

University of Stirling: Stirling, Scotland
The University of Stirling offers two genealogy courses through its summer school. Scottish Family History, a five-day, noncredit course, provides opportunities for practical research using original records (church, governmental, legal, and local) and published information. Students receive group and individual guidance and have time to conduct research. The course is well suited to students at all levels of experience. The Certificate in Scottish Family History Studies, also offered by the summer school but extended over nearly a year, is earned through a five-day course in August, a three-day workshop in the spring, and four distance-learning packages

A progressive scheme of instruction and study, combined with a series of assessments and certificates, allows IHGS graduates to acquire professional credentials.

completed during the interim. Students submit three assignments and a final project. Successful students receive not only the certificate but also two notional undergraduate credits toward a B.A. degree at the university (two units being one-eighth of the total needed to complete degree requirements). Other United Kingdom universities may also recognize the credits. Students of all levels are admitted, and participants from other countries are welcome; adaptations are made for those unable to attend the spring seminar. The curriculum includes the study of paleography, legal documents (with an emphasis upon interpretation), and family and community life and history, as well as hands-on research and the preparation of research reports. The Association of Scottish Genealogists and Record Agents recognizes the course as fulfilling one of the requirements for membership.

Canada

The genealogical community in Canada is organized along provincial lines, with no national groups, conferences, or programs. Many Canadians attend U.S. conferences and educational sessions of other types. As in the States, genealogical societies in various provinces and cities of Canada also host conferences and seminars of modest size. One major educational effort deserves special note below.

Genealogical Institute of the Maritimes

This organization's goal is the improvement of genealogical practice in the Maritime Provinces. Through lectures, publications, and other educational forums, it encourages excellence in research methodology and increased professionalism. Its education committee has published guidelines for instruction aimed at standardizing a core curriculum in basic methods for beginning researchers. Its dual purpose is to promote public teaching of "scientific" genealogy and to ensure more uniform approaches and outcomes for those seeking basic knowledge of genealogical research. The institute also conducts Canada's oldest certification program. (See chapter 3.)

New Zealand

Genealogical education in New Zealand follows much the same pattern as in Australia, centering primarily upon publications and congresses sponsored by societies. The major training program is that of the Genealogical Research Institute of New Zealand, which offers a four-part, independent-study course. Successful completion of the program earns for the student a certificate that represents professional credentials in New Zealand. (See chapter 3.)

Summary Concepts

Accountants, doctors, lawyers, teachers, and other professionals are expected to make a lifelong commitment to education. As genealogists, we should expect

> The institute's education committee has published guidelines for instruction aimed at standardizing a core curriculum in basic methods for beginning researchers.

nothing less of ourselves. Professional integrity assumes there will be continued study and learning. In our field, that pursuit follows at least two paths: *(a)* progressive development of research skills, including an understanding of changes wrought by rapidly advancing technology; and *(b)* deeper knowledge of such related fields as genetics, geography, heraldry, history, language, and law, which influence genealogy and allow individuals and families to be placed in a broader social context.

Obviously, this instruction is not neatly packaged in any series of courses or conferences. The treated programs lay the necessary groundwork for us to become professionals—and some go well beyond that. But we inevitably face the need to reach further, searching creatively and energetically for the educational resources to help us achieve and maintain professional-level expertise. In that process, we help to earn respect and recognition for the professional label *genealogist*.

Professional integrity assumes there will be continued study and learning.

NOTES

Many program administrators and other colleagues graciously provided information for this chapter: Marthe Arends, Bellevue Community College; Dr. Richard C. F. Baker, Institute of Heraldic and Genealogical Studies; Carlene Brown, University of Washington; Dr. John Philip Colletta, Washington, D.C.; Mary Lou Delahunt, Genealogical Institute of Mid-America; Dr. Patricia Dice, University of Alabama–External Degree Program; David Dobson, St. Andrews, Scotland; Yves du Passage of the Chambre Syndicale des Généalogistes et Héraldistes de France; Dr. Alice Eichholz, CG, Norwich University; Albert Frank, Moravian Archives; James L. Hansen, FASG, State Historical Society of Wisconsin; Cynthia Hightower, U.S. National Archives; Dr. Ronald A. Hill, CG, Boise, Idaho; Dr. John Forster Holt, Australasian Association of Genealogists and Record Agents; Edith James, U.S. National Archives; Dr. Thomas W. Jones, CG, Gallaudet University; Elizabeth Kelley Kerstens, CGRS, Plymouth, Michigan; Sarah Thorson Little, University of Washington; Lynn C. McMillion, CLS, and Marie Varrelman Melchiori, CGRS, CGL, National Institute on Genealogical Research; Kory L. Meyerink, AG, Utah Genealogical Association; Gordon W. Miller, James Madison University Library; Dr. Gary B. Mills, University of Alabama, History Department; Dr. Joan Kirchman Mitchell, Institute of Genealogy and Historical Research, Samford University; Marilyn Miller Morton, FIGRS, Birmingham, Alabama; Suzanne Murray and Robert Naylor, National Genealogical Society; Michael John Neill, Carl Sandburg College; Vernon Nelson, Moravian Archives; Eileen O Dúill, CGRS, Dublin, Ireland; Margaret O'Sullivan, Genealogical Research Institute of New Zealand; Constance Potter, U.S. National Archives; Dr. David H. Pratt, AG, Brigham Young University; Joy Reisinger, CG, Board for Certification of Genealogists; David E. Rencher, AG, British Institute of Genealogy and Historical Research, Samford University; Marsha Hoffman Rising, CG, CGL, FASG, Springfield, Missouri; Dr. Allen B. Robertson, CG(C), Genealogical Institute of the Maritimes; Marie-Antoinette Rohan, Brittany, France; George R. Ryskamp, J.D., AG, Brigham Young University; Cornelia Schräder-Müggenthaler, Lake Garda, Italy; Jane Schwerdtfeger, New England Historic Genealogical Society; Paul F. Smart, AG, Family History Library; Kip Sperry, AG, CG, CGI, FASG, Brigham Young University; Margery Stirling, University of Stirling; Jean Thomason, Institute of Genealogy and Historical Research, Samford University; Elisabeth Thorsell, Federation of Swedish Genealogical Societies; Constantine Tsatso, Smithsonian Associates; Nick Vine Hall, DipFHS (Hons.), Society of Australian Genealogists and Australasian Association of Genealogists and Record Agents; Shirley Langdon Wilcox, CG, National Genealogical Society; and John Vincent Wylie, GENTECH.

1. Donald Lines Jacobus, FASG, *Genealogy as Pastime and Profession*, 2d rev. edition (1968; reprinted, Baltimore: Genealogical Publishing Co., 1986), 44. Emphasis added.

2. Cameron Allen, J.D., FASG, "Developments in the American Society of Genealogists: A Reconsideration of 'What is FASG?'," *Association of Professional Genealogists [APG] Quarterly* 12 (June 1997): 54. Allen's quote is from the ASG constitution.

3. For further discussion of the differences between certificate courses and certification, see

EDUCATIONAL
PREPARATION

It is the studying you do
after your school days that
really counts. Otherwise
you know only that which
everyone else knows.

—*Henry L. Doherty*[13]

Thomas W. Jones, Ph.D., CG, "Certification—What Does it *Really* Mean?" *APG Quarterly* 14 (December 1999): 166–68.

4. Ed Neal, "Distance Education: Prospects and Problems," *National Forum: Phi Kappa Phi Journal* 79 (Winter 1999): 41. Illustrating public wariness of online education is the experience of the highly touted and politically backed Western Governors University, where "rapture . . . surpassed reality in terms of numbers of students enrolling." Offering 130 virtual courses in 1998–99, WGU drew fewer than 120 students. See Associated Press release "Program without Bytes," reported in Business & Technology Section, *Tuscaloosa (Alabama) News,* 23 August 1999, p. 5B.

5. Among the institutions that provide this copying service are the National Genealogical Society Library in Arlington, Virginia; the Allen County Public Library in Fort Wayne, Indiana; and the Monroe County Local History Room in Sparta, Wisconsin.

6. Giles E. Dawson and Laetitia Kennedy-Skipton, *Elizabethan Handwriting: 1500–1650: A Guide to the Reading of Documents and Manuscripts* (New York: W. W. Norton, 1966).

7. Ronald A. Hill, Ph.D., CG, "Interpreting the Symbols and Abbreviations in 16th and 17th-Century English Documents," *Genealogical Journal* 21 (1993): 1–13.

8. Silvain Bertoldi, *Lire les écritures anciennes: Comment s'etrainer* (Angers: Archives Municipales d'Angers, n.d.). Information on the course is available online at the Archives Municipales d'Angers' website.

9. Ronald E. Latham, *Revised Medieval Latin Word-List from British and Irish Sources* (London: Oxford University Press, 1983).

10. Eileen A. Gooder, *Latin for Local History: An Introduction,* 2d edition (London: Longman, 1978).

11. Charles Trice Martin, *The Record Interpreter: A Collection of Abbreviations, Latin Words, and Names Used in English Historical Manuscripts and Records* (1892; reprinted, Sussex, England: Phillimore and Co., 1982).

12. Conrado Morterero y Simón, *Apuntes de iniciación a la paleografía española de los siglos XII a XVII* (Madrid: Hidalguía, 1979).

13. Quoted in Ted Goodman, *The Forbes Book of Business Quotations: 14,173 Thoughts on the Business of Life* (New York: Black Dog and Leventhal Publishers, 1997), 794.

FURTHER STUDY

Association of Professional Genealogists [APG] Quarterly 12 (June 1997): 43–56, for several feature articles dedicated to the subject of genealogical education.

Eichholz, Alice, Ph.D., CG. "The Adult Degree Program." *APG Quarterly* 8 (June 1993): 37–38.

Greenwood, Val D., AG. *The Researcher's Guide to American Genealogy.* 3d edition. Baltimore: Genealogical Publishing Co., 2000. Chapter 1, "Understanding Genealogical Research."

Mills, Elizabeth Shown, CG, CGL, FASG. "Academia *vs.* Genealogy: Prospects for Reconciliation and Progress." *National Genealogical Society Quarterly* 71 (June 1983): 99–106.

———. "Genealogists and Archivists: Communicating, Cooperating, and Coping!" *Society of American Archivists Newsletter* (May 1990) and *National Genealogical Society [NGS] Newsletter* 16 (June 1990): 73, 85–86.

"Professional Debates." *APG Quarterly* 4 (Spring 1989), consisting of Sandra Hargreaves Luebking, "Genealogical Education Is Not for Teachers Only," 17–18; Charles D. Townsend, "Genealogical Education: A Response," 18–19; and Elizabeth Shown Mills, "Genealogical Quality Is Not a Professional Concern Only [response to Townsend]," 21–22.

Rising, Marsha Hoffman, CG, CGL, FASG. "Concepts in Advanced Genealogical Education." *APG Quarterly* 5 (Winter 1990): 84.

Sperry, Kip, AG, CG, CGI, FASG. "Family History at Brigham Young University." *NGS Newsletter* 22 (November/December 1996): 158–60.

Stratton, Eugene A., FASG. *Applied Genealogy.* Salt Lake City: Ancestry, 1988. See especially chapters 13, "Academia and Genealogy," and 15, "The Organization of Genealogy."

Taylor, Robert M., and Ralph J. Crandall, eds. *Generations and Change: Genealogical Perspectives in Social History.* Macon, Georgia: Mercer University Press, 1986.

3

**CERTIFICATION
AND ACCREDITATION**

**CERTIFICATION
AND ACCREDITATION**

Keynotes

Certification and Accreditation

by Elizabeth Shown Mills, CG, CGL, FASG
Paul F. Smart, AG
Jimmy B. Parker, AG
Claire Mire Bettag, CGRS

Skill and ethics. In every hobby and profession, practitioners are measured by their skill and their ethics. Genealogy is no exception. As family historians, as well as professionals, we depend upon thousands of people we do not personally know. We exchange research with others. We extract data from countless publications, databases, and archival collections, whose validity we must appraise. We hire other professionals to do our legwork in distant areas, trusting that they will be able to solve problems outside our area of access or expertise.[1]

Over time, as professionals we develop a network of colleagues whom we know—through professional reputation, if not personal experience—to be highly skilled. But what of the genealogical consumer who lacks our "inside information"? How do family historians who are careful in their own data collection safeguard against misinformation or missed clues when they employ a professional, write a repository for help, or use a published work? How can the neophyte, enthusiastic but unfamiliar with the standards and practices of this field, judge the skill and ethics of those who offer genealogical services or products?

Professional Choices

Academic degrees, a major standard in other professions, say little about the qualifications of a genealogist. Chapters 1 and 2 make clear two points: degree programs in genealogy are exceedingly rare, and most people come into our profession after training for and practicing in another field. Thus, while most of our academic degrees attest the discipline of our intellect and our appreciation for education, they are no measure of genealogical expertise.

Associational membership is an equally problematic standard—especially in the United States, where professional organizations have an open-membership structure. North America's two primary groups, the Association of Professional Genealogists (APG) and the Genealogical Speakers Guild (GSG), welcome any and all who are interested in professional standards and participate in some activity related to genealogy. APG also requires its members to abide by a code of ethics. However, neither organization imposes any competency test. Instead, they encourage their members to seek credentials from a legitimate certifying or accrediting body. The distinctions between guild membership and tested credentials were clearly made in a 1996 article coauthored by the presidents of the Association of Professional Genealogists and the Board for Certification of Genealogists.[2]

Professional credentials, in genealogy as in all fields, are the most obvious safeguard the public has. They are the best assurance we can offer our clients, customers, patrons, readers, and students.

Professional credentials are the most obvious safeguard the public has. They are the best assurance we can offer our clients, customers, patrons, readers, and students.

U.S. Credentialing Bodies

Consumer protection and peace of mind, in most fields, are offered by public-service programs that conduct competency tests and impose codes of ethics upon their associates. For genealogists, two such agencies exist in the United States and serve the international community to varying degrees. One was launched in 1964; the other is rooted in a program initiated that same year. Their basic purposes are the same: to set and maintain standards of quality in researching, teaching, and publishing genealogy. Their tests, procedures, and focuses are different, although both require a broad knowledge of sources and repositories. For one, applicants submit projects conducted in whatever repositories are appropriate to their specialties. The other emphasizes using materials of the Family History Library at Salt Lake City, Utah.

Board for Certification of Genealogists

Incorporated in Washington, D.C., in 1964, BCG is independent of any organization; however, its trustees have always been national leaders. Like many American programs for educational and professional excellence in family history, its founders were fellows of the American Society of Genealogists (our field's scholastic honor society). They also included other prominent scholars who followed the Jacobus School of thorough research, careful documentation, and skilled analysis of evidence.

To hold certification in the United States, we must pass qualifying tests and subscribe to the BCG Code of Ethics, reproduced in appendix B. Certification is granted for only a five-year period. At the end of that time, we must demonstrate anew—by passing a renewal examination—that we continue to meet the latest standards of quality and ethics. As associates of the board, we may tailor our professional specialty, first, by choosing a certification *category* and, then, developing ethnic, geographic, or subject *focus areas* of our choice.

BCG CATEGORIES

Certification categories reflect the types of *activities* genealogists pursue. Each category carries its own credential. In brief:

Certified Genealogical Record Specialist^{SM}

The CGRS category—which represents the most commonly sought credential—appeals especially to those who

- specialize in *records* of a particular geographic area, subject, or ethnic group.
- compile record abstracts or repository guides for publication.
- assist patrons of libraries and archives who seek their ancestry.
- answer research queries for local genealogical societies.
- edit society newsletters or magazines.
- publish family periodicals or single-surname magazines.
- operate genealogical bookstores.
- write genealogical columns for their area newspapers.
- help clients who prefer to direct the searches they commission.
- provide genealogical assistance to heir-searching agencies and legal firms.

Certified Genealogist^{SM}

Certified Genealogist^{SM}
The CG category appeals most to those who frequently

- resolve difficult lineage problems for others.
- compile whole-family genealogies for self or clients.
- edit scholarly journals.
- work with genetic research projects.
- assist legal firms that require court appearance as an expert witness.

Certified Lineage Specialist^{SM}
The CLS category is designed for those who enjoy tracing extended lines of ascent and descent—proving relationships at each link—rather than compiling whole-family genealogies. The CLS may choose to be a generalist or may apply for one of two focus areas, as follows:

HEREDITARY SOCIETY APPLICATIONS—for those who

- are active in lineage societies.
- help others prepare lineage applications.

NATIVE AMERICAN LINEAGES—for those who

- specialize in documenting Native American lineages.
- help "unrecognized" Native American groups prepare petitions for federal recognition.

Certified Genealogical Lecturer^{SM}
The CGL category is designed for those who

- regularly speak to genealogical societies, lineage organizations, and civic groups.
- already hold certification in one of the research categories (CG, CGRS, or CLS).

Certified Genealogical Instructor^{SM}
The CGI category is designed for those who

- teach full-scale, structured genealogical courses.
- already hold certification as a CG.

BCG PROCEDURE
Prospective applicants first contact the Board and request a preliminary application. They are supplied with an official form and other informational literature. Upon returning this preliminary application, they receive a full set of instructions and application materials. Applicants have a year to complete the work and return their portfolios. It is not necessary to travel to a testing site. Costs are exceedingly modest in comparison to similar programs in other professions. But the standards are high.[3]

BCG EXAMINATION
The BCG evaluation is based upon portfolios that applicants submit to demonstrate expertise. Specific materials required for each portfolio depend upon the chosen category and the requested geographic or ethnic specialty.

It is not necessary to travel to a testing site. Costs are exceedingly modest in comparison to similar programs in other professions.

CERTIFICATION
AND ACCREDITATION

Requirements for all BCG applicants:

- *Document work:* Transcribe, abstract, evaluate, and develop work plans for each of two documents BCG supplies.
- *Evidence discussion:* Prepare 150- to 300-word essays discussing the strengths and weaknesses of two types of primary materials important to the geographic area, subject, or time period in which the applicant normally works.
- *Evidence evaluation:* Critically evaluate two derivative sources common to one's areas of special interest.
- *Research reports:* Submit two research reports (prepared in response to an authorized research project—whether pro bono or fee-based) that demonstrate knowledge of, and skill in using, a variety of records relating to the areas in which the applicant normally works.

Additional requirements, by category:

CGRS:

- *Document work:* Transcribe, abstract, evaluate, and develop work plans for each of two documents of one's choice. (This requirement is in addition to similar work on two documents of the board's choice, as discussed above for all applicants.)
- *Evidence discussion:* Select and cite two sources or source types considered reliable enough to have evidentiary value in projects one typically conducts; then, in 150–300 words, discuss the role of that material in a genealogical research plan and assess the strengths and weaknesses of each, giving explicit examples.
- *Extended research report:* Submit one report of an extended research project that seeks a solution to a genealogical problem, not just a particular document; reflects the use of a wide variety of sources for both primary and secondary information; includes at least four photocopies of supporting documents; and does not treat ancestors of the applicant (or spouse)—or, at least, none closer than a grandparent.

CG:

- *Descending genealogy:* Compile a completely documented genealogy that traces *all* descendants of a chosen ancestor, including full biographical data for three generations and identifying information on all members of the fourth. The first two generations should have lived and died beyond memory of descendants living when research began; the fourth generation should not be closer than the applicant's (or spouse's) grandparents, if one of their families is used. Evidence should come heavily from original sources with primary information. Each person in the first three generations should be placed into appropriate historical context relevant to the era, locale, and circumstances. This compilation is a substantial project that typically runs from several dozen to a hundred or so pages.
- *Complex evidence problem:* Present a fully discussed and completely documented case study in which a difficult research problem is resolved by analyzing, correlating, and weighing complex evidence—as when *(a)* direct evidence from primary informants directly state contradictory information; *(b)* a persuasive conclusion can be drawn from an accumulation of indirect evidence of high quality; or *(c)* a body of indirect evidence can be assembled to convincingly disprove direct evidence. Some cases may involve multiple types of evidentiary problems.[4]

> Evidence should come heavily from original sources with primary information. All individuals in the first three generations should be placed into appropriate historical context relevant to their era, locale, and circumstance.

CLS:
- *Reconstructed lineage—generalist:* Trace five consecutive generations in one bloodline, coming forward from a remote ancestor or tracing backward from a recent person. All other criteria applying to the CG's compiled genealogy apply to this compilation.
- *Reconstructed lineage—hereditary-society focus:* Submit two hereditary society applications—each for a different society—that *(a)* do not relate to the applicant's (or spouse's) ancestry; *(b)* do not begin or end with the same person or repeat a person iEv n any generation; *(c)* do not rely on previously approved applications for any society; *(d)* are not based in whole or significant part on published works; and *(e)* follow the society's instructions. Attachments should include all photocopies, etc., submitted to the society and all relevant correspondence with the society.
- *Reconstructed lineage—Native American focus:* Submit two Native American lineages (usually shorter than five generations) that trace the ancestry of a living person (other than applicant or spouse) to an individual born prior to 1850—one identified as a Native American of a specific tribe by a reliable, primary-information source. For each person, the account should provide reasonably sufficient information on birth, marriage, and death, with full source citation and photocopies of supporting documentation.
- *Complex evidence problem (all CLS applicants):* Prepare a complex-evidence case study, as described for the CG.

CGL:
- Hold certification in one category above; and
- Submit audiocassettes of two lectures on genealogical methods or sources, together with supporting handouts, visual aids, and bibliographies.

CGI:
- Hold certification as CG; and
- Submit a syllabus for a full-scale course of instruction; cassette tapes of two class sessions, with student participation; and samples of completed student projects.

BCG STANDARDS
In evaluating a portfolio, BCG heavily considers two areas: the applicant's knowledge of sources within his or her chosen specialty; and the ability to document all research, soundly evaluate evidence, and report findings in a clear and professional manner.

BCG EVALUATION
BCG maintains a panel of several dozen judges who are nationally recognized authorities in wide-ranging specialties. Each portfolio is evaluated by three to four judges, each acting independently of the other. There is no pro forma review by BCG officers or trustees. Recommendations from BCG associates are neither necessary nor considered—candidates are judged on their abilities, not their contacts. Applicants receive a completed evaluation sheet, scoring their performance in thirty to fifty different skill areas, as well as a written analysis of their strengths and weaknesses.

Applicants who do not pass may appeal to the full board of trustees if they feel their portfolio has been inappropriately judged. Most prefer to address the problems noted by the judges and reapply. There is no mandatory waiting period.

BCG heavily considers the applicant's knowledge of sources and the ability to document research, soundly evaluate evidence, and report findings in a clear and professional manner.

CERTIFICATION
AND ACCREDITATION

BCG TRAINING

The board assists prospective applicants in two ways.

- It publishes an educational newsletter (*OnBoard*) three times a year, offering skill-building advice on wide-ranging topics and specific advice on the preparation of applications. Subscriptions are open to any person, library, or society.

- It conducts many workshops each year at national, state, and local conferences and institutes. For example, at national conferences in 1996 and 1999, certified associates presented intensive 18- to 21-session skillbuilding tracks to consistently packed audiences. Special educational packets containing the taped lectures, the accompanying syllabus material, and the essential visual aids were developed for ongoing distribution by the conference taper, Repeat Performance, to benefit genealogists who could not attend the sessions.

BCG ADVERTISING

The services of certified associates are advertised by the board in a variety of ways. A published roster is supplied to all state archives and major genealogical libraries nationwide and is available to the public at a nominal cost. It provides extensive detail on the skills and specialties of each certified person. State-level lists of certified associates are often complimentary at the BCG booth at major conferences and supplied to many courthouses and libraries nationwide. Certified associates are listed, by geographic regions and special interests, on the board's website.

BCG PUBLIC-ASSURANCE POLICY

BCG views its credentials as a public assurance that its associates have been tested; have demonstrated professional-level skill at research, analysis, and writing; and have agreed to abide by its strict Code of Ethics. Should any member of the public be dissatisfied with the genealogical work or conduct of a certified person, BCG should be informed of the problem and provided supporting evidence, for appropriate action.

For the protection of the public, BCG's credentials are legal service marks that can be used under license, for a term of five years, by associates who meet the board's standards of expertise and ethics. Use of these credentials by any individual who has not passed a board examination in the designated category is a legally actionable infringement of the proprietary rights that the board has held for many decades.

BCG offers arbitration services to any member of the public sector who employs a certified person and feels the results were inappropriate. The board reserves the right to discipline associates or revoke certification, for just cause, after a confidential hearing in which all affected parties are entitled to present their own evidence and review all materials under consideration.

International Commission for the
Accreditation of Professional Genealogists

Based in Salt Lake City, Utah, and incorporated in 2000, the International Commission for the Accreditation of Professional Genealogists (ICapGen) was created as a successor to the accreditation program offered since 1964 by the Genealogical

> For the protection of the public, BCG's credentials are legal service marks that can be used only under license by associates who meet the board's standards of expertise and ethics.

Society of Utah (GSU). Currently sponsored by the Utah Genealogical Association, ICapGen plans for independent status when legal and financial details can be finalized. The program was born of GSU's mission to help members of The Church of Jesus Christ of Latter-day Saints (LDS) accomplish their ancestral pursuits—a fundamental obligation of the Mormon religion being to identify ancestors as far back in time as possible. For nearly four decades, accreditation was administered by GSU and its successor, the LDS Family History Department; at the suspension of the Department's involvement in 2000, Accredited Genealogists were offered dual options. By special arrangement with the Board for Certification of Genealogists, they could transfer to BCG (assuming a BCG credential), or they could transfer to ICapGen, a new agency independent of the LDS, that would continue the accreditation credential.

Accreditation through ICapGen, as in the LDS program, is granted for renewable five-year periods. Candidates for renewal must demonstrate continued proficiency and a current awareness of developments in their specialty areas.

ICAPGEN PROCEDURE
Potential applicants initiate the process by contacting ICapGen by postal mail or through its website. They receive a brochure explaining the program and the geographic and subject areas offered. There is only one category of accreditation: Accredited Genealogist. The ICapGen examination is a three-stage process. There is a modest fee, and stages two and three are pursued only in Salt Lake City. Applicants should plan to spend two or more days there for the tests.

ICAPGEN EXAMINATION

Stage one: application
After reviewing the preliminary materials, prospects may request an official application form, to be completed and returned with a number of items. These consist of

- a pedigree chart of three to four generations prior to 1875 in the geographic area;
- family group records for the same three to four generations;
- a research log showing the sources searched in compiling the information; and
- a research report written to a client or written as if it were to be sent to a client.

Applicants who show promise are invited to proceed with the next two stages.

Stage two: written examination
The second step consists of a six-part evaluation of knowledge and skill. It requires a time commitment of about eight hours in Salt Lake City and assumes that the applicant has a working knowledge of the Family History Library. The parts are as follows:

- *Handwriting:* applicants are asked to read (or translate for foreign research) one or more records relative to the area and time period of their geographic specialty.
- *Document recognition:* applicants are presented with sample documents and reference sources important for their specialty and are asked to identify them.
- *LDS Church records:* applicants are tested on their knowledge of materials prepared by the Family History Department, such as the Ancestral File™ and the International Genealogical Index® (IGI).

The ICapGen examination is a three-stage process. Stages two and three are pursued only in Salt Lake City.

**CERTIFICATION
AND ACCREDITATION**

- *Brief pedigree evaluations:* applicants are to analyze a research problem, list sources to be searched for resolving that problem, and explain the expected results.
- *Pedigree research problem:* applicants are given a pedigree problem on which they will carry out research in the library and compile a client report detailing the results of the search, with suggestions for future research.
- *General questions and answers:* applicants are tested on a knowledge of facts pertaining to the history and records of the chosen area—including such items as historical events affecting research, types of records, time period covered by them, and their content and availability.

These written examinations are created and revised by two or more area specialists who hold accreditation.

Stage three: oral examination
If candidates pass the written examination, an oral exam is scheduled—usually two hours in length. Applicants sit before three or more area specialists and are expected to satisfactorily defend the pedigrees they submitted with their applications. Weaknesses noted in the written examination may be reviewed at this time also.

ICAPGEN STANDARDS
Accredited Genealogists are expected to have sufficient knowledge and experience to assist clients in compiling accurate and complete pedigrees and family group records in a timely and efficient manner. They are also expected to be able to compose a well-written research report.

> Accredited Genealogists are expected to have sufficient knowledge and experience to assist clients in compiling accurate and complete pedigrees and family group records.

ICAPGEN EVALUATION
Examination materials are appraised by members of ICapGen. Successful applicants must make a score of 90 percent or more on the written examination. Those who fail may retake the exam after a minimum of three months and after delineating their efforts to improve.

ICAPGEN TRAINING
No specific training is given by ICapGen to become accredited. Potential applicants may better prepare themselves for accreditation by

- gaining as much practical experience as possible in their geographic focus area.
- consulting with experienced researchers in their chosen specialty.
- taking genealogical courses at institutions such as Brigham Young University (or their own local college or university) or through home-study programs such as those offered by BYU and the National Genealogical Society. (See also chapter 2.)

ICAPGEN ADVERTISING
Accredited Genealogists who wish to have their names published as a service for individuals seeking professional help may request a listing on ICapGen's website. This roster, on which Accredited Genealogists appear by their area specialty, will be provided as part of the services offered by ICapGen to its members.

ICAPGEN PUBLIC-ASSURANCE POLICY

Accredited Genealogists sign a statement agreeing to adhere to the field's standard Code of Ethics (originally developed by the Board for Certification of Genealogists) and to work with ICapGen. When problems occur between a client and an accredited researcher, ICapGen is always willing to try to mediate. However, it is not responsible for the performance of the Accredited Genealogist.

International Credentialing Bodies

The 1960s-era movement toward certification and accreditation of genealogists was not limited to the United States. However, the international scene has progressed more slowly toward the establishment of credentials or associations that attest genealogical expertise. At this writing, programs have been identified for Australia, Canada, England, France, Ireland, New Zealand, and Scotland. The Canadian models, not surprisingly, bear more resemblance to the U.S. programs—being independent tests of demonstrated ability rather than the culmination of a specific course of study provided by the accrediting body.

Elsewhere, "credentials" of a surrogate nature can be achieved by membership in a professional guild. In these cases, we usually find a concurrent emphasis in ongoing training. As in the U.S., specific educational prerequisites are not prescribed, by and large. The prevailing custom is for genealogists to devise an educational regimen for themselves through independent readings, participation in local or regional conferences, and distance education. This last approach includes subscriptions to independent-study courses offered by Brigham Young University in Provo, Utah, where the proffered subjects include the British Isles, Germany, Latin America, Scandinavia, and Southern Europe. Some genealogists in countries without credentialing bodies— as well as some international professionals with research interests or a client base in North America—also seek credentials from the two U.S. agencies. In short, the international scene is seeing significant growth in both professional ties and cooperative efforts that transcend national bounds. All share a common goal: enhancing the profession and the qualifications of those who practice it.

The remainder of this chapter surveys formal credentialing programs and screening bodies that exist outside the United States.

> The international scene is seeing significant growth in both professional ties and cooperative efforts that transcend national bounds.

Australia

Two credentialing bodies have been active in Australia for nearly a quarter century— one tied to an educational program, the other to a professional membership organization.

AUSTRALASIAN ASSOCIATION OF GENEALOGISTS AND RECORD AGENTS

Founded in 1977 and based in Australia, AAGRA acts as a professional organization for genealogists in both Australia and New Zealand. It does not require any specific educational background and admits members in two categories:

- *Genealogists (G):* Those who compile family histories and genealogies for clients and are often responsible for effecting the publication of the finished project.

CERTIFICATION

AND ACCREDITATION

- *Record Agents (RA):* Those who specialize in the knowledge of records and sources and the researching of these.

Admission to AAGRA depends largely upon the applicant's research ability and knowledge of sources. Also important is skill in writing a professional-quality research report that is judged by credentialed peers on such skills as citation, use and analysis of evidence, range of sources, manner of reporting, and clarity of expression. Applicants are required to submit samples of their work. Members are listed in a publicly distributed brochure and on the AAGRA website under the postnomial *(G)* or *(RA)* and must subscribe to the AAGRA code. (See appendix B.)

SOCIETY OF AUSTRALIAN GENEALOGISTS

Since 1974, this open-membership society has offered a Diploma in Family Historical Studies, not just to professionals but to any genealogist who aspires to maintain the highest standards possible in genealogical research. The process of earning the credential is rigorous, the society's standards exacting, and the subject matter challenging. To receive the diploma, candidates must complete a comprehensive two- to three-year course, prepare a major and minor thesis, and pass a three-hour written examination. Professors of Australian history assess the exams and theses. Those awarded the diploma are entitled to use the credential *DipFHS* after their names.

Canada

Genealogical activity in Canada is organized on a provincial rather than national basis. Several provinces have begun to set up their own certification programs, with educational components. The Maritime Provinces led the movement; separate (but smaller) programs have followed in Quebec, Saskatchewan, and other provinces. All these programs—demonstrating the ethics expected of professional organizations— have been careful to avoid duplicating or encroaching upon the distinctive credentials established by earlier groups. Canada's two principal programs are discussed below.

GENEALOGICAL INSTITUTE OF THE MARITIMES (GIM)

Established in 1983 as a nonprofit organization, the institute conducts a rigorous examination leading to one of two credentials that are somewhat comparable to those used by the older American board. (To avoid confusion, the Maritime credentials always include the word *Canada* or—for the postnomial—a parenthetical *C.*) In brief, the Maritime program distinguishes its two categories by the following criteria:

GRS(C)
The Genealogical Record Searcher (Canada) is a genealogist who

- on behalf of clients examines records for genealogical or biographical information and reports the results;
- can devise an appropriate plan to solve a client's problem; and
- understands wide-ranging documentary materials, capably reads old handwriting, properly cites sources, prepares professional-quality reports, and exhibits ethical conduct.

CG(C)

The Certified Genealogist (Canada) is one who

- meets all the requirements of the GRS(C);
- has a "complete knowledge" of genealogical research principles and well-honed skills in evaluating evidence and resolving problems; and
- can prepare a genealogy manuscript, based on standard formats, for clients or for publication.

Maritime certification is a three- or four-step process, as follows:

- The preliminary application asks for information on education, classes taught, research experience, participation in genealogical organizations, and works published. Responses are graded by a system well explained in the institute's instruction manual. Applicants who score at least seven points are eligible to submit a full application for GRS(C). Those who score at least fourteen points may apply for CG(C).
- The full application requires one submission in each category: candidates for GRS(C) submit one research report on a problem of their choosing; CG(C) candidates submit a compiled family history of not more than twenty pages, with complete documentation of all facts.
- Those whose work sample passes the second step then take a written examination. Candidates appear in person, at a site convenient to them and the institute's representative, for a two-hour test that measures their knowledge of some or all of the following components: handwriting; research methods; and genealogical sources, terminology, and theory. A score of 80 percent on the written exam earns certification.
- Those who score in the 70–80 percentile sit for an oral exam to discuss strengths and weaknesses. A satisfactory performance at this stage qualifies the applicant.

Unlike the U.S. programs, GIM does not require periodic retesting of those whom it certifies. However, members are strongly encouraged to continue their education in the field, in accordance with professional expectations.

BUREAU QUÉBÉCOIS D'ATTESTATION DE COMPÉTENCE EN GÉNÉALOGIE (BQACG)

The BQACG was created as a service agency in 1990 by the Fédération québécoise des sociétés de généalogie (Quebec Federation of Genealogical Societies)—a nonprofit agency that dates to 1984. The bureau recognizes three categories of professionals:

M.G.A.	Maître Généalogiste Agréé	Master Genealogist–Solicitor
G.R.A.	Généalogiste Recherchiste Agréé	Genealogical Researcher–Solicitor
G.F.A.	Généalogiste Filiation Agréé	Lineage Genealogist–Solicitor

Genealogists earn these credentials when they pass evaluation by three of the fifteen judges who serve the bureau. Candidates are judged upon a genealogical dossier that includes family lines researched, lectures, published works, and other related genealogical accomplishments.

Unlike the U.S. programs, GIM does not require periodic retesting of those whom it certifies.

**CERTIFICATION
AND ACCREDITATION**

AGRA's screening process is less formal than that of similar organizations elsewhere. Nonetheless, its membership roll is highly selective.

England

Genealogists seeking professional credentials in England also have multiple options. One program is based upon specific educational training; the other is a peer-evaluated membership organization.

ASSOCIATION OF GENEALOGISTS AND RECORD AGENTS

Since 1968, this association has served the British professional community and consumers internationally. AGRA's screening process is less formal than that of similar organizations in Australia and elsewhere in the British Isles, in that it does not require the submission of work samples. Nonetheless, its membership roll is highly selective; and listings are granted only to those recommended by present AGRA members who attest that the candidates are well qualified and experienced. All AGRA members are required to subscribe to a code of conduct. (See appendix B.)

INSTITUTE OF HERALDIC AND GENEALOGICAL STUDIES

This Canterbury-based nonprofit, educational trust, founded in 1961, offers credentials in conjunction with IHGS course work and examinations. After proceeding successfully through several levels of instruction and after satisfying the institute examiners, professionals may be awarded a certificate or diploma that carries the weight of professional credentials. The various ranks granted are as follows:

- *Part I Certificate:* granted to those who have progressed through course levels A to D and successfully sat for an exam at each stage.
- *Part II Certificate:* granted to Part I holders who take additional course work on-site or by correspondence and demonstrate wide practical experience.
- *Record Agent Certificate:* granted to those who hold a Part II Certificate and pass two assignments set by IHGS—*(a)* research of a problem provided by the institute and submission of a report in prescribed format; and *(b)* submission of a portfolio of materials reflecting the scope and depth of the candidate's accumulated experience. Holders of this award are eligible for membership in AGRA, above.
- *Diploma in Genealogy:* granted to those who hold a Record Agent Certificate and demonstrate thorough understanding of heraldry and its application to demography, genealogy, history, intestate succession, and overseas research. An oral exam treats Latin or English records from the sixteenth century forward.
- *Graduate Member of the Institute:* a status awarded to those who have earned the Diploma and complete an application specifically for Graduate Member status.
- *Licentiateship (L.H.G.):* granted to Graduate Members past the age of twenty-five, with at least five years of genealogical experience, who submit an approved, fully referenced thesis or research dissertation of roughly 15,000 to 50,000 words. Additional requirements may be imposed in some cases.

France

In France a clear distinction is made between *la généalogie familial* (family history) and *la généalogie successorale* (heir searching). All references here are to the former. The profession is still only loosely organized, with no government regulation and no peer group administering competency examinations. Practitioners voluntarily belong to different professional organizations, one of the oldest of which has taken initial steps toward self-regulation:

CHAMBRE SYNDICALE DES GÉNÉALOGISTES ET HÉRALDISTES DE FRANCE

This membership organization, founded in 1980 with both membership rules and a code of conduct (see appendix B), has launched a serious effort to address the question of professional regulation and qualification, with the goal of establishing the equivalent of a certification program. Its members, a mix of family historians and genealogists, must complete the baccalaureate (high-school degree) and three years of higher education, preferably toward a degree in history. Although the organization conducts no classes, it holds informational meetings for prospective members.

Ireland

In 1988, with the support of the Chief Herald of Ireland and approval of Ireland's Genealogical Office, professional genealogists founded a regulating body to encourage high standards among its members and to protect the interests of clients.

ASSOCIATION OF PROFESSIONAL GENEALOGISTS IN IRELAND

Membership is open to all professional genealogists in Ireland who are not permanently employed in another field. APGI's Board of Assessors evaluates work samples submitted by applicants, as well as background information on their experience. Members subscribe to a code of ethics. (See appendix B.) Any dissatisfaction with the services provided by APGI members is investigated when reported to the Honorable Secretary of the Genealogical Office.

New Zealand

A significant spurt of interest in genealogy in the Southern Hemisphere has spawned two programs that award credentials to professional researchers in New Zealand:

AUSTRALASIAN ASSOCIATION OF GENEALOGISTS AND RECORD AGENTS

For this program, which serves both Australia and New Zealand, see page 53.

GENEALOGICAL RESEARCH INSTITUTE OF NEW ZEALAND

GRINZ awards a Diploma in Family History that carries the weight of a professional credential. Genealogists who aim to pursue family history at the advanced level progress through a four-part, independent-study program. The credential is intended to ensure high standards of personal and professional genealogical research and teaching. Holders of the diploma are authorized to use the acronym *GRINZ* after their name, as a formal credential.

Scotland

As elsewhere in the British Isles and Europe, the Scottish genealogical community has no independent testing body with a formal exam structure. However, professionals

> GRINZ awards a Diploma in Family History that carries the weight of a professional credential.

**CERTIFICATION
AND ACCREDITATION**

have created a self-regulating membership organization, with a view toward consumer protection. That body and its policies are as follows:

ASSOCIATION OF SCOTTISH GENEALOGISTS AND RECORD AGENTS
Since ASGRA's birth in 1981, membership has hinged upon the submission of work samples for approval by the association. Those whose expertise is deemed sufficient remain members in good standing so long as they adhere to ASGRA's Code of Practice. (See appendix B.) Their services are advertised in the association's "Information Leaflet and List of Professional Searchers."

Summary Concepts

The search for family and identity is a major force in the lives of many people around the globe. It is now a significant consumer investment, a popular profession, and an important adjunct to academic and other professional fields. As with any legitimate endeavor that moves from an obscure pastime to a major enterprise, it has developed standards of quality and professional conduct that bear remarkable resemblance across many national bounds. In this changing climate, accreditation and certification are important elements of consumer protection. Neither is required in our field, and many good genealogists are still uncredentialed. But the existence of these programs—with some four decades of experience and service behind the movement—has done much to elevate research standards, promote integrity by hobbyists and professionals alike, and otherwise improve the public image of genealogy itself.

> The existence of these programs has done much to elevate research standards, promote integrity by hobbyists and professionals alike, and otherwise improve the public image of genealogy.

NOTES

Appreciation is due to several program administrators and colleagues for their assistance with this chapter: Dr. Richard C. F. Baker, Institute of Heraldic and Genealogical Studies; Yves du Passage, Chambre Syndicale des Généalogistes et Héraldistes de France; Dr. Duncan B. Gardiner, AG, CG, of Ohio, a leading authority on research in Slovakia and the Czech Republic; Dr. John Forster Holt, Australasian Association of Genealogists and Record Agents; Eileen O Dúill, CGRS, of Dublin, Ireland; Margaret O'Sullivan, Genealogical Research Institute of New Zealand; Dr. Allen B. Robertson, CG(C), Genealogical Institute of the Maritimes; Cornelia Schräder-Müggenthaler of Lake Garda, Italy; Elisabeth Thorsell, Federation of Swedish Genealogical Societies; and Nick Vine Hall, DipFHS (Hons.), creator of the diploma program of the Society of Australian Genealogists and longtime leader of the Australasian Association of Genealogists and Record Agents.

1. Portions of the program descriptions in this chapter appeared in Elizabeth Shown Mills and Paul F. Smart, "Research Ethics: Genealogical Accreditation and Certification," *Ancestry* 15 (March–April 1997): 14–19, and are used here with the publisher's permission.

2. Elizabeth Shown Mills and Kay Germain Ingalls, CGRS, "Have Checkbook—Am a Professional," *OnBoard* [educational newsletter of the Board for Certification of Genealogists] 2 (September 1996): 17–18.

3. All prospective applicants should study *The BCG Genealogical Standards Manual* (Orem, Utah: Ancestry Publishing and Board for Certification of Genealogists, 2000), as well as the board's applications guide.

4. For model case studies demonstrating all these complex evidence situations—as well as a sound grounding in genealogical evidence—see *Evidence: A Special Issue of the National Genealogical Society* (September 1999).

4

**THE
ESSENTIAL
LIBRARY**

Keynotes

Keynotes (cont.)

The Essential Library

by Joy Reisinger, CG

A personal library is an essential tool of every professional. As genealogists, we use the written word on a daily basis for information about unfamiliar locales and repositories, as well as for source material. The size and nature of our in-house collection depend on many factors—not the least of which are our specialties, our distance from a good reference library, and the premium we place on convenience or economy. This chapter has two purposes. The first is to suggest criteria by which each of us can appraise our needs and then proceed to build our library in stages. The second is to identify the body of literature that many of today's best genealogists consider sound and essential for all researchers, whatever their interests, as well as those for the most common geographic and ethnic specialties.

Selection Criteria

Education, efficiency, and reliability are hallmarks of a good professional library. Budgets, space limitations, and poor choices are its nemeses.

Education, efficiency, and reliability are the goals of a good professional library. Budgets, space limitations, and poor choices are its nemeses. The guidelines offered in this section are designed to help us build a quality library within our personal limits and to minimize our risk of making choices we'll later regret. The suggestions are both specific and general—reflecting the standards of the field and the highly personalized nature of genealogical research.

Education

As beginning family searchers, we probably thought of a "genealogical library" as a collection of materials in which to look up names. As professionals, we are more apt to view it as a collection of materials *from which we learn*. Toward that end, the essential library is a balance of three types of media: books and journals we can regularly study to broaden our knowledge base; reference works that yield facts on demand; and source materials that further our research on a specific area, ethnicity, or topic. In other words:

INSTRUCTIONAL WORKS: Guides to methods, sources, and genealogical principles. Periodicals that discuss these essentials and provide exemplary case studies.

GENERAL REFERENCES: Atlases, dictionaries, gazetteers, and legal codes.

SOURCE MATERIALS: Books, CDs, microforms, and source-oriented periodicals.

Efficiency

In all professions and trades, efficiency demands that we have at hand the tools we regularly need to perform our tasks. If we accept client commissions and our personal library is inadequate, we must charge the client unnecessarily for time spent in consulting basic works elsewhere. Whether we assist others or conduct research for our own publications, classes, or lectures, a failure to have material readily at hand will interrupt our workflow—creating wasted time and lost trains of thought. By contrast, personal ownership of the material most relevant to our work enables us to improve upon our "tools of the trade." We may highlight important or recurring passages, add bookmarks, or make additions and corrections so that these materials, at every use, will provide us with the most accurate and up-to-date information possible.

Reliability

By word of mouth, we may already know which of the *classics* are trustworthy. Avoiding a bad purchase from the enticing stream of *new* offerings may be more difficult. Good genealogists (like good public and university libraries) turn first to the scholarly journals—the ones that give candid critiques instead of "sweetheart" reviews—for objective evaluations; and most of these journals try to assess major offerings within nine months or so. When our need is more urgent, we might borrow a copy to evaluate, if we know a colleague who has gambled already on the purchase. Or we can volunteer to critique the book for a local or regional publication, thus acquiring a review copy. (Note: As a rule, the major journals do not accept volunteered reviews; they prefer to seek out the most authoritative and unbiased reviewers possible for each work.)

Obviously, choosing works unseen and unreviewed, on the basis of a publisher's enticing flyers or ads, is a gamble; and gambling is a sure way to waste both funds and shelf space. Even though the major genealogical publishers are serious about quality control, regrettable mistakes still happen. Our field has also been "discovered" commercially by suppliers who do not understand our standards. That increases our risk. Too, candor demands that we acknowledge problems in our own ranks: a multitude of family histories and local records published by well-intentioned people with more enthusiasm than experience. All things considered, it is more crucial than ever that we build our professional libraries upon the same safeguard major genealogical libraries use: *check the reviews before writing the check*—but look to quality journals for reliable guidance.

A Purchasing Plan

Budgets and space are very real restraints on our ability to acquire all the works we want and need. Thus, to build a quality library we need more than just attention to quality. We need a *purchasing plan*. There is no one-size-fits-all model for our field, given the endless diversity of our interests. However, many professionals apply the priorities outlined in figures 1 and 2 and discussed below.

The basic shelf

The core collection of any professional's personal library is affordably small—twenty or so reference works and a minimum of two to four periodicals. Most of us

FIG. 1
SELECTION CRITERIA

*Do I really need
to buy this?*

- Is this a major guide I will need to restudy periodically?

- If I do not have this at hand, will the lack of it interrupt my workflow when it is needed?

- Is this easily available at a nearby repository?

- Have I used (and copied from) this more than three times?

- If I have not personally studied this item, how do reviewers appraise it? Can I borrow a copy to assess its value?

- Does it cite its sources?

- Is it available online?

*Check the reviews before
writing the check!*

THE ESSENTIAL LIBRARY

FIG. 2
PURCHASING PLAN
(U.S. MODEL)*

*For an effective
professional library*

TYPE OF PUBLICATION	PRIORITY LEVELS		
	1 BASIC SHELF	**2** ESSENTIAL MATERIALS	**3** USEFUL BUT DISCRETIONARY ITEMS
Instructional Works			
Comprehensive manuals	✓		

EXAMPLES:
    BCG Genealogical Standards Manual
    Greenwood, *Researcher's Guide*
    Mills, *Evidence!*
    NARA, *Genealogical Research*
    Szucs and Luebking, *The Source*			

"Popular" magazines/newsletters national level (at least 1)	✓		
Professional magazines/newsletters	✓		
Scholarly journals (at least 1)	✓		
Specialty guides (national level)		✓	

EXAMPLES:
    Hone, *Land & Property Research*
    NARA, *Guide to Federal Records*			

Specialty studies in adjunct areas			✓
General References			
National/international overviews	✓		

EXAMPLES:
    Black, *Black's Law Dictionary*
    Eichholz, *Red Book*
    Kemp, *Vital Records Handbook*			

Specialty works		✓	
EXAMPLE: Reisinger, *Index to . . . Syllabi*			
Specialty references in adjunct areas			✓
Source Materials			
Basic national databases/indexes	✓		

EXAMPLES:
    PERSI
    *SS Death Benefits Index***
    Family History Library Catalog			

Works that treat our ethnic specialty	✓	✓	
our geographic specialty	✓	✓	
areas that supplied migrants to our geographic specialty area		✓	
Statewide or specialty indexes		✓	
Statewide or specialty databases			✓
Statewide or specialty source books			✓

  * International genealogists would substitute whatever comparable, national-level guides serve their country.
** This and similar basic databases are sometimes found online at no cost or by subscription.

have these basics long before we decide to "turn professional." To this shelf, most of us would add a highly personal selection of source books so crucial to our specialty that it would be difficult to operate professionally without them. The works recommended below form an excellent basic shelf for American researchers and some are equally valuable to international genealogists. Similar selections for many international areas appear in the Essential Titles section of this chapter.

GENERAL REFERENCES

The personal library of all serious genealogists has certain items that are almost too fundamental to mention. A collegiate or universal dictionary, a thesaurus, a world and national atlas, and a state or provincial atlas that shows current boundaries for counties, towns, or other political divisions lead the list. An up-to-date legislative directory for the researcher's area is also essential because professional genealogists often have to get politically involved with legislation affecting vital records. In the United States, the classic Everton's *Handy Book** and the newer work, *Ancestry's Red Book*, are basic to identifying sites and the records that exist for them. (Both works are necessary, since each has weak sections in which the other is more reliable.) *Black's Law Dictionary*; Kemp's *International Vital Records Handbook*; Thorndale and Dollarhide's *Map Guide to the U.S. Federal Censuses;* Curran, Crane, and Wray's *Numbering Your Genealogy;* and the professional directories published by the Association of Professional Genealogists and the Board for Certification of Genealogists round out this category.

Internationally, aside from Kemp's handbook, the range of works is far too broad to single out examples, but many are included under Essential Titles.

INDEXES TO SOURCE MATERIAL

Certain indexes are indispensable for effective, efficient library work—items that enable us to plan our research before we reach a crowded facility. Researchers who have to travel any distance to a Family History Center and don't have access to it via the Web <www.FamilySearch.org> should own the microfiche of the Family History Library Catalog for their area of expertise. (Used microfiche readers often can be purchased inexpensively, or the fiche may be taken to a local library.) The *Periodical Source Index (PERSI)*, the mammoth ongoing finding aid covering thousands of periodicals for the period 1847 to date, is a tremendous time-saver that's affordable for virtually every professional, now that it is available on CD-ROM. It is also accessible online through a subscription database from the CD-ROM publisher.

PERSI is a tremendous time-saver that's affordable for virtually every professional, now that it is available on CD-ROM.

INSTRUCTIONAL WORKS

The manuals in this category do double duty as both teaching tools and ongoing references. Absolutely essential is a guide to the citation of sources and evaluation of evidence, both conventional and online. The new standard, applicable inter-

---

* All works mentioned in this introduction are fully cited in the Essential Titles section.

THE ESSENTIAL LIBRARY

nationally with the same type of modification U.S. researchers use to differentiate between regional records, is Mills's *Evidence! Citation & Analysis for the Family Historian.* Equally vital is *The BCG Genealogical Standards Manual,* which defines quality for all types of genealogical work. Professionals also need the most comprehensive, most reliable, most current guidebook possible for methods and sources in their nation—one that teaches research principles and helps us *understand* the records, as opposed to lists of repositories and collections. In the United States, the major work in this category is Greenwood's *Researcher's Guide to American Genealogy.* On the Basic Shelf, it is augmented by Szucs and Luebking's revision of *The Source,* Meyerink's *Printed Sources,* and the *Guide to Genealogical Research in the National Archives.*

POPULAR MAGAZINES AND NEWSLETTERS

As professionals, we regularly read the informal magazines and newsletters for two reasons: in order to know what our clients are learning, and to keep abreast of genealogical trends and problems. The U.S. bimonthlies *Ancestry, Everton's Genealogical Helper,* and *Heritage Quest* have the largest global following in the magazine category—and at least one should be represented in our library. For current events in the U.S., the Federation of Genealogical Societies news magazine (*Forum*), the National Genealogical Society's *NGS Newsmagazine,* and the New England Historic Genealogical Society's *New England Ancestors* are equally essential and difficult to choose between—combining news with short, informative articles on resources and repositories. Equally important, for its continuing-education value, is *OnBoard,* the educational newsletter of the Board for Certification of Genealogists (whose circulation is not limited to Board associates).

SCHOLARLY JOURNALS

The essential tool most often overlooked by those new to the field—quality journals—is an important source of continuing education. Professional researchers should subscribe to at least one major journal, add all the others to their "library reading list," and then religiously do that reading. The *National Genealogical Society Quarterly,* the *New England Historical and Genealogical Register, The American Genealogist,* and *The Genealogist* are the standard-bearers in the field. Articles in scholarly journals may not treat our specific families, but the methodologies demonstrated by their writers can open doors for us when we apply them to our own problems; and their source citations constantly point us to new material. None of these journals restricts itself to American families.

SPECIALTY WORKS

The final element of a basic library is totally dependent upon the area or specialties in which we work—and upon the volume of material produced on that subject. At the least, we need *(a)* basic guidebooks to our specialty; *(b)* source books, periodicals, and CD-ROM and Internet databases that provide essential abstracts, transcripts, or indexes; and usually *(c)* statewide indexes from our geographic specialty that enable us to peg individuals into a specific county or town. While good professionals rely most heavily upon original source materials rather than

Articles in scholarly journals may not treat our specific families, but the methodologies demonstrated by their writers can open doors for us when we apply them to our own problems.

published copies or extracts, derivatives remain indispensable as finding aids. Modern ones provide every-name indexes that enable us to identify not only the individuals who created records but also the "hidden names" within church, courthouse, and town-hall documents.

The expanding library

Expanding our basic shelf is an equally personal venture, shaped by the nature of the work we typically do. As we add to ours, we give special consideration to the titles discussed in the next section. All are works that have been tested daily—and are deemed essential—by leading professionals around the globe.[1] Some are out of print but might be found through used-book dealers.[2]

Essential Titles

Figure 2 presents a model for building a sound personal and professional library in affordable stages:

Level 1:   Basic Shelf items that all professionals need
Level 2:   Essential items we should acquire as our means permit
Level 3:   Useful items to acquire after the essential library has been established

The titles that follow all fall into levels 1 and 2. There are many other excellent guides, references, and databases from level 3 that you will want to add, as your resources permit. For ease of use, the list below flags Basic Shelf items with a bookshelf symbol in the margin, as shown at right.

U.S. materials

ADDRESS GUIDES

Bentley, Elizabeth Petty. *The Genealogist's Address Book.* Current edition. Baltimore: Genealogical Publishing Co. [periodically revised]. Many gaps exist because not all agencies responded to the questionnaire.

———. *County Courthouse Book.* Current edition. Baltimore: Genealogical Publishing Co. [periodically revised]. A useful supplement to Everton's *Handy Book* and Eichholz's *Red Book,* it may be more accurate for your area of interest.

See also ADOPTION for Culligan, Johnson; SOURCE GUIDES for Eichholz, Kemp.

ADOPTION AND TWENTIETH-CENTURY GUIDES

Askin, Jayne, and Molly David. *Search: A Handbook for Adoptees and Birthparents.* 2d edition. Phoenix, Arizona: Oryx Press, 1998. Best adoption methodology book on the market. Excellent sample letters to adoption agencies, archives, courthouses, and libraries.

Culligan, Joseph J. *Adoption Searches Made Easier.* Miami, Florida: FJA, 1996. Primarily an address book for courthouses, genealogical and historical societies, vital-record bureaus, and other offices. Very little methodology.

THE ESSENTIAL LIBRARY

Johnson, Richard S. *How to Locate Anyone Who Is or Has Been in the Military: Armed Forces Locator Directory*. 8th edition. Burlington, North Carolina: MIE Publishing, 1999. Excellent source for addresses of veterans organizations and information on open or closed military records.

Hinckley, Kathleen W., CGRS. *Locating Lost Family Members & Friends: Modern Genealogical Research Techniques for Locating the People of Your Past and Present*. Cincinnati: Betterway Books, 1999. Unsurpassed. Basic Shelf.

AFRICAN-AMERICAN GUIDES AND CATALOGS

Gutman, Herbert. *The Black Family in Slavery and Freedom, 1750–1925*. New York: Pantheon Books, 1976. A classic for historical perspective.

National Archives Trust Fund Board. *Black Studies: A Select Catalog of National Archives Microfilm Publications*. Washington: NATFB, 1996.

Newman, Debra L. *Black History: A Guide to Civilian Records in the National Archives*. Washington: NATFB, 1984.

Rose, James, and Alice Eichholz, CG. *Black Genesis*. Detroit: Gale Research Company, 1978. Annotated bibliography, covering census records, deeds, manumissions, military records, etc. Still valuable, though it needs updating.

Streets, David H. *Slave Genealogy: A Research Guide with Case Studies*. Bowie, Maryland: Heritage Books, 1986. Step-by-step guide to tracing slaves. Focuses on Wayne County, Kentucky, but demonstrates methods and types of analyses.

Woodtor, Dee Parmer. *Finding a Place Called Home: A Guide to African-American Genealogy and Historical Identity*. Rev. edition. New York: Random House, 1999.

ATLASES AND MAPS

Thorndale, William, and William Dollarhide. *Map Guide to the U.S. Federal Censuses, 1790–1920*. Baltimore: Genealogical Publishing Co., 1987. Maps show county boundary lines for each state, in each federal census year—superimposed upon current boundaries. Basic Shelf.

See also ELECTRONIC SOURCES for *US GeoData*.

COLONIAL NEW ENGLAND MATERIALS

Anderson, Robert Charles, FASG. *The Great Migration Begins: Immigrants to New England, 1620–1633*. 3 vols. Boston: New England Historic Genealogical Society [NEHGS], 1995. This series, with other volumes for later years, offers reconstructed biographies of single men and family heads known for the first waves of New England settlement, with a critical analysis of sources.

Melnyk, Marcia. *Genealogist's Handbook for New England Research*. 4th edition. Boston: New England Historic Genealogical Society, 1999. Provides "genealogies" of towns; repository addresses, hours, phone numbers, and important information about their vital records, deeds, and probate files.

Sanborn, Melinde Lutz, FASG. *Supplement to Torrey's New England Marriages Prior to 1700*. Baltimore: Genealogical Publishing Co., 1991. 2d supplement, 1995. Additions and corrections primarily from journal articles and ongoing research.

Torrey, Clarence Almon. *New England Marriages Prior to 1700*. Baltimore: Genealogical Publishing Co., 1985. Extracted from more than 2,500 volumes of material, published through about 1960. Torrey's manuscript, available at NEHGS and on microfilm elsewhere, cites his sources. The published volume does not. For relevant entries, one checks the manuscript for source data.

See also ELECTRONIC SOURCES for *New England Historical and Genealogical Register.*

DICTIONARIES

Black, Henry Campbell. *Black's Law Dictionary: Definitions of the Terms and Phrases of American and English Jurisprudence, Ancient and Modern.* 6th edition. St. Paul, Minnesota: West Publishing Co., 1990. The 4th edition (1957) has more obsolete terms; the abridged 7th edition (1999) is less useful. Basic Shelf.

Get

DIRECTORIES

Association of Professional Genealogists. *APG Directory.* Denver, Colorado: APG, current edition. Use to help find other professionals. Also online. Basic Shelf.

Board for Certification of Genealogists. *Certification Roster.* Washington: BCG, current edition. Use to find tested experts in the region where you need help. Also online. Basic Shelf.

ELECTRONIC SOURCES*

Ancestry Reference Library. CD-ROM. Salt Lake City: Ancestry, 1998 edition. Contains the full text of *The Source, Ancestry's Red Book, The Archives,* and other significant works. The whole is fully searchable.

Civil War CD-ROM. Carmel, Ind.: Guild Press of Indiana, 1996—. Contains fully searchable text of *The War of the Rebellion: A Compilation of the Official Records of the Union and Confederate Armies* (127 vols. published by Congress, 1880–1901); William F. Fox's *Regimental Losses in the Civil War, 1861–1865* (Albany, New York: Albany Publishing Co., 1889); Frederick H. Dyer's *Compendium of the War of the Rebellion,* 2 vols. (1908; reprinted, New York: Thomas Y. Yoseloff, 1959); and Alan and Barbara Aimone's *A User's Guide to the Official Records* (Shippensburg, Pennsylvania: White Mane Publishing Co., ca. 1993).

Family History SourceGuide. 1 CD-ROM. Salt Lake City: Family History Department, 1998. Contains all the Family History Library's *Research Outlines.*

National Genealogical Society Quarterly, vols. 1–85 (1912–97). 1 CD-ROM. Arlington, Virginia: NGS and Brøderbund, 1997. Offers images, search engine, and every-name index.

The New England Historical and Genealogical Register, vols. 1–148 (1847–1995). 9 CD-ROMs. Boston: New England Historic Genealogical Society, 1996. Offers image copies, search engine, and every-name index.

Periodical Source Index [PERSI]. 1 CD-ROM. Salt Lake City: Ancestry and Allen County Public Library. An electronic version of the ongoing hard-copy series, which indexes the subject matter of thousands of periodicals since 1847.[3]

U.S. General Land Office. *Automated Records Project.* CD-ROM series. Washington: General Land Office, 1993—. State-by-state databases of all original land entries in many federal (public-land) states. An extremely valuable and economical series.

U.S. Geological Survey. *US GeoData: GNIS, Geographic Names Information System.* 1 CD-ROM. Washington: Dept. of the Interior. Also available online.

HISPANIC GUIDES

Platt, Lyman D. *Hispanic Surnames.* Baltimore: Genealogical Publishing Co., 1997.

---

* Electronic editions of valuable reference works are being produced at an explosive rate, on CD-ROM, online, or both. The above list is merely representative of publishers and their offerings.

THE ESSENTIAL LIBRARY

Putney-Beers, Henry. *Spanish and Mexican Records of the American Southwest.* Tucson: University of Arizona Press, 1979.

Ryskamp, George R., J.D., AG. *Finding Your Hispanic Roots.* Baltimore: Genealogical Publishing Co., 1997.

See also INTERNATIONAL: CUBA, LATIN AMERICA, MEXICO, PORTUGAL, SPAIN.

INSTRUCTION MANUALS

Board for Certification of Genealogists. *The BCG Genealogical Standards Manual.* Orem, Utah: Ancestry, 2000. For everyone—not just for certification. Basic Shelf.

The Chicago Manual of Style: The Essential Guide for Writers, Editors, and Publishers. 14th edition. Chicago: University of Chicago Press.1993. Basic Shelf.

Curran, Joan Ferris, CG; Madilyn Coen Crane; and John H. Wray, Ph.D., CG. *Numbering Your Genealogy: Basic Systems, Complex Families, and International Kin.* Arlington, Virginia: National Genealogical Society, 2000. For clarity and accuracy in organizing data; the only guide for numbering genealogies with complex international migration and step-kin/adoption situations. Basic Shelf.

Greenwood, Val D., AG. *The Researcher's Guide to American Genealogy.* 3d edition. Baltimore: Genealogical Publishing Co., 2000. The classic guide. Basic Shelf.

Hatcher, Patricia Law, CG. *Producing a Quality Family History.* Salt Lake City: Ancestry, 1996. Covers formats, typefaces, layouts, indexes, and publishing process. Basic Shelf.

———, and John V. Wylie. *Indexing Family Histories: Simple Steps for a Quality Product.* Arlington, Virginia: National Genealogical Society, 1994.

Hone, E. Wade. *Land & Property Research in the United States.* Salt Lake City: Ancestry, 1997. Helps to understand the complexities of land research in both state-land states and public-land states. Also cites locations of many records.

Jacobus, Donald Lines, FASG. *Genealogy as Pastime and Profession.* 2d rev. edition 1968. Reprinted, Baltimore: Genealogical Publishing Co., 1986. Recommended reading for every serious genealogist. Basic Shelf.

Kemp, Thomas Jay. *The American Census Handbook.* Wilmington, Delaware: Scholarly Resources, 2000.

Leary, Helen F. M., CG, GGL, FASG, ed. *North Carolina Research: Genealogy and Local History.* 2d edition. Raleigh: North Carolina Genealogical Society, 1996. Excellent discussions of data evaluation, research techniques, and other topics valuable for professionals—not just for North Carolina research.

Meyerink, Kory L., AG, ed. *Printed Sources: A Guide to Published Genealogical Records.* Salt Lake City: Ancestry, 1998. Basic Shelf.

Mills, Elizabeth Shown, CG, CGL, FASG. *Evidence! Citation & Analysis for the Family Historian.* Baltimore: Genealogical Publishing Co., 1997. Part 1 explains the processes of citation and analysis. Part 2 provides over 300 models for citing standard and electronic sources in bibliographies and footnotes/endnotes, together with short forms of those citations. Includes many genealogical sources that are omitted from other, more general citation manuals. Basic Shelf.

National Archives and Records Administration. *Guide to Federal Records in the National Archives of the United States.* 3 vols. Washington: NARA, 1995.

———. *Guide to Genealogical Research in the National Archives.* Rev. edition. Washington: National Archives Trust Fund Board [NATFB], 1985. Basic Shelf.

Rose, Christine, CG, CGL, FASG, and Kay Germain Ingalls, CGRS. *The Complete Idiot's Guide to Genealogy.* New York: Alpha Books, 1997. Professional genealogists are frequently asked to recommend a beginner's guide—this is it. Despite its "mass market" title, it is also a good reference for the more experienced.

Ross-Larson, Bruce. *Edit Yourself: A Manual for Everyone Who Works with Words.* Rev. edition. New York: W. W. Norton, 1996.

Get

Rubincam, Milton, CG, FASG. *Pitfalls in Genealogical Research.* Salt Lake City: Ancestry, 1987. Recommended reading for every professional.

Sperry, Kip, AG, CG, FASG. *Reading Early American Handwriting.* Baltimore: Genealogical Publishing Co., 1998.

Stevenson, Noel C., J.D., FASG. *Genealogical Evidence: A Guide to the Standard of Proof Relating to Pedigrees, Ancestry, Heirship, and Family History.* Rev. edition. Laguna Hills, California: Aegean Park Press, 1989. Some concepts are outdated.

Szucs, Loretto D. *They Became Americans: Finding Naturalization Records and Ethnic Origins.* Salt Lake City: Ancestry, 1998.

——, and Sandra Hargreaves Luebking. *The Archives: A Guide to the National Archives Field Branches.* Salt Lake City: Ancestry, 1988.

——, eds. *The Source: A Guidebook of American Genealogy.* Rev. edition. Salt Lake City: Ancestry, 1997. Chapters by 16 leading genealogists. Basic Shelf.

JEWISH GUIDES

Kurzweil, Arthur. *From Generation to Generation.* New York: HarperCollins, 1994. A beginner's guide.

——, and Miriam Weiner, CG, eds. *The Encyclopedia of Jewish Genealogy: Sources of Jewish Genealogical Information in the United States and Canada.* Northvale, New Jersey: Jason Aronson, 1991.

Mokotoff, Gary. *How to Document Victims and Locate Survivors of the Holocaust.* Teaneck, New Jersey: Avotaynu, 1996. Also lists published *Yizkor* books by town.

——, and Warren Blatt. *Getting Started in Jewish Genealogy.* Bergenfield, New Jersey: Avotaynu, 1999.

Zubatsky, David S., and Irwin M. Berent. *Jewish Genealogy: A Sourcebook of Family Histories and Genealogies.* Teaneck, New Jersey: Avotaynu, 1996. A finding aid to published and manuscript genealogies. Arranged by surname.

See also **INTERNATIONAL MATERIALS: EASTERN EUROPE; FRANCE,** Bernard; **ISRAEL**

JOURNALS (STANDARD-BEARERS)

National Genealogical Society Quarterly. Ed. by Elizabeth Shown Mills, CG, CGL, FASG. Emphasizes advanced research methods and guides to little-known resources. Also publishes annual models of compiled genealogies. Founded 1912. A Basic Shelf choice.

Get + new

The American Genealogist. Ed. by David L. Greene, Ph.D., CG, FASG; Robert Charles Anderson, FASG; and Joseph C. Anderson III, CG, FASG. An independently produced quarterly journal founded by Donald Lines Jacobus, FASG, in 1922 as the *New Haven Genealogical Magazine.* Emphasizes early Atlantic colonies and British and Medieval lineages. A Basic Shelf choice.

The Basic Shelf needs at least one of the four items in this group of journals.

Many serious genealogists subscribe to all.

The Genealogist. Ed. by Charles Hansen, FASG, and Gale Ion Harris, Ph.D., FASG. Semiannual journal of the American Society of Genealogists, formerly published by the Association for the Promotion of Scholarship in Genealogy. An eclectic collection of all types of compiled genealogy and resolved genealogical problems, emphasizing studies too lengthy for other journals. A Basic Shelf choice.

The New England Historical and Genealogical Register. Ed. by Henry B. Hoff, J.D.,

THE ESSENTIAL LIBRARY

FASG; Helen S. Ullman, CG, Associate Editor. Quarterly publication of the New England Historic Genealogical Society. Emphasizes compiled accounts of early New England families. Founded 1847. A Basic Shelf choice.

MILITARY MATERIALS

Heitman, Francis B. *Historical Register and Dictionary of the United States Army from Its Organization, September 29, 1789 to March 2, 1903.* 2 vols. 1903; reprinted, Gaithersburg, Maryland: Old Soldiers Books, 1988. Lists Regular Army officers.

National Archives Trust Fund Board. *Military Service Records: A Select Catalog of National Archives Microfilm Publications.* Washington: NATFB, 1985. Basic reference work for identifying federal military and benefits records available on microfilm.

Neagles, James C. *U.S. Military Records: A Guide to Federal & State Sources, Colonial America to the Present.* Salt Lake City: Ancestry, 1994.

See also ELECTRONIC SOURCES for *Civil War CD-ROM.*

NATIVE-AMERICAN MATERIALS

Carter, Kent. *The Dawes Commission and the Allotment of the Five Civilized Tribes, 1893–1914.* Salt Lake City: Ancestry.com, 1999.

Hill, Edward E. *Guide to Records in the National Archives of the United States Relating to American Indians.* Washington: National Archives and Records Service, 1981. Federal records are the backbone of research on this ethnic group.

National Archives Trust Fund Board. *American Indians: A Select Catalog of National Archives Microfilm Publications.* Washington: NATFB, 1995.

SOURCE GUIDES AND CATALOGS

G6

Eichholz, Alice, Ph.D., CG, ed. *Ancestry's Red Book: American State, County & Town Sources.* Rev. edition. Salt Lake City: Ancestry, 1992. State-by-state lists of county and city offices, their holdings, and creation dates; general discussions of resources within the states. There are errors and omissions, but there are also valuable chapters. The revised edition corrects a goodly number of problems noted by reviewers of the original edition, but some chapters remain plagued. Use in conjunction with Everton's *Handy Book;* each corrects the other on particular points. Basic Shelf.

Everton, George Sr., ed. *The Handy Book for Genealogists: United States of America.* 9th edition. Logan, Utah: Everton Publishers, 1999. State-by-state and county-by-county addresses of genealogical societies and courthouses, together with data on county formation and record availability. This work should be used with Eichholz's *Red Book,* because each corrects errors in the other. Basic Shelf.

Filby, P. William, comp. *A Bibliography of American County Histories.* Baltimore: Genealogical Publishing Co., 1985. The work is not intended to be complete because it omits county histories that cover multiple counties.

———, comp. *American & British Genealogy & Heraldry: A Selected List of Books.* 3d edition. Boston: New England Historic Genealogical Society, 1983. Arranged by subject and locality, with many little-known sources.

Kemp, Thomas Jay. *International Vital Records Handbook.* 4th edition. Baltimore: Genealogical Publishing Co., 2000. Contains addresses, application forms, and ordering information for vital records in the U.S., Canada, and other countries. Basic Shelf.

Lainhart, Ann S. *State Census Records.* Baltimore: Genealogical Publishing Co., 1992. State-by-state listing of state-level enumerations, with descriptions.

Matchette, Robert B., et al. *Guide to Federal Records in the National Archives of the United States.* 3 vols. Washington: National Archives and Records Administration [NARA], 1995. Also available at NARA's website.

National Archives and Records Administration. *National Archives Microfilm Resources for Research: A Comprehensive Catalog.* Washington: NARA, 1996. Also available at NARA's website.

———. *Diplomatic Records: A Select Catalog of National Archives Microfilm Publications.* Washington: NATFB, 1986.

———. *Federal Court Records: A Select Catalog of National Archives Microfilm Publications.* Washington: NATFB, 1987.

———. *Federal Population Censuses, 1790–1890: A Catalog of Microfilm Copies of the Schedules.* Washington: NATFB, 1998.

———. *Genealogical & Biographical Research: A Select Catalog of National Archives Microfilm Publications.* Rev. edition. Washington: NATFB, 1991.

———. *Immigrant and Passenger Arrivals: A Select Catalog of National Archives Microfilm Publications.* Washington: NATFB, 1991.

———. *Military Service Records: A Select Catalog of National Archives Microfilm Publications.* Washington: NATFB, 1985.

———. *1900 Federal Population Census: A Catalog of Microfilm Copies of the Schedules.* Washington: NATFB, 1996.

———. *The 1910 Federal Population Census: A Catalog of Microfilm Copies of the Schedules.* Washington: NATFB, 1996.

———. *The 1920 Federal Population Census: Catalog of National Archives Microfilm.* 2d edition. Washington: NATFB, 1992.

Reisinger, Joy, CG. *Index to NGS and FGS Conferences and Syllabi.* Washington and Salt Lake City: National Genealogical Society and Federation of Genealogical Societies, 1993. Use to find syllabus materials prepared for major conferences by dozens of leading genealogists, on a wide variety of specialized topics. Available from either organization.

Schreiner-Yantis, Netti and Marian Hoffman, comps. *Genealogical & Local History Books in Print.* 1st–4th editions, plus two supplements, by Schreiner-Yantis; Springfield, Virginia: Genealogical Books in Print, 1975–92. 5th edition, 4 vols., by Hoffman; Baltimore: Genealogical Publishing Co., 1996–97. Each edition is radically different.

STYLE GUIDES

The Chicago Manual of Style. 14th edition. Chicago: University of Chicago Press, 1993. Generally considered the "definitive" treatment of editing and assembling publications, although it does not address genealogy per se.

Mills, Elizabeth Shown, CG, CGL, FASG. *Evidence! Citation & Analysis for the Family Historian.* Baltimore: Genealogical Publishing Co., 1997. Part 2 provides over 300 models for citing standard and electronic sources in bibliographies and footnotes/endnotes, together with short forms of those citations. Covers many types of genealogical materials omitted from *The Chicago Manual of Style, MLA Handbook,* and other style guides. Basic Shelf.

International materials

AUSTRALIA

Gray, Nancy. *Compiling Your Family History*. Sydney: Society of Australian Genealogists and Australian Broadcasting Corporation, 1993. A brief how-to guide aimed at beginners, but it offers contact addresses for each state and territory.

Rogers, Ruth. *Family History for Beginners*. Canberra: Heraldry and Genealogy Society of Canberra, 1994. Probably the best introductory guide to Australian sources.

Vine Hall, Nick, DipFHS (Hons.). *Parish Registers in Australia: A List of Originals, Transcripts, Microforms & Indexes of Australian Parish Registers*. 2d edition. Middle Park, Australia: privately printed, 1990.

————. *Tracing Your Family History in Australia: A Guide to Sources*. 2d edition. Albert Park, Australia: privately printed, 1994. The only national source guide in print. Summarizes early-European settlement in each region and includes a 110-page bibliography.

CANADA

Department of the Secretary of State of Canada. *The Canadian Style: A Guide to Writing and Editing*. Toronto: Dundurn Press, 1985.

Family History Library. *Research Outline: Canada*. Rev edition. Salt Lake City: Family History Department, 1993.

Fellows, Robert F. *Researching Your Ancestors in New Brunswick, Canada*. Fredericton: Provincial Archives, 1979. Necessary for research in the province, although outdated.

Hillman, Thomas A. *Catalogue of Census Returns on Microfilm: Catalogue de recensements sur microfilm, 1666–1891*. Ottawa: Public Archives of Canada, 1987. Use as a place-finder, as well as for reel numbers.

————. *Catalogue of Census Returns on Microfilm, 1901*. Ottawa: National Archives of Canada, 1992.

Jonasson, Eric. *The Canadian Genealogical Handbook*. N.p.: Wheatfield Press, 1978. Still the best guide, although addresses and fees are outdated. Essential for reel numbers to the microfilmed ships' passenger arrival lists.

Merriman, Brenda Dougall, CGRS, CGL. *Genealogy in Ontario: Searching the Records*. 3d edition. Toronto: Ontario Genealogical Society, 1996. One of the best.

Punch, Terrence M. CG(C). *Genealogical Research in Nova Scotia*. 3d edition. Halifax: Petheric Press, 1985. Excellent.

————, and George F. Sanborn Jr., FASG, eds. *Genealogists' Handbook for Atlantic Canada Research*. 2d edition. Boston: New England Historic Genealogical Society, 1997. Each chapter is by an expert on the province covered.

Taylor, Ryan. *Books You Need to Do Genealogy in Ontario: An Annotated Bibliography*. Fort Wayne, Indiana: Round Tower Books, 1996. Very helpful for literature surveys.

CUBA

Carr, Peter E. *Guide to Cuban Genealogical Research: Records and Sources*. Chicago: Adams Press, 1991.

A library is not a luxury but one of the necessities of life. A little library, growing each year, is an honorable part of a man's history.

—*Henry Ward Beecher*[4]

———. *Censos, Padrónes y Matrículas de la Población de Cuba: Siglos 16, 17 y 18* (Censuses [and Other Lists] of the Population of Cuba: 16th, 17th, and 18th Centuries). San Obispo, California: Cuban Index, 1993.
See also **LATIN AMERICA, SPAIN;** and **U.S. MATERIALS: HISPANIC GUIDES.**

EASTERN EUROPE
Mokotoff, Gary, and Sallyann Amdur Sack. *Where Once We Walked: A Guide to the Jewish Communities Destroyed in the Holocaust.* Teaneck, New Jersey: Avotaynu, 1991. A gazetteer of 21,000 Central and Eastern European localities, arranged alphabetically and phonetically under the Daitch-Mokotoff Soundex System, so that various spellings can be readily found.
Weiner, Miriam, CG. *Jewish Roots in Poland: Pages from the Past and Archival Inventories.* New York: YIVO, 1998.
———. *Jewish Roots in Ukraine and Moldova: Pages from the Past and Archival Inventories.* Clifton, New Jersey: Routes to Roots Foundation, 1999.
See also **U.S. MATERIALS: JEWISH GUIDES;** and **INTERNATIONAL MATERIALS: GERMANY, POLAND**

ENGLAND
Colwell, Stella. *Family Roots: Discovering the Past in the Public Record Office.* Rutland, Vermont: Charles E. Tuttle Co., 1991. Covers materials in the Public Record Office (PRO), with case studies focusing on particular families.
Cox, Jane, and Timothy Padfield. *Tracing Your Ancestors in the Public Record Office.* 5th edition by Amanda Bevan. Kew, England: Public Records Office Handbooks no. 19, 1999. A key reference work to understanding genealogical material in the PRO, with an appendix of useful addresses for other archives.
Dawson, Giles E., and Laetitia Kennedy-Skipton. *Elizabethan Handwriting: 1500–1650: A Guide to the Reading of Documents and Manuscripts.* New York: W. W. Norton, 1966. Discussed at length in chapter 2.
Herber, Mark D. *Ancestral Trails: The Complete Guide to British Genealogy and Family History.* Stroud, England: Sutton Publishing, in association with the Society of Genealogists, 1997; Baltimore: Genealogical Publishing Co., 1998.
Humphery-Smith, Cecil, ed. *The Phillimore Atlas and Index of Parish Registers.* Rev. edition. Sussex, England: Phillimore and Co., 1995. Includes Scotland. Combines atlas with guide to parish registers and probate jurisdictions.
Martin, Charles Trice. *The Record Interpreter: A Collection of Abbreviations, Latin Words, and Names Used in English Historical Manuscripts and Records.* 1892; reprinted, Sussex, England: Phillimore and Co., 1982. Discussesd at length in chapter 2.
Moulton, Joy Wade, CG. *Genealogical Resources in English Repositories.* Columbus, Ohio: Hampton House, 1988. Also available from Genealogical Publishing Co., Baltimore, with supplements of 1992 and 1996. A county-by-county guide to record offices and other research facilities, with detailed treatment of London.
Reid, Judith Prowse, and Simon Fowler. *Genealogical Research in England's Public Record Office: A Guide for North Americans.* 2d edition. Baltimore: Genealogical Publishing Co., 2000.
Rogers, Colin D. *The Family Tree Detective: A Manual for Analysing and Solving Genealogical Problems in England and Wales, 1538 to the Present Day.* Manchester?: Manchester University Press, 1983. A problem-solving approach to research and records.

Good as it is to inherit a library, it is better to collect one.

—*Augustine Birrell*[5]

THE ESSENTIAL LIBRARY

Wagner, Anthony Richard, Sir, FASG. *English Genealogy*. 3d edition. Sussex, England: Phillimore, 1983. English social history as a background for genealogical research; history of the records; history of genealogy and heraldry.

FRANCE

Astorquia, Madeline, et al. *Guide des sources de l'histoire des états-unis dans les archives françaises*. Paris: France Expansion, 1976. Comprehensive and detailed.

Bernard, Gildas. *Les familles juives en France: XVIe–1815: Guide des recherchces biographiques et généalogiques*. Paris: Archives Nationales, 1990.

————. *Les familles protestantes en France: XVIe siècle–1792: Guide des recherches biographiques et généalogiques*. Paris: Archives Nationales, 1987.

————. *Guide des recherches sur l'histoire des familles*. Paris: Archives Nationales, 1988. The definitive work, quite detailed. Treats many types of archives and records. Also covers the distinctive French Republican calendar. If a library can have only one book in this category, this is it.

Commission de coordination de la documentation administrative. *Comment éditer une publication*. Paris: Documentation française, ca. 1980.

Dubost, Jean François. *Les Étrangers en France: XVIe siècle–1789*. Paris: Archives Nationales, 1993. A comprehensive treatment of methods and sources.

Pontet, Patrick. *Ancestral Research in France*. Andover, Hampshire, England: Anglo-French Family History Society, 1998.

————. *Ancestral Research in Paris*. Andover, Hampshire, England: Anglo-French Family History Society, 1998.

————. *A–Z Genealogical References and Sources*. Andover, Hampshire, England: Anglo-French Family History Society, 1998. An alphabetical listing and explanation of French materials and their content, location, and terminology.

Valynseele, Joseph, ed. *La généalogie: Histoire et pratique*. Paris: Larousse, 1991.

Vuillet, Bernard, et al. *Sur les traces de vos ancêtres à Paris: la recherche des origines*. Paris: Archives de Paris, 1997. An excellent guide for research at the Archives of Paris, the combined facility for the city and the department of Seine.

GERMANY

Brandt, Edward R., et al. *Germanic Genealogy: A Guide to Worldwide Sources and Migration Patterns*. 2d edition. St. Paul, Minnesota: Germanic Genealogy Society, 1997. Covers a broader region than just present-day Germany, with maps and discussions of geography and history. Some consider this the best guide of all to German research, in any language.

Jensen, Larry O. *A Genealogical Handbook of German Research*. 2 vols. Pleasant Grove, Utah: Privately printed, 1980; vol. 1, revised 1983. Includes handwriting samples, examples of records, and some methodology advice.

Quester, Erich [Bearbeiter]: *Wegweiser für Forschungen nach Vorfahren aus den ost deutschen und südetendeutschen Gebieten sowie aus den deutschen Siedlungsräumen in Mittel-, Ost- und Südosteuropa*. 4th edition. Neustadt an der Aish: Verlag Degener and Co., 1995. The classic work for research in former East Germany and the other specified regions.

Ribbe, Wolfgang, and Eckart Henning. *Taschenbuch für Familiengeschichtsforschung*. 11th edition. Neustadt an der Aish: Verlag Degener and Co., 1995. Covers many basic and advanced topics, with bibliographies.

A library book is not an article of mere consumption but of capital, and often in the case of professional men, setting out in life, is their only capital.

—*Thomas Jefferson*[6]

IRELAND

Begley, Donal E., ed. *Irish Genealogy: A Record Finder.* 1981; reprinted, Dublin: Heraldic Artists, 1987. Each chapter is written by an authority on the subject.

Falley, Margaret Dickson, FASG. *Irish and Scotch-Irish Ancestral Research: A Guide to the Genealogical Records, Methods, and Sources in Ireland.* 2 vols. 1962; reprinted, Baltimore: Genealogical Publishing Co., 1988. The Bible of Irish how-to books, with comprehensive explanations of sources and repositories. Use recent guides to update record locations. For the advanced.

Family History Library. *A Genealogical Research Guide for Ireland.* Rev. edition. Salt Lake City: Family History Department, 1994. A genealogical how-to guide focusing on resources in the FHL collection.

Grenham, John. *Tracing Your Irish Ancestors: The Complete Guide.* 2d edition, Dublin: Gill and MacMillan; Baltimore: Genealogical Publishing Co., 1999. Covers basic and lesser-used sources (by county), Catholic parish maps, etc.

Handran, George B., CG, ed. *Townlands in Poor Law Unions: A Reprint of Poor Law Union Pamphlets of the General Registrar's Office.* Salem, Massachusetts: Higginson Book Co., 1997. Particularly valuable for using FHL's International Genealogical Index™ (IGI), because indexes of civil registrations (post-1864) use registration district for birthplace in lieu of exact townland. Also useful for Valuation Office research, census work, and historical demographic data.

Helferty, Seamus, and Raymond Refaussé, eds. *Directory of Irish Archives.* 3d edition. Dublin: Four Courts Press, 1999. Addresses, telephone numbers, hours of operation, and a summary of major holdings for archives throughout Ireland.

Her Majesty's Stationery Office. *General Alphabetical Index to the Townlands and Towns, Parishes and Baronies of Ireland, Based on the Census of Ireland for the Year 1851.* Dublin, 1861; reprinted, Baltimore: Genealogical Publishing Co., 2000. Not a gazetteer, but still definitive for locating place names and their jurisdictions of baronies, counties, parishes, poor law unions, and townlands.

Lewis, Samuel. *A Topographical Dictionary of Ireland.* 1837; reprinted, Baltimore: Genealogical Publishing Co., 1995. A classic for Irish research; one can find the various religious-parish names by searching Lewis's civil parish data.

MacLysaght, Edward. *The Surnames of Ireland.* Dublin: Irish Academic Press, 1991. Definitive authority on the origin and meaning of Irish surnames. Due to tribal origins of many Irish surnames, this work can point to possible origins of an Irish immigrant.

McCarthy, Tony. *The Irish Roots Guide.* Dublin: Lilliput Press, 1991. Emphasizes the study of ancestors in the context of social position. Primarily addresses Irish Catholic families, but many of the sources pertain to other Irish families.

Mitchell, Brian. *A Guide to Irish Churches and Graveyards.* Baltimore: Genealogical Publishing Co., 1990.

———. *A Guide to Irish Parish Registers.* Baltimore: Genealogical Publishing Co., 1988.

———. *A New Genealogical Atlas of Ireland.* Baltimore: Genealogical Publishing Co., 1986.

Prochaska, Alice. *Irish History from 1700: A Guide to Sources in the Public Record Office* [England]. London: British Records Association, 1986. Detailed summation of the record categories pertaining to Irish material.

Public Record Office of Northern Ireland. *An Irish Genealogical Source: Guide to Church Records.* Belfast: Ulster Historical Foundation, 1994. Definitive guide

A great library contains the diary of the human race.

—*George Mercer Dawson*[7]

to the location of church records for Northern Ireland. Cites microfilm numbers at PRONI and identifies records still in local custody. Includes standard christenings, marriages, and burials, as well as communicant rolls, membership registers, minutes, preachers' books, vestry registers, etc.

Ryan, James G., ed. *Irish Church Records: Their History, Availability, and Use in Family and Local History Research.* Glenageary, County Dublin: Flyleaf Press, 1992. Excellent coverage of Baptist, Catholic, Church of Ireland, Huguenot, Jewish, Methodist, Presbyterian, and Quaker records.

———. *Irish Records.* 2d edition. Glenageary: Flyleaf Press, 1997; Salt Lake City: Ancestry, 1997.

ISRAEL

Sack, Sallyann Amdur. *A Guide to Jewish Genealogical Research in Israel.* Teaneck, New Jersey: Avotaynu, 1994. Detailed guide to the accessibility and holdings of each agency. Appendixes include *Yizkor* books and *landsmannschaften* listed at the Yad Vashem Library and a list of towns represented at 1981 World Gathering of Holocaust Survivors.

See also U.S. MATERIALS: JEWISH GUIDES.

ITALY

Cole, Trafford R. *Italian Genealogical Records: How to Use Italian Civil, Ecclesiastical, and Other Records in Family History Research.* Salt Lake City: Ancestry, 1995. Discusses history and development of Italian recordation and describes the records.

Colletta, John Philip. *Finding Italian Roots: The Complete Guide for Americans.* Baltimore: Genealogical Publishing Co., 1993. Takes the researcher from American records to Italian records in an easy-to-understand format, explaining record categories, content, and availability.

Fucilla, Joseph G. *Our Italian Surnames.* Baltimore: Genealogical Publishing Co., 1987. Useful for determining areas where certain Italian surnames are common.

LATIN AMERICA

Platt, Lyman D. *Una Guía Genealógica-Histórica de Latinoamerica.* Ramona, California: Acoma Books, 1978.

See also CUBA, MEXICO; U.S. MATERIALS: HISPANIC GUIDES.

MEXICO

Archivo de Simancas, Secretaria de Guerra, *Hojas de Servicios de América.* Valladolid: Patronato Nacional de Archivos Historicos, 1958.

Bolton, Herbert E. *Guide to Materials for the History of the United States in the Principal Archives of Mexico.* 1913; reprinted: Millwood, New York: Kraus Reprint Co., 1977.

García de Miranda, Enriqueta, and Zaida Falcon de Gyves. *Nuevo Atlas Porrua de la República Mexicana.* 9th edition. Mexico City: Editorial Porrua, 1993.

Gerhard, Peter. *A Guide to the Historical Geography of New Spain.* Cambridge, England: Cambridge University Press, 1972.

———. *The North Frontier of New Spain.* Norman: University of Oklahoma Press, 1982.

Every library should try to be complete on something, if it were only the history of pinheads.

—Oliver Wendell Holmes[8]

———. *The Southeast Frontier of New Spain.* Norman: University of Oklahoma Press, 1993.

Herrera Huerta, Juan Manuel, and Vicente San Vicente Tello. *Archivo General de la Nación, México: Guía General.* Mexico City: Archivo General, 1990.

Magdaleno, Ricardo. *Catálogo XX del Archivo General de Simancas: Títulos de Indias.* Valladolid: Patronato Nacional de Archivos Históricos, 1954.

Naylor, Thomas H., and Charles W. Polzer. *Northern New Spain: A Research Guide.* Tucson: University of Arizona Press, 1981.

Platt, Lyman D. *Serie de Investigaciónes Genealógicas del IGHL: México.* Salt Lake City: Instituto Genealógico-Histórico Latinoamericano, 1991. See especially: vol. 2, *Guía General: Divisiónes Políticas;* vol. 3, *Guía General: Divisiónes Eclesiásticas;* and vol. 4, *Guía de Investigaciónes Genealógicas.*

Rodriguez Ochoa, Patricia. *Guía general de los archivos estatales y municipales de México.* Mexico City: Sistema Nacional de Archivos, 1988.

See also LATIN AMERICA; and U.S. MATERIALS: HISPANIC GUIDES.

NEW ZEALAND

Bagnall, A. G. *New Zealand National Bibliography.* 5 vols. Wellington: Government Printer, 1967–85. A handy finding list for published material.

Bromell, Anne. *Tracing Family History in New Zealand.* Auckland: Godwit, 1996. National coverage, but only a brief list of "useful addresses."

NORWAY

Andresen, Harald. *Norsk Lokalhistorie: En Bibliografi.* Oslo: Universitetsforlaget, 1969. Guide to farm/family histories.

Hansen, Morten. *Norske Slektsbøker.* Oslo: H. Aschehoug, 1965. A bibliography of Norwegian family histories.

Nedrebø, Yngve. *How to Trace Your Ancestors in Norway.* Oslo: Royal Norwegian Ministry of Foreign Affairs, 1996. Available free from any U.S. Norwegian consulate office; includes addresses for state archives in Norway.

Solem, Jan Fredrik. *Norsk Slektshistorisk Bibliografi, 1963–1984.* Oslo: Statens Bibliotekhøgskole, 1985. A supplement to the 1965 Hansen volume.

Stoa, Nils Johan, and Per-Øivind Sandberg. *Våre Røtter: Håndbok I slektsgransking for nybergynnere og viderrekomne.* Oslo: J. W. Cappelens Forlag, 1992. Perhaps the definitive guide for Norwegian genealogical research.

POLAND

Chorzempa, Rosemary A. *Korzenie Polskie, Polish Roots.* Baltimore: Genealogical Publishing Co., 1993. Basic guide to Polish research.

Ortell, Gerald A. *Polish Parish Records of the Roman Catholic Church.* Milwaukee: Polish Genealogical Society of America, 1996. Helpful to non-Polish-speaking researchers who know village of origin in Poland and use filmed parish records. Offers basic Polish and Latin genealogical vocabulary, examples of register entries, and explanations of basic social systems and church organization.

PORTUGAL

Azevedo, Pedro A. de, and Antonio Baiao. *O Arquivo da torre do Tombo.* 1905; reprinted Lisbon: Arquivo Nacional da Torre do Tombo-Livros Horizonte, 1989.

My books are my tools, and the greater their variety and perfection, the greater the help to my literary work.

—*Tryon Edwards*[9]

THE ESSENTIAL LIBRARY

Church of Jesus Christ of Latter-day Saints. *Basic Portuguese Paleography, Resource Papers*, ser. 2. Salt Lake City: LDS, 1976.

———. *Word List: Portuguese and Latin*. Salt Lake City: LDS, 1995.

Cruz, António. *Paleografia Portuguesa: Ensaio de Manual*. Porto: Universidades Portucalense, 1987.

Diccionário chorográphico de Portugal, continental e insular. 12 vols. Porto, Portugal: n.p., 1929–49.

Mariz, Jose. *Inventario Colectiveo dos Registos Paroquiais*, vol. 1, *Centro e Sul*. Lisbon: Secretária de Estado da Cultura, 1993.

———. *Inventário Colecteveo dos Registos Paroquiais*, vol. 2, *Norte*. Lisbon: Secretária de Estado Da Cultura, 1994.

Serrão, Joel. *Roteiro de Fontes da História Portuguesa Contemporânea, arquivos de Lisboa: Arquivo Nacional da Torre do Tombo*. 2 vols. Lisbon: Instituto Nacional de Investigação Científica, 1984.

———. *Roteiro de Fontes da História Portuguesa Contemporânea, arquivos de Lisboa: Arquivos do Etado, Arquivos da C.M.* Lisbon: Instituto Nacional de Investigação Científica, 1985.

See also **U.S. MATERIALS: HISPANIC GUIDES.**

SCOTLAND

Irvine, Sherry, CG. *Your Scottish Ancestry: A Guide for North Americans*. Salt Lake City: Ancestry, 1997.

Moody, David. *Scottish Local History*. London: B. T. Batsford, 1986. Good instruction on placing ancestors in their communities; better than the author's *Scottish Family History,* because it discusses a greater variety of records.

Sinclair, Cecil. *Tracing Your Ancestors in the Scottish Record Office*. Edinburgh: Her Majesty's Stationery Office, 1990. Also Sinclair, *Tracing Scottish Local History* [same publisher], 1994. Both are essential for learning extant records. *Local History* incorrectly assumes some records are irrelevant to genealogists.

Smout, T. C. *A Century of Scottish People, 1830–1950*. 1986; reprinted, London: Fontana Press, 1987.

———. *A History of the Scottish People, 1560–1830*. 1969; reprinted, London: Fontana Press, 1989. Essential to understanding early-modern Scots and those who emigrated in the seventeenth through early-nineteenth centuries.

SPAIN

Atlas Gráfico de España. 16 vols. Madrid: Aguilar, 1969.

Bermudez Plata, Cristobal. *El Archivo General de Indias de Sevilla, sede del americanismo*. Madrid: n.p., 1951.

Bores, Angel de Plaza. *Archivo General de Simancas. Guía del Investigador*. 4th edition, rev. Madrid: n.p., 1992.

Crespo Noguera, Carmen. *Archivo Histórico Nacional: Guía*. Madrid: Ministerio de Cultura, 1989.

Guía de Archivos Militares Españoles. Madrid: Ministerio de Defensa, 1995.

Guía de fuentes para la historia de Ibero-América conservados en España. 2 vols. Madrid: Dirección General de Archivos y Bibliotecas, 1965, 1969.

Guía de los Archivos Estatales Españoles: Guía del Investigador. 2d edition. Madrid: Ministerio de Cultura Dirección General de Bellas Artes y Archivos, Subdirección de Archivos, 1984.

A library should be the delivery room for the birth of ideas—a place where history comes to life.

—*Norman Cousins*[10]

Guía de los Archivos y las Bibliotecas de la Iglesia en España. 2 vols. León: Asociación Española de Archiveros Eclesiásticos, 1985. vol. 1, *Archivos;* vol. 2: *Bibliotecas personal.*

Madoz, Pascual. *Diccionario geográfico-estadístico-histórico de España y su posesiónes de ultramar.* 16 vols. 1845–50; reprinted, Almendralejo, Badajoz: Centro Cultural Santa Ana, 1992–96.

Millares Carlo, Agustín. *Tratado de Paleografía Española.* 3 vols. Madrid: Espasa-Calpe, 1983.

Ministerio de Educación y Ciencia, Dirección General de Archivos y Bibliotecas [DGAB]. *Censo-Guía de Archivos Españoles.* Madrid: Ministerio de Educación, 1962.

Oficina General de Información y Estadística de la Iglesia en España. *Guía de la Iglesia en España.* Madrid: Oficina General, 1954; three supplements, 1955–57.

Sánchez Belda, Luis. *Archivo Histórico Nacional: Bibliografía de archivos españoles y de archivística.* Madrid: Dirección General de Archivos y Bibliotecas, 1963.

———. *Guía del Archivo Histórico Nacional.* Madrid: Dirección General de Archivos y Bibliotecas 1958.

See also **CUBA, LATIN AMERICA, MEXICO;** and **U.S. MATERIALS: HISPANIC GUIDES.**

SWEDEN

Johanson, Carl-Erik. *Cradled In Sweden.* Rev. edition. Logan, Utah: Everton Publishers, 1995. This is the book to have if you are serious about Swedish research.

Pladsen, Phyllis J., and Joseph C. Huber. *Swedish Genealogical Dictionary.* 2d edition. N.p.: Pladsen-Huber Press, 1993. Includes old words found in records before the spelling reform of 1906; more useful than a modern Swedish-English dictionary.

SWITZERLAND

Familiennamenbuch der Schweiz: Les noms de familles suisses; I nomi di famiglia svizzeri (Swiss Family Surname Book). Zürich: Polygraphischer Verlag, 1971. An alphabetical listing of surnames, giving villages where they are found.

Suess, Jared H. *Handy Guide to Swiss Genealogical Records.* Logan, Utah: Everton Publishers, 1978. Includes French and German word lists and sample letters.

Wellauer, Maralyn A. *Tracing Your Swiss Roots.* Milwaukee: privately printed, 1988. Overlaps somewhat with Suess but adds other material.

WALES

Ifans, Dafydd, ed. *Cofrestri Anghydffurfiol Cymru; Nonconformist Registers of Wales.* Aberystwyth: National Library of Wales, 1994. Lists all nonconformist registers that have been deposited in a Welsh record repository; the major drawback is that a vast number have not yet been deposited.

Istance, Jean, and E. E. Cann. *Researching Family History in Wales.* Birmingham, England: Federation of Family History Societies/Association of the Family History Societies of Wales, 1996. Not a how-to book, but a very detailed guide to the location and access of Welsh records—including addresses, opening hours, and costs.

Rowlands, John, and Sheila Rowlands, eds. *Second Stages in Researching Welsh Ancestry.* Baltimore: Genealogical Publishing Co., 1999.

Never lend books, for no one ever returns them; the only books I have in my library are books that other folks have lent me.

—*Anatole France*[11]

THE ESSENTIAL LIBRARY

TIP

The locality guides prepared by the Family History Library for many countries and all U.S. states are a valuable, low-cost collection for every genealogical shelf.

―――. *The Surnames of Wales for Family Historians and Others*. Baltimore: Genealogical Publishing Co., 1996. Major new work based on years of research and name studies. Shows how surnames are used and how they can be both a stumbling block and an aid to research.

―――. *Welsh Family History: A Guide to Research*. 2d edition. Birmingham, England: Federation of Family History Societies, 1993; Baltimore: Genealogical Publishing Co., 1999. Standard reference work on Welsh research. Over 20 chapters written by various academic and family historians deal with such subjects as the Court of the Great Sessions, parish registers and bishop's transcripts, nonconformity church records, Welsh surnames and place names, and wills and estates.

Williams, C. J., and J. Watts-Williams, eds. *Cofrestri Plwyf Cymru/Parish Registers of Wales*. Aberystwyth: National Library of Wales, 1986. Lists locations of all parish registers for the Established Church in Wales—generally at a county record office or the National Library of Wales.

NOTES

1. Many colleagues deserve recognition for their recommendations of essential works: Robert Charles Anderson, FASG, for England; Claire Mire Bettag, CGRS, for French guides; Curtis Brasfield, CGRS, for African Americans; Sharon DeBartolo Carmack, CG, for Italy; Donn Devine, J.D., CG, CGI, for legal references; George B. Handran, J.D., CG, for Ireland; James L. Hansen, FASG, for Native Americans; Patricia Law Hatcher, CG, FASG, for colonial New England; Blaine Hedberg, for Norway; Dr. Ronald A. Hill, CG, for England and Latin script; Dr. Helen Hinchliff, CG, for Scotland; Kathleen W. Hinckley, CGRS, for adoption and twentieth-century; Birdie Monk Holsclaw, for electronic sources; Dean Hunter, AG, CGRS, for Wales; Karen Livsey, for Sweden; Suzanne McVetty, CG, for Ireland; Marie Varrelman Melchiori, CGRS, CGL, for the American military; Elizabeth Shown Mills, CG, CGL, FASG, for Cuba, France, Mexico, and Latin America; Gary Mokotoff for Israel and Jewish Americans; Eileen Polakoff for Israel and Jewish Americans; David E. Rencher, AG, for England and Ireland; George R. Ryskamp, J.D., AG, for Mexico, Portugal, and Spain; Henning Schröeder, for Germany; Beth Stahr, CGRS, for Poland and Switzerland; and Nick Vine Hall, DipFHS (Hons.), for Australia and New Zealand.

2. Two large networks of used-book dealers can be tapped online at <www.bibliofind.com> and <www.bookfind.com>, both sites that consolidate inventories from thousands of dealers of "old, rare, and used books in the U.S. and abroad."

3. For an instructive review of the electronic edition of PERSI, see Kathleen W. Hinckley, reviewer, "Periodical Source Index (PERSI)," *Association of Professional Genealogists Quarterly* 13 (June 1998): 68–69.

4. Henry Ward Beecher (1813–87), American clergyman and writer, quoted at *Quotations about Libraries and Librarians,* website <www.nlc-bnc.ca/ifla/I/humour/author.htm>, downloaded 3 January 1998.

5. Augustine Birrell (1850–1933), British essayist and statesman, ibid.

6. Thomas Jefferson (1743–1825), American president, ibid.

7. George Mercer Dawson (1849–1901), Canadian explorer, ibid.

8. Oliver Wendell Holmes (1809–94), American physician and man of letters, ibid.

9. Tryon Edwards (1809–94), American theologist and editor, ibid.

10. Norman Cousins (1912 or 1915–90), American editor and professor of medical humanities, ibid.

11. Anatole France, pen name of French novelist Jacques Anatole François Thibault (1844–1924), ibid.

Ethics and Legalities

5

**ETHICAL
STANDARDS**

Keynotes

Ethical Standards

by Neil D. Thompson, LL.B., Ph.D., CG, FASG

Ethics are a system of moral principles and practices generally accepted as binding within a particular field. For professional genealogists, two sets of ethical standards prevail: those that pertain to research scholarship, and those related to business matters.

The academic world has developed effective standards for proper research and fair use of intellectual materials. The business world—law, medicine, and accountancy, for example—has established canons of conduct that govern relationships between client and practitioner. In both worlds, accepted ethical standards have been tested in the courts and may now have the force of law, as well as the power of custom. This is not the case in our field. No statutory rule or body of precedent (case law) binds the ethical practice of professional genealogy. While it is true that many of us work within the legal freedoms and restrictions of employment agreements or client contracts, we should not confuse legalities with ethics. Silently incorporating the non-copyrighted work of someone else into our own research report, for example, may be legal but it is not ethical.

Codes of conduct have long been in place for genealogists who are certified or accredited and for those who belong to various associations of professional genealogists. (See appendix B.) Because sanctions for violation include termination of credentials or membership, compliance hinges upon an individual's desire to remain identified with the particular organization. Without the force of law *requiring* them, both credentials and memberships are optional. Ethics are not.

Any discussion of ethical obligations tends to read like a litany of *thou shalt nots;* but guidelines, if they are to be helpful, should distinguish clearly between behaviors the community deems acceptable and those it disapproves. The underlying principle that generates the litany, of course, is the Golden Rule: Do unto others as we would have them do unto us. Thus: we do what we undertake to do, and we do it as well as we can. We are honorable and trustworthy in our dealings with clients and others who benefit from our work. And we treat fellow professionals as colleagues rather than competitors.

Within this framework, we consider here three aspects of ethics for the professional genealogist: client relationships, colleague relationships, and community relationships.

Client Relationships

Our clients may be individual researchers, family or surname groups, genealogical or hereditary societies, or government or private agencies. They may be paying clients or we may assist them pro bono. Regardless, our relationships with them begin with soliciting or accepting employment and end with delivery of and payment for our work product. Ethics are our guidelines for defining and maintaining an equitable balance between the value given and the value received.

> For professional genealogists, two sets of ethical standards prevail: those that pertain to research scholarship, and those related to business matters.

It is unethical to educate ourselves at a client's expense. We do not charge our time for learning techniques or sources.

Soliciting and accepting assignments

No ethical standard requires us to sit in an empty office, waiting for clients to seek us out. Although common sense dictates that soliciting and accepting employment is necessary, professional ethics place restraints on when, where, and how we do it. We do not troll for clients among those we serve as a volunteer or paid employee, for example; so we do not include in our communications with them our personal business cards or book-promotion fliers. We do not solicit employment from applicants to a lineage society for which we are the approving genealogist. We do not approach the patrons of a research facility with offers of for-a-fee advice or assistance. When a patron approaches us, we limit the contact to setting an appointment for discussion elsewhere and at a time when we are no longer on a client's "clock."

PERSONAL LIMITATIONS

We refrain from misleading or ambiguous statements about our expertise or credentials in all public and private advertising. Ethics require that we represent ourselves honestly, all the time and under all circumstances. So rigorous is this requirement that we do not accept paid commissions beyond our training and experience, lest it imply we have qualifications we know we don't have. As a general rule, we decline projects when

- we are not fluent in the language or handwriting of records likely to be needed.
- their focus is within a legal, social, ethnic, or recordkeeping system with which we are unfamiliar.
- the effective analysis of our findings is likely to require a technique we have not yet mastered.

It is true that the only way to gain experience for future commissions is to accept some now that will broaden our knowledge. However, it is unethical to educate ourselves at a client's expense. Thus, we do not charge our time for learning land-platting techniques or twentieth-century sources, for example, to the client whose work requires them. Nor do we use that time as an excuse for unexpected delay of the research report. When we know in advance that a particular commission is beyond our current capabilities, we inform the client and, by declining the assignment altogether or by placing clearly worded conditions on our acceptance, we leave the person free to hire someone else. When we realize in mid-project that completing it will require capabilities we do not have, we compile a report of work done to that point and offer the client the option of continuing with another genealogist. Misrepresenting ourselves by statement or implication may provide some temporary satisfaction, but it is far outweighed by the permanent (and often public) dissatisfaction of a disappointed client.

ACCESS LIMITATIONS

Clients often assume, albeit illogically, that professional genealogists have immediate access to every record that might solve their research problems. Popular misconceptions about what is (and is not) on the Internet exacerbate this tendency.

We know, however, that records do not float in the ether waiting for us to pluck out whichever ones we desire—our access is circumscribed by their location and form. Consequently, it is unethical to solicit or accept commissions from clients who are unaware of these limitations. At the outset, we explain, without ambiguity, that work on the project will be affected by time (e.g., for microfilm orders) or expense (e.g., for travel to distant repositories) and refer the client to someone who is better situated for the assignment. If it becomes apparent after the investigation has begun that the trail is headed for records beyond our immediate access, we inform the client and offer alternatives. Not only ethics but economics dictate that we do not undertake additional time or expense without additional authorization. We are free to solicit such authorization, based on our knowledge of the ancestors' behavior or activities and the records needed to document it; but if we imply that there is nobody else capable of continuing, we have crossed the line into unethical behavior.

REFERRALS

When we refer most clients to another professional, it is helpful (although not an ethical requirement) to be reasonably specific. A generalized "I can't" leaves them without effective recourse. We might suggest a particular colleague or a source for lists of other researchers, but we should take care to recommend only those we know are reliable. Our own reputations suffer when we give bad advice. It is also unethical, of course, to solicit or accept any kind of payment, or "kickback," from colleagues in exchange for our referrals.

> We should take care to recommend only those we know are reliable. Our own reputations suffer when we give bad advice.

If our suggestion of other researchers is in reply to an inquiry letter, it is well to return whatever materials the prospective client sent us—particularly anything that may be difficult or expensive for the client to duplicate as he or she proceeds to find help elsewhere. When we have already completed a portion of the work and the client chooses a successor (whether or not the choice is at our recommendation), we cooperate in the change by supplying—promptly and at the client's reasonable expense—materials in our possession that will be needed to complete the project. In such situations, it is unethical to withhold or falsify these materials.

REPLACEMENTS

Inevitably, some clients ask us to take projects previously handled by others. It is not unethical to do so, provided we have not intentionally lured them into our net. Clients have a right to select their genealogists, at any time and for any reason. But we do not prey upon a colleague's client base with promises of speedier results, more erudite reports, cheaper rates, or other benefits—even if our promises are based on fact. Sometimes we are asked to work simultaneously with another genealogist, rather than as a replacement. Again, there is nothing untoward in accepting the commission, although wisdom suggests clarifying the ground rules first.

Agreeing on terms

Because professional ethics require that we do whatever we agree to do, the terms

ETHICAL STANDARDS

of each client commission are of paramount importance. In the negotiations that precede an agreement or contract, we are honest about our timing, charges, and reporting methods. We expect the client to be honest about the nature of the research assignment, its scope, and its goal. Defining the terms of a mutually beneficial agreement is a *mutual* obligation.

OBJECTIVES

The ultimate responsibility for ensuring that we have adequate information about a proposed commission rests with us—we are obliged from the outset to determine the client's needs and wishes. We need to know whether we are to examine specific, identified records; extend a family line; solve a stubborn ancestral problem; complete a series of small assignments (e.g., answering a society's "please help me" letters, or verify applicants' research and citations); or contribute to a broad-based project (as with medical research or historic-site investigation). When a prospective client's definition of the commission is vague or contradictory, we ask for clarification. We do not simply choose some convenient aspect of it and proceed.

FINANCIAL LIMITS

Financial terms also need to be agreed upon in advance and in writing. For individual and family-group clients, a simple form letter can suffice, provided we ask the client to countersign and return an extra copy that we supply. Although the client's initial payment in response to our offer of services may stand as legal proof of acceptance, it is best to avoid the possibility of future problems by clear, well-designed procedures in the beginning. We specify in advance any additional charges for record copies, usage fees, out-of-town travel, or the hiring of record agents in distant areas. If we anticipate a need to subcontract or use research assistants, we inform the client ahead of time and request permission. The client, after all, has chosen *us* and may have good reasons for not taking the problem to a different party.

> If we anticipate a need to subcontract or to use research assistants, we inform the client ahead of time and request permission. The client, after all, has chosen *us*.

Our fee schedule is a complex matter—one that chapter 10 covers in more depth. Just a few points need mentioning here from the purview of ethics. When our fees are based on an hourly rate, we work with the client to establish a per-report or entire-project budget that reflects a reasonable estimate of the time needed. When we request a retainer before beginning, we establish at the outset whether the unused portion will be returned with the report or kept as a deposit for further work. When our fee is a lump-sum payment for a specified work product (a search of census indexes, perhaps; or a lecture, course of instruction, journal article, or book-length manuscript), we take care that the client's expectations and our own reflect the realities of our commitment. We do not make extravagant promises or agree to specifications we know we cannot meet. Regardless of how and when we will be paid, sound business practice as well as professional ethics should preclude the unexpected, both for ourselves and for our clients.

DELIVERY DATES

When time limitations are put upon completion of a project, our agreement should state them clearly. Otherwise, convention or law may assume we will exert our best efforts to complete the task within a "reasonable" time—and reasonable may mean different things to the researcher who faces normal delays and the client who eagerly scans each day's mail for a report. When we provide an estimate of the time needed to complete an assignment or to provide interim reports, we do so fairly. Underestimating time and costs in order to attract clients, and then demanding that they pay extravagant fees upon completion of the project, is called "low-balling." It is unethical in any profession.

Fulfilling the commission

Many clients seek our help only after exhausting the resources available to them, often the same ones available to us. Some may have already discovered records that contain the needed proof but do not grasp their significance. Our obligation to the client includes designing and carrying out an efficient and intelligent research plan based on the data they have collected already. Consequently, beginning a project without first asking for a report of prior findings is incompetent at best and unethical at worst. In those cases when we follow another genealogist, we gracefully accept our predecessor's contribution and refrain from undue remarks about its general quality. If, however, the work was so incompetent that the client's welfare demands our comment, we provide it dispassionately.

After a careful review of all previous work, regardless of who did it, we establish with the client a valid starting point for our investigation. We do not begin by "verifying" findings that are patently reliable. If we suspect that revisiting a record may be productive, we point that out. If, on the other hand, our review discloses that the earlier search was exhaustive and the conclusions inevitable, we report our analysis and advise the client that further efforts are unlikely to produce different results. When we do not ask for and respect our clients' input, they are justified in complaining that our research reports tell them nothing they did not know or that we copied records they already had.

Having received sufficient information about the investigation's purpose, scope, and background, our work and our report must be responsive to the client's authorization. We do not examine 1760s-era church registers for proof of an 1840s-era marriage, nor do we send abstracts to the client who wishes authenticated document copies. We follow the lineage society's rules meticulously when we fill out a client's application papers. We use standard genealogical and citation formats when we compile a client's family history for publication. We prepare ourselves thoroughly and our documents precisely when we appear in court as an expert witness. And if our authorization is for eight hours, we do not bill for ten. If we have actually worked ten hours, two of them are at our own expense.

Reporting results

Our reports—hard-copy, online, on-disk, or oral—accurately reflect the work done and whether the goal has been met. Sometimes our client will be disappointed, for every search does not solve a problem. If additional research is likely to meet the

> Beginning a project without first asking for a report of prior findings is incompetent at best and unethical at worst.

goal or another one acceptable to the client, we provide a reasonable, reliable estimate of the records remaining and the additional time needed. Seeking to enlarge our commission by recommending work unlikely to be productive is unethical.

Irregular behavior exists in the best of families, and genealogical research frequently uncovers colorful matters that suggest a need for discretion. Illegitimacy, crime, and miscegenation are common situations. An ancestor's military service may be on the "wrong" side of a conflict, or proof emerges that the client does not descend from the elegant ancestor of family lore. A suspicion on our part that a client may not appreciate the finding does not justify our withholding or whitewashing facts. Once we have reported them, however, we respect the client's wishes regarding them—provided that our own ethical standards will not be violated in doing so. Naturally, we do not publicize the embarrassing information; but we do not participate with the client in preparing fraudulent lineage-society papers or publishing a family history we know to be based on falsified data.

Maintaining confidentiality

Regardless of twists and turns in judicial interpretations of copyright law and the rules of fair use, the ethical standard for professional genealogists is this: work done for a client is the property of that client. The matter at issue is *client rights* to the information we were authorized to collect versus *our right* to disseminate what may be our intellectual property. Without our client's permission, we do not publish or circulate our findings in any way. Whether the research problem was simple or complex, we do not use our findings to illustrate lectures or case-study articles, as classroom teaching aids, or in the reports we send to other clients. Clients must be free to discuss their research—and family skeletons—with us, and confidentiality is the only atmosphere in which that freedom can flourish.

In some cases, our obligation to maintain confidentiality is clear and incontrovertible. If clients wish to publish their family history, for example, it is obviously and grossly unfair for us to beat them into print. Nevertheless, few areas of professional research generate as many "what ifs" as this one. To consider some common dilemmas, what if

1. a prospective client wishes us to pursue an inquiry we have already completed for another client?

2. the client dropped a project that we then pursued to an imaginative and instructive solution that would help others, if shared?

3. the solution to the client's problem resulted from creative analysis and correlation of evidence on our part, not from the mere location of records that state needed data?

4. we have permission to publish only our own part of the work (the analysis and compilation, for example), but it rests on client-supplied information (from a family Bible or letters, perhaps)?

5. the client dies, becomes ill, or simply moves away before we can obtain permission to publish the solution to a longstanding problem or one involving a family of public interest?

> Regardless of judicial interpretations of copyright law and rules of fair use, the ethical standard for professional genealogists is this: work done for a client is the property of that client.

6. we have full permission from the client, but the project involved the work of a previous or subsequent genealogist also hired by the client?

7. the client did not pay in full for the research we wish to use in a case study or methodology lecture?

8. we want to help future genealogists by contributing the results of our career-long efforts to a manuscript collection?

The keys to threading our way through the "what if" minefield are these: the Golden Rule and Wise Foresight.

DILEMMA 1

When we look at an ethical difficulty from the client's point of view and consider what we would want done to us under the same circumstances, the solution often becomes apparent. For example:

- If we were the new client, would we want to be informed that the research we envision had already been done for somebody else—or would we want the genealogist to simply rebill us the full original fee and mail us a duplicate of the prior report?

- If we were the prior client, would we want the genealogist to distribute our reports, perhaps to fellow researchers with whom we were in conflict—or would we want to be notified of a second researcher working on the problem and have our permission sought before the solution is shared?

In many cases, the simplest resolution of a second-client–same-problem difficulty is to put the two researchers in touch with each other (with the permission of both, of course) and let them sort out the report-sharing themselves. Wise Foresight suggests that such situations be anticipated and covered by a clause in the routine letter of agreement.

One misconception should be corrected before leaving this subject. Genealogists who work within a narrow geographic region and time period usually become familiar with just about everybody in that society. Using neighbors and in-laws to distinguish among people of the same name is a common (and recommended) technique. Often, we are approached by a client who wishes direct work done on a family we traced only peripherally for an earlier report. In these cases, we may reuse our own research notes without notifying the earlier clients or seeking their permission—for the new project has a different goal and will undoubtedly lead in a different direction. Without permission, however, we may not reuse any of the material an earlier client sent us, such as the reports of previous genealogists, data from private family papers, or the client's unpublished compilation.

DILEMMA 2

If we were the client whose genealogist had continued beyond our commission, would we want to be notified that the solution had been found? Would we appreciate an opportunity to purchase the subsequent work or receive it in exchange for permission to publish? Or would we prefer to see the solution in print shortly after our own stated "no solution possible" went to press? Of course, the genealogist in

Without permission, we may not reuse any material an earlier client sent us.

ETHICAL STANDARDS

these circumstances must avoid any hint of extortion; such an offer must be made fairly and generously. If the solution required no extended effort—perhaps the chance discovery of a pertinent tombstone or a misfiled public document—simply giving it to the client is advisable. That generates the kind of goodwill no amount of advertising can duplicate.

DILEMMA 3
Isolating creativity from results is tricky. On the one hand, clients pay for our time *and* our expertise: that expertise includes knowledge, skill, *and* creativity. They do not pay for information, because that may not exist no matter how much time and skill we put into the search. On the other hand, if, in the course of one client project, we develop or employ a technique that works miracles, the client has not purchased all future rights to our *methodology* so that we cannot use that approach again. It may well be possible to use the problem as a teaching example, by carefully creating an illustration that duplicates all elements at the same time that it masks all detail likely to identify the client, the ancestral family, or the specific solution to the client's problem. While this approach is regularly used in lectures, it would not be acceptable as a case study for journals, where a citation of evidence is needed for every stated fact. Before proceeding to use the case anonymously, it is also courteous to discuss parameters with the client.

DILEMMAS 4–6
Wise Foresight can avoid most disclosure-permission difficulties. Our agreement with each client should include a clear statement of the boundaries within which we are free to reuse our own work and any client-supplied materials. With written permission in hand, we need not worry when a client dies or cannot be located. For living and locatable clients, common courtesy dictates that we notify them of our intention to publish (perhaps allowing them a preview) and send them a copy of the final article, book, classroom exercise, or lecture tape. Our working agreement should also stipulate how and whether the client will be cited as our source: some prefer that they not be mentioned, others welcome the acknowledgment. We may need additional permissions from the holders of family papers before we cite those documents. Without their permission, but with client's approval, we limit our citation to "photocopy received from [*client identity*]."

Finally, our agreement with the client should include a statement concerning any other reuse permissions granted in the past or envisioned for the future. If another genealogist has received or will be granted an okay to publish his or her portion of the work, we will need to contact that genealogist, perhaps to collaborate on the publication or perhaps to obtain permission to publish it ourselves. Otherwise, we cannot use the material.

DILEMMA 7
Wise Foresight also can eliminate most difficulties with clients who do not pay for the work they have commissioned. We might want to convert from a budget-and-invoice system to one based on retainers or prepayments. If nonpayment by

> Our agreement with each client should include a clear statement of the boundaries within which we are free to reuse our own work and any client-supplied material.

disappointed clients arises from our specialization in an area replete with record losses, we can prepare clients for possible frustration by letting them know ahead of time that missing records may preclude a successful outcome.

DILEMMA 8

What to do with our files—what *can* be done ethically—can be resolved by Wise Foresight as well. We may make provision by will that they be deposited in an institution willing to receive them or sold to another genealogist. In either case, we take care to remove from the files any personal information about a client and the records of our financial dealings with them. These data should remain private. We clearly identify the files (or parts of files) for which we have not obtained permission for reuse, because all rights to that material remain with the client who authorized its collection. Since we may need to keep such papers as long as we are in business, our literary executor will need precise instructions about which set of files is which and how to dispose of each. We can place restrictions on our donation to an institution or rely on the repository's own rules to safeguard the integrity of our work. But in the long run, we must entrust it to the ethical and scholarly standards of future genealogists who use our papers.

Colleague Relationships

It is peculiar among professional genealogists that we tend to view as "colleagues" only those engaged in the same kind of work we do ourselves. If we are lineage society specialists, for example, we may not naturally count among our colleagues those who are book publishers and distributors, editors, heirship and adoption researchers, lecturers, librarians, program planners, agency personnel, teachers, and writers—not to mention those who work on specific historical, legal, medical, preservation, and psychological projects. The oversight exists in all combinations.

Conflicting goals and personalities inevitably cause stress and disagreement. Ambition and competition can easily gallop out of control if a conscious rein is not applied. Many chapters in this manual stress the need to advertise and market our talents, but there's a distinct line between "selling ourselves" and pushing ourselves on others—or over them. As with client relationships, ethics are our guidelines for defining and maintaining a responsible balance between our own ambitions, needs, and standards and those of our fellow professionals.

> Ethics are our guidelines for defining and maintaining a responsible balance between our own ambitions, needs, and standards and those of our fellow professionals.

Working together

Bad manners and poor taste are not unethical. They are simply foolish, especially within a business context. Ethical colleague relationships, therefore, do not depend on being "nice"; they depend on being honorable. We are not required to like each other, but we are obliged to treat each other fairly.

TEAM RELATIONSHIPS

When two or more of us are assigned to a different aspect of the same project, we

ETHICAL STANDARDS

generously share our background data, findings, and conclusions—offering suggestions diplomatically but with appropriate energy. We do not seek to dominate each other with a demonstration of superior insight, intellect, or vocabulary; but we do not acquiesce in inferior work merely to bolster the confidence of a weaker colleague. In those occasional cases when a client wishes two or more genealogists to work independently on the same aspect of a problem, we do not consult the others about our findings or the timing of our reports. Doing so might defeat the client's purpose, since some use this method to test our diligence or reporting methods or to collect interpretative nuances within the records. In these cases, we might take extra pains with our writing and report format, but we do not falsify our abilities or otherwise compete unfairly by taking extraordinary measures. Hiring a temporary proofreader or typist for such a report—when we do not normally use the services of one—or concealing the number of research hours or expense that went into it is unethical.

STAFF-PATRON RELATIONSHIPS

Those of us who work in public and private agencies deal impartially with genealogical entrepreneurs who use our facilities. We neither favor the ones we like nor obstruct those we do not. If we are application judges, journal editors, or publishers, we do not turn down a colleague's otherwise acceptable work product simply because we find that person unattractive; nor do we approve inadequate work because it comes from a friend. Those of us on the other end of the transaction do not importune our friends for uncommon privileges or exceptional consideration. Nor do we impugn the motives of those whose own business, ethical, or scholarly standards must cause us disappointment.

MENTORING RELATIONSHIPS

Mentoring the less-experienced is a worthy enterprise relatively free of ethical considerations, but a few deserve note. Our work with a protégé is confidential: we do not regale our comrades with beginners' bloopers or with the stunning perspicacity of our advice to them. We do not even disclose the fact that we are acting as mentor, without either the protégé's permission or some overriding consideration related to the circumstances of our role. We do not actively participate in work that will come before us for official approval, and we take pains that any advice we give in connection with it is general and universally applicable. We do not offer deliberately misleading or excessively cynical advice; and if we inadvertently do so, we hasten to correct ourselves. In all cases, our guidance is aimed at helping a protégé join us among the ranks of effective, reputable genealogists.

We do not actively participate in work that will come before us for official approval.

AUTHOR-EDITOR RELATIONSHIPS

Another colleague relationship that sometimes causes concern is that between author and editor. Aside from the question of plagiarism, addressed below, ethics demand that our manuscript not infringe anyone's copyright or privacy right. We guarantee that we have examined all sources indicated and have not suppressed relevant facts or distorted their significance.

It is unethical, without due notice, to offer the same or similar material to multiple publications at the same time. (The literary scene, in which agents widely distribute manuscripts in an attempt to generate bidding wars, is a world foreign to scholarship.) Quality publishers invest much time and expense in evaluating manuscripts and preparing them for press—peer review, fact checking, citation verification, copyediting (even substantive editing), typesetting, and proofreading. No journal, society, or publishing house looks kindly upon shelving a project because we have tardily "remembered" that we sent our manuscript elsewhere. No editor enjoys the stress of hurriedly filling blank pages because material scheduled for press is about to be published (or has already appeared) elsewhere. We send our literary efforts to one publication at a time. It may delay the publication; but caution in this matter is not only more ethical, it is safer. Once burned, editors and publishers have very long memories.

Critiquing peers

Critical reevaluation of existing "knowledge" in our field is beneficial, even necessary, to its general health. Without the kind of growth encouraged by sharp-eyed critics, our genealogical reports, lectures, syllabi, and publications soon descend beyond inaccuracy into irrelevance.

For some of us, our role as critic is an official or quasi-official one. As reviewers, lecturers, or teachers, we are called upon to evaluate the writings of our colleagues. We do so honestly. We do not mask major errors with vague generalizations or diminish the value of good work with lists of minor shortcomings. The community relies on our responsible and informative judgments. Our obligation is to *all* fellow genealogists, not to the single colleague involved. We do not use a review to praise unjustly the work of someone whose influence will advance our career. We do not seize the opportunity to "get even" with someone who has offended us. If our critique must be negative, we refrain from cleverly worded vitriol or personalized attacks on motives, morals, and abilities. It is the work product we are critiquing, not the personality of its producer. We are wise to remember, in fact, that arrogant condemnation of another's honest mistakes leaves us defenseless when our own are uncovered—as they inevitably will be.

In some cases, our critique is offered privately, often directly to the individual who produced the work. As proofreaders, application judges, or journal-article previewers, for example, we provide specific, helpful comments. We point out mistakes without condescension, identifying areas capable of improvement. Our remarks remain private; disclosure is limited to those with a direct "need to know." In other cases—conference lectures, for example—our critique is anonymous and takes the form of filing a preprinted form or casting an evaluation ballot. Stuffing the ballot box is unethical, as it is in any other kind of voting. Finally, if a public critique is called for, as when we discover errors in the existing literature or a charlatan in our midst, we do not turn a blind eye to the problem, even though doing so might be safer and kinder. Abandoning our ethical responsibilities by ignoring manifest incompetence or fraud makes us a willing party to the offense.

> As reviewers, we do not mask major errors with vague generalizations or diminish the value of good work with lists of minor shortcomings.

In this area, responsibilities to the client and the community can easily conflict. What if, for example, the erroneous article, book, or lecture is produced by a client and is based on misinterpretation, misrepresentation, or misunderstanding of our reports? Our first obligation is to the client. If an increasingly firm series of requests for a published retraction brings no result, our responsibility then shifts to the community. We must publish the correction ourselves. We do not do so with bitterness or scathing comments, and we refrain from mentioning our professional relationship with the author. A straightforward, unemotional discussion of the genealogical issues is called for, not an attack or a plea for sympathy. Wise Foresight can often sidestep problems by including in our initial contract a clause that we be given the chance to preview any publication based on our work.

Giving due credit

Omitting the source for a genealogical fact is a failure in scholarship. Neglecting to mention that our work is based on research done by somebody else is a failure in ethics. Appropriating as our own the work of another is universally condemned, in our field as in others. Neglecting to give due credit can also be professionally fatal, because discovery is inevitable. It is far preferable to acknowledge aid, even when that aid was of a minor or tangential nature.

The prohibition against claiming another's work, or permitting the impression of such a claim to prevail, applies to all areas of genealogical endeavor. It is unethical and injurious to put our name to a publication that incorporates, in whole or in part, the prior research of another genealogist who is not treated as a joint author. The fact that it was done a century ago by someone long dead, or that we found it with a vacated copyright (or none at all), does not relieve us of responsibility. The fact that it was done at our behest by an agent or subcontractor does not mitigate our obligation. The fact that it was contributed by a client with full permission to publish, or developed as part of a group effort, does not eliminate our need to include appropriate attribution. (Giving specific credit, where due, is also a matter of self-protection; to put one's name to the work of another—as in a "coauthor" relationship with a client, in which the professional has not verified the accuracy of the research previously done by the client—is to accept the blame, as well as legal liability, for any and all errors the client may have made.)

Even if we completely redo the research, examining each record ourselves, we *must* acknowledge the other's research plan—if we would not have found the same records or arrived at the same conclusions without its aid. Citing an original source when we have seen only someone's abstract of it is not only unethical, it is dangerous; we thereby accept the blame for any errors therein. Whether we use another's analysis, compilation, research, or merely "the gist of the thing" in a publication or an unpublished report, we lay ourselves open to a charge of plagiarism. In scholarly circles, there is no worse charge—short of murder or treason—and punishment for the crime is swift and permanent.

The same principle extends to oral presentations. We do not deliver another's lecture (or any part thereof) or distribute its handout without first obtaining the

> Citing an original source when we have seen only someone's abstract of it is not only unethical, it is dangerous.

author's permission and including appropriate acknowledgment. Some truths, of course, are universal—no matter who says them, when, or in what words. But arrangement, illustration, and manner of presentation are unique to each speaker. "Borrowing" from a colleague without permission is a form of theft. We do not "borrow" their discoveries to illustrate our lectures—nor do we use their anecdotes, their bibliographies, or their lecture titles. Furthermore, we do not help, or even quietly acquiesce, in such behaviors by others.

Safeguarding reputations

Each of us is entitled to the reputation we have earned, be it good or bad. We do not seek to protect our standing by blaming colleagues for our mistakes, nor do we expect them to shield us from the consequences. We accept the blame for our failings and make appropriate apology for them. But we are also entitled to the glory of our successes, and no one has a right to deprive us of the approval our efforts have generated. By the same token, we do not have a right to damage or destroy another's reputation, particularly with unfounded or exaggerated allegations. We do not spread rumors; we do not join in witch-hunts. We do not disparage a colleague's value to the field because we dislike his or her personal habits, traits, or preferences. And we do not seek to build a reputation for intellectual or ethical rigor on the ashes of a colleague's good name.

On the other hand, we cannot skip along in the sunshine, refusing to acknowledge that some of our colleagues are less than competent, others less than strictly ethical, and still others quarrelsome and difficult. When we are asked for our opinion of a colleague by someone with a need to have it (an editor considering a manuscript, a program planner considering a speaker, or a client considering an alternative researcher), we are obliged to be candid or to remain silent. There is no middle way to answer the question. If we speak, it is only from direct personal knowledge. We do not exaggerate minor failings or minimize major ones. We give full credit and praise when it is due; when it is not, we refrain from sweeping condemnation. If we know of mitigating circumstances that may have affected the colleague's performance, we may explain them. We tell the truth, and we devoutly hope that those who are asked about us will do the same.

Community Relationships

The genealogical community is far more inclusive than our clients, colleagues, and employers. It also encompasses those who buy our books and tapes, enroll in our classes, read our articles, register for our workshops, and subscribe to our journals. It includes those who encounter our reports long after we have forgotten the contents. Elected and appointed officials of genealogical, hereditary, and historical societies, as well as their members, are part of the community. Lurkers and flamers on the Internet and visitors to our websites are also part of a fellowship that includes all who have studied, are studying, or will study family relationships. Few groups care as passionately or work as ferociously as genealogists do. Naturally,

> Arrangement, illustration, and manner of presentation are unique to each speaker. "Borrowing" from a colleague without permission is a form of theft.

> We concern ourselves with the welfare of the whole, not with benefits to one faction at the expense of others.

conflicts develop, personalities clash, and open warfare results sometimes. Our ethical responsibility to the community dictates that we enter the fray (if we enter it) as peacemakers, not as combatants. We concern ourselves with the welfare of the whole, not with benefits to one faction at the expense of others. We refrain from sly digs and bitter confrontations that cause dissension.

Sometimes situations develop that are not covered by established ethical guidelines, and it is difficult to find our way through a maze of conflicting opinion. But as we strive to refine our own ethical sensibilities, we must not forget those of the community. Ethics apply to everybody. Our standards should not be murmured privately in hushed whispers. They should not be taken for granted. We should not allow them to be preempted by an elite who lays down the law for the rest of us. A healthy community requires that standards be promulgated and that they be debated openly—by everyone affected.

Summary Concepts

Ethics. Commandments. Injunctions. Proscriptions. By nature, discussions of ethics are strewn with negatives. But the personal application of ethics is really a positive-negative balancing act. We avoid misrepresentation by fully disclosing facts and generously giving credit. We protect the rights of our clients by putting their interests first—recognizing that, in doing so, we build our own reputation and business. We conduct a professional life that is a credit and not a detriment to the high calling of *genealogist*. We give back to the field in full measure for the benefits we receive—by sharing our research in print, our expertise at the podium, and our talents in professional organizations. The breadth and scope of these positive aspects, which are more fully developed in many chapters of this manual, far exceed the negatives on which this chapter necessarily dwells.

NOTES

The author thanks Helen F. M. Leary, CG, CGL, FASG, for her substantive contributions to this chapter, based on issues and problems raised by students over the ten years she has conducted the Professional Genealogy track of the Samford University Institute of Genealogy and Historical Research.

FURTHER STUDY

Christians, Clifford G., ed., and Mark Fackler. *Media Ethics: Cases and Moral Reasoning*. New York: Longman Publishing Group, 1997.

Leary, Helen F. M. "Application Strategies: Observing the Code." *OnBoard* 4 (May 1998): 11–12.

National Federation of Paralegal Associations. *Model Code of Ethics and Professional Responsibility and Guidelines for Enforcement*. Published at the federation's website.

Peterson, Marilyn R. *At Personal Risk: Boundary Violations in Professional-Client Relationships*. New York: W. W. Norton, 1992.

Roberts, Gary Boyd. "A Professional Code for Genealogical Libraries and Librarians." *National Genealogical Society [NGS] Quarterly* 67 (March 1979): 11–13.

Sheppard, Walter Lee Jr., CG, FASG. "Professional Ethics in Genealogical Research." *NGS Quarterly* 67 (March 1979): 3–10.

6

**EXECUTING
CONTRACTS**

Keynotes

Chapter 6

Executing Contracts

by Patricia Gilliam Hastings, J.D.

What can a written contract do? Will it help us in business matters to put our agreements for professional work in writing? These threshold questions may generate different answers in different cases. This chapter reviews, in very broad terms, ways that written agreements can protect our rights; and it offers sample contracts. It cannot give specific legal advice—attorneys can do so only in individual cases and then only with regard to a particular set of facts. If details change, the advice may also change. Because all of us have highly personalized situations, each of us may require departures from the general suggestions presented here.

Contracts range from oral agreements to the most formal of written documents. Some agreements do not have to be in writing to be enforceable as contracts; but legally defining the terms of an oral agreement can be difficult after a dispute arises, if parties swear to different understandings. Written agreements, too, have various degrees of formality. The word *contract,* used in this chapter, includes various written forms of agreement. The principal (though not exclusive) focus is on research performed for clients in exchange for a fee; the same principles apply to other forms of professional work, including writing, lecturing, or consultation.

Weighing Options

Professionals must balance the need for formal, contractual protection with the circumstances of each situation. There is no one-size-fits-all agreement. Generally speaking, the genealogical world is a gentler, kinder place than the one attorneys usually inhabit. Most clients are honest and pay their bills on time. With many commissions, perhaps most of them, the professional requests a retainer and then bills the client as services are performed. Thus, the financial consequences of a default are small enough that the professional would seldom spend time and money to enforce payment in court. However, the rights that a genealogist needs to protect often go far beyond mere money. We may need, for example, an agreement with clients over such vital matters as the use of our work product. Clearly, more complicated and sophisticated situations call for more formal agreements.

Benefits and limitations

Benefits of a written contract range from financial and legal protection to good client relations and peace of mind. In particular, a contract can

- specify exactly what services we will perform, exactly when and in what amount our client will compensate us, and exactly what expenses the client will reimburse.

- record any exceptions, disclaimers, or conditions we wish to attach to our work.

- establish in advance the kind of future use we or our client may make of our work product.

Benefits of a written contract range from financial and legal protection to good client relations and peace of mind.

- give us rights enforceable by binding arbitration or in a court of law.
- shift to the other party any legal fees and court costs we may incur in enforcing the agreement.
- specify the forum in which any litigation will take place and the state whose law will be applied.

Conversely, a contract also binds us, not just our client. If we breach an agreement, our client can enforce his or her contractual rights against us. We will be liable for any resulting damages the client incurs, just as clients are responsible for damages caused by any breach they commit.

Of course, a contract itself does not assure performance by either party. If a client fails to pay for services rendered, we have to take that client and the contract to arbitration or to a court of proper jurisdiction and ask for an order to pay. If either finds that we have done what we agreed to do and that our client has wrongfully failed to perform, it can award money damages and sometimes other relief—perhaps an order forbidding the client from doing some act that is under way or threatened. If the client ignores the arbitrator or judge's order, we may have to go back to court to discover what assets the client has that can be used to pay our judgment or to charge the client with contempt for refusing to obey the order. The losing party can also appeal the order of the trial court, adding delay and legal expense. With arbitration, however, there is no appeal.

Common sense and business judgment

Contractual rights are never a substitute for good business judgment. For example, if a potential client, in our initial contact, complains mightily of poor service or value from a string of previously hired genealogists, it is wise to consider whether we, too, may find that client difficult to please. Or if a client begins our relationship by forgetting to pay the advance or requesting immediate work with a promise of payment to follow, it may well be a sign of slow payments to come.

Will a contract scare away a potential client? It might. This, too, calls for a business judgment. Should we give up the advantages gained from a written contract in exchange for not alarming (and possibly losing) a potential client? If a client would be intimidated by a written agreement, might this client also be ambivalent about performing his or her end of the bargain?

The general rule is that agreements, whether written or oral, are enforceable. Yet a longstanding requirement, dating from the 1600s, requires certain types of contracts to be in writing in order for them to be enforced. To avoid the legal analysis necessary to decide whether a written contract is mandatory in each case, it is simpler and safer to put our terms in writing as a matter of habit. Should it ever become necessary to prove the terms of the agreement, that written contract is far superior to a swearing contest.

Should it ever become necessary to prove the terms of the agreement, that written contract is far superior to a swearing contest.

Less-formal alternatives

Many professionals prefer to spell out their terms in a letter—trusting that the client's responding letter of authorization constitutes an acceptance of the terms. Yet it can be tricky to express, in ordinary letter format, all the elements we may need for protection. For example, one bit of boilerplate usually included in formal contracts (discussed more fully on pages 111–12) is the merger clause—stating that there are no other agreements, oral or written, except those contained in the present document. Including this clause prevents a party from coming into court and saying, "Well, this contract is only part of our agreement; we had an oral agreement on the side"; or, "There were other terms covered by a different letter." Few professional genealogists include the merger clause in letters of agreement, because it sounds unnatural in a letter. They take a risk. Because only one party writes and signs a letter, a client with larceny in his or her heart could easily create another letter, purporting to be a later agreement.

If properly drafted and executed, an engagement letter can be just as binding but less intimidating than a formal contract. The letter should contain all the necessary elements; it should specify that it contains the entire agreement between parties; and it should ask the client to sign at the bottom to indicate his or her acceptance of the terms covered by the letter. Should a client refuse or neglect to sign, we are at least alerted to potential problems. We can then choose whether to establish a professional relationship or to decline the commission. Obviously, if we decide that any provisions of a formal contract are too esoteric for the letter of agreement, then we will be denied the benefit of those provisions if or when a conflict develops.

If we feel clients may be intimidated by legalities such as those raised by the samples provided in this chapter, an auxiliary suggestion may help to alleviate client concern. A warm but businesslike cover letter can point out that the contract or letter of engagement is requested in accordance with professional practices recommended by *Professional Genealogy: A Manual for Researchers, Writers, Editors, Lecturers, and Librarians.*

Drafting Contracts

There is nothing magic about legal training that endows an attorney with a special ability to draft contracts, although more complex situations certainly call for more legal oversight. Drafting a contract is no different from drafting any other document, be it a lecture or a client report. We determine what topics we should include and we write the provisions in unambiguous terms. Even if we hire an attorney to draft our prototype, we still participate, because someone of limited familiarity with our profession cannot easily anticipate every business complication that might develop. When we meet with an attorney, we go armed with a list of subjects to cover in the agreement and a list of problems we and our colleagues encounter. The attorney can then, with our help, draft provisions or recommend business practices designed to prevent the recurrence of those problems.

There are significant advantages to being the party who prepares the first draft of the contract. We get to define the issues, include all the provisions we need to protect ourselves, and provide the basic framework of the document. For example:

If we feel clients may be intimidated by legalities, a cover letter can point out that the contract or letter of engagement is requested in accordance with professional practices recommended by *Professional Genealogy*.

Many people, presented
with a proposed contract,
will simply sign it without
attempting to negotiate
any of the terms.

- In a research commission, we may feel it impossible to accurately project a completion date. Thus, we can insert a stipulation that both parties understand the difficulty of predicting how many competing projects may arrive on our desk at the time this client authorizes the commission and that we can only approximate the time needed for our performance.

- In a lecture contract, we will likely want a provision reimbursing us for any prepaid expenses, such as airfare, should the event be canceled for any reason that is not our own cause. The sponsors will likely not offer that clause if they initiate the draft.

Another advantage to being the one who drafts the document is that many people, when presented with a proposed contract, will simply sign it without attempting to negotiate any of the terms.

On the other hand, there are potential disadvantages to being the drafting party. A major one is that courts, as a matter of policy, often construe ambiguous portions of a document against the party who drafted it. The reasoning is that if there is ambiguity, the person who drafted the agreement was in the best position to prevent the misunderstanding from arising. The advantages of being the one who writes the initial draft, however, are almost always greater than any disadvantages.

Fundamental principles

In deciding upon terms to include in our agreement, we should weigh the burden each provision poses. Would any given clause be onerous to ourselves or appear onerous to our clients? For example:

- We may wish to require that any legal action be brought in our home state, but would it be fair to the client to require him or her to bring suit against us there? For both parties, it might be less burdensome and expensive to submit disputes to binding arbitration and agree to court enforcement of the decision.

- We may have particular concerns about confidentiality. Do we feel strongly that we have a scholarly responsibility to correct, in print, previously published errors—and wish to ensure that the client's concept of confidentiality does not preclude this?

Where we draw the line is a business decision, not a legal one—because we surely would not seek to include an unconscionable item. But the line must be drawn on issues of this type as part of the drafting process.

In more general terms, whether we use a letter of agreement or a more formal document, we should

- use specific, clear, and concise language.
- use shorter sentences rather than longer ones.
- avoid complex provisions, double negatives, and exceptions to exceptions.
- arrange the provisions logically, keeping related matters together.
- use captions to label the topics to be discussed.

- avoid ambiguity or incompleteness. (For example, if we intend for the sponsor of our lecture to provide an overhead projector and a screen, we don't say that the sponsor "should" furnish these items if we really mean "shall." While the word "should" will probably sound less threatening to the sponsor, it signifies a less-than-certain responsibility for performance.)

- avoid expressing the same thought using different words. (Doing so will raise questions about the significance to be drawn from the difference in expression. Untold numbers of judges have had to decide just which alternative the parties really intended when a contract used inconsistent language.)

Essential elements

IDENTITIES
Logically, the names of the parties are the first essential. In more formal agreements, identification includes the place of residence for each. If either party is not a natural person, the contract should describe its nature—corporation, partnership, professional association, etc.—and the state under which it is organized.

DATE
The date of the contract may indicate whether the agreement supersedes an earlier one, as well as the time when work performed (or money owed) becomes subject to the agreement. There's nothing wrong with having a contract cover work performed before the contract is executed, so long as both parties agree. For example, the contract could be executed on July 5 but be effective as of the prior April 15.

CONSIDERATION
The consideration (what each party bargains for and exchanges with the other—typically, the client's payment for our research time, or a society's honorarium in exchange for the program we present) needs to be specifically stated. Consideration must involve giving and taking on both sides, to be legally enforceable. A promise by one party to give another a gift, with nothing in return, would not qualify. A more formal agreement usually states the parties' agreement that the consideration is legally sufficient.

SCOPE OF SERVICES RENDERED
In clear, concise, and complete language—predicated on a good knowledge of the business—this section should cover three perspectives: the actions the client will perform (other than payment); the service or product we will provide the client; and the standards to which we will perform. More specifically:

Client commitments
Depending upon the situation, this may not be a factor; but, typically, researchers do expect certain actions from the client. The client may need to provide specific information or materials relating to earlier research, in order to prevent duplication

> A contract's consideration must involve giving and taking on both sides to be legally enforceable.

EXECUTING CONTRACTS

of previous work. We may require that clients call us only during certain office hours. Such points are spelled out here.

Professional commitments

The wording of this section needs to be crafted with particular care in order to preserve our status as independent contractors. Client control of *how we work* could be interpreted as creating an employer-employee relationship, with the client responsible for employer taxes. (Client control of *where* we work could also suggest employer status, if we are working with materials that are available in the same form in multiple locations, such as microfilmed censuses or published books.) Thus, we avoid all details of *how* we will do the work. Instead, we describe *what* we intend to accomplish and *what form* our final product will take. For example:

Consultation and research services: Will we provide a preliminary evaluation, in which we appraise the quality and meaning of the information the client has already gathered? Will we locate and provide photocopies of specified documents? Will we conduct general research, including an analysis of our findings? Will we report negative findings—searches that generated no information—or will we restrict our reports to only those materials containing useful data? Will we make recommendations for further research by us, by the client, or by other professionals? Will we enter our findings into a genealogical database or update family group sheets for the client?

Lecturing services: How long will our lecture(s) be? What subject(s) will we cover? Will we provide handouts or syllabus materials—if so, at whose expense? May attendees tape our lecture? May a sponsoring society or library film it for later use by members or patrons?

Writing or editorial services: Will we organize the client's research notes in preparation for a family history? Will we edit a client's manuscript—if so, will we limit ourselves to copyediting or will we also perform substantive editing (verification and correction of facts, etc.)? Will we employ other researchers on a subcontracting basis and compile their findings into a family history?

Performance standards

Unless we specify otherwise, our services or product will be expected to comply with standards of the profession—both formally adopted codes and prevailing practice. Therefore, if time or cost limitations imposed by the client—or any other good reason—require us to deviate from accepted standards, we should state the exception. This is also the place to spell out the most important standards and practices, if we think our client may not be familiar with them, or to refer to copies of them as attached exhibits. Beyond this, if we have given our client a written proposal in some other form or a schedule of fees, its details may be incorporated by referencing it in the contract and attaching a copy of it as an exhibit to the agreement.

TIME FOR PERFORMANCE

The client deserves some idea of when the service will be provided. It is best to tie the date of completion to the date the contract is executed—and to the provision of

> Unless we specify otherwise, our services or product will be expected to comply with standards of the profession—both formally adopted codes and prevailing practice.

any material the client is to furnish. Otherwise, a client who procrastinates about signing or following through on the agreement can seriously disrupt our schedule. In arriving at this date, we should consider whether we have or anticipate a backlog of other work. We will also want to ensure that the client realizes the uncertainty and costs involved in finding a particular piece of information or using certain resources within a limited time period. We may also want to provide for an automatic extension, perhaps requiring ourselves to notify the client in writing and to state our reasons for any delay that activates the extension.

COMPENSATION

If we have a statement of fees and expenses that we provide in response to inquiries, we can incorporate it by reference and attach a copy. Otherwise, numerous factors will shape this provision in our contract. Do we charge by the hour? Do we expect an advance or a retainer? If so, is any of it refundable? Will progress payments be required? Do we charge for travel time or mileage? Will we be reimbursed for the cost of photocopies, certificates, postage, meals, lodging, parking, telephone calls, or other expenses? Will we charge for time spent reviewing and evaluating research materials provided by the client? Will we bill the client for time spent in telephone consultation and report writing? How soon is payment due after billing the client?

Unless we are prepared to comply with federal and state truth-in-lending laws—which require rigorous disclosure of the terms of credit and prescribe specific provisions to protect the debtor—we should not assess late fees, finance charges, interest on the unpaid amount, or any other penalty that makes us look like a creditor. If we decide to charge penalties and have little or no experience with these regulations, we should have our attorney draft the appropriate provisions.

CONFIDENTIALITY

Of all the issues to be covered by a professional-client contract in genealogy, confidentiality is one of the murkiest. There is no doubt that the best position from the standpoint of legal protection—as well as federal laws regarding copyright and works for hire—is dramatically at odds with the ethical position the field of genealogy has traditionally taken. A blanket promise of confidentiality is dangerous—raising a risk of liability for the genealogist who agrees to keep confidential papers or facts known to or discoverable by others. Arguably, the only materials that the genealogical professional should pledge to hold confidential are

- those not a matter of public record, or which cannot be rightfully obtained from another nonconfidential source.
- those no one else has independently developed—subject, of course, to the researcher's scholarly and professional responsibility to correct errors in previously published books and articles.
- those the client has not disclosed to other people.

Material that does not meet these criteria can easily surface from other sources within the genealogical community. Even though we are not the ones who reveal it, the client may conclude that we did and charge us with breaching our agreement.

A blanket promise of confidentiality is dangerous, raising a risk of liability for the genealogist who agrees to keep confidential papers or facts known to (or discoverable by) others.

To effectively use dis-
claimers, we should think
about situations in our
practice in which clients
have not understood how
genealogical lecturing, research, or writing works.

Cases in which our work may be used in legal proceedings, contemplated or already under way, pose additional risks for us if our confidentiality clause is not carefully worded. Even if we have entered into an agreement to keep information confidential, a court can still compel us to disclose it. Should we refuse, that court could even jail us until we decide to cooperate—under which conditions we would soon discover that breach of contract is less to be feared than contempt of court. Can the client still bring a suit for breach of contract? Certainly. Whether the client would prevail depends upon the facts in the case. Thus, we may want to include a provision releasing us from confidentiality restrictions if a court orders us to provide information.

DISCLAIMERS

A disclaimer is a notice of refusal to accept responsibility for something. The first paragraph of this chapter is an example. In order to effectively use disclaimers in client agreements, we should think about situations in our practice in which clients have not understood how genealogical lecturing, research, or writing works. Those who are unfamiliar with the techniques and methods involved especially need to be informed that it may not be possible to conclusively prove relationships or other facts. A specific disclaimer not only protects us from the negative consequences that can stem from client disappointment; it also puts the client on notice that the discovery of specific facts cannot be ethically guaranteed.

DELEGATION OF DUTIES

Some professionals routinely subcontract with others to do research for clients; some do so only if research moves beyond certain bounds. The general rule of contracts is that assignment (subcontracting) is allowed, although contractors remain liable for work done by agents—unless clients specifically agree to the substitution. However, contracts for personal services, like those a genealogist supplies, are a clear exception to the general rule. The test is whether performance under the contract is so dependent upon the abilities and reputation of the contractor that assignment of the responsibility would be unfair to the client.

The more prominent our reputation and ability as a professional genealogist, the more likely a contract will be deemed a "personal service contract." Arguably, our professional reputation is the factor that attracted the client in the first place. Still, our agreement can include a clause permitting us to subcontract work to others. If the client signs, he or she assents to subcontracting. We may want to give the client reassurance by restricting assignment to persons holding certain professional credentials and by providing that we will be responsible for an agent's work. The latter provision is not necessary, though; we are responsible whether or not we include the statement.

FUTURE USE OF WORK PRODUCT

The information and files we create in the course of our work as independent contractors belong to us under current copyright law. However, ethical considerations place some limits on our future use of it—as, for example, charging

another client for the same report without the original client's consent. We can also place limits on how the client uses the written report we provide. As the creator of a written work, we own the copyright; but by agreement we can transfer any of our rights to the client and specify how it may or may not be used. For example, we may require the client to submit to us for approval the form in which any proposed use of our work might appear. Chapters 5 and 7 provide fuller discussions of prevailing ethical and copyright considerations.

Again, however, it takes more than contracts to prevent clients from publishing our work as their own—even if they misstate our findings or conclusions. We must still take the contracts and the clients to an arbitrator or court of proper jurisdiction, ask for an order prohibiting them from further distributing the work, and specify any damages to which we feel entitled as a result of their breach.

REMEDIES
Generally, either party's remedy for breach of contract is *compensatory damages* (money) for the resulting injury. However, where our reputation may be at stake—as with misrepresentation or wrongful use of our work product, or attributing to us conclusions or works that are substantially someone else's—it is beneficial to include a provision authorizing *injunctive relief,* as well. If, for example, a client published our work in violation of our agreement, a court could issue an injunction requiring the client to stop. An *order for specific performance* requires the party in breach to actually perform what he or she has promised to do, such as obtaining approval before publication, rather than paying money damages which could not really compensate us for the injury. Disobedience of an order—including an arbitrator's decision—is contempt of court and can be punished by jail or fine until the offender obeys. Although a contractual provision is not required for a judge to issue an injunction or order specific performance, the inclusion of such a provision surely makes the judge's decision easier, should it come to that.

We can attempt to limit our own liability for breach of contract by including a clause in this remedy section. For example, our client's entire recovery might be limited to the return of money paid us. Whether an arbitrator or a court upholds such a provision would probably depend on the magnitude of the client's injury.

Boilerplate, a term laypersons often equate with items of legal mumbo jumbo in which they see little substance, is unfairly maligned.

BOILERPLATE
Boilerplate, a term laypersons often equate with items of legal mumbo jumbo in which they see little substance, is unfairly maligned. Attorneys include stock wording only when there is a reason to do so, and they review each clause each time a new contract is drafted to determine whether it is appropriate to include. We should do the same. The key considerations in the common boilerplate concepts for contracts are these:

> *Merger.* A merger clause states that the written document contains the entire agreement between the parties and that no modification or amendment is valid unless it is in writing and signed by all or both parties. The merger clause is vital to the integrity of a written contract, even if the words must be softened for use in the less formal letter of engagement. Without it, we may have difficulty

EXECUTING CONTRACTS

excluding all other correspondence except the one document *we* consider to be our agreement.

Survival of terms and conditions. This clause specifies that the terms and conditions of the contract will continue beyond the time of performance. For example, if our client has agreed that we must approve any future use of our work product, we want that provision to survive even after both of us have completed performance—that is, after we have done the work and our client has paid us.

Choice of jurisdiction, venue, forum and law. The general rule is that defendants must be sued in their home county and state, unless they have sufficient contacts with another location to make it reasonable to be sued there. However, parties to a contract can agree in advance as to where any dispute would be litigated or whether to make binding arbitration the sole forum. They can also agree upon which state's law will apply. There will be significant expense for us if we and our attorney have to travel to a distant locale to file suit for our fee or to answer a lawsuit—or if we have to retain counsel licensed in that jurisdiction. Two don't come for the price of one!

Third parties. Most contracts contain a clause saying that the agreement is binding on heirs, legal representatives, successors, and assigns. Thus, if the client should die, his or her estate would still be liable for payment of our fee. Before including such a provision, however, we should consider what would happen if we die before completing the work. If our heirs and assigns are bound, who will assume responsibility for performance? Should the client's money be returned? Should only a portion of that advance be returned if we have already done some of the work? Who will decide what percentage should be returned? Should our agreement allow us (or our heirs) to subcontract to have the work done? These are questions not addressed by the usual stock language. Conceivably, too, our client might have a third party publish our work or copublish it. If such a publication requires our agreement, we need to have the third party bound to the agreement as well.

Arbitration. We may want to require our client to submit any disputes to binding arbitration by a professional association to which we belong or by some other specified provider of arbitration services. Arbitration can save money in attorneys' fees. Should we decide to require it, we should provide in the contract that the decision of the arbitrators may, at the election of either party, be entered as a judgment in a court having jurisdiction over the parties. Otherwise, because an arbitrator or sponsoring entity has no inherent enforcement power over nonmembers, we may find ourselves without the power of a court to enforce an arbitration award. If nothing is said about arbitration in a contract, it is presumed that the parties do not intend to engage in arbitration.

Attorneys' fees and court costs. In the absence of a statute or an agreement otherwise, the general rule is that each party is responsible for his or her own legal costs. A contract can shift that burden to the other party or to the losing party.

Execution by parties. All parties to be bound should sign at the end of the contract. If we use a letter of agreement, we should place the word "Accepted" and a signature line at the end, and then be sure to have the client sign it.

> There will be significant expense for us if we and our attorney have to travel to a distant locale to file suit for our fee or to answer a lawsuit.

Generally speaking, signatures to a contract do not need to be notarized unless the document will be recorded. However, the standard wording for acknowledgment before a notary includes an explicit statement that the notary personally knows the parties or has ascertained their identities, and that the persons present before the notary are the ones who signed the document. Thus, there is an official witness in case the client later claims that his or her signature is a forgery. As professionals, we balance the likelihood of such an event against the inconvenience to the client of finding a notary.

Summary Concepts

A written agreement can give us rights that are enforceable in a court of law. We should remember that we, as well as the client, are bound to the terms—and that the contract itself does not make either party perform. A contract is especially valuable to us, as professional genealogists, if we have an established professional reputation to protect or if we undertake a project of substantial size. Among the most crucial topics that a contract should address are

- date and identity of the parties.
- scope of the services to be rendered.
- compensation to be paid.
- expenses to be reimbursed.
- information to be treated as confidential.
- disclaimer of assured results.
- future use of the work product.
- merger of all prior agreements into the written one.
- choice of law and forum for dispute resolution.

> A contract is especially valuable to us if we have an established professional reputation to protect or if we undertake a project of substantial size.

Three sample contracts appear in figures 4–6; however, they are only examples, not forms to be rigidly followed. The more valuable or unique the rights we seek to protect, the more we need an attorney to assist us in drafting our agreement. It is important for us to become actively involved in the drafting of our contract, even if we have legal counsel, and we must continue to refine our document. For a small project there may not be enough at stake to justify the time, cost, and client trepidation that a formal contract entails, compared to an informal agreement contained in a letter that states the terms of the engagement. As a caveat, however, if a letter is used in place of a more formal contract, both parties should sign and the genealogist should consider which of the other elements discussed in this chapter should be included as well. In any event, a contract is never a substitute for good business judgment.

FURTHER STUDY

Fishman, Stephen. *Consultant & Independent Contractor Agreements*. Berkeley, California: Nolo Press, 1998.
————. *Hiring Independent Contractors: The Employer's Legal Guide*. 3d edition. Berkeley, California: Nolo.com, 2000.

EXECUTING CONTRACTS

FIG. 3
SUMMARY GUIDELINES

Don't

- Blindly accept the suggestions in this chapter. We should apply our own common sense and contact a professional if we need more help. The facts in our own individual case may dictate a departure from the general principles discussed, or the applicable law may vary from place to place. Law and practice may also change over time, leaving this discussion out of date.

- Agree orally to anything not in the document (if a formal contract or letter of agreement is used). Instead, we should amend the written agreement, getting everyone's signatures to the amendment.

- Include finance charges or penalties for late payment. If we do, we should be prepared to comply with complex federal truth-in-lending laws.

Do

- Learn from mistakes. When we get burned, we should think about how we could have prevented it from happening. If a contract provision would have helped, we should add it to our future contracts.

Remember

- The same contract won't work for every situation. We treat the basic document as a draft, amending it as necessary. Boilerplate provisions should not be tacked on without carefully evaluating their applicability to the terms under contract.

- The more valuable the rights we want to protect, or the more unusual the work we agree to perform, the more reason there is to consult our own attorney rather than rely on this general treatment.

- If our client is more legally sophisticated than we are or submits a contract for our signature, we need to consult our own attorney—unless we are confident our education and expertise will let us adequately protect ourselves.

- If our client presents us with a prepared contract and we choose not to involve our attorney, we may treat the document as a proposal and negotiate until we have included the provisions we need to protect ourselves. We should consider also whether the client has the expertise to draft a comprehensive and binding contract.

- The higher our professional profile and standing, the more we need a contract to protect our reputation. If we're not yet at that level, let us remember that today's obscure genealogist may be tomorrow's blazing comet. After all, success and respect in this profession *are* what we're trying to accomplish.

- A contract is never a substitute for sound business judgment.

FIG. 4
CONTRACT FOR
GENEALOGICAL
LECTURING SERVICES

THIS AGREEMENT is made this the ____ day of _____ 20__, by and between Ann E. Boddie, Certified Genealogist (hereinafter called "Speaker") of [*cite address*], and Wishwenew Genealogical Society (hereinafter called "Society") of [*cite address*].

WHEREAS, Speaker is engaged in providing genealogical lecture services, and

WHEREAS, Society wishes to present an educational seminar or event ("Event") and desires to employ the services of Speaker therein,

NOW THEREFORE, in consideration of the mutual promises contained herein, the sufficiency of which is hereby acknowledged, the parties agree as follows:

1. Date, Time, and Place of Event. Event shall take place in the city of _____, at an appropriate place to be selected by Society, on __ _____ 20__, between the hours of 9:00 a.m. and 4:00 p.m.

2. Content of Program. Speaker shall provide four one-hour lectures on topics selected by Society, from a list provided by Speaker. Speaker shall, however, have final approval of the combination of topics selected and the sequence of presentation. Parties must agree on the topics on or before __ _____ 20__. If Society chooses, Speaker shall additionally offer, at no extra charge, a question-and-answer session for the personal problems of attendees. If elected, such session shall be scheduled as the last offering of the day.

3. Lecture Enhancements. Speaker shall produce lecture enhancements (such as outlines, bibliographies, maps, glossaries, or other appropriate matter) of approximately four pages per one-hour lecture, for distribution only to the registrants. Speaker shall provide camera-ready masters for each set of lecture materials and shall submit them to Society on or before __ _____ 20__. Society shall duplicate copies of the materials in numbers commensurate with the number of advance registrants and anticipated walk-in registrants. Speaker retains the copyright to all lecture enhancements. Speaker grants Society a one-time license to copy the material and disseminate it subject to the following conditions: (*a*) materials shall not be sold or otherwise distributed to nonattendees; and (*b*) materials shall not, without the prior written approval of Speaker, be bound with advertisements of other individuals or firms, by which combination the other individuals or firms might appear to have the endorsement of Speaker.

4. Equipment. Society shall supply the equipment listed below, to be set up in working order (with spare bulbs and batteries) at the hour that doors open for the registration of attendees: (*a*) slide projector (carousel, front projection; with remote control); (*b*) overhead projector (not opaque), to be placed within reach; (*c*) large screen (at least 6' in small rooms; 10' to 12' for larger rooms, meeting halls, and auditoriums); (*d*) lectern (equipped with light); (*e*) lapel microphone; (*f*) pointer (light or laser); (*g*) table (for Speaker's materials); and (*h*) water pitcher and glass.

5. Facilities. Society shall be responsible for selecting and preparing the meeting site. In choosing a site, Society shall consider not only the number of registrants that Society customarily draws but also the number that Speaker typically attracts at all-day, single-speaker events (i.e.: ____ to ____ registrants, with ____ being average). Seating arrangements should ensure that all attendees face the Speaker and the screen upon which visual aids are projected. Lighting should permit comfortable viewing of visual aids without excessive darkness or screen washout caused by sun glare from undraped or stained-glass windows. Society shall locate vendors and other activities outside the lecture room or, if in the same room, shall ensure that such vendors or activities are discontinued during Speaker's presentations.

6. Taping. Speaker agrees to permit audiotaping by individual attendees for their private use, with the proviso that tapes are not to be duplicated, transcribed, or otherwise disseminated. No taping shall be done for commercial purposes or by Society for distribution to nonattendees, Society members, or library patrons. Private tapes may not be used for other meetings of Society or for meetings of any other group. Society shall inform attendees of this policy in publicity materials and shall announce this policy from the podium after attendees are in their seats and before Speaker is introduced.

[*Alternative to* **Taping**. No tape or video recording shall be permitted.]

7. Publicity. Speaker shall provide Society with one or more black-and-white glossy photographs,

Note:

This and the following two examples are not fill-in-the-blanks, one-size-fits-all models. They merely illustrate issues that need considering. Some matters are handled differently from one example to the other. Each of us should tailor the specifics to our own circumstances, with individualized advice from an attorney.

Fig. 4 is adapted from a model presented by Elizabeth Shown Mills as "Letter of Agreement," *Genealogical Speakers Guild Newsletter* 1 (November 1992): 5–6.

EXECUTING CONTRACTS

FIG. 4 (CONT.)
CONTRACT FOR
GENEALOGICAL
LECTURING SERVICES

a professional biography, and other publicity materials. Society shall provide Speaker an advance copy of any publicity prepared for distribution and shall not disseminate any material without Speaker's prior approval. "Publicity" includes, but is not limited to, fliers that announce themes, topics, and services. Society shall begin publicity efforts at least six to nine months prior to Event and shall extend such efforts to other societies and potential attendees within at least a two-hour driving range.

8. Lecture Fees. Society shall pay Speaker a base fee of $_____ for four one-hour lectures, plus $____ for each attendee in excess of 150. Should Society and Speaker agree to additional lectures in conjunction with this seminar, compensation shall be at the rate of $_____ per one-hour lecture. Society shall pay Speaker on the day of Event.

9. Travel Expenses. Society shall reimburse Speaker for round-trip travel by air (coach class, advance purchase) or (if more economical and feasible) by automobile at the rate of ____ cents per mile. Automobile travel shall be deemed "not feasible" if the distance between Speaker's location on the morning before Event and the destination (city in which seminar is to be held) is more than 200 miles. If Society requests that air reservations be made more than a month in advance of Event, then Speaker shall submit receipts for immediate reimbursement by Society. If air reservations are made by Speaker one month or less in advance of Event, then Society may delay reimbursement until the day of Event.

10. Personal Accommodations. Society shall provide Speaker with hotel or motel accommodations beginning the night immediately preceding Event and continuing through the night immediately following Event. Such accommodations should include a no-smoking [*or smoking*] room in a reasonably quiet, standard-class facility. Society shall handle all financial arrangements directly with the hotel or motel. Meals en route or on-site, not otherwise covered by the air carrier or Society's scheduled functions, shall be billed to Society and shall not exceed $____ per meal. Society shall provide transportation to and from airport to motel, and to and from motel to meeting place, or reimburse speaker for the expense of such transportation.

11. Cancellation. This agreement may be canceled if (1) a natural or public disaster should render Event unfeasible; or (2) serious illness or family death should incapacitate Speaker. If a natural or public disaster requires cancellation, Society shall not be responsible for Speaker's fee but shall reimburse Speaker for any sums already expended for nonrefundable airfare. In the event that Speaker should be unable to fulfill her obligations, she agrees to assist Society in finding a comparable replacement and shall not be reimbursed by Society for any advance sums she may have expended.

12. Merger. This document contains the entire agreement of both parties. It supersedes all oral and written proposals and all other prior agreements, understandings, or communication. Its terms may not be altered or changed except by a writing signed by both parties.

13. Survival of Terms and Conditions. The terms and conditions of this contract shall survive its performance.

14. Jurisdiction, Venue, and Controlling Law. The parties agree that this agreement shall be construed in accordance with the laws of the state of [*Speaker's state*].

15. Severability. If any portion of this agreement shall be declared invalid or unenforceable by a court with jurisdiction over the parties, the remaining portions not so declared shall remain valid and enforceable.

16. Titles. The titles of the sections of this agreement are descriptive and are inserted for convenience of location only and do not define or limit the material contained thereunder.

17. Third Parties. This agreement shall be binding on the legal representatives, successors, and assigns of the parties. Should Speaker die before this contract has been performed, Society's sole remedy shall be the reimbursement of any expenses already advanced to Speaker.

18. Notices. All notices under this agreement shall be in writing and shall be deemed to be given five days after deposit in the U.S. mail, postage prepaid, and addressed as set forth in the first paragraph of this agreement. Should either party wish to have his or her place of notice changed, he or she shall send the new address by certified mail to the other party.

19. Execution in Counterpart. The parties acknowledge that two copies of this agreement are being executed. Each is deemed to be an original, but they constitute one and the same instrument.

20. Performance of Actions Necessary to Complete Transaction. Both Society and Speaker shall be required to execute any documents or take any actions that may reasonably be required to effectuate the transactions contemplated herein.

21. Waiver of Breach. The waiver of a breach of any provision of this contract shall not be construed as a waiver of any prior or subsequent breach.

22. Legal Costs. If a dispute arises in connection with this agreement, the losing party shall pay any and all reasonable attorneys' fees and court costs that the prevailing party has incurred in connection with the enforcement of this agreement.

IN WITNESS WHEREOF, the parties have signed this agreement on the day and date following their names, below.

<table>
<tr><td>_____</td><td>_____</td></tr>
<tr><td>Ann E. Boddie, Certified Genealogist, Speaker</td><td>for Wishwenew Genealogical Society</td></tr>
<tr><td>Telephone no. _____</td><td>Telephone no. _____</td></tr>
<tr><td>Fax no. _____</td><td>Fax no. _____</td></tr>
<tr><td>E-mail _____</td><td>E-mail _____</td></tr>
<tr><td>Date _____</td><td>Date _____</td></tr>
</table>

FIG. 4 (CONT.)
CONTRACT FOR
GENEALOGICAL
LECTURING SERVICES

EXECUTING CONTRACTS

**FIG. 5
CONTRACT FOR
GENEALOGICAL
RESEARCH SERVICES**

THIS AGREEMENT is made this the ___ day of _____ 20__, by and between Ann E. Boddie, Certified Genealogist (hereinafter called "Genealogist"), of [*cite address*], and Clyde Curious (hereinafter called "Client") of [*cite address*].

WHEREAS, Genealogist is engaged in providing professional genealogical services, and

WHEREAS, Client has the need for and desires to engage Genealogist for such services,

NOW THEREFORE, in consideration of the mutual promises contained herein, the sufficiency of which is hereby acknowledged, the parties agree as follows:

1. Services to be Rendered. [*List specific work that will be performed here. Amend it to suit the specific situation, but avoid specifying details of how work shall be performed, which could suggest an employer-employee relationship.*]

[*Example:* Genealogist shall analyze information now in Client's possession and research appropriate ancestral lines to determine client's eligibility for membership in the Guild of St. Margaret of Scotland. If eligibility is found, Genealogist shall prepare application papers with complete documentation for Client's use. If not found, Genealogist shall prepare a report on the extent of the research, with documentary support of the conclusions.]

2. Condition Precedent and Effective Date. Client shall provide to Genealogist a summary of information known to him about matters covered in the scope of services, to include copies of previous research reports or summaries, copies of significant documents, and lists of sources or collections previously searched. This Agreement shall become effective only after receipt of such information, copies, and lists, and upon receipt of the retainer fee described in Section 4.

3. Time of Performance. Genealogist shall provide the research services detailed in Section 1, above, on or before ___ weeks [*or months*] after the effective date in Section 2, unless she earlier notifies Client (as provided in Section 17) of the need for an extension. Upon such notification, she shall be automatically entitled to an additional sixty (60) days.

4. Compensation. Client shall pay $___ per hour for Genealogist's time and authorizes up to ___ hours of work. The hourly fee shall be applied to time spent appraising and surveying Client's prior work, in addition to research time and time spent preparing society-application papers or the alternative report. Client shall pay an advance of $_____ , which shall be applied to the authorized hourly fees. When the authorized maximum has been reached, Genealogist shall provide Client with the work product specified in Section 1. Additional research, if Client requests it, shall be authorized only by an amendment in writing, signed by both parties to this agreement. Client understands that if he delays in deciding whether to authorize additional research, Genealogist will have to spend additional time reacquainting herself with the facts of his case. Should Client's execution of the present contract be delayed by six months, Client understands that the stated fee may need to be renegotiated.

5. Expense Reimbursement. Client shall reimburse Genealogist for costs she incurs for certificates, photocopies, parking expenses, telephone toll calls, and other necessary out-of-pocket expenses, provided she submits an itemized bill and provided that the total of expenses does not exceed $_____ . If Genealogist anticipates that expenses may exceed this $_____ maximum, she shall notify Client in writing and obtain his agreement, also in writing, to the reimbursement of additional expenses.

6. Confidentiality. Client understands and agrees that Genealogist shall hold confidential his name, address, telephone number, and other identifying information about him, unless he authorizes their release in writing. Genealogist shall also accord confidentiality to all material furnished by Client which contains (*a*) information that is not a matter of public record or which cannot be rightfully obtained from another nonconfidential source; (*b*) information that no one else has independently developed; and (*c*) information that Client has not disclosed to anyone else except under a strict, written, confidentiality agreement that has the effect of preventing disclosure by any other person or entity. Client understands that even though Genealogist may agree to keep certain information confidential, a court can compel Genealogist to disclose that information.

Note:

Different approaches to issues covered in all the examples, like compensation or dispute resolution, illustrate some of the options to be considered. The approach shown in an example is not a specifiic recommendation for its use in that type of contract.

[*Supplemental provision, Alternative 1:* Genealogist shall treat with discretion, even if they are matters of public record, matters that concern living persons, their parents, or immediate families, and the following matters designated by Client as sensitive: (*list specifics*). Client understands that even though Genealogist may agree to keep said information confidential, a court can at any time compel Genealogist to disclose that information.]

[*Supplemental provision, Alternative 2:* Genealogist shall not publish or otherwise share results of research performed for Client without Client's agreement in writing, except for limited submissions to genealogical journals to correct previously published errors.]

7. Disclaimers. Client understands and agrees that Genealogist can make no guarantees regarding what information, if any, may be found or what conclusions may be drawn from it. Client further understands and agrees that Genealogist cannot predict in advance the time needed to find information or prove facts or relationships, and that the risk of nondiscovery, or of discoveries contrary to those desired, is on Client, not Genealogist. [*Add other disclaimers here that are necessary for professional protection or for client education.*]

8. Delegation of Duties. Client agrees that Genealogist may delegate certain research duties of her choosing to other qualified researchers. Genealogist represents that she will not engage any agent to perform research duties unless that agent (1) holds credentials from a professionally recognized certifying or accrediting agency in the field of genealogy; or (2) has been researching for others for at least ____ years and has a reputation, known to Genealogist, for quality work.

9. Future Use of Work Product. Client understands that Genealogist must protect her professional reputation. In that regard, he agrees that he shall obtain Genealogist's consent, in advance, to any publication of any portion of her work product. Should she not consent, Client may not publish her work. Genealogist shall respond to a request for publication within thirty (30) days from the date Client delivers material specifically designated as proposed for publication. Genealogist's reply shall indicate any specific sentences or sections to which she objects, as well as the reason(s) for objection. She shall also submit recommended changes at no cost to Client, and Client shall be required to make said changes to the manuscript as a condition of her consent to publication. Client shall incur no expense for Genealogist's time spent in studying or responding to material proposed to be published. Genealogist shall not unreasonably withhold her consent to publication.

10. Remedies. If the parties are unable to agree on any matter arising out of this contract, the issues shall be submitted to the arbitration process of the [*name of appropriate professional organization or other provider of arbitration services*]. The parties expressly agree that the arbitration decision may, at the election of either party, be entered as a final judgment in any court of law or equity having jurisdiction over either of the parties. The arbitration process and its enforcement under this section shall be the only remedy which either party shall have with respect to any controversy concerning this agreement; and the finding of the arbitrator shall be final, permanent, and binding on both parties.

11. Merger. This document contains the entire agreement of the parties. It supersedes all oral or written proposals and all other prior agreements, understandings, or communication. Its terms may not be altered except by a writing signed by both parties.

12. Survival of Terms and Conditions. The terms and conditions of this contract shall survive its performance.

13. Jurisdiction, Venue, and Controlling Law. The parties agree that this agreement shall be construed in accordance with the laws of the state of [*Genealogist's state*] and that neither party will resort to the courts of any jurisdiction to resolve disputes arising out of this agreement, except for the purpose of entering as a final judgment an arbitration decision rendered pursuant to Section 10 of this agreement.

14. Severability. If any portion of this agreement shall be declared invalid or unenforceable, the remaining portions not so declared shall remain valid and enforceable.

15. Titles. The titles of the sections of this agreement are descriptive and are inserted for convenience of location only and do not define or limit the material contained thereunder.

FIG. 5 (CONT.)
CONTRACT FOR
GENEALOGICAL
RESEARCH SERVICES

EXECUTING CONTRACTS

FIG. 5 (CONT.)
**CONTRACT FOR
GENEALOGICAL
RESEARCH SERVICES**

16. Third Parties. This agreement shall be binding on the heirs, legal representatives, successors, and assigns of both parties. Should Genealogist die before this contract has been performed, Client's sole remedy shall be the return of any unearned fee.

17. Notices. All notices under this agreement shall be in writing and shall be deemed to be given five days after deposit in the U.S. mail, postage prepaid, and addressed as set forth in the first paragraph of this agreement. Should either party wish to have his or her place of notice changed, he or she shall send the new address by certified mail to the other party.

18. Execution in Counterpart. The parties acknowledge that two copies of this agreement are being executed. Each is deemed to be an original, but they constitute one and the same instrument.

19. Performance of Actions Necessary to Complete Transaction. Both Client and Genealogist shall be required to execute any documents or take any actions that may reasonably be required to effectuate the transactions contemplated herein.

20. Waiver of Breach. The waiver of a breach of any provision of this contract shall not be construed as a waiver of any prior or subsequent breach.

21. Dispute Resolution Costs. If a dispute arises in connection with this agreement, the losing party shall pay any and all reasonable arbitration costs, attorneys' fees, and court costs that the prevailing party has incurred in connection with the enforcement of this agreement.

IN WITNESS WHEREOF, the parties have signed this agreement on the day and date following their names, below.

_____   _____
Ann E. Boddie, Certified Genealogist   Clyde Curious

Telephone no. _____   Telephone no. _____
Fax no. _____   Fax no. _____
E-mail _____   E-mail _____
Date _____   Date _____

[Letterhead of Genealogist]

[Date]

[Client name and address]

Dear _____ :

You have asked me to undertake professional genealogical services for you. This letter, with the accompanying Schedule of Fees and Expenses, describes the agreement between us regarding these services. If you agree with the terms, please sign both copies in the space provided at the end and return one to me.

I will undertake to [*State client objectives. Describe briefly the problem and scope of the work and any applicable time constraints. Don't specify how work will be done, to avoid suggesting an employer-employee relationship.*].

So that I will not duplicate work already done, you will provide me with the information you already have on the matter, including copies of reports or summaries of previous research touching on the problem, copies of significant records, and notes on sources or collections already searched.

Our agreement will become effective, and I will begin work, when I have received (*a*) that material; (*b*) a copy of this letter, with your signature accepting it; and (*c*) your check for the initial retainer of $____. This retainer is not refundable but will include up to ____ hours of work before you will be charged an hourly fee. You have authorized a maximum of ____ hours for this initial assignment, in accordance with the attached schedule of fees and expenses, and will authorize any additional time in writing.

>   [*The nonrefundable provision is included here to eliminate any need to hold
>   the retainer in a separate account until it is earned through hourly charges.*]

I will perform this work as an independent contractor in accordance with prevailing professional standards in genealogy, including the Code of Ethics of the Association of Professional Genealogists, the Code of Ethics adopted by the Board for Certification of Genealogists, and the Standards recommended by the National Genealogical Society, copies of which are attached.

After I have analyzed your problem, completed the research, and reached my conclusions, I will provide you with [*Describe desired product. Examples: "a documented report describing my findings and the basis for my conclusions," or "copies of relevant documents with full source citation," or "a completed society-application form, accompanied by necessary documentation, ready for your signature and submission," or "an edited manuscript," or "camera-ready copy."*].

I will hold confidential any information you provide that is not already a matter of public record or public knowledge. I will treat with discretion, even if they are already matters of public record, issues that concern living persons, their parents, or immediate families, as well as the following items that you have specifically noted as sensitive: [*List any such items*]. Otherwise, I retain the right to make further use of the results of work done at your request, including publication in articles or books, with acknowledgment of your sponsorship of the research, unless you request anonymity. However, I will not accept fees to provide these results to other interested persons but will, with your consent, refer them to you for the information and allow you to determine the terms under which you may decide to share it.

You agree that if you distribute to others or publish any information taken from my report, including my findings and conclusions, you will report them accurately, you will include any qualifiers (for example, the words *probable* or *possible,* when accompanying a conclusion), and you will credit my report as the source. I retain the copyright to the report and the manner in which I have expressed the information in it. You may make a limited number of personal copies as a "fair use" of the copyrighted report, but you agree that you will not otherwise publish or make multiple copies of the report without my written permission.

**FIG. 6
ENGAGEMENT LETTER
FOR GENEALOGICAL
RESEARCH SERVICES ∗**

∗ *Contributed by
Donn Devine, J.D., CG, CGI*

Although it is less formal in appearance, an agreement in letter form, with a client's signed acceptance, is a binding contract. This example, like the preceding ones, is illustrative only. Decisions on provisions to include in an actual engagement letter should be made with legal advice.

EXECUTING CONTRACTS

FIG. 6 (CONT.)
ENGAGEMENT LETTER
FOR GENEALOGICAL
RESEARCH SERVICES

We both agree that if any dispute arises out of this agreement, we will use the arbitration services of [*Specify an appropriate professional organization or other provider of arbitration services.*] and accept as final and binding on both of us the arbitration decision, and we both consent to the entry of the decision as a final judgment in any court that may have jurisdiction over either of us.

This letter and the accompanying fee schedule reflect the full scope of our agreement and replace any earlier, tentative commitments by either of us. Any changes will be effective only if they are also made in writing.

Thank you for the opportunity to be of service.

Sincerely yours,

_____

Genealogist

ACCEPTED:

_____

Client

_____

Date

7

**COPYRIGHT
AND FAIR USE**

Keynotes

Chapter 7

Copyright <u>and</u> Fair Use

by Val D. Greenwood, J.D., AG

Familiarity with basic copyright issues is a must for the professional genealogist. These issues can affect our own creative work, as well as the manner and extent to which we can use the work of others. Copyrights are not a modern concept. The United States Constitution grants Congress "power . . . to promote the progress of science and useful arts, by securing for limited times to authors . . . the exclusive right to their respective writings."[1] Various laws and amendments over the two centuries since have kept copyright provisions abreast of economic, intellectual, social, and technological advances.[2]

Because legal privileges and restrictions vary internationally, this chapter focuses upon U.S. practices. However, many of the issues discussed here are broadly applicable, regardless of where one lives. Since 1988 the United States has conformed with the international Berne Convention, which contributes greatly to our protection of literary rights. Over seventy other countries have also signed the Berne Convention, meaning that authors in any of those countries enjoy rights in all of them. More detailed information is available in circulars published by the U.S. Copyright Office, some of them referenced in this chapter. A complete list, as well as the full text of current versions, may be read or downloaded from the U.S. Copyright Office website on the Internet or from corresponding offices in other nations.

> Over seventy countries have signed the Berne Convention, meaning that authors in any of those countries enjoy rights in all of them.

General Concepts

Definitions

COPYRIGHT

A copyright is a package of exclusive legal privileges, including control of the reproduction, publication, and sale of protected works, whether published or unpublished.[3] For general works, these include the rights to

- reproduce copies,
- prepare derivatives (condensations, translations, etc.) based on the original, and
- distribute copies to the public.

For literary (as well as choreographic, dramatic, and musical) works, they include the rights to

- perform the work publicly and
- display it publicly.

Because copyrights are personal property, owners are free to transfer all or any of those rights to others. Although the rights are said to be exclusive, important limitations exist. One of the main exceptions, *fair use,* is discussed later in this chapter. Perhaps the most misunderstood provision is this: a copyright protects the

COPYRIGHT AND FAIR USE

A copyright protects the form in which a creative idea is expressed, but it does not protect the idea itself or its informational content.

form in which a creative idea is expressed, but it does not protect the idea itself or its informational content.

PUBLICATION

Although both are fully protected by copyright, the law still distinguishes between published and unpublished material. A work is considered "published" if

- copies are distributed to the public by some means like lease, loan, rental, sale, or subscription.
- copies are shared, with no restrictions on further use of its contents.
- copies are offered for public display or further distribution. However, public display alone does not constitute publication, no matter how many people see or hear it. For example, a lecture to a genealogical audience is not published if the lecturer does not make it available for distribution.

We should also bear in mind that putting a work on the Internet is publication of that work. If, for example, a genealogical society decided to put several years of its periodical onto such a site, it should do so only with the consent of those who own the copyrights—usually, the authors of the various articles.

Ownership

A copyright comes into existence when a work is created. At that point it belongs exclusively to its creator or author. Only the author or those who derive their rights from the author can rightfully claim protection. In the case of a "work made for hire," the employer (which may be a company or an organization, as well as an individual) is considered the author. Thus, the employer owns the copyright, rather than the employee who actually created the work.

Works made for hire are those prepared by employees within the scope of employment. They may also be specially commissioned for use in collective works, compilations, or texts—if the creators sign agreements to consider such as works made for hire. The creative product of an independent contractor is not considered "made for hire" unless very specific requirements are met, including a signed agreement specifying that result. Typically, those of us who conduct research for clients and operate as sole proprietors or partners (see chapter 8) are independent contractors. As such, we own the copyright to our creative work. This proviso is somewhat at odds with traditional ethics in the practice of genealogy, wherein many professional researchers have felt that ownership should belong to the clients who commission us. The seeming conflict can be resolved by assigning some or all of our rights to the client. Chapters 5 and 6 offer more detailed guidance on ethics, contractual assignment of rights, and our personal protection against misrepresentation when those rights are assigned.

Joint authors hold the copyright as co-owners unless some other appropriate agreement is reached between or among them. They might agree in writing that the work will be considered one made for hire, as above; or they might otherwise assign their individual rights to others.

Periodicals and anthologies pose a special case. The copyright to an individual article is distinct from that of the collective work in which it is included. Copyrights to articles belong initially to authors or contributors, who may grant publication rights to a society or an individual—commonly the right of first publication or exclusive publication for a specified period. But ownership of a manuscript or the authority to print and distribute it does not constitute copyright ownership.

Eligibility

Only "original works of authorship" can be protected by copyright. Various classes of works are eligible. Those by genealogists and family historians most frequently are classed as *nondramatic literary works*—a term defined broadly enough to include compilations, computer programs, and correspondence. Audio and video tapes are protected under another class. Apart from the literary form in which they are expressed, names, slogans, or titles have no copyright protection. These items, if and when they meet certain criteria for distinctiveness, fall under the trademark process[4]—as well as the purview of ethics, as discussed in chapter 5.

Prior to 1978, a work had to be either published or registered to be protected. For pre-1978 publications without a copyright notice, the opportunity to claim copyright protection was lost forever. Unpublished works created before the effective date of the 1978 law—if they were neither copyrighted nor in the public domain— were automatically copyrighted when the statute went into effect. The current law covers practically all unpublished works produced in the United States and published works if the author wants it. Our labors are even covered during the creation process, because any "completed" part is protected. Works not copyrighted are said to be "in the public domain." Within this broad framework, special situations exist.

GOVERNMENT PUBLICATIONS

Official government publications are not eligible for copyright in any form by anyone. As lecturers, publishers, researchers, teachers, and writers, we may incorporate this material into our own copyrighted material without any specific approval; but those portions remain uncopyrighted, and ethical issues still must be considered. At the same time, the works of private authors, even if published by the government, have full protection under the law.

TRANSCRIPTS AND INDEXES

This category, of particular interest to genealogists, carries severe limitations. Because copyrights are granted for *creative authorship or arrangements,* not informational content, our transcripts and indexes may not be copyrightable or they may be just partially protected. Either the selection of the data or the arrangement of the elements must involve judgment or creativity. If we include every possible item and exercise no selectivity, then a creative arrangement is necessary. Such common treatments as chronological, numerical, and alphabetical listings do not qualify—no matter how much effort goes into our compilation. For example:

Official government publications are not eligible for copyright in any form by anyone.

- An alphabetical index to the names in an old church record or census schedule will likely not be accepted for registration unless we can prove a creative contribution—perhaps the interpretation of old or difficult handwriting, the addition of explanatory notes, or the translation from another language.

- Transcripts pose an even greater difficulty. By definition, transcripts are not originals; they are copies of existing works. A book titled or described as a transcript is obviously a *derivative* work—reproduced from someone else's original. To copyright a derivative, we must satisfactorily explain how interpretive judgment went into its creation. Mere skill in copying will not suffice.[5]

As professional genealogists, we are seriously impeded by these restrictions. Faithfulness to the original—to its sequence of information and its precise wording—is essential to genealogical quality. Some suggested ways to work around this problem appear later in this chapter.

Fair use

Fair use is an old common-law concept that the latest copyright law specifically addresses. It puts significant limits on the exclusive nature of copyright protection, permitting certain uses without violating the owner's legal rights. Those uses are usually associated with commentary, criticism, news reporting, research, scholarship, and teaching. *Commentary* and *criticism* include book reviews. *Teaching* includes making multiple copies of limited portions for classroom use. In some cases, entire chapters might legally be copied and distributed to students. Whether a particular use is fair varies from case to case. The criteria set forth in the current statute originated in the courts, where the fair-use concept was a common defense in infringement cases. Specifically, fair use considers[6]

- the purpose and character of the use, including whether it is of a commercial or nonprofit educational nature;

- the type and content of the work itself;

- the amount and substantiality of the portion used in relation to the work as a whole; and

- the effect of the use on the potential market for or value of the work.

As genealogists, we have several interests in this fair-use exception. It generally lets us photocopy limited portions of a work for our personal use. It also lets us quote to some extent in our writings, if we properly attribute the material. Because copyright law is intended to protect the owner's financial return, as one means of promoting "the progress of Science and useful Arts," any use so extensive that it cuts into sales, subscriptions, or profits is illegal. At the same time, materials distributed under the fair-use exception usually broaden the market for the work and promote sales.

Libraries and archives enjoy special privileges under the fair-use exception, in order to advance research and scholarship. These institutions may reproduce and

Fair use considers the amount and substantialness of the portion used in relation to the work as a whole.

distribute single copies of a copyrighted work if

- the reproduction or distribution is not made for direct or indirect commercial advantage;
- the collection of the library or archives is (*a*) open to the public, or (*b*) available to researchers in a specialized field, whether or not they are affiliated with that institution; and
- the reproduction or distribution of the work includes a notice of copyright.[7]

For libraries, this exception applies to an *unpublished* work only if the copy is made for security reasons or for an interlibrary loan. It applies to a *published* work only if a single article from a collection or periodical is involved, the copy is for scholarly purposes, and it becomes the property of the user. An exception applies to an entire work when the original is out of print or otherwise unobtainable at a fair price.

Genealogical Applications

There are many questions we might ask about how copyright laws apply to our work products. The answers may be as varied as our employment. Most professional genealogists still conduct research on commission; yet most who accept client assignments also engage in other professional genealogical activities—commonly authoring or compiling books and articles, lecturing or teaching, and publishing or selling genealogical materials. From the standpoint of copyrights, the client research reports, compiled books and articles, lecture materials, and reprinted works are the work products most likely to be affected.

Client research reports

There is no doubt that our research reports are copyrighted, if we want them to be, and that we own the copyright. As independent contractors rather than employees of our clients, we are not producing a *work for hire* under the copyright law, unless we have defined our work as such in a written contract. However, we do not own any of the facts or ideas contained in our writing—we own the copyright, which covers only the literary form in which our findings are expressed.

PROFESSIONAL LIMITATIONS
The simple truth is that our written product has no significant monetary value apart from the facts and ideas that comprise it. We cannot ethically sell it to someone else. Certainly as professional genealogists, we have the right to use the facts disclosed by our research to write whatever we wish, for whatever purpose. But ethics, courtesy, and good judgment suggest that we should not publish information and conclusions the client paid us to produce, unless we have the client's written consent. This is true even though we own the copyright to the written material in which we include that information.

Ethics, courtesy, and good judgment suggest that we should not publish information and conclusions the client paid us to produce, unless we have the client's written consent.

CLIENT LIMITATIONS

Our clients also have every legal right to use the facts we report to them—in any way they choose, within bounds. They cannot legally and ethically publish our writings as their own. Nor can they alter the facts or conclusions we supply and publish that alteration with us cited as the author. Copyright law explicitly gives us the right "to prevent the use of [our] name as the author of the work . . . in the event of a distortion, mutilation, or other modification of that work which would be prejudicial to [our] honor or reputation."[8] By the very nature of what we do as genealogists and our desire for accuracy, we usually expect our clients to use our research product without alteration, no matter who owns what rights.

SAFEGUARDING RIGHTS

In the final analysis, our principal interest is not ownership but fairness—to the client and to ourselves. We can best achieve this through a written agreement or contract before we begin research, as described in chapter 6. When developing a research contract, we should consider the result that both we and our client desire. We will want a clear understanding of the limits, rights, and expectations on both sides. For example, we may reserve the right to review and approve (and perhaps edit) any materials prepared for publication that are based on the results of our research. In some cases, that may even include the right to prevent publication until agreement is reached on what is to be published and how our original findings may have been affected by later research.

If our clients are professionals—perhaps attorneys or other genealogists—who may pass our reports on to clients of their own, we may want a contract provision requiring that the secondary client be given a full copy of the report we prepare on the matter—perhaps with notice of our copyright. Or we might reserve the right to review and approve any summaries or reports prepared for secondary clients based on our research. If we wish to be identified when the facts produced by our research are published or passed on to others, we can stipulate that, too, in a contract.

Some clients may not fully understand copyright principles and may not realize that they have bought our time—not our work product. In such cases, it may be important to specifically reserve our right to use our research results in books or journal articles, with credit given to the client for sponsoring the research. The issue is one we broach carefully, not because of copyright law but out of sensitivity for the feelings of the client, who has paid for the research. Concern here is important—not only to our reputation and ongoing success as a professional, but also to the image of the genealogical profession in general.

Compilations and indexes

As professional genealogists, we are seriously impeded by the restricted eligibility for copyright of compilations and indexes. Fundamental to the practice of our field is faithful reproduction of facts as they appear in an original document—faithfulness to both sequence of information and precise wording. If we are

> Some clients may not fully understand copyright principles and may not realize that they have bought our time—not our work product.

reluctant to invest labor and funds into publishing quality transcriptions, lest our investment be copied and reproduced for sale by others, we might consider the value of substantially annotating our work. We would, of course, observe the cardinal rule that annotations must be clearly distinguished from the text of the original—commonly through the use of square brackets, indentation, or footnotes or endnotes to set off the added data. Within this context, we might, for example:

When copying records

- add footnotes or indented paragraphs amid text to cross-reference other available material on various people; add personal data on individuals named on cemetery markers; provide origin or migration data for parties involved in land conveyances; or identify relationships between deceased individuals and buyers at their estate sales. For any such added data, we would, of course, supply the proper documentation.

When compiling indexes

- include topical entries (subject entries), not just names and places. (See chapter 26.)

- consolidate entries for individuals whose names are variously spelled—*if* we know enough about those individuals to make these matches *correctly.*

- add identifying information in brackets beside the names of individuals. Common amplifications include names of husbands, wives, or parents; ethnic identifiers; and dates of birth and death.

Substantial "creative" additions of this type—documented and *clearly separated from our meticulously faithful transcriptions*—may earn copyright registration for our book and protection for our "original" parts. True, the transcriptions themselves would remain uncovered, and the truly unscrupulous might still extract, retype, and publish our highly skilled transcripts under their names. Yet for all practical purposes, our partial copyright will normally discourage reproduction. Obtaining copyrights for compilations or indexes under any circumstance hinges upon the effectiveness with which we explain to the Copyright Office the nature and extent of our creative contribution.

Lecture materials

As lecturers, our work products take at least two forms: oral presentations (which may or may not be audio- or videotaped) and written materials (which are disseminated to audiences or displayed as visual aids in the course of the lecture). Both forms are covered by the copyright law. Most of the general rights and exceptions previously made in this chapter apply to these two forms. In brief:

- It is not necessary to formally request registration each time we write a lecture. Indeed, that practice is commonly discouraged, especially since most professional lectures are in a continual state of revision.

- The information we impart is not copyrightable, only the exact words in which

> Obtaining copyrights for compilations or indexes hinges upon the effectiveness with which we explain to the Copyright Office the nature and extent of our creative contribution.

we say it—assuming that arrangement of words is original to us in the first place. (If it's not, it should be!)

- Our written materials are protected, even if we do not affix the copyright symbol or the word "copyright." As a practical matter, however, it is wise to do one or the other—to "warn off" potential violators who may not be familiar with copyright law. It is a lot simpler and cheaper to warn than to sue.

- Our visual aids are protected, as artwork or as literary works, so long as they originate with us. That protection is also limited to the arrangement of words or graphic elements, rather than informational content.

- We may quote from the copyrighted work of others, so long as we (a) stay within the bounds of fair use; (b) use the material for commentary, critique, or instructional purposes; and (c) properly identify the material's author or creator. In general, this provision includes limited use of artwork and cartoons, as well as literary work.

- If our oral presentations are audio- or videotaped, we may also expect archives, libraries, and other lecturers to use them in accordance with educational exceptions made by the copyright law. This includes the lending of tapes by libraries and other nonprofit institutions, but not by individuals.

Reprinted works

Genealogical publishers provide a valuable service to the field, not only by introducing new works but also by reissuing rare and out-of-print ones. If we decide to reprint a rare volume—or to launch a publishing house specializing in facsimile copies—we would naturally check each book's status with the Copyright Office. The fact that a work was first created over ninety-five years ago does not necessarily mean that its copyright has expired. As in all aspects of our professional lives, we are also wise to lean toward caution in all legal matters. While the copyright law generally denies protection to materials published without a copyright notice before 1978, some authorities contend that a "common-law right" still exists. Authors of such pre-1978 works who are still alive—or their heirs—may choose to defend their rights. Even if they don't, ethics and courtesy suggest that their permission should be sought. More than a few professionals, legally assured that certain works had no copyright protection, have damaged their professional reputations by marketing the works without permission of living authors or heirs. When in doubt, we should consult an attorney.

Protection Processes

Three elements combine to perfect the copyright on a specific work—*notice, registration,* and *deposit.* Each is examined below, together with other considerations that affect the copyright over its term.

Notice

A copyright notice is a written statement placed on the work itself. A proper

More than a few professionals, legally assured that a work had no copyright protection, have damaged their professional reputations by marketing the works without permission of living authors or heirs.

notice consists of three elements:

- The copyright symbol © or the word *Copyright*—it is not necessary to use both (for sound recordings the symbol is ℗ on the recording medium or the label);
- The year of first publication; and
- The name of the copyright owner.

Neither registration nor permission from the Copyright Office is needed to place this notice on a work. Recognizable abbreviations or alternative designations for the owner's name are acceptable. These three elements normally appear together in the notice, as shown in the following example:

© 2000, John Doe

The Berne Convention made notice an optional step. For works published since 1 March 1989, the author's rights are preserved with or without a notice affixed.[9] Nonetheless, notices are still strongly recommended.

The primary purpose of copyright notice is to advise the world of the owner's rights and to prevent claims that any infringement was unintentional. Thus, notice should be placed where it is easily seen. If we are not yet experienced in this area, we might study the placement of notices on similar works to get an idea of general practice. Statements like "All rights reserved" and "Unauthorized reproduction in any manner is prohibited" add nothing to the owner's rights, although they often appear for emphasis. The existence of the notice on the work bars use of an "innocent infringement" defense if a suit is filed. Variant forms of notice should usually be avoided.

Although unpublished work is now protected without notice, we cannot prosecute an infringement if we have not proceeded to the second stage: registration. To avoid the possibility of our material being inadvertently published before we feel it is ready, we are wise to add a copyright notice to any copies that leave our control. For example:

Unpublished work © 2000, John Doe

Registration

Registration with the Copyright Office is necessary to protect ownership rights only if *(a)* the work was published before 1 March 1989; or *(b)* it lacks a proper copyright notice—as when there is either an omission or error in the date or name. However, even though registration is not required on contemporary works, it is a good idea. It creates a public record of the owner's claim; and it is a prerequisite to bringing an infringement suit if the work is of U.S. origin. There are also other incentives for registration:

- If a work is registered within five years after publication, the registration is prima facie evidence of the validity of the copyright and of the facts stated on the certificate. That is, of itself the certificate is adequate to establish the fact of copyright or raise the presumption of fact, unless it is disputed.

Although unpublished work is now protected without notice, we cannot prosecute an infringement if we have not proceeded to the second stage: registration.

COPYRIGHT AND FAIR USE

FIG. 7
COPYRIGHT FORMS
COMMONLY USED
BY GENEALOGISTS

Form PA
For original registration of works relating to the performing arts—e.g., musical, dramatic, and audiovisual works such as videotaped family histories.

Form SE
For original registration of works issued or intended for issue in a series on an indefinite basis—e.g., journals, magazines, newsletters, or newspapers.

Form SR
For original registration of sound recordings—that is, taped interviews and/or lectures.

Form TX
For original registration of nondramatic literary works, published or unpublished—for example: written articles, compilations that meet originality requirements, family histories, or translated works. Automated databases and computer programs with copyrightable screen displays are also classed as nondramatic literary works and are registered using this form.

- If a work is registered within three months after publication, or before any infringement within that period, statutory damages and attorneys' fees can be claimed in an infringement suit. Otherwise, only actual damages and lost profits may be claimed.

A work may be registered at any time during the life of the copyright, and both published and unpublished works may be registered. If an unpublished work is registered, it need not be reregistered upon publication—but can be, if desired. Registration requires

- a properly completed registration form,
- a filing fee, and
- two copies of the best edition—as first published. (If the work is unpublished or was first published outside the United States, only one copy need be filed.)

Different registration forms exist for various types of works, as shown in figure 7. The required fee is stated on each form. Short versions of many of these forms are available for easier registration. The short forms can be used if

- the author is living,
- there is only one author,
- the author is the sole owner of the copyright,
- the work is completely new, and
- the work is not a work made for hire.

Other forms of more limited applicability—including renewals of pre-1978 copyright and corrections to previous registrations—are listed on the Copyright Office website. Copies of registration forms can be downloaded via the Internet by connecting to that website. To print the forms, we may need to download special software from the Internet site. We may also obtain the forms via postal mail or via fax-on-demand by phoning the Copyright Office—Publications Section; the website provides current addresses and phone numbers.

Registration forms must be typed or neatly hand printed in black ink. Legible photocopies are also acceptable, if on white paper and if the reverse side of the form is printed in the same direction as the front (head to head). Because the registration certificate is prepared from the form, those not meeting these requirements are returned. Applications may be submitted by

- the author—the creator(s) or the organization or person for whom the work was made for hire,
- the copyright claimant—either the author or any organization or individual claiming ownership of *all* rights that initially belonged to the author, or
- the owner of any exclusive right—a person or organization claiming any of the exclusive rights relating to the copyright that are listed at the beginning of the chapter under Definitions.

We submit all completed forms and all related materials to the Register of Copyrights at the Copyright Office. "Related materials" include the filing fee and the deposit copies. If these materials are received separately, they are usually returned. If published copies are received without the registration form and fees, those copies may be sent to the Library of Congress as a donation, and additional copies will need to be submitted with the registration form and filing fee. Each mailing must include our return address (with zip code) and a daytime phone number. We do not need an attorney to file our registration form. We may pay our fees in U.S. dollars by check, bank draft, or bank money order made payable to the Register of Copyrights.

The Copyright Office does not acknowledge receipt of registration forms. If materials are in proper order, the office sends a certificate of registration within sixteen weeks. If problems exist or if the registration cannot be accepted, the office phones or sends an explanatory letter within that same period. If we need to know when the office receives our materials, we can send our submission by registered or certified mail, with return receipt requested. We should allow at least three weeks for return of the receipt.

Registration is effective the day the Copyright Office receives all required items in acceptable form. We do not need to have the registration certificate in hand before publishing the work or placing a copyright notice on it.

Deposit

Although registration is not mandatory, the law requires that two complete copies of the "best edition" of any and all works published in the United States be deposited in the Library of Congress within three months after publication. One copy of unpublished works is required.[10] We would not forfeit our copyright by failure to deposit the required copies, but we may suffer fines and penalties. Submitting the registration form, deposit copies, and filing fee together satisfies both registration and deposit requirements.

Related Matters

Duration of protection

Before 1978, the period of protection was twenty-eight years from the date of publication—or, if unpublished, from the date of registration. The copyright could be renewed for one additional term of twenty-eight years, anytime during the final year. Terms vary by category for works created since 1 January 1978. The 1998 Sonny Bono Copyright Term Extension Act added twenty years to each of the original 1978 terms. As amended, the duration for each category is as follows:[11]

Anonymous (or pseudonymous) works
Protection extends for ninety-five years from the date of first publication or for one hundred and twenty years from the date of creation. Lacking death information, when the ninety-five or one hundred and twenty years have elapsed, the Copyright Office assumes that authors have been dead for seventy years.

The law requires that two complete copies of the "best edition" of any and all works published in the United States be deposited in the Library of Congress within three months after publication.

Authored works
Protection lasts for the life of the author plus seventy years, regardless of who owns the copyright. In the case of jointly authored works, the seventy-year period begins with the death of the last survivor.

Works created before 1978
(Those not previously published without copyright notice.) Protection lasts a maximum of ninety-five years for published works—extended from the pre-1978 maximum of fifty-six years. No such copyrights will expire before the end of 2002.

Works made for hire
Protection follows the rules for anonymous and pseudonymous works.

All works in the public domain before the 1978 act remain in the public domain. No copyright protection remains on any work created more than ninety-five years ago, except unpublished works—these being automatically covered by the 1978 statute. The Register of Copyrights keeps a file on authors' deaths. Evidence of a death—or the fact that the author is still living on a particular date—may be filed by any person with a valid interest in the copyright. A filing must identify the person making it, the nature of that person's interest, and the source of the information.

Renewal of copyrights

Copyrights on works created before 1978 must still be renewed. If not, the work passes into the public domain after the original twenty-eight-year term. The copyright renewal period is now sixty-seven years—providing a total ninety-five years of potential protection. To renew, Form RE must be completed and submitted to the Copyright Office, together with the filing fee, before the end of the twenty-eighth calendar year. Works previously renewed had their renewal period automatically extended by the new statute and its amendments to sixty-seven years. There is no renewal for works created since 1978.

Transfers and licenses

We may assign or transfer any or all of the *exclusive rights* listed at the beginning of this chapter. But a transfer is valid only if we (as owners) or our agent signs it. (An exception exists for transfers that take place by operation of law, as by will or inheritance.) Notarization is not required but is recommended. Nonexclusive transfers, called *licenses,* need not be in writing; but written documents are recommended. If written and signed, a license has priority over later transfers of exclusive rights. An example of a nonexclusive transfer is a license to publish a copyrighted work without transferring exclusive ongoing ownership of that right.

Because copyright is a personal-property right, it is subject to the contract laws and the personal-property ownership and transfer laws of the individual

No copyright protection remains on any work created more than ninety-five years ago, except unpublished works—these being automatically covered by the 1978 statute.

states. We should consult an attorney when we have questions relating to the transfer of copyright ownership in a specific state.

The Copyright Office will record documents relating to copyright transfers, although the transfers are effective without recording. In fact, we may record almost any document relating to a copyright if it is accompanied by the proper fee and meets the following legal requirements:

- It must contain the actual signature(s) of the person(s) who executed the document. (In some stated exceptions, sworn or official certification of copies is acceptable.)

- It must be complete by its own terms—that is, any related documents or materials must be included.

- It must be legible and capable of being reproduced legibly in microform.

Recordation is not mandatory, but it has advantages. It can establish priorities in case of conflicting claims, and it provides notice to the world of copyright ownership. However, recording a document does not guarantee that the content of the document is accurate or legal. If we choose to have a document recorded, we should mail it, along with two copies of its Document Cover Sheet, to the Copyright Office—Documents Unit. The office will record the cover sheet and any other submitted papers, then return the originals.

Copyright Office publications

The Copyright Office is the best source for additional details on most matters discussed in this chapter—aside from our discussions of specific genealogical applications. In addition to the previously discussed forms, the office publishes numerous circulars, information kits that include the circulars, and announcements on various types of work; figure 8 introduces some of them. We may obtain these materials free of charge via the Internet, by fax-on-demand, or by postal mail.

Copyright searches

Questions frequently arise about existing works and their status. If we discover a valuable, out-of-print work and would like to reprint it or quote from it extensively, we need to know two things: *Is there a current copyright? If so, who owns it?* Generally speaking, we can obtain this information by

- examining a copy of the work for a copyright notice, place and date of publication, author, and publisher; and

- searching Copyright Office catalogs and other records; or

- having the Copyright Office make a search.[12]

The government-documents section of many public and university libraries—as well as law libraries—has the Copyright Office's *Catalog of Copyright Entries*, which is a good place to begin an investigation, though it has limitations.[13] (Among

---

**FIG. 8
INFORMATION KITS
COMMONLY USED BY
GENEALOGISTS**

Subject	Kit no.
Books	100
Computer Programs	113
Copyright Searches	116
Fair Use	102
International Copyright	100
Mini Copyright Information	118
Renewals	117
Serials	114
Sound Recordings	121
Useful Articles	103

Copyright laws help us defend our property rights and avoid infringing upon the rights of others. A working knowledge of these laws is essential to every genealogical researcher, writer, lecturer, or publisher.

its other omissions, it does not include assignments of copyrights.) Issued as a serial since 1891, the *Catalog of Copyright Entries* exists in printed form through 1978 and on microfiche for 1979–82. Post-1982 copyright data are available only online, via the Copyright Office's website. If we ask the office to make the search, we pay the statutory fee. Requests for searches should be addressed to the Copyright Office—Reference and Bibliography Section.

Summary Concepts

Because the issue of copyrights is perceived to be complicated, many professional genealogists avoid involvement with its details. But an understanding of basic concepts and rules greatly enhances our professionalism. Copyright laws throughout the world serve the progress of civilization in four respects: they encourage creativity, they protect financial investments in that creativity, they prevent unjust damage to reputations caused by misrepresentation of professional work products, and they foster education within a fair and legal framework. More personally, copyright laws help us to defend our property rights and to avoid infringing upon the property or moral rights of others. A working knowledge of these laws is essential to every genealogical researcher, writer, lecturer, or publisher.

NOTES

1. Article 1, Section 8.
2. For the 1978 copyright law, with current amendments, see *Act for the General Revision of the Copyright Law, U.S. Code,* Title 17, chapters 1 through 8; also on the Copyright Office website. Subsequent citations of section numbers are drawn from Title 17.
3. These are listed in Sec. 106.
4. For an introduction to trademark regulations, see Kate McGrath and Stephen Elias, with Sarah Shena, *Trademark: How to Name a Business and Product; A Friendly Guide to the Laws that Govern Commercial Names* (Berkeley, California: Nolo Press, 1992); or Mark Warda, *How to Register Your Own Trademark* (Naperville, Illinois: Sourcebooks, 1997).
5. "Copyright Office Letter to Members of the National Genealogical Society," *National Genealogical Society Newsletter* 15 (May–June 1989): 67–71.
6. Sec. 107.
7. Sec. 108.
8. Sec. 106A.
9. Sec. 405.
10. Sec. 407.
11. Sec. 102, as amended by Public Law 105-298, the 1998 Sonny Bono Copyright Term Extension Act, adds twenty years to each of the terms under the 1978 law. The amendments in this act in large part address needs perceived by the entertainment industry.
12. See Circular 22, *How to Investigate the Copyright Status of a Work,* p. 3.
13. *Catalog of Copyright Entries* (Washington: Copyright Office, serialized 1891–1982).

FURTHER STUDY

Fishman, Stephen. *The Copyright Handbook: How to Protect & Use Written Works.* 5th edition. Berkeley, California: Nolo Press, 1999.
———. *Copyright Your Software.* 2d edition. Berkeley, California: Nolo Press, 1998.

Career Management

8

**ALTERNATIVE
CAREERS**

ALTERNATIVE CAREERS

Keynotes

Alternative Careers

by Elizabeth Kelley Kerstens, CGRS

We're all entrepreneurs at heart. The definition of the word was almost designed with the professional genealogist in mind: *a person who organizes, manages, and assumes responsibility for a business or other enterprise.* Entrepreneurs seek to combine their education, interests, and talents into specially crafted career opportunities. Many of our colleagues have done exactly that, branching out as authors, book dealers and publishers, forensic and genetic researchers, photographers, software developers, talk-show hosts, and translators—to name just a few. Some combine traditional client research with other career options; some have left research commissions and consultations behind as the demands of a new focus become dominant. The beauty of being an entrepreneur is that our choices are limited only by our imagination—and to a lesser degree, our resources.

If you are already a successful entrepreneur, congratulations! This chapter is not for you. But if you have a career idea brewing that needs just a gentle shove, read on. This discussion will

- help you focus on a specific career path,
- highlight a variety of career options available,
- provide tips and strategies for making the transition,
- point out pitfalls encountered by others along the entrepreneurial road, and
- list references for further research.

This chapter does *not* treat the conventional careers—research, lecturing, teaching, and traditional genealogical writing. Given their dominance, those options are discussed in depth in separate chapters. Career options that require advanced degrees or licensing—such as accountants, lawyers, or librarians—are also excluded. We should look to the literature of those fields for thorough guidance. This discussion is for those who want to translate a specialized skill or talent into a not-so-common genealogical profession.

> Two roads diverged in a wood. I took the one less traveled by, and that has made all the difference.
>
> —*Robert Frost*[1]

Career Options

Before we abandon one livelihood for another, we should thoroughly analyze our motivations, resources, and talents. (The materials suggested under FURTHER STUDY provide valuable guidance here.) Jumping into a venture without this self-scrutiny poses considerable risks. We might choose a path that doesn't suit our personality type or our long-term goals—or worse. Complete honesty and objectivity about our capabilities and desires will help us find a profitable niche that we enjoy. We should not limit ourselves to the sampling of choices below or to the more established fields. Rather, we should let our analysis point the way—perhaps even to a pioneer trail. Our career choice does not have to parallel our educational background, either. Many of us develop talents outside that formal training; and we obtain our degrees in youth, before we experience the activities that now intrigue us. Our career in genealogy should be one that excites us and one that motivates us to achieve and grow—intellectually, financially, and professionally. But we should plan to spend many hours building this new business and not be disappointed if the financial rewards come slowly. Genealogy is a specialty market that has produced few millionaires.

Once we have discovered our niche, we need to develop a business plan and a marketing plan. Later chapters will help us with both. Here, we want to mull some of the less traditional options, consider the experiences of colleagues who have made niches for themselves, and weigh the requirements.

Artifact genealogist

Genealogical research does not have to center upon families. Just as people have lineages, so do artifacts. An item found on a battlefield—a musket, bayonet, sword, or uniform—belonged to some soldier at some time in history. Marie Varrelman Melchiori, CGRS, CGL, of Vienna, Virginia, has found a market researching Civil War artifacts to prove historical ownership. The Civil War memorabilia shows and conventions that are held throughout the country have an avid and large following. Most vendors book booth space to sell collectibles, reproductions, and similar consumer goods; but Marie offers consultations on research methods and sources. Her now-loyal clientele bring her repeat business, to research military veterans and document their artifacts through her intimate familiarity with military records at the National Archives.[3] Other researchers specialize in furniture, letters, pictures, quilts, samplers, or sports items. The rich variety of human interests is every bit as historical as it is contemporary.

MINIMUM REQUIREMENTS

Considerable research skill is a given. We also must be familiar with (and have convenient physical access to) a wide range of records relating to the type of artifacts in which we choose to specialize. Attention to detail and an ability to see relationships between seemingly unconnected records are equally essential. There are no extraordinary financial requirements, other than purchasing a basic research library, a specialty library, and the office equipment needed to conduct business. These items are frequently acquired over time as the genealogist becomes familiar with the needs of his or her chosen specialty.

HOW TO BEGIN

If this idea intrigues us, we are probably already experienced with this type of research. We might build a following by volunteering at an appropriate library, museum, antiquarian association, or genealogical society. Most can use help answering queries, if not with the artifacts and actual records. We write articles for targeted publications, read Internet mail lists, and offer suggestions to those seeking answers. We attend gatherings related to our specialty—Civil War shows or roundtables, for example. We join networking organizations or history associations. We concertedly study this specialty and develop an ongoing education program that allows us to keep up to date. Then we prepare and disseminate marketing materials that highlight our services.

Author—popular press

About 75 percent of the population, we're told, feel their experiences are worth at least one book. Translating this into income is not so easy. Genealogical publishers don't underwrite the production of family histories, and some don't pay advances for the titles they do publish. The popular press is more generous, but selling ideas to it can be an uphill battle. So why bother? Because we may be the needle in a haystack that those editors are looking for.

A key to success here is the ability to transform our niche knowledge into material for a general market. A number of modern genealogists have written books that appear on the shelves of trendy bookstores. Tony Burroughs, owner of the Chicago research firm Black Roots, recently stepped into the popular-press realm when his agent convinced Simon and Schuster to publish his *Black Roots: A Beginners' Guide to Genealogical Research*. Tony has climbed his way to the top of a specialized niche, African-American genealogical research, via a degree in education, a career as an elementary and high school teacher, experience as a computer consultant, and a sideline as a genealogy instructor in adult education.[4] With experience and initiative, he transformed his *idea* into a widely marketable product.

MINIMUM REQUIREMENTS

The obvious requisites for this career choice are a talent for writing, a marketable specialty, and considerable experience. (This last ensures that we impart correct and fresh information, rather than recycling or misconstruing what colleagues have already put into print or on tape.) Tony admits, "Writing for the popular press is not for everyone—the market is not that big. But things are opening up. We have to be the best in a niche market and need good luck and timing. The first is earned with a lot of hard work and perseverance. The last two are a combination of being prepared to accept opportunity when it knocks and recognizing it when it does."[5] A large financial investment is not normally required when pursuing this type of career, but another source of livelihood usually is. Significant income is unlikely before publication and uncertain afterwards. A computer and printer are the only required equipment, at least initially. A good reference library is essential, and should include the current edition of *Writer's Market*.[6]

HOW TO BEGIN

We simply start writing about our specialty—*now!* We keep writing. We join writers groups and societies in our area of interest. We pen articles that highlight our specialty and submit them to appropriate genealogical journals, magazines, or newsletters. Then we *rewrite* our articles, imagining a more general audience; and we submit those to niche magazines. We take continuing-education writing classes. We learn to craft proposals that sell our ideas to editors. We prepare writing samples. We practice, practice, practice. We won't get rich overnight in this career; but the more experience we gain, the better are our chances of success.

Ideas won't keep; something must be done about them.

—*Alfred North Whitehead* [7]

Book publisher

It has happened to us all. We're searching a library's card catalog. We find a reference to something that might supply answers to all our riddles. But the work resides in a rare-book room and cannot be photocopied. Robert Griffin, owner of Bergen Historic Books in Englewood, New Jersey, founded his company after one such frustration a few years ago.[9] Bob runs a mail-order business out of his home, selling books he has reprinted and reselling other books that pertain to his niche market—history and genealogy in northern New Jersey and southern New York. He came into publishing with a Bachelor of Arts degree in English, a Master of Business Administration in business policy, and many years of corporate experience and professional genealogical work.[10]

Bob, who shared his publishing adventures and concerns in a two-part series featured in the *APG Quarterly*[11] is quick to point out that this career choice is time-consuming. But he truly relishes that time spent working with grateful customers, increasing his personal knowledge of published resources, creating books that are useful in his own library, networking with libraries and librarians he might not otherwise have access to, and filling invitations to speak and write.

MINIMUM REQUIREMENTS

The financial investment is significant, but it varies according to the nature of the books to be published. Experience in retail sales and bookkeeping is a plus. A computer and laser printer, fax machine, and photocopier are essential. Software includes word-processing (or page-layout) and database (or mailing list) programs. We also should check with our local government to see what types of licensing our municipality requires for running a business from our home.

HOW TO BEGIN

Thorough research into the various aspects of publishing can prevent unpleasant surprises. We need to decide the types of books we will specialize in and identify our target market, making certain our specialty is not so narrow that we attract insufficient orders. Then we develop a business plan based on our research. We line up manuscripts or reprintable books (unencumbered by copyrights) that apply to our target market. We add indexes to works that lack them, to increase their marketability. We shop for a printing house that is best equipped to handle our type of publications at the most economical price; and we determine the lead time that company requires—from the day a manuscript is received by the printer to the day the finished product is delivered. We need to know the format in which the printer accepts submissions—electronic disks, online transmissions, or camera-ready mechanicals (paper copies). Prudence suggests that we offer prepublication sales to test interest in our product or begin by publishing just one book. We might consider having other vendors retail our product until we have more titles to offer. An online search for book vendors can yield a lengthy list of potential outlets, even in a field as specialized as genealogical bookselling. As with other career choices, we learn by trial and error—though the lessons here can be costlier.

Outside of a dog, a book is a man's best friend. Inside of a dog, it's too dark to read.

—*Groucho Marx*[8]

Book vendor

Of all the choices presented in this chapter, bookselling has the potential for being either the most prosperous or the most disastrous business venture. Books, software, and microforms are popular goods for a genealogical market. Some vendors have storefronts, some sell by mail-order catalogs, and some rely solely on the Internet. Many vendors buy booth space at the various national, regional, and local conferences to increase contact with their primary market. Success stories of all types are not hard to find, but one theme runs throughout: the successful book dealer is a versatile entrepreneur.

Sherry Irvine, CG, and Mic Barnette are book vendors with "brick and mortar" sites. Sherry owns a bookshop in Victoria, British Columbia; Mic is situated in an antique mall in Houston, Texas. Both businesses are open five days a week; and both owners find that consulting, lecturing, and writing are natural companions to bookselling. Sherry writes books; Mic is a genealogical columnist for the *Houston Chronicle*. Sherry teaches through the Samford University Institute of Genealogy and Historical Research's British Institute; Mic has taught at three campuses of Houston Community College. Before venturing into retail, Sherry earned a B.A. in history, taught for several years, worked in another bookstore, and held various management positions in volunteer organizations. Mic's pre-retail background includes a B.A. in history and political science, an earlier career in commercial sales and advertising, and years of conducting genealogical research.[12]

Craig R. Scott, CGRS, founded a small publishing company and expanded into an Internet bookstore, Willow Bend Books, which soon acquired Family Line Publications, a well-known genealogical publishing house, catalog retailer, and storefront in Westminster, Maryland. Like Mic and Sherry, Craig was not totally dependent upon book sales—dividing his time between research clients (his research specialty is military records), writing, lecturing, and publishing. Prior to launching Willow Bend Books, Craig earned an M.A. in human-resources management; retired from a twenty-year Naval career in medical administration; and invested years in genealogical lecturing, research, and writing.[13]

MINIMUM REQUIREMENTS

Business savvy and experience in the retail environment are logical for anyone starting out in sales. Conflict-resolution skills are beneficial, as is a personal knowledge of the products to be sold. Perhaps the largest obstacle is a financial one—all three vendors indicated the need for substantial starting capital (at least $15,000 to be safe). We should plan to reinvest profits in the business, as it struggles to survive and grow. Initial equipment purchases would include a fax machine, photocopier, computer, printer, and microform reader. A comprehensive personal reference library is also helpful.

HOW TO BEGIN

Irvine offers sage advice for would-be retailers: "When you begin your own retail business you must have absolute faith in yourself and a willingness to work hard. You need to know your strengths and weaknesses and your comfort level where

I am opposed to millionaires, but it would be dangerous to offer me the position.

—*Mark Twain*[14]

risk is involved. Each of us sets a personal level where risk is seen to change into opportunity."[16] When Sherry started out, she committed to a lease with regular monthly rent after determining that the opportunity outweighed the risk.

If our business will be a storefront, we need to gather information from all our local, state, and federal regulatory agencies concerning business licenses, employment regulations, insurance requirements, and taxes. If our business will be on the Internet, we *still* will be subject to some of the same regulations. Various government agencies provide free publications to assist small-business owners, and many have web pages with the information readily available for downloading. Chapter 9, "Structuring a Business," is absolutely essential study for anyone considering this type of career.

More personally, we need to create a network of contacts within several different spheres in order to stay abreast of the latest developments in the retail, genealogy, and publishing worlds. Organizational memberships, not only in APG but also in our local chamber of commerce and other retail-merchant groups, guide our progress and expand our idea bank. We should also get to know all the publishers that distribute books and other media in our specialty areas and continually study the catalogs of adjunct fields for titles of genealogical value.

640K ought to be enough for anybody.

—*Bill Gates, 1981*[15]

Desktop designer/typesetter

The digital revolution has spawned many new career choices for enterprising individuals. Of these, "desktopping" is a natural for genealogy, where so many people envision a family history, are inexperienced at publishing, and often find traditional printing houses beyond their financial means. Even among those with computers, many genealogists are still awestruck by the power of the programs and need a skilled artisan to assist them in page layout and design. Our colleague Ann P. Brown points out that genealogists who succeed in desktop publishing are usually creative, original thinkers, with multiple skills in design, grammar, and computer usage.[17] Some have degrees in art, computer science, journalism, or marketing. Others transferred from more traditional publishing trades—typesetting and graphic design. But no particular one of these is necessary.

As this chapter's author, I yield to temptation here and offer myself as an example. A bachelor's degree in journalism and a master of arts in public relations led to twenty years as a public-relations practitioner. I have no degree in the graphic arts; but in a dozen concurrent years of self-taught, personal-computer use, I have focused upon editorial and graphic services. As a genealogist, what could be more natural for me than to apply those experiences to a niche that both individuals and organizations need: editing, design, and market consulting? It has been a rewarding choice—leading to the editorship of the *APG Quarterly,* the BCG newsletter *OnBoard,* and then *Genealogical Computing.* The Board certification that I acquired along the way—which at first blush seems irrelevant to design or marketing—is still an important professional credential, one that enhances my credibility among genealogical colleagues and reassures clients that I well know the market (and standards) to which we advertise their services.

MINIMUM REQUIREMENTS

At the risk of stating the obvious, a state-of-the-art computer and laser printer are mandatory. So are a fax machine; a flatbed scanner; a high-speed or cable modem with Internet access; a photocopier; and graphics, page-layout, photo-composition, and word-processing software. Optional (but highly desirable) are a color inkjet printer, a graphics tablet, a microform reader, and a notebook computer and printer. The initial financial outlay can be quite substantial, if all of the above items need to be purchased. Equipment and software upgrades require significant investments on a continual basis. A shelf of desktop-publishing references is expected—starting with a dictionary, grammar book, thesaurus, style guide (commonly the current edition of *The Chicago Manual of Style*),[18] and citation manual (the standard is now Mills's *Evidence! Citation & Analysis for the Family Historian).*[19]

HOW TO BEGIN

If we are not thoroughly familiar with software programs for sophisticated layout and design, classes will help the software work for us. We subscribe to design and desktop-publishing magazines, such as *Dynamic Graphics* and the *National Association of Desktop Publishers Journal*[20]—and study them regularly. We study ads, billboards, and brochures, as well as book and magazine layouts; and we build idea files, annotating samples with positive and negative aspects of their design elements. Our public career begins with our own brochure, business card, and stationery. We design several versions, with dramatically divergent elements, and pick the one that works best for our image. We offer to design items for friends—an offer that serves two purposes. First, our talents improve if we ask those friends for honest critiques and accept their opinions without taking them personally. Second, if our friends like our work, they tell others about our services. Word-of-mouth advertising is one of the most effective methods of acquiring new clients. Once we determine what our desktop-publishing niche will be, we advertise our services to the target market. Success will probably not come overnight; but practice, persistence, and patience nurture both our business and our talent.

Editor/writing consultant

Perhaps we have a flair for the written word. If we enjoy writing—or polishing the prose of others—a career in literary services might be our calling. As genealogical societies upgrade their standards and their publications, a growing number are contracting for the services of a professional editor. Major publishers, as they expand their lists of genealogy titles, seek freelance copy editors, or "technical editors" (those with considerable expertise in subject matter, as well as grammatical skills). Throughout the field, the exploding numbers of hobbyists who want to compile a family history have seen a corresponding increase in those who want a quality product and have the money to pay for whatever help they need to accomplish that. Those needs cover the gamut from simple proofreading, copyediting, or indexing of their manuscripts to full-scale writing of a family history, using materials the client has accumulated.

I am returning this otherwise good typing paper to you because someone has printed gibberish all over it and put your name at the top.

—*English professor, Ohio University*[21]

149

ALTERNATIVE CAREERS

Dawne Slater-Putt, CG, who owns and operates Heritage Pathways of Wake Forest, North Carolina, brings appropriate training and experience into her career as a genealogical writer and editor. With a B.A. in journalism, and master's degrees in history and library science, Dawne edited the highly regarded *Indiana Genealogist* through its first six years, supervised the compilation of the mammoth series *PERSI* for the Allen County Public Library, and now serves the *National Genealogical Society Quarterly* as its indexer.[23] Since launching her own business, Dawne has been the proverbial entrepreneur, providing a full range of literary services in addition to lecturing and leading group research tours. This diversity has the added advantage of letting her select the projects that are most intriguing to her, and it creates a schedule that is anything but routine.[24]

MINIMUM REQUIREMENTS

Extensive writing and editing experience is obviously needed. Attention to detail and a good organizational sense are absolutely vital. An appropriate educational background is expected—along with a wide-ranging expertise in genealogy. While some clients may seek mere copyediting services, genealogical editors should also be capable of catching and correcting factual problems as well as infelicitous grammar. (If we count on securing clients who are only interested in our geographic or ethnic specialty, our market may be too narrow for career survival.) Shelves of reference manuals on editing, proofreading, and grammar are a must—alongside a well-rounded library of genealogical reference materials. A computer with word-processing software, a laser printer, and a photocopier are the minimal equipment needs. Virus-protection programs are essential, considering that editors frequently work with electronic submissions. A scanner with superior text-recognition software is useful for material that does not arrive electronically. A fax machine and e-mail service expedite the continual questions for which editors need answers from their authors. Financial requirements go beyond advertising and marketing budgets. We need ready access to a wide variety of not-so-basic genealogical and historical reference works, as well as counterparts in related fields (law, geography, economics, etc.) that genealogists use to put family history into context. Internet capability (for Library of Congress catalog access, etc.) is basic.

HOW TO BEGIN

As with any type of literary career, we should step up our production of articles for journals, magazines, and newsletters—writing often and on a variety of topics. We should not expect remuneration, however. Some commerical publications offer small honoraria, but genealogical-society publications rarely pay for their content. Writing for the national genealogical journals is an educational experience in itself. Their editors generally submit incoming manuscripts to peer review before making a publication decision. If our work is accepted, it may still need major revision or editing to conform to the standards and style of a particular journal. If writing is a new venture for us and we cringe at the thought of being edited, it is good to remember two things. First, all writers need editors—even editors, when they write, value the "outside" editorial eye that refines their work impartially.

You've got to continue to grow or you're just like last night's cornbread—stale and dry.

—*Loretta Lynn*[22]

Second, the editing process is not personal. Working harmoniously with a discriminating editor, to hone our words into the best possible product, is an experience we all need before we attempt to red-pencil the work of others. It is also valuable experience to edit a genealogical society's publication—and to apply to it the same standards that the major journals apply. All these forums will help build our reputation, as well as our capability, before we hang out our shingle.

Photographer

Photography plays a major role in genealogy—whether for documentation of historic sites, homes, or gravestones or for matching ancestors' faces with their names. In the age of cable television and multimedia computers, our world is daily becoming more dependent on visual images. In several ways, genealogists with a bent for photography can apply those talents to a commercial enterprise.

PHOTO RESTORATION

Photo restoration—the copying of an original image and the removal of blemishes— is a service that has proliferated since the advent of computer technology. Opportunities still exist for work of the old-fashioned ilk (using the darkroom and an airbrush), but that process is slower and generally more costly than digital services that rely upon scanners and photoediting software. The skills required for darkroom and airbrush work are very different from those required for digital restoration. The former requires training in traditional photographic techniques, with more advanced training or experience in restoration. The latter requires expertise in scanning and digital photographic editing; experience in photography is desirable but not required.

PHOTO COPYING AND ENHANCEMENT

This specialty, which stops short of actually repairing damaged areas, can also be offered digitally or through traditional darkroom techniques. The process is similar to restoration; one makes a negative or digital image of the original and provides a copy to the customer from the negative or digital version. Advanced techniques in image restoration are not necessary.

ON-SITE PHOTOGRAPHY

A number of genealogists today offer people the opportunity to obtain images of their ancestral homes, graves, or other sites (as well as local scenery) at a fraction of the cost of travel to the location. Genealogical photographers usually provide a choice of traditional negatives and photographs or digital images, enabling consumers to import images into many of the currently marketed genealogy programs. It is not necessary to own a digital camera to offer digital images, however. Some image-processing companies will transfer exposed negatives to a CD-ROM as part of the development process.

MINIMUM REQUIREMENTS

The type of service we choose to provide usually determines the skills and investment we need. Educational degrees in photography are uncommon, though

What was any art but a mould in which to imprison for a moment the shining elusive element which is life itself—life hurrying past us and running away, too strong to stop, too sweet to lose.

—Willa Cather[25]

ALTERNATIVE CAREERS

available at some institutions; other schools offer minors or specialty certificates in photography, within a broader discipline such as journalism. Regardless of educational background, practical experience is a must. Whatever form of services we choose, the investment in equipment will be intensive. Traditional photographic services require good-quality camera equipment, including lenses and bodies, filters, a tripod and copying stand, lights, darkroom equipment, and supplies as needed. Digital photographic services require an investment in state-of-the-art computer equipment, including a scanner, a backup system, very large hard drives, and photoediting software. At a minimum, while we train, we need a good-quality 35-mm camera with more than just a 50-mm lens. (We might consider buying used lenses while in the training stage.) A photographic business can incur a large initial outlay of cash, which may require creative financing.[27]

HOW TO BEGIN
As with writing and editing, we begin by intensifying our practice. We shoot scenery, people, close-ups, and gravestones; and we shoot lots of them. We concentrate on different ways to compose images and learn how to turn the camera so we are shooting angled shots. If there is a continuing-education course in photography available, we might want to take it; then ask the instructor to critique some of our work. If we plan to do photographic enhancements or restoration, we might offer our services to friends for the cost of our materials. Well-done work will prompt others to spread the word about our abilities. If we plan to take photos for hire, we might try selling some of our work to companies that purchase stock photography. Or we could volunteer to take shots for our community newspaper or chamber of commerce. Most important, we need to find a photographic niche that interests us. Photography is an art form and a way of communication. We communicate much more effectively if we feel intensely about what we do.

Probate or heir searcher

Many people die intestate each year, leaving unclaimed estates with no apparent heirs. Genealogists who specialize in tracing family branches of intestate decedents are variously called probate or heir searchers and legal or forensic genealogists. If we are competitive, enjoy the thrill of the chase, can launch assignments immediately, are willing to work long hours without immediate financial reward, and make skillful witnesses in court cases, this may be our career choice. Many times, heirs who live out of the state or country are not aware of a relative's death; and we could be the conduit through which they learn of their entitlement and secure the proof of kinship necessary to claim their inheritance.

Eileen M. O Dúill, CGRS, is a legal genealogist in Dublin, Ireland. Eileen holds both a bachelor's and a master's degree in history and specializes in Irish research. She turned her interest to probate matters after working on a family intestacy case in New York, preparing the Irish documentation and testifying in America. Now, she performs these services for families and heir-locator firms in the United States, Britain, and France. She also conducts genealogical research for clients to

Fate tried to conceal him by naming him *Smith*.

—*Anonymous*[26]

keep a steady income, because probate cases may not pay until the estate is settled—an event that can take two years from the time next of kin are located.[28] In contrast, Robin R. Alexander, Ph.D., CG, of Alexander Genealogical Services in Austin, Texas, also works as a probate searcher. Robin (whose doctorate is in art education) specializes in Texas, particularly nineteenth- and twentieth-century families. Prior to hanging her shingle as a probate searcher, Robin honed her organizational skills as a teacher for nineteen years and refined her interviewing and research abilities while pursuing her doctorate. She also accepts "traditional" research assignments.[29]

MINIMUM REQUIREMENTS
Eileen and Robin agree that a college education is essential for someone entering this career. Robin also adds, and many colleagues agree, that even though certification is not required, the courts are aware of genealogy's credentialing processes and prefer experts who have been tested by their peers. According to Edward H. Little, CALS, who discussed "Estates and Missing Heirs: An Unfolding Opportunity" in the *APG Quarterly,* heir searchers who are certified can easily establish credentials with a court, "since examination to defined standards has been conducted by at least three acknowledged genealogical experts."[30] (The same respect logically applies to any of the credentials earned through legitimate genealogical-testing programs.) Eileen also suggests paralegal training to better prepare for international probate work.

Regardless of educational background, a thorough knowledge of pertinent court records and experience in nineteenth- and twentieth-century research are mandatory. Little suggests two other requirements: good interviewing skills, because we eventually have to interview living people; and the ability to travel quickly, in order to avoid delays in obtaining records. Equipment requirements include the standard office fare: computer, laser printer, notebook computer and printer for travel, photocopier, microform reader, fax machine, Internet access, and e-mail address. Standard reference works for our area—such as telephone books, local how-to guides, and maps—are also necessary. The financial commitment varies, depending on the amount of equipment that needs to be purchased, the existence of supplemental-income sources, and the promptness with which our cases are settled.

HOW TO BEGIN
Eileen suggests that beginning heir searchers study prevailing legal codes for handling unclaimed funds. Then we should frequent local courthouses, become thoroughly familiar with the probate filing system, and introduce ourselves to our local probate judge. With this grounding, we should read local legal lists for probate cases and unclaimed bank accounts, select small cases, and try to locate next of kin. We should also join organizations such as local, state, and national genealogical societies and bar associations (if we are eligible), as well as APG. With experience and contacts, we are ready to prepare marketing materials targeted toward estate attorneys and heir-locator firms. We should also consider doing some work pro bono to hone our skills, as well as to demonstrate them—although the joy of reuniting families with long-lost relatives can be its own reward.

Difficulties are meant to rouse, not discourage.

—*William Ellery Channing*[31]

Software developer

Personal computers have invaded our lives in full force. A cursory survey of genealogical publications unearths myriad references to software designed to assist us with accounting, indexing, platting, and—naturally—tracking ancestors and descendants. Somebody has to design this software. If we have a knack for ones and zeros, that somebody could be any of us. The market's oversaturation with lineage-linked databases suggests that, as enterprising software developers, we will explore the marketplace, determine where voids exist in the current offerings, and develop the next "essential" product.

Barney Tyrwhitt-Drake, owner and programmer of Drake Software Associates in Great Missenden, Buckinghamshire, England, has developed computer programs in the scientific and genealogical fields since 1965. Barney holds a master's degree in pharmacology. His thirty years of worldwide experience in medical research, development, and marketing are applied to the main portion of his business: creating scientific and medical software. But amid his lifelong pursuit of family history he discovered a significant void in Britain's genealogical-software market that he is well positioned to fill.[33]

Ira J. Lund, who similarly operates Cumberland Family Software in Clarksville, Tennessee, dates his interest in genealogy to his teenage years. While studying computers at the University of Texas, Ira began developing his own lineage-linked genealogy program. In 1991 he released the first version of Cumberland Family Tree as shareware and continues to improve his product, based on input from customers worldwide. His program fills a niche within lineage-linked genealogy software by providing the capability to print reports in twelve different languages, with more language support planned for the future. Ira has a B.S. in computer science and works as a market analyst in his full-time job.[34]

Is a strong background in computer science or programming a prerequisite? Not necessarily. Perceiving another void, I plunged into software development with no formal instruction but some years of self-instruction and experience in a range of programs, from page layout to databases. Along the way I learned programming, built the elements of a genealogical records-organization program, and eventually marketed a cohesive package that has been well received.[35]

MINIMUM REQUIREMENTS

Essential or not, an educational or practical background in some form of computer science will greatly benefit us, if we look to this field. Comprehensive genealogical-research skills and an understanding of the process are crucial to building a following; it is our edge in a market dominated by megacorporations. The ability to write and document computer programs, a state-of-the-art hardware system, and the software and accessories needed to accomplish programming tasks are a must. How-to books for using those tools will line our bookshelves—and should be read! The financial outlay could be substantial if equipment and software need to be purchased or upgraded, and we should budget for the up-front costs of product distribution. Fortitude and a strong sense of commitment are essential personality traits during those fledgling days when there is no light at the end of the tunnel.

Everything that can be invented has been invented.

—*Charles H. Duell,*
U.S.Commissioner
of Patents, 1899[32]

Soberly, Ira adds a warning: we need to be "interested enough in genealogy and programming to work long hours, more as a hobby, with little pay for three to five years before receiving any substantial income."

HOW TO BEGIN

As we evaluate our objective and draft a business plan, a market analysis is crucial to narrow our options. We should experimentally design small programs that accomplish minor tasks and give them to friends to test. Barney suggests that we join our local genealogical society and help train members in the practical aspects of using personal computers in family-history research. "This alone will teach much about market needs, expectations, and gaps in the range of current products." We can also volunteer to beta-test software for both large and small companies. An Internet search for "beta testing" will help us find software that interests us. Once we discover our program niche and have a design in mind, we should set up a reasonable production schedule that includes lots of excess development time to allow for electronic catastrophes and unforeseen circumstances. And we should prepare to spend much time in front of a monitor as we create and design and test and debug. It helps to network with other programmers in the field and ask for tips. We may want to hire independent contractors to do parts of the work for us—preparing marketing materials or packaging the final product, perhaps. That expense pays off in a reduction of stress and allows us to devote our time to our ultimate objective—creating software that the genealogical market wants and needs.

Storyteller

Storytelling has been around since prehistory—at least that's what we're told! Much of our knowledge of prehistory has been passed down by bards, lyricists, poets, and others with the ability to weave fact and fiction into memorable tales. Storytellers differ from authors or filmmakers; they have the singular ability to captivate audiences with spoken words and no props. Commenting upon the growth of storytellers worldwide, Jeannine Pasini-Beekman concludes that technology "has made storytelling more popular because people don't have as many opportunities for human contact. When they spend so much time in front of a computer screen, they need to get that human interaction that happens even when a person is telling a story to 2,000 people."[36] With our love of history, we genealogists have the potential to be enchanting storytellers. Our colleague Nancy Kavanaugh has found success as a part-time storyteller and instructor in a community arts program. While she has a college degree and a strong business background, she feels that personal experience, good stories, and specific classes or workshops in storytelling as an art form are more important tools for success in this career field.[37]

MINIMUM REQUIREMENTS

The ability to delight an audience is a necessity. No special materials or equipment are needed, and the financial investment is minimal. A collection of myths, legends, and fairy tales is a useful stock-in-trade for us. Our bookshelf should also

It is the easiest thing in the world to tell a story—and the hardest to be a fine storyteller.

—*Ruth Sawyer*[38]

The wireless music box has no imaginable commercial value. Who would pay for a message sent to nobody in particular?

—*David Sarnoff, 1920s*[39]

include *Storytelling Professionally* or *The Storyteller's Start-up Book*.[40] And we should spend a lot of time creating, developing, and personalizing our lore.

HOW TO BEGIN

Beyond classes and workshops in the art of storytelling, we seek out performances and festivals. We practice, practice, practice. We hone our talent by trial and error, adapting popular approaches to our own unique personality. The National Storytelling Association, which can be contacted online, will help us network with others who are successful in the business. As with all genealogical fields, we need marketing materials—brochures and business cards. And we invariably find that volunteering in civic forums, libraries, and schools will be one of our best forms of advertisement.

Talk-show host

A great speaking voice, a command of language, quick recall, and a desire to help beginning researchers can be channeled into more careers than just public speaking or storytelling. With these talents, we might consider creating our niche as a talk-show host. The market potential is great, even if the profit presently isn't. While the concept of genealogy talk shows has not caught on rapidly in most countries, encouraging examples exist.

Australia's Nick Vine Hall, DipFHS (Hons.), created celebrity status for himself through a half-hour talk show aired nationally, with an audience of about one million. When Nick goes on air, he is prepared to answer just about any type of question—a laptop at his fingertips houses a large reference database, and he lugs a case of reference books to the studio for topics not addressed in his database. Nick's visibility supports a full-time genealogical practice, including instructional stints aboard cruise ships. Unlike some colleagues in this special field, Nick's background is not in broadcasting, although it has well prepared him. He holds a Diploma in Family Historical Studies and served ten years as the executive director of the Society of Australian Genealogists.[41]

Laura Bradley hosts a weekly, one-hour genealogy program on WBLQ 88.1 FM in Westerly, Rhode Island. As a volunteer at the radio station, she receives commissions from the airtime she sells. Laura keeps the show fresh by inviting a variety of guests and encouraging call-ins. Because she runs the studio while she's on air, she must know how to operate the radio console; sign in and get off the air on time; and run commercials, station identifications, and public service announcements. (Stations in larger markets frequently have an engineer at the console, freeing the host to concentrate on stimulating dialogue and banter.) In contrast to Nick, Laura has a B.S. degree in business and an M.A. in marketing, sold radio airtime for another station in the past, and had another talk show before this one. When she proposed her first genealogy program, the station's management accepted the idea because of her experience in radio.[42]

Ronald Bernier hosts the half-hour radio show "Your Family's History Today" on KFNX Phoenix every Friday evening from his home in Salt Lake City. With experience in French Canadian and U.S. genealogical research, as well as adoption and missing heir searches, Ron says the radio show opportunity was a "lark." The station wanted a host for a genealogy program and contacted a number of companies in their search. Ron was tapped through his company, Genealogical Resource Institute, and was interviewed along with a number of other people. He was picked because of his personality and broadcast voice. The show, still new at this writing, is expected to expand into other markets. He has different themes for each broadcast, although callers often determine the direction each night's discussion takes.[43]

MINIMUM REQUIREMENTS

Successful genealogical talk-show hosts need wide experience in genealogical research, touching on most record types and situations. Otherwise, they quickly lose credibility with the audience.[44] A background in public speaking, broadcasting, and writing will significantly benefit us, if we choose this route. Unless we have a benefactor or are extremely lucky, we should not expect to make a living in this career choice. While we may not have to incur a large financial outlay initially, neither will we be paid much—if anything—for our efforts. Nick reports spending $10,000 a year on his personal library so that he has the best and latest references at his fingertips. Laura had to purchase her own headphones, an item that ranges in costs from $25 to $200. Ron is paying for his airtime but is reimbursed by sponsor time. Obviously, our own requirements will vary, depending on the support available from the sponsoring radio station.

HOW TO BEGIN

Without a degree in broadcasting, we should plan to commit a significant amount of time to self-education. The websites of both the National Association of Broadcasters and the Radio and TV News Directors Association recommend excellent books that can help prepare us. Once we are convinced we have what it takes to pursue this potential, we should contact radio stations in our area and offer to appear as a guest to discuss topical issues in genealogy. Any number of current matters can become provocative subjects. For instance, the Australian government conducts a population census every five years and disposes of the originals after it gleans the information it needs. According to Nick, census time prompts genealogists and historians to protest destruction of these important records—presenting timely opportunities for him to address the media. Once we earn a guest slot, we should contact area genealogical societies, alert them to our broadcast time, and rally their support for publicity. With localized experience as a guest, we might list ourselves with a talk-show registry and test our abilities in more demanding situations.[45] Once we build the background to earn a local hosting slot, we will probably turn to current rosters of the Association of Professional Genealogists, the Board for Certification of Genealogists, and the Genealogical Speakers Guild for a talent pool of potential guests. Talk-show hosting is a demanding field; but if we are sufficiently innovative, confident, and persistent, we can crack the market open and create a niche.

The greatest pleasure in life is doing what people say you cannot do.

—*Walter Bagehot*[46]

Summary Concepts

Genealogy is no longer an "elitist" hobby. Its rewards—as either a pastime or a profession—are no longer a well-kept secret. Surveys within the United States show it to be a major interest of the American population, growing exponentially; and global growth is impressive. Genealogical opportunities have been noted everywhere from the business daily *Wall Street Journal* to the trade publication *Target Marketing.* Large corporations and conglomerates are now creating projects for, and directing their marketing toward, family-history enthusiasts.

All of this spells opportunity, from which professionals can carve out a profitable and rewarding market. Several chapters in this manual explore "traditional" careers in depth. The alternative career choices presented in this chapter merely suggest the breadth of potential that exists—from heraldic art and design to historic-site documentation. As genealogists, we are uniquely positioned at the threshold of a burgeoning field. The personal success each of us finds here is confined only by the limits we impose upon ourselves.

Whatever the career we choose, we face a significant risk as we make the transition from hobbyist to professional. It is difficult for many of us to separate the fun of research from the reality of a viable business; but if we don't, our business will suffer. As we conduct our market research, appraise our talents, fill gaps in our knowledge base, volunteer to gain experience, and begin testing the viability of our product or service, we will do well to remember the counsel of Beth Duncan, an entrepreneurship specialist with the Mississippi State University Extension Service: "People have a hobby they're good at and reach a point where they try to sell it. But they've still got their hobby hat on. Unless [they] take the hobby hat off and throw it away, [they] won't be successful."[48] In genealogy, the common signs of that hobby hat are a reluctance to set fees that are commensurate with our offering, an overcommitment of time to all those organizations that need us, and weak skills in financial management and marketing. Several subsequent chapters in this manual provide valuable guidance in all these areas.

You miss 100 percent of the shots you never take.

—*Wayne Gretsky*[47]

NOTES

1. Robert Frost (1874–1963), American poet, quoted in Mike Rosenberg, "The Quotation Guide," at website Mike's Home Page <life.bio.sunysb.edu/ee/msr/quotes2.html> (State University of New York, Stony Brook), downloaded 3 January 1998.

2. Lily Tomlin (1939), American comedian, quoted in ibid.

3. Marie Varrelman Melchiori, GRS, CGL, responding to a survey of professionals in preparation for this chapter. Kathleen W. Hinckley, "Profile of a Professional: Marie Varrelman Melchiori," *Association of Professional Genealogists [APG] Quarterly* 5 (Fall 1990): 63–64.

4. Tony Burroughs, survey response. Suzanne McVetty, "Profile of a Professional: Tony Burroughs," *APG Quarterly* 12 (September 1997): 98–100.

5. Burroughs, survey response.

6. Joe Feiertag and Mary Carmen Cupito, *The Writer's Market Companion* (Cincinnati: Writer's Digest Books, 2000).

7. Alfred North Whitehead (1861–1947), English philosopher and mathematician, quoted in Rosenberg, "The Quotation Guide."

8. Groucho Marx (1890–1977), American actor and humorist, quoted in "Quotations about Libraries and Librarians," at website *International Federation of Library Associations and Institutions* <www.nlc-bnc.ca/ifla/I/humour/author.htm>, downloaded 3 January 1998.

9. Robert D. Griffin, "From Consumer to Printer, Part I," *APG Quarterly* 12 (March 1997): 16.

10. Griffin, survey response.

11. Griffin, "From Consumer to Printer, Part I," and its sequel, Part II, *APG Quarterly* 13 (March 1998): 10–12.

12. Sherry Irvine, CG, survey response; Mic Barnette, survey response.

13. Craig R. Scott, CGRS, survey response.

14. Mark Twain (1835–1910), American humorist, quoted in Rosenberg, "The Quotation Guide."

15. Bill Gates (1955–), Chairman, Microsoft Corp., quoted in *Timely Quotes* <www.worldtrans. org/pos/timely.html>, downloaded 3 January 1998.

16. Irvine, survey response.

17. Ann P. Brown, "Adding Desktop Publishing to Your Genealogical Services," *APG Quarterly* 7 (December 1992): 92.

18. *The Chicago Manual of Style,* 14th edition (Chicago: University of Chicago Press, 1993).

19. Elizabeth Shown Mills, CG, CGL, FASG, *Evidence! Citation & Analysis for the Family Historian* (Baltimore: Genealogical Publishing Co., 1997).

20. At this writing, both have websites that provide contact information.

21. Rosenberg, "The Quotation Guide."

22. Loretta Lynn (1935–), country music singer and songwriter, quoted in Criswell Freeman, ed., *The Book of Southern Wisdom: Common Sense and Uncommon Genius from 101 Great Southerners* (Nashville, Tennessee: Walnut Grove Press, 1994), 48.

23. *Periodical Source Index, 1848–1985,* 15 vols., and annual supplements to date (Fort Wayne, Indiana: Allen County Public Library, 1988—).

24. Dawne Slater-Putt, CG, survey response.

25. Willa Cather (1873–1947), American writer, quoted in Phillip Bower, "Quotations from the Daily Miscellany, *The Daily Miscellany* <www.geocities.com/Athens/Forum/1327>, downloaded 3 January 1998.

26. Rosenberg, "The Quotation Guide."

27. The Small Business Administration, treated more fully in chap. 9, "Structuring Your Business," also offers advice for building start-up capital. For the SBA website, see <www.sba.gov>.

28. Eileen M. O Dúill, CGRS, survey response.

29. Robin R. Alexander, Ph.D., CG, survey response.

30. Edward H. Little, CALS, "Estates and Missing Heirs: An Unfolding Opportunity," *APG Quarterly* 9 (March 1994): 5–6.

31. William Ellery Channing (1780–1842), American clergyman, quoted in Rosenberg, "The Quotation Guide."

32. *Timely Quotes.*

33. Barney Tyrwhitt-Drake, survey response. See also the Drake Software Associates website.

34. *About Cumberland Family Software* <www.cf-software.com/author.htm#early>; also e-mail correspondence from Ira J. Lund to author, 19 November 1997.

35. See Clooz® software at Ancestor Detective® website.

36. Audrey Galex, "Storytelling: An Old Tradition Gets a New Life On-line," *CNN Interactive* <www-cgi.cnn.com/TECH/9511/storytelling/index.html>, issue dated 27 November 1995.

37. Nancy Kavanaugh, survey response.

38. Ruth Sawyer, *The Way of the Storyteller* (New York: Penguin Books, 1977), quoted at home page of *The Art of Storytelling* <www.seanet.com/~eldrbarry/roos/art.htm>, downloaded 3 January 1998.

39. David Sarnoff (1891–1971), Russian-American broadcasting pioneer, quoted in *Timely Quotes.*

40. Harlynne Geisler, *Storytelling Professionally: The Nuts and Bolts of a Working Performer* (Englewood, Colorado: Libraries Unlimited Press, 1997); Margaret Read MacDonald, *The Storyteller's Start-up Book* (Des Moines: August Home Publishing, 1993).

41. Douglas R. G. Sellick, "Talkback Genealogy," in *How to Trace Your Family Tree in Six Easy Steps* (Surrey Hills, New South Wales, Australia: Century Publishing, 1988), 6–7; Nick Vine Hall, Dip. FHS (Hons.), survey response.

42. Laura Bradley survey response (1997) and e-mail of 13 February 2000 <LBrad16686@aol.com>.

Work and play are words used to describe the same thing under differing conditions.

—*Mark Twain*[49]

ALTERNATIVE CAREERS

43. Author's interview with Ronald Bernier, Salt Lake City, 24 February 2000.

44. Nick Vine Hall, "Radio Talk-Back Shows about Genealogy," *APG Quarterly* 6 (Winter 1991): 90–91.

45. For one example, see the website *National Talk Show Guest Registry*.

46. Walter Bagehot (1826–77), English economist, quoted in Rosenberg, "The Quotation Guide."

47. Wayne Gretsky (1961–), Canadian athlete, quoted in *Clint Greenleaf: Quotations Page* <cgi.geocities.com/Athens/Oracle/6517/417.htm>, downloaded 3 January 2000.

48. Cynthia E. Griffin, "Crafting a Business," *Entrepreneur Magazine Online*, September 1996—quoting Professor Beth Duncan, from "Home Based & Micro Businesses in Mississippi," *Mississippi State University Cooperative Extension Service: Family and Consumer Education Resources* <www.ext.msstate.edu/fce/home bus/hbmb.html>. Despite its localized name, the MSU site offers information of value to any entrepreneur, starting with its "Frequently Asked Questions."

49. Mark Twain, quoted in Joe Moore, *Have You Ever Noticed?* (New York and London: Pocket Books, 1985), 125.

50. Quoted by Moore, ibid., 126.

People willing to roll up their sleeves seldom lose their shirt.

—*Anonymous*[50]

FURTHER STUDY

Dynamic Graphics. Bimonthly magazine, rich with design ideas for products and publications.

Entrepreneur Magazine. Monthly. Available at newsstands.

Fishman, Stephen. *Software Development: A Legal Guide.* 3d edition. Berkeley, California: Nolo.com, 2000.

Jacobus, Donald Lines, FASG. *Genealogy as Pastime and Profession.* 1930. 2d rev. edition, 1968; reprinted, Baltimore: Genealogical Publishing Co., 1987.

Kersey, Cynthia. *Unstoppable.* Naperville, Illinois: Sourcebooks, 1998. Offers inspirational stories of entrepreneurs who persevered against all odds.

Kramer, Felix, and Maggie Lavaas. *Desktop Publishing Success: How to Start and Run a Desktop Publishing Business.* Homewood, Illinois: Business One Irvin, 1991.

Mills, Elizabeth Shown, CG, CGL, FASG. "Equipping Ourselves for Quality Service: Physical Plant and Continuing Education—BCG Survey Results." *OnBoard* [educational newsletter of the Board for Certification of Genealogists] 3 (May 1997): 9–10, 14.

Montgomery, Erick D. "Historic Site Documentation." *Association of Professional Genealogists [APG] Quarterly* 4 (Winter 1989): 79–83.

Otterbourg, Robert K. *Retire & Thrive: Remarkable People Share Their Creative, Productive, and Profitable Retirement Strategies.* Washington: Kiplinger Books, 1999. Includes such helpful chapters as "Starting All Over Again," which addresses starting a business and making career changes, and "Back to School," which treats acquiring or adding degrees.

Pino, Laurence J. *Finding Your Niche.* New York: Berkley Publishing Group, 1994. This book provides work sheets to help us zero in on our career specialty through analyzing the market and our business and personal identities.

Powers, Mike. *How to Start a Business Website.* New York: Avon Books, ca.1999.

———. *How to Start a Mail Order Business (The 21st Century Entrepreneur).* New York: Avon Books, 1996.

Ross, Marilyn Heimbert and Tom Ross. *Jump Start Your Book Sales: A Money-Making Guide for Authors, Independent Publishers, and Small Presses.* Buena Vista, Colorado: Communication Creativity, ca. 1999.

———. *The Complete Guide to Self-Publishing.* Cincinnati: Writers Digest Books, 1994.

National Storytelling Membership Association, *StoryNet Home Page.* This site contains links to many related sites, including storytellers and stories.

Sturdevant, Katherine Scott. "Documentary Editing for Family Historians." *APG Quarterly* 5 (Fall 90): 51–56.

Vine Hall, Nick, Dip. FHS (Hons.). "Radio Talk-Back Genealogy." *Council of Genealogy Columnists Newsletter* 7 (June 1994): 1–2.

Watson, Bruce. "The Storyteller Is the Soybean . . . The Audience Is the Sun." *Smithsonian Magazine* 27 (March 1997): 60–69.

9

**STRUCTURING
A BUSINESS**

Keynotes

Keynotes (cont.)

Structuring a Business

by Melinda Shackleford Kashuba, Ph.D.

Anyone can start a business. There are no entrance exams. The critical information about our business—its finances, market analysis, and sales strategy—can be carried around in our heads. My husband's great-grandfather was such a businessman. He came to the Island of Maui from China in 1881 with nothing. He labored for many years, first as a cane cutter and then a meat cutter for Haleakala Ranch on Maui. Seeing opportunity in the tiny town of Makawao, where there was no butcher, he opened his own shop. He carried the information about his business around in his head for forty-seven years, until he retired. From public records, we know he mortgaged the family home twice to pay off business debts. Operating from hand to mouth, he never took his shop past the point of breaking even. Although many of his thirteen children worked with him, he had almost nothing to pass on to them—just a few knives and tools. When he died, the business died with him. In retrospect, it is easy to see why. Many genealogists also run their businesses in just this manner, with minimal planning or documentation, and they wonder why opportunities seem to elude them!

There are certainly no guarantees in the business world. Barbara Brabec, author of *Homemade Money*, reports the following statistics on business failure:[1]

> 55–60% of all small businesses fail in five years or less.
> 95% of all these failures are due to poor management.

These numbers should sober but not frighten us. Anyone who contemplates self-employment should know the realities of the business world. The best hedge against failure is to do our research, craft an effective plan, and manage our business accordingly. That plan will change over time, as our experience grows and we gain confidence in our managerial abilities. For those of us with minimal exposure to the world of business and entrepreneurship, this chapter introduces many of the nettlesome details of setting up shop and operating a profession the "proper" way—that is, with commitments on paper that define our enterprise and sketch a blueprint for its future.

> Many genealogists run their businesses with minimal planning or documentation, and they wonder why opportunities seem to elude them.

Options

Personal factors

Each of us knows better than anyone else the unique talents and experiences we can draw upon to make our business successful. Posing a series of questions at this point can help us define them. Ideally, we should set aside at least a two-hour block of time in a quiet place away from our usual environment—no distractions, children, or spouses—just us alone with our thoughts. We need to think and dream *concretely* about our personal goals, visions, qualifications, strengths, weaknesses, and fears. Here, we appraise the present and decide the future of our business.

To begin with, answers probably will come slowly and with some difficulty. The first two hours may net us very little in the way of direction. So we try again. Each time we try, we will coax more information from inside our minds and hearts. *We cannot skip this step*—even if we are already in business for ourselves (the insights that come from this exercise will probably differ from the ones we had when we began our business). Above all, we should bear in mind that all good entrepreneurs are dreamers. So let's identify our dream and the elements that will convert it to reality. The answers to these questions will help us focus on our visions and provide the motivation that carries us through the rough times every business has.

GOALS

Why do we want to go into business for ourselves? Are we tired of working for someone else? Do we want freedom? Do we need extra income? Are we looking for something that excites passion and great interest? Do we want to be rich or "just comfortable"? Do we want to contribute something special to society?

VISIONS

What does our dream business look like? Let's close our eyes. Let's focus on what we want our business to look like at the end of three years—or five. Are we working alone or do we have a staff? Are we operating out of a home office or a commercial suite? Are we spending most of our time in libraries and archives? Do we have clients? Are we writing books and articles? Teaching classes or lecturing at national meetings? Publishing the work of others? Operating a mail-order business? Or are we juggling a combination of several or all of these things? Do we see ourselves as the renowned expert in [*let's name that dream!*]? While our visions are in sharp focus, let's write them down. But let's be sure to concentrate on what "feels right" to *us*—not what we think others expect. We may need to try this exercise several times until we truly reach that "feels right" stage.

TRAITS

Are we entrepreneurs at heart? There are a number of self-assessment books available on the market to identify our natural entrepreneurial talents. Almost every guide to starting our own business includes tests designed to identify business acumen. Several are listed in this chapter's notes and bibliography. Most define seven broad traits that define the entrepreneur:[2]

Seeks opportunity
Successful entrepreneurs see an unfulfilled need in the marketplace and strive to fill that void. Often, the product they offer is a common one tailored to fit the need of the consumer, rather than an original contribution to the marketplace.

Is self-disciplined
The ability to work long, focused hours on a pet project is one of the defining attributes of entrepreneurial characters. These individuals do not burn out quickly but work well beyond the limit where most people become bored, distracted, or tired of a project.

All good entrepreneurs are dreamers. So let's identify our dream and the elements that will convert it to reality.

STRUCTURING A BUSINESS

Works hard
Long hours—into the night, over weekends, and during holidays—reflect the entrepreneur's desire to succeed against all odds. Rather than watching the clock, they tally successes. Still, it is important that entrepreneurs learn to balance the needs of business with other elements in their lives—kin and friends, recreation, spirituality, for example.

Values independence
Entrepreneurs are often perceived as stubborn and hardheaded. Many are fired for insubordination when working in large corporations. Once on their own, they appear to "calm down" and focus their energies on more positive avenues. To the surprise of many, these individuals may become exemplary team players after starting their own businesses.

Possesses self-confidence
Intense belief in one's ability to succeed against daunting odds is another hallmark of entrepreneurs. To many, this smacks of naïveté akin to Mary Poppins or "Unsinkable" Molly Brown, but a knack for picking oneself up after a failure and starting all over again is a valuable talent.

Practices flexibility
Entrepreneurs also adapt easily to new circumstances. As their businesses develop and grow, they anticipate (and change along with) the marketplace. In the beginning, they may do all of the work themselves; but successful entrepreneurs quickly delegate as their businesses grow. Genealogists, for example, may start out wearing a dozen hats—from research to marketing, writing to bookkeeping, speaking to filing. As their enterprise grows, they may assign some of these duties to assistants or consultants. Yet, over time, our successful colleagues adeptly switch in and out of all these tasks, at different stages of their growth, amid seemingly conflicting demands.

Makes intelligent decisions
Intuition and native intelligence make for good decision making—but so does a team of capable advisors. Entrepreneurs must often render decisions quickly, even when they do not understand all aspects of the situation that demands their decision. Without expert advice, those decisions might not be sound. With a graphic artist and an accountant, an attorney, and an insurance agent on their team—all chosen *prior to need* rather than during a crisis—genealogical entrepreneurs not only render decisions more quickly and intelligently but also position themselves to seize unforeseen opportunities.

Intuition and native intelligence make for good decision making—but so does a team of capable advisors.

SUPPORT
What is our personal situation—our financial and human support system? How much can we afford to spend to begin our business? How much can we afford to lose? Will we be able to pay our bills while our business takes root? Can we wait as long as two years before we take a salary? Are other people involved? If so, have we thoroughly discussed our business ideas with them? Do we have the support of our family and friends in this endeavor? How will we handle finances and schedules if we do not have their complete backing? Will they commit to our plan for however long it may

take before the business becomes successful? Without either moral or financial support—if not both—entrepreneurial dreams are infinitely harder to achieve.

TRAINING

What expertise have we developed? Are we confident that we do indeed meet public expectations for a professional genealogist? By what professional barometers do we measure our abilities? Are we committed to professional growth through regular attendance at both seminars and conferences, where we can network and stay abreast of resources and methodology? Do we routinely read journal articles in our focus area(s)? Will we commit ourselves to continued training, even after our business expands and we become successful?

EQUIPMENT

Do we have access to the equipment necessary to practice our profession or produce our product? In comparison to other types of enterprises, service businesses require a minimal investment in equipment, but we do need access to at least a personal computer, telephone answering machine, and a fax machine—if not a laptop and modem. In today's era of instant communication, many clients and customers expect e-mail or Internet contact. How will our clients communicate with us? How will we reach them, especially when we are traveling for research on their behalf?

OUTSIDE RESOURCES

Have we identified resources that can answer our questions regarding business management? Have we checked our local college for business courses or spoken with representatives of our area Chamber of Commerce, Service Corps of Retired Executives (SCORE) office, Small Business Administration (SBA) office, or local chapter of a national association dedicated to small businesses? Have we searched the Internet for its rich array of guidance?

FEARS

What is holding us back? What is the worst thing that can happen if our business *succeeds*? And the worst if it *fails*? Whatever fears we have about success or failure, let's write them down. After contemplating our worst nightmares, we are ready to ask: what will make us feel comfortable enough to move ahead and to begin our business or expand our existing one into new areas?

STRENGTHS AND WEAKNESSES

What are our strengths and weaknesses? Have we drafted a professional resume based upon our training and experience in *genealogy*? Here, many of us need to honestly confront one fact of life: impressive degrees acquired in other fields often do not equate to genealogical expertise. We must ask ourselves, "What special genealogical knowledge and skill do I have to offer, to assure a client that I will find all possible records, interpret them correctly, and recognize hidden clues? Would certification or accreditation reinforce my claims to expertise? Do I have experience managing time, projects, and people? To a great extent, our success in this field will depend upon the degree to which we are honest with ourselves in identifying our strengths and our shortcomings. We do not have to be the perfect manager or an internationally

To a great extent, our success in this field will depend upon the degree to which we are honest with ourselves in identifying our strengths and our shortcomings.

> No one can build a successful business out of vanity and self-delusion.

renowned expert to begin a business. But we must be willing to acknowledge our shortcomings and commit ourselves to improving or eliminating them. No one can build a successful business out of vanity and self-delusion.

FOLLOW-UP

Have we set the date on our calendar for reevaluation of self and situation? If not, let's pick that date now—perhaps six months or a year away at most. Procrastination is self-defeating because we will never be less busy than we are today. Reevaluation is important to the management of our company. It will keep us in touch with the *operation* of our business and force us to appraise its strengths and weaknesses. It will show us how far we have come and how far we may need to go to become a viable business or to survive amid competitive and technological changes. Review should become an annual habit. Help is available. SCORE, for example, offers an excellent "Checklist for Going into Business." It covers nearly all aspects of decision making, from a market analysis to a financial inventory.[3]

Amid these preliminary evaluations, we'll also want to consider some fundamental and even unique traits of genealogy that also affect the structure of our business.

Peculiarities of the field

Professional + Client + Problem + Document = Analysis and Report

Would that our business could be so simple! In reality, genealogists wear a variety of hats: author, conservationist, consultant, instructor, librarian, researcher, and tour leader—just to name a few. Yet there are a few qualities that are common to all our enterprises, as well as those in the larger and even more diverse service industry.

Our product is usually service.
Most of us provide help, not goods. Client satisfaction is paramount to our survival as a business.

Our product is often intangible.
Clients of the service industry—as pointed out by Rhonda Abrams in *The Successful Business Plan: Secrets & Strategies*—buy "a process, advice, or result, rather than a tangible item."[4] No genealogist should be so bold (or so naive) as to guarantee a *result*. The client purchases our special knowledge and experience related to a particular type of record. Our reports document the search process, the records found, and the significance of their facts; and they provide advice in the form of recommendations for future research.

Our product is perishable.
We sell our time—the most perishable of all commodities. Abrams asks us to consider "the ways our 'product' is constrained by time."[5] How many records can we search in an hour? A day? How many reports can we produce in a day or a week? Can we efficiently arrange work for several clients at a particular repository on a given trip? Are we comfortable using independent contractors to hunt for specific records while we work on more complex aspects of a client's problem? Are there other feasible ways for us to save time?

Customers purchase our product infrequently.
Most clients hire us for research or problem analysis and advice. It is unusual for one to retain our services for months or years on end. We usually do not provide regular, recurring services to a particular client—as do gardeners or maid services. A client may use us a few times over a five-year period, or only once.

The person who performs the service determines the quality.
Unlike the standard of quality one might expect in a consumer product like a refrigerator or a computer, the quality one receives from a service-sector firm is based upon the experience and knowledge of the individual who actually performs the work. This probably will be a major concern of ours, once business builds to the point that the demand exceeds the time we have available. Eventually, most of us consider expansion—a prospect that, in a service field, means adding personnel. When that day comes, we inevitably ask ourselves three questions.

> The person who performs the service determines the quality.

- *Will we be able to employ assistants whose level of expertise matches our own?* Realistically, *no*—not usually. Given the independent nature of those who practice genealogy professionally, most people consider "working for someone else" only until they develop the training and expertise to be successful on their own.

- *If we use less experienced help to perform our "legwork" and reserve our time for "more difficult analysis," can we reach conclusions with complete confidence that our searchers did not overlook any clues in records they examined and dismissed as irrelevant? Can we reach reliable conclusions if important details were overlooked?* Any answers here are debatable.

- *Are we willing to put our names to a report based on decisions made by less experienced searchers?* Even with proper acknowledgment of an assistant's work, one fact remains: the person who performs the service determines the quality.

Subjective perceptions of quality guide client satisfaction.
Our clients often have no objective measures for judging the quality of research on their behalf. Therefore, we educate them about standards—beginning, perhaps, with the ethical guidelines set by the Association of Professional Genealogists, the Board for Certification of Genealogists, or one of the other organizations whose codes and standards appear in appendix B. We also strive to appear as professional as we can in all client communications—providing clear and neatly typed correspondence, reports, and expense statements. In short, the business we structure must win confidence and inspire trust.

Blueprints

Every successful business is based on two foundations: a mission statement and a business plan. Many genealogists think—wrongly—that these formalities are necessary only if one applies for bank financing or a grant. To the contrary, a mission statement and a business plan are the heart and soul of our business. They define the path we intend to follow. They sum up—in one package—the *who, what, why, where, when,* and *how* of our efforts. Once written, they enable us to recite the salient points of our service to anyone in fewer than five sentences. That result is a powerful tool indeed, because clients do not have the time, patience, or inclination to listen to lengthy descriptions of how wonderful we are. They want brief essentials about our service, our offering, and its costs.

A mission statement and a business plan convert our vision into concrete blueprints—a "brain book," some call it, because together they centralize all important documents in one place for easy reference. For us, they will be "living documents" that we'll use often, to help discern real opportunities from the superficial temptations of fads or crises. But those blueprints will change and mature as our business develops into directions we could never anticipate. Together with our monthly cash-flow statements and quarterly financial reports, they will provide a foundation for annual reviews of performance and policies. Preparing these documents is a long-term investment of our knowledge, skill, time, and spirit. The return on that investment, if we make it wisely, will be the success of our dream.

Mission statement

A mission statement can be pragmatic or philosophical, but it should not be negative and it should not be about money.

A mission statement captures in a few sentences the nature of our business. It states the meaning and significance of what we are doing and why we are doing it. It is highly personal. It can be pragmatic or philosophical, but it should not be negative ("I don't want to work for someone else") and it should not be about money. If we place money at the center of our mission statement, then we are bound for disappointment. (When was the last time we heard a genealogist say that he or she came into this field because "the money is so good"?) The final form of our mission statement is seldom arrived at quickly. Indeed, it may take months to coax from our deepest thoughts, desires, and spiritual center. Once written, it does not tend to change as frequently as other aspects of our business plan.

Many entrepreneurship guides—and the SBA as well—recommend a break in our planning at this stage. If we are launching a new business, it is wise to test our mission statement against a preliminary analysis of the marketplace and our competition. The opening pages of chapter 11 provide excellent advice for making these appraisals and deciding the position or niche we want to occupy. The result should encourage us one way or the other—that is, it may excite us over the prospects available or it may suggest more viable alternatives. In either case, trial marketing will provide the insight we need to draft the rest of our blueprints.

Business plan

A well-written business plan is a paradox: it is both flexible and restrictive. It permits us to respond to short-term opportunities but reminds us of our long-term business goals. Many popular texts treat the subject. A browse through the shelves of our local bookstore or library will turn up at least one whose author's voice and experience appeal to us. Each text has its own method and suggested outline. The one followed here is the one most often presented by the SBA.[6] Our individual plan will evolve over time into a more sophisticated document—particularly if we seek funding from banks, equity investors, or institutions. At the present point, our need is simply to commit the essentials to paper.

OVERALL PRESENTATION

The overall look of the document should be professional and well organized. We will want to produce it on quality stock and nicely bind it with a cover from a print shop or office-supply store. If we take the attitude *"Why worry about looks? No one will see it but me,"* then we are likely to settle for second-best efforts in all of its preparation.

COVER PAGE

The cover page should identify the document; state the name of our company; and provide our business's street or post office address, e-mail and web-page addresses, and telephone and fax numbers.

EXECUTIVE SUMMARY

A synopsis placed at the beginning of our plan informs readers of the most important aspects of our business, without their having to read through the entire document. Initially, the average business plan is ten to twenty pages in length. As the business develops, a forty- to fifty-page plan is not extraordinary. The SBA model calls for us to place our financial projections in the summary; other models present those numbers only within the context of our financial documents. Before choosing one option or the other, we should consider the audience that may review the plan. If we submit it to a banker or potential investor, then our financial needs, application of funds, earnings projections, and potential return to investors should be treated here in this initial abstract.

This executive summary is clear and concise—one to two pages at most. It includes the name of the business; its location, products and services; and the relevant experience of the owner. (For the genealogist, perhaps research, writing, lecturing, sales, and management.) The summary also includes the mission statement as well as the business's present status and future plans. Last, the executive summary of a business plan written to obtain funding will explain why we seek a loan, how much we need, and why our business will be successful.

TABLE OF CONTENTS

The table of contents provides an overview of topics covered in the document—clearly and accurately reflecting the location of information in the business plan. The content and sequence should flow in a logical manner.

COMPANY DESCRIPTION

This section provides both general information and specific details. A general statement, based upon our business research during test marketing, briefly describes our business within the context of the genealogy industry. In our specific details, we try to give readers insight into the day-to-day operation of our company by describing

- the legal structure we have chosen (sole proprietorship, partnership, or corporation).

If we take the attitude *"Why worry about looks? No one will see it but me,"* then we are likely to settle for second-best efforts in all of its preparation.

STRUCTURING A BUSINESS

- our business's history, present status, and future projections.

- our product(s) or service(s). If we produce an item for sale, we will discuss its marketability. If we provide a service, we will state why or how it is unique.

- our planned accomplishments over the next few years.

- details of management and staffing. Actual resumes of individuals involved in the business will go in the SUPPORTING DOCUMENTS section discussed later in this chapter. Here in the company description, we briefly identify who will do what work; and we cite their qualifications, responsibilities, and salaries.

- procedures for record keeping—how records are maintained, who keeps them, and how they are used to manage the business. Chapter 12 offers quite a bit of helpful advice on this subject. For questions that arise beyond this, we will turn to our accounting advisor, who knows our personal situation and stays abreast of current laws.

- insurance details—policies, carriers, coverages, limits, and costs.

- inventory procedures—the tracking of purchases and sales.

- safeguards for security and confidentiality. If we are researchers and lecturers and our client contracts address these issues, we should include a copy of the contract in our supporting documents—along with ethics statements from organizations of which we are a member, such as those appearing in appendix B.

INDUSTRY DESCRIPTION AND ANALYSIS

> We analyze our competition, its qualifications, its location, its services, its pricing, and its length of time in business. Then we detail a plan for fair and effective competition.

Here, we analyze the results of our marketing research: our competition, its qualifications, its location, its services, its pricing, and its length of time in business. Then we detail a plan for fair and effective competition. We identify our target market and the share of that market we expect or need to acquire. If our trial marketing included client questionnaires, demographic data, or similar tools, we include that in the SUPPORTING DOCUMENTS section.

MARKETING AND SALES STRATEGIES

Concrete details are needed. If part of our marketing strategy depends upon our physical location—proximity to a record source or institution—then we state the importance of this factor. We also describe the pricing of our product or services and any warranties that may be applicable, as well as any copyrights or patents that protect our products. A useful addition would be information on industry trends and how our business can meet the challenge of future changes in the marketplace.

FINANCIAL DOCUMENTS

If we are just starting a business, this section will discuss our personal financial situation. If ours is an existing business, then we include the following to document its performance history:

- *Balance sheet*—a statement showing the condition of the business on a given date: assets, liabilities, and net worth.

- *Income statement*—an account that shows profits and losses over an appropriate period of time (monthly, quarterly, or annually). If we have no profit-and-loss history, then we construct an operating plan that forecasts profit and loss projections. This is a powerful assessment tool that shows what has happened (or should happen) in our business.

Sample spreadsheets to portray these statements and projections can be found in almost every small-business text. They are also available from the local SBA or SCORE office. A simple spreadsheet design places months of the fiscal year across its top horizontal axis, while its left vertical axis lists such categories as Revenue (sales), Cost of Sales, Gross Profits, Expenses (advertising, depreciation, insurance, interest on debt, rent, salary, supplies, telephone, utilities, etc.), and Total Expenses. The last category, located in the bottom left corner of the spreadsheet, is Net Profit.

- *Financial history*—a document that tracks the flow of money through our company *from its inception*.

This same information is incorporated into loan applications. As part of our financial documentation, we should add a section regarding projections of profits and losses based upon our past and present performance. This information translates into long-term goals for the operation of our business. If we have no past or present performance to assist us in formulating long-term goals, then we need to document the assumptions on which we base our projections. As we work in our business every day, crises of the moment tend to erase projections from our mind. Our best insurance against a faulty memory is to write down our assumptions, no matter how sketchy or unsophisticated they may later prove to be. The paper trail we create through this documentation will be needed in the future if we apply for a loan, and it will help us in the analysis of our business performance during the annual review.

- *Break-even analysis*—a graph that depicts the point at which our company begins (or should begin) to make a profit.

Some business writers debate the usefulness of a break-even analysis within a business plan, arguing that it's usually built upon guesswork and is highly idiosyncratic and subject to the bias of the preparer. Others see it as valuable— and it can be, if we are honest with ourselves. The graph is simple in design. Its horizontal axis again ticks off the months of our fiscal year; its left vertical axis lists dollar amounts incrementally. To create a break-even analysis, we plot here our actual (or projected) income by month. On a separate line, we plot the total costs (fixed and variable) of our business—including our salary. The intersection of these two lines is known as the *break-even point*—the dollar amount required to meet all our expenses in a given month. Let us not despair if that point is months, or even a year or two, away. All in all, the break-even analysis is a potent visual image of how hard we must work to be successful in our business.

> The break-even analysis is a potent visual image of how hard we must work to be successful.

SUPPORTING DOCUMENTS

Depending upon the audience, format, and purpose of our business plan, supporting documentation might include a wide variety of items—logically assembled in the same order as the corresponding sections of the report. Commonly, these would include

- our resume and those of our staff;
- financial statements and credit reports (personal ones, if we are starting a new business);

- letters of reference;
- cash-flow and profit-and-loss statements;
- balance sheets and a break-even analysis;
- copies of pertinent agreements (e.g., leases or client contracts);
- documents pertaining to our legal structure, insurance, property titles; and
- other materials referenced in the business plan—such as client contracts, codes of conduct, demographic information, and marketing plans.

Once we have a clear blueprint of who we are, what we want to be, and where we are on the path to those goals, we must choose a legal structure for our business.

Legal Structures

Genealogists who stand on the threshold of professionalism rarely visualize themselves as a *company* and usually give little thought to the legal structure they need to establish. They are caught up in the vagaries of records and methodology, the excitement of the search, the desire to help others, and the concept of "hanging out a shingle." More often, the profession foists itself upon us, as the "genealogical grapevine" spreads the word of our expertise in a particular area and a growing number of inquirers ask us for help. Odds are good that most of us could benefit now from a review of the advantages and disadvantages of the various legal structures under which we can and must operate.

The legalities that follow are those that exist in the United States. Internationally, some of the same policies—but also many different ones—apply. Just as the American genealogist is urged throughout to consult qualified legal and financial advisors, our international colleagues will want to do the same.

The three basic forms of business in the United States are: Sole Proprietorship, Partnership, and Corporation. The Corporation form (also known as a C Corporation) can be further divided into S Corporations and Limited Liability Companies. If we are just now venturing into professional genealogy, we need to carefully consider each option and later revisit them as our company and its assets grow. In all cases beyond the simplest form of Sole Proprietorship, we should consult an attorney and a tax accountant. The advice presented in this slim section could never be sufficient. Many whole books exist to guide us through the process, and several of them are suggested in the section FURTHER STUDY at the end of this chapter. As genealogists we tend to feel at ease with legal documents, so the necessary filing of forms for incorporation may not intimidate us. However, various states view these structures differently. Our accountant or tax attorney will make certain we understand how our state or municipality handles various types of businesses. Armed with this information on the advantages and disadvantages of each form of business, we can make an informed decision as to the type that best suits our situation.

Sole proprietorships

Legal simplicity, economy, and autonomy tend to make sole proprietors of most

Genealogists who stand on the threshold of professionalism rarely visualize themselves as a *company* and usually give little thought to the legal structure they need to establish.

genealogists. We may need to file only a simple form with our city or county clerk and—voila!—we are in business. As sole proprietors, we are the proverbial rulers of our domain. We control its money, its decisions, and its day-to-day management. We endure fewer government regulations and less taxation. We do not have to file separate tax returns for our business, because its profits are considered our personal income. We can use Schedule C, Profit and Loss from a Business or Profession, and file it with our standard federal 1040 (individual) tax return. But there are special taxes and tax planning we should not overlook—particularly self-employment tax and quarterly filing of estimated taxes. Henry Hoff, a Certified Genealogist and Certified Public Accountant, discusses both of these (and more) in an article published by the *Association of Professional Genealogists [APG] Quarterly*.[7]

Given the advantages of sole proprietorships, why does this chapter not end here? Because there are also risks and limitations involved—particularly the following:

- As sole proprietors, we are liable for all our business debts and obligations—a point that seems fair and just. When we just start out and have little or no assets, this form of company appears ideal. But let us recall the assets inventory we completed earlier, when crafting our business plan. Can we afford to lose those items in the event of a lawsuit—not only our microfilm reader and computer but also *our house, car, and bank accounts?*

- We should also consider what will happen to our business in the event of our death, physical disability, or mental incapacitation. In most cases, our business—and income—terminates. No child, spouse, or other designated person can pick up a sole-proprietorship business and legally run it.

- Financial institutions may not consider our sole proprietorship very "professional," in comparison to other forms of business enterprise. Sole proprietorships commonly have few assets. Bankers know that anyone with substantial assets would not risk that loss by selecting this type of company. If we choose certain genealogical enterprises that involve substantial start-up costs or maintenance, a lack of collateral may make it difficult to obtain financing or long-term loans.

Partnerships

As defined by American law, a partnership is "an association of two or more persons to carry on as co-owners of a business for profit."[8] Such individuals are also termed *general partners*. Partnerships usually require the writing of Articles of Partnership. This document, which is usually filed with the Secretary of State (or its counterpart) in our state of residence, will define (among other things) the

- percentage of contributions made by each partner at start-up or at a later date (contributions may include managerial and material assets as well as money);
- duration of the partnership;
- method of accounting;
- division of profits and losses;
- role of each partner;
- management of employees and operations;

> As sole proprietors, we are the proverbial rulers of our domain. We control its money, its decisions, and its everyday management.

STRUCTURING A BUSINESS

- provisions for settling disputes;
- instructions upon the absence, disability, or death of a partner; and
- terms by which the partnership may be modified, sold, or dissolved.[9]

One advantage of a partnership is its comparative ease of formation. There are fewer documents to file than with a corporation. Income and losses are reported on tax returns of the individual partners. Partnerships may more easily attract money from lending institutions because they operate under a more formal structure than a sole proprietorship. With an equally committed partner, we gain another reservoir of experience, another point of view, and a sounding board for our brainstorms—all valuable commodities.

The downside of a partnership is steep. We forfeit independence in management and decision making. We each assume unlimited liability for business debts, commitments, and activities of every other partner. As with a sole proprietorship, our personal assets may be at risk. Should our partner die or depart, then our business is terminated unless the articles make other provisions. Should we be the only surviving partner, the business can proceed under rights of survivorship; but we must find a new partner or else legally restructure our business. (Partnership or "key man" insurance can be obtained to protect against financial disaster in the event of a loss of a partner, a point discussed more fully in the insurance section of this chapter.)

A popular type of partnership in the past was the LP, the "limited partnership," in which designated partners agreed to risk only the investments they made in the business. Limited partners did not enjoy the same rights or exercise the same control as general partners—or else they risked the loss of limited-liability status. This type of partnership also prevented the public disclosure of certain sensitive information about the company. However, that protection no longer exists, and this form has largely been replaced by the limited-liability company discussed later in this chapter.

Corporations

Corporations are "living entities," separate and apart from the individuals who found, own, manage, or hold shares in them. The main reason to form a corporation is to limit personal liability. Should a business fail, the personal assets of shareholders cannot be touched by creditors, unless a lawsuit successfully proves that company officers flagrantly disregarded the law. Forming a corporation absolutely requires consultation with an attorney and a tax accountant prior to filing forms, because each state has its own regulations. After reviewing our particular situation, our attorney will help us decide the type of corporate legal structure that fits our management style, financial circumstances, and company goals.

Forms and guidelines for incorporation are available from our state's Office of the Secretary of State. Filling out the paperwork is not difficult—once our attorney has helped us decide the appropriate structure. That attorney should also review our documentation to make sure we have included all required information, as well as important clauses to protect our interests. He or she will also advise us concerning

> The main reason to form a corporation is to limit personal liability. Should a business fail, the personal assets of shareholders cannot be touched by creditors.

existing contracts we may have acquired while operating as a sole proprietor or partnership—or apprise us of state laws regarding the transfer of certain licenses and contracts from one form of business to another. We will also need to obtain a "corporate seal" from our Secretary of State's office. This emblem includes the name of the company and the state in which it is incorporated.

Three types of corporations are possible under current U.S. law. The following discussion of C Corporations (popularly called C Corps) is limited to general remarks that are basic to all corporative structures. Separate sections add a few specifics about the S Corporations (S Corps) and Limited Liability Companies (LLCs).

C CORPORATIONS

A corporation may own assets and incur debts. Shareholders neither own those assets nor hold responsibility for those debts. Shareholders merely own stock (equity) in the corporation. Their interests can be bought and sold like any other type of asset. The application of these fundamental principles can be confusing in small companies that are owned by a few people or by one person who acts as the corporate director, officer, and sole employee. In such cases, roles *must* be understood and respected. If a corporation is run sloppily, without attention to corporate structure or control—or if the sole shareholder, sole director, and sole employee are indistinguishable in activity and act as one and the same without respect to the corporation's charter—a court may set aside the legal protection created by incorporation. If that corporation is ours, we may become personally liable for its debts and commitments.

Paul Adams, in *155 Legal Do's (and Don'ts) for the Small Business,* outlines a four-factor test used by the IRS to distinguish a corporation from a noncorporation (a partnership, for example). To pass this test, a company must possess three of the following four characteristics:

- Does the firm have limited liability?
- Does it have centralized management?
- Does it have a limited life in the event of the death or departure of a principal?
- Are ownership interests freely transferable?[10]

Advantages

Aside from limits on personal liability, incorporation offers other advantages. Corporations persist as legal entities after the death or incapacitation of a principal, because they have a formal management structure that includes directors and officers. They can raise money through the sale of stock. Financial institutions view them as more favorable loan risks than other types of businesses, because they typically are more substantial and more professionally run. Corporations often pay lower tax rates than other types of businesses.

Incorporation forces a business to follow its charter (a document issued by the Secretary of State that outlines the powers and limitations of the corporation). Once a quarter, directors are expected to convene for a review of *(a)* the quarterly financial statement rendered by the company's accountant, *(b)* goals achieved or failed in the prior quarter, *(c)* short-term goals for the coming quarter, and *(d)* long-term goals.

If the sole shareholder, sole director, and sole employee are indistinguishable in activity, a court may set aside the legal protection created by incorporation.

This exercise is not merely an odious formality. It is a positive benefit that prompts (or forces) periodic business evaluations and decisions. We should also take minutes during our board meetings. This evidence that our company behaves as a corporation can provide protection in the event of a lawsuit.

Disadvantages

A corporative structure limits our business activities to parameters set by the laws of the state in which we are incorporated. Local, state, and federal regulations add up to numerous filings, including periodic financial statements that include balance sheets. We may also be subject to taxes on corporate earnings as well as a personal income tax, if earnings are distributed to shareholders as dividends. This "double taxation" is one of the common complaints against the C Corp business structure. Also, our state may have laws regarding the transfer of certain licenses and contracts from one form of business to another.

S CORPORATIONS

S Corps, formally known as Subchapter S Corporations, differ somewhat from the above description of the standard C Corp. The S Corp has attributes of both the C Corp and the partnership—chief among which is the fact that profits (dividends) and losses are taxed to the shareholders, not to the corporations, as personal income. This circumvents the "double taxation" dilemma most C Corps face. Several stringent conditions must be met in order for us to use the S Corp form. One common pitfall is the failure of many S Corps to file the required IRS Form 2553 (Election by a Small Business Corporation) within the mandated two and a half months after filing articles of incorporation at the state level. Failure to submit this form can cost us the S Corp tax advantage and render us unable to file a new election status for five years. To avoid such problems, we should not neglect to consult an attorney prior to filing for S Corp status.

LIMITED-LIABILITY COMPANIES

This new breed of corporation—validated in almost every state of the United States—is popular because it limits liability, similar to a regular corporation, while providing flexibility and taxation benefits similar to a partnership. Its articles of organization also function like a partnership agreement (particularly the old limited partnership), outlining the rights and responsibilities between "members." As with other types of corporations, if we choose this form we must file the operating agreement with the Secretary of State in our state, pay the minimum tax or annual maintenance fee if our state levies one on corporations, and apply for a federal taxpayer identification number. In some instances, professionals who are required to be licensed (e.g., physicians, engineers, or barbers) cannot use this form of business. In most areas, genealogists are unaffected by these restrictions, although some genealogical activities may be in certain locales (e.g., private-detective work). Obviously, we should consult an attorney familiar with the requirements of the LLC in our state.[11]

"Double taxation" is one of the common complaints against the C Corp business structure.

Business Regulations

Local and state ordinances

In many areas, a business cannot legally operate without a license or without complying with specific (often unanticipated) regulations. Each locality is different. Before "hanging out our shingle" or placing advertisements for our services, we should check with the appropriate clerks of our city, county, or other applicable jurisdiction. The following general information, provided by SCORE and the SBA, should not be deemed complete for our own particular jurisdiction.

BUSINESS LICENSES

Some localities require payment of an annual fee. Some require licensing only if the business needs policing (this probably would not apply to a genealogy business). For caution, we should inquire at all jurisdictional levels.

ZONING RESTRICTIONS

Running a business legally from our home also requires us to research and comply with local restrictions on home-based businesses. Discretion suggests that we do not contact the local zoning office to ask specifically about "home-based businesses," but rather inquire about the zoning classification of our residence. The clerk's office should be able to supply us with copies of ordinance requirements stating whether home-based businesses are allowed in our neighborhood. If we find that our residence is not zoned for business enterprises, we should consult an attorney to discuss the ordinance requirements and the manner in which they are enforced. Then we must decide how we want to proceed and what risks we are willing to assume. If the zoning ordinance does not permit the operation of our business, we might apply for one of the following—depending upon the requirements of our local government:

- *Zoning changes* are permanent alterations in the zoning classification of *our residence.* They often involve a very lengthy process of legally mandated steps—public hearings held, legal notices published, and environmental clearances obtained.

- *Variances or conditional-use permits* allow us to operate a business in a location not normally zoned for business activity. Obtaining these can take up to ninety days, if we are successful, and may involve public notices or environmental clearances.

Zoning appeals also require payments of fees—from tens to hundreds of dollars—to the local government agency that processes the paperwork.

Zoning cautions also apply to physical changes in our office: new construction, remodeling, purchases of new buildings, or leasing property to operate a business. Because changes to the structure may also require a building permit, we should inquire prior to construction. Zoning is the way a community ensures that land uses are harmonious with each other. Most concerns fall into three categories: traffic, parking, and signage. A genealogical business probably would not run afoul of any of these issues, except in neighborhoods where parking is scarce. If ours is such a case, we

If we find that our residence is not zoned for business enterprises, we should consult an attorney to discuss the ordinance requirements and the manner in which they are enforced.

should ensure that clients who visit us are given parking instructions and that delivery trucks arrive and depart in a manner safe to the neighborhood. Genealogists who strive to be a good neighbor seldom suffer neighborhood concern over the operation of a home-based business.

FICTITIOUS BUSINESS-NAME STATEMENTS (DBAs)

The business name we choose may invoke other regulations. Sole proprietorships and partnerships that do not use the last name of their owners—or companies whose names imply ownership by others—must file a statement of Fictitious Business Name or DBA ("doing business as") with the city or county clerk. Wisdom suggests making a preliminary check with this same office, prior to filing, to confirm that the name is not already in use. The filing fee varies between jurisdictions. Publication of a legal notice usually follows the filing. Clerks of some jurisdictions place the ads and include the charge in the filing fee. DBA statements are not necessary for corporations because the documents of incorporation serve the same identification purpose.

TAXES AND SALES PERMITS

Business taxes are volatile in nature. Most states and some local jurisdictions tax not only income but also sales or rentals of tangible personal property. Some states tax the sale of services as well. Traditionally, companies have paid income and sales taxes to states in which they had a "physical presence"—that is, an address, inventory, or employee or representative based there. But that definition of physical presence is changing. States that do not have reciprocal agreements with each other may require us to file in each state where we earn money in excess of a certain amount. (As a genealogical example, this could apply to a speaker who is paid for out-of-state lecturing.) Insofar as sales taxes are concerned, we might follow the counsel of Bob Adams in *Streetwise Small Business Start-Up,* who contends that "the safest route . . . is to simply collect sales tax in every state where [we] sell products or services."[12] In the long run, considering the range of taxes and penalties that exist, advice from an accountant or tax attorney could spare us many legal and financial problems.

> Considering the range of taxes and penalties that exist, advice from an accountant or tax attorney could spare us many legal and financial problems.

PROPERTY TAXES

If we own real estate, we expect to pay taxes on our home or on commercial or industrial property. But we may be surprised to learn that some localities impose a property tax on the inventory, equipment, and furniture a business owns. Although the percentage of estimated value is quite small with this type of tax, penalties for noncompliance may be substantial. The point is another to add to our growing list of issues we should discuss with our legal or financial advisor.

Federal ordinances

FEDERAL TRADE COMMISSION

Any business that operates across state lines or advertises in other states falls under the scrutiny of the Federal Trade Commission. One of the more common regulations applicable to a genealogical business is the prohibition against selling any article at less than cost in order to harm a competitor. Other laws deal with truth in advertising; "bait and switch" selling; withholding of refunds or deposits paid by clients; and the misrepresentation of warranties, guarantees, or quality. Genealogical businesses that sell by mail must obtain a copy of FTC regulations and review them.

INTERNAL REVENUE SERVICE

Corporations—as well as sole proprietorships or partnerships with employees—must obtain a "taxpayer identification number" from the IRS. This number functions as an identifier similar to our personal Social Security numbers; it must be used for corporate tax returns, as well as for filing employee withholding on federal and state tax forms. To obtain the taxpayer ID number, we simply contact the IRS to request Form SS-4 and then submit the completed form. There is no charge. While requesting the form, we might also ask for Publications 334 (Tax Guide for Small Business) and 583 (Starting a Business and Keeping Records). All are available by calling the IRS or by visiting its website, which allows keyword searches for all publications, rulings, and public statements. See figure 9 for a list of other IRS publications of interest to small-business entrepreneurs. Of considerable value, too, is the summary of taxes and allowable expenses in Hoff's previously mentioned article.[13]

Employee-contractor distinctions

Genealogists who use an assistant or subcontractor, even occasionally, should be aware of another issue of major concern to the IRS: the distinction between employees and independent contractors. For *employees,* we must properly process a payroll; withhold employee taxes; pay Social Security and Medicare assessments, unemployment insurance, and workers' compensation out of our own revenue; and possibly provide other benefits. We are spared these costs and much onerous bookkeeping if we engage *independent contractors*—individuals who perform services for a lump sum or an hourly fee that includes their "overhead."

As business owners, we may not freely choose to assign our workers to one status or another. The IRS strenuously—yet nebulously—defines distinctions between the two categories, and it rigorously enforces those distinctions. For any independent contractor to whom we pay a total of $600 or more over the course of a calendar year, we must submit a federal Form 1099 and report the full sum paid. Failure to file this report subjects us to penalties. Should federal and state tax authorities rule that our independent contractor is actually an employee, we could be forced to pay not only the back taxes owed but also employee benefits, interest, and penalties.

There is no one test to determine the difference between employees and independent contractors in all situations. Basic guidelines that the IRS uses to determine independent-contractor status include, but are not limited to, the questions below. Not all of these guidelines have to apply in every case; but if a significant percentage do not apply, then the IRS or the tax courts are likely to rule that the "contractor" is actually an employee.The consequences of a negative ruling are grave enough to encourage us to take these distinctions seriously. The IRS criteria fall into three categories:[14]

FIG. 9
USEFUL IRS
OFFERINGS

The following forms and publications can be ordered from IRS or downloaded from its website.

Forms

1040-ES	Estimated Tax for Individuals
1099-MISC	Miscellaneous Income
2553	Election by a Small Business Corporation
8829	Expenses for Business Use of Your Home
SS-4	Application for Employer ID Number

Publications

334	Tax Guide for Small Business
463	Travel, Entertainment, Gift, and Car Expenses
508	Education Expenses
509	Tax Calendar for [year]
533	Self-Employment Tax
535	Business Expenses
541	Tax Information on Partnerships
552	Recordkeeping for Individuals
560	Retirement Plans for the Self-Employed
583	Starting a Business and Keeping Records
587	Business Use of Your Home
910	Guide to Free Tax Services
917	Business Use of Your Car
946	How to Depreciate Property

Those that should generate a "yes" answer:
- Does the independent contractor have control over his or her work?
- Does the independent contractor have his or her own business license?
- Does the independent contractor have his or her own business cards, letterhead, and a business address?
- Does the independent contractor have a business bank account?
- Does the contractor perform work for—and receive pay from—other entities?

Those that should generate a "no" answer:
- Does the independent contractor have the right to terminate a work agreement without liability?
- Does the company or the independent contractor determine when, where, and how the work is performed?
- Does the independent contractor work full-time for the company?
- Does the independent contractor work on the company's premises?
- Does the company train the independent contractor?
- Does the independent contractor have an investment interest in the company—receive a share of profits or incur losses?
- Does the company supply any materials or equipment to the independent contractor that are necessary to perform the work?

Those that involve miscellaneous considerations:
- How does the company hire or discharge independent contractors?
- How is the independent contractor paid—hourly, weekly, or monthly?

Payroll and income taxes

Even if we have just one employee, we need assistance from an accountant or payroll service experienced with small-business management. Ideally, this person or service should handle both our payroll calculations and our filings. Taxation and employee laws at the federal and state levels are very complex. The chances for mistakes, such as withholding too little from each check, are high. So are the penalties. Should we fail to file payroll taxes in a timely manner, for example, the IRS can collect a 50 percent penalty, plus the back taxes owed. This type of debt cannot be discharged through bankruptcy proceedings. Hence, many small businesses, confused by the morass of regulations, find themselves out of business but still owing a large debt, with interest, to the federal government.

The IRS may also expect us to make quarterly tax payments on our estimated income for the fiscal year—starting in our second year of business. Many states have similar requirements, although they may not use the same income basis or payment schedule as the federal government. Our accounting advisor can help us weigh the advantages and disadvantages of making these payments and ensure that we meet all the applicable deadlines.

Unemployment insurance

Unemployment insurance becomes an issue only if we have employees, as opposed to

Even if we have just one employee, we need assistance from an accountant or payroll service experienced with small-business management.

independent contractors. The amount we pay depends on a variety of factors such as salaries, our company's balance, the date we hire an employee, and the condition of our state's unemployment-insurance account.

Workers' compensation
As soon as we issue the first paycheck to a full-time or part-time employee, we must pay at least a minimum level of worker's compensation. Payment is mandatory, and failure to pay on time invites a lawsuit with serious penalties. Courts can collect overdue worker's compensation directly from shareholders and corporate officers—corporation status does not shelter personal liability here. Some states sponsor their own programs. Others require the purchase of a policy through an insurance agent. We may also purchase additional workers' compensation coverage through agents and brokers, to bolster our financial protection.

Resource Management

Beyond laws and agency regulations, a successful business pays considerable attention to its three major resources: time, people, and money. A separate chapter in this book deals exclusively with time management. This chapter should raise some pointed questions on the last two issues, because safeguards for these resources should be built into every business from its inception.

Client resources

"Everyone is in the business of customer satisfaction, and the customer is always right. Successful businesses have an obsession with customer service." So warns Brian Tracy, in his *Universal Laws of Success*.[15] Jay Conrad Levinson's immensely popular Guerrilla Marketing series similarly touts the importance of customer service and its relationship to successful promotion of our products and services, pointing out that satisfied customers are repeat customers.[16]

MAXIMIZING CLIENT SATISFACTION
According to the most common recommendations for making client satisfaction an integral part of our business structure, we should

- be timely in our responses to clients. If we are not able to do the work, we can either subcontract it to an independent contractor or refer the client to someone else with appropriate expertise or access to the record sources.

- be timely in the delivery of our work product. With the advent of fax machines and e-mail, many clients expect speedier service, and many will pay more for it. However, the quality of our work should not be sacrificed on the altar of haste.

- stay in touch with our clients, even though there may be long periods of time before they need us again.

- maintain a file of past client contacts. During lulls in business, we can drop them a note or a copy of an article on a subject related to some aspect of their problem.

Clients expect speedier service, and many will pay more for it. However, the quality of our work should not be sacrificed on the altar of haste.

STRUCTURING A BUSINESS

This communication helps build trust and expresses our honest concern with their needs—and it builds repeat orders. People like to do business with those they know.

- schedule special promotions, limited-time offers, or discounts during any slow season we may have.

- encourage clients to contract with us several months in advance of holiday or reunion events at which they want to share findings with relatives.

- develop standards of performance for independent contractors we employ. Wisdom suggests that we also spot-check their work to ensure that those standards of quality and accuracy are being met.

- integrate our business or service with other related enterprises. For example, we might develop an alliance with a local graphic artist who can create lovely heritage charts, a photographer who can copy and restore our client's photographs, or a company that sells acid-free scrapbook supplies.

- cultivate a network of other genealogists upon whom we can rely or to whom we can subcontract when our work load is heavy or the client's problem falls outside our area of expertise.

RESPONDING TO CLIENT CONTACTS

As businesspersons, we also need to consider how we can maximize our time while providing a high level of client service. Of all the time drains that the genealogist reports, daily communication is the most common. How can we most efficiently respond to our messages? How can potential or current clients reach us, especially when we are at the archives, traveling between destinations, or actually in our office but trying to concentrate on a difficult project? Regardless of our business structure, a variety of options exists—each with advantages and disadvantages. Some appear more professional than others, and some are costlier:

Answering machine
The simplest investment is an answering machine attached to our residential telephone line or dedicated business line. Its major advantage, aside from costs, is that it permits us to screen calls when deadlines are tight but important calls are expected. However, if we attach other communication devices (fax machines, modems, etc.) to the same phone line, we could experience compatibility problems.

Voice mail
This more professional (and more expensive) option comes in various forms. We may choose to install a software program in our personal computer, which requires us to keep the computer active around the clock. Or we may purchase a "voice mail-box" from a supplier of telephone services.

Live voice
A live voice that accepts calls, directs them to the proper person, or takes a message definitely creates the most professional impression. We may hire an answering service or enlist a family member or friend to help us during our published office hours. As our business grows, we might consider a part-time or full-time receptionist or assistant to answer calls. It should go without saying, but home business guides repeatedly point to a problem here: we should never try to change our voice and pretend that we are the receptionist as well as the genealogist!

> Of all the time drains the genealogist reports, daily communication is the most common. How can we most efficiently respond to our messages?

Pager/cellular phone (with voice-mail or e-mail capability)
If we are frequently away from the office, we may want to consider a pager or cellular phone. It is up to us whether we give the number to everyone or just certain clients. One or the other device may be vital if our business includes obtaining records at particular repositories for clients who need immediate response.

E-mail
If we maintain an e-mail address for client contact, we should take care to use a reliable service. E-mail addresses from economy providers that do not function reliably are frustrating to potential clients (and us) and will cost us business. We should strive to answer our e-mail as promptly as we do our other calls—within twenty-four hours of the message posting, if not sooner.

Website
A Web presence is an increasingly viable and popular option. Regardless of whether we sell products or services, a website can provide instant information to any inquirer—details of our qualifications, services, and (if we choose) rates. We may post tip sheets, special promotions, or other helpful literature that attracts clients without continual (and interruptive) personal contact. A time investment is still necessary to create and maintain the data. Again, our computer must remain on around the clock or we must pay a commercial service to maintain our site.

The bottom line on communications is this: let us not get caught up in the hype of buying the best system on the market, but focus on what gets the job done for our business at the best price. What really matters is efficiently handled contacts that inspire client confidence and trust, while saving us time.

Financial resources

PHYSICAL PLANT

One of the most common issues raised by those who launch a business for the first time is that of equipment. Specifically: *new* vs. *used* and *purchased* vs. *leased.* Equipment decisions are personal ones that must be based upon the financial resources we have available. The latest and best are beyond the reach of most new businesses. The fundamental question is *What can I live with—and live without?* The most recent survey of genealogists—albeit dated now—clearly shows that the professionals in the field invest significantly in technology that must be continually upgraded—particularly computers (with quality printers), microform readers, photocopiers, fax machines, and computer peripherals. (See figure 10.) Beyond this, abundant shelving and numerous filing cabinets—as well as the ubiquitous desk—are all vital.

Today's marketplace offers a variety of means by which we can economize. Both local businesses and major catalog companies offer used business furniture and reconditioned equipment. Want ads alert us to business-liquidation auctions. Sound construction in furniture and factory warranties for equipment are major points to consider. For genealogists, chic (and expensive) designs are not common considerations, because clients typically do not come to our offices. Quality research

**FIG. 10
ESSENTIAL
OFFICE EQUIPMENT**

Rankings reflect the percentage of professional genealogists who considered each item essential, in a survey conducted by the Board for Certification of Genealogists.

Computer	90%
Microfilm/fiche reader	79
Photocopier	70
Modem	53
CD-ROM player	49
Fax machine	45
Typewriter	45
Scanner	19

SOURCE: "Equipping Ourselves for Quality Service," *OnBoard* 3 (May 1997): 9.

STRUCTURING A BUSINESS

reports are in no way enhanced by a designer desk; they can be prepared just as well on a door laid across a pair of two-drawer file cabinets. "Instant" shelves of 1-by-10-inch boards, straddling stacked-brick supports, hold books just as well as polished, wall-to-wall built-ins; and ordinary plastic dish tubs organize supplies or files as well as fancier baskets and crates from office-supply stores.

With so much used business furniture on the market, renting furniture does not make sense. However, equipment leasing is an option worth exploring—particularly for computers that are so soon obsolete. Leasing can help stretch our available cash, if we critically compare prices. One business-management guru suggests another option: if friends or relatives hesitate to loan us money for our business but want to help somehow, we might have them purchase equipment items and lease them to us, while retaining ownership.[17]

Lease agreements are typically complex and their many clauses must be scrutinized prior to signing. The *Small Business Advisor* offers a helpful list of comparisons that basically fall into four categories:[18]

- *Cost.* This includes the down payment, length of lease or loan, balloon payments, warranty, and total cost of the lease or loan.
- *Cash flow.* Amid seasonal surges in business, do we have money to make monthly payments on the loan or lease, while meeting costs of maintenance and insurance?
- *Possible tax benefits.* For example, we should check current tax laws to see whether we qualify for income-offsetting depreciation or whether there are tax advantages to our personally purchasing equipment (or property) and leasing it to our business.
- *Obsolescence.* How long will the item be operable? What is its technological life—and its cost divided by the number of useful years we can reasonably expect?

Other lease terms we will want to weigh carefully (and possibly discuss with our accounting or legal advisor) include

- period or term of lease;
- rate or lease payment;
- financial details related to payment;
- residual value of the item or purchase option;
- description of the specific value of the item;
- designation of who maintains, insures, and receives tax credit;
- obsolescence and replacement of the item as technology advances;
- renewal provisions;
- termination-of-lease provisions; and
- security deposits, warranties, or any "hidden" fees.

INSURANCE

Can our business sustain a major loss or lawsuit?

Amid all the work of starting our business, it is important to consider the protection of our investment. The minutiae involved here—and the time expenditure—hardly reflect the reasons why most of us chose a genealogy business. But still we must ask ourselves: *Can our business sustain a major loss or lawsuit?* More to the point: *Can we personally sustain endless legal expenses, a significant loss of billable hours, and the added stress?* The answers should inspire us to action.

Primary insurance needs

In most cases, our risks go far beyond the "what if lightning strikes my computer" thoughts that typically come to mind. As genealogists offering primarily service, we may anticipate that our economic hazards will include at least the following:

Property replacement insurance

Our equipment, office furniture, and storage facilities are obviously at risk—to lightning, fire, flooding, and similar damages. If our office is in our home, we often can cover these risks with a rider to our homeowner's policy. If we occupy an office elsewhere, obtaining insurance may be more problematic. In California, for example, severe earthquakes of late have made small-business policies more difficult to obtain. What of our personal library and our working files? The value of both is likely to be significant.

Vehicular insurance

Any vehicles used in business activities need special consideration. We should check our existing policies for limits and restrictions they place upon business operation and augment those policies in whatever ways necessary.

Liability insurance (nonvehicular)

Liability insurance can be both difficult to obtain and expensive to purchase for the small-business owner. Yet many companies will not allow independent contractors to work on the premises—nor will they sign a contract with one—without proof of liability-insurance coverage. Two types are available.

- *General-liability coverage* protects us, up to a certain dollar amount, against generic liability suits (e.g., someone trips over our doormat or we accidentally cause an injury). Home-based businesses can sometimes purchase general liability insurance from the company that provides their homeowner insurance.

- *Specific-liability coverage* is a more complex concern. Traditionally, only licensed professionals with clear standards of conduct and operation (e.g., doctors and lawyers) had to obtain liability insurance. But now, small businesses, independent contractors, and downsized managers have changed the liability-insurance landscape. Specific liability coverage is appraised according to several criteria: the annual dollar amount earned by the business, the number of years the owner has been in business, his or her expertise in the field, the number of employees, and the size of the client businesses being served. In essence, the more trade a company does and the larger its clientele, the more opportunities exist for a situation in which a lawsuit might be filed.

- *Errors-and-omissions insurance* is the one type of specific liability coverage that most concerns genealogists. What if we misidentify a client's ancestor and construct an erroneous lineage—thereby wasting considerable client funds? What if we misidentify a long-lost sibling and inflict emotional damage? What if we publish incorrect information that causes someone to file inaccurate lineage papers and suffer the embarrassment of rejection? Errors-and-omissions insurance can provide coverage for sky-high legal costs. Other types of specific insurance coverage include libel in print and online, invasion of privacy, and

> Many companies will not allow independent contractors to work on the premises—nor will they sign a contract with one—without proof of liability-insurance coverage.

intellectual-property issues. Each business is unique. The challenge to our insurance underwriter is to understand as much as possible about the type of business we operate, the services we offer, and the nature of our clients.

Partnership or "key man" insurance
Although seldom considered by genealogists, "key man" insurance is common among small companies in other fields, to protect a business against the death or disability of an important, or key, employee. Both life insurance and disability insurance are available for employers. Unlike the other types of insurance discussed above, key man insurance is not a deductible business expense. The cash value of such a policy—as with ordinary life insurance—is also an asset of the business that can be borrowed against as value accumulates over time. The interest and dividends are not subject to income tax as long as the policy remains active.[19]

Obtaining coverage
Determining our insurance needs is a three-step process. First, we inventory the risks our business faces. Second, for each identified hazard or potential threat, we specifically list the items or conditions that need coverage—at least over and above the amounts already carried under our current homeowner's and vehicular policies. Finally, we formulate a research plan (this should sound familiar) to search for the best coverage at the lowest rates. Typically, this includes

- comparing the price of new equipment against our current insurance to ensure that the replacement coverage of our policy is accurate;

- reviewing the literature of the professional associations in which we hold memberships, to identify those that offer member insurance; and

- contacting a number of brokers who are familiar with insuring small businesses.

The FURTHER STUDY section of this chapter cites an excellent series by Dale D. Buss, who offers much other insight into the nuances of this important and often overlooked (until too late) aspect of business.

Personal resources

Clients are vital, yes; but they are (theoretically) replaceable. We are not.

Each of us is the most important person in our business. Clients are vital, yes; but they are (theoretically) replaceable. We are not. And there are no paid "sick days." To be a top-functioning executive of our company, we must pay attention to our physical and mental health. Solving research problems, writing books and articles, preparing classes and speeches, meeting performance deadlines, and maintaining constant responsiveness to clients are all energy-intensive activities. Coupled with the legal and financial demands of running our own business, these stresses are a potent "double whammy." Add to that the other aspects of our lives—spouses, children, house and tuition payments, etc.—and our physical and mental resources can seriously suffer. In one *APG Quarterly* issue, William B. Saxbe, a physician and Certified Genealogist, reminds us of important common-sense measures to protect our health.[20]

As we plan the structure of our genealogical business, wisdom (as well as Saxbe and other writers on the subject) suggests that the following practices be ingrained from Day 1:

- Regular physical activity, even if it's just walking around the block.

- Regular meals, with limited intake of caffeine, sweets, and fat—especially if we are not particularly active. Caffeine and sweets can set our nerves on edge, and an overly "fatty" lunch can make us feel sluggish and sleepy in the afternoon.

- Brief physical breaks every hour or two—especially when we work at the computer or microform reader. Vision problems, pinched nerves, and tedium are sure companions otherwise.

- A half-hour nap or meditation break amid long hours of intense concentration. Clearing our mind will make our performance sharper when we resume work.

- Membership in home-business support groups or a local chapter of a professional association. These forums introduce us to new people and stimulating exchanges of ideas.

- Weekly lunch dates with friends. Cabin fever is a real threat to those whose primary place of business is a home office.

- Periodic vacations—even if just for a long weekend. After hours of constant work, the batteries in our laptop computers need recharging. So do those in our minds and bodies.

- Regular attendance at national conferences and institutes. Our knowledge base needs to stay current. We need to network and keep our passion for genealogy alive.

- Regular, undivided attention to our family or friends. They are, after all, the most important support network that we have.

Summary Concepts

Planning a successful business structure that will shelter and nourish our professional dreams is, arguably, the most daunting task we face as genealogists. Legal regulations are many, and ramifications are serious. Yet we have no alternative but to comply—cautiously, carefully, and completely—if we pursue our entrepreneurial itch. The time invested initially in research and planning is steep, but the returns can be even more impressive. Whatever our goals and dreams as professional genealogists, they can be reached if sound business planning and management keep company with our determination to produce the highest-quality service and products.

Planning a successful business structure that will shelter and nourish our professional dreams is, arguably, the most daunting task we face as genealogists.

NOTES

1. Barbara Brabec, *Homemade Money: The Definitive Guide to Success in a Home Business* (Cincinnati, Ohio: Betterway Publications, 1997), 169–70.

2. Ken Malone, *Introduction to the Business Plan*, lecture syllabus (Santa Ana, California: Service Corps of Retired Executives, 1996), appendix A.

3. Service Corps of Retired Executives, *Checklist for Going into Business,* Management Aid Number MP12 (Washington: U.S. Small Business Administration, n.d.).

4. Rhonda M. Abrams, *The Successful Business Plan: Secrets & Strategies,* 2d edition (Grants Pass, Oregon: Oasis Press/PSI Research, 1993), 278.

5. Ibid., 278–79.

6. Santa Ana (California) Chapter, Service Corps of Retired Executives, *Business Plan Outline* (Santa Ana: SCORE, n.d.), a pamphlet.

STRUCTURING A BUSINESS

7. Henry B. Hoff, CPA, CG, FASG, "Taxes and the Professional Genealogist," *Association of Professional Genealogists* [APG] *Quarterly* 11 (December 1996): 110.

8. Bob Adams, *Streetwise Small Business Start-Up: Your Comprehensive Guide to Starting and Managing a Business* (Holbrook, Massachusetts: Adams Media Corp., 1996), 306.

9. Ibid., 335, for a lengthy list of types of articles found in a partnership agreement, etc.

10. Paul Adams, *155 Legal Do's (and Don'ts) for the Small Business* (New York: John Wiley and Sons, 1996), 23–24.

11. Ibid., 27.

12. Adams, *Streetwise Small Business*, 306.

13. Hoff, "Taxes and the Professional Genealogist," 110.

14. Adams, *155 Legal Do's (and Don'ts)*, 151–55; Adams, *Streetwise Small Business*, 348.

15. Brian Tracy, *Universal Laws of Success* (Franklin Lakes, New Jersey: Career Press, 1997), 87.

16. Jay Conrad Levinson, *Guerrilla Marketing Attack: New Strategies, Tactics, and Weapons for Winning Big Profits from Your Small Business* (Boston: Houghton Mifflin, 1989).

17. Adams, *Streetwise Small Business*, 382.

18. *The Entrepreneur Magazine Small Business Advisor* (New York: John Wiley and Sons, 1995), 113–20.

19. Mark R. Greene, *Insurance Checklist for Small Business,* Management Aid Number 2.018 (Washington: U.S. Small Business Administration, n.d.), unpaginated.

20. William B. Saxbe Jr., M.D., CG, "Live Right, Live Better, Live Longer: How To Be a Healthy Genealogist," *APG Quarterly* 12 (September 1997): 78–80.

21. Lido "Lee" A. Iacocca (1924–), American auto executive, quoted in Bob Phillips, *Phillips' Book of Great Thoughts, Funny Sayings* (Wheaton, Illinois: Tyndale House Publishers, 1993), 55.

> In the end, all business operations can be reduced to three words: people, product, and profits. People come first.
>
> —*Lee Iacocca*[21]

FURTHER STUDY

Bowman, Sally-Jo. "How to Weigh Your Options: Freelancing Full Time." *Writer's Digest* 76 (November 1996): 23–25.

———. "Launching Your Business." *Writer's Digest* 76 (December 1996): 36–39.

Burstiner, Irving. *The Small Business Handbook: A Comprehensive Guide to Starting and Running Your Own Business.* 3d edition. New York: Simon and Schuster, 1997.

Buss, Dale D. "Equipment Insurance: Coverage Against Catastrophes." *Home Office Computing* 15 (September 1996): 68–74.

———. "Health Insurance: Shop Before You Drop." *Home Office Computing* 15 (August 1996): 56–64.

———. "Liability Insurance: So Sue Me." *Home Office Computing* 15 (October 1996): 68–74.

Covello, Joseph A., and Brian J. Hazelgren. *Your First Business Plan: Learn the Critical Steps to Writing a Winning Business Plan.* 3d edition. Naperville, Illinois: Sourcebooks, 1995.

Edwards, Paul and Sarah. *Working from Home.* New York: Jeremy P. Tarcher/Putnam, 1999.

Kashuba, Melinda. "Small Business Alphabet Soup." *APG Quarterly* 10 (September 1995): 84–86.

Small Business Handbook: Laws, Regulations, and Technical Assistance Services. Washington: U.S. Department of Labor, 1993.

Smalloffice.com: From the Editors of Home Office Computing/Small Business Computing. Website <www.smalloffice.com>. This site offers, among much else, numerous timely articles from back issues of both magazine sponsors.

Turner, Marcia Layton. *The Unofficial Guide to Starting a Small Business.* New York: Macmillan, 1999.

U.S. Small Business Administration. *Business Plan for Small Service Firms.* Management Aid No. MP11/2.022. Washington: U.S. Government Printing Office, undated leaflet.

Waymon, Lynne. *Starting and Managing a Business from Your Home.* Washington: U.S. Small Business Administration, 1986.

10

**SETTING
REALISTIC FEES**

Keynotes

Setting Realistic Fees

by Sandra Hargreaves Luebking

"As to reward, my profession is its own reward; but you are at liberty to defray whatever expenses I may be put to, at the time which suits you best." So said Sherlock Holmes to a new client as he began "The Case of the Speckled Band."[1]

Mr. Holmes's generosity is stirring, but our logic is affronted by his apparent inattention to the most elementary of business details: establishing a fee system. Perhaps Sherlock has no need of income or does not realize that profit is essential to maintain his practice. He does appear to recognize the value of recovering expenses. But leaving the time of reimbursement to the client's discretion seems somewhat risky, even in the nineteenth century.

Some of us in the field of genealogy manage twentieth-century research practices in this very manner. We resist the idea of profiting from work we enjoy or see no need to recoup costs of doing business when we are "only working out of our own home." We may dislike collecting fees. Or, perhaps, we are unsure of how to arrive at a fair recompense. In short, we are too often uncomfortable imposing any financial structure on our work and would quite prefer to have remuneration managed by someone else—perhaps a Dr. Watson or a Mrs. Hudson.

This is a luxury few of us can afford. Most of us need income, even for work we enjoy. The U.S. Internal Revenue Service agrees, according to Certified Public Accountant Frank T. Hales. The IRS Code "specifies that no deduction will be allowed with respect to an activity unless the activity is engaged in for profit." Hales encourages us to write a plan of operation and profit intent. "If the business is not established from the beginning to make a profit, it is considered a hobby, and no deduction is allowed for normal operating expenses in excess of income."[2]

Establishing a fee system is not only good business sense, it is a signal to the IRS. How do we develop a schedule that provides the needed income without pricing services beyond the reach of potential clients? A fee-setting formula, patterned after that used in other service occupations, will help us establish a rate that is both reasonable and realistic. This chapter focuses upon the concerns of genealogists who conduct client research, edit, or perform desktop publishing services and similar work that is billed by the hour. (In contrast, genealogists who teach or lecture commonly find that stipends for those activities are set by the sponsoring organizations and are seldom commensurate with the hours invested. As in many professions, the resulting time deficit for these activities is commonly charged to "advertising costs" or "professional contributions."[3])

> The Internal Revenue Code specifies that no deduction will be allowed with respect to an activity unless the activity is engaged in for profit.
>
> —*Frank T. Hales*, CPA

The Formulas and the Process

The basic formulas for setting a fee are simple: (1) *Salary + Expenses + Profit = Targeted Income;* and (2) *Targeted Income ÷ Billable Hours = Hourly Fee.* The process is a bit more complex, but it breaks down into six steps.

SETTING REALISTIC FEES

1. *Identify annual salary need.*
   Our beginning figure is the amount of money we must have to achieve or maintain our desired standard of living.

2. *Determine annual expenses.*
   Expenses are our costs to run an office, maintain our professional skills, and conduct research.

3. *Establish profit margin.*
   Profit, over and above wages, provides us with fuel and a safety net for a growing practice.

4. *Determine billable hours.*
   Billable hours are those we actually spend in client work. This number (averaged daily, weekly, or monthly) determines our hourly fee.

5. *Apply the formula and divide.*
   (Salary + Expenses + Profit) ÷ Billable Hours = Hourly Fee.

6. *Evaluate this figure.*
   After measuring the fee against basic evaluators, we decide upon adjustments.

Each of these several steps involves numerous considerations.

Identifying salary needs

Our fee system originates with a simple question: what do we need or want to earn annually, before taxes? If we support a family, our income needs may be greater than those of a retiree who is supplementing a pension. If we have a single, long-range goal, as did the Chicago researcher who sent three daughters through college almost simultaneously, our annual salary might be based on, say, triple tuition. Taking our needs and desires into consideration, we can arrive at an annual figure. Is it $10,000? $50,000? $80,000? More?

If we haven't a clue as to an income goal, we might investigate annual salaries for comparable professions. What is a typical income for title searchers in our area? What do detectives earn? How much do attorneys pay their paralegals? We may also check income survey reports available at numerous Internet sites worldwide—where fees are frequently broken down by locale and educational background, as well as job title. Surveys posted in mid-1998, for example, reported average hourly rates of $40 to $80 for U.S. paralegals (up to $150 in California and Hawaii).[4] Among other posted survey results for consultants were the following average annual pre-tax incomes for 1998–2000: graphic designers, at a median of $41,000–$45,000; technical writers at an average advertised salary of $54,460 or $32.99 hourly on a contract basis; and consultants of all types at a median $61,000–$75,000.[5] The message is clear; we should not underestimate our income potential.

Calculating expenses

After establishing salary needs, we must identify the annual expenses of a research practice. Expenses fall into two categories: indirect costs and direct costs.

Our fee system originates with a simple question: what do we need or want to earn annually, before taxes?

194

INDIRECT COSTS

This set of expenses covers the equipment, products, or professional counsel that enables us to provide service or goods. Such costs are often termed *overhead*. An estimate of indirect expenses begins with such basics as office supplies and the printing of our business cards and stationery. To this, we must add personal items adapted to client use—perhaps office equipment, furniture, and utility bills. While we would undoubtedly acquire some such items to pursue genealogy as a hobby, the usage becomes considerably greater once genealogy becomes a professional practice. The number of file cabinets, the amount of space needed to house them, the size of hard drives on our computer, and the amount of energy used to operate our equipment for longer hours—all surge significantly as we move from the hobby to the professional phase. A portion of these increased operational and replacement costs becomes part of our business expenses.

As professionals, we also must anticipate purchases that may become necessary as our business grows. While we may not yet foresee a need for a portable paper shredder or an automatic call router, we should find value in a modem, an answering machine, and at least one dedicated business-communications line. We will consider specialized computer software and a laser printer to produce "high-tech" family charts as well as professional-quality reports, ads, and perhaps publications. Our goal is to provide the best research and support services possible, including state-of-the-art data retrieval, word processing, and even graphics.

Indirect costs will include some less obvious payouts, as shown in figure 11. We should consider membership dues that stem from our business status—such as those for our local chapters and national associations of professional genealogists—or certification and licensing fees. We compute our outlay for the last national conference, the one where we attended lectures on writing business reports or maintaining proper tax records, rather than topics of personal research interest. Are our bookshelves laden with works such as this manual, purchased to help us professionally? These are all business expenses. Marketing, which is critical to every enterprise, is a support cost. Management experts recommend that one-third of our fee be used to attract new business. This figure must be added to our expenses.

Yet another significant indirect cost is our benefits package. Because we are self-employed, we must provide our own health and disability insurance, sick-leave support, vacation pay, and retirement fund—none of which comes cheaply. One New York researcher lamented to the *APG Quarterly* that she paid $3,000 a year for medical-insurance premiums through a group plan (a single-person policy), pushing her hourly fee well beyond the $20 some of her colleagues then charged. "At $20 per hour, I'd have to work and bill for 150 hours just to pay these premiums," she reported.[6] On reflection, at that rate she would have to work considerably more hours than 150 to clear the needed $3,000, after expenses and income and other taxes have been deducted.

DIRECT COSTS

Direct costs are the easily identifiable charges incurred as we provide a service or

---

FIG. 11
COMMON INDIRECT COSTS TO CONSIDER WHEN COMPUTING EXPENSES

Equipment:
Answering machine
Cellular phone
Computer
Copy machine
Fax machine
Microfilm/fiche reader
Modem
Pager
Printer
Scanner

Other office costs:
Box rental
Computer software
Desks/file cabinets
Equipment maintenance
Office cleaning/decorating
Office supplies
Printing/photography
Postage
Rent or mortgage
Telephone/online services
Utilities

Professional costs:
Advertising
Legal/financial counsel

Other costs:
Auto/maintenance
Books/subscriptions
Client entertainment
Conferences/courses
Insurance
    disability/health
    liability
    life
    property
    vehicle
Legal/financial counseling
Membership dues
Retirement pay
Self-employment taxes
Sick-leave pay
Vacation pay
Workers' compensation

FIG. 12

COMMON DIRECT COSTS (WHICH MAY OR MAY NOT BE ITEMIZED FOR CLIENT)

Postal fees:
Express mail
Foreign postage
Bulky package charges

Travel costs:
Meals for overnight trips
Mileage to distant sites
Motel/hotel expenses
Parking/transit fees

Other costs:
Access fees
Clerk/notary fees
Copies on site
Fax charges
Film/book rentals
Other user fees
Toll calls

product to our clients. Some—such as excess postage, copy charges, long-distance calls, and certificate fees—may be billed to the client whose request generated them. When billed separately from our hourly rate, these items are not computed in our cost of doing business (insofar as calculating our hourly fee, although those expenses certainly would be computed at tax time). Other direct costs may be difficult to allocate to a single client—such as mileage, parking, and access fees at research sites when we undertake multiple projects.

One option is to factor these charges and bill a portion directly to each of several clients. Or we can incorporate these amounts into our general expenses, so that the total cost is shared by all clients paying the hourly rate. Examples are transportation outlays, which can amount to a hefty $20–$30 per day for an urban-based searcher, and such routine activities as the copying of client reports for our own files. (See figure 12 for other similar expenses.) If our standard operating procedure is to spread nonallocated expenses among our clients, these charges become part of our base cost of doing business.

Indirect and direct costs not billed as separate items to a client compose our expenses. When added to our salary figure, we have two of the three components of our fee-setting formula. The third is profit.

Setting a profit margin

Yes, Sherlock, not only do we need a salary, we need a profit. Profit is our reward for the risk of being self-employed, as opposed to collecting a guaranteed paycheck each week. Profit enables us to upgrade our services and equipment, thereby maintaining a high level of performance. Profit makes our business grow. Profit—not salary—is funneled back into the business, allowing us to keep pace with future client demands.

Most service-provider businesses allow from 10 to 20 percent of the fee for a profit factor. If our wages and expenses total $40,000 annually, a 20 percent profit would bring the annual amount to $48,000. These three components, *Salary + Expenses + Profit,* are equal to the amount of money our research practice must generate every year. That figure, divided by the number of billable hours available to us, will dictate the necessary hourly fee.

Determining billable hours

Billable hours are those hours we charge to a client. Most professionals are seldom able to bill for a forty-hour week. Instead, large amounts of time are spent in nonbillable activities. Some of these tasks may eventually generate income: the hours spent marketing our services, answering research inquiries, reading (and writing for) journals, preparing lectures and audiovisuals, networking, or attending to administrative details. Often in genealogy, nonbillable time also includes volunteer work that has little or no direct client potential. In the latest survey conducted by the Board for Certification of Genealogists (BCG), respondents who identified themselves as full-time professionals reported working only 20–30 billable hours per week and another 14–20 nonbillable/volunteer hours. (Significant variations were reported by those who were certified and those who were not—with those holding dual certifications logging the maximum for both billable and nonbillable hours.)[7]

If we are committed to managing a business in a professional manner, we must look seriously at volunteer activities. We must be realistic about the actual number of hours absorbed by those organizational offices, those unpaid editorships, or those teaching or consulting positions that carry no compensation. While these opportunities may provide us with enormous educational and goodwill benefits, they drain time and energy from our business pursuits.

Some activities delude us. They pay stipends that are a reliable source of income, but they do not adequately compensate for the time taken from our business. One national organization provides $11,000 as an annual stipend for editing its quarterly. This may seem attractive until we compute the hours required for sorting and responding to mail; soliciting, fact checking, and editing manuscripts; and data entry and proofreading. Careful timekeeping shows that the $11,000 annual stipend equates to under $3 per hour—for work that does not directly produce clients.

> Some activities delude us. They pay stipends that are a reliable source of income, but they do not adequately compensate for the time taken from our business.

A professional genealogist may enjoy the work and satisfaction of contributing to the field. But if the post requires ten hours per week that could be billed at $35 each, our professional is losing $350 per week of potential income (ten billable hours). Meanwhile, operational costs may remain the same and may even be increased by the extra tasks. It is unlikely that any business could survive this degree of volunteer commitment.

As professionals, we determine our volunteer time. Perhaps we need to "just say no" or set more restrictions. This may mean, for example, speaking without charge to just one group every other month, or being an officer in only one or two organizations each year. Once our limit is met, then we do no more.[8] Meanwhile, we must adjust our time and rates to compensate for the resulting nonbillable hours.

Applying the formula

Remember the formulas? *Salary + Expenses + Profit = Targeted Income* and *Targeted Income ÷ Billable Hours = Hourly Fee?* To apply the elements, we might consider these two representative (but fictional) examples:

Case One

As a new professional, Lemuel Samuels determines that he needs a pretax salary from genealogy of $19,000 to supplement a retirement pension. Lemuel estimates that his annual expenses will be $5,500 in the first year; to this $24,500, he adds the 20 percent profit he must reinvest in his business each year to keep it viable. The annual pretax income that his business must generate is $29,400.

Next, Lemuel determines the number of billable hours he can spend per week at business activities. Due to many commitments, he decides that ten hours a week, fifty weeks a year, is realistic. Dividing his pretax income need of $29,400 by 500 billable hours gives Lemuel the hourly fee he must charge: roughly $60.

While Lemuel mulls the prospect of charging $60 per hour, let's visit Nola Bonaparte as she establishes her fee.

Case Two

Nola, having no supplemental income and no dependents, requires $34,000 in annual pretax wages. Her costs of doing business are greater than Lemuel's for two reasons. First, she resides in an urban area where the costs of rent, products, and transportation—as well as photocopies and communications—are far more than in Lemuel's community. Second, Nola intends to work full time, which will multiply her expenses.

All things considered, Nola arrives at a "costs" figure of $14,000. When she adds a 20 percent profit to wages and expenses ([$34,000 + $14,000 = $48,000] x .20), she finds an annual income requirement of $57,600. Although Nola intends to work full-time at genealogy, she has studied the BCG survey and projects that no more than thirty weekly hours can be considered billable time—particularly during her first year of business, in which she will be occupied with learning effective management skills and establishing office routines.

Nola also knows she cannot realistically plan to produce this amount of billable work for all fifty-two weeks a year. Allowing for a one-week vacation and three weeks for facility closures, holidays, and possible illness, Nola determines that 48 weeks times 30 hours gives her 1,440 billable hours per year. That number, divided into the $57,600 annual income, results in an hourly fee of $40.

Evaluating the results

Should either fee surprise us? Do we worry that it may scare away clients? Before we slash it in panic, we should consider the words of *Working from Home* authors Paul and Sarah Edwards: "Underpricing is one of the most frequent mistakes home-based businesses make."[9]

Underpricing often results from a misconception of what people will pay. We may find it difficult to charge for work we enjoy doing, or perhaps we underrate our own talents. But we should consider this: clients do not pay us to simply log research time or type reports. They pay also for the time, effort, and expense we have invested in developing the expertise we apply to their problems. They hire us to work more quickly and more skillfully than they could. It is our knowledge, skill, and efficiency—as well as time—that we are selling. Combined, that is our product.

Wisdom suggests that we also measure our fee against those of others in our specialty and geographic area. For this comparison, we choose others who are similarly competent and professional in the field of genealogy. But we use this guideline cautiously. Our colleagues may subsidize their businesses by other means, making it unrealistic for us to match their low prices. That attempt might leave us financially strapped. We should consider, too, the psychological consequences of fee dropping. Consultant and author Howard Shenson states, "Setting your fees too low conveys the message that you don't value your services adequately. It may also communicate that you may not be able to provide quality."[10]

Clients do not pay us to simply log research time or type reports. They pay also for the time, effort, and expense we have invested in developing the expertise we apply to their problems.

If we simply cannot justify the fee we have calculated, what are our options?

- We can adjust our annual income (a tricky matter if our wage was based on need rather than want).
- We can reduce our costs (do we absolutely need that fax machine?).
- We can increase our billable hours, thereby decreasing the cost per hour (which may mean giving up some volunteer activities we enjoy).

Once our hourly fee is set, we continue to test it as our business evolves. Our income needs may change or our expenses may increase. Our profit margin, sufficient at first, may become inadequate to maintain a high level of service. Fee setting is not a once-in-a-lifetime decision; rather, it is an ongoing process. A realistic hourly rate reflects our ability, area conditions, client demand, and a wide range of other changing factors. Most important, the hourly fee we charge reflects the fee-setting formula: *Salary + Expenses + Profit = Targeted Income.*

Administrative Policies

Now that we have arrived at a fee, we will need to examine some practical means of administering several variables—particularly advances, retainers, refunds, and special fees for out-of-ordinary circumstances. Many home-based service providers find fiscal sanity in this credit policy: "100% down, no monthly payments!"[11] Whether we agree or not, retainers and advances can simplify money management. To clarify the difference: *Retainers* are the initial fees that clients pay to secure the services of professionals. *Advances* are moneys accepted for ongoing services, once the initial contract has been met.

Our fee policy should be defined in our first response to research inquiries. That policy should specify a total number of hours for research, evaluation, and preparation of the client's report. (Because we always include report-preparation time in our billing statements, it is well to acquaint prospective clients with this practice before their projects are under way.) We should be firm and consistent in our requests for retainers and advances. We also should allow ourselves time not only to receive and deposit a payment but also to have the check clear the client's bank. The time and costs saved in collections are well worth losing a few prospects who may resist prepayment. Occasionally, potential clients ask for exceptions, citing a need for immediate work. They assure us the fee will be sent promptly upon receipt of the report. Rather than compromise our policy, we might encourage them to send a cashier's check or money order via overnight mail.

> Our fee policy should be defined in our first response to research inquiries.

Retainers

Retainers are an accepted business practice—particularly, though not exclusively, for those engaged in freelance activities. Retainers insure that the initial costs of a project are met without resorting to collection procedures. Retainers provide a cash flow to keep our business healthy. The amount we set depends on our hourly fee and the nature of the assignment. By way of example, we might consider another pair of hypothetical situations:

Case One

We receive an inquiry from a client who has collected no records. Our response may read, "The hourly rate is $40 for research and report preparation. An initial retainer of $200 is required to begin work. This provides you with three to four hours of research in selected sources and a report that will include recommendations for future action. Should you decide to continue the research, you may authorize four- to eight-hour increments, making advance payments for each increment."

Case Two

An inquiry comes from a potential client whose prior research led to the proverbial brick wall. Such projects justify larger retainers, because they require evaluation of materials already collected by the clients and the preparation of analytical reports that could take many hours. Thus, our response might read, "The hourly fee is $50 for research and report preparation. A $500 retainer is required to evaluate research performed by you or others, along with copies of all documents you have acquired. A detailed report will summarize the evaluation and present options for extending the line. Should the analysis not require the full advance, the remainder will be credited toward future research."

Advances

Once the retainer has been used, we may or may not wish to request advances for ongoing work. Typically, the choice depends upon the length of time authorized and the total fee that is at risk. Commissions for two to three hours, from a repeat client, might be handled by sending a bill with the report. If the client authorizes ten hours, let us say, prudence suggests an advance—perhaps 50 percent of the authorized time—before we continue.

If the nature of that ten-hour assignment requires short blocks of work— perhaps two to three hours—then we might report and bill at regular intervals, applying any balance or remainder to the final report. This is our protection against mounting costs that may not be reimbursed. It also provides a more practical payment plan for our client, who may authorize ten hours without the full realization that, at $40–$50 per hour, he or she is responsible for a $400–$500 payment—plus expenses.

If our assignment is one of a problem-solving nature that requires extensive research and correlation of evidence before a report can be made on a single research segment, then a retainer and advances become even more imperative. In such complex cases, with ongoing clients, many genealogists adopt a split-fee approach. They request an advance of half the estimated fee, plus anticipated expenses, with the remainder payable upon receipt of the report.

Small-job rates

Woe unto us if we lower our hourly fee for what appears to be a quick or simple

Woe unto us if we lower our hourly fee for what appears to be a quick or simple search!

search! The client who wants us to "just copy a page from a book" or "obtain just one death certificate" is often the client who has an incorrect title, page number, or date of demise. These seemingly easy requests can absorb billable time that should be earning our usual fee. We may reasonably offer a small-job rate for searches that do take under one hour. But this fee should never be less than one hour's minimum. Even on a search of ten minutes, a standard compensation of one hour at our usual fee is necessary to help defray the costs of doing business—from our initial reading of the client's letter of inquiry, to our response, to the client's letter of authorization (with more ancestral detail for us to study), to our fulfillment of the request, and then our final response, plus postage. A small-job assignment should be paid for in advance.

Refunds

Refunding is a reasonable option when a project has absorbed more than one hour but less time than was authorized. Many professionals find it best to explain in a cover letter or billing statement attached to the final report, "The research agreed upon is now completed. There remains a credit on your account of $25.95. This may be applied to future research or a refund will be sent in thirty days, as you instruct." If instructions are not received, we send the refund as stated. Our policy may be to refund only unused portions of advances, not retainers. If this is our intent, we should make that clear in our initial contract, letter, or e-mail response to the client's inquiry about our services.

Summary Concepts

The fee-setting formulas *Salary + Expenses + Profit = Targeted Income* and *Targeted Income ÷ Billable Hours = Hourly Fee* are basic to every professional practice. Applying that formula and judiciously managing retainers, advances, small-job fees, and refunds are all essential to establishing and maintaining a viable research business. Although we may sometimes wish to provide our services free, as did Sherlock Holmes, reality dictates otherwise. To operate in a professional and businesslike manner, we must devise a fee system that is fair to our clients, ourselves, and our profession.

> To operate in a professional and businesslike manner, we must devise a fee system that is fair to our clients, ourselves, and our profession.

NOTES

1. Sir Arthur Conan Doyle, *The Adventures of Sherlock Holmes* (Hertfordshire, England: Wordsworth Editions, 1995), 215.
2. Frank T. Hales, "Good Record Keeping: The Key to a Successful, Tax-Wise Business," *Association of Professional Genealogists [APG] Quarterly* 6 (Winter 1991): 87–89.
3. A reality check for those who lecture can be found in Elizabeth Shown Mills, "Economics of Genealogical Lecturing," *Federation of Genealogical Societies Forum* 3 (Summer 1991): 4–7. While the figures for both income and expenses are out-of-date, the ratio between them and the number of hours invested remains starkly realistic.

SETTING REALISTIC FEES

Rule No. 1:
Never lose money.

Rule No. 2:
Never forget Rule No. 1.

—*Warren Buffett*[12]

4. Website, *National Federation of Paralegal Associations: Survey* <www. paralegals.org>, downloaded 10 March 1998 and 11 November 2000; the 1998 survey provided more breakdowns.

5. Websites, *Salary Zone: The Compensation Resource for Internet Professionals* <www. zdnet.com/enterprise/salaryzone/>, and *Salary Ticker* <www.computerjobs.com/content/ticker>, downloaded 11 November 2000. Printed sources of guidance on fee-setting vary widely. Many journals published by professional organizations in other fields also report surveys of relevance to the genealogist. For example, those who offer editorial services might study rates published periodically by the *National Association of Desktop Publishers Journal,* whose categories include editing and proofreading as well as graphics work.

6. Eileen Polakoff, responding to the "Question of the Quarter: Earning a Living," *APG Quarterly* 6 (Winter 1991): 101.

7. Elizabeth Shown Mills, "Professionalism and Fees: BCG Survey Results," *OnBoard* [educational newsletter of the Board for Certification of Genealogists] 3 (January 1997): 3.

8. Desmond Walls Allen, "Saying No," *APG Quarterly* 7 (June 1992): 20.

9. Paul and Sarah Edwards, *Working from Home: Everything You Need to Know About Living and Working under the Same Roof* (Los Angeles: Jeremy P. Tarcher, 1997), 123.

10. Howard L. Shenson, *The Contract and Fee-Setting Guide for Consultants and Professionals* (New York: John Wiley and Sons with University Associates, 1996), 1.

11. Bernard Kamoroff, *Small-Time Operator: How to Start Your Own Small Business, Keep Your Books, Pay Your Taxes, & Stay Out of Trouble!,* rev. edition (Willits, California: Bell Springs Publishing, 1996), 50.

12. Warren Buffett (1930–), American investor and financier, quoted in Ted Goodman, ed., *The Forbes Book of Business Quotations: 14,173 Thoughts on the Business of Life* (New York: Black Dog & Leventhal Publishers, 1997), 583.

FURTHER STUDY

Billingsley, Carolyn Earle. "Billing the Client." *APG Quarterly* 8 (December 1993): 87.

———. "Business or Pleasure?" *Professional Genealogists of Arkansas, Inc., Newsletter* 4 (November 1991): 9.

"Fees: Responses to the Fall 1990 Question of the Quarter." *APG Quarterly* 6 (Spring 1991): 8–16. Although the rates are now considerably dated, the issues and views are still quite relevant.

"Financial Matters: Are Your Rates Too Low? Find Out How to Evaluate Your Services." Website <www.smalloffice.com/miser/archive>, consulted 28 January 2000.

"How to Price Your Products and Services." U.S. Small Business Association website <www.sba. gov/SCORE/ca/pricing.html>, consulted 28 January 2000

Harper, Stephen C. *The McGraw-Hill Guide to Starting Your Own Business: A Step-By-Step Blueprint for the First-Time Entrepreneur.* New York: McGraw-Hill, 1991.

Mills, Elizabeth Shown. "Making a Living at Genealogy: Analyzing Our Problems and Our Options." *APG Quarterly* 7 (December 1992): 87–91.

Mississippi State University Cooperative Extension Service website. "FAQ2: How Do I Price My Product and Services?" <www.ext.msstate.edu/fce/homebus/q2.html>, consulted 28 January 2000.

Remington, Gordon L. "Will Work for Food: Economic Realities of Subcontracting in Salt Lake City." *APG Quarterly* 7 (June 1992): 31–37.

Rising, Marsha Hoffman. "Is There Any Such Thing as a Professional Hobbyist?" *APG Quarterly* 8 (March 1993): 3–6.

Rowe, Barbara, and Alma J. Owen. *Pricing for Profit.* West Lafayette, Indiana: Purdue University, 1996.

Stern, Linda. *Money-Smart Secrets of the Self-Employed.* New York: Random House, 1997.

———. "Why Give It Away?" *Home Office Computing* (February 1994): 24.

Warren, Paula Stuart, and James W. Warren. "Communicating with Clients: The Information and Rate Sheet." *APG Quarterly* 7 (June 1992): 42–44.

11

**MARKETING
STRATEGIES**

MARKETING STRATEGIES

Keynotes

MARKETING STRATEGIES

Keynotes (cont.)

Marketing Strategies

by Elizabeth Kelley Kerstens, CGRS

Marketing is a mystery to many of us in the small-business world. When we took the plunge and hung that proverbial shingle, few of us realized the multitude of business skills needed to keep even the smallest venture viable—accounting, management, marketing, purchasing, and tax planning, just to name a few. Some professional genealogists have the luxury of turning away clients, while the rest of us scratch our heads trying to figure out how these lucky few are so successful. Although this chapter does not include an analysis of how specific genealogists become overwhelmed with commissions and sales, it is reasonable to speculate one likely way: effective marketing. Some established professionals may never have spent one marketing dollar; their practices depend on hard-earned and well-deserved reputations that foster word-of-mouth advertising—a business's best friend. Others have used various approaches to build name recognition, such as placing advertisements in carefully targeted publications (the ones they know are regularly read by their desired clientele).

So how do we get from here to there? This chapter covers the basics of putting together a marketing program for a small genealogical practice or specialty trade. Each of us will tailor the information to fit our particular situation. Marketing can be as complicated or as simple as we want to make it. Yet we cannot overlook the importance of advertising and professional promotion. Family history has become a competitive industry, with many interests tugging at the genealogical dollars available. Our creativity and innovation may be the difference between our success and failure in this marketplace.

Marketing Plans

A marketing plan is a well-thought-out blueprint for how we implement advertising techniques during a specified period, such as a calendar year. It should be part of our overall business plan. (We *do* have one of those by now, don't we?) As with most undertakings, tools exist to help us start. Myriad books at libraries and bookstores contain sample strategies.[1] Software programs can walk us through the logistics.[2] An Internet search points to various organizations that provide free marketing advice—such as the Mississippi State University Cooperative Extension Service[3] and the Small Business Administration.[4]

Is all this *really* necessary? If our livelihood depends on the success of our business, a marketing plan is crucial! Creating it compels us to focus on the scope of our activities. It makes us analyze and define our target clients. It forces us to discover the *best methods* for marketing our specific products or services. And it requires us to prepare a workable *budget*.[5] Without a blueprint, our advertising efforts will be haphazard at best and probably misdirected. So, yes, we take the time to create a plan and we stick to it, confident that we will be rewarded in the long run.

If our livelihood depends on the success of our business, a marketing plan is crucial! Without a blueprint, our advertising will be haphazard at best and probably misdirected.

Specialization

Whether we conduct research, lecture, teach, or pursue a less traditional career in genealogy, we need a specialization. If we are not already expert in a geographic area, ethnic group, specific repository, or certain type of records, attaining that expertise is a first priority. Generalists are a dime a dozen. As specialists, we can carve a niche for ourselves and define a specific population that is interested in our services or products.

That niche may already be apparent. Perhaps we are fascinated with land records and the mountains of information they contain. We well know the intracacies of the resources available in our locale and are ready to establish ourselves as "the land-record expert in [*name it*]." Or we have a knack for compiling lineage-application papers that are routinely approved. That's our niche! That's where we want to concentrate our efforts.

The flip side of the niche dilemma is determining whether there are sufficient consumers who need our services. If we narrow our specialty so much that we appeal to just a handful of people, both now and in the foreseeable future, our business prospects dim. "People buy results, not products" is a common adage.[6] Although researchers can never promise that a problem will be solved, clients still buy the results of our search. Even if we do advertise a product, our customers are not likely to buy the product to sit on their shelves; they are paying for the results that our product might help them achieve. Thus, our offering has to provide a perceived value to the consumer, or our message will be lost in the cacophony of marketing appeals directed at them daily.

To determine our niche, we might ask ourselves the following questions:

- What facet of genealogy most intrigues me?
- In what areas am I willing to constantly learn and grow?
- What type of activity has the potential to bring in repeat business?
- Is there a demand for what I would like to do?
- What can I offer consumers that no one else can?
- Who is my competition?
- Who are my potential clients or customers?

> Generalists are a dime a dozen. As specialists, we can carve a niche for ourselves and define a specific population that is interested in our services or products.

Image

Every successful entrepreneur has a business identity. This can be as simple as using our name and a phrase that describes our activity: for example, *Donald MacDougal, Research Down Under*. Or, we can choose a business name that tells our target market what our business sells: *Worldwide Maps*. It is wise to spend the time and a little extra money on developing an attractive logo that uniquely symbolizes what we plan to offer. Both logos and business names foster recognition through multiple exposures. While we're creating our business image, we also think about other tangibles and intangibles associated with it.

STATIONERY

What type of stationery will we use for our business cards, envelopes, and letterhead?

We choose this carefully to ensure that color and quality convey the image we are building. Recycled paper may be perfect for an "earth-friendly" business, but it may not have the professional appearance we seek. What typeface will we use on our communications? All our materials should use one font family. Obviously, cartoon letters are not a good choice, but a distinctive typeface sets us apart from the crowd. We want to present a unique, unified, professional, and well-planned image on all products that go to our target audience.

SELLING POINTS

What are our best qualities? Let's list our assets on a piece of paper and tape it to our computer. Then we can use items from the list as often as possible in all our marketing messages and materials—including stationery. For instance, what makes us the local expert on land records? How many years of experience do we have with these records? Are we certified or accredited? What formal or informal training have we received in our niche area? Are we stable—that is, will we continue to live in the same geographic area for the foreseeable future? What kind of access do we have to the pertinent records? If we live in Montana but claim to be an expert on Nova Scotia, how can we support that claim and how can we access the necessary records on a timely and cost-efficient basis? What success *have* we had in these records? How do we publicly document that success?

SERVICE LEVEL

What type and level of service can we accurately advertise? Customer service is one of the most important aspects of a viable business. We have to determine how we will provide that service and whether we can sustain the type of patron we seek with the service we promise. For instance, if our cover letter to prospective clients assures them that they will receive their heraldic artwork within two weeks of receiving their down payment, will we be able to follow up on that claim? Promising more than we can deliver is a surefire way to alienate clients.

Competition

Who else is active in our specialty? What do they offer—or not offer—our potential clients? Researching our competition is crucial to a successful marketing program. If we live in Salt Lake City and we advertise general research services, we will be trying to attract the same clients as a legion of other professionals doing research at the Family History Library. But if that's where we live and what we do, we need to conduct *business* research to position ourselves competitively. This calls for creativity, but we are careful to avoid any approach that hints of impropriety. Our competitors are our colleagues as well; we treat them as honestly and openly as we want them to treat us.

Researching our competition is crucial to a successful marketing program. But we are careful to avoid any approach that hints of impropriety.

As a rule, professionals in most fields do not publish their fees, do not provide annual reports to the public, and do not run publicly traded companies. Thus, there are few statistics available of the type that could be studied for more commercial businesses. Yet other approaches can be used:

- We study the ads of our competitors to see what—not necessarily how—they advertise. We cannot determine the success of any advertising campaign by just looking at ads, but we should be able to identify the areas in which our competitors specialize. Then we use this information to find ourselves a niche that is not already crowded.

- We study the current rosters of the Association of Professional Genealogists (APG), the Board for Certification of Genealogists (BCG), the Genealogical Speaker's Guild (GSG), and others available in our geographic area.[7] We identify competition by specialty and locale and then analyze their genealogical credentials and activities, educational background, and other relevant data—taking care to appraise this as impartially as would a client who knows none of us.

- We study genealogical periodicals for accomplishments by these colleagues. This includes the quarterly publications of the three organizations above,[8] as well as other national-level magazines and newsletters. All carry news of members. Then we extend the search to the major genealogical journals, where our competition may be putting their success stories into print as powerful proof of their abilities.

- We surf the Internet. Many genealogists have websites. Some list their services with commercial directories that are fee based, without criteria. Others are membership based—such as the APG, BCG, and GSG online rosters—or complimentary, such as *Cyndi's List of Genealogy Sites on the Internet: Professional Researchers, Volunteers, and Other Research Services*.[9] We should not worry much about the services offered by those who offer free "lookups." We cannot compete with their "prices," so they are not our competitors. Yet it is obvious that our qualifications and our publicity have to convince the market of the value of paying for our services.

Position

Within our personal universe, the people we know can probably describe us in a variety of ways. We may be someone's spouse, neighbor, or teacher. Each of these relationships conjures up stereotypical images. We also have the ability to influence how we are perceived, or *positioned,* in a relationship: we may introduce ourselves as "Mark's *favorite* sister" or "Jane's *long-term* protégée." The same holds true in the business world. One software firm, for example, positions its product as "the no. 1 selling genealogy software." It bases that slogan on sales figures. Another major product does not lead in sales but positions itself as "the easiest and fastest software," on the basis of testimonials and reviews by leading genealogists.

So what is our business position in relation to our competition? Are we the "only Certified Genealogist in Newcastle"? Are we the only area specialist who can (or cares to) read the obsolete penmanship of our region's earliest records? Even a casual scan of print and electronic advertising turns up numerous genealogists consciously positioning themselves in particular niches with slogans that promise "prompt retrieval of federal records" or "thoroughness you can trust," and such business names as *Census Searches—Today!*

Marketing guru Alexander Hiam suggests a three-step process for positioning our business:[10]

> Positioning is not about what you are, but how people see you, and how they see you in context.
>
> —*Allan H. Rouse*[11]

1. *We select our target group of clients.* They may belong to a specific ethnic group, or fall between certain ages, or seek membership in a particular lineage society. Whichever, we need to define them and divide them into manageable segments for more effective marketing.

2. *We design our positioning strategy.* Whether we contrast our business against our competitors or emphasize a unique consumer benefit, we succinctly state that position. Hiam advises, "Think of the positioning statement as a marketing plan so compact that [we] can put it on a scrap of paper and keep it in [our] wallet."[12]

3. *We capture that position through our marketing program.* All elements of our advertising must incorporate our positioning strategy in order for our business to gain recognition in the consciousness of our target clients.

Marketing Tools

Business cards

Among genealogical professionals, a business card is frequently the sole marketing tool. With a little effort, it will be just the first item in our tool kit. Essential elements of any business card are

- business name and/or individual name,
- mailing address,
- telephone and fax numbers (if applicable), and
- e-mail address (if applicable).

Additional elements might include our

- logo,
- positioning statement, and
- Internet address.

These elements can be arranged in any number of effective designs within the 2-by-3½-inch bounds of the standard business card. But we don't stop there! The card has a back side that is prime real estate, rarely used. We should resist the temptation to put *essential elements* on the back, so that larger print can be used on the front—after all, cards are tiny and type that is not proportionately small creates an unprofessional, "homemade" look. Instead, we use the back for special offers—perhaps a booth number at a conference where the cards are to be distributed, or a list of our services, or a miniature view of our home page. We can also make cards for even more specific occasions. For example, if we speak to a group about the pros and cons of secondary research using CD-ROMs, we might offer a limited-time discount on a quality search of the CD-ROMs we own.

Business cards are quite easy to produce, using any word-processing or desktop-publishing program and laser or ink-jet sheets of perforated or peel-off cards. This approach allows us to produce just the amount we need. If we are unsure of our design skills, we can hire someone to create an attractive template we can reuse with

Business cards are quite easy to produce using any word-processing or desk-top-publishing program.

our own software. Business cards are the most flexible and least expensive element of our marketing program. Let's maximize their potential.

Brochures

A brochure picks up where our business card leaves off, and it is a popular marketing tool for genealogists. (The Genealogical Speakers Guild even provides its members with booth space to display their personal brochures at national conferences.) Usually designed around folded panels that fit comfortably within a no. 10 (U.S.) or DL (international) envelope, brochures serve several purposes. They can list or describe our products or services, provide ordering information, offer helpful tips, feature testimonials by satisfied customers, or announce new services or products. Brochures should be creatively designed to attract attention, but they need to harmonize with other elements of our marketing package.

PAPER STOCK

We select the paper stock carefully, keeping in mind the business image we want to convey. Loud colors and wild fonts usually attract the wrong kind of attention. For many projects, white or light pastel, 60-pound weight (or *28-pound*, using other measuring scales) is quite effective. Textured paper such as linen can add class without dramatically increasing costs. Depending on the amount of text and the brochure's design, we can use either letter- or legal-size paper to create three or four folded panels.

COLOR

Attractive, affordable color can be added in various ways. For example:

* Using a light-colored paper and a complementary color ink (other than black), we can produce a quality, two-color brochure for the price of one ink color. (For this, we use our local printer rather than a quick-copy shop.) The Third Irish Genealogical Congress Committee printed an attractive brochure on a light gold, 60-pound, legal-size sheet with a linen texture and green ink. Very economical—and very Irish!

* For a more "full-color" look, our pale paper stock can carry design elements in several screens of the same ink color, ranging from light to dark.

* Specialty papers in mail-order catalogs come preprinted with a wide array of attractive designs.[13] Using these has both a downside and an upside. If we need more than one or two hundred copies, the cost is significantly higher than with the two approaches above. In any case, our text will have to be planned around the brochure's preprinted layout—an inconvenience for some. If we well match our fonts, point sizes, and other specialized elements to the commercial product, the result can be outstandingly professional. However, because these *are* commercial papers, with very distinct designs, we run the risk of discovering that competitors are also marketing themselves with "our" image.

When using either of the first two options, we should plan our promotion with timelessness in mind; brochures cost more to produce than any other item in our marketing tool kit. There is no rule that says we can't have more than one brochure, however. Whatever our target clientele, we may find various ways to create promotions aimed at that group.

Business cards are the most flexible and least expensive element of our marketing program. Let's maximize their potential.

Fliers

Unfolded, single-sheet, quick-copy fliers are economical and effective for time-specific events or offerings. We plan the design to harmonize with our other products, but they need not be fancy. They are "throwaways." We use them for large mailings or for stacks placed on "freebie" tables at conferences. The object here is to get our message out—cheaply but effectively. We distribute them where our target audience will find them (obviously not at the grocery store).

As with brochures, we can enhance the appeal of our fliers by selecting colored paper. Brights and neons are nice, but usually a tad more expensive than pastels. Very intense colors defeat our goals; many people have trouble reading text on such stock as electric blue, Chinese red, or forest green. It's wise to remember, too, that if our product appeals to people, they may wish to make copies for others in their network; those intense colors do not photocopy well, either. Black is commonly the ink of choice; our economical quick-copy mart may have no other color. Many shops offer quantity discounts for copying, but we should order only what we need. These *are* throwaways!

Marketing Methods

Direct advertising

Purchased advertising is a risky facet of marketing. Too many people create ads and place them everywhere, without any effort to determine the effectiveness of the ad campaign as a whole or any forum in particular. Others simply fill a rectangle with all the fine print it will hold and trust that every subscriber to every periodical is going to pore over every word. If we do not have the time to create a killer ad and track its success or failure, we'd probably be better off not advertising in the first place. Without feedback, we simply donate our hard-earned money to someone else's publication.

Obviously, well-done and well-placed advertisements can produce results. Without an unlimited marketing budget (who has that?), it's prudent to start with a small item in one carefully selected periodical. Here, we have two goals. First, we target our ad to the clientele we want to reach. For example, if we prefer short-term research projects under the specific direction of clients, it is logical to place display ads in local and commercial magazines that cater to the hobbyist. On the other hand, if we enjoy challenging and long-term projects, our professional ads might more successfully target readers of the advanced-level journals in our field. Our second goal is to make our ad stand apart from others of similar size and content. Graphic designer Elaine Floyd suggests the following ideas:[14]

- Design the ad with heavy top and bottom borders—don't worry about the sides.

- Include an eye-catching visual. (This also can be text used as a graphic—that is, individual letters, overscaled or set in a complementary font.)

- Keep copy to a minimum to save room for a large headline and good-sized contact

> Without an unlimited marketing budget, it's prudent to start with a small item in one carefully selected periodical.

information. (This bears repeating: *keep copy to a minimum.* Ads are definitely one of those places where *less is more!)*

- Run the ad in the form of a coupon with a dashed border.

- Give readers a reason to respond.

- Code each ad so you know which one works. We can do this by adding a "department number" to a post office box address, or by developing a number code that we place discreetly in a lower corner of a coupon.

Indirect advertising

WORD-OF-MOUTH ADVERTISING

Billions of dollars are spent worldwide, annually, on commercial ads—but that isn't even the most effective approach. What works best? Word of mouth. We all shop that way, for both goods and services. Unless we are totally impulsive, we do comparison shopping for large or out-of-the-ordinary purchases. We ask friends for recommendations. Sometimes we seriously consider buying a product until friends tell us about their bad experience with it or its producer. Or, on a friend's suggestion, we may try something we had never considered. Often, little or no commercial advertising entered into this decision. It was purely word of mouth.

Obviously, reputation can work for *or against* us, without our direct control over either. If we provide excellent service or a spectacular product, word will spread. But if we don't respond to a book order or lecture invitation for a month or we send out a report with poor documentation, we invite (and get) bad press. Numerous studies show that if people are satisfied with a product or service, they will tell someone else; if they are dissatisfied, they will tell at least nine other people. It is clearly in our best interest to ensure that grapevine broadcasts are favorable ones. How do we influence word of mouth? For starters, we

- don't offer something we are unprepared to deliver. If we claim that we always find results for a client, and we fail even once, criticism will fly. Customer service should be constantly on our mind.

- ask for testimonials from satisfied clients. These can be used in our marketing tools to highlight our services. Obviously, a testimonial needs to offer something positive and specific, and we always identify the satisfied client.

- find ways to get others to give us positive publicity. For instance, *Eastman's Online Genealogy Newsletter*[15] and *Missing Links*[16] are popular weekly e-mail newsletters targeted to genealogists. The editors of both watch for new and interesting subjects. Their large reach (25,000 and 400,000 weekly readers respectively in early 2000) make them "decision influencers." By persuading such people to write a positive piece about us or our services, we reach a significant audience with little effort on our part. The challenge is to find reasons why editors or columnists would want to write about us.

In word-of-mouth advertising, our goal is referrals. This method is the most economical and can be the most far-reaching. With a bit of creativity, we can find other ways to positively increase our visibility among our target clients.

Word of mouth is the single most powerful form of marketing. It has more sway over purchase decisions than advertising or any other form of marketing promotion.

—Alexander Hiam[17]

MARKETING STRATEGIES

PROOF-IN-THE-PUDDING ADVERTISING

Print and broadcast advertising can (and should) involve more than just promises or claims. Another powerful form of publicity is "proof in the pudding." For genealogists, this means lecturing and writing. We develop a specialty that truly sets us apart from others—expertise with a unique type of record or a challenging ethnic group or an exceptional ability at problem solving, perhaps. Then we identify appropriate forums in which to showcase our expertise in a manner that helps other researchers. Both the podium and the press have their particular advantages.

Lecturing

The podium may or may not have remuneration attached. Even when societies offer honoraria, as with most state and national conferences, the stipends may scarcely cover the costs of visual aids or partial expenses for conference attendance. The time we take from billable hours to spend on lecture development can only be considered an investment. The return that we hope for (aside from the unbankable satisfaction of contributing to our field) is increased business. That investment can also yield long-term dividends, since lectures at most major conferences are taped and marketed by a commercial firm. As those tapes continue to be sold, royalties will be negligible; but every catalog distributed by the firm will advertise us as an authority in our chosen area—as will future editions of Reisinger's *Index to . . . Conferences and Syllabi*, which is published and marketed by both the National Genealogical Society and the Federation of Genealogical Societies.[18]

Writing articles

The press offers both similar and different opportunities for proof-of-the-pudding advertising of four different types:

Commercial family-history magazines
These publications actually pay (modestly) for good material. Most seek short and relatively light fare, creating an excellent opportunity to further our name recognition among the masses with minimal time investment.

Genealogical-society magazines and newsletters
Whether local, regional, or family oriented—whether in print or online—society publications compete in basically the same market as the commercial ones, but they do not pay. These typically feature compiled record abstracts or general "how-tos." Here again, we can brand our name upon a certain type of research in the public mind with limited expenditure of time; and this is an especially valuable option if we prefer record-searching commissions.

Major journals
The journals that are standard-bearers in our field also do not pay for material, but their dividends can be far more powerful. Here, where longer articles are the norm and sound scholarship is expected, we can create a really rich pudding—displaying in depth our knowledge of a subject area or our ability to solve the seemingly unsolvable. If we yearn for those elite and seemingly mythical clients—the ones with a sophisticated appreciation of all that good research involves, who confidently offer us a blank check and a free rein—we are far more likely to find

> The time we take from billable hours to spend on lecture development can only be considered an investment. The return we hope for is increased business.

them among readers of the major national journals. Far more than popular magazines, quality journals have a permanent shelf life in libraries internationally, multiplying our audiences exponentially and extending our promotion indefinitely. Most journals also let writers purchase attractive offprints in bulk at reasonable prices. These special copies (containing just our articles, not full issues) can then be distributed to those who inquire about our services and describe similar or equally difficult cases. With offprints, we can offer potential clients more than promises. We can send them *proof* of our skill and expertise.

Professional magazines and newsletters
These do not cut us checks either. Yet, like service to the field in all other ways, by contributing our expert knowledge to these forums we build a reputation among colleagues, who can give us valuable referrals.

> With offprints, we can offer potential clients more than promises. We can send them *proof* of our skill and expertise.

Direct mail

Guerrilla Marketing expert Jay Levinson describes direct mail as advertising "intended to produce profits without a face-to-face meeting."[19] It may or may not be a worthwhile marketing method for professional genealogists. As with other approaches treated here, the success of a direct-mail campaign is linked to how well we target our message and how much creativity we employ. Before we lick the first stamp, we should determine what we want to accomplish. We've already spelled this out in our marketing plan, right? Now, we go a step further: we define what we want *this mailing* to accomplish. For instance, if we are American researchers and we offer free consultations on the Pennsylvania Dutch, we can expect queries about research in Germany and the Netherlands as well. Careful phrasing helps to prevent inappropriate requests to which we must respond.

Envelopes and flats
Most people hate junk mail. So how do we avoid having our carefully prepared piece end up in a recycling bin? For our first effort, we should try mailing to a small group of potential clients whose needs and attitudes we understand. Buying a mailing list is rarely the way to go, because we strive to identify quality over quantity in prospective clients. A more effective approach is to cull a client list from the query sections of genealogy magazines and newsletters pertaining to our niche. Once we've developed our targeted mailing list, the following tips can help us prepare the content:

- We concentrate on one key reason why the recipient should use our service or product.

- We repeat the key consumer benefit at least three times.

- We make the benefit meaningful to the recipient. We are specific rather than general. How can our service improve his or her life?

- We add credibility to the key consumer benefit—using testimonials from previously satisfied clients—but we don't go overboard.

- We let potential clients see the personality of our business. We are conversational, not stuffy. We show our humanness. We use mail-merge capabilities in word-processing programs to personalize our mailings.

MARKETING STRATEGIES

- We assume that readers want to know about our service, so we tell them enough for them to make an informed decision. Some marketing guides even say not to worry about length—that recipients who are interested will read what we have to say.

- We use "trigger areas" to capture the reader's attention—e.g., the lower left corner of an envelope or the front panel of our brochure.

- We use a colorful or odd-sized envelope. We use a stamp instead of a postage meter, to avoid having our material look mass-mailed. We might consider addressing each envelope by hand or use more than one stamp per envelope to heighten the impression of a personalized letter. Old stamps or ones theme-related to our service or product can attract attention.

- We put a money-saving, limited-time, or free-gift offer on the outside of the envelope.

- We try to snare a memorable address or phone number—Box 1812, perhaps, if we specialize in the War of 1812.

- We always use a postscript. Research shows this is the most read portion of a letter!

- We can offer free gifts or bonuses that don't have to be costly—a copy of a historical map or an inexpensively produced research guide.

Frequent mailings keep our name before our market. While particular individuals may not be interested in our first mailing, they may respond to the second or the sixth. Studies show that our message needs to be repeated at least seven times to be really heard.

Postcards
Economical to print and mail, cards serve nicely for that all-important follow-up. They can also be used for coupons, announcements, and special offers. Postcards come in several different sizes. Photographs or colorful graphics can fill one side, as long as the image relates to our message. The postcard becomes a coupon when we encourage the reader to "mail back the postcard by [*date*] and receive a [*gift*]."

E-mail and faxes
E-mail announcements are an iffy approach and faxes are virtually verboten. Some people appreciate receiving commercial e-mail for items in which they are interested, and some professionals or companies swear by the results. But e-mail users are increasingly irritated with "junk" messages, and legislative action—which already exists for unsolicited fax advertising—is likely. The Direct Marketing Association, which offers a convenient website, has e-mail marketing guidelines that we need to monitor if we choose this route.

Regardless of the approach, one direct-mail campaign will not be useful to the next, if we don't test the responses. What type of response constitutes success *for us?* We need to establish a setpoint or goal. As we continue our marketing, we should experiment with layouts and promotions to determine which type garners the best results. We test continually, to hone our message and method; but we test only one

> Frequent mailings keep our name before our market. Studies show that our message needs to be repeated at least seven times to be really heard.

idea per mailing. Otherwise, we cannot determine which change improved or reduced our response rate.

Newsletters

An effective and relatively inexpensive way of retaining clients, newsletters can also attract new business. They allow us to keep in continual contact with our customers, reminding them of our value. Periodic newsletters can give updates on the repositories we visit, describe success stories we have generated for our clients (with their permission, naturally), and advise people of changes in our services or fees. We can mail to just our current client base or expand the mailing to include potential ones. We even have a choice now of formats: mail via traditional means (postal service), electronic transmission, or website posting. Newsletters are flexible and inexpensively produced with word-processing, page-layout, or website-editing software. How can we maximize results if we try this approach? These ways help:

- We title our newsletter creatively. It should relate to our service or business and should appear prominently on the front page.

- We decide the frequency of publication and stick with it. We might want to start out quarterly, rather than monthly or bimonthly. Production time always exceeds expectations.

- We keep the newsletter short—two to four letter-sized pages.

- We match the look of our newsletter to our stationery, business cards, and other items used for our business image.

- We use narrow columns and short paragraphs (newspaper style) and prune our prose tightly, to provide more information.

- We keep the newsletter informational. It's okay to talk briefly about our services, but that is not our primary purpose. If the newsletter does not benefit our readers, they will lose interest.

- We include free offers or coupons for our services, to test effectiveness.

- We use letters from happy clients as "letters to the editor," but we don't overdo it.

- We use graphics, headings, and generous amounts of white space to break up paragraphs of text. The experts are unanimous: Few people read material that is crammed margin to margin with unrelieved blocks of type.

- We increase distribution beyond our current client list—taking copies to conferences, or encouraging readers to share their copies with friends.

- We use first-class postage, so the newsletter will arrive promptly and avoid association with the junk-mail image.

Direct-mail newsletters are *not* considered junk mail and are more likely to be read than direct-mail brochures. E-mail newsletters could be seen as junk if recipients are not approached cautiously. The first e-mail should announce the newsletter, provide a sample, *and require readers to reply if they want to receive future issues.* (The new "push marketing" ploy used by some Internet providers, which dumps mail on recipients unless they go to each website and specifically ask to be deleted from a

> We test continually; but we test only one idea per mailing. Otherwise, we cannot determine which change improved or reduced our response rate.

MARKETING STRATEGIES

company's database, is not a way to build a supporting client base in genealogy.) If we do not get a reply, we promptly take that person off our potential subscriber list. Junk e-mail is politically incorrect. By contrast, home-page newsletters or e-zines are available for anyone to look at anytime they care to visit our site. We can also set up requests for e-mail newsletters from our e-zine's web page—a matter more fully discussed below.

Internet advertising

Is our business ready for a home page on the World Wide Web? We should determine this in our marketing plan. If we want to attract new clients, the Internet provides a method for endless numbers to learn about us and contact us. If we want the page there "just for information," we have to change our content regularly to keep people coming back. Most important, though, are we prepared for a potential onslaught of interest in our product or service? Can we check our e-mail every day, or even twice a day, for responses? People who use e-mail expect quick replies—a perfect opportunity to impress potential clients or turn them off. We may already be on the Web, but if we are not, we should ask ourselves the following questions before we follow the hype onto the Internet.

> Are we prepared for a potential onslaught of interest in our product or service? Can we check our e-mail every day, or even twice a day, for responses?

COST

Can we afford it? According to one authority, "Many newcomers to the Web are frustrated with the actual results their presence has produced, though they seem willing to wait and see and to make adjustments in their pages to position themselves better."[20] A Web presence means cash expenditures for the registration of our domain name, monthly online charges, and software. It means time expenditures for keeping up with computer technology—as well as keeping our home page fresh. Can our business absorb the up-front and ongoing costs?

LOCATION

Where will our home page be located? Do we have an Internet service provider? If so, what services does it offer and how much space does it make available for our pages? How much traffic can the server manage? How current is its technology? If we don't have a server, we investigate this market carefully. It might be prudent to start with one that has gained recognition as a quality service provider; we can always change servers later—at a cost.

PROGRAMMING

Are we going to learn the programming languages of the Internet—or will we hire someone to prepare our page? There are many free tutorials on the Web for HTML and JAVA (the two major programming languages), but is it worth our time to create our site ourselves? Many new products have hit the market recently to assist with web-page design. We can research the latest offerings in such forums as *PC Magazine* or *PC Magazine Online* to find out which programs are worth the money and the learning curve.[21]

LINKS

Are we willing to spend the time looking for other pages to link to—and vice versa? Linkages are the key to Internet success. The phrase *If we build it, they'll come* is not necessarily true on the Web, if "they" don't know we're there. We will need to include our web-page and e-mail addresses on all marketing materials so we can be found. We also need to identify other related sites, and contact them to inquire whether they will add us as a link to their site.

CONTENT

What content will our site contain? If we are trying to attract genealogical clients, we might consider putting some of our own family research online for potential clients to examine. Of course, we choose our best and most thoroughly documented work. We can attract a following if our home page includes free tidbits from our own research experience. If we have information to share, we might consider creating an e-zine on our site, or offering an electronic newsletter by e-mail subscription. Graphics enliven our pages, but we should not go overboard. Many people still use slow modems, and we lose their interest fast if our pages take too long to download. Parameters for the "acceptable" kilobyte size of a page or an individual graphic will continually change, as technology advances, so specifics here would be obsolete tomorrow. Before designing a page, we should seek guidance on file size from computer-magazine literature or we can study other websites. Many of them identify the number of kilobytes in a graphic before it downloads; and a browser's "temporary Internet files directory" typically records the sizes of specific pages we have visited. By timing a download and comparing it to the file size, we soon learn how much is *too* much for a page to carry.

COMMITMENT

Will we be committed to the web page? We may not see results instantly. If we don't and we get discouraged, it is tempting to close down the site. As providers of a public service, we need to be very patient with an Internet presence. Web surfers are accustomed to receiving information for free and may not be interested in paying for our services. If we establish a site solely to make money, this marketing tool will likely fail us. If we establish a Web presence as just another element of a broader marketing package, we may ultimately be rewarded; our target market will come to recognize our name and the quality service we symbolize.

> If we establish a site solely to make money, this marketing tool will likely fail us. If we establish a Web presence as just another element of a broader marketing package, we may ultimately be rewarded.

MARKET

Are our potential clients using the Web? A 1997 survey by the Association of Professional Genealogists revealed that of the APG members who responded, 95 percent use computers but only about 33 percent conduct research online. In a fall 1996 survey by the Board for Certification of Genealogists, mailed to a comparable number of associates and applicants, 60 percent of respondents reported regular online activity. (More recent surveys, if available, would likely show a near universal online presence.) While most of these respondents conduct research professionally and probably are not our targets, the surveys suggest the current technical capabilities of the marketplace.[22]

If we choose the Internet route, we need to find other ways to be responsive to our market, once that home page is established. If we notice questions being asked repeatedly in e-mail requests, we might develop a link from our home page to added pages of "Frequently Asked Questions." Still, we should not be surprised at the number of surfers who ignore or overlook those FAQ sheets—finding it easier to send an e-mail query. We should also plan to update our information regularly and add new features to keep visitors coming back.

Library, agency, and society lists

If we seek research commissions, free advertising is often available in a more old-fashioned form: inclusion on lists that many libraries, government agencies, and societies distribute in response to requests for help. In the 1996 BCG survey, 60 percent of respondents reported inclusion on the lists of local agencies and libraries and 51 percent also had their names on a list distributed by their state archive or state library.[23]

Others maximize their potential by joining organizations that distribute member directories—for example, the Association of Professional Genealogists and the Genealogical Speakers Guild—or they seek certification or accreditation. The lists maintained by APG, BCG, and GSG all include international as well as U.S. genealogists. The APG and BCG rosters are formally published every two years or so and distributed or sold to major libraries (as well as individuals) globally. All three groups include their rosters on their websites and offer members or associates the option of e-mail hotlinks through which interested surfers can instantly contact the professional. The Salt Lake City–based accreditation program—like most of the international credentialing programs—does not formally publish a directory, but it provides free lists to all inquirers and some have online rosters. BCG, for its various conference booths, often prepares up-to-the-minute lists with associates grouped by states—attractive fliers that have been popular giveaways. Considering that the major conferences routinely draw 1,500 to 2,500 attendees, these lists are also a significant "member service."

On the downside, an increasing number of libraries, archives, government agencies, and societies impose selection criteria for inclusion on their lists. Some seek to minimize liability by recommending only those who have earned professional (tested) credentials. When we approach an agency to seek a listing, we should first inquire as to their policy.

Summary Concepts

As an entrepreneur, we wear many hats. One of those needs to be "Marketing Director," if we want our business to grow and thrive. Marketing principles don't have to be intimidating or overwhelming. Those of us who simply don't like this aspect of entrepreneurship might consider using a part-time assistant to handle publicity and promotions. Whether we assume this role ourselves or assign it to an employee,

An increasing number of libraries, archives, government offices, and societies impose selection criteria for inclusion on their lists. Some seek to minimize liability by recommending only those who have earned professional (tested) credentials.

the important thing is to begin that marketing today. All suggestions offered in this chapter will not fit each of our individual molds. None of us will be able to implement all usable ideas at once or even in the near future. But today *is* the first day of the rest of the life of our business. Let's use it to creatively design an effective marketing plan and then put those ideas into action. Otherwise, in the long run, this day will *not* be a truly profitable one.

> Today is the first day of the rest of the life of our business. Let's use it to creatively design an effective marketing plan.

NOTES

1. James C. Makens, *The Marketing Plan Workbook* (Englewood Cliffs, New Jersey: Prentice-Hall, 1985), guides us through the elements of a plan that we tailor to our business. Although it's now a "vintage" publication, it's still in print because it's still valuable. David F. Ramacitti, *Do-It-Yourself Marketing* (New York: American Management Association, 1994), also helps small businesses design marketing strategies.

2. For example, see Jian Software's *Marketing Builder* (Mountain View, California: Jian, ongoing editions); website available. Also useful is Jian's *BizPlanBuilder,* which has been the best-selling business-plan program for the last ten years.

3. Mississippi Department of Economic and Community Development, "Small Business Marketing," at website *Mississippi State University Cooperative Extension Service* <www.ext.msstate.edu/pubs/Toolkit/mdecd-8.htm>, consulted 30 January 2000. While the site name is specific to one locale, the information offered is of value to any entrepreneur.

4. Service Corps of Retired Executives, Orange County, California, Chapter, "The Business Plan: Marketing Plan," at website *Small Business Administration* <www.sba.gov/SCORE/ca>; at the California homepage, follow keywords for "Business Plan" and "Marketing Plan" to access lists of questions that assist in putting together a marketing plan.

5. The SBA site, above, also helps with budgeting.

6. "Small Business Marketing," at website *Mississippi State University Extension Service.*

7. All the major societies that publish directories or lists of professional associates can be contacted online or by correspondence with the address cited at their websites.

8. These are the *Association of Professional Genealogists [APG] Quarterly; Speak!* newsletter of the Genealogical Speaker's Guild; and *OnBoard,* newsletter of the Board for Certification of Genealogists.

9. Cyndi Howells, "Professional Researchers, Volunteers, and Other Research Services," at website *Cyndi's List of Genealogy Sites on the Internet.*

10. Alexander Hiam, *Marketing for Dummies* (Foster City, California: IDG Books World-wide, 1997), 49–52. A no-nonsense approach to marketing for those without a large corporation or marketing department behind them, Hiam's book is well worth the money!

11. Allan H. Rouse, "White Fawn or Galloping Buffalo: Marketing Yourself," *APG Quarterly* 5 (Spring 1990): 3; reprinted, *APG Twentieth Anniversary Issue* (1999): 100.

12. Hiam, *Marketing for Dummies,* 49–52.

13. Examples are *(a)* Impact Idea Art; Post Office Box 291505; Nashville, TN 37229-1505; *(b)* Paper Showcase; Post Office Box 8465; Mankato, MN 46002-8465; and *(c)* Paper Direct; 100 Plaza Drive; Secaucus, NJ 07094-3606.

14. Elaine Floyd, "Marketing Madness: Using Technology to Brighten Your Image," *Technique* 2 (Special Issue: 1995): 20–26.

15. Richard Eastman's *Eastman's Online Genealogy Newsletter* is available by subscription, with automatic delivery; and archived issues are available at this writing. Current contact information is available online.

16. Julia Case and Myra Vanderpool Gormley, CG, eds., *Missing Links;* this online newsletter is available by subscription for automatic delivery. Current contact information is available online.

17. Hiam, *Marketing for Dummies,* 181.

18. Joy Reisinger, CG, *Index to NGS and FGS Conferences and Syllabi* (Washington and Salt Lake City: National Genealogical Society and Federation of Genealogical Societies, 1993).

MARKETING STRATEGIES

19. Jay Conrad Levinson, *Guerrilla Marketing Attack: New Strategies, Tactics & Weapons for Winning Big Profits from Your Small Business* (Boston: Houghton Mifflin, 1989), 140.

20. Stephen Beals, "Getting Your Web Feet Wet," *Desktop Publishers* 8 (September 1996): 36–38.

21. *PC Magazine,* available at newsstands; also *PC Magazine Online.*

22. Elizabeth Kelley Kerstens, "Who Are We?" *APG Quarterly* 12 (March 1997): 5–8; Elizabeth Shown Mills, CG, CGL, FASG, "Equipping Ourselves for Quality Service: Physical Plant and Continuing Education—BCG Survey Results," *OnBoard* 3 (May 1997): 2.

23. Elizabeth Shown Mills, "Client Assignments—Quality and Quantity: BCG Survey Results," *OnBoard* 3 (September 1997): 20.

Blessed are the flexible, for they shall not be bent out of shape.

—*Anonymous*

FURTHER STUDY

Adler, Elizabeth. "Get Your Document Read." *Technique* 2 (October 1995): 22–23. Discusses methods of making your marketing materials stand out from the crowd.

Albert, Richard. "Marketing for the Home-Based Entrepreneur." *Home Business* 4 (January–February 1997): 8–24. A basic discussion of marketing—including direct mail, positioning, and printed materials.

Dynamic Graphics. Bimonthly magazine, with ideas galore for designing all types of advertisements, marketing aids, products, and publications.

Gosney, Michael, John Odam, and Jim Schmal. *The Gray Book: Designing in Black & White on Your Computer.* Chapel Hill, North Carolina: Ventana Press, 1990.

Guerrilla Marketing Online. A highly recommended weekly magazine, put together by the organization behind the *Guerrilla Marketing* books.

Holsclaw, Birdie Monk. "Going Online: The Internet for Professional Genealogists." *APG Quarterly* 11 (June 1996): 54–57. An excellent, nontechnical discussion of the utility of the Internet to professional genealogists.

Levinson, Jay Conrad. *Guerrilla Advertising: Cost-Effective Tactics for Small-Business Success.* Boston: Houghton Mifflin, 1994.

———. *Guerrilla Marketing: Secrets for Making Big Profits from Your Small Business* (Boston: Houghton Mifflin, 1998).

———. *Guerrilla Marketing Weapons: 100 Affordable Marketing Methods for Maximizing Profits from Your Small Business.* New York: Plume Books, 1990. See particularly chapters 2 (for creating client mailing lists), 5 (for newsletters), and 8 (for direct mail).

——— and Charles Rubin. *Guerrilla Marketing Online: The Entrepreneur's Guide to Earning Profits on the Internet.* Boston: Houghton Mifflin, 1997.

——— and Seth Godin. *Guerrilla Marketing for the Home-Based Business.* Boston: Houghton Mifflin, 1995. A must-read for small businesses—and the *first* that should be read of all the Levinson manuals. *Guerrilla Marketing* series. The many ideas discussed, with examples, are mind-boggling.

Michaels, Nancy, and Debbi J. Karpowicz. *Off-the-Wall Marketing Ideas.* Holbrook, Massachusetts: Adams Media Corp., 2000. Offers many effective and innovative suggestions, with actual examples of successful entrepreneurs.

Mills, Elizabeth Shown. "How to Market Yourself as a Lecturer." *APG Quarterly* 9 (December 1994): 98–101. A six-step plan designed specifically for the genealogical lecturer.

Stopke, Judy, and Chip Staley. *An Eye for Type.* 3d expanded edition. Ann Arbor, Michigan: Promotional Perspectives, 1992.

White, Jan V. "Why Design Is Important." *Technique* 2 (August 1995): 14–16. Advice for using design to attract attention to our marketing tools.

Women's Business Center. Cosponsored by the U.S. Small Business Association, this agency offers much excellent material relating to marketing, management, procurement, technology, and other business interests. See website.

12

**BUSINESS
RECORD KEEPING**

BUSINESS RECORD KEEPING

Keynotes

Keynotes (cont.)

Business Record Keeping

by Helen F. M. Leary, CG, CGL, FASG

Every business activity generates records. If we don't pay attention to them, they'll grow like kudzu, smothering our office and eventually strangling the business itself. Cultivation of one kind of record while allowing the rest to run rampant can be disastrous, too. Focusing exclusively on cash-flow records may leave us with little more than a detailed description of our road to bankruptcy. If we focus instead on the work flow, our road may lead to the same point but we're likely not to notice until we're there. Business record keeping is a management tool, not merely a housekeeping chore or a storage problem; and it's an important protection against legal difficulties. Good control of our business requires quick, reliable access to all its records—access that can be provided only when they are kept in a well-designed, faithfully maintained system.

System Overview

Unless we can afford to hire an expert, we will design our own record keeping system. To do this well, we focus on three things: *(a)* standards of retrievability and ease of use; *(b)* organization of records into logical groups; and *(c)* filing arrangements that fit our office space. Our system should be a reflection of our sense of order and the way we work. But, as a management tool, it must recognize also the nature of our business and the way we *ought* to work.

Standards

Organizational gurus tout all sorts of systems, from motivational to mnemonic, labyrinthine to high-tech. A sampling are cited under FURTHER STUDY. But an effective system need not be complicated, sophisticated, expensive, or esoteric. Insofar as standards go, our system should address five points: completeness, intuitiveness, interdependence, simplicity, and disposability.

Completeness
All the different kinds of records generated by a profitable, long-term business must be accommodated within our system.

Intuitiveness
The system itself should dictate where to put each record and where to look when we need it again. It should not tempt us to file data randomly or require that we search the entire haystack to find a particular straw.

Interdependence
A good filing system is one that suggests logical cross-references. Whenever one record is retrieved, its label or location should suggest others that may be needed for the best use of the one at hand. This is particularly important for analyses of income and related expenses.

> The system itself should dictate where to put each record and where to look when we need it again.

BUSINESS RECORD KEEPING

Simplicity
The system should be simple enough to maintain quickly and reliably. In most cases, we will have sole responsibility for filing and retrieval. We need a system that will eat up as few nonbillable hours as possible.

Disposability
Regular and systematic culling is equally essential. We need not only the ability to retrieve files but also an effective policy for disposing of records that have outlived their usefulness. Some records are ephemeral; they can be disposed of almost immediately (e.g., telephone callback notes). Some are permanent and should be kept for the lifetime of the business (its legal records). Some are temporary; their useful life will end after something else has happened (our computer's service contract after it or the computer has expired).

Organization

In order to design a recordkeeping system that meets these criteria, we need to analyze how our business works. This is best done by following the old riddle *How do you eat an elephant? One bite at a time.* Let's break down our business into its component parts, sort the parts, and assign them their proper places. In short, we produce an organizational chart that depicts the various business functions we perform and the relationships that exist between them. That chart will be the basis upon which we organize our records.

Odds are, our chart—even for a "one-person operation"—will suggest kinship to General Motors or IBM. Big business divides responsibilities among company officers. If we're the only officer our company has, then we wear all those hats. As president, for example, we start the business and continue to dictate its direction. As secretary, we answer the mail and telephone. As treasurer, we manage the financial affairs. And, as manager or vice-president of one division or another, we govern our workflow. Figure 13 shows a sample organizational chart for a full-fledged, multifaceted genealogical business. It is the basis for the sample system this chapter presents. Each of our charts (and systems) will vary, but the sample still serves. Let's visualize ourselves moving from office to office to perform different activities. This helps us see the records in context and encourages a system design that will serve well for decades.

Filing arrangements

Filing takes time. We should schedule that time as a regular part of our business day or week—if we plan to do it when we're "not so busy," we'll always be too busy to do it. Then we'll find ourselves needing papers that aren't where logic says they should be. *Ah, yes! They're in one of those stacks waiting to be filed!* The next thirty minutes we spend sifting through those stacks will put us even more behind.

Filing takes time. If we plan to do it when we are "not so busy," we will always be too busy to do it.

FOLDERS
Whatever the document, it deserves to be in a folder. That folder needs to be labeled. The whole needs to be in proper alphabetical or chronological sequence amid related

BUSINESS RECORD KEEPING

FIG. 13
ORGANIZATIONAL CHART

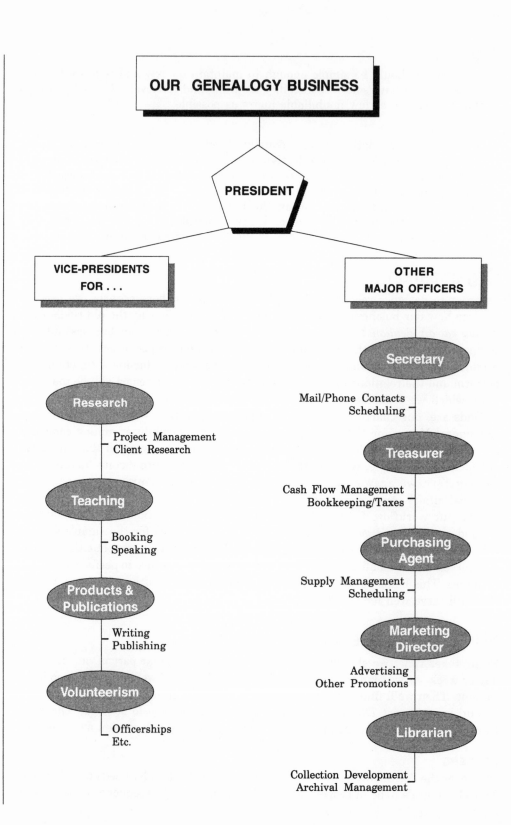

BUSINESS RECORD KEEPING

files in a drawer, crate, or storage file box. The contents of each file deserve to be subdivided as soon as the file becomes so thick we need more than a minute or two to find what we want. Computer files are organized similarly, into directories—sometimes called *folders*—and subdirectories. Backup disk files are more accessible if they are grouped on the diskette by subject or date; the diskettes should then be labeled and filed in disk trays in the sequence used for paper folders.

Today's array of filing supplies absolutely begs us to be efficient. Tailoring these materials to our system makes filing and retrieval physically easier.

- Hanging-folders on file racks (freestanding or inside file-cabinet drawers) allow sorting through numerous files easily and quickly. When one or more are removed, the rest do not collapse on themselves in an untidy heap.

- Bulky client-research or writing projects and overhead transparencies filed with lecture notes can be accommodated best in box-bottom folders.

- Legal-sized documents are happier flat-filed in legal-size folders and containers than folded to fit within letter-size ones.

- Odd-sized bits and pieces of paper, such as client correspondence and financial receipts, are more secure in pocket folders.

- Vinyl or pressboard folders are best for permanent or often-consulted files and for the pending section of our system (see below). From there the papers are moved elsewhere when appropriate, but folders usually remain in place.

- Color-coding gives us an instant visual overview of system contents. Assigning color codes should be done systematically and with future expansion in mind. Supplies that are normally in stock at nearby office-supply houses are best for areas that rapidly expand (client research files, correspondence, etc.). Supplies in glamorous, special-order colors should be reserved for systems likely to expand slowly or not at all. Logically, files for each "officer" on our organizational chart would have their own distinctive color.

FILING SPACE

Because physical files must occupy physical places—and because we use some records more often than others—we divide our filing space into three areas:

Pending
Here we place files that are waiting for something to happen (for the end of the month, perhaps) or for someone to do something (for the mail-order house to send the supplies we requested, etc.). Pending files need to be close at hand, so the records can be reviewed frequently for follow-up action.

Working
Current files should be clearly divided by business function. Subdivisions might reflect different stages through which a series of records moves toward final resolution. For example, under Client Research, we might have subdivisions for Waiting to be Analyzed and Ready for Research.

Storage
Files that are no longer active should be moved to a site that is still handy, but no longer "under foot." Periodically, many of their items will need to be retrieved.

> The contents of each file deserve to be subdivided as soon as the file becomes so thick we need more than a minute or two to find what we want.

A diagram of our filing system belongs permanently with our business plan. When we modify our system, the design should be updated.

Former clients contact us after several years, wanting to resume where we left off. Old book manuscripts need revising for a new edition. But in the interim, we will work much more efficiently if inactive materials are removed to storage.

Sample System

General principles almost always sound logical. That's why people suggest them. Why is it, then, that so many of us get frustrated when we try to apply those perfectly sensible rules? It's the exceptions, the variances, and the endless cases of *What if?* and *Should I?* and *But this could fit HERE or THERE!* The sample system outlined below can provide a helpful blueprint, as we consider the varied activities, functions, records, and roles common to professional genealogists.

President

FUNCTION 1: START-UP

Preliminary inventory of assets
The contributions we bring into our business, to ensure its success, are of two types, tangible and intangible.

- *Tangible assets*
  These are the books, equipment, and office furnishings we have on hand and their monetary value at the time this business starts, not their value at the time they were purchased. The total, plus what we take out of our personal bank account to open our business account, is our initial *capital investment*.

  > FILING TRACK: *Working Files>PRESIDENT>Start-up>Assets.*

  > RETENTION: Permanent.

  > CROSS-REFERENCE: A copy of the Tangible Assets Inventory should go in *Working Files>TREASURER>Start-up>Tax Support.*

- *Intangible assets*
  Our training, talents, interests, experience, and contacts—who we are, not what we have—are our intangible assets. They need to be inventoried and evaluated also. The fact that they are intangible makes it difficult to place a monetary value on them, but they are crucial to many phases of our planning, marketing, and development.

  > FILING TRACK: *Working Files>PRESIDENT>Start-up>Assets.*

  > RETENTION: Permanent.

Mission statement and business plan
Presumably we have already created both of these, following the guidelines covered in chapter 9. Now we need a permanent home for the documents.

  > FILING TRACK: *Working Files>PRESIDENT>Start-up>Mission Statement* [or *Business Plan*].

  > RETENTION: Permanent.

Legal documents
These also fall into two broad types of materials, permanent and temporary.

• *Permanent*
This category includes (where applicable) our articles of incorporation or partnership agreement, fictitious business name statement (DBA), sales tax permit, or zoning exceptions for office use of our home.

> FILING TRACK: *Working Files>PRESIDENT>Start-up>Legal Documents>Permanent.*

> RETENTION: Permanent.

• *Temporary*
This category includes the items that are periodically renewable: business licenses, certification or accreditation files, equipment or office leases, insurance policies, and postal permits.

> FILING TRACK: *Working Files>PRESIDENT>Start-up>Legal Documents>[Type of Document].*

> RETENTION: Permanent.

> CROSS-REFERENCE: Enter renewal dates on the Secretary's Calendar (see page 233).

FUNCTION 2: SUPERVISION

Annual reports
Formal or informal, these are generated by our comparison of the Treasurer's Income and Expenses Statements with our financial goals. They include any adjustments we plan for increasing profits (such as cutting expenses, increasing billable hours, or raising our hourly fee).

> FILING TRACK: *Working Files>PRESIDENT>Supervision>Annual Reports.*

> RETENTION: Three-year minimum.

New projects
Here we file notes and letters dealing with new ideas or activities we are contemplating.

> FILING TRACK: *Pending Files>PRESIDENT>Supervision>New Projects [or Idea File]*

> RETENTION: Move to Working Files or to Wastebasket, as appropriate.

Secretary

FUNCTION 1: MAIL AND TELEPHONE CONTACTS

Inquiries and replies
The potential client's letter of inquiry about our services (or our notes on the phone conversation) should be stapled to a copy of our answer and held until the work is authorized or until there is little chance that it will be. Its home would depend upon the nature of the document.

TIP

We can use the blank backs of outdated papers for rough notes and drafts. When both sides are full, we recycle.

BUSINESS RECORD KEEPING

> FILING TRACK:
> Correspondence: *Pending Files>SECRETARY>Telephone [or Mail] Contacts.*
> Postal receipts: *Working Files>TREASURER>Receipts.*
> Return-receipt cards: *Working Files>CLIENT RESEARCH>[Client name].*

> RETENTION: Keep in Pending Files until the work is authorized, or for two years if no authorization follows.

> CROSS-REFERENCE:
> 1. Note postal charges for specific clients on Time-and-Charges Log (see page 241).
> 2. Many professionals also maintain (and record inquiries on) a Secretary's Correspondence Log.

Authorizations (written)

The Secretary retrieves the prior inquiry and reply, acknowledges the authorization, and begins a new file or updates an old one.

> FILING TRACK: *Working Files>CLIENT RESEARCH>[Client Name].*

> CROSS-REFERENCE: Enter estimated time for work on Secretary's Calendar (page 233).

Other correspondence

Typically, this consists of communications with colleagues, our accountant, our attorney, or other professionals.

> FILING:
> 1. Recycle ephemeral correspondence.
> 2. Route the rest to appropriate Working File or Pending File. (If we create a Miscellaneous Correspondence File, it will tempt us to mix important papers with trivia.)

Telephone notes

The simplest method for keeping track of *incoming* calls and messages is a spiral-bound message pad that produces two copies. One can be torn out, the other is a "fail-safe" record, in case the tear-off copy is misplaced.

> FILING:
> 1. Ephemeral messages go to Wastebasket. For important messages, the original tear-off copy is transferred appropriately.
> 2. If the contact involves a future obligation, create an appropriately labeled Activity Folder and insert the tear-off copy of the message.

> CROSS-REFERENCE:
> 1. Note the obligation on the Secretary's Calendar.
> 2. If the call is a client consultation, record length of call (we will bill for that time), then file the note in the appropriate Client Research File (page 241).

Phone log

A chronological list of *outgoing* phone calls is an important business tool. For convenient comparison with the phone bill, we might enter data in the same order (date, city, state, phone number), identify the person called, and note the reason for calling. When the bill arrives, we add to the Phone Log entries whatever time and charges will be billed to clients or organizations for whom we made the calls.

TIPS

After a year, a pending file needs reexamining. If a prospective client sent anything resembling an original record or "only copy," we can return it with a brief note. This might spark a reply that would not have come otherwise.

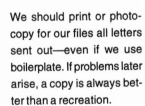

We should print or photocopy for our files all letters sent out—even if we use boilerplate. If problems later arise, a copy is always better than a recreation.

Some phone contacts need a followup letter, confirming details of the conversation—for example, when clients phone to assign work or to alter instructions laid out in their contracts or letters of authorization.

> FILING: The Phone Log might be a computer file or a paper document—or kept on the same pad with incoming calls, as long as the two are separate entities.

> RETENTION: At the end of the year, we move it (or a computer printout) into *Working Files>TREASURER>Tax Support Records.*

Contact lists

A file of frequent and potential contacts is essential to every business operation; often the file consists of several lists, each specific to an area of our activity. Whatever system we use should be capable of alphabetical insertions and cross-references (example: Bank, see First Moneyplace*).*

> FILING: Keep in a computer file, or as a book or Rolodex™ on the desktop.

FUNCTION 2: SCHEDULING

Secretary's calendar

Whether maintained on paper or on computer, our calendar should include three essentials:

- All activities and estimated time for completing each. This calendar should also include both business and personal activities. As a general rule, we try to draw every line possible between our business and personal lives to forestall challenges by tax agencies. However, if we don't integrate our personal and business schedules we'll wreak havoc, because the self-employed seldom are able to confine their business activities to the "normal" workday and workweek (9:00–5:00, Monday through Friday).

- Blocks of time for office management—bookkeeping, correspondence, filing.

- Blocks of time for staying current in our field—reading, attending conferences, taking courses, etc.

> FILING: If paper calendars are used, keep with Telephone Notes and Log on desktop.

> RETENTION: Permanent. These chronicle our business history. (They will also be fun to read ten years from now.)

Project planner

This tool is necessary only if we work with others on a regular basis. Similar to a calendar, it tracks extended-time assignments.

> FILING: Same as Secretary's Calendar.

> RETENTION: Same as Secretary's Calendar.

Treasurer

FUNCTION 1: CASH FLOW MANAGEMENT

Outgoing invoices

These billings cover time and expenses, other services, or products. This discussion

TIPS

If we use our personal line for office calls, writing a monthly business check to the home account for that part of the bill will reinforce distinctions between our business and personal expenses.[1]

If we maintain our contact lists on the computer, naming the file ADDRESS.BK, rather than PHONE.BK, will put it at the top of the directory listing, for quicker access.

BUSINESS RECORD KEEPING

assumes that our business finances are on a *cash basis* for tax reporting—that is, income is ours when we receive the check or cash, and expenses are ours when we pay for the goods or service. We would use different invoicing and bookkeeping methods if our tax advisor recommended an *accrual basis* (that is, we enter Income into Account Books, below, when we send out bills and enter Expenses when we incur them).

> FILING TRACK:
> Prior to payment: *Pending Files>TREASURER>Unpaid Invoices.*
> After payment: *Pending Files>TREASURER>Paid Invoices.*

> CROSS-REFERENCE:
> 1. Keep a copy in the paper file for the activity that generated the bill.
> 2. Enter received checks in Account Books.

Incoming bills

The above comments for Outgoing Invoices also apply to Incoming Bills. Recommendations here are based on the premise that bills are paid just once or twice a month rather than immediately upon arrival.

> FILING TRACK:
> Prior to payment: *Pending Files>TREASURER>Unpaid Bills.*
> After payment: *Pending Files>TREASURER>Paid Receipts.*

> CROSS-REFERENCE: Enter payments in Account Books.

FUNCTION 2: BOOKKEEPING

Account books

This record of our income and expenses can be kept on paper or on computer. The same standards of documentation are used in bookkeeping as in genealogical reporting; in short:

- Every statement of fact (in this case, mathematical fact) must have a citation to its *income source* (where the money came from) or its *outgo destination* (where the money went).

- Income and outgo are divided into a series of "accounts." Income accounts might be Lecturing or Book Sales. Outgo accounts might be Photocopies or Supplies. Figures 11 and 12 in chapter 10 itemize numerous expenses that warrant treatment as separate accounts. Or we may follow the income and expense breakdowns that are standard on Schedule C of IRS Form 1040.

In choosing commercial software, the typical genealogist needs nothing beyond the basics. The most popular accounting programs for home or personal finances and tax preparation have all the bells and whistles the sole proprietor needs, unless involved in sales of books or products. (This is one area where our business has *nothing* in common with General Motors or IBM!) However, whatever we use, wisdom suggests that we consult our tax advisor when we set up Account Books and recheck with him or her a few months later to make certain they (and we) are working correctly.

TIP

This chapter's discussion of taxation cites U.S. tax laws and forms. The discussion is descriptive enough that international users of this manual should be able to transpose the suggestions to their own tax situations.

Account Books should be capable of producing the information we need for financial management—for example, monthly and annual Profit and Loss Statements so we can plan and test our budget, while making competent judgments about the use of our business time. Our Account Books must also be capable of producing the summaries we need for taxpaying. Basically, these would be

- Periodic year-to-date statements of taxable income and expenses, as a basis for evaluating our quarterly liability for Estimated Taxes (see chapter 9).

- Annual statements of income from all business sources.

- Annual totals for each category of business expense we can deduct from our income at tax time.

- Annual totals for capital expenses, such as equipment purchases.

> FILING TRACK: *Working Files>TREASURER>Account Books.* (We keep these near our desktop and use them frequently.)

> RETENTION: Close out annually, but keep in *Storage Files>TREASURER>Tax Support Records* for at least seven years, to be prepared in case of an IRS audit. Some professionals prefer to keep them permanently, because there is no statute of limitations if the IRS suspects fraud (even unjustifiably). A photocopy of our return and its canceled tax-payment check(s) should be kept indefinitely to prove that the return was filed and *received*.

Expense and auto logs

These daily accounts are required by the IRS. Instructions for the self-employment form of our annual tax return state the basic requirements. Expense Logs keep track of the *amounts* and *purposes* for which we spend cash (photocopies, meals, tips, etc.) or pay for such things as entertainment and travel. Auto Logs keep track of either our actual vehicular expenses (gas, tires, etc.) or our business mileage (to the courthouse, post office, bank). We might also note the client or agency on whose behalf we incur each expense.

> FILING:
  1. The Auto Log belongs in our car. The Expense Log can be combined with it, or kept in our pocket or purse. A pocket-size notebook works well.
  2. At year's end, move to *Working Files>TREASURER>Tax Support Records.*
  3. After tax return for the year is completed, move to *Storage Files> TREASURER>Tax Support Records>[Year].*

> CROSS-REFERENCE: At least monthly, transfer data from Logs to Account Books. (If we wait until the end of the year and tackle this chore all at once, we regret it. In the meantime, we don't have the necessary data to make accurate projections for quarterly returns of Estimated Tax.)

Receipts

Two categories of records are common here: our paid bills and those odd-sized, multicolored bits of paper that accumulate in the wallet, the pocket, and the glove compartment of our vehicle. Because these expenses are entered promptly into Account Books, some professionals feel it is not necessary to sort receipts by type of expenditure also.

TIP

For business use of our personal car, it is easier to document mileage as an expense if, once a month, we multiply business miles by the current IRS allowance and write a check to our household account for that amount.

BUSINESS RECORD KEEPING

> FILING TRACK:
> 1. *Working Files>TREASURER>Tax Support Records>Receipts*.
> 2. After tax return for the year is completed, move to *Storage Files> TREASURER>Tax Support Records>[Year]*.

> RETENTION: Keep for seven years.

Banking records
We immediately reconcile canceled checks and bank statements with Account Books, making sure to enter bank charges and interest into Account Books as well.

> FILING:
> 1. *Working Files>TREASURER>Tax Support Records>Banking Records*.
> 2. After tax return for the year is completed, move to *Storage Files> TREASURER>Banking Records>[Year]*.

> CROSS-REFERENCE: Match deposit slips against Paid Invoices and Account Books to make sure all income is documented. Tax agencies frown seriously on underreporting. Mistakes are both expensive and dangerous.

FUNCTION 3: TAX PREPARATION
We might as well bite the bullet and do this ourselves. Although we consult our tax advisor, we serve our interests best by doing enough background reading of our own to prepare a return. We are the ones who make the financial decisions in our businesses. If we are not aware of their tax consequences, we make costly mistakes. Computer tax-preparation software can help. If we are afraid of making a Horrible Mistake, we can take our records and completed return to our tax advisor for review. Then we should be certain we understand any changes that our advisor recommends. The key records we maintain in this category are as follows:

Income tax return and special schedules
We keep copies of every form submitted with the federal and state returns, as well as a photocopy of our cancelled payment check(s).

> FILING TRACK: *Storage Files>TREASURER>Tax Preparation>[Year]*.

> RETENTION: Keep for at least seven years.

Tax support records
This category includes virtually all our financial papers—in general:

• Annual statements of interest earned; any Form 1099 (Miscellaneous Income) we receive from a person or entity for whom we worked or lectured.

• Books, logs, paid invoices, and receipts.

• Applicable worksheets completed in accordance with tax instructions (though not submitted with the return) and our own scratch or practice sheets.

• State, county, and municipality tax forms and supporting documents.

• Sales-tax reporting forms.

TIP

Consider using accordion portfolios for receipts. They fit our file drawers but have sides so nothing falls out. Those with twelve pockets will separate receipts by month and make a convenient bundle for storage when we finish our tax return.

- Employee tax and Social Security reporting forms.

  > FILING TRACK: *Storage>TREASURER>Tax Preparation>[Year]*.

  > RETENTION: Keep for at least seven years.

Purchasing Agent

FUNCTION: SUPPLIES AND EQUIPMENT MANAGEMENT

Stationery items

As purchasing agent, we maintain (and possibly design) masters for our letterhead, envelopes, business cards, brochures, mailing labels, etc. These files should be stored flat in a stiff envelope within an appropriately labeled folder. If we are certified, this set of files logically includes the master copy of our certification seal.

  > FILING TRACK: *Working Files>PURCHASING>Stationery [or Brochure, etc.]*.

  > RETENTION: Permanent—or until redesigned.

  > CROSS-REFERENCE: We may want to archive one copy for our business history.

Serial-, model-, and stock-number lists

Lists of these numbers are needed for both repairs and replacement of supplies—not to mention cases of fire or theft.

  > FILING TRACK: *Working Files>PURCHASING>Serial [etc.] Numbers*.

  > RETENTION: Discard when equipment is replaced.

  > CROSS-REFERENCE: If we buy supplies locally, we may want to keep a card list of model and stock numbers in our wallet, day planner, or Expense Log.

Capital purchase records

Two kinds of documents are commonly kept here: consumer research files and paperwork for products bought.

- **Consumer research files.** These would include ads, new product reviews, and written estimates of what we need and can afford.

  > FILING TRACK: *Pending Files>PURCHASING>Capital Purchase Plans*.

  > RETENTION: After a decision is made, destroy or recycle all but the ones for the product chosen.

  > CROSS-REFERENCE: Move to *Working Files>PURCHASING>Capital Purchase>[Specific Item]*, as below.

- **Paperwork for products bought**. For each acquired item, we also keep our purchase or lease contract or receipt, service contracts, warranty, and technical manuals.

  > FILING TRACK: *Working Files>PURCHASING>Capital Purchases>[Specific Item]*.

  > RETENTION: Destroy or recycle when product is replaced.

TIPS

Each year, we should compare our present return with those of the recent past, noting

- our general patterns of income and expense; and

- any excess deductions or payments we need to bring forward to this year's return.

We should also keep our reporting methods as uniform as possible from year to year.

The professional printer who prepares our letterhead and matching stationery supplies may keep our masters on file so we can reorder by phone. If so, wisdom suggests that we keep backup duplicates in our own files.

BUSINESS RECORD KEEPING

TIP

The calculations needed to amortize costs of major our equipment purchases (which often have different "lives" for tax purposes) are most helpful if those calculations are made on or attached to the Treasurer's copy of the purchase document. They can be checked off each year until the deduction is exhausted or the equipment is replaced.

> CROSS-REFERENCE: Put photocopy of purchase contract or receipt in *Working Files>TREASURER>Tax Support Documents.*

Marketing Director

FUNCTION: BUSINESS PROMOTION

Advertisements
For efficient management of our promotional efforts, we keep copies of our design masters, published advertisements, related correspondence, and any statistics we generate by coding our ads (see chapter 11, Marketing Strategies).

> FILING TRACK: *Working Files>MARKETING>Advertisements.*
> RETENTION: Three years is a reasonable period during which the ad might generate responses.
> CROSS-REFERENCE: A copy of the ad, stapled to its corresponding bill, should go in *Working Files>TREASURER>Receipts.*

Professional resume
Ideally, we should maintain both a detailed resume and an abridged version. If we produce brochures that describe our services or biographical sketches for publication, they belong in this file also.

> FILING TRACK: *Working Files>MARKETING>Resume [or Brochures, etc.].*
> RETENTION: Destroy or recycle out-of-date resumes, biographies, or brochures, to avoid confusion.
> CROSS-REFERENCE: We may want to archive copies of each for our business or personal history.

Review-copy log
If we are publishers, we will want to keep a log of copies sent out for review—identifying the book, the recipient, the date mailed, and the cost of the book (a tax deductible expense).

> FILING:
A. At end of the year, move to *Working Files>TREASURER>Tax Support Records.*
B. After preparing tax return, move to *Storage>TREASURER>Tax Support Records<[Year].*
> RETENTION: Keep at least seven years.

Librarian

FUNCTION 1: COLLECTION DEVELOPMENT

Purchasing plan and publication reviews
As librarian for our enterprise, we will maintain files of published reviews for books and CD-ROM that we are likely to use—and may actually buy. While the master copy of our purchasing plan remains in the President's permanent files,

that purchasing plan is inseparable (or should be!) from any covetous designs we may have on capital investments. Therefore, it is logical that a copy of the purchasing plan be maintained in close proximity to those product reviews.

> FILING TRACK: *Pending Files>LIBRARIAN>Reviews [or Purchasing Plan].*

> RETENTION: After a purchasing decision is made, transfer reviews to *Working Files>LIBRARIAN>Archival Management>Reviews.* (Even if we do not buy a particular book or product that is relevant to our specialty, as we proceed to use it in the future we will likely reconsult the review to refresh our memory of its strengths and weaknesses.)

Receipts

> FILING: Route to *Working>TREASURER>Receipts* for proper action.

FUNCTION 2: ARCHIVAL MANAGEMENT

Offprints and media

Photocopies and audio- or video tapes are commonly archived by professional genealogists for future consultation. Diverse subjects usually cover business ethics, computer maintenance and software tips, copyright and right-to-privacy issues, genealogical methods and sources, historical and legal discussions that help interpret research findings, and tax and investment concerns.

> FILING TRACK: *Working Files>LIBRARIAN>Business Resources>[Subject].*

> RETENTION: Purge regularly. Out-of-date advice is dangerous.

Forms and templates

These typically include form letters, report and invoice templates, boilerplate explanations to merge into form letters, bibliographic lists, style sheets, and similar oft-repeated materials.

> FILING TRACK: *Working Files>LIBRARIAN>Form Files>[Subject].*

Vice-President for Research

FUNCTION 1: PROJECT MANAGEMENT

Tracking file

A master record of all clients, past and present, can be kept on individual sheets or cards or maintained in a computer data base. We begin a Client Tracking Form (see figure 14) when a new authorization is received. We follow the project from initial contact to closing. We note billing details, time, instructions, present status of work, and the path names of associated computer files. New authorizations by past clients can be added to their old Client Tracking Form, even if work treats a different problem. To be a useful tool, the Client Tracking Form must be up to date.

> FILING TRACK: *Working Files>RESEARCH>Tracking File>[Client Name].*

> RETENTION: Permanent.

BUSINESS RECORD KEEPING

FIG. 14
CLIENT TRACKING FORM

DEERE

CLIENT .... | Jane Doe Deere   (Mrs. Buck)
                                      | Phone: 123-123-1234   12345 Northwoods
                                      | Fax: 123-123-1235   Grand Mountain, US 00000
                                      | e-mail: jdeere@info.com

FILE NAME .... | Research / DEERE-Jane / Report 1 (also Report 2, Report-3)

STATUS .... | 10 July 1996   Project authorized by client letter
                                      | $35 per hour + expenses
                                      | 30¢ per mile, out-of-town travel   Advance: $560.00
                                      | Work 16 hours; report after each 8
                                      | Begin: late August–early September

                                      | 29 Aug 1996   Mailed interim Report 1
                                      | Worked 8 hours   Balance: $280.00

                                      | 10 Sep 1996   Mailed final Report 1
                                      | Worked 8 hours
                                      | Expenses: $18.00, photocopies   Due: $ 18.00

                                      | 17 Sep 1996   Invoice paid in full   Balance: $ 00.00
                                      | Authorization to continue: 8 hours

                                      | 23 Sep 1996   Mailed Report 2
                                      | Objective reached in 7 hours
                                      | Client invoiced   Due: $245.00

                                      | 30 Sep 1996   Invoice paid in full   Balance: $ 00.00
                                      | "Thank You: No new research needed."

                                      | **CLOSED**   **Records removed to Storage**

NEW PROJECT .... | 03 May 1998   Phone authorization: 8 hours
                                      | "Please try adjacent ABC County"
                                      | Fee quoted: $440.00 (same expenses)
                                      | Letter of confirmation mailed for signing

STATUS .... | 20 May 1998   Advance & signed letter received   Balance: $320.00
                                      | Begin: 1 July

NOTE:

This tracking system can be maintained on computer, manually in a log book, or in a card file as shown at left.

Time-and-charges log

This file is begun before we analyze the client problem or do any research. Here, we record the time and money spent on a client's project—and we record it at the time each occurs; we don't guess when we prepare the invoice. Before billing, we add the entries previously made (at the time they occur) in our Auto Log, Expense Log, or Telephone Log.

> > FILING TRACK: *Working Files > RESEARCH > [Client Name] > [File Subdivision].*

> > RETENTION: Permanent—both electronic and hard copy. Safety suggests that the electronic copy on the hard drive be backed up by an archived floppy disk.

> > CROSS-REFERENCE: At billing, attach a copy permanently to the Unpaid Invoice.

FUNCTION 2: RESEARCH

Client research files

The Secretary begins this file with the initial inquiry, authorization, and client-supplied research notes—then assigns a file name (the client's name or the primary ancestral surname). As the project progresses, we generally add other types of data, as below. If we perform more than one assignment for the client, it may be necessary to subdivide these files, as follows:

- Our analysis and research plan (see chapter 14).

- Later correspondence with the client or with others on his or her behalf.

- Research notes and photocopies.

- Reports to the client and corresponding invoices.

- Appendixes—such as ancestor charts, family group sheets, and maps.

- Printouts of related Computer Files. (When we change hardware or software, or as technology advances, we may lose access to the electronic files.)

> > FILING TRACK: *Working Files > RESEARCH > [File Name] > [File Subdivision].*

> > RETENTION: Permanent.

Vice-President for Teaching

FUNCTION 1: BOOKING AND TRAVEL ARRANGEMENTS

Event files

This master file of all bookings, past and present, can be kept on individual sheets or index cards, or maintained in a computer database—in the same manner as our Client Tracking Files. An Event File is begun when an invitation is proffered and the date is tentatively blocked on our schedule pending a final agreement. It follows arrangements from initial contact to paid invoice. It includes the contract and all subsequent correspondence or telephone notes.

It is professionally dangerous and inefficient to send out reports without keeping a full file copy of the report and all attachments. If clients were to question our work, we'd lack the needed materials to consult. If they lodged a complaint, we could not defend ourselves. If they later asked us to resume the project where we left off, we would not have the complete file. If the client suffered a record loss and came back to us, we could not help without redoing the entire work.

BUSINESS RECORD KEEPING

> FILING TRACK:
> 1. *Working Files>TEACHING>[Event or Sponsor Name]*.
> 2. After payment, transfer invoice to *Working Files>TREASURER>Paid Invoices*.

> RETENTION: Permanent. Many societies issue return invitations after some years elapse; then we need to identify our prior contacts, topics, and special situations involved. Or another society in the same region may invite us, in which case we enhance our drawing power by not repeating topics from the earlier event.

> CROSS-REFERENCE:
> 1. Enter income appropriately in Account Books.
> 2. Enter date of event on Secretary's Calendar.

Short-term travel documents

As a booking agent, we arrange travel (if the sponsor does not) and maintain tickets; confirmations; and receipts for such miscellaneous expenses as meals, parking, and taxi.

> FILING TRACK:
> Before event: *Pending Files>TEACHING>Travel>[Event or Sponsor Name]*.
> After event: Transfer to *Working Files>TREASURER>Tax Support Documents*. The income is entered appropriately in Account Books.

> CROSS-REFERENCE: Income and Expenses are entered in Account Books.

Long-term travel documents

Frequent-flyer program records; auto-, hotel- and discount-club plans; and similar materials fall within this category; but their filing and retention differ from documents that pertain to only one event.

> FILING TRACK: *Working Files>TEACHING>Travel>[Program]*. Frequent-flyer-program records may be subdivided by airline, if we participate in multiple programs.

> RETENTION: Purge regularly. Upon expiration, most can be destroyed. If frequent-flyer miles are taxable in our jurisdiction, we should transfer used award documents to *Working Files>TREASURER>Tax Support Records>Income: Miscellaneous*.

> CROSS-REFERENCE: Consult IRS instructions for Schedule C, Form 1040, to determine whether mileage awards must be reported as income.

FUNCTION 2: LECTURING

Lecture materials

Handout masters, lecture notes, and visual enhancements may be foldered, placed in notebooks, clipped into report covers, or boxed and placed on bookshelves; but they still need to be arranged systematically.

> FILING TRACK: *Working Files>TEACHING>[Topic]>[Type of Material—Handout Masters, Lecture, Visuals, etc.]*.

> RETENTION: Permanent—or until lecture or supplemental material is revised.

TIP

Paying by business check or credit card, whenever possible, provides an ideal receipt. If cash outlays are necessary, we should be extra careful to enter the amount and purpose of each in our Expense Log, which should be with us on the trip.

Vice-President for Products and Publications

FUNCTION 1: WRITING

Manuscripts

Working drafts are ephemeral. In most cases, they are redundant as soon as the next one is finished. Major revisions, however, should be kept until we are certain that we have finished writing. If we use a computer, it is wise to copy each draft and work on the copy until a final draft is produced.

> FILING TRACK: *Working Files>PUBLICATIONS>Manuscripts [Title of Work]*.

> RETENTION: Permanent. After publication, transfer both electronic and paper copies to Storage for later production of new versions or editions.

Contracts, copyrights, and registrations

See chapters 6 and 7 for Contracts and Copyrights and chapter 27 for International Standard Book Numbers [ISBN] and International Standard Serial Numbers [ISSN] that publishers and bookstores use to identify book and periodical (serial) titles, respectively.

> FILING TRACK:
> 1. Copyrights and ISBN/ISSN requests: *Pending Files>PUBLICATIONS>[Type of Request]>[Title of Work]*.
> 2. Approved requests: *Working Files>PUBLICATIONS>[Type of Registration]> [Title of Work]*.
> 3. Contracts: *Working Files>PUBLICATIONS>[Type of Registration]>[Title of Work]*.

> RETENTION: Permanent. When terms of these items expire, remove to Storage.

> CROSS-REFERENCE: Record year of copyright renewal in "Long-range Dates" on Secretary's Calendar.

Financial records

These vary according to whether our writing earns income and whether the income is from royalties or direct sales. Incidental expenses for producing the final draft (paper, toner, etc.) are part of general office expenses, and need not be entered separately in Account Books. When we publish and sell the material ourselves or through a distributor, we should follow the guidelines in Function 2, below.

> FILING: Transfer to *Working Files>TREASURER>Receipt [or Paid Invoice]*.

> CROSS-REFERENCE: Set up a Royalties account in Account Books.

FUNCTION 2: PRODUCING, PUBLISHING, OR SELLING

Capitalization expense records

Under current regulations, expenses related to payments for producing books—for example, typesetting and graphic services, printing, binding, and shrink-wrapping— or other items for sale (forms, novelties, etc.) must be apportioned among all the

TIP

Many costs incurred in the production of books may not be tax-deductible in the year we actually pay those expenses. We should carefully study tax law on this point.

BUSINESS RECORD KEEPING

copies or products produced and deducted from income product by product.

> > FILING TRACK: *Working Files>TREASURER>[Name of Book or Product]*.

> > RETENTION: After the last item of a product is sold and the taxable income is reported, keep the file in Storage for seven years.

Inventory

The IRS requires that we prepare an annual list that cites, for each book or product, the number and value of items or copies produced and the number and value of items or copies remaining unsold. (If we use small-business accounting software for billing, our inventory figures should stay up to date without an actual book-by-book count each year.)

> > FILING TRACK: *Working Files>TREASURER>Inventory*.

> > RETENTION: After completion of the year's tax return, move to Storage and retain with other tax files for seven years.

> > CROSS-REFERENCE: Copy the print-run/production and unsold figures onto next year's Inventory Form, before removing to Storage.

Sales accounts

Here we keep records of when and to whom we ship orders, the income from each sold item, any refunds we make, and the marketing expenses we incur. If we have numerous titles or items for sale, we need a more sophisticated bookkeeping system than is normal for a research business. A tax advisor is essential.

> > FILING TRACK: *Working Files>TREASURER>Sales>[Name of Book or Product] >Income [or Expenses]*.

> > RETENTION: Same schedule as other Treasurer accounts.

Customer lists

In addition to a basic mailing list, this file should track sales customer by customer, rather than item by item—something that standard small-business accounting software can do with ease. Maintaining a separate list of standing-order customers lets us print their mailing labels immediately.

> > FILING TRACK: *Working Files>PUBLISHING>Customer Lists*.

> > RETENTION: Permanent.

Vice-President for Volunteerism

FUNCTION: ORGANIZATIONAL ACTIVITIES

Volunteer records are often the quickest to get out of hand. Control is essential, but it can be difficult to judge what to keep or throw away. The following guidelines may help.

Organizational records

Keep the minutes, financial reports, and final reports issued by officers of the organization for which we donate time, work, or advice. We may wish to keep files

TIP

If we use a distributor to warehouse our stock and fill orders, our contract should require annual inventory reports.

for controversial issues as well. Unless space is abundant, we eliminate preliminary reports, proposals that are not implemented, and out-of-date lists of officers and members.

> > FILING TRACK: *Working Files > VOLUNTEER > [Name of Organization] > [Type of Document]*.
> > RETENTION: Keep as long as we remain active in the organization.

Personal administrative records

As officers or chairs we create other materials—some of longtime importance, others not. For the duties we fill and the files we pass on to others, we keep the kind of records we wish our predecessor had given us!

> > FILING TRACK: *Working Files > VOLUNTEER > [Name of Organization] > [Type of Document]*
> > RETENTION: At the end of our service, we pass essential records to our successor and dispose of the remainder (generally: ordinary correspondence, notes, and our own preliminary reports) if we lack storage space.

Personal records

For our personal and business history, we want to maintain a selection of materials that illustrate our accomplishments—such as award certificates, diplomas, magazine and newspaper articles that document our contributions to the field, membership cards for professional organizations, photographs that capture our activities live, printed programs for conferences and other events at which we were featured, recordings of lectures or events, and resumes at various stages of our professional life.

> > FILING TRACK: *Working Files > VOLUNTEER > [Name of Organization] > Personal Records*.
> > RETENTION: Remove to Storage, at end of service.

Summary Concepts

Competent business management requires quick and reliable access to business records. This can be accomplished only within a comprehensive system for acquiring and keeping needed information in paper or electronic form. An effective system design is based on our business's Organizational Chart—a diagram that depicts the hierarchy and relationships of its divisions (President, Secretary, Treasurer, etc.) Records are grouped correspondingly into logical series (based upon function or duties). Available filing space is divided into three usage areas: Pending, Working, and Storage. Computer disk space is similarly subdivided into subdirectories and backup diskettes. To be effective, the entire system must be precisely and faithfully maintained. Obviously, our system will be a reflection of our sense of order and the way we work. But, as a management tool, it must recognize also the nature of our business and the way we *ought* to work.

For the duties we fill and the files we pass on to others, we keep the kind of records we wish our predecessor had given us!

BUSINESS RECORD KEEPING

Order is a lovely nymph, the child of beauty and wisdom; her attendants are comfort, neatness, and activity; her abode is the valley of happiness: she is always to be found when sought for, and never appears so lovely as when contrasted with her opponent, disorder.

—*Samuel Johnson*[3]

NOTES

1. This tip, of course, presumes that we maintain a separate business account. However, many banks will not open a business account without evidence of a local business license; and many locales won't issue business licenses for certain residential addresses (as discussed in chapter 9).

2. Bookstores offer a number of good commercial taxpaying guides, all tax-deductible. We may wish to purchase several until we find the ones that best suit our needs.

3. Samuel Johnson (1709–84), English author, lexicographer, and conversationalist; quoted in Tryon Edwards, *The New Dictionary of Thoughts: A Cyclopedia of Quotations,* Ralph Emerson Browns, ed. (1852; revised edition, N.p.: Standard Book Co., 1962), 458.

FURTHER STUDY

Entrepreneur Magazine's Complete Guide to Owning a Home-Based Business. New York: Bantam Books, 1990. A comprehensive, still relevant discussion that is particularly applicable to genealogical businesses.

Department of the Treasury, Internal Revenue Service. *Tax Guide for Small Business.* Publication 334. A free booklet available at most IRS offices. It includes a list of subsidiary publications that relate to specific aspects of business taxpaying.

Hales, Frank T. "Good Record Keeping: The Key to a Successful, Tax-Wise Business." *Association of Professional Genealogists [APG] Quarterly* 6 (Winter 1991): 87–89.

Hoff, Henry B., CPA, CG, FASG. "Taxes and the Professional Genealogist." *APG Quarterly* 11 (December 1996): 110–15.

Litman, Laurie. "Recordkeeping," *How to Start a Business,* website of the San Joaquin Delta College Small Business Development Center. Revised 3 January 2000. An award-winning "online book."

Pinson, Linda, and Jerry Jinnett. *Keeping the Books: Basic Recordkeeping and Accounting for the Small Business.* 3d edition. Chicago: Upstart, 1998.

"Record Keeping for Small Business." *The Alberta Business Advantage.* Website of Alberta Economic Development and Tourism. The Alberta Economic Development is a rich source of papers on numerous aspects of home-based and other small businesses—advice that transcends national bounds.

SCORE—Counselors to America's Small Businesses, website. One of the best online sites for all types of small-business help.

"The SOHO Guidebook." Website *CCH Business Owner's Toolkit,* copyright 2000. Sponsored commercially, this Internet publication offers thousands of pages on almost every conceivable aspect of small business management.

13

TIME MANAGEMENT

TIME MANAGEMENT

Keynotes

Time Management

by Patricia Law Hatcher, CG, FASG

Time. Money. Genealogists rarely have enough of either. We talk about them as if they are the same: "spending time," "saving time," "time is money." But they aren't the same. There is a significant difference. We can earn money; we can receive it as a gift; we even can *win* it—but our day always contains exactly twenty-four hours. Thus, time management is not about managing time. It's about managing what we put into those inelastic twenty-four hours. It's about choices. We must choose what consumes those precious hours and what does not.

This chapter is not for the organized person looking for a few more tips—those lucky folks may skip to the next chapter. It is for the disorganized genealogist who is chronically overcommitted, behind schedule, and frazzled.

Management Problems

Time management is an ongoing activity. Dozens of times each day we make decisions—consciously or unconsciously—to begin, continue, or terminate various activities. Many of the time management problems genealogists face do not have solutions, but if we recognize the problems, we can make more informed decisions.

Problem 1: Creating boundaries

The biggest problem a professional genealogist has is the mixing, even merging, of vocation and avocation. Almost any one of us, if given eight hours and told that we must use it for something we really want to do, would—guess what—use it for genealogy. Other professions are marked by boundaries of time, place, and activity: their workdays begin at a particular hour, at a particular location, by performing an activity that is identifiably "work." Our boundaries are fuzzy. In genealogy, we share the problem of time and place boundaries with other professionals who are independent contractors or who operate home-based businesses; but the problem of setting activity boundaries is a matter peculiar to genealogy.

SOCIAL BOUNDS

If we are to be professional, we must control digressions from the work at hand, whether we are preparing a client report, writing a newsletter article, creating a lecture, or doing our filing. All deserve our full and uninterrupted attention. It can be difficult to persuade our family, friends, neighbors, and pets that we really are working and cannot routinely be interrupted for nonbusiness matters. But there is a difference between being accessible and being at someone's beck and call.

PHYSICAL BOUNDS

Before we can identify boundaries for others, we must establish them clearly for ourselves. If we have a home office, we need a clearly defined office space with

> The biggest problem a professional genealogist has is the mixing, even merging, of vocation and avocation.

TIME MANAGEMENT

physical boundaries, preferably with a door. We'll benefit from higher productivity. If we take a home-office tax deduction, the Internal Revenue Service requires that clearly defined space.

TEMPORAL BOUNDS

We need to establish an identifiable beginning and ending to our workday. We can set office hours and post them to remind ourselves and others. We should answer the telephone in a businesslike manner, without the telltale sounds of a television or a radio in the background. We should, somewhat literally, put on work clothes, go to the office, and close the door.

Problem 2: Identifying clients

"But I don't have clients, because I don't do research for pay." Wrong! Anyone reading this book probably has clients. There are many kinds of clients. We are professional genealogists *not* because we crank a microfilm reader for monetary gain, but because we have agreed to produce something for someone. In the consulting business, this is called a *deliverable*. We must identify our deliverables and our clients (paying or otherwise), in order to identify how we fill our time.

Let's see how many clients we really have. On a sheet of paper, let's write *Client List* in big letters at the top, then divide the paper into four columns. The first column needs the label *Client*, the second *Deliverable*; the others can stay blank. We'll use them later. For now, let's ask ourselves,

Are we

- *writing an article?* We enter the editor's name as the client and the article title as the deliverable.

- *compiling a book for press?* The camera-ready copy is the deliverable; the client may be another individual, a society, or even ourselves. If the book is personal, our publishing company is the client.

- *preparing a lecture?* The society is the client.

- *working on certification?* The Board for Certification of Genealogists or the Genealogical Institute of the Maritimes, perhaps, is the client.

- *preparing an extra-large pedigree chart for Mom's family reunion?* Mom's the client now.

- *generating an electronic file for a researcher who shares our problem line?* That person is the client; the file is the deliverable.

We have a lot more clients than we thought, don't we? But probably not quite enough to explain where our time goes. So, let's add three more entries.

Our business, for which the deliverable is "office tasks." This incorporates all those mundane, time-consuming chores such as paying bills, buying file folders, and making backup copies of computer files.

> We are professional genealogists not because we crank a microfilm reader for monetary gain, but because we have agreed to produce something for someone.

Our profession, for which the deliverable is "education." Education encompasses reading books and journals; exploring online sources of information; and attending lectures, conferences, and workshops.

Our own research, whose obvious deliverables may be as important professionally as personally. We are an important client, not only because we need to be nice to ourselves but also because we research our own families differently. Most of us spend infinitely more time and pursue our own elusive ancestors with considerably more diligence and persistence than is feasible for a paying client. As a result, we explore pathways we would otherwise never have entered—led by an ancestor who didn't bother to ask if we *wanted* to learn about Kentucky's criminal court records before he rode off on a horse he neglected to pay for. Ultimately, our experiences in researching our own ancestors will benefit our clients, whether they are readers, lecture or radio audiences, patrons of our library or bookshop, or people who ask us to do research.

Problem 3: Organizing time

Our days are already five hours too short; where are we going to find time to organize? We have no choice. The one factor common to every time-management program is a formal system of organization—setting goals, listing tasks, identifying priorities, and marking completions. Those who teach time management are convinced that *the key to having enough time is taking time to organize our time.*

So, back to the Client List. After adding *Date Due* and *Estimated Hours Required* at the head of the two remaining columns, we need to complete the information and prioritize the listed items. Our desks should be clear of *all* papers, except those related to the top priority item. Everything else goes out of sight; if an eye can see them, the mind will wander from the task at hand. (The Client List, not the stack of paper, should be our reminder.) Tackling the first project, we complete it in one sitting, if possible. The startup time required to return to that project at a later date is much greater than most of us realize.

Problem 4: Planning for unbillable time

We know everything takes time, but do we acknowledge and plan for it? How long does it take to buy stamps, learn a computer program, or take out the trash? Do we routinely allow for that time when planning our day? How often have we said, "I can write that report in three hours," only to find that it took well over four. Why? The difference may be due to optimism—or it may be due to the difference between *lapsed time* and *applied time.*

How many *external* interruptions were there—phone calls, plumbing repairs, questions from family members or colleagues, or neighbors who stopped by to chat? Maybe we did "keep on working," but we simply can't do two things simultaneously at full efficiency. (Anyone who can wouldn't be reading this chapter.) How many *internal* interruptions were there—misplaced papers or unrelated matters that caught our attention? And, finally, how long does it actually take to do the routine,

> One factor common to every time-management program is a formal system of organization: setting goals, listing tasks, identifying priorities, and marking completions.

TIME MANAGEMENT

auxiliary tasks the project requires—to record time and expenses, label a file folder, type an invoice, make file copies, address and stamp an envelope, and file the report? For a few days, we should keep a log—using a timer to track *applied* rather than *lapsed* time for every task. The results can be surprising.

Problem 5: Cutting time waste

Although time management is about making choices, there is one choice that we should never make. We should never choose to waste time. Five minutes watching cardinals at the bird feeder—is that wasted time? No. It may provide a needed rest for computer-weary eyes or let us return to a difficult problem with a fresh perspective. It certainly adds to the quality of life. Choices shouldn't be based merely on whether something is productive or lucrative; fun is okay.

What then is wasted time? For starters, most of us can remember a time (or lots of them!) we spent thirty minutes looking for a mislaid paper or file. That time was neither productive nor lucrative, and it definitely wasn't fun. (Odds are, it also made our blood pressure rise.) There is not a single positive benefit from using time in that manner—and it is *totally unnecessary*. If a task must be done, there is a most efficient time to do it. In the case of filing that lost paper, the moment had passed, never to be recovered. One key to managing time is managing paper. Stacks labeled (literally or mentally) "to be filed" are big time wasters. Once we have picked up a piece of paper, we should *not* put it down anywhere other than in its final resting place.

Waiting until the last minute to complete a letter or report, an article or lecture, or handouts or transparencies creates a rash of opportunities for wasted time. It can force an extra trip to the copy center and another to the post office to dispatch overnight mail. Those extra trips are wasted time. A rush job is more likely to be a botched job that needs corrections—more wasted time (not to mention embarrassment for us and time loss for the recipient). It is difficult to proofread material we have just written. We need to allow time for it to get "cold" and give ourselves the opportunity to correct or improve it *before* presenting the final copy. That's saving time.

Problem 6: Identifying procrastination

Procrastination is easy to identify. It's putting off tasks until the last minute. Or is it? What if there simply isn't enough time before then? Is that procrastination or merely a reasonable ordering of priorities? If the task is unpleasant, we probably are procrastinating. But what if the task is, say, writing a lecture that we volunteered to give? Surely unpleasantness isn't the problem.

There is another cause of procrastination. Perfectionism. Given the attention to detail required for genealogical research, it is no surprise that many of us are perfectionists. We often have difficulty accepting anything less than a perfect presentation from ourselves. By postponing the project until the last moment, we provide ourselves with a built-in excuse for any imperfections in the result: "I had to write it on the plane," or "I've been so busy, I only had three hours to put it

> Most of us can remember a time (or lots of them!) we spent thirty minutes looking for a mislaid paper or file. That time was neither productive nor lucrative, and it definitely wasn't fun.

together." Sometimes we *know* we'll do a good job (some of us could probably ad-lib the entire talk and get a great response), and we've probably been mentally planning it for months. Yet a rushed final execution often means late handouts; transparencies with typos; and unnecessary worry for the program chairperson, syllabus editor, or others involved. If we are procrastinating perfectionists, we should consider how our actions affect others.

Problem 7: Making time for growth

Being professional requires continual education. Much of it is acquired by reading. National journals help us improve our methodology. Regional and local publications inform us about records in our areas of interest. Business and computer publications help us increase our business efficiency. And books, journals, and articles in nongenealogical fields—such as archaeology, history, law, religion, and sociology—remind us that an ancestor is more than a name and three dates on a chart.

Reading takes time, lots of it. The key is not to let it stack up. We should *schedule* breaks for reading. In nice weather we can take a cup of coffee and our journals to the patio or porch, away from the telephone and desktop clutter. We'll be more relaxed, and our "must-read" stack will quickly shrink. We needn't stop there, either. We can double-up our time. If we keep current newsletters in the car, we can read them at the bank's drive-through line or in the dentist's waiting room. We might keep some by the telephone, for when the tech-support line puts us on hold. Many lectures at national conferences are taped. We can use those tapes to "attend" lectures during our daily walk or weekly drive to the archives.

Education also means networking. At conferences, workshops, and professional round tables, the discussions of research in general—and difficult cases in particular—help us grow, whether we are professionals or hobbyists. The new friends and contacts we make will prove valuable through the years. We should remember, though, that other genealogists have time-management problems, too. Let's respect *their* time, as well. Contact with peers can be a constant exchange, so we look for ways to do it efficiently. We might, for example:

- keep a stack of stamped postcards at hand and use them for brief notes to colleagues and clients. "Great article. I learned a lot about that record group." Or, "Next time you are at the archives, would you please verify this date for me? Thanks, I owe you." Or, "Received the file Friday. I'll begin the work at the Historical Society on the 15th."

- respond to colleagues' queries on their original letters and keep photocopies for our file. A brief handwritten note that says, "I read that date as the '14th day of September A.D. 1748'," is always better than a nonexistent typed response.

- use the telephone more often. Many of us are penny wise and pound foolish about long-distance calling. Which costs less—thirty minutes of nonbillable time to create a letter (let's be realistic about the time involved) plus the cost of letterhead, envelope, and stamp—or $1 for a ten-minute daytime call? Of course, when we call we must also control the chitchat.

> A rushed final execution often means late handouts; transparencies with typos; and unnecessary worry for the program chairperson, syllabus editor, or others involved.

Problem 8: Saying "no"

Like the gal in *Oklahoma!,* many of us have a great deal of difficulty uttering a simple two-letter word. Why is this so difficult? We feel pressured to say "yes." The source of the pressure may be the requestor or it may be ourselves because, by nature, we want to please. Effective time managers practice saying *"No!"* out loud until it sounds right. Some put a large sign over their telephone that says *"No!"* and another on their calendar. And they are wary of offering before they are asked.

We also have difficulty saying "no" to ourselves. We have a great idea for an article we *want* to write or a lecture we *want* to give. Should we say "no" or should we put it on our priority list? It helps to remember that we haven't miraculously added a twenty-fifth hour to our day. If we place the item on the list, we demote every item below it, and one of them must fall off. We have, in effect, said "no" to that bottom item. We shouldn't delude ourselves. We really can't do everything we want to do. We must take control. We must choose *which* project deserves that "no." We must be realistic when assessing how long a project will take. A lecture may involve only an hour of speaking, but it probably involves forty hours of preparation and from four hours to two days surrounding the presentation, depending on where it is given.

Ironically, one thing to which we have difficulty saying "no" isn't even a person. It's a thing—the telephone. We do not have to answer the phone just because it rings. The voice on the other end can usurp an immense amount of our time— time we can't replace. The answering machine is a wonderful tool for screening phone calls.

Problem 9: Giving away time

Most professional genealogists want to give time to the field. We know how much we benefit from the efforts of others. Genealogy is based on sharing. Without that sharing and giving, our success rates would be minimal—and the work considerably less enjoyable. We want to give back in fair measure; but we shouldn't do it just because someone asks, no matter how worthy the request. The issue isn't *should* we give time. Rather, it's *How much time can we offer without jeopardizing other projects? It's Are we giving it to the right tasks?* And *Are we investing it in the right places?* To be professional means to give our time where we can benefit genealogy and genealogists the most.

Suppose we are researchers in a "black hole" county. We'd like to help our local society. The seminar chair asks us to do vendor letters. An inner voice should cry *Stop!* What are our *strengths?* We can type those letters, but so can half a dozen other members. What they cannot do, but we can, is write an article on alternate resources for the burned records in that county. As professionals, we should *recognize and emphasize our strengths,* not our abilities. Lawyers do not dust their own bookshelves. Doctors do not schedule their own appointments. If we can contribute from a strength instead of an ability, we've made far better use of our time.

To be professional is to give our time where we can benefit genealogy and genealogists the most.

We could, of course, do both the article and the vendor letters, but what then would we push off the priority list? Maybe we can delay the research for that elderly lady in California. *Stop!* She may have spent five years looking for a competent researcher in our neck of the woods. She may be *very* elderly. We may be able to find the answer that is the high point of her genealogy this year. Now why was it that we should type those vendor letters?

Problem 10: Controlling the inquiring mind

Ironically, the trait that makes good genealogists *very* good also makes behind-schedule genealogists even more behind. The constantly open, curious, inquiring mind occasionally helps us crack a tough case, generally broadens our knowledge, and almost always wreaks havoc with our carefully constructed schedules.

The inquiring mind. It wonders why a particular name is *here* or another name isn't. It leads us to read the patent medicine ads next to the obituaries, to study tombstone carvings and carvers, to learn a foreign language, to read all items on an estate inventory and research an unfamiliar term. It prompts us to track down the biography of an ancestor's preacher, to chart extended families, to determine naming patterns, or to seek the ancestry of an entire community. The inquiring mind defies organization, but it makes us better genealogists.

How do we control the inquiring mind? *Should* we control it? Not necessarily. But before it leads us away from our charted path, we should look again at the schedule it's about to upheave. Will we be displacing personal research with no fixed deadlines—or client work that's already overdue? Therein rests the decision as to whether we should follow that siren call or install earplugs and forge ahead on scheduled tasks, after making a note for the future.

Summary Concepts

Can the disorganized, overcommitted, behind-schedule, and frazzled genealogist miraculously become a model of organization and efficiency? No. How about more organized, less overcommitted, less behind schedule, and less frazzled? Yes! Once we realize that it is our own responsibility to make our own decisions about what does—or does not—make it into our precious, inflexible, twenty-four hours. They were given to each of us individually, and *we* should control their use.

NOTES

1. Horace Mann (1786–1859), American educator, quoted in Edmund Fuller, ed., *6200 Wise Cracks, Witty Remarks, & Epigrams for All Occasions* (New York: Wings Books, 1971), 280.

FURTHER STUDY

Every issue of the *Association of Professional Genealogists [APG] Quarterly* features articles, discussions, and tips that can help with the decisions we must make. In particular, the June 1992 issue (vol. 7) treats many problems described in this chapter. Seminars on time management, often

Lost yesterday, somewhere between sunrise and sunset, two golden hours, each set with sixty diamond minutes. No reward is offered for they are gone forever.

—*Horace Mann*[1]

TIME MANAGEMENT

> A time management system must feel comfortable to us, or we'll quickly abandon it.

focused upon an organizer product, are popular with busy business people. Bookstores and libraries have numerous books and tapes on time management, and new ones appear each year. We should look for one that strikes a familiar chord. A time management system must feel comfortable to us, or we'll quickly abandon it. The following resources can serve as a beginning point in this quest.

Eisenberg, Ronni. *The Overwhelmed Person's Guide to Time Management.* New York: Plume, 1997.

Ferner, Jack D. *Successful Time Management: A Self-Teaching Guide.* New York: Wiley, 1995.

Haynes, Marion E. *Practical Time Management: How to Make the Most of Your Most Perishable Resource.* Los Altos, California: Crisp Publications, 1991.

Home Office Computing. See website for subscription data.

Kanarek, Lisa. *Organizing Your Home Office for Success: Expert Strategies That Can Work for You.* 2d edition. Dallas, Texas: Blakeley Press, 1998.

Klein, Ruth. *Where Did the Time Go?: The Working Woman's Guide to Creative Time Management.* Rocklin, California: Prima Publications, 1994.

Mayer, Jeffrey J. *Time Management for Dummies.* Foster City, California: IDG Books Worldwide, 1999.

Mindell, Phyllis. *Power Reading: A Dynamic System for Mastering All Your Business Reading.* Englewood Cliffs, New Jersey: Prentice Hall, 1993.

"Responses to the September 1994 Question of the Quarter: Time-Saving Tips." *APG Quarterly* 10 (March 1995): 23–26.

Scott, Dru. *Time Management and the Telephone: Making It a Tool and Not a Tyrant.* Los Altos, California: Crisp Publications, 1998.

Silber, Lee T. *Time Management for the Creative Person.* New York: Three Rivers Press, 1998.

Small Business Computing & Communications. By subscription from <www.SmallOffice.com>.

Smith, Hyrum W. *The 10 Natural Laws of Successful Time and Life Management: Proven Strategies for Increased Productivity and Inner Peace.* New York: Warner Books, 1994.

Stapinski, Helene, "Beat the Clock." *Home Office Computing* (May 1998): 64–68. Nine strategies to overcome time-crunches and streamline our operations.

The Get Organized News. Monthly newsletter. See website for subscription data.

The Small Business Journal. At newsstands. Also see website for subscription data.

Professional Research Skills

14

PROBLEM ANALYSES
AND
RESEARCH PLANS

**PROBLEM ANALYSES
AND RESEARCH PLANS**

Keynotes

Problem Analyses and Research Plans

by Helen F. M. Leary, CG, CGL, FASG

Family genealogists have a straightforward goal: to solve whatever problems their ancestors present. As professional genealogists, we have a different goal: to fulfill the terms of our contract with the client. Two clauses of that contract form the basis for this chapter: the research problem and the time limit. Within that limit—expressed as a specified number of hours, a sum of money, or a deadline—we must

- analyze the problem;
- develop a plan for solving it;
- conduct the investigation; and
- write the client report.

The efficiency of our analysis and the precision of our plan are keys to the success of our business—just as important as our knowledge of records.

> The efficiency of our analysis and the precision of our plan are keys to the success of our business—just as important as our knowledge of records.

Problem Analyses

Analysis is a process of disassembly—breaking down a composite into its constituent parts. This process illuminates the nature of the object or subject. It helps us identify the essential features, the relationships between them, and the roles each plays within the whole. In some fields, analysis is an end in itself; in genealogy, it is the means to the end—the mechanism by which we make reliable judgments about facts, theories, or courses of action.

For professional genealogists, the problem analysis that precedes research is conducted in two stages: the preliminary analysis and the detailed analysis. Although each stage has a different purpose, the process remains the same: applying to the problem a series of tests or questions that are so narrowly focused they cannot be evaded with generalities.

Preliminary analysis

When a potential client requests help, our immediate need is a sound decision in favor of accepting or declining the commission. Thus, our preliminary analysis focuses on three things: the nature of the research problem, the terms of the contract, and the likely consequences of the decision.

RESEARCH PROBLEM

Prudent professionals first compare the request to their business plan. (See chapter 9.) Do the business criteria include the type of work required to fill the client's need— perhaps complex problem-solving, consultation, database assistance, record retrieval, or compilation of a family history? Does the research problem lie in the geographic area and time period defined by our business plan?

PROBLEM ANALYSES
AND RESEARCH PLANS

CONTRACT TERMS

If the scope of an assignment appears compatible, other particulars need to be weighed. Does the time limit suggest a reasonable chance of success, or does the client expect a lineage traced to the unknown immigrant ancestor in three hours of work? Does the proposed timing and the amount of payment meet the fee schedule set for our business? Can our schedule accommodate the project?

DECISION CONSEQUENCES

In all analyses, it is wise to remember the old saw: *the devil is in the detail*. Great potential for future distress lies in hidden complexities. A problem that seems narrowly defined and fairly easy to solve can be the disguised tail of a tiger. Once grasped, it may be hard to turn loose. Multiple men of the same name may have to be better identified and sorted out before a "simple" question can be answered. Records that normally would provide direct answers may not have survived or may not have been created at all. Before making a final decision, we are wise to skim our personal library—refreshing our memory about record availability in the problem area and checking census indexes or similar "people finders" for the incidence of same-name persons. Other factors to consider include these:

- Does anything about the problem definition suggest that it might be more complex than it appears? For example, a client's statement, "I've looked everywhere and can't find John's wife," might stem from the client's inexperience or it might be an accurate account of an exhaustive search of all appropriate records. If true, the latter might foretell a wide-ranging probe of esoteric and unindexed sources or, perhaps, the need to build a case on indirect or circumstantial evidence. We might save ourselves grief, in this preliminary stage, by evaluating the client's manner of describing problems and documenting details. Therein may lie hints of the skill and thoroughness that underlie the information we're now asked to build upon.

- Does the commission imply special circumstances that need consideration? Might court testimony be required, for example?

- Do we have an overriding reason to accept a commission that may not fit our business plan or schedule? If so, what will we move aside or where may we skimp to make time for both the project and the necessary skill development?

- If we accept the commission, do we need anything further from the client—perhaps a more complete description of the problem? Does the client need to furnish source data for stated facts; or a notarized client-permission letter to conform to right-to-privacy laws; or photocopied documents, application blanks, and society instructions; or authorization to contact family members?

- If we decline the commission, can we recommend other researchers?

Detailed analysis

Once an assignment is accepted—before research begins in our home library, in any repository, or online—we should make a detailed analysis of all data the client provided. Our objective at this point is to create a well-directed research plan, appropriate to the scope and time limit of the commission. The client's problem may

We might save ourselves grief by evaluating the client's manner of describing problems and documenting details. Therein may lie hints of the skill or thoroughness that underlie the information we're now asked to build upon.

come to us as a terse letter, a short summary of known data, or a file of prior research notes. Regardless, in our analysis of this data, we should create for ourselves a set of instructions—each on an individual sheet. (This might be done in a computer file or on paper. The medium is less important than the method, although data entered into the computer can be integrated into later stages of our work without retyping.) One sheet, perhaps, might be headed *Ask client;* another, *Find out,* another, *Check,* and another, *Collect and compare.* As our analysis proceeds, we will create work lists on each sheet. By way of example:

Ask client
- why does client state that Barnabas cannot be John's father?
- are the family Bible entries all in the same hand, or do they appear to be written by various people across three generations?

Find out
- legal age brackets for poll-tax payment, militia service, and public labor.
- whether and/or when John left the county.

Check
- county militia rolls.
- county tax rolls and delinquent tax lists.
- county road-order books.

Collect and compare
- signatures and signature marks.
- cattle brand marks.
- all Doright land transactions, 1750–1825.

At this stage, we call heavily upon our background knowledge of sources—it is useless to instruct ourselves *Check marriage records,* if there are none extant for that place and time. We also need experience with effective methods so that we can make sound projections. For example, correlating all those Doright land transactions may be desirable but impossible within the time limits our client set.

Our goal, in this analysis process, is to probe the data for reliability, insight, and direction. We check to see if each piece of information is properly documented. We weigh the logic of each statement in the client's summation. We analyze the details to wrest additional clues regarding potential activities or behavior, associations, or records. When a question cannot be answered from the given data—and if the client's response is not satisfactory—we frame another instruction for our work lists.

Test 1: Focus
To identify the starting point for the research and aim it in the right direction, we ask three main questions:

Who is the principal person in the problem?
Although several people may be mentioned in the client's data, one is typically the key figure. That person is the starting point. Normally, our focus will be the client's earliest *proved* ancestor, not the person the client hopes to claim. Thus, if a problem is defined as "I have my lineage back to the colonial immigrant, but cannot prove the

Normally, our focus will be the client's earliest *proved* ancestor, not the person the client hopes to claim.

**PROBLEM ANALYSES
AND RESEARCH PLANS**

connection between my grandfather John and his father, Ben," the principal person in the problem is almost always John—not Ben or the immigrant. It is John's records that will most likely provide clues to or proof of his paternity. (Exceptions do exist, of course. Occasionally, but rarely, a surname is so uncommon that virtually all who bear it are traceable to a single immigrant. If we know this to be the case, we might feasibly work from both ends of the broken lineage to see if it will close.)

What identifiers distinguish this person from all other human beings?
Typically, the prime identifiers include

- name: given, middle, and family (or patronymic) names; nicknames; initials.
- birth facts: date, place, unusual circumstances (adopted, orphaned, etc.).
- marriage facts: date, place; also spouse's name, parentage, and personal facts. (List multiple marriages separately.)
- death facts: date, place, testacy (or intestacy), unusual circumstances.
- residence(s): colony, territory, state, county, town, or township (as appropriate); specific parcel of land; length of residence. (List multiple residences separately.)
- children: known detail.
- parentage: known detail.

What major life event is the focus of the client commission?
Typically, a client's need will focus on a birth, marriage, or death—or on a biographical circumstance such as kinship, literacy, migration, property ownership, public service, religion, or wealth. Because an event is also a composite of details, subsidiary questions would include

- where did the event take place, or the circumstance arise, or the relationship originate?
- when did it occur (specific or estimated date or duration)?
- who else should have been involved?

Test 2: Evidence

Somewhere within the client's data lies the key to the problem's solution. The objective is to identify that key. If the problem is complex, we may find several keys, each of which deserves its own round of research. The second test consists of questions grouped according to the type of information each of them addresses:

How reliable is the source or sources from which the data come?
Chapter 17, Evidence Analysis, describes the tests that are needed here.

How reliable is the client's handling of data from those sources?
Clients display wide disparity in skill levels. Their search patterns and their interpretation of the materials they use can seriously affect the reliability of the information upon which they tell us to base our search.

Crucial test questions relating to client-data reliability can be grouped into several types of analyses, as follows:

Clients display wide disparity in skill levels. Their search patterns and their interpretation of materials they use can seriously affect the reliability of the information upon which they tell us to base our search.

**PROBLEM ANALYSES
AND RESEARCH PLANS**

MATHEMATICAL ANALYSIS

Inconsistencies often appear when we simply calculate the ancestor's age at various events. For example:

- The client states: "Revolutionary War Colonel John Doright was born in 1760 or 1768." If born in 1760, he would have been sixteen when the war erupted in 1776. The possibility that he was appointed or elected a colonel at that age is virtually nil. By 1782, however, he would have been twenty-two; his reputed service is possible, although still not probable. If born in 1768, it is highly unlikely that he served in any capacity—except, perhaps, as a drummer boy.

- The client states: "John Doright was born 1792; he was apprenticed in 1800, to serve until age twenty-one; and he married in 1810." The details are questionable. At the time of his indenture, he would have been about eight years old; his service would have expired in 1813. Rarely did masters permit a bondservant to marry before the term expired. If all facts stated by the client are correct, then an explanation is needed. Thus, the instructions we write for ourselves might include

    Check date and terms of the apprenticeship.

    Find out if John's wife was the master's daughter.

    Find out how soon John's first child was born after his marriage.

TIME-LINE ANALYSIS

By creating a full-scale time line of events in the ancestor's life, we may spotlight other problems. This chronological list or chart would include

- every known situation, major and minor, in which the ancestor participated—not just births, marriages, and deaths, but such activities as administering estates, changing residence, petitioning for a ferry, serving as a pallbearer, or witnessing a deed.

- place and date for each entry, with calculation of the ancestor's age at that time.

- source(s) for each detail—some of which may need identifying or reexamining.

- circumstances surrounding the event that indicate age or civil condition (for example, whether married or single; minor or adult; enslaved, indentured, or apprenticed).

- Legal, religious, or social requirements for each event on this time line (for example, "parental permission required for brides under age [—]," might be noted beside the ancestor's marriage event).

Close scrutiny of the completed time line may reveal

- obvious inconsistencies—as when the ancestor had to have been in two places at the same time. Or, if parental permission is filed with the ancestor's marriage certificate and the bride (by the client's calculations) was twenty-four at the time, something is amiss.

- missing events—as when land ownership was required for jury duty. The man's jury service must have been preceded by a land purchase, grant, or inheritance.

> By creating a full-scale timeline of events in the ancestor's life, we may spotlight other problems.

**PROBLEM ANALYSES
AND RESEARCH PLANS**

When peculiarities appear, we note this on our work sheets. In the jury problem, for example, it might be *Check deeds, grants, and probate records.*

LOGICAL

PSYCHOLOGICAL ANALYSIS

Some events should not have occurred because of the place, time period, or conditions of an ancestor's life. Others might appear illogical on the surface but could be true under certain conditions that we should investigate. For example:

- If John is said to have been the governor's son, but he signed his will with an "X" and owned just fifty acres on Pauper's Swamp, we should note the incongruity: *Consider possibility that two men of same name are merged into one.*

- If John's wife conceived a child while he was with his military unit an impossible distance away, then multiple circumstances might exist. Either he was not with the unit as believed or his wife had some serious explaining to do when he returned. In either case, if their society permitted divorce, the likelihood of one demands an entry on our work lists: *Check for divorce and separation records after date of John's return.*

- If a chronic debtor is said to have purchased 300 acres of good land, an inconsistency may or may not exist. The possibility that John inherited the purchase money would trigger a high-priority entry on our lists: *Check for parental will or estate packet, circa 1803—John paid Richard Roe £600 for 300 acres, Prettyplace Creek (client cites Deed Book 10:335).*

Sometimes a client's information simply does not "sound right," and we are justified in flagging the point for verification and possible correction. A Connecticut-born boy of 1875, named Jefferson Davis, would be an anomaly; a German immi-grant who wrote impeccable English would be rare; a death at age 107 would be even more so. We'd be remiss *not* to question such items.

CLIENT-SKILL ANALYSIS

Typically, the client not only provides details of the problem but also proposes a plan of action. Prudence suggests that we test the extent and the efficiency of the client's research and the conclusions upon which the client's plan is based. Common problems within the information supplied by clients include

- *Overlooked records.* Our experience with the time and place may point to relevant materials the client has not searched. If so, then we should enter on our work lists an instruction to remedy the oversight.

- *Faulty use of records.* Those examined by the client may not have been used to full advantage. The published abstract that the client provides for "proof" may be obviously missing crucial information (the legal land description, for example). Or the client may have searched under just one spelling of an ancestral surname—overlooking key variants. In either case, we enter an instruction to reexamine the records.

- *Too-narrow search.* One of the most frequent shortcomings in a client's search pattern is an omission of (or skimpy data for) the ancestor's collateral kin, in-laws, neighbors, bondsmen, and witnesses—and fellow members of the same fraternal order, graduating class, inspection staff, jury, or militia unit—as well

Sometimes a client's information simply does not "sound right," and we are justified in flagging the point for verification and possible correction.

as others who played peripheral roles in the ancestor's life. Appropriate entries on the work lists might be *Reexamine census, Re-abstract land records,* or *Check manuscript collections for [—].*

- *Faulty interpretation.* Our experience with the ethical, legal, religious, and social systems that governed the ancestor's era, ethnicity, gender, and place should prompt us to evaluate whether the client has correctly interpreted the records. Handwriting may have been misread. Inheritance and marital-property laws may have been ignored. Denominational baptism regulations may have been misunderstood. If so, we may instruct ourselves, *Collect and study photocopies of the relevant documents.*

Test three: Methodology
If the client's data are sufficiently extensive, we can apply a third set of tests. (If not, we will later find this approach useful for appraising our own research findings and correlating them with the client's original data.) The pertinent methodology often includes three types of even more detailed analyses:

HANDWRITING STUDY

From available records, we collect and compare penmanship samples, signatures, and marks. These often establish whether all writers were the same person, or they help us distinguish between or among them, if they were not the same.[1]

LAND-RECORDS STUDY

Analysis and correlation procedures for land records are time-consuming, but they can provide such definitive proof of relationship that further research is unnecessary. Or they can shortcut research by pointing us to a probable parent. Useful analyses include

- correlating purchases and sales to pinpoint primary residences and inheritances.[2]

- platting land to establish that one parcel of land is the same as another, or that it was part of a larger tract—or to reassemble a neighborhood and identify nearby cemeteries, churches, roads, and other landmarks.[3]

If the client's data permit this level of study prior to our research, then we may add appropriate entries to our work list: *Focus on Ben, the likely father (he owned same tract as John, thirty years earlier).* If the client's file provides only abstracts that omit full legal descriptions and the length of the assignment allows for this level of work, we instruct ourselves: *Search tract books for [—]* or *Photocopy deeds for land descriptions.* If we will need the client to authorize additional hours to conduct this land study, our self-instruction at the present point might be: *Check land indexes for approximate number of relevant records.* We will need a reasonable time estimate before we can make the recommendation.

WHOLE-FAMILY (OR NEIGHBORHOOD) STUDY
This technique is by far the most time-consuming; but, if followed relentlessly, it is a well-proved method.[4] Especially diligent clients may have performed this work before contacting us. If not, our self-instruction statement might be something like this: *Collect extensive reliable data about everybody of the ancestral surname in the*

area (and/or collect same data on all neighbors and associates). Track to their destinations any who moved away. Track back to their origins any who moved into the known ancestral area.

Test 4: Deductions

All of the foregoing tests focus upon information explicitly provided in the records that our client supplies. Beyond this, we may *deduce* valuable information from these materials as well. For example, the client problem might be "find John Doright's father." We then might phrase various hypotheses that begin with the statement, *Because John was born 1820–24,*

- his father died no earlier than March 1819 [nine months before January 1820]. If that father was at least twenty when John was born and lived to be about eighty, then our instructions might read: *Look for Doright wills (father of John), ca. 1819–84.*

- his parents likely married by 1824. So our instructions would be: *Look for Doright marriages in or before 1824,* and *Look for a Doright female in wills or estate records of a non-Doright who died 1819–24 or later.*

- he was under age until 1845. In this case, our instructions would be: *Look for Doright households with a male aged six to ten in 1830 and sixteen to twenty in 1840;* and *Check guardian and apprenticeship records, 1820–45.*

Supporting documentation

For projects that involve anything beyond a simple record search or retrieval, various types of supporting documentation are needed. Several were introduced above amid the detailed analysis: work lists, time lines, land plats, and land-transaction summaries. We may need still others: ancestor or descendant charts; detailed lists of associates, collateral kin, in-laws, and neighbors; plats assembled into neighborhoods; or maps annotated to show migration routes.

Upon completion of our analysis, we may be ready to compile our research plan. On the other hand, if our client specified a plan and our evaluation of the problem or the client's data convince us that the requested procedure is premature or unwise, we have a complication to resolve before research begins. Our objective, as stated in the opening paragraph of this chapter, is to fulfill the client contract. We may have agreed to the client's procedure, because it appeared feasible at the time of the initial inquiry—*before* the client sent all supporting information. In this case, it would be best to contact the client, tactfully explain the conclusions drawn from the newly supplied evidence, and request permission to pursue the research plan generated by our skilled analysis.

The process of preparing that plan is basically as follows.

If our client specified a plan and our evaluation of the problem or the client's data convince us that the requested procedure is premature or unwise, we have a complication to resolve before research begins.

Research Plans

Plan refers to the process of thinking through our purposes and procedures before research begins. Because our purpose is defined in the client's authorization, we tailor a plan as precisely as possible to the commission. The research problem dictates its content; the time determines its extent. From a professional standpoint, however, the research problem is not the client's *overall* genealogical quest; it is only the portion identified in the client's letter of authorization. Normally, unless the commission has no time limit, the resolution of the client's broader needs goes beyond the scope of the present contract.

Plan development

An efficient research plan is developed in three stages: analysis, refinement, and logistics. Each stage has the same objective: systematic, precisely targeted research. In its final form, the plan consists of detailed, prioritized lists of

- the records we intend to search at each repository we visit;
- the data we will seek in each;
- any unusual techniques needed to analyze and correlate the findings (perhaps land-records analyses); and
- any particular form or format needed to report our findings (possibly a lineage-society application blank).

STAGE 1: ANALYSIS
See the discussion on pages 261–68.

STAGE 2: REFINEMENT
Once we complete the analysis, we review and refine the "instructions" we wrote for ourselves. Those that relate to *kinds* of data, we reduce to a list of sources likely to produce that data. If some instructions are redundant, or were su-perseded as the analysis progressed, we drop them. If several research institutions need to be visited, we list each beside the relevant source(s). We then prioritize our lists of self-instructions, deciding which of them promise the most direct and reliable completion of the client's contract. If, for example, the client needs an identification of an ancestral spouse, the instruction statement *Check marriage register* naturally belongs ahead of *Find out who the neighbors were and check their wills and estate packets,* because a bridal surname found in the register would delimit the neighborhood search.

STAGE 3: LOGISTICS
The final step is to regroup instructions by research facility. If, at this point, we realize it is impractical to visit the place where a "best source" is located, we identify more accessible alternatives.

We prioritize our lists of self-instructions, deciding which of them promise the most direct and reliable completion of the client's contract.

Although our plan identifies the sources most likely to provide the required information, we cannot predict that they will yield it. We cannot project the nature of anything we might find. Therefore, our plan should be flexible enough to allow for a certain amount of correction and expansion as research progresses. Laboriously itemizing every possible alternative—just in case the likeliest ones prove

**PROBLEM ANALYSES
AND RESEARCH PLANS**

unproductive—wastes time and blurs the precision of the plan. If the likeliest sources do not produce the expected information, that fact constitutes a new problem and requires another round of research. If the client's time has almost expired, we use the remainder of the time to report as much of the solution as found and itemize recommendations for the next round. If sufficient time remains, we may launch the next round (or series of rounds)—beginning each with a fresh analysis and plan, as defined by the previous round's findings.

Plan documentation

Our strategy needs to be recorded in some manner on paper. Sometimes the project is so narrowly defined or so limited in time that we can just underline parts of the client's letter and attach a "sticky note" upon which we pen our self-instructions. For projects of greater complexity, the plan can be typed directly into a computer file and printed for reference while the research is done. If we use a portable computer on site, we can integrate our research notes, then subsequently edit the whole and create the client report.

Plan support

Two types of files, both developed during the research phase of a client project, can provide support for future research planning: source lists and a relational database.

SOURCE LISTS
When projects involve successive rounds of research on the same problem, we build a Project Source List that is the equivalent of a research log. We note the source citation, the date and place each record was examined, and a brief comment about what was sought and whether it was found. From individual project lists, we can develop a Master Source List for all our research—with annotated citations giving data about access restrictions, gaps in coverage, and likely contents. When the Master Source List is arranged by geographic area, the citations themselves can act as a reminder of records that should be included in future plans for research in the same areas.

RELATIONAL DATABASE
For projects that include complex problem-solving, a relational database manager is a wise investment. But we also have to invest the time needed to design a template for numerous, highly variable research-plan elements. A typical database sets up fields in which we distribute the following types of information:

- Dates—the date of the plan, of project deadlines (for interim and final reports), of events that are the target of the research (birth, death, marriage, enlistment, etc.), and of events documented in client-supplied and researcher-located records.
- Names—given or surnames of key individuals, known or potential kin, etc.;
- Geographic locations—creeks, counties, townlands, etc.
- Militia or military units.

Projects that involve successive rounds of research on the same problem call for an annotated, master source list.

- Documents—types or collections.
- Clients—names and addresses.
- File names—notes or reports.

A well-designed template can be used for future projects with little or no amendment. Such a template can also be designed to include fields from the Project Source List. When those fields are the same in both the Project and Master lists, citations and notations can be copied from one to the other without retyping.

Summary Concepts

The analysis procedures outlined in this chapter are not designed for a three-hour, just-find-this-divorce-case assignment. Few professionals worthy of the label need real assistance for projects of that type; their experience and record familiarity will swiftly focus their search for them. Rather, this chapter focuses upon the more challenging assignments wherein professionals are asked to identify a wife (when no marriage record exists), or parents (when no clues are known), or some potential ancestor with lineage-society eligibility, or an immigrant forebear remote in time.

The entire process of analyzing the research problem and developing a plan has one objective: accurate, efficient, and responsive research. That means we must tailor the level of our analysis to the nature and extent of the contract we execute with the client. It is folly to launch a search without an appropriate plan. It is unwise to base a search upon unreliable information, even if the client provided it. It is prudent to glean all possible clues from the client's data before beginning a new investigation. Consequently, many researchers who specialize in resolving difficult problems routinely build two things into their contracts: *(a)* they ask the client to provide working copies of all supporting data, rather than overviews or problem summaries that reflect only the client's interpretation of the data; and *(b)* they specify that the first assignment will consist solely of an analysis of the client's data and the preparation of a research plan.[5]

Whatever approach we take, we must resist the temptation to spend *undue* quantities of time in the office before leaving for the research facility. Inappropriately exhaustive analyses, plans, or computerized documentation will inordinately delay completion of the client commission. The degree to which we achieve an effective balance between time allotted to analysis, planning, and research is also a measure of our professional skill.

> The degree to which we achieve an effective balance between time allotted to analysis, planning, and research is also a measure of our professional skill.

NOTES

1. For example, see Ronald A. Hill, Ph.D., CG, "Identification through Signatures: Using Complex Direct Evidence to Sort Colwills of Cornwall," *National Genealogical Society [NGS] Quarterly* 87 (September 1999): 185–98; and Kay Rockett, "Signatures, Penmanship, and Name Variations: Identifying Reverend Mr. Jacob Ware," *NGS Quarterly* 86 (September 1998): 218–22.

2. For example, see Elizabeth Shown Mills, CG, CGL, FASG, "Backtracking Hardy Hunter: A Case Study in Genealogical Problem Solving via the Preponderance of Evidence Principle,"

PROBLEM ANALYSES
AND RESEARCH PLANS

Problems are just opportunity in work clothes.

—*Henry Kaiser*[6]

Association of Professional Genealogists [APG] Quarterly 1 (Spring 1986): 1–19 and (Summer 1986): 1–19. Part 2, the summer installment, illustrates the technique of correlating purchases and sales to identify inheritances and parental identity.

3. For example, see Ge Lee Corley Hendrix, CG, FASG, "John Bond vs. John Bond: Sorting Identities via Neighborhood Reconstruction," *NGS Quarterly* 79 (December 1991): 268–82; and Elizabeth Shown Mills, "Applying the Preponderance of the Evidence Principle to a Southern Frontier Problem: William Medders of Alabama," *NGS Quarterly* 82 (March 1994): 32–49, for problem resolution via family reconstitution using different land survey systems.

4. For example, see Gerald M. Haslam, Ph.D., "Family Reconstitution as a Means of Individual Identification: Ole Anderson Kolvien of Voss, Norway," *NGS Quarterly* 81 (December 1993): 283–92; and Cameron Allen, J.D., FASG, "Corralling a Family's Woods-Colts: Some Strassers (Strawsers) of Ohio," *NGS Quarterly* 85 (March 1997): 5–24.

5. A late 1996 survey conducted by the Board for Certification of Genealogists (the only such data available) reveals that 30–40 percent of certified professional researchers require an analysis as the first assignment. Record specialists were the least likely to set this prerequisite; lineage specialists the most likely. See Elizabeth Shown Mills, "Client Assignments—Quality and Quantity: BCG Survey Results," *OnBoard* (September 1997): 17–20, particularly 19.

6. Henry J. Kaiser (1882–1967), American industrialist, quoted in Rhoda Thomas Tripp, comp., *The International Thesaurus of Quotations* (New York: Thomas Y. Crowell, 1970), 507.

FURTHER STUDY

Leary, Helen F. M., and Lee Albright. "Designing Research Strategies," in Helen F. M. Leary, ed., *North Carolina Research: Genealogy and Local History,* 2d edition. Raleigh: North Carolina Genealogical Society, 1997. Pages 17–67.

Mills, Elizabeth Shown. "Ten Steps to a Solution: How to Analyze a Problem and Develop a Research Strategy," *New England—Bridge to America,* 2000 Conference Syllabus, National Genealogical Society. Arlington, Virginia, NGS, 2000. Session T-68. (Or see similar item by Mills in *Unlock Your Heritage with Creative Problem Solving,* 1997 Conference Syllabus, Federation of Genealogical Societies. Dallas, Texas: Federation of Genealogical Societies, 1997. Session T-24.)

Rising, Marsha Hoffman, CG, CGL, FASG. "Problem Analysis and Strategy Planning." *Traveling Historic Trails: Families on the Move,* 1996 Conference Syllabus, National Genealogical Society. Arlington: NGS, 1996. Session W-2.

Rose, Christine, CG, CGL, FASG. "Solving the 'Problem' in 25 Hours or Less On-Site." *Rocky Mountain Rendezvous,* 1998 Conference Syllabus, National Genealogical Society. Denver: NGS, 1998. Session T-90.

15

**RESEARCH
PROCEDURES**

RESEARCH PROCEDURES

Keynotes

Research Procedures

by Linda Woodward Geiger, CGRS, CGL

As professional genealogists, we typically choose areas of specialization—ethnic, geographic, or topical. One foundation for this choice should be the availability of research facilities and resources—original records as well as publications. Most of the materials we need should be handily available. A specialty in an area or collections distant from our home may require different strategies and frequent travel; such delays and costs can seriously diminish our client base. At the least, it is a given that we should know the government structure, history, settlement patterns, and topography of any locality involved in our specialization. Above all, we must know the record sources—what exists, where to find them, and how to use and interpret them.

Regardless of our specialty, effective research on any specific project comes from long-range preparation, followed by a literature survey and an actual on-site search. This chapter provides strategies for identifying available resources, determining their locations, using electronic finding aids, and otherwise preparing ourselves before we arrive on site. Finally, it offers suggestions for the research itself—both good work habits and goodwill builders. We should, of course, adapt these recommendations to each particular project and to our individual, professional style.

Long-range Preparation

Efficient and thorough research begins with long-range preparation. It requires a time investment that is not billable directly to any client, but it repays huge dividends. It enables us to target each research effort precisely—a timesaver for us and our clients. It provides a relevant checklist for each project—even computer-based templates or boilerplate material for preparing research plans. On site, the results of this preparation are obvious—conveying to record custodians the image of expertise, knowledge, and preparedness that professional genealogy should convey.

General guides

The kind of long-range preparation that is the hallmark of the professional begins with the compilation of two resource guides for our professional practice.

REPOSITORY GUIDE

A repository guide is a notebook or a vertical file with information on each record-holding facility that serves our specialty—those close enough to be accessible on a daily basis and those that are more distant but still essential. Our guide should consider every possibility: government agencies (every level from local to national), libraries and archives (private and public); and specialized collections of businesses, churches, fraternal organizations, museums, and societies (genealogical and

On site, the results of preparation are obvious—conveying to record custodians the image of expertise, knowledge, and preparedness that professional genealogy should convey.

RESEARCH PROCEDURES

A truly useful repository guide consists of an inventory of holdings for each facility, supported by relevant logistical data.

historical). A truly useful repository guide consists of an inventory of holdings for each facility, supported by relevant logistical data—with the whole arranged either geographically or alphabetically by agency.

INVENTORY OF HOLDINGS
to include

- specific record collections—noting subject, time frame, medium (bound publication, CD-ROM, database, manuscript, map, microprint, photographs, etc.), collection size, and condition;
- card catalogs, indexes, and other finding aids;
- access restrictions, if any; and
- online catalogs, if available.

LOGISTICAL DATA
to include

- hours of operations, online addresses, telephone numbers;
- directions to the repository and a map, if necessary;
- parking arrangements and/or access by public transportation;
- availability of snack bars or restaurants, on site or nearby;
- special rules or procedures for the research area—hours for ordering original documents; limits on materials allowed in search room (for example, notebooks or loose papers only, camera, laptop computer, or scanner); regulations for photocopying;
- fees—for use of facilities or for document copies—and whether these may be paid by check or must be tendered in cash; and
- research services provided by the repository, if any.

LOCALITY GUIDE

A locality guide, organized in much the same way as our repository guide, focuses upon the geographic areas crucial to our specialty. If we restrict our work to one county, our locality guide will be brief. If we work a wide-ranging area, it could be quite extensive, as we set up individual sheets or files on a town-by-town, county-by-county, or even region-wide basis. Locality guides typically cover the following:

- historical background—date established, seat of government, names of "parent" jurisdictions;
- record losses—dates, extent, and nature;
- extant records—by type and inclusive dates, including location of originals and/or filmed copies;
- newspaper indexes, newspapers, and repositories that hold these;
- published sources (including repository for each) and online abstracts and databases;
- lists of jurisdictional boundary changes—including dates of changes and names of the other jurisdictions involved; and
- area maps.

Information sources

Material for both the repository and locality guides can be gleaned from an almost endless array of resources. For starters, the courthouse or town hall, a local library, and the state or provincial archives can offer a variety of finding aids, in published and manuscript form. The challenge is not so much finding information as in staying current. Once assembled, our guides will need continual updating, as new materials are located or discovered and more books and articles are published. Beyond this, the following approaches will yield a valuable body of material.

LOCAL RESOURCES

Through a basic search of the city directories, Yellow Pages, and miscellaneous materials in the reference section of our local library we can usually glean a sizable list of agencies with research value, as well as finding aids. Local government offices may have inventories of their holdings. The county engineer may have maps. The local chamber of commerce usually maintains its own lists of area societies and cultural facilities—as well as area maps and location data on cemeteries and historical sites. (In our contacts with this source, we might also include inquiries about any miscellaneous materials of a historical nature that the chamber might hold. For example, the Sandersville, Georgia, Chamber of Commerce sent me a free typescript of burials and plot-site data for that community's Old City Cemetery.)

PUBLICATIONS

The Family History Library in Salt Lake City offers inexpensive research outlines for locations worldwide. Its locality catalog (available at the Salt Lake City facility, its thousands of Family History Centers worldwide, and online) specifically itemizes holdings by country; by internal divisions such as province, state, or county; and by town and parish. Major published works for many countries offer essential overviews, including both historical narrative and detailed listings of repositories. In the U.S., specifically, Szucs and Luebking's *The Source*[1] and Meyerink's *Printed Sources*[2] both focus on materials. Everton's *Handy Book*[3] and Eichholz's *Red Book*[4] are arranged by geographic region—first by state, thereunder by county and/or by town. On a state-specific level, excellent guides are randomly available.[5] Internationally, Vine Hall's *Tracing Your Family in Australia: A Guide to Sources*[6] and Stoa and Sandberg's Norwegian guide, *Våre Røtter: Håndbok I slektsgransking for nybergynnere og viderrekomne,*[7] are excellent examples. Chapter 4, The Essential Library, lists similar guides for many countries in which genealogists are active. Also useful are the lectures on various large repositories presented at national conventions and congresses. Many professionals routinely comb the conference syllabi, photocopying lecture materials that relate to repositories and geographic areas, for insertion in their personal resource notebooks or files.

PERSONAL RECONNAISSANCE

Once we have compiled a master list of possible research facilities for our area of interest, we should telephone, write, or visit each of them. Ideally, we make a personal visit to all repositories within convenient traveling distance. The objective is twofold.

> Once we have compiled a master list of possible research facilities for our area of interest, we should telephone, write, or visit each of them.

RESEARCH PROCEDURES

We want to thoroughly familiarize ourselves with the resources in each repository; and we want to introduce ourselves to staff members, whose assistance we will periodically need. If the repository has prepared printed guides to their collections, we need copies. If these exist but are not available for sale, we can usually acquire permission to make our own photocopies; if not, we should compile our own general survey. We should also expect *not* to learn everything on this first visit. Our inventory will expand as we become more familiar with each facility.

ONLINE AIDS

The past several years have seen a phenomenal, worldwide Knowledge Revolution—equal in significance to the Industrial Revolution that changed society so drastically for our ancestors of the nineteenth century. Today, a legion of computers with mammoth storage capacity forms an invisible network (the Internet or the World Wide Web), on which individuals, agencies, and companies post files of data. The extent and breadth of electronic material mushrooms daily. But, as in a traditional library, the quality of the available information varies wildly.

Genealogists who care about producing sound work use the Web to locate primarily five types of information:

- Catalogs posted by major libraries worldwide, such as the U.S. Library of Congress's catalogs to its book and manuscript holdings.

- Access information (hours, fees, contact data, etc.) posted by thousands of archives, government agencies, libraries, and museums.

- Record-availability data posted worldwide by genealogical and historical societies.

- Maps of distant locales.

- (To a limited and highly selective extent) databases; indexes; record files; and even digital images of documents, maps, and photographs. (See pages 280–82.)

Obviously, no resource guide could be complete without combing and culling the information available online. Yet discretion remains the watchword.

Special strategies

Every region has distinct characteristics, all of which could never be addressed in a single chapter. However, three particular research situations merit a brief mention because they require innovative strategy.

LARGE URBAN AREAS

Record offices in large metropolises often store noncurrent primary materials in out-of-the-way warehouses off-limits to researchers. City clerks commonly know nothing about their historical records or where these might be located—they are challenged enough by maintenance of contemporary records in their immediate physical custody. For additional strategies and suggestions, urban researchers will find Szucs's "Tracking Urban Ancestors" in *The Source* informative reading.[8]

> The extent and breadth of electronic material mushrooms daily. But, as in a traditional library, the quality of the available information varies wildly.

VERY RURAL AREAS

Sparsely populated rural areas may present a different set of problems. Their government offices may be in isolated places, with few amenities that researchers typically expect. Such areas commonly lack an adequate genealogical or historical library. In rural settings particularly, a retired official or an old-timer who is an unofficial purveyor of local lore may be a tremendous source of information— sometimes oral, sometimes documentary.

AREAS OF HEAVY RECORD LOSS

Fires, floods, and other natural disasters have destroyed untold numbers of records; but rumors of this destruction often exaggerate the damage or consequences. Alternate sources may exist for lost originals—for example, copies prepared for another agency; or records created in (or removed to) jurisdictions previously cut away from the ill-fated one; or appeals court collections, with files transferred from the lower level where the destruction later occurred. In other cases, local officials sometimes recreated registers from documents in private collection. In the best of cases, the damage occurred in modern times *after* officials filmed many of the originals. These and other approaches are discussed in greater detail by Mills's several versions of "The Battle of the 'Burned Courthouse'."[9]

When we launch a specific client project, we turn first to our resource and locality guides to craft a general research plan (as outlined in chapter 14). The resulting research will be conducted in one or two stages—depending upon the client's authorization: (1) a survey of published materials; and (2) in-depth research, on site, in an appropriate repository.

Literature Surveys

Stage One research, the literature survey, has a rather checkered reputation among genealogists. Many researchers seldom progress beyond it—though this surely includes no professional worthy of the name (the Board for Certification of Genealogists, we note, has no Certified Book Searcher category). Genealogists who restrict themselves to published sources risk branding themselves as amateurs and—far worse—risk dead ends and woeful mistakes. Not only is there an infinite amount of documentary materials that have never been processed and disseminated, but published sources are notorious for transcription errors and omissions.

Yet the literature survey is essential. Reinventing the wheel is as dumb an idea in genealogy as in any other aspect of life. As a rule, published materials—in a library, online, or reproduced on CD-ROM for use on personal computers—provide indexes more complete than those available for manuscripts, church archives, or courthouse records. Electronic indexes are shortcuts that can suggest a likely solution to our problem. They help us narrow our target for time and cost efficiency on site. In some cases, they may be our only option—as older records deteriorate from so much use.

> Stage One research, the literature survey, has a rather checkered reputation among genealogists. Yet the literature survey is essential.

RESEARCH PROCEDURES

The hallmark of a skilled professional, so far as published materials are concerned, is the ability to use these resources *wisely*. As general guidelines, we

- comb census indexes, compiled genealogies, local histories, published abstracts, and periodical literature—extracting all material of value.

- consult original records or quality reproductions to (*a*) confirm the accuracy of relevant findings in the published sources; and (*b*) mine the often-abundant lodes of local materials that remain undisseminated in any form.

Published materials exist today in three principal forms: print, CD-ROM, and online. The latter two require special consideration.

CD-ROM

A 1996 survey conducted by the Board for Certification of Genealogists reveals that 90 percent of the surveyed professionals felt computers are essential, 53 percent felt modems are, and 49 percent felt the same about CD-ROM drives.[10] A current survey would undoubtedly show even higher figures, especially for the latter two. Compact discs are now a medium of choice for many publishers and researchers. They hold great quantities of data and are far less expensive to produce than paper publications. However—and many consumers are not aware of this—CD-ROM manufacturers currently project only a ten-year life cycle for these products. As name indexes, these products offer advantages—most permit using a "wild-card option" to ferret out spelling variants. On the other hand, producers seldom recognize the need for the topical or locality indexes that good print publications often provide.

The CD market offers a panoply of wonders, but it's a hazard course studded with destructive snags. As professionals, we must recognize the difference. Chapter 4 cites several offerings worthy of a professional library—including census indexes, the PERSI database (for periodical literature),[11] and the name-indexed graphic images of a century or so of major journals such as the *National Genealogical Society Quarterly* and the *New England Historic Genealogical Register*. Such finding aids, consulted prior to visiting a library, can save much valuable research time. On the other hand, CD indexes contain just as many errors as (and, in some cases, more than) their printed counterparts. By far the greatest risk is incurred with commercial databases and "family trees"—most of which make no effort to verify or document their "facts."[12]

> The CD market offers a panoply of wonders, but it's also a hazard course studded with destructive snags.

ONLINE OPTIONS

The Internet carries even greater risk—given the existence of tens of thousands of sites created by individuals with more enthusiasm than professional experience in either genealogy or publishing. We distinguish between them in the same manner that we appraise quality in any genealogical offering—for example, by the presence of reliable documentation, the absence of obvious contradictions and typos, and the semblance of thoroughness and logical reasoning.

Illustrative of the offerings that can be essential to preparatory work are the nine websites that follow.[13]

RESEARCH PROCEDURES

GOVERNMENT SITES

- *Bureau of Land Management* (U.S.). This site is an excellent example of the power and value the Internet already provides. BLM offers, free of charge, both a database and images of every patent issued by the federal government in various American states. We can search by the name of the patentee, by the legal description, by the date of the application for land, or by patent numbers. With patent data in hand, we can place a mail order with the National Archives for the corresponding land-entry files that offer additional information—all without expensive on-site research.

- *General Register Office* (Scotland). The GRO's website is the launch pad for searching adoption, birth, death, divorce, and marriage registers created in Scotland since 1553, as well as censuses for the open-access period, 1841–91. Visitors to the GRO site learn of many available types of records and have the option of seeking their own personal data, requesting a search for records relating to others, or purchasing microfilm copies of collections that are already filmed.

- *Library of Congress* (U.S.). This extraordinary site has so much it defies description. Its Research Tools page provides a link to the library's online catalogs by which we may search for books or manuscripts by authors, titles, and keywords (including places). In addition to identifying relevant materials, we may check LC's Copyright Office databases to determine whether specific books are still protected; or we may download the full text of current copyright laws or print out copyright forms for registering our own books and serials. Other offerings range from transcribed slave narratives to an online version of the National Union Catalog of Manuscript Collections (NUC-MC) and thousands of photographs. This site also links us to other catalogs or access-policy statements of dozens of libraries internationally.

- *Library of Virginia* (U.S.). The Digital Library created by Virginia's state library-archives is a major repository for research. Online already are more than 600,000 scanned images of family pages from Bibles, maps, colonial and military records, and many indexes to other LV holdings.

- *National Archives and Records Administration* (U.S.). Here we find instructions for using the National Archives and its regional facilities—hours of operation, types of available records (with many links and indexes), and specific itemization of materials that researchers may take into the research areas. We can read or download the new three-volume *Guide to Federal Records in the National Archives of the United States* and essential catalogs identifying the hundreds of thousands of reels of microfilm NARA has published. An additional feature of the site is NAIL (NARA Archival Information Locator)—a pilot database of selected holdings in NARA's regional archives across the country. A recent NAIL search for the surname *Wood(w)ard,* for example, resulted in 102 different hits—including references to Wood(w)ard enrollments on the Guion Miller Rolls of the Bureau of Indian Affairs and to appearances in criminal cases heard by the notorious "hanging judge" of the U.S. District Court for the Western District of Arkansas. Using the citations NARA provides for these database entries, we may order the full records from the appropriate NARA facility.

Visitors to the GRO site have the option of seeking their own personal data, requesting a search for records relating to others, or purchasing microfilm copies of collections already filmed.

RESEARCH PROCEDURES

ORGANIZATIONAL SITES

- *USGenWeb*. One section of this website is indispensable for professional-level research; another is increasingly useful as it grows. The first is the county-by-county, state-by-state links on which local volunteers post access information for area repositories and societies, summarize record holdings in the courthouse or town hall, and randomly enter other data of value. A second component is the USGenWeb Archives with some 100,000 pages of abstracted records arranged by state and county. As with any abstracts, quality varies according to the skill of each individual who made the abstracts.

- *WorldGenWeb*. This international counterpart to USGenWeb has host sites for every continent and over half of the world's nations. Its offerings are similar to those of USGenWeb, in form and content.

PRIVATE SITES

- *A Barrel of Genealogy Links*. This privately produced site offers links to a vast array of vital websites—including the U.S. National Archives and Records Administration's Manuscripts from the Federal Writers' Project (which allows surname searches of WPA-era manuscripts), as well as Library Information Servers on the Web. Shortcuts to a hundred or so Civil War sites that are open to visitors yield information on specific regiments (U.S. and Confederate), the Virginia Military Institute Archives, Grand Army of the Republic, lists of women discussed in Civil War books, and details of regimental battle flags from the War between the States. This site provides much concrete information on the availability of records and specific repositories.

- *Cyndi's List*. At this site, the Internet guru Cyndi Howells offers a gateway to virtually everything genealogical that exists on the Web. For those who are not intimidated by size and do not lose their way amid a maze of directories and subdirectories, *Cyndi's List* is a link to societies of more than a hundred different ethnic interests; to professionals and publishers; to articles, books, and electronic databases; to adjunct fields; to archives and libraries; and to individual home pages—among much else.

In short, valuable material exists online, but no Web search can replace the use of physical repositories containing primary records.

Valuable material exists online, but no Web search can replace the use of physical repositories containing primary records.

On-site Research

General preparation

Preparedness is the watchword for on-site research. Chapter 14 details an excellent program for analyzing the research problem and developing a plan of research—both built upon the repository and locality guides discussed in the present chapter. From the standpoint of preparedness, several points from chapter 14 bear repeating or amplifying. We should

- prepare a list of spelling variations for each surname in our project and an alphabetized list of all names for which we'll search.
- double-check our research plan to be sure it is clear and precise—and that it spotlights the records most likely to provide the answers we seek.
- organize compact notes for each family group or neighborhood.
- acquaint ourselves with state or local laws regarding record access.
- prepare a fallback strategy to implement if and when we are denied access to records that should be open for public use.
- assemble a portable packet of essential supplies—pencils, paper clips, etc.

Beyond these basics, we plan the physical aspects of our research to comply with the regulations of the repository. In some facilities, researchers cannot bring into the search room such personal containers as boxes, briefcases, portfolios, and purses. If we arrive with such possessions, we may have to store them in lockers. The archives may provide paper and pencils, or it may simply post its policy that pens are banned. Some facilities allow loose-paper research notes (a limited amount, usually), laptop computers, approved scanners, hand-held wallets, or coin purses—all subject to inspection when we enter or leave the research complex.

Goodwill builders

On site, we have only one chance to make a good first impression on the record-keepers whose goodwill we need. If we dress professionally and conduct ourselves in a professional manner, we are far more likely to be treated as professionals. In record offices, we will want to blend in with the attorneys and legal aides. At libraries and archives, we should appear to be the scholars that we are. Courtesy and a pleasant demeanor encourage the staff to help us if we need it. Proper etiquette also means that we treat the materials carefully. (See NGS Standards for Use of Records, Repositories, and Libraries, in appendix B.)

Here, as elsewhere, the responsibility for our research lies with us. We don't expect staff members to do it for us. Occasionally, we will need assistance—perhaps, access to records relegated to some attic, basement, or outbuilding. If we have established good rapport with the staff, they are more likely to give gracious help than lame excuses. Rarely, we may need to remind a clerk (courteously, of course) of the applicable regional as well as national "freedom of information" acts. On the other hand, if we are new to a particular facility, access to out-of-the-way materials may be more difficult to obtain. Until we become known to the staff, we may consider hiring another researcher—one familiar to, and respected by, the staff—to come with us and open doors for us, figuratively speaking.

> If we dress professionally and conduct ourselves in a professional manner, we are far more likely to be treated as professionals.

Good work habits

PHOTOCOPYING

If Hamlet were a genealogist, his famed question would probably be *To photocopy or not to photocopy—which should I do?* The answer depends upon the circumstances.

RESEARCH PROCEDURES

Some small record offices or libraries may not even offer this option—their one machine is restricted to official use. If our research has taken us into an "overflow" storage area, there may be no photocopying machine there at all. In other situations, the per-copy cost may be prohibitive; or the individuals in our search may have executed dozens to hundreds of records. In other cases, the age or fragility of materials prompts the repository to post no-copying signs or to require that visitors, prior to copying, present each document to the staff for inspection and approval. Otherwise, general guidelines call for photocopying

- actual signatures or signature marks—excluding record-book copies, unless the principal parties actually signed the record book.

- documents that provide proof of identity, relationship, or vital information (birth, marriage, or death dates and places).

- documents with voluminous details that cannot be abstracted (condensed) without losing valuable data—for example, property inventories, probate sales, and lengthy or complex court cases.

- documents with elements or wording we don't understand or can't clearly read.

Quality photocopying requires that we also observe three other principles:

- If a document has multiple pages, we should promptly clip them together (using the supply of clips we brought with us—borrowing supplies from the repository does not convey an image of preparedness and professionalism).

- If an oversized page must be photocopied in parts, we should immediately label the copies "page __, top" (or middle or bottom), as appropriate.

- If an adequate margin exists, we should neatly pen in that margin a complete citation of the book name/number/page or file name/number, repository name, and location. If the margin is not adequate, we should place this identification on the back of the photocopy. (The front side is preferable, because reverse-side identification may be overlooked by clients who make copies for others.)

NOTE TAKING

Good work habits are essential, whether we are conducting the literature survey or delving into one-of-a-kind manuscripts. Note taking on site may be problematic. Not all facilities supply such amenities as worktables, good lighting, and comfortable chairs. Yet even if we are working by flashlight in a basement—balancing an open, thirty-pound record book precariously on top of a rusted-out oil can, while we hold our battery-operated laptop with one hand and type with the other—standards remain the same.

In general, reliable notes have four parts:

- the citation,
- the physical analysis of the record,
- the abstract or transcription, and
- the content analysis of the record.

> Good work habits are essential, whether we are conducting the literature survey or delving into one-of-a-kind manuscripts.

Citation

Expert documentation is not an option. Careless documentation is a guarantee (bona fide insurance!) that a research effort will hit a brick wall, self-destruct, or mislead others for generations to come. Every time we retrieve a book, a manuscript, a microform, or a register (deeds, estate records, and such), we need to

- note full identification in standard, academic format for genealogical research. If we need a handy reminder, *Evidence! Citation & Analysis for the Family Historian* is a portable, user-friendly guide with format models for wide-ranging types of genealogical materials.[14]

- record every bit of data—it is better to have too much information than too little. We should develop the habit of recording our source *before* we begin to review the material or take notes.

- read all relevant, supporting material. The introduction to a book, for example, may not contain the name of the individual we seek; but a well-prepared book will use its introduction to give us essential background on the subject and the records. In some record books, scribes may pen background information at the front or the back—notations, for example, that this register is actually a transcription of a damaged original.

Physical analysis of record

Good genealogists "listen to what the document is trying to say." The physical condition of a manuscript—or the fact that a published family history does or does not cite its own sources—may later assume immense importance as we analyze the credibility and accuracy of our information. (*Evidence!* offers sound advice in this regard as well.) Common questions that we should pointedly ask of the documents include these:

- Who had jurisdiction over this particular record?

- Why was the record created?

- Are there breaks in the series of records to which this one belongs?

- Is the binding of the book so tight that some words cannot be read at the ends of each line?

- Is the document legible—or is the page damaged, the ink faded, and the penmanship a scrawl?

- Does the style of handwriting match the era in which the record was created?

- Is this a modern, typewritten index? Is this index comprehensive, or is it a plaintiff-only or groom-only index?

In response to these questions, we record a clear description of the record, its contents, its reason for being, and any other insights we glean from it.

Abstract or transcript

Chapter 16 addresses at length the procedures and qualities that make a well-crafted abstract or transcript. Only a few generalities need mentioning in the present chapter. Basically, we should

> Expert documentation is not an option. Careless documentation is a guarantee (bona fide insurance!) that a research effort will hit a brick wall, self-destruct, or mislead others.

RESEARCH PROCEDURES

- read the document carefully in its entirety before we start our notes.

- include every stated circumstance, date, event, fact, name, or place.

- replicate the marks or signatures as faithfully as possible, if actual signatures or signature marks appear and photocopying is not possible. Depending upon the nature and condition of the record, it may or may not be possible to trace the original. If the record is fragile, we should not attempt a tracing. If the archives does not have a stated policy regarding writing on top of documents, but the record appears in sound shape, we might ask for permission. Using an acid-free plastic transparency and a felt-tip pen (assuming foresight prompted us to bring them) can help us make an accurate tracing with minimal pressure on the original document.

- write all dates from standard calendars as day/month/year. If the original uses a nonstandard date such as those of the French Revolution, the Quaker calendar, or ecclesiastical systems, the exact word/number string should be copied, with quotation marks before and after.

- copy the signatures of witnesses in exact order: in church records, particularly, the position of a signature can speak to certain relationships.

- copy all abbreviations exactly—whether they represent words or names—placing quotation marks around them to emphasize that these appear in the originals and are not of our own invention.

- limit our own use of abbreviations to standard ones—perhaps just *co.* for *county*, *adm^r/exec^r* for *administrator/executor* (or *adm^x/exec^x* for *administratrix/executrix)*, and *wit.* for *witness*, in addition to the common *b., m.,* and *d.* for *birth, marriage,* and *death*.

- flag any unclear letters or words by underscoring them and immediately following them with a question mark placed in square brackets.

- note precisely any overwritten text, strikeouts, or interlined additions made by the scribe.

If taking notes manually, we should

- use a notebook, rather than loose sheets that can flutter off a makeshift work station and be lost.

- number each page immediately.

- write on just one side of each sheet of paper.

Content analysis of record

Each abstract or transcript should close with a thoughtful appraisal of the record's *content*. Is it missing material that *usually* appears in this type of document? Does a will refer to "my beloved wife" although the document does not actually name her? Does the clerk's recorded copy carry no recording date or no date for the original execution of the document? Several "Skillbuilding" articles in the Board for Certification's educational newsletter, *OnBoard,* constitute an excellent refresher course.[15]

Each abstract or transcript should close with a thoughtful appraisal of the *content* of that record.

OTHER CONCERNS

Avoiding legal and ethical problems

Before taking any note or approaching a photocopying machine, we should pause to consider copyright law and scholarly ethics. Almost without exception, the serious problems that writers and lecturers have faced in both regards trace directly to lazy or careless note taking.

COPYRIGHT AND FAIR USE

Work published under a copyright date prior to 1918 is considered to be in the public domain; we may copy from these as extensively as we want. Modern international law automatically creates a copyright when a work is drafted; copying limits are severe. Still, a small amount of copying may be allowed in certain circumstances under the "fair use" doctrine. For more detailed information on this complex subject, see chapter 7.

ATTRIBUTION AND PLAGIARISM

Beyond copyright lie the problems of inadequate attribution and plagiarism. Neither is regulated by federal laws or penalties, only by professional reputation. Ethics in all research fields require two things:[16]

- *Careful use of quotation marks.* First, if we borrow the words of another—even a two-or-three-word turn of phrase (clichés excluded, of course)—we are obliged to put quotation marks around those words and properly attribute them (identify their author and publication data). Obviously, we must be careful in our note taking to set off in quotation marks *all* words that we copy directly, even short phrases. For that matter, whether we copy a phrase exactly from a document or whether we abstract it can later be a crucial issue in our analysis of this evidence. Oversight or carelessness in the matter of quotation marks can result in erroneous or unreliable judgments.

- *Careful paraphrasing or abstracting of material.* Particularly when copying from books or articles, insufficient paraphrasing (expressing the author's information or opinions in our own words) can later bring charges of plagiarism against us. If an original paragraph, for example, contains five sentences and each develops a particular point, we cannot copy those thoughts, tinker with a word or two here and there, and satisfy ourselves that we have *paraphrased* the author. Plagiarism is the copying of someone's *thoughts*. A determination of plagiarism not only considers the number of words changed or unchanged and the similarity in sentence and paragraph structure, but also the extent to which the original author's thoughts are "borrowed" without attribution. Again, to keep us safe, our note taking habits must be meticulous in the use of quotation marks around even the shortest strings of words that we copy.[17]

> If an original paragraph contains five sentences and each develops a particular point, we cannot copy those thoughts, tinker with a word or two here and there, and satisfy ourselves that we have paraphrased the author.

Maintaining research logs on site

Thorough research also calls for a research log—sometimes called a *research calendar* or an *annotated, master source list* (the term used in chapter 14). By whatever name, it is a list (perhaps in tabular format) of materials we have consulted. Some pieces of information we record may reflect our personal needs and preferences; but some are constants. On the list below, the first three are the absolute essentials.

- Citations for all sources consulted, including those that yielded *negative results*—that is, no obvious information of relevance. Without this notation, we or our client may one day waste time studying that fruitless resource again.

- Time period covered by the materials we actually searched—if using original record collections.

- Date the source was used.

- Name of the repository where source was housed.

- Comment column identifying the individuals or families sought in that source—including variant spellings of their names.

- Comment column stating positive or negative results.

- Cross-reference to file location of our research notes.

- Notation as to whether photocopies were made from each source—with specific identification of page(s) copied and file location of the copy.

- Time frame covered by the records.

When our project is lengthy and involved, it may be beneficial to divide our log by categories. Or we may create a distinct log for each locality (county and/or state) with divisions by subject (census, estate, etc.). Here again, computers wonderfully ease the chore of creating and maintaining these files.

Using technological tools to advantage

Technology provides several types of portable equipment that can expedite research and—if used properly—enhance the quality of our work. Digital cameras, hand-held scanners, laptop computers, and portable printers are increasingly popular research tools. Most facilities do permit them, although some place restrictions. Repositories that depend upon photocopies for income may disallow hand-held scanners; others may prohibit their use on fragile documents. Small record offices on limited budgets may frown on electronic equipment that does not have its own battery supply. Obviously, goodwill suggests that if a facility does not have a posted policy for the use of personal equipment on site, we should ask before we plug in or use anything we bring with us.

Laptops, where permitted, offer many advantages. If a facility bars research files or loose paper (or the research plan we carefully constructed in conformity to chapter 14's guidance), then the inability to periodically consult our notes can seriously hamper the success of our search. Not so, if we have those files on our computer. When our research produces a lengthy list of index entries, for each of which we must locate the original record book or file, we may divide the screen on our laptop and view the index entries while entering notes from the record book. When certain items need flagging, we may boldface them or box them in. When we return home, our research notes are already keyed in—ready for annotating, editing, and incorporating into the client report.

Goodwill suggests that if a facility does not have a posted policy for the use of personal equipment on site, we should ask before we plug in or use anything we bring with us.

As laptop users, we can create templates of common forms we use—preparing them in either a database or a word-processing format and heading them with our name and address. When we need them, we can access them by a few keyboard strokes. Good genealogists use forms judiciously, avoiding them in situations that would require rearranging or condensing data—as with deeds, wills, and estate records. Yet abstract forms can be beneficially employed in copying data from standardized and highly structured records such as censuses, city directories, grantor-grantee indexes, and some tax-digest tables.

A few cautions are also in order. We should

- proofread each abstract, entry, or note as soon as we type it—transposed dates and misspelled names happen so easily.

- back up our data every few minutes to a floppy disk, to avoid loss if the power fails or the computer crashes.

- exert extra care when executing a cut-and-paste function—accidents here are a frequent cause of lost or garbled research notes.

> Good genealogists use forms judiciously, avoiding them in situations that require rearranging or condensing data—as with deeds, wills, and estate records.

Summary Concepts

The reliability of our research depends upon the skill we apply to the process. As professionals, we are expected to know the sources that exist for our specialty—their whereabouts and their peculiarities. We are expected to know the collections held by all repositories relevant to our specialty. We are expected to know and observe the regulations imposed by those facilities. We are expected to achieve an appropriate balance between the use of original materials and the databases, publications, and transcripts derived from those originals. And we are expected to expertly record the particulars of all material we consult and all information we extract.

On-site research is especially challenging, educational, and exciting. As a rule, it is tremendously rewarding. It is also a necessity for professional genealogists. To protect ancient and fragile original documents—as well as for convenience—we first use digitized images, microforms, and traditional publications to every extent feasible. But not everything is, or probably ever will be, reproduced for widespread distribution or ease of access. Even when published versions exist, we cannot forget that each new layer of processing increases the chance of data error or data loss. When reproductions or their information appear questionable, we should examine the source, if access is possible. There is still no shortcut for proper research methodology, using original materials based on primary information. As helpful as they may be, modern publishing modes cannot eliminate the professional need for well-prepared, well-organized, and well-conducted on-site research.

NOTES

1. Loretto Dennis Szucs and Sandra Hargreaves Luebking, eds., *The Source: A Guidebook of American Genealogy,* revised edition (Salt Lake City: Ancestry, 1997).

RESEARCH PROCEDURES

2. Kory L. Meyerink, AG, ed., *Printed Sources: A Guide to Published Genealogical Records* (Salt Lake City: Ancestry, 1998).

3. George Everton Sr., *The Handy Book for Genealogists: United States of America,* 9th edition (Logan, Utah: Everton Publishers, 1999).

4. Alice Eichholz, Ph.D., CG, ed., *Ancestry's Red Book: American State, County & Town Sources,* revised edition. (Salt Lake City: Ancestry, 1992).

5. For example, *A Guide to Local Government Records in the South Carolina Archives* (Columbia, South Carolina: University of South Carolina Press for the South Carolina State Archives, 1988); and Kip Sperry, AG, CG, FASG, *Genealogical Research in Ohio* (Baltimore: Genealogical Publishing Co., 1997). See also the National Genealogical Society's Research in the States Series for contextual guidance to the resources of selected states.

6. Nick Vine Hall, DipFHS (Hons.), *Tracing Your Family History in Australia: A Guide to Sources,* 2d edition (Albert Park: Privately printed, 1994).

7. Nils Johan Stoa and Per-Øivind Sandberg. *Våre Røtter: Håndbok I slektsgransking for nybegynnere og viderekomne*; Our Roots: Genealogical Handbook for Beginners and Professionals (Oslo: J.W. Cappelens Forlag, 1992).

8. Loretto Dennis Szucs, "Tracking Urban Ancestors," *The Source,* 654–83. Also see Suzanne McVetty, CG, and Roger D. Joslyn, CG, FASG, "Tactics for Metropolitan Areas," *Association of Professional Genealogists [APG] Quarterly* 13 (December 1998): 120.

9. Elizabeth Shown Mills, CG, CGL, FASG, "The Battle of the 'Burned Courthouse': Alternate Approaches to the South's Classic Genealogical Problem," *APG Newsletter* 4 (December 1982): 1–5. Mills provides various other strategies in several national conference lectures titled "Battle of the Burned Courthouse"; for the most recent syllabus materials, see *Rocky Mountain Rendezvous, National Genealogical Society 1998 Conference, . . . Program Syllabus* (Arlington, Virginia: NGS, 1998): 412–15.

10. "Equipping Ourselves for Quality Service: Physical Plant and Continuing Education—BCG Survey Results," *OnBoard* [educational newsletter of the Board for Certification of Genealogists] 3 (May 1997): 9.

11. *Periodical Source Index* [PERSI], CD-ROM (Salt Lake City: Ancestry and Allen County, Indiana, Public Library, 1997—) is a regularly updated, electronic version of the ongoing hardcopy series, which indexes the subject matter of thousands of periodicals since 1847.

12. For pertinent cautions, see Elizabeth Shown Mills and Gary B. Mills, Ph.D., CG, "Databases: Research Heaven, Hell, or Limbo?" Editors' Corner, *National Genealogical Society Quarterly* 86 (June 1998): 83.

13. Two currently popular guides to genealogical resources on the Internet are Barbara Renick and Richard S. Wilson, *The Internet for Genealogists,* 3d edition (Cincinnati: Betterway Books, 1998), and Thomas Jay Kemp, *Virtual Roots: A Guide to Genealogy and Local History on the World Wide Web* (Wilmington, Delaware: Scholarly Resources, 1997). The smaller and more economical Renick-Wilson guide offers addresses and descriptions of more than 200 major genealogical sites, which then link us to others. The Kemp guide offers far more sites, but no descriptions.

14. Elizabeth Shown Mills, *Evidence! Citation & Analysis for the Family Historian* (Baltimore: Genealogical Publishing Co., 1997).

15. Kathleen W. Hinckley, CGRS, "Skillbuilding: Analyzing City Directories," *OnBoard* 2 (May 1996): 16; Elizabeth Shown Mills, "Skillbuilding: Analyzing Wills for Useful Clues," *OnBoard* 1 (May 1995): 16; and "Skillbuilding: Analyzing Deeds for Useful Clues," *OnBoard* 1 (January 1995): 8.

16. Elizabeth Shown Mills, "That Awful P-Word: Plagiarism," *OnBoard* 4 (September 1998): 17–20.

17. Other enlightening examples of plagiarism and improper paraphrasing can be found in Joseph Gibaldi, *MLA Handbook for Writers of Research Papers,* 4th edition (New York: Modern Language Association of America, 1995), 26–29.

18. Kory L. Meyerink in synopsis of his lecture, "The Future of FamilySearch® for the Genealogist," *1995 Conference Program, Federation of Genealogical Societies* (Salt Lake City: FGS, 1995), 9.

An excellent genealogist knows the limitations of each tool, while a poor genealogist expects the tools to do the work by themselves.

—*Kory L. Meyerink,* AG[18]

16

**TRANSCRIPTS
AND
ABSTRACTS**

TRANSCRIPTS
AND ABSTRACTS

Keynotes

Transcripts <u>and</u> Abstracts

by Mary McCampbell Bell, CALS, CGL

Reliable research, reliable conclusions, reliable reports, and reliable publications all rest on one foundation: skill at note taking. Chapter 15 addresses the subject from a broad perspective. This chapter focuses upon the two most essential note-taking skills: transcribing and abstracting. Both require familiarity with the mechanics of editing words. Both require us to understand the records we use and the boilerplate we find in them. For abstracts, we must also be able to distinguish between crucial details and excess verbiage. Toward that end, this chapter reviews note-taking principles and presentation styles. Examples from a variety of legal documents demonstrate how to transcribe and abstract—with step-by-step illustrations of how an abstract evolves.

Basic Distinctions

Transcribe and *abstract* are, themselves, words that are often misunderstood. They are confused with each other and they are confused with similar words that involve other processes: *translate* and *extract*. Briefly, the distinctions are these:[1]

Transcribe *vs.* translate

DEFINITIONS

To *transcribe* (to make a *transcription*) is to copy a document literally, word for word—with all spelling, grammar, and punctuation copied *exactly* as found. *Transcribe* should not be confused with *translate*, which means to convert a document from one language to another, as faithfully as language differences allow.

GUIDELINES

A transcript—a faithful copying of a document, word for word and punctuation mark for punctuation mark—adheres to the following principles:

- If names, numbers, or words are abbreviated, we do not spell them out.

- If diacritical marks appear—as, for example, the tilde (~) or the straight line above words that past scribes used to indicate the omission of certain letters—we reproduce those diacriticals.

- If superscript is used to indicate the omission of letters, we reproduce the superscript. Failure to do so can alter meanings and identities. A female whose name is written as *Mar*^{y} is likely to be *Margery*. If we do not preserve the superscript, we change her name to *Mary*.

- If we need to add something to a document for clarity, we place our comments in square brackets—never parentheses. Square brackets are a typographical warning device that tells our readers: *I have added this. It's not in the original.*

Transcribing and abstracting require us to understand the records we use and the boilerplate we find in them.

- If we are in doubt about a word or phrase, we flag it with a question mark in square brackets. If only part of a word is clear, we underline the unclear part. If several words appear unclear, we note the number of words. If a passage is unreadable, we indicate the length of the passage.

- When making transcriptions amid research notes or client reports, we enclose the copied text in quotation marks. At publication stage, if the transcription is woven into our narrative, then we may follow the typographical convention for long quotes that are set off by indented paragraphs. (Also see chapter 22, Record Compilations.)

All rules have their exceptions. Where the "faithfulness" of transcriptions is concerned, two are common: *(a)* We can type transcripts, even though the originals are handwritten; and *(b)* We reproduce certain obsolete letterforms in their modern style, just as we do with all antiquated penmanship. The principal three are these:[2]

- The so-called *double-f* appearing at the start of names (often mistakenly copied as *Ffrancis*) is not a *double-f*. It is an early form of the single, uppercase *F.*

- The long-tailed *double-s,* which appears to be a lowercase *p,* should be written as what it was meant to be: *ss.*

- The seemingly peculiar use of *"y"* in such words as "ye olde . . . " is not a *y.* It is a *thorn,* an obsolete letter of the English language that represented the sound *th.* Today, that sound is written as *th.*

Abstract *vs.* extract

DEFINITIONS

Abstracts are *summaries* that record all important detail from a whole document. *Extracts* are *word-for-word* copies of *selected portions* of a piece of writing.

GUIDELINES

Because an *extract* is a quotation, it is set off by quotation marks. Because an *abstract* is our summary in our own words, an abstract uses no quotation marks. However, much confusion is created by the fact that *abstracts* of documents frequently contain *extracts*, when phrases, sentences, or paragraphs seem so important that we hesitate not to copy them word for word. Amid abstracting land records, for example, we should copy verbatim the legal description of the land, or we may encounter a portion of a document whose meaning is so unclear that we dare not summarize it, lest we make a wrong interpretation.

When our abstracts contain significant extracts, we place quotation marks around that material we have copied word for word—using *exact* spelling, punctuation, and abbreviation inside those quotation marks. Why? Because, after we leave that record behind, return home, and proceed to analyze our findings, we frequently discover that the meaning of a statement or a situation hinges upon an exact turn of phrase. A failure to distinguish an extract from abstracted material—by using those simple quotation marks—can affect the reliability of our analysis. It may also open us to charges of plagiarism, if and when we or our heirs publish the results of our research. Other guidelines for compiling reliable abstracts include the following:

A failure to distinguish an extract from abstracted material—by using those simple quotation marks—can affect the reliability of our analysis. It may also open us to charges of plagiarism, if and when we or our heirs publish the results of our research.

- Proper abstracts preserve the exact arrangement of data. Therefore, the careful abstractor does not use the abstract forms often recommended in beginning genealogy classes. These forms require us to rearrange the contents of a deed, will, or other document to fit the order of the blanks on the form. Doing so shifts words out of context and frequently changes a document's meaning. No two documents are alike, and forms rarely allow (or adequately so) for the unusual in a document.

- Names should be copied exactly. If they are abbreviated, we do not spell them out. If they are spelled out, we do not abbreviate to save space or time. If a string of names carries no internal punctuation—as when a testator says, "To Mary Susan Katie Jones: all my wearing apparel." We cannot guess whether the testator is referring to one female of the surname Jones, or two, or three. To clarify, we may add a comment in square brackets: [*no commas used between names*]. Alternatively, we might *suggest* the appropriate position of commas by placing them in square brackets[,] as used here, but only if we are reasonably certain of the identity.

- Signatures and signature marks are faithfully reproduced. If a signature or mark appears to be an original, we note that—using square brackets around the note.

- When the word *jurat* appears beside the name of a witness, we include that word with the signature. It indicates which witness(es) attested the authenticity of the document when it was presented for filing.

- When words denote race or color, we do not alter the terminology to comply with modern preferences. Words of the past often had different meanings, and genealogical clues lurk within them.

As with transcripts,

- if we feel it necessary to add (usually for clarity) any information or explanation that is not in the original document, we place that addition in square brackets.

- When uncertain of a word or phrase, we flag it with a question mark in brackets.

> If we feel it necessary to add any information or explanation that is not in the original document, we place that addition in square brackets.

Essential Elements

Format

Both transcripts and abstracts commonly follow a basic pattern:

1. Documentation:
   - Identification of the record (e.g., John Smith Will).
   - Location (name of agency, office, or repository).
   - Source citation (typically, book/volume/liber and page/folio number; or collection name and file or number).[3]
   - Dates the document was written, filed, and recorded.
2. Body of the document (which differs with each record type).
3. Witnesses and signatures.
4. Legal addenda such as notarizations, attestations, proofs, and dower relinquishments.

**TRANSCRIPTS
AND ABSTRACTS**

TIP

Typographical conventions
exist for good reasons, as
Benjamin Franklin himself
pointed out . . .

"Lately, another Fancy has
induced some printers to
use the short round 's,'
instead of the long one,
which formerly served well
to distinguish a word readily
by its varied appearance.
Certainly . . . omitting this
prominent Letter makes the
Line appear more even; but
renders it less immediately legible; as the paring [of]
all Men's Noses might
smooth and level their
Faces, but would render
their Physiognomies less
distinguishable."[4]

The combination of upper-
and lowercase letters in
typed text serves the same
role (distinguishability). A
decision to ignore its utility
should not be made lightly.

Style

Abstracting is as much an art as a science. Transcribing is a more rigid process. In both cases, however, the genealogist has at least some options to choose among, as a reflection of personal tastes. Whether abstracts or transcripts are used for client reports, personal research, or publication, we should give some thought to the appearance of our product:

- Should our transcription break each line at exactly the same point as the original, or should it conserve space by wrapping lines within the margins set for our typescript?

- Should the abstract be created in paragraph or outline style?

- Is white space important to the overall appearance of the abstract?

- Will a brief abstract serve the same purpose as a longer, more detailed one?

- Should we abbreviate words? Lightly? Heavily? At all? Often abstractors use unnecessary abbreviations that do not save the space they anticipated.

- Should we present names in all capital letters? If so, just surnames or full names?

To the last line of questioning, typographers say *no*—emphatically. A page of abstracts filled with names rendered totally in uppercase letters is a page with line spacing so cramped that it is both hard to read and typographically repugnant. Moreover, the combination of tall and short letters that is standard in many languages is far easier for the eye and mind to grasp quickly than are blocks of letters all the same height. Genealogists have reached no such consensus. Some say *yes*. This convention (left over from the days when few publications had indexes, and typewriters offered no means of emphasis other than capitalization) helps them spot names. Some genealogists say *no*—that the use of all uppercase destroys evidence of the original manner of capitalization. (Was *DEVILLE* actually written as *DeVille* or *Deville* in the original? Was *TERHUNE* written *Terhune* or *terHune?*)

For those who prefer using "all caps," a compromise is possible so long as two conventions are followed:

- We can reduce the size of the capital letters by using "small capitals," available with many fonts, or by reducing the size of regular capitals by one or two points: GALLAGHER, rather than GALLAGHER, will still stand out in the text—without screaming. (The FINAL ABSTRACT examples in this chapter use a two-point reduction.)

- We can use a combination of capital-letter sizes to show distinctive capitalization within names that begin with particles—i.e., DEVILLE or TERHUNE. In these two examples, the capitals are reduced by one point, with a further reduction to two points to indicate lowercase letters in the particles. The results are still inelegant but represent a serviceable compromise.

The Process

Figure 15 presents the 1849 will of Frances Field of Culpeper County, Virginia.

FIG. 15
RECORDED WILL:
A MODEL FOR
ABSTRACTING
AND TRANSCRIBING

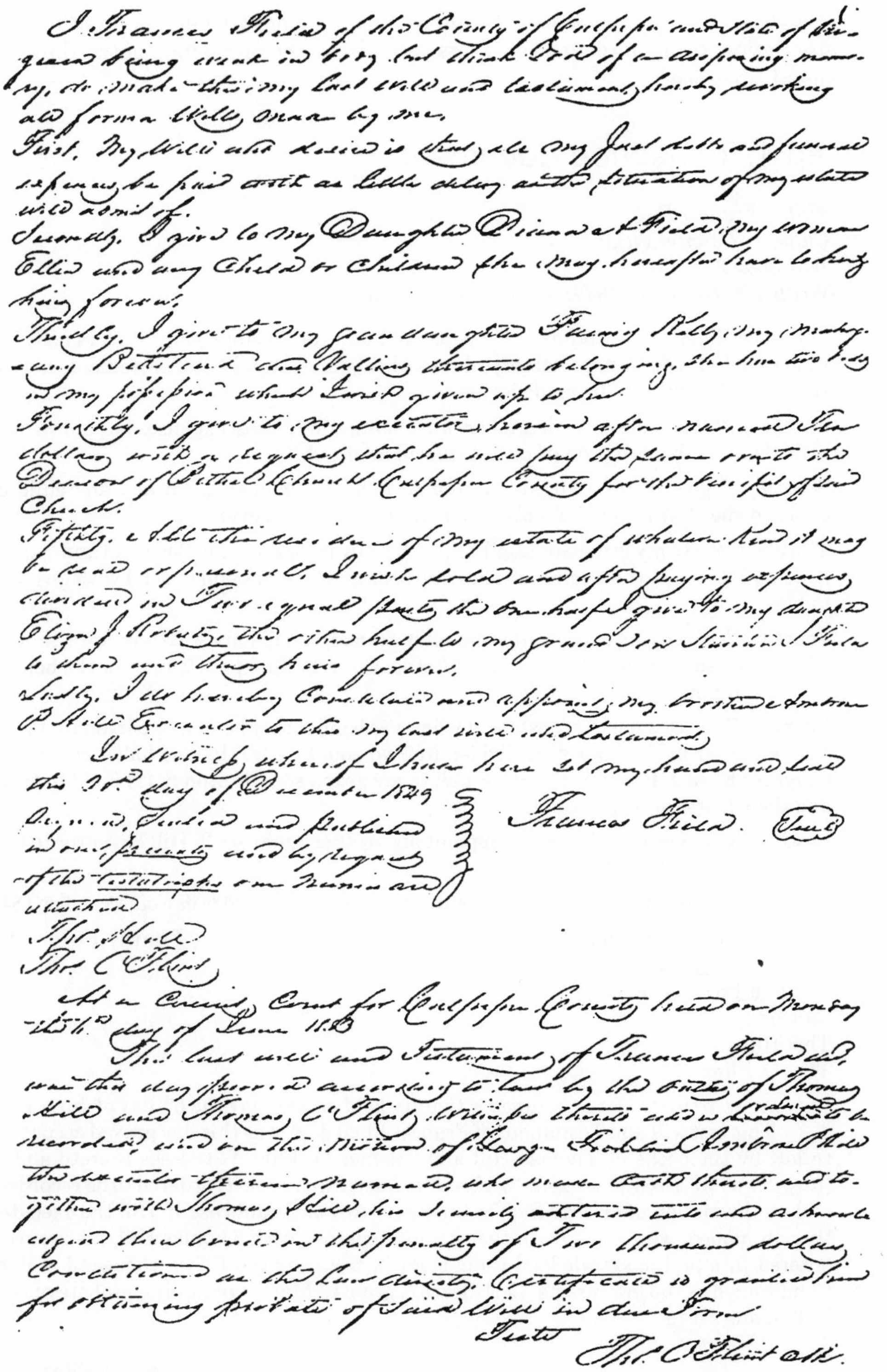

TIP

When details need to be added to typed transcriptions, many copyists prefer to place the added matter in italics to make it typographically distinct from the wording of the original. The transcript at right provides two examples of this practice:

- the header that identifies the document, its source, and its relevant dates; and

- the insertion of question marks, spelling corrections, and explanations of textual irregularities—all placed inside of square brackets.

Through a series of steps, we will follow this document from the creation of a transcription, through removal of excess verbiage, to the production of two different styles of abstracts.

Step 1: Transcribe document

Will of Frances Field
Culpeper County, Virginia
Will Book 2:69
Written 20 December 1849; proved 6 June 1853

"I Frances Field of the County of Culpeper and State of Virginia being weak in body but thank God of a disposing memory, do make this my last will and testament, hereby revoking all former Wills made by me,

First, My Will and desire is that all my Just debts and funeral expenses be paid with as little delay as the situation of my estate will admit of.

Secondly, I give to my Daughter Diana A. Field my woman Ellin and any child or children she [*Ellin*] may hereafter have to her & heirs forever.

Thirdly, I give to my grandaughter Fanny [*?*] Kelly my mahogany Bedstead and Vallins [*valance*] thereunto belonging, she has two beds in my possession which I wish given up to her.

Fourthly, I give to my executor herein after named Ten dollars with a request that he will pay the same over to the Deacon of Bethel Church Culpeper County for the benefit of said Church.

Fifthly, All the residue of my estate of whatever Kind it may be real or personall, I wish sold and after paying expenses divided in Two equal parts, the one half I give to my daughter Eliza J. Roberts, the other half to my grand son Stanton S. [*?*] Field to them and their heirs forever.

Lastly, I do hereby constitute and appoint my brother Ambrose P. Hill Executor to this my last will and Testament.

In witness whereof I have here set my hand and seal this 20th day of December 1849

Signed, Sealed and published   }   Frances Field (seal)
in our presents and by request   }
of the testatrixes our names are   }
attached
Thos Hill
Thos O. Flint

At a Circuit Court for Culpeper County held on Monday the 6th day of June 1853
This last will and Testament of Frances Field decd, was this day proved according to law by the oaths of Thomas Hill and Thomas O. Flint Witnesses thereto and is [*illegible word crossed through; "ordered" is interlined above it*] ordered to be recorded, and on the motion of ~~George Ficklin~~ [*name crossed out*] Ambrose P. Hill the executor therein named, who made Oath thereto and together with Thomas Hill, his security entered into and acknowledged their bond in the penalty of Two thousand dollars Conditioned as the law directs. Certificate is granted him for obtaining probate of said Will in due Form

Teste

Thos O. Flint, clk"

Step 2: Remove excess verbiage

The next process is to cross out unnecessary, superfluous, or boilerplate language that will not be included in the abstract. Most boilerplate can be eliminated; but we must know and watch carefully for the exceptions, lest we lose important facts or clues.

Will of Frances Field
Culpeper County, Virginia
Will Book 2:69
Written 20 December 1849; proved 6 June 1853

"I Frances Field of the County of Culpeper and State of Virginia being weak in body but thank God of a disposing memory, do make this my last will and testament, hereby revoking all former Wills made by me,

First, My Will and desire is that all my Just debts and funeral expenses be paid with as little delay as the situation of my estate will admit of.

Secondly, I give to my Daughter Diana A. Field my woman Ellin and any child or children she may hereafter have to her & heirs forever.

Thirdly, I give to my grandaughter Fanny [?] Kelly my mahogany Bedstead and Vallins [valence] thereunto belonging, she has two beds in my possession which I wish given up to her.

Fourthly, I give to my executor herein after named Ten dollars with a request that he will pay the same over to the Deacon of Bethel Church Culpeper County for the benefit of said Church.

Fifthly, All the residue of my estate of whatever Kind it may be real or personall, I wish sold and after paying expenses divided in Two equal parts, the one half I give to my daughter Eliza J. Roberts, the other half to my grand son Stanton S. [?] Field to them and their heirs forever.

Lastly, I do hereby constitute and appoint my brother Ambrose P. Hill Executor to this my last will and Testament.

     In witness whereof I have here set my hand and seal this 20th day of December 1849

Signed, Sealed and published   }   Frances Field (seal)
in our presents and by request   }
of the testatrixes our names are   }
attached
Thos Hill
Thos O. Flint

     At a Circuit Court for Culpeper County held on Monday the 6th day of June 1853 This last will and Testament of Frances Field decd, was this day proved according to law by the oaths of Thomas Hill and Thomas O. Flint Witnesses thereto and is [*illegible word crossed through; "ordered" is interlined above it*] ordered to be recorded, and on the motion of ~~George Ficklin~~ [*name crossed out*] Ambrose P. Hill the executor therein named, who made Oath thereto and together with Thomas Hill, his security

TIP

When photocopying a document from a record book or collection—with plans to transcribe or abstract it later—we should still take time, right then and there, to read every word of it. Should we have trouble reading any words or passages, we should then copy and study other specimens of that scribe's penmanship.

entered into and acknowledged their bond in the penalty of Two thousand dollars Conditioned [?] as the law directs. Certificate is granted him for obtaining probate of said Will in due Form

                                          Teste
                                              Thos O. Flint, clk"

Figure 16 explains the rationale upon which the highlighted passages were excised from this will.

Step 3: Review remaining text

Will of Frances Field
Culpeper County, Virginia
Will Book 2:69
Written 20 December 1849; proved 6 June 1853

"I Frances Field of County of Culpeper and State of Virginia . . . give to my Daughter Diana A. Field my woman Ellin and any child or children she [*Ellin*] may hereafter have. . . . I give to my grandaughter Fanny [?] Kelly my mahogany Bedstead and Vallins [valence] . . . she has two beds in my possession which I wish given up to her. . . . I give . . . my executor . . . Ten dollars . . . that he will pay the Deacon of Bethel Church Culpeper County. . . . All the residue of my estate . . . real or personall, I wish sold and after paying expenses divided in Two equal parts, the one half I give to my daughter Eliza J. Roberts, the other half to my grand son Stanton S. [?] Field. . . . I . . . appoint my brother Ambrose P. Hill Executor . . . . 20 December 1849. . . .

Thos Hill   Frances Field (seal)
Thos O. Flint

. . . Circuit Court for Culpeper County . . . 6 . . . June 1853, . . . will . . . of Frances Field decd, was this day proved . . . by the oaths of Thomas Hill and Thomas O. Flint Witnesses . . ., and on . . . motion of ~~George Ficklin~~ [*name crossed out*] Ambrose P. Hill the executor . . . made Oath with Thomas Hill, his security enter[ing] into . . . their bond . . . of Two thousand dollars. . . ."

Step 4: Create abstract

After removing the excess verbiage, we create an abstract that reflects our chosen style. Two samples are produced on the facing page, and two differences between them are worth noting:

- Both use all capitals for names; but sample 1 reduces their size by two points.
- Sample 1 spells out all words, while sample 2 heavily abbreviates.

Yet both abstracts contain exactly the same number of lines! A question is obvious here: *if heavy abbreviating does not save significant space, is it worth the loss of clarity and readability?* Does the reduction of point size for "all caps" make names any more or less difficult to pick out?

    The following samples also use a generous amount of white space, sample 1 being closer to the preferred format of the writer. By contrast, the examples labeled FINAL ABSTRACTS used throughout the rest of this chapter sometimes use space more conservatively, to illustrate other style choices.

If heavy abbreviating does not save significant space, is it worth the loss of clarity and readability?

FIG. 16
PROBATE RECORDS:
SPECIAL GUIDELINES
FOR ABSTRACTING

Basic principles

- Use the same language as the testator. If the testator says "I give," do not change the meaning by converting it to "he gives." Sometimes the exact wording of the will is abstruse enough that we could easily change meanings and intent in the conversion process.
- Keep the original sequence as written by the testator.
- Separate the bequests for clarity. A semicolon or period makes it clear when one bequest ends and another begins.
- Name all persons listed in the will—maintaining, if possible, the order in which they were named. Children *might* be listed by the testator in age order, or some other revealing sequence.
- Excise legal language judiciously. Obviously, we need to be familiar with inheritance laws of the time and place or else preserve all legal phrases until we examine the law. (For example, in the Field will, if the testator had left slave Ellin "to my Daughter Diana and *the heirs of her body* forever," rather than to her "& heirs forever," the added words would have changed the future of that inheritance from the common situation to special treatment under the law.[5])
- Never say a will was "proved" unless the recording information says it was. Otherwise, we only know that the will was *filed* or *presented* for probate on a certain date.

Essential items

- Identification of the record (e.g., John Smith Will).
- Source citation (typically, book/volume/liber and page/folio number; or collection name, file name or number, and document number).
- Location (name and place of agency, office, or repository).
- Dates the document was written, proved, filed, and recorded.
- All named individuals, with their signatures and any stated roles or relationships.
- Addenda such as notarizations, attestations, and dower relinquishments.

Other inclusions

Rule of thumb: anything that is described or traceable must be included, with all detail given in the original document. For example:

- Slaves—names, ages, skills, infirmities, racial composition, relationships, residences, etc.
- Land—legal description, if given (copy it exactly—it may be the only surviving document with that description, or the recorded copy of the deed or grant might be in error).
- Memorabilia or unusual items such as carriages, family Bibles, pictures, silver goods, or watches—also items suggesting literacy or occupation (e.g., books, blacksmith tools).
- Animals with names or distinctive markings; also branding irons.

Watch for

- Religious clues. If the will does not begin with "In the name of God Amen" or a similar oath, the testator may have been a member of a pacifist group such as the Quakers. It is helpful to point out this clue by noting "[*Will does not begin with 'In the name of God'*]."
- Slave manumissions. Depending upon the circumstances and the wording, such manumissions could *suggest* (but not *prove*) antislavery sentiments or paternity of slave children.
- Clues in the recordation data. The probate of a will several years after its draft might imply that the testator had recently died. Sometimes, amid the recording information, it is noted that an executor or witness had died. Sometimes, a female witness's surname appears here in a different form from that on the witness line, implying her marriage in the interim.

SAMPLE ABSTRACT 1

This version uses no abbreviations, reduces capitalized names by two point sizes, and judiciously adds minimal punctuation for grammatical clarity.

> Will of FRANCES FIELD
> Culpeper County, Virginia, Will Book 2:69
> Written 20 December 1849; proved 6 June 1853
>
> I, FRANCES FIELD of Culpeper County: to my daughter, DIANA A. FIELD, my woman ELLIN and any children ELLIN may have; to my granddaughter, FANNY [?] KELLY, my mahogany bedstead and her two beds in my possession; to executor, $10 to pay Deacon of Bethel Church of Culpeper County. Rest of estate sold to pay expenses; balance divided in two equal parts between my daughter, ELIZA J. ROBERTS, and my grandson, STANTON S. [?] FIELD. I appoint my brother, AMBROSE P. HILL, my executor.
>
> Witnesses: THOS. HILL, THOS. O. FLINT.   [Signed] FRANCES FIELD
>
> Proved, 6 June 1853, on oaths of THOMAS HILL and THOMAS O. FLINT, witnesses. On motion of ~~GEORGE FICKLIN~~ [sic] AMBROSE P. HILL, Executor, Hill posted bond of $2,000, with THOMAS HILL as his security.

SAMPLE ABSTRACT 2

This version uses standard (and quite overpowering) capitals, as well as many abbreviations.

> Will of FRANCES FIELD,
> Culpeper Co., Va., WB 2:69
> Writ. 20 Dec. 1849; prov. 6 Jun. 1853
>
> I, FRANCES FIELD of Culpeper Co., to my dau., DIANA A. FIELD, my woman ELLIN and any child ELLIN may have; to my grdau., FANNY [?] KELLY, my mahogany bed-stead and her two beds in my possession; to exec^r $10 to pay Deac. of Bethel Ch. of Culpeper Co. Rest of est. sold to pay expenses and bal. div. into two eq. parts btw. dau., ELIZA J. ROBERTS, and my grson., STANTON S. [?] FIELD. I appt my bro., AMBROSE P. HILL, my exec^r.
>
> Wit. THOS. HILL, THOS. O. FLINT   [Signed] FRANCES FIELD
>
> Prvd. 6 June 1853 by oaths of THOMAS HILL and THOMAS O. FLINT, wits. On motion of ~~GEORGE FICKLIN~~ [sic] AMBROSE P. HILL, Exec^r, Hill posted bond of $2,000 with THOMAS HILL as his sec.

Obviously, the rampant abbreviations saved no line space.

A Sampler of Models

Appraisal or inventory

Genealogical instruction manuals differ somewhat in their advice regarding the extent to which property inventories should be abstracted. As general guidelines: when research leads to an inventory—commonly in an estate file or a mortgage record—we should photocopy the full record, if the repository permits. If not, and the inventory is that of a known ancestor, then a full or partial transcript is in order, depending upon the circumstances. At times, our style depends upon our purpose:

When research leads to an inventory, we should photocopy the full record, if the repository permits.

- For a client, we might abstract any boilerplate introductory or closing matter but fully transcribe the details of the property.

- For a compilation of published record abstracts, we might justify providing condensations that preserve the basics: any and all names, dates, and relationships; the total amount of the inventory; and the nature of the property. In such a case, we would always indicate that the full document has more detail.

The following illustrates the mechanics of making a full transcription and the essentials for a highly condensed abstract.

STEP 1: TRANSCRIBE

Antoine Coton-Maïs, f.m.c., Inventory and Appraisement[6]
Natchitoches Parish, Louisiana
Succession [Probate] vol. 14:41–43
Drawn 17 February 1840; filed [no date given]

"Be it remembered, that on this seventeenth day of february in the year one thousand Eight hundred and forty, in pursuance of an order of the court of Probate of the parish of Natchitoches in the State of Louisiana, and after due notice to that effect given to all the parties interested, I, Charles E. Greneaux, parish Judge and ex officio Judge of the Court and notary public, proceeded to take an inventory of the property belonging to the Succession of Antoine Coton-Maïs, a free man of color late of the said Parish, deceased. The said Inventory was taken at the request of the heirs and legal representatives of the said Antoine Coton-Maïs, and in their presence, and in the presence of Henry Hertzog, Esquire, attorney appointed by the said County [parish] to represent one of said heirs, who is absent, as represented in the petition presented to that effect.

"Louis Morin and Henry Octave Deronce, free men of color, having been duly appointed and sworn to that effect, apraised [*sic*] the property, to wit:

5 plows $1—5 dº $4—1 do $2	$7.00
1 Lot hoes, spades &c $1—dº 50¢— 1 lot axes $5	6.50
2 new Plows $16—12 cotton baskets .75	16.75
2 Beef hides $1—2 saddles $12	13.00
1 Lot, Bedstead, spinning wheels, scales &c	2.00
1 Lot, Pots, andirons & Buckets	6.00
1 Lot Tools $2/ 1 cart body & axle ton/ tombereau [cart] & rein [?]	8.00
1 ox cart $40—1 gig & harness $50	90.00
1 Keg nails $4—1 barrell containing empty Bottles $.50¢	4.50
1 Lot earthen jars containing Seltz water	1.00
1 Demijohn & 1 basket Bottles	3.00
1 Lot Shingles $8—1 coil Rope, cross cut Saw & Scythe $6	14.00
1 Bedstead & bedding $5—1 do $4— 1 dº $4	13.00
1 Trunk $.50—1 Jar $1— 4 Rushbottom chairs $2	3.50
3 Tables $3.00—1 Bureau toilette $10	13.00
1 clock $5—1 sack oats $.50—2 looking glasses $2	7.50
	$208.75

1 small Bedstead & Bedding, spinning wheel &c	$2.00
1 grey mare & colt $10—1 grey colt $7	17.00
1 paint horse $7—1 Bay horse $40	47.00
1 Dun mule $35—1 Brown mule $35	70.00
2 Black Dº together $35	35.00
1 yoke oxen $25—1 dº $15	40.00
1 pr. unbroken dº $15—1 cow & calf $6	21.00
1 cow & calf $6—1 dº $4—1 do $4	14.00
1 cow $3—4 yearlings $5	8.00
24 Bales cotton @ $15 pr. Bale	360.00

Slaves

Robbin,	negro man,	aged	42	years	500.00
Henry Whitehead,	dº	"	23	"	600.00
Mark	dº	"	26	"	600.00
Allick	dº	"	25	"	500.00
Henry	dº	"	25	"	550.00
Harry	dº	"	15	"	400.00
Betsy	negress	"	40	"	350.00
Jenny	dº	"	30	"	600.00
Ellen	dº	"	30	"	

and her three children, Raphaël, aged about nine years, Jim, aged about four years, and Marguerite, aged about one year, appraised together at   700.00
Celesie   negress, aged 20 years   600.00

TIP

When transcribing an appraisement, we should "add up" the stated figures while the original is still at hand, to check the accuracy of our transcriptions. (Alas, some record clerks should have done the same.)

TRANSCRIPTS

AND ABSTRACTS

<u>Lands</u>

All that certain tract of land or Plantation on which the deceased resided,
situate in the said Parish of Natchitoches, containing five arpents, more
or less, front on the left bank of Red
River, with all the depth and privileges thereto belonging, and all the
buildings and improvements thereon, bounded above by lands of Jean
François Hertzog, and below by
lands of Florentine Conant and
Jerome Sarpy, appraised at Seven
Thousand Dollars   7,000.00

[*Balance brought forward*]	13,222.85
22 Bales Cotton in New Orleans @ $15	330.00

<u>Papers</u>

In Bank notes	159.00
Note of Louis Balthazard	100.00
Note of Louis Monet paid to	
Mr Roubieu	105.86
Receipt of Jacques Porter $150	.00
Note of Antoine Aubuchon	121.16
Nérès Pierre Metoyer, account	112.00
	$14,150.77

TIP

When abstracting individ-
ual documents (as for
clients or our own files),
our abstract should identify
the official(s) involved.

When abstracting an entire
series of documents by a
single official (as for publication), it is not necessary
to repeat that person's
identity in each abstract;
rather, we make that identification in our preface or
section heading.

There being nothing else belonging to the said succession to be inventoried, I have
closed the present Inventory, and have signed the same with the parties interested,
and appraisers, in presence of the undersigned witnesses, at the Parish of Natchitoches,
aforesaid, on the day and year first above written. /signed/ Marie X Delpiche her mark
— Marie Louise Coton-Maïs X her mark — Désirée Coton-Maïs X her mark — Arsène
Coton-Maïs X her mark — Marie Suzette Coton-Maïs X her mark — Charles Coton-
Maïs X his mark; Louis Monete X his mark — Louis Mulon X his mark, all declaring
they know not how to write — Antoinette Coton May — L^s Balthazar — François
Metoyer fils — Henry Hertzog attorney — C. N. Rocques — appraisers: Louis Morin
— H^y O^{ve} Deronce — witnesses: E. Dupré — F. B. Sherburne — C. E. Greneaux, parish
judge & ex officio Judge of Probate."

STEP 2: REMOVE THE EXCESS

Antoine Coton-Maïs, f.m.c., Inventory and Appraisement
Natchitoches Parish, Louisiana
Succession [Probate] vol. 14:41–43
Drawn 17 February 1840; filed [no date given]

"Be it remembered, that on this seventeenth day of february in the year one thousand
Eight hundred and forty, in pursuance of an order of the court of Probate of the parish
* of Natchitoches in the State of Louisiana, and after due notice to that effect given to
all the parties interested, I, Charles E. Greneaux, parish Judge and ex officio Judge of
the Court and notary public, proceeded to take an inventory of the property belonging
to the Succession of Antoine Coton-Maïs, a free man of color late of the said Parish,
deceased. The said Inventory was taken at the request of the heirs and legal
representatives of the said Antoine Coton-Maïs, and in their presence, and in the
presence of Henry Hertzog, Esquire, attorney appointed by the said County [*parish*]
to represent one of said heirs, who is absent, as represented in the petition presented
to that effect.

---

* In abstracts made for publication, this boilerplate is typically eliminated. However, the
statement here is important from a research standpoint, because it refers to prior court
actions we should locate for a full accounting of this estate settlement. At the same time,
while it may be interesting that the parish judge was physically present for the inventory
at the home of the deceased, his was a routine appearance of no legal or social significance
in that society.

"Louis Morin and Henry Octave Deronce, free men of color, having been duly appointed and sworn to that effect, apraised [*sic*] the property, to wit:

5 plows $1—5 d° $4—1 do $2	$7.00
1 Lot hoes, spades &c $1—d° 50¢—	
1 lot axes $5	6.50
2 new Plows $16—12 cotton baskets .75	16.75
2 Beef hides $1—2 saddles $12	13.00
1 Lot, Bedstead, spinning wheels,	
scales &c	2.00
1 Lot, Pots, andirons & Buckets	6.00
1 Lot Tools $2/ 1 cart body & axle ton/	
tombereau [cart] & rein [?]	8.00
1 ox cart $40—1 gig & harness $50	90.00
1 Keg nails $4—1 barrell containing	
empty Bottles $.50¢	4.50
1 Lot earthen jars containing Seltz water	1.00
1 Demijohn & 1 basket Bottles	3.00
1 Lot Shingles $8—1 coil Rope,	
cross cut Saw & Scythe $6	14.00
1 Bedstead & bedding $5—1 do $4—	
1 do $4	13.00
1 Trunk $.50—1 Jar $1—	
4 Rushbottom chairs $2	3.50
3 Tables $3.00—1 Bureau toilette $10	13.00
1 clock $5—1 sack oats $.50—2 looking	
glasses $2	7.50
	$208.75
1 small Bedstead & Bedding,	
spinning wheel &c	$2.00
1 grey mare & colt $10—1 grey colt $7	17.00
1 paint horse $7—1 Bay horse $40	47.00
1 Dun mule $35—1 Brown mule $35	70.00
2 Black D° together $35	35.00
1 yoke oxen $25—1 d° $15	40.00
1 pr. unbroken d° $15—1 cow & calf $6	21.00
1 cow & calf $6—1 d° $4—1 do $4	14.00
1 cow $3—4 yearlings $5 8.00	
24 Bales cotton @ $15 pr. Bale	360.00

Slaves

Robbin,	negro* man,	aged	42 years		500.00
Henry Whitehead,	d°	"	23	"	600.00
Mark	d°	"	26	"	600.00
Allick	d°	"	25	"	500.00
Henry	d°	"	25	"	550.00
Harry	d°	"	15	"	400.00
Betsy	negress*	d°	"	40	"	350.00
Jenny	d°	"	30	"	600.00
Ellen	d°	"	30	"	600.00

and her three children, Raphaël, aged about nine years, Jim, aged about four years, and Marguerite, aged about one year, appraised together at 700.00

Celesie negress, aged 20 years 600.00

Lands

All that certain tract of land or Plantation on which the deceased resided, situate in the said Parish of Natchitoches, containing five arpents, more or less, front on the left bank of Red River, with all the depth and privileges thereto belonging, and all the buildings and improvements thereon, bounded above by lands of Jean François Hertzog, and below by lands of Florentine Conant and Jerome Sarpy, appraised at Seven Thousand Dollars 7,000.00

[*Balance brought forward*]	$ 13,222.85
22 Bales Cotton in New Orleans @ $15	330.00

Papers

In Bank notes	159.00
Note of Louis Balthazard	100.00
Note of Louis Monet paid to	
Mr Roubieu	105.86
Receipt of Jacques Porter $150	.00
Note of Antoine Aubuchon	121.16
Nérès Pierre Metoyer, account	112.00
	14,150.77

TIP

Accurately transcribing inventories from the past often requires us to use unabridged or specialized dictionaries to identify obsolete words.[7]

There being nothing else belonging to the said succession to be inventoried, I have closed the present Inventory, and have signed the same with the parties interested, and appraisers, in presence of the undersigned witnesses, at the Parish of Natchitoches, aforesaid, on the day and year first above written. /signed/ Marie X Delpiche her mark

---

* Some words used in historical records are out of vogue (or considered insensitive) today. However, historical researchers have an obligation to accurately reproduce the past, without personal judgment. The terms *negro* and *negress* are important to maintain here, because in this society they often suggest not only gender but specific racial composition—if the slaves in question had been part Indian or white, other terms likely would have been used.

— Marie Louise Coton-Maïs X her mark — Désirée Coton-Maïs X her mark — Arsène Coton-Maïs X her mark — Marie Suzette Coton-Maïs X her mark — Charles Coton-Maïs X his mark; Louis Monete X his mark — Louis Mulon X his mark, all declaring they know not how to write — Antoinette Coton May — L^s Balthazar — François Metoyer fils — Henry Hertzog attorney — C. N. Rocques — appraisers: Louis Morin — H^y O^{ve} Deronce — witnesses: E. Dupré — F. B. Sherburne — C. E. Greneaux, parish judge & ex officio Judge of Probate."

Inventories typically include many items that may or may not need to be copied, depending upon the purpose of the abstract.

STEP 3: REVIEW WHAT REMAINS

Inventories typically contain many items that may or may not be copied, depending upon the purpose of the abstract. A published volume of county probate (or parish succession) records is likely to eliminate the items shaded above in step 2, on the premise that researchers interested in any particular estate will obtain a copy of the full document for the inherent value all these details possess. However, a useful abstract still does not ignore the existence of such items. The common practice is to replace the itemizations with a generic (group) identification and, perhaps, note the quantity of items involved.

Thus, this review of the information left by step 2 uses editorial additions in square brackets to represent the consolidated items.

Antoine Coton-Maïs, f.m.c., Inventory and Appraisement
Natchitoches Parish, Louisiana
Succession [Probate] vol. 14:41–43
Drawn 17 February 1840; filed [no date given]

". . . seventeenth . . . of february . . . one thousand Eight hundred and forty, . . . inventory of . . . property belonging to . . . Succession of Antoine Coton-Maïs, . . . free man of color . . . of said . . . Parish, deceased. . . . taken at . . . request of . . . heirs and legal representatives . . . and in their presence, and in . . . presence of Henry Hertzog, Esquire, attorney appointed by the . . . [parish] to represent one of . . . heirs, who is absent, as represented in . . . petition presented to that effect.

"Louis Morin and Henry Octave Deronce, free men of color, . . . apraised [sic] the property . . . [a summary follows; individual valuations are not copied]:

[Farm tools, carts, and supplies]
[4 beds, other household and kitchen furnishings]
" 1 gig & harness
  1 clock
  24 Bales cotton

Slaves

Robbin, negro* man 42
Henry Whitehead, d° 23
Mark   d°   26
Allick   d°   25
Henry   d°   25
Harry   d°   15
Betsy   negress 40
Jenny   d°   30
Ellen   d°   30 and her three children
    Raphaël, nine
    Jim, four
    Marguerite, one
Celesie   negress 20

Lands

Plantation on which the deceased resided, in Parish of Natchitoches, containing five arpents, front[ing] on left bank of Red River, bounded above by Jean François Hertzog and below by Florentine Conant and Jerome Sarpy.

22 Bales Cotton in New Orleans

Papers

Bank notes
Note of Louis Balthazard
Note of Louis Monet paid to Mr Roubieu
Receipt of Jacques Porter
Note of Antoine Aubuchon
Nérès Pierre Metoyer, account

[Total] $14,150.77"

". . . /signed/ Marie X Delpiche her mark — Marie Louise Coton-Maïs X her mark — Désirée Coton-Maïs X her mark — Arsène Coton-Maïs X her mark — Marie Suzette Coton-Maïs X her mark — Charles Coton-Maïs X his mark; Louis Monete X his mark — Louis Mulon X his mark, all declaring they know not how to write — Antoinette Coton May — L^s Balthazar — François Metoyer fils — Henry Hertzog attorney — C. N. Rocques — appraisers: Louis Morin — H^y O^ve Deronce — witnesses: E. Dupré — F. B. Sherburne — C. E. Greneaux, parish judge. . . . "

STEP 4: CREATE FINAL ABSTRACT

Antoine Coton-Maïs, f.m.c., Inventory and Appraisement
Natchitoches Parish, La., Successions, 14:41–43
Drawn 17 February 1840; filed [no date given]

In presence of legal heirs and HENRY HERTZOG, attorney for one absent heir, the property of COTON-MAÏS, free man of color, was inventoried and appraised by LOUIS MORIN and HENRY OCTAVE DERONCE, also free men of color. *Personal property [summarized here]:* farm tools, carts, and supplies; 4 beds and other household and kitchen furnishings (including a clock); 1 gig and harness—also 20 bales of cotton on the premises and 22 bales [*at market*] in New Orleans. *Slaves:* ROBBIN (male), 42; HENRY WHITEHEAD, 23; MARK, 26; ALLICK, 25; HENRY, 25; HARRY, 15; BETSY, 40; JENNY, 30; ELLEN, 30 (with her three children: RAPHAËL, 9; JIM, 4; MARGUERITE, 1); and CELESIE, 20—all called "negroes" except for Ellen's children, race unstated. *Land:* plantation on which deceased resided in Natchitoches Parish, containing 5 arpents fronting on left bank of Red River, bounded above by JEAN FRANÇOIS HERTZOG and below by FLORENTINE CONANT and JEROME SARPY. *Papers:* bank notes; notes and accounts on LOUIS BALTHAZARD, LOUIS MONET ("paid to MR. ROUBIEU"), JACQUES PORTER, ANTOINE AUBUCHON, and NÉRÈS PIERRE METOYER. *Total value:* $14,150.77.

Signed by mark: MARIE LOUISE COTON-MAÏS, DÉSIRÉE COTON-MAÏS, ARSÈNE COTON-MAÏS, MARIE SUZETTE COTON-MAÏS, CHARLES COTON-MAÏS, LOUIS MONETE, LOUIS MULON. By signature: ANTOINETTE COTON MAY; L^s BALTHAZAR; FRANÇOIS METOYER[,] "the son"; HENRY HERTZOG, attorney for absent heir; C. N. ROCQUES. Also by signature: appraisers LOUIS MORIN, H^y O^ve DERONCE; witnesses E. DUPRÉ, F. B. SHERBURNE; and parish judge C. E. GRENEAUX.

Bill of sale

English common law makes a distinction between a bill of sale and a deed. The former is traditionally used for personal property, the latter for realty. Genealogists frequently encounter bills of sale for such items as ships, slaves, and vehicles—even "improvements" on land the grantor did not actually own. Of all records that may be found in a deed book, a bill of sale can be the simplest to transcribe and abstract.

STEP 1: TRANSCRIBE

Howel to Bradshaw, Bill of Sale
Jefferson County, Tennessee
Deed Book H:60–61
Drawn 10 April 1806; registered 5 August 1806

[*Marginal notation*]

All types of legal records require us to carefully and knowledgeably analyze the language, lest important information be missed.

TRANSCRIPTS

AND ABSTRACTS

Genealogists frequently encounter bills of sale for such items as ships, slaves, and vehicles—even "improvements" on land the grantor did not actually own.

"Paul Howel to }   B of sale
Jnº Bradshaw   }   for his possession of land &c in Jefferson County
Registered August 5ᵗʰ 1806

[Body of document]
"KNOW all men by these presents that I Paul Howel of the State of Tennessee and County of Jefferson hath bargained and sold, and by these presents doth bargain and sell unto John Bradshaw of the said state and County his heirs and assigns forever My Improvement and claim of land, and my house where I now live, and all my premises adjacent thereto: for and in consideration of the sum of Twenty Dollars to me in hand paid by sᵈ John Bradshaw the receipt whereof I do hereby acknowledge; and I the said Paul Howel against myself my heirs &C to him the said John Bradshaw his heirs &C shall and will warrant and forever Defend. As witness my hand and seal this 10ᵗʰ day of April 1806

test   Paul + Howel
Joseph Coppock   mark

State of Tennessee}
Jefferson County } July Sessions 1806
Then was the within Bill of sale duly proven in Court & recorded. Let it be registered.
                              Test   Jhamilton clk
                                          By D. Barton DC [Deputy Clerk]"

STEP 2: REMOVE THE EXCESS

Howel to Bradshaw, Bill of Sale
Jefferson County, Tennessee
Deed Book H:60–61
Drawn 10 April 1806; registered 5 August 1806

[Marginal notation:]
"Paul Howel to }   B of sale
Jnº Bradshaw   }   for his possession of land &c in Jefferson County"
Registered August 5ᵗʰ 1806

[Body of document:]
"KNOW all men by these presents that I Paul Howel of the State of Tennessee and County of Jefferson hath bargained and sold, and by these presents doth bargain and sell unto John Bradshaw of the said state and County his heirs and assigns forever My Improvement and claim of land, and my house where I now live, and all my premises adjacent thereto: for and in consideration of the sum of Twenty Dollars to me in hand paid by sᵈ John Bradshaw the receipt whereof I do hereby acknowledge; and I the said Paul Howel against myself my heirs &C to him the said John Bradshaw his heirs &C shall and will warrant and forever Defend. As witness my hand and seal this 10ᵗʰ day of April 1806

test   Paul + Howel
Joseph Coppock   mark

State of Tennessee }
Jefferson County   } July Sessions 1806
Then was the within Bill of sale duly proven in Court & recorded. Let it be registered
                              Test   Jhamilton clk
                                          By D. Barton DC

STEP 3: REVIEW WHAT REMAINS

Howel to Bradshaw, Bill of Sale
Jefferson County, Tennessee
Deed Book H:60–61
Drawn 10 April 1806; registered 5 August 1806

". . . Paul Howel of . . . Tennessee and County of Jefferson . . . sell . . . to John Bradshaw
of . . . said state and County . . . My Improvement and claim of land, and my house where
I now live, and all my premises adjacent thereto . . . for Twenty Dollars . . . 10 . . . April
1806

test   ^{his}
                                        Paul + Howel
Joseph Coppock   ^{mark}

State of Tennessee   }
Jefferson County   } July Sessions 1806
. . . Bill of sale . . . proven in Court & recorded. . . . "

STEP 4: CREATE FINAL ABSTRACT

The bill of sale can now be reduced to just six lines, as the text is smoothed out for a
concise, readable abstract that still uses abbreviations judiciously.

Howel to Bradshaw, Bill of Sale
Jefferson Co., Tenn.; Deed Book H:60–61
Drawn 10 Apr. 1806; registered 5 Aug. 1806

PAUL HOWEL to JOHN BRADSHAW, both of Jefferson Co. Sale by HOWEL for $20, of "My
Improvement and claim of land, and my house where I now live." * [Signed] Paul Howel, +
"his mark." Witness: JOSEPH COPPOCK. Proved and recorded: July Sessions, 1806.

Deed (warranty)

Deeds tend to have more boilerplate than other records. The usual result is an abstract that is briefer than a will or inventory but more complex than a simple bill of
sale. All types of deeds require us to carefully and *knowledgeably* analyze the legal
language, lest important information be missed. Their boilerplate shows considerable
variety, and the distinctions between certain phrases that are used (or not used) can
have implications for resolving genealogical problems. The land-records chapters of
The Researcher's Guide to American Genealogy provide an excellent foundation in the
significance of deed terminology.[8] Case studies in major genealogical journals illustrate
the problem-solving potential of skillfully preserving boilerplate we find in deeds.[9]
Figure 17 summarizes the essentials for abstracting all types of land records, while
figure 18 itemizes the major types of deeds.

TIP

Quality abstracts try to
follow the same rules of
grammar and syntax that
apply to all other types of
writing.

---

* Quotation marks are added here to the phrase "My Improvement . . . where I now live" because
Howel wrote in the first person, beginning with "I, Paul Howel. . . ." If we eliminate the opening
"I," we change the voice of the passage to third person, which violates syntax when coupled with
"*my* improvement." Yet when grantors and testators refer to "*my* property where *I* now live," "*my*
children," etc., if we change the pronoun to "he" or "his" to avoid a voice shift (as rules of good
grammar admonish us to do in narrative writing), we may create ambiguity in the identity of the
referenced person. If we retained the "I " so that "my improvement" maintains syntax, a problem
would still arise when the pronoun later shifts to "*his* mark." As a less-than-perfect compromise in
abstracts, we should at least use quotation marks around the phrase that creates this shift in voice.

TRANSCRIPTS
AND ABSTRACTS

The following deed is the most common type—one usually called a *warranty deed* (although that term did not prevail in this time and place), meaning that the sellers held and granted a full and unconditional title to the property.

STEP 1: TRANSCRIBE

Mayo to Brookes, Warranty Deed
Middlesex County, Virginia
Deed Book 3, part 2:251–52
Drawn 4 June 1711; proved 5 June 1711

"TO ALL CHRISTIAN people to whom__ [?] these presents shall Come we Vallentine Mayo and Anne my Wife of the County of Middlesex send greeting in our Lord God everlasting KNOW YEE that wee Vallentine Mayo and Anne my Wife as well for and in Consideration of the naturall affections which wee have and bare unto our well beloved Cuzen Jonathan Brooks of the aforesade County as also for divers other good Causes and Considerations at this present Espetially moveing have given and granted and by these presents do give and grant and Confirm unto the sade Jonathan Brookes and his heires thirty nine Acres of Land Situate Lying & being in the County of Middlesex and bounded as followeth Viz—beginning at a Red oack Corner Tree of the Land of Thomas Obrissel deced and running West one hundred & Sixty Seven Poles along an old Line of the Land of John Stamper deced to a Corner white oack of the said Stampers and Henry Tugwell thence north six Poles to an ash and beach by the Run of a Swamp Called—Micklebourroughs Swamp Jast above the horse Bridg thence down and along the sade swamp run one hundred and Eightey Poles to the Land granted by Pattent to John Bourk deced to a white Oack thence along the said Land granted by Patent to the sade John Bourk its several Courses to the Land of the sade Thomas Obrissle deced and lastly West along the sade obrissles Land to the Place it begun att the s^d Land being granted by Patent to the sade Vallentine Mayo in the year 1702—TO HAVE AND TO HOLD the sade Land and Premises with all and Singular its Rights Members and appurtenances thereunto belonging or in any wise appertaining together with all houses orchards Swamps and Marshes woods underwoods ways Meadows & <u>seed</u>ings [?] whatsoever to the sade hereby granted sd Land and other the premises belong or in any wise appertaining to the sade Jonathan Brooks and his heirs or Assigns forever freely and quiately without any matter of Challenge Claim or Demand of us the sade Vallentine Mayo & Anne my Wife or our heirs Exec^rs administrators or assignes or any other person or persons whatsoever for our use in our name or by our Cause means or procurement or without any Money or other thing therefore to us yealeded payd or done to us the sade Vallintine Mayo and Anne my Wife our heires Exec^rs or administrators but shall and will Warrant and forever defend by these presents the

FIG. 17
LAND RECORDS:
SPECIAL GUIDELINES
FOR ABSTRACTING

Essential items: land-record abstracts

- Identification of the record (e.g., John Smith–James Brown Deed of Trust).
- Source citation (volume/liber and page/folio number; or collection name and file or number).
- Location (name and place of agency, office, or repository).
- Dates the document was written, proved, filed, and recorded.
- Grantor (seller) and grantee (buyer).
- Other named individuals and their signatures, with stated roles and relationships.
- Place(s) of residence for all parties to instrument, when given.
- Consideration (the amount and terms of payment)
- Land description—physical (waterways, etc.) and legal; adjacent landowners, if named.
- Miscellaneous information—chains of title, information on witnesses, dower release, etc.

sade Jonathan Brooks and his heires executors administrators and assignes forever against us the sade Vallintine Mayo & Anne my Wife or any other person or persons whatsoever laying any Claime to the sade Land or anything belonging thereto and lastly that the Sade Vallintine Mayo and Anne his wife at the time of the ensealing & delivery of these presents hath good Right full power and Lawfully authority to give grant and Confirm the sade Land and premises to the s^d Jonathan Brooks and his heires or assignes forever EN WITNESS whereof the sade Vallintine Mayo and Anne his wife hath hereunto Set their hands and fixed their Seals this 4 day of June 1711

Signed Sealed & delivered in th^e presents of us—

John Lewis
Henry (H) Ball his mark
Jno (X) Bone, his mark

Vallentine Mayo {seal}
Anne (A) Mayo her mark {seal}

At a Court held for Middlesex County the 5th day of June 1711 Valentine Mayo Came this day into Court presents & acknowledged the within deed to Jonathan Brooks & which at the said Brookes Motion is admitted to record.

Test Wil Stanard Cl Cur [*Clericus Curia—i.e., Clerk of Court*]
Record^r Test Wil Stanard Cl Cur

Anne Mayo also the wife of the said Vallentine this day appeared in Court and being first examined freely and Voluntarily relinquished her Right of Dower in th^e Land Conveyed by this Deed to the said Brooks which is hereby Certyfied—

Test Wil Stanard Cl Cur
Record. p^r Wil Stanard Cl Cur

That livery and seizin of the within premises was mayde by the within menchened Valantine Mayo and Anne his Wife to Jonathan Brooks this 4 Day of June 1711 in the presents of us

John Lewis
Henry (H) Ball his mark
Jno (X) Bone, his mark

Vallantin Mayo
Anne (A) Mayo

At a Court held for Midd_x County th^e fifth day of June 1711 The above written was acknowledged in Court by Vallentine Mayo and Anne his Wife and admitted to Record

Test Wil Stanard Cl Cur
Record^r Test Wil Stanard Cl Cur"

STEP 2: REMOVE THE EXCESS

Mayo to Brookes, Warranty Deed
Middlesex County, Virginia
Deed Book 3, part 2:251–52
Drawn 4 June 1711; proved 5 June 1711

"TO ALL CHRISTIAN people to whom ___ [?] these presents shall Come wee Vallentine Mayo and Anne my Wife of the County of Middlesex send greeting in our Lord God everlasting KNOW YEE that wee Vallentine Mayo and Anne my Wife as well for and in Consideration of the naturall affections which wee have and bare unto our well beloved Cuzen Jonathan Brooks of the aforesade County as also for divers other good Causes and Considerations at this present Espetially moveing have given and granted and by these presents do give and grant and Confirm unto the sade Jonathan Brookes

FIG. 18
COMMON TYPES OF DEEDS

(Each of which has its own genealogical significance)

- Deed of division
- Deed of gift
- Deed of partition
- Deed of release
- Deed of trust
- Quitclaim deed
- Warranty deed

TRANSCRIPTS
AND ABSTRACTS

Never omit the metes and
bounds of a legal land description. We use these to

- plat land so adjacent
  tracts can be properly
  identified and fitted
  together;
- prove whether any
  piece of land is the
  same as another of
  similar acreage and
  landmarks;
- prove the subdivision
  of larger tracts;
- prove identity of own-
  ers and relationships
  between consecutive
  owners;
- and much more!

and his heires thirty nine Acres of Land Situate Lying & being in the County of Middlesex and bounded as followeth Viz—beginning at a Red oack Corner Tree of the Land of Thomas Obrissel deced and running West one hundred & Sixty Seven Poles along an old Line of the Land of John Stamper deced to a Corner white oack of the said Stampers and Henry Tugwell thence north six Poles to an ash and beach by the Run of a Swamp Called—Micklebourroughs Swamp Jast above the horse Bridg thence down and along the sade swamp run one hundred and Eightey Poles to the Land granted by Pattent to John Bourk deced to a white Oack thence along the said Land granted by Patent to the sade John Bourk its several Courses to the Land of the sade Thomas Obrissle deced and lastly West along the sade obrissles Land to the Place it begun att the s^d Land being granted by Patent to the sade Vallentine Mayo in the year 1702—TO HAVE AND TO HOLD the sade Land and Premises with all and Singular its Rights Members and appurtenances thereunto belonging or in any wise appertaining together with all houses orchards Swamps and Marshes woods underwoods ways Meadows & seedings [?] whatsoever to the sade hereby granted sd Land and other the premises belong or in any wise appertaining to the sade Jonathan Brooks and his heirs or Assigns forever freely and quiately without any matter of Challenge Claim or Demand of us the sade Vallentine Mayo & Anne my Wife or our heirs Exec^rs administrators or assignes or any other person or persons whatsoever for our use in our name or by our Cause means or procurement or without any Money or other thing therefore to us yealeded payd or done to us the sade Vallintine Mayo and Anne my Wife our heires Exec^rs or administrators but shall and will Warrant and forever defend by these presents the sade Jonathan Brooks and his heires executors administrators and assignes forever against us the sade Vallintine Mayo & Anne my Wife or any other person or persons whatsoever laying any Claime to the sade Land or anything belonging thereto and lastly that the Sade Vallintine Mayo and Anne his wife at the time of the ensealing & delivery of these presents hath good Right full power and Lawfully authority to give grant and Confirm the sade Land and premises to the s^d Jonathan Brooks and his heires or assignes forever EN WITNESS whereof the sade Vallintine Mayo and Anne his wife hath hereunto Set their hands and fixed their Seals this 4 day of June 1711
Signed Sealed & delivered in th^e presents of us—

John Lewis   Vallentine Mayo {seal}
Henry (H) Ball his mark   Anne (A) Mayo her mark {seal}
Jno (X) Bone

At a Court held for Middlesex County the 5th day of June 1711 Valentine Mayo Came this day into Court presents & acknowledged the within deed to Jonathan Brooks & which at the said Brookes Motion is admitted to record.
        Test Wil Stanard Cl Cur
     Record^r Test Wil Stanard Cl Cur

Anne Mayo also the wife of the said Vallentine this day appeared in Court and being first examined freely and Voluntarily relinquished her Right of Dower in th^e Land Conveyed by this Deed to the said Brooks which is hereby Certyfied—
        Test Wil Stanard Cl Cur
     Record^r & Wil Stanard Cl Cur

That livery and seizin of the within premises was mayde by the within menchened Valantine Mayo and Anne his Wife to Jonathan Brooks this 4 Day of June 1711 in the presents of us
John Lewis   Vallantin Mayo
Henry (H) Ball his mark   Anne (A) Mayo
Jno (X) Bone, his mark

At a Court held for Midd$_x$ County th^e fifth day of June 1711 The above written was acknowledged in Court by Vallentine Mayo and Anne his Wife and admitted to Record
Test Wil Stanard Cl Cur
Recordr Test Wil Stanard Cl Cur"

STEP 3: REVIEW WHAT REMAINS

Mayo to Brookes, Warranty Deed
Middlesex County, Virginia
Deed Book 3, part 2:251–52
Drawn 4 June 1711; proved 5 June 1711

". . . wee Vallentine Mayo and Anne my Wife of the County of Middlesex . . . for . . . naturall affections which wee . . . bare unto our well beloved Cuzen Jonathan Brooks of the aforesade County . . . give . . . to the sade Jonathan Brookes and his heires thirty nine Acres of Land . . . in the County of Middlesex . . . Viz—"beginning at a Red oack Corner Tree of the Land of Thomas Obrissel deced and running West one hundred & Sixty Seven Poles along an old Line of the Land of John Stamper deced to a Corner white oack of the said Stampers and Henry Tugwell thence north six Poles to an ash and beach by the Run of a Swamp Called—Micklebourroughs Swamp Jest above the horse Bridg thence down and along the said swamp run one hundred and Eightey Poles to the Land granted by Pattent to John Bourk deced to a white Oack thence along the said Land granted by Patent to the sade John Bourk its several Courses to the Land of the sade Thomas Obrissle deced and lastly West along the sade obrissles Land to the Place it begun . . . the s^d Land being granted by Patent to . . . Mayo in the year 1702$_{[.]}$." . . . Mayo and Anne . . . will Warrant and forever defend . . . against . . . any . . . persons whatsoever laying any Claime to the sade Land or anything belonging thereto$_{[.]}$ . . . 4 . . . June 1711 in . . . presents [presence] of . . .

John Lewis	Vallentine Mayo (seal)
Henry (H) Ball his mark	Anne (A) Mayo her mark (seal)
Jno (X) Bone, his mark	

. . . 5 . . . June 1711 Valentine Mayo Came . . . into Court . . . & acknowledged the within deed to Jonathan Brooks. . . .

Anne Mayo . . . wife of . . . Vallentine this day appeared . . . and Voluntarily relinquished her Right of Dower in th^e Land. . . . livery and seizin of . . . premises mayde by . . . Mayo and Anne . . . to Jonathan Brooks . . . 4 . . . June 1711 in presents of . . .

John Lewis	Vallantin Mayo
Henry (H) Ball his mark	Anne (A) Mayo
Jno (X) Bone	

. . . fifth June 1711 The above written was acknowledged in Court by Vallentine Mayo and Anne his Wife. . . . "

STEP 4: CREATE FINAL ABSTRACT

Even with excess verbiage removed, the remaining detail is lengthy and intimidating to many family researchers. It is tempting to reduce the abstract further by eliminating the surveying "rigmarole" that describes the land. Let's squelch that impulse! In many genealogical ways, this land detail is needed. Therefore, the final abstract created from this warranty deed illustrates the inclusion of an *extract* (being the long and precisely quoted land description) within an *abstract*.

TIPS

If we omit words from a passage enclosed by quotation marks, we show the omission via ellipses.

When we quote several paragraphs from a document, we should put quotation marks at *(a)* start of document, *(b)* start of each new paragraph, and *(c)* end of document.

**TRANSCRIPTS
AND ABSTRACTS**

When we add punctuation
to anything within quotes,
we should enclose those
added marks in square
brackets.

Mayo to Brookes, Warranty Deed
Middlesex Co., Va.; Deed Book 3, pt. 2:251–52
Drawn 4 June 1711; proved 5 June 1711

VALLENTINE MAYO and wife ANNE of Middlesex Co., for natural affection give to "our well beloved Cuzen [cousin] JONATHAN BROOKS," of same place, thirty nine Acres of Land in Middlesex, described as

> "beginning at a Red oack Corner Tree of the Land of THOMAS OBRISSEL decd and running West one hundred & Sixty Seven Poles along an old Line of the Land of JOHN STAMPER decd[.,] to a Corner white oack of the said STAMPERs and HENRY TUGWELL[;] thence north six [?] Poles to an ash and beach by the Run of a Swamp Called—MICKLEBOURROUGHs Swamp Jast above the horse Bridg[;] thence down and along the said swamp run one hundred and Eightey poles to the Land granted by Pattent to JOHN BOURK deced[.,] to a white Oack[;] thence along the said Land granted by Patent to the sade JOHN BOURK [for] its several Courses[,] to the Land of the sade THOMAS O⁽ⁱⁱ⁾BRISSLE decd[.;] and lastly West along the sade OBRISSLES Land to the Place it begun[.]"

MAYO was granted the land by patent in 1702. MAYO & ANNE warrant title against "any . . . persons whatsoever laying any Claime to the sade Land or anything belonging thereto."[Signed] VALLENTINE MAYO; ANNE MAYO (A) "her mark." Witnesses: JOHN LEWIS; HENRY BALL (H) "his mark"; JNO BONE (X) "his mark."

4 June 1711, property delivered by MAYO and ANNE to BROOKS, in presence of LEWIS, BALL, and BONE.

5 June 1711, acknowledgment by MAYO and dower release by ANNE.

Deed (quitclaim)

In the preceding example, the Mayos conveyed land under an unconditional deed—meaning that they had full title and could warrant (or guarantee) it unconditionally. A quitclaim deed has a core of boilerplate different from that of the warranty deed, because the quitclaimer's title is incomplete or potentially cloudy. The research implications inherent in this distinction should be self-evident; genealogical implications may exist as well—as when the grantor quits (or gives up) his claim to property that he and several other heirs had jointly inherited. The following example also illustrates a case in which the document is an original in private hands.

STEP 1: TRANSCRIBE

Bennett to Bennett, Quitclaim
Lauderdale County, Mississippi
Drawn 29 July 1872; recorded [no data shown]
Photocopy of document sent by [client's name]
  to Mary McCampbell Bell; Arlington, Virginia
Location of original unknown

"State of Mississippi   }   July 29ᵗʰ 1872
Lauderdale County   }

"Know all men by these presents that we W. H. Bennett and wife Elisabeth Bennett of said county & State in consideration of the sum of Three Hundred Dollars to us paid by O. P. Bennett of Thomas County Georgia the receipt where of is hereby acknowledged do by these presents grant, remise, release, and forever quit-claim unto the said O. P. Bennett his heirs and assigns all our right title, interest, and estate in and to the following tract or parcell of land situate in the County of Anson & State of North Carolina and lying on the waters of Jones Creek and described in the Division of the Estate of J. C. Bennett Decd Lot No 5 and bounded as follows to wit

"Beginning at a pile of rocks in the edge of the Wadesboro Road 2nd corner of Lot No 4 and runs up said road 20 chs & 50 links to a large Post oak, Lucas's corner, then No 32 W with said road 10 chs & 70 links to a stake near a large Post oak, Leaks corner in the edge of sd road, then So 55 West 18 chs to a Red oak stump, Hinsons corner then So 57 West 31 chs & 50 links to Jones Creek, then down the various courses of sd creek to a Black Gum on the bank 3 corner of Lot No 4 Sweet Gum pointers, then with said line No 56 E 55 chs to the beginning containing one Hundred & fifty four acres more or less. To have and to hold the above released premises to him the said O. P. Bennett his heirs and assigns and to his and their use and behoof forever, so that neither we the said W. H. Bennett and wife Elisabeth Bennett nor our heirs nor any other person or persons in the name right or stead of us or them shall, or will by any way or means have claim or demand any right or title to the above release premises or to any part or parcel thereof forever, In witness whereof we the said W. H. Bennett and wife Elisabeth Bennett have hereunto set our hands and seals this 29th day of July A. D. 1872

W. H. Bennett   (seal)   E. Bennett   (seal)"

STEP 2: REMOVE THE EXCESS

Bennett to Bennett, Quitclaim
Lauderdale County, Mississippi
Drawn 29 July 1872; recorded [no data shown]
Photocopy of document sent by [client's name]
*   to Mary McCampbell Bell; Arlington, Virginia*
Location of original unknown

"State of Mississippi }   July 29th 1872
Lauderdale County   }

"Know all men by these presents that we W. H. Bennett and wife Elisabeth Bennett of said county & State in consideration of the sum of Three Hundred Dollars to us paid by O. P. Bennett of Thomas County Georgia the receipt where of is hereby acknowledged do by these presents grant, remise, release, and forever quit-claim unto the said O. P. Bennett his heirs and assigns all our right title, interest, and estate in and to the following tract or parcell of land situate in the County of Anson & State of North Carolina and lying on the waters of Jones Creek and described in the Division of the Estate of J. C. Bennett Decd Lot No 5 and bounded as follows to wit

"Beginning at a pile of rocks in the edge of the Wadesboro Road 2nd corner of Lot No 4 and runs up said road 20 chs & 50 links to a large Post oak, Lucas's corner, then No 32 W with said road 10 chs & 70 links to a stake near a large Post oak, Leaks corner in the edge of sd road, then So 55 West 18 chs to a Red oak stump, Hinsons corner then So 57 West 31 chs & 50 links to Jones Creek, then down the various courses of sd creek to a Black Gum on the bank 3 corner of Lot No 4 Sweet Gum pointers, then with said line No 56 E 55 chs to the beginning containing one Hundred & fifty four acres more or less. To have and to hold the above released premises to him the said O. P. Bennett his heirs and assigns and to his and their use and behoof forever, so that neither we the said W. H. Bennett and wife Elisabeth Bennett nor our heirs nor any other person or persons in the name right or stead of us or them shall or will by any way or means

TIP

When land descriptions say "on waters of…creek" rather than simply "on… creek," we need to preserve that distinction. The first means the land lies within the *watershed* of the creek; the latter means the land is actually bounded by the creek itself.

TRANSCRIPTS

AND ABSTRACTS

have claim or demand any right or title to the above release premises or to any part or parcel thereof forever. In witness whereof we the said W. H. Bennett and wife Elisabeth Bennett have hereunto set our hands and seals this 29ᵗʰ day of July A. D. 1872

W. H. Bennett   (seal)   E. Bennett   (seal)"

STEP 3: REVIEW WHAT REMAINS

Bennett to Bennett, Quitclaim
Lauderdale County, Mississippi
Drawn 29 July 1872; recorded [no data shown]
Photocopy of document sent by [client's name]
    to Mary McCampbell Bell; Arlington, Virginia
Location of original unknown

"State of Mississippi }   July 29ᵗʰ 1872
Lauderdale County   }

". . . W. H. Bennett and wife Elisabeth Bennett of said county & State in consideration . . . of Three Hundred Dollars . . . paid by O. P. Bennett of Thomas County Georgia . . . forever quit-claim unto the said O. P. . . . all our right title, interest, and estate in . . . land situate in the County of Anson & State of North Carolina . . . lying on the waters of Jones Creek and described in the Division of the Estate of J. C. Bennett Decd Lot No 5[:]

"Beginning at a pile of rocks in the edge of the Wadesboro Road 2ⁿᵈ corner of Lot No 4 and runs up said road 20 chs & 50 links to a large Post oak, Lucas's corner, then No 32 W with said road 10 chs & 70 links to a stake near a large Post oak, Leaks corner in the edge of sd road, then So 55 West 18 chs to a Red oak stump, Hinsons corner then So 57 West 31 chs & 50 links to Jones Creek, then down the various courses of sd creek to a Black Gum on the bank 3 corner of Lot No 4 Sweet Gum pointers, then with said line No 56 E 55 chs to the beginning containing one Hundred & fifty four acres. . . . 29 July 1872

W. H. Bennett (seal)   E. Bennett (seal)"

STEP 4: CREATE FINAL ABSTRACT

Bennett to Bennett, Quitclaim
Lauderdale Co., Miss.
Drawn 29 July 1872; recorded [no data shown]
Photocopy of document sent by [client's name]
    to Mary McCampbell Bell; Arlington, Virginia
Location of original unknown.

W. H. BENNETT and wife ELISABETH BENNETT of said county, for three hundred dollars paid by O. P. BENNETT of Thomas County, Georgia, quitclaim to O.P. "all our right title, interest, and estate" in Lot No. 5 of J. C. BENNETT Estate division in Anson County, North Carolina. The lot, lying on the waters of Jones Creek, is described as:

"Beginning at a pile of rocks in the edge of the Wadesboro Road 2ⁿᵈ corner of Lot No 4 and runs up said road 20 chs & 50 links to a large Post oak, LUCAS'S corner[;] then No 32 W with said road 10 chs & 70 links to a stake near a large Post oak, Leaks corner in the edge of sd road[;] then So 55 West 18 chs to a Red oak stump, HINSONS corner[;] then So 57 West 31 chs & 50 links to Jones Creek, then down the various courses of sd creek to a Black Gum on the bank 3 corner of Lot No 4 [at] Sweet Gum pointers[;] then with said line No 56 E 55 chs to the beginning." 154 acres.

29 July A. D. 1872. [signed] W. H. BENNETT; E. BENNETT.

TIP

Deeds that specify *first party, second party,* and *third party,* are often conditional deeds that deserve special attention.

Deed (trust)

Both of the foregoing deeds have *two* principal parties—grantor (a married couple in each case) and grantee (each an individual). Other deeds and indentures have *three* parties—grantor, grantee, and a trustee who holds the deed pending certain action. Trust documents were drawn for various reasons—commonly to provide security for debt or to set aside property for a married daughter in a manner that would legally separate it from that of her husband. The latter situation prompted the document below, which is actually a memorial (recitation) of terms from an original agreement.

STEP 1: TRANSCRIBE

Lyster to Palmer, Trust Document
Registry of Deeds, Dublin
Book 130:128–29, no. 88250
Drawn 7 October 1746; filed 30 April 1748

[*Heading*]
"To the Register appointed for registering Deeds Conveyances and Wills

[*Marginal notation*]
Lyster & ano[r] to Palmer & ano[r]
Reg[d] the 30th of April 1748 at 12 o'Clock at Noon

[*Body of document*]
A Memorial of Indented Articles dated the Twenty Seventh day of Oct[r] one thous[d] Seven Hun[d] and forty six made or ment[d] to be made by & between Thom[s] Lyster of Grange in th[e] County of Roscomon Esq[r] of the first part, Remy Carroll of Ardagh in the C[o] of Gallway Esq[r] and Marg[t] Carroll his Eldest Dau̅r of the Second part & Roger Palmer of Palmerstown in the C[o] of Mayo & James Carroll of Killway [?] in the Co. of Galway Esq[rs] of the third part for & concerning a Marriage agreed to be had between the s[d] Thomas Lyster & th[e] s[d] Margarett Carroll whereby the said Remy Carroll did Cov[t] and agree with the s[d] Thomas Lyster to Assign & make over to th[e] said Roger Palmer & James Carroll the securitys in S[d] articles ment[d] for the sum of one Thousand five Hundred pounds as a Marriage portion with the said Marg[t], as Trustees to th[e] uses therein ment[d] and the said Tho[s] Lyster did thereby Cov[t] and agree that he would in consid[n] of the S[d] Marriage & Marriage portion & in order to make a Suitable provision for the S[d] Margaret in case She should Survive the Said Tho[s][, and] for th[e] Issue of th[e] S[d] Marriage[,] Execute two bonds to the said Roger Palmer & James Carroll for the purposes therein ment[d] of the principal Sum of two Thousand pounds each with warr[t] of Atty [?] to Confess Judgem[t] thereon for the purposes therein ment[d] and it is by Said Articles recited that th[e] s[d] Thomas Lyster had a Demand of one thousand pounds principall money due on th[e] Estate of Howard Egan Esq[r] dec̅ed & of a Considerable Arrear of Interest due thereon & had a Suite then depending for the Same[,] it was thereby concluded & agreed upon by all the parties to th[e] S[d] articles that in Order to make a provision for th[e] s[d] Margarett in case she Survived the S[d] Thomas & for th[e] issue of S[d] Marriage the S[d] one Thousand five Hundred pounds portion agreed to be paid by th[e] Said Remy with the Said Marg[t] or the Securitys for the Same & also the two Bonds for the principall Sums of Two thousand pounds each agreed to be Executed by th[e] S[d] Thomas Lyster as afores[d] & also th[e] s[d] one thousand pounds with all th[e] Interest then or thereafter to become due thereon shou'd when recovered be Lodged in the hands of the S[d] Trustees for th[e] purposes therein ment[d] & for no other use or

TIP

Trust deeds are not always labeled as such—either in the index or the margin of the record. Usually, they are identifiable by the presence of someone called "party of the third part" or "trustee," as seen in this document.

purpose wᵗsoever & it was thereby further agreed that if the Sᵈ Thomas Lyster shou'd dye & thᵉ Sᵈ Margarette Survive him that She Should yearly receive during her Life one hundred & fifty pounds for her Support & Maintenance in full Lieu Satisfaction & Barr of all dower & thirds which she might be intitled to out of the real or personal Estate of the Said Thoˢ which he then was or should be thereafter Seized or possessed of & that Said one Hundred & fifty pounds Should be paid her yearly out of the Said Sevˡˡ Sums or Securitys Lodged with the Sᵈ Trusttees as aforsᵈ and it was thereby further agreed that if the said Lyster Should dye Leaving Issue by the Said Margᵗ a Son & one or more Daũrs that then the Sᵈ two Sevˡˡ Sums of two thousand pounds Should be for the benefitt of Such issue paying thereout to the said Margᵗ if she should Survive thᵉ Sᵈ Thomas Seventy five pounds a year during her Life out of the Intˢᵗ arising on Sᵈ bonds as aforesᵈ & one Thousand pounds₍,₎ part of Sᵈ Fifteen Hundred pounds part₍,₎ and thᵉ Sᵈ Sum due on Egans Estate & agreed to be Lodged with Sᵈ Trustees as aforesᵈ Shall be for the uses in Sᵈ Articles mentᵈ with Sevˡ other Clauses and Covᵗˢ in the Sᵈ Articles mentᵈ which Said Articles are witnessed by Mathew Lyster of the City of Dublin Esqʳ Christʳ Fallon of Ballandeeccy [?] in the Cᵒ of Roscomon Gent. and Wᵐ Ousley of the Sᵈ City Gent and this Meml is also witn'd by Henry Garvey of Woodfield in the Cᵒ of Mayo Gent and by the said Wᵐ Ousley Gent—Remy Carroll (Seal) — Signed & Sealed in presence of us, Hen: Garvey—Will Ousley. The above named Wᵐ Ousley came this day before me & made oath that he Saw the above named Thoˢ Lyster Remy Caroll Margarett Carroll [*her name is interlined*] & James Carroll duly Seal & Execute the above mentᵈ Articles [*interlined word illegible*] of wᶜʰ the above writing is a Memˡ & also Saw thᵉ sᵈ Remy Carroll Sign & Seal thᵉ Sᵈ Memorial [*a whole interlined line is illegible*] & that he delivᵈ the Same to Me, James Saunders Dep Regʳ on the 30th day of April 1748 at or near Twelve o'Clock at Noon—Will: Ousley — Sworn the 30th of April 1748 before

James Saunders Dep Regʳ."[10]

STEP 2: REMOVE THE EXCESS

Lyster to Palmer, Trust Document
Registry of Deeds, Dublin
Book 130:128–29, no. 88250
Drawn 7 October 1746; filed 30 April 1748

[Heading]
"To the Register appointed for registering Deeds Conveyances and Wills

[Marginal notation]
Lyster & anoʳ to Palmer & anoʳ
Regᵈ the 30th of April 1748 at 12 o'Clock at Noon

[Body of document]
A Memorial of Indented Articles dated the Twenty Seventh day of Octʳ one thousᵈ Seven Hunᵈ and forty six made or mentᵈ to be made by & between Thomˢ Lyster of Grange in thᵉ County of Roscomon Esqʳ of the first part, Remy Carroll of Ardagh in the Cᵒ of Gallway Esqʳ and Margᵗ Carroll his Eldest Daũr of the Second part & Roger Palmer of Palmerstown in the Cᵒ of Mayo & James Carroll of Killway [?] in the Co. of Galway Esqʳˢ of the third part for & concerning a Marriage agreed to be had between the sᵈ Thomas Lyster & thᵉ sᵈ Margarett Carroll whereby the said Remy Carroll did Covᵗ and agree with the sᵈ Thomas Lyster to Assign & make over to thᵉ said Roger Palmer & James Carroll the securitys in Sᵈ articles mentᵈ for the sum of one Thousand five Hundred pounds as a Marriage portion with the said Margᵗ, as Trustees

to the uses therein mentd and the said Thos Lyster did thereby Covt and agree that he would in considn of the Sd Marriage & Marriage portion & in order to make a Suitable provision for the Sd Margaret in case She should Survive the Said Thos [and] for the Issue of the Sd Marriage[, does] Execute two bonds to the said Roger Palmer & James Carroll for the purposes therein mentd of the principal Sum of two Thousand pounds each with warrt of Atty [?] to Confess Judgemt thereon for the purposes therein mentd and it is by Said Articles recited that the sd Thomas Lyster had a Demand of one thousand pounds principall money due on the Estate of Howard Egan Esqr deced & of a Considerable Arrear of Interest due thereon & had a Suite then depending for the Same[.] it was thereby concluded & agreed upon by all the parties to the Sd articles that in Order to make a provision for the sd Margarett in case she Survived the Sd Thomas & for the issue of Sd Marriage the Sd one Thousand five Hundred pounds portion agreed to be paid by the Said Remy with the Said Margt or the Securitys for the Same & also the two Bonds for the principall Sums of Two thousand pounds each agreed to be Executed by the Sd Thomas Lyster as aforesd & also the sd one thousand pounds with all the Interest then or thereafter to become due thereon shou'd when recovered be Lodged in the hands of the Sd Trustees for the purposes therein mentd & for no other use or purpose wtsoever & it was thereby further agreed that if the Sd Thomas Lyster shou'd dye & the Sd Margarette Survive him that She Should yearly receive during her Life one hundred & fifty pounds for her Support & Maintenance in full Lieu Satisfaction & Barr of all dower & thirds which she might be intitled to out of the real or personal Estate of the Said Thos which he then was or should be thereafter Seized or possessed of & that Said one Hundred & fifty pounds Should be paid her yearly out of the Said Sevll Sums or Securitys Lodged with the Sd Trusttees as aforsd and it was thereby further agreed that if the said Lyster Should dye Leaving Issue by the Said Margt a Son & one or more Daũrs that then the Sd two Sevll Sums of two thousand pounds Should be for the benefitt of Such issue paying thereout to the said Margt if she should Survive the Sd Thomas Seventy five pounds a year during her Life out of the Intst arising on Sd bonds as aforesd & one Thousand pounds[,] part of Sd Fifteen Hundred pounds part[,] and the Sd Sum due on Egans Estate & agreed to be Lodged with Sd Trustees as aforesd Shall be for the uses in Sd Articles mentd with Sevl other Clauses and Covts in the Sd Articles mentd which Said Articles are witnessed by Mathew Lyster of the City of Dublin Esqr[,] Christr Fallon of Ballandeeccy [?] in the Co of Roscomon Gent. and Wm Ousley of the Sd City Gent. and this Meml is also witn'd by Henry Garvey of Woodfield in the Co of Mayo Gent and by the said Wm Ousley Gent—Remy Carroll (Seal) — Signed & Sealed in presence of us, Hen: Garvey—Will Ousley. The above named Wm Ousley came this day before me & made oath that he Saw the above named Thos Lyster Remy Caroll Margarett Carroll [her name is interlined] & James Carroll duly Seal & Execute the above mentd Articles [interlined word illegible] of wch the above writing is a Meml & also Saw the sd Remy Carroll Sign & Seal the Sd Memorial [a whole interlined line is illegible] & that he delivd the Same to Me, James Saunders Dep Regr on the 30th day of April 1748 at or near Twelve o'Clock at Noon—Will: Ousley — Sworn the 30th of April 1748 before

James Saunders Dep Regr."

TIP

In many locales that have suffered record loss, the only proof of a marriage may come from a trust deed of this type—another reason for doing thorough land research, even when the objectives are simply vital dates.

STEP 3: REVIEW WHAT REMAINS

Lyster to Palmer, Trust Document
Registry of Deeds, Dublin
Book 130:128–29, no. 88250
Drawn 7 October 1746; filed 30 April 1748

TRANSCRIPTS
AND ABSTRACTS

TIP

When we are uncertain of the reading of a word, it should be boldfaced, italicized, or underscored—with a square-bracketed question mark following it. If only part of a word is unclear, we highlight just that part.

"A Memorial of . . . Articles . . . dated the Twenty Seventh day of Oct[r] one thous[d] Seven Hund and forty six . . . between Thom[s] Lyster of Grange in . . . County . . . Roscomon Esq[r] of the first part, Remy Carroll of Ardagh in . . . C[o] . . . Gallway Esq[r] and Marg[t] Carroll his Eldest Daur of the Second part & Roger Palmer of Palmerstown in . . . C[o] . . . Mayo & James Carroll of Killway [?] in . . . Co . . . Galway Esq[rs] of the third part . . . concerning a Marriage agreed to . . . between . . . Thomas Lyster & . . . Margarett Carroll[.] . . . Remy Carroll did . . . agree with . . . Lyster to Assign . . . to . . . Palmer & James Carroll the securitys . . . for . . . one Thousand five Hundred pounds as a Marriage portion with Marg[t], as Trustees to the uses therein ment[d] [&] . . . Lyster did . . . agree to make a Suitable provision for . . . Margaret in case She should Survive . . . Tho[s] [and] for . . . Issue of S[d] Marriage[, does] Execute two bonds to . . . Palmer & James Carroll for . . . two Thousand pounds each with warr[t] . . . and it is . . . recited that . . . Lyster had a Demand of one thousand pounds . . . due on . . . Estate of Howard Egan Esq[r] dec[ed] & . . . Considerable . . . Interest due thereon[, a] Suite then depending for . . . Same[.] . . . if . . . Thomas . . . shou'd dye & . . . Margarette Survive him . . . She Should yearly receive during her Life one hundred & fifty pounds for her Support & Maintenance in full . . . Satisfaction . . . of all dower & thirds she might be intitled to out of real or personal Estate of . . . Tho[s] . . . & that Said one Hundred & fifty pounds Should be paid her yearly out of the Sev[ll] Sums or Securitys Lodged with Trusttees[,] . . . if . . . Lyster Should dye Leaving . . . by . . . Marg[t] a Son & one or more Daur̃s . . . then the S[d] two . . . Sums of two thousand pounds Should be for benefitt of Such issue paying to . . . Marg[t] . . . Seventy five pounds a year during her Life out of Int[st] arising on S[d] bonds . . . & one Thousand pounds[,] part of S[d] Fifteen Hundred pounds[,] and S[d] Sum due on Egans Estate & agreed to be Lodged with Trustees as afores[d] Shall be for the uses in S[d] Articles ment[d]. . . . Articles . . . witnessed by Mathew Lyster . . . of Dublin Esq[r][,] Christ[r] Fallon of Ballandeeccy [?] in . . . C[o] . . . Roscomon Gent.[,] . . . W[m] Ousley of . . . S[d] City Gent. [M]emorial . . . witn'd by Henry Garvey of Woodfield in . . . C[o] . . . Mayo Gent and . . . W[m] Ousley Gent—Remy Carroll {Seal} —Signed . . . Hen: Garvey—Will Ousley. . . . Ousley made oath that he Saw . . . Tho[s] Lyster Remy Caroll Margarett Carroll . . . & James Carroll . . . Execute . . . Articles . . . & also Saw . . . Remy Carroll Sign & Seal . . . Memorial . . . & that he deliv[d] the Same to Me. . . on 30 . . . April 1748. . . . Sworn 30 April 1848 before James Saunders Dep Reg[r]."

STEP 4: CREATE FINAL ABSTRACT

Lyster to Palmer, Trust Document
Registry of Deeds, Dublin
Book 130:128–29, no. 88250
Drawn 7 October 1746; filed 30 April 1748

27 October 1746, articles of agreement: THOM[S] LYSTER, ESQR. of Grange, Co. Roscomon, of the first part; REMY CARROLL, ESQR. of Ardagh, Co. Gallway, and MARG[T] CARROLL his eldest daughter, of the second part; to ROGER PALMER, ESQR. of Palmerstown, Co. Mayo & JAMES CARROLL, ESQR. of Killway [?], Co. Galway, of the third part. THOMAS & MARGARETT are to marry. REMY promises THOMAS he will assign to PALMER & JAMES CARROLL, as trustees for MARGARET, a marriage portion of £1500. Thomas, to provide for MARGARET (in case she survives him) and for any of their children, similarly assigns to PALMER & JAMES CARROLL two secured bonds for 2000£ each, along with £1000 due him from estate of HOWARD EGAN, ESQ[R.], with the considerable overdue interest, for which he has sued. If MARGARET survives THOMAS, she will receive, out of funds held by trustees, £150 annually for her support, in full satisfaction of all "dower and thirds" she might have received from THOMAS'S estate. If THOMAS dies before MARG[T], leaving by her a son and one or more daughters, then the £2000 shall be for their benefit and MARGARET will receive £75 a year out of the interest generated by remaining funds. Witnesses to

articles of agreement: MATHEW LYSTER, ESQR. of Dublin; CHRIST_R FALLON, GENT. of Ballandeeccy [?] in Co. Roscomon; witneses to later memorial: HENRY GARVEY, GENT. of Woodfield in Co. Mayo, and W_M OUSLEY, GENT—REMY CARROLL (seal) — Signed HEN: GARVEY—WILL OUSLEY.

30 April 1748, OUSLEY delivered the memorial to JAMES SAUNDERS, Dep. Registrar, and made oath that he saw THO_S LYSTER, REMY CAROLL, MARGARETT CARROLL, and JAMES CARROLL execute the articles and saw Remy Carroll sign the memorial.

Mortgage

When property owners have pledged realty or personal goods as security for a debt, they often have done so via a mortgage—another type of conditional deed. If the terms of the debt are met, the mortgage is voided or canceled. Under common law (the basis for legal codes in most English-speaking countries), if land was pledged the person who held the mortgage actually had the legal right to take possession of the land. In most American states and colonies, that was not actually the custom. In America also, researchers frequently find mortgages executed by those who did not own land—instead they pledged cattle, crops, and household furnishings. A mortgage deed can be as complex as the previous trust document or it can be relatively simple, as the following example shows.

STEP 1: TRANSCRIBE

Lee to Campbell, Mortgage
Washington County, Virginia
Deed Book 1:38
Drawn 13 February 1786; proved 15 August 1786

"THIS INDENTURE made the thirteenth day ~~day~~ [*sic*] of February one thousand seven hundred and eighty six; between Peter Lee of the County of Washington and commonwealth of Virginia on the one part and Arthur Campbell Esq_r of the aforesaid County and Commonwealth of the other part Witnesseth that for and in consideration of the sum of one hundred pounds lawful money of Virginia in hand paid to the aforesaid Peter Lee by the abovementioned Arthur Campbell, the receipt whereof I do hereby acknowledge have bargained and sold and by these presents, according to due form of law, do bargain, sell and deliver unto the said Arthur Campbell a certain tract or parcel of land lying in said County of Washington and containing two hundred and fifty acres as by Grant from said Commonwealth bearing date the fifth day of July one thousand seven hundred and eighty five will more full appear. To have and to hold the said bargained premises unto the said Arthur Campbell his heirs or assigns for ever. And I the said Peter Lee for myself my Executors and Administrators the said bargained premises unto the said Arthur Campbell his heirs Executors and Administrators the said bargained premises unto the said Arthur Campbell his heirs Executors or Administrators [*sic*] and assigns will warrant and defend by these premises against all persons whatsoever. PROVIDED nevertheless that if I the said Peter Lee, do and shall well and truly pay or cause to be paid unto the said Arthur Campbell or his Executors and Administrators one hundred pounds like lawful money as above, as per Bond bearing date the same day with these presents, for redemption of the bargained premises, then this present deed of Mortgage shall be void and of no effect but if default be made in the payment of the

TIP

The Latin term *sic,* placed in square brackets, is a transcriber's notation that means "this anomaly appeared exactly this way in the original."

TRANSCRIPTS
AND ABSTRACTS

said one hundred pounds in part or in whole, contrary to the manner and form aforesaid that then it shall remain and be in full force and virtue: in witness whereof, I have hereunto set my hand & seal the day and year above written—

Sealed and delivered in presence of   Peter Lee (seal)
David Carson }
P. Campbell   }
John Houston }

At a Court held for Washington County August 15th 1786
This deed of Mortgage from Peter Lee to Arthur Campbell Esqʳ was exhibited in Court and proved by the oaths of David Carson and Patrick Campbell Witnesses thereto and Ordered to be recorded.

Test John Campbell C.W.C."

When we find a mortgage on file, we should look for a later cancellation. Occasionally a mortgage was not recorded until the debt was cleared, in which case the voiding of the mortgage may be added to the bottom of the document. Usually, a mortgage was recorded promptly. If and when cleared, a marginal notation may have been added to the original recording or the clearance may have been registered at a later point in the record books.

STEP 2: REMOVE THE EXCESS

Lee to Campbell, Mortgage
Washington County, Virginia
Deed Book 1:38
Drawn 13 February 1786; proved 15 August 1786

"THIS INDENTURE made the thirteenth day ~~day~~ [*sic*] of February one thousand seven hundred and eighty six; between Peter Lee of the County of Washington and commonwealth of Virginia on the one part and Arthur Campbell Esqʳ of the aforesaid County and Commonwealth of the other part Witnesseth that for and in consideration of the sum of one hundred pounds lawful money of Virginia in hand paid to the aforesaid Peter Lee by the abovementioned Arthur Campbell, the receipt whereof I do hereby acknowledge have bargained and sold and by these presents, according to due form of law, do bargain, sell and deliver unto the said Arthur Campbell a certain tract or parcel of land lying in said County of Washington and containing two hundred and fifty acres as by Grant from said Commonwealth bearing date the fifth day of July one thousand seven hundred and eighty five will more full appear. To have and to hold the said bargained premises unto the said Arthur Campbell his heirs or assigns for ever. And I the said Peter Lee for myself my Executors and Administrators the said bargained premises unto the said Arthur Campbell his heirs Executors and Administrators the said bargained premises unto the said Arthur Campbell his heirs Executors or Administrators and assigns will warrant and defend by these premises against all persons whatsoever. PROVIDED nevertheless that if I the said Peter Lee, do and shall well and truly pay or cause to be paid unto the said Arthur Campbell or his Executors and Administrators one hundred pounds like lawful money as above, as per Bond bearing date the same day with these presents, for redemption of the bargained premises, then this present deed of Mortgage shall be void and of no effect but if default be made in the payment of the said one hundred pounds in part or in whole, contrary to the manner and form aforesaid that then it shall remain and be in full force and virtue: in witness whereof, I have hereunto set my hand & seal the day and year above written—

Sealed and delivered in presence of   Peter Lee (seal)
David Carson }
P. Campbell   }
John Houston }

At a Court held for Washington County August 15th 1786

This deed of Mortgage from Peter Lee to Arthur Campbell Esqʳ was exhibited in Court and proved by the oaths of David Carson and Patrick Campbell Witnesses thereto and Ordered to be recorded.

Test John Campbell C.W.C."

STEP 3: REVIEW WHAT REMAINS

Lee to Campbell, Mortgage
Washington County, Virginia
Deed Book 1:38
Drawn 13 February 1786; proved 15 August 1786

"...thirteenth...of February one thousand seven hundred and eighty six; between Peter Lee of... County of Washington... commonwealth of Virginia... and Arthur Campbell Esqʳ of... aforesaid County[.]... in consideration of... one hundred pounds... paid to ...Lee by...Campbell,...[Lee does] sell...to...Campbell...land...in...County of Washington... containing two hundred and fifty acres as by Grant from... Commonwealth bearing date the fifth... of July one thousand seven hundred and eighty five.... Lee... will warrant... these premises against all persons whatsoever. ...if ...Lee.. shall...pay...the one hundred pounds... as per Bond bearing date the same day with these presents,... this... deed of Mortgage shall be void....

...in presence of   Peter Lee (seal)
David Carson }
P. Campbell   }
John Houston }

...Washington County, August 15ᵗʰ 1786
...proved by oaths of David Carson and Patrick Campbell Witnesses....."

STEP 4: CREATE FINAL ABSTRACT

Lee to Campbell, Mortgage
Washington Co., Va.; Deed Book 1:38
Drawn 13 Feb. 1786; proved 15 Aug. 1786

PETER LEE of Washington Co. to ARTHUR CAMPBELL ESQᴿ of same. In consideration of £100 paid to LEE by CAMPBELL, LEE conveys to CAMPBELL 250 acres in Washington County, a Commonwealth grant dated 5 July 1785 and warrants the title. If LEE pays the £100 as due by bond bearing present date, the mortgage shall be void. [Signed] PETER LEE. Witnesses: DAVID CARSON, P. CAMPBELL, JOHN HOUSTON.

15 August 1786, proved in court by oaths of DAVID CARSON and PATRICK CAMPBELL witnesses.

Summary Concepts

When most laypeople encounter legal boilerplate, their eyes glaze. Tedious repetition, outmoded phrasing, obscure technical words, and sentences that seem to run on forever—all these characteristics of legal records create an urge to skip and skim. Serious genealogists thoroughly rein in those impulses. Much of the boilerplate *can* be eliminated, as the examples in this chapter illustrate. Yet before we can safely cut and cull, whittle or lop, we must lay four personal cornerstones. We must know the

Tedious repetition, outmoded phrasing, obscure technical words, and sentences that seem to run on forever—all these characteristics of legal records create an urge to skip and skim. Serious genealogists thoroughly rein in those impulses.

TRANSCRIPTS

AND ABSTRACTS

FIG. 19

TRANSCRIBING

TOMBSTONE

INSCRIPTIONS*

General procedures
- Allow ample time—much more than you planned.
- Record the date you read the stones.
- Record the cemetery's precise location (if urban, give street address; if rural, then cite highway number or road name and distance or direction from closest town—ideally with township-range-section numbers or a Global Positioning System reading).
- Map the burial ground, if the cemetery office has no plat map; depict lanes and other landmarks; number or letter the rows.
- Take photographs or drawings of each stone, if possible, for help when preparing the material for publication.
- Be alert for completely or partially buried stones. (Leave no stone unturned, literally.)
- Do not overlook very small stones with only initials listed. These could represent small children—or footstones, in cases where headstones have been lost.
- Look for inscriptions on every side of each stone.
- Do not leave the cemetery in worse condition than it was when you arrived.

Taking notes
- Read stones one row at a time, if possible—numbering the transcriptions by row, in original order.
- Copy the inscription as precisely as possible. Clearly indicate illegible or inferred portions. If necessary to the interpretation of the text, sketch the layout of the inscription to indicate relative position of text and graphic elements.
- Use an underscore or another symbol to indicate inscriptions that are incomplete—e.g., "died in 19__."
- Include notations about unreadable stones and their relative position to other stones.
- Include location data (both lot and stone) with each inscription. If a numbering system does not exist for the cemetery or cannot be devised, include enough geographic detail to make each stone locatable.
- Reproduce insignias as closely as possible by drawing, photographing, or rubbing. Avoid using a verbal description as a substitute for an actual design.

Overcoming legibility problems
- Try reading at different times of the day or on different days.
- Make rubbings or tracings, using large kraft or tracing paper and a broad crayon.
- If cleaning is needed, touch should be gentle and cleaner should be mild, nonchemical, and nonabrasive.

Augmenting the inscriptions
- Consult sexton records, if they exist—especially to locate unmarked graves.
- Clearly separate tombstone data from that supplied by the sexton's records.
- Consult auxiliary sources (for example, church burial registers or memorials in church minute books, death certificates, newspaper obituaries, and probate files) that may reference other interments in that cemetery.
- Do not intermingle inscription data with auxiliary data. Use square brackets, footnotes, or other standard editorial devices to set apart the additions.

Preparing final manuscript
- Do not alphabetize inscriptions; leave them in original order to preserve clues inherent in their location and sequence.
- Prepare a separate section for burials without stones.
- Prepare an index to help users check for names of interest.

* *Contributed by Michael John Neill*

terminology (something we learn from legal dictionaries), we must know the genealogical implications of various types of records (something we learn from methodological lectures and case studies in major journals), we must know editing conventions (something this manual provides throughout), and we must practice, practice, practice. Whether we are working with legal records, tombstone data (see figure 19), or other record forms, skilled transcripts and abstracts are the very foundation upon which reliable research is built.

Skilled transcripts and abstracts are the very foundation upon which reliable research is built.

NOTES

1. Helen F. M. Leary, CG, CGL, FASG, "Skillbuilding: Converting Records into Reliable Copies," *OnBoard* [educational newsletter of the Board for Certification of Genealogists] 5 (May 1999): 20; Elizabeth Shown Mills, CG, CGL, FASG, "Skillbuilding: Producing Quality Research Notes," *OnBoard* 3 (January 1997): 8; Mills, "Skillbuilding: Transcribing Source Materials," *OnBoard* 2 (January 1996): 8; and Val D. Greenwood, J.D., AG, "Abstracting Wills and Deeds," *The Researcher's Guide to American Genealogy*, 3d edition (Baltimore: Genealogical Publishing Co., 2000). Greenwood also gives examples of various abstracts.

2. For more on this subject, see Leary, "Skillbuilding: Converting Records into Reliable Copies," and *The BCG Genealogical Standards Manual* (Orem, Utah: Ancestry, 2000).

3. For specifics of source citation according to type of record, a useful guide is Elizabeth Shown Mills, *Evidence! Citation & Analysis for the Family Historian* (Baltimore: Genealogical Publishing Co., 1997).

4. Quoted in Michael Quinion, *World Wide Words* 105 (25 July 1998). For subscription and archives to this weekly e-mailed newsletter, see its website.

5. For example, see Curtis Brasfield, " 'To My Daughter and the Heirs of Her Body': Slave Passages as Illustrated by the Smithwick-Latham Family," *National Genealogical Society [NGS] Quarterly* 81 (December 1993): 270–82.

6. Contributed by the editor. The abbreviation "f.m.c." used in this document was a standard postnomial in records of that era and locale; it meant *free man of color*.

7. For example, Richard M. Lederer Jr., *Colonial American English, a Glossary: Words and Phrases Found in Colonial Writing, Now Archaic, Obscure, Obsolete, or Whose Meanings Have Changed* (Essex, Connecticut: Verbatim Book, ca. 1985); and Dr. Penelope Christensen, *What Did They Do?* (Toronto: Heritage Productions, 1997).

8. Greenwood, op. cit.

9. For example, see Margaret Hickerson Emery, CG, "The Adeustone-Rogers Families of Virginia: Tracing a Colonial Lineage through Entailment and Naming Patterns," *NGS Quarterly* 77 (June 1989): 89–106; and Katherine E. Harbury, CG, "Revisiting William Young of Essex County, Virginia—All of Them!" *NGS Quarterly* 79 (September 1991): 194–206.

10. Eileen M. ODúill, CGRS, of Dublin, Ireland, is due thanks for locating this complicated document and assisting with the reading of portions of it.

11. (Sidebar, p. 326) Chuang-tse (386?–?286 B.C.), Chinese philosopher and teacher, quoted in Eugene E. Brussell, ed., *Webster's New World Dictionary of Quotable Definitions* (New York: Webster's New World, 1988), 610.

FURTHER STUDY

ABSTRACTING AND TRANSCRIBING:

Freidel, Frank, ed. *Harvard Guide to American History.* London, England, and Cambridge, Massachusetts: Belknap Press, 1974. See chapter 1, section 1.3, and all of chapter 2.

Geiger, Linda A. Woodward, CGRS, CGL. "Techniques for Transcribing and Abstracting Documents: A Refresher Course." *Association of Professional Genealogists [APG] Quarterly* 10 (September 1995): 87–88.

Leary, Helen F. M. "Abstracting," in Leary, ed., *North Carolina Research: Genealogy and Local History,* 2d edition. Raleigh: North Carolina Genealogical Society, 1996.

TRANSCRIPTS

AND ABSTRACTS

INTERPRETATION OF HANDWRITING:

Bertoldi, Silvain. *Lire les ecritures anciennes: Comment s'etrainer.* 3 vols. Angers, Bertoldi, n.d. The author of this self-teaching course is an archivist, paleographer, and curator of the Archives of the City of Angers.

Cruz, António. *Paleografia Portuguesa: Ensaio de Manual.* Portu: Cadernos Portucale, 1987.

Dawson, Giles E., and Laetitia Kennedy-Skipton. *Elizabethan Handwriting: 1500–1650: A Guide to the Reading of Documents and Manuscripts.* New York: W. W. Norton, 1966.

Hill, Ronald A., Ph.D., CG. "Interpreting the Symbols and Abbreviations in 16th and 17th-Century English Documents." *Genealogical Journal* 21 (1993): 1–13.

Johnson, Arta F., Ph.D. *How to Read German Church Records without Knowing Much German.* N.p.: Privately printed, 1980.

Kirkham, E. Kay. *The Handwriting of American Records for a Period of 300 Years.* Logan, Utah: Everton Publishers, 1981.

Millares Carlo, Agustín. *Tratado de Paleografia Española.* 3 vols. Madrid: Espasa-Calpe, 1983.

Schweitzer, George W., Ph.D. "Deciphering Old German Script," in *Exploring a Nation of Immigrants—Houston Style.* Syllabus, 1994 conference, National Genealogical Society. Arlington, Virginia: NGS, 1994.

Sperry, Kip, AG, CG, CGI, FASG. *Reading Early American Handwriting.* Baltimore: Genealogical Publishing Co., 1998.

Stryker-Rodda, Harriet. *Understanding Colonial Handwriting.* Baltimore: Genealogical Publishing Co., 1986.

INTERPRETATION OF RECORDS:

Black, Henry Campbell. *Black's Law Dictionary: Definitions of the Terms and Phrases of American and English Jurisprudence, Ancient and Modern.* 6th edition. St. Paul, Minnesota: West Publishing Co., 1990. The 4th edition (1957) is good for more obsolete terms.

Drake, Paul, J.D. *What Did They Mean by That? A Dictionary of Historical Terms for Genealogists.* Bowie, Maryland: Heritage Books, 1994.

Evans, Barbara Jean. *The New A to ZAX: A Comprehensive Genealogical Dictionary for Genealogists and Historians.* 2d edition. Champaign, Illinois: Privately printed, 1990.

Ryskamp, George R., J.D., AG. "Common-Law Concepts for the Genealogist: Real-Property Transactions." *NGS Quarterly* 84 (September 1996): 165–81.

———. "Fundamental Common-Law Concepts for the Genealogist: Marriage, Divorce, and Coverture." *NGS Quarterly* 83 (September 1995): 165–79.

Winslow, Raymond Jr. [Numerous chapters in] Helen F. M. Leary, ed., *North Carolina Research: Genealogy and Local History.* 2d edition. Raleigh: North Carolina Genealogical Society, 1996. Principally see 97–105 and 151–290.

Words are used to express meaning; when you understand the meaning, you can forget about the words.

—*Chuang-tse*[11]

INTERPRETATION OF WORDS:

Gooder, Eileen A. *Latin for Local History: An Introduction,* 2d edition. London: Longman, 1978.

Latham, Ronald E. *Revised Medieval Latin Word-List from British and Irish Sources.* London: Oxford University Press, 1983. A handbook of words coined in England and Ireland through the Medieval period. Includes entries not found in dictionaries of classical Latin, also numerous word variations common to documents of the period.

Martin, Charles Trice. *The Record Interpreter: A Collection of Abbreviations, Latin Words, and Names Used in English Historical Manuscripts and Records.* 1892. Reprinted, Sussex, England: Phillimore and Co., 1982.

Ortell, Gerald A. *Polish Parish Records of the Roman Catholic Church.* Milwaukee: Polish Genealogical Society of America, 1996. Offers basic Polish and Latin genealogical vocabulary, examples of register entries, and more.

Pladsen, Phyllis J., and Joseph C. Huber. *Swedish Genealogical Dictionary.* 2d edition. N.p.: Pladsen/Huber Press, 1993. Includes old words found in records before the spelling reform of 1906; more useful than a modern Swedish-English dictionary.

17

EVIDENCE
ANALYSIS

Keynotes

Evidence Analysis

by Donn Devine, J.D., CG, CGI

Determining the significance of the information we've found is the heart of our work as genealogists. Some discussions of the subject tend to present it as a great mystery comprehended only by the elect. In reality, we just seek satisfactory answers to four questions:

- What does the information tell us?
- Can we be confident that it reflects actual fact?
- Does it pertain to the individual or issue in which we're interested?
- What conclusion can we draw from it?

We need adequate answers to the first three questions before we can answer the final one. Obviously, if the information is not interpreted correctly and it is not relevant or dependable, a reliable conclusion can't be drawn.

Family historians have been answering these questions for as long as genealogy has been around. They've done so by studying records and matching the information found there with the particular individual in which they are interested. But not until relatively recent times have *most* genealogists become cautious about noting *the information's source* and the *bases for their conclusions*. Donald Lines Jacobus and his followers of the mid-twentieth century made source citation and critical evidence analysis the measures for acceptable genealogical studies, as it long had been in law and social science.[1]

Amid another spurt of genealogical scholarship at the close of the twentieth century, genealogy has become a discipline of its own. In borrowing standards of analysis from other fields, Jacobus and his followers found it necessary to adapt and redefine the established terms, but those alterations conflicted with concepts in the fields from which they were borrowed. Similarly, patterns of citation that worked efficiently for other learned fields fell short of genealogical needs. The result, in the 1990s, was a spate of cooperative efforts to

- define an appropriate genealogical proof standard;[2] and
- identify the elements of source citation that are crucial to the analysis process.[3]

In short, the genealogical treatment of sources has moved from mere *identification* (so that material can be reconsulted if need be) to *analysis* (so that findings can be accurately interpreted and only the best evidence accepted as "proof").

The genealogical treatment of sources has moved from mere *identification* (so that material can be reconsulted if need be) to *analysis* (so that findings can be accurately interpreted and only the best evidence accepted as "proof").

Genealogical Proof Standard

Simply put, we meet the Genealogical Proof Standard when our evidence fulfills the following tests:[4]

- Our research has been systematic and exhaustive.

- The evidence is reliable and correctly interpreted.

- Any contradictory evidence is soundly rebutted.

- Each statement of fact is scrupulously documented.

- Every deduction is clearly reasoned and persuasively explained.

However, two cautions also apply:

- The genealogical proof standard describes the *minimum* weight of evidence we need to convince ourselves and others that our conclusions reflect past reality.

- Our "proof" is always subject to reevaluation whenever new evidence arises.

This chapter explores the means by which genealogy arrived at its standard of proof and the concepts that underpin it.

Evolution of Standards

The lawyer and genealogist Noel C. Stevenson—a fellow and later president of the Jacobus school's American Society of Genealogists—brought the term *evidence* into widespread genealogical use through his 1979 volume *Genealogical Evidence: A Guide to the Standard of Proof Relating to Pedigrees, Ancestry, Heirship, and Family History.*[5] Stevenson's analytical treatment was a major sequel to the scholarly and critical approach pioneered by his predecessors at ASG. He explained at length the legal concepts of admissible and inadmissible evidence and the reasons that specific types of evidence are permitted or excluded in trials. He also recommended the legal rules as a basis for selecting genealogical evidence—a major deviation from the traditional view of genealogy as the "handmaiden of history."

Adoption of legal terminology

Stevenson also created a significant change in the terminology used to describe genealogical standards. While many family historians had traditionally referred to documentary evidence as *proofs*—especially documents submitted with lineage-society applications—that usage declined after Stevenson's book presented the subject of *evidence* in such depth. The three legal concepts that Stevenson emphasized were

- *absolute or conclusive proof,* which is seldom possible to achieve, because informants may have made hard-to-discover misrepresentations. In genealogy, absolute or conclusive proof is perhaps attainable only through DNA testing.

- *proof beyond a reasonable doubt,* which is the standard necessary for conviction in criminal courts. This high bar is occasionally possible to obtain in genealogical issues, when all the significant evidence is both convincing and in agreement, but it is an impractical goal for most genealogical investigations.

In genealogy, absolute or conclusive proof is perhaps attainable only through DNA testing.

- *proof by a preponderance of the evidence,* which is the standard applied to most issues in civil court trials. Stevenson advocated this standard for genealogical evidence. In his view, genealogical proof requires that the conclusion carry conviction and satisfy the conscience, but it need only be supported by the greater weight of the evidence—that is, a conclusion can be simply more probable than not.

Stevenson did not discuss a fourth legal standard that is intermediate between the second and third:

- *proof by clear and convincing evidence,* as it is called in some jurisdictions. This standard, used in civil trials where the outcome affects life or liberty rather than property, is actually closer to the level with which most genealogists are comfortable.

The preponderance of the evidence

Stevenson's proposal to weigh genealogical evidence according to the rules applied in American courts was only partially successful. Genealogists adopted his preferred term—the preponderance of the evidence—but applied two modifications. They raised its threshold to approach that of clear and convincing evidence, and they broadened the concept to describe the process of analyzing and weighing a complex body of evidence and drawing conclusions from it. In a 1987 article, another ASG leader, Walter Lee Sheppard Jr., succinctly described the new, higher genealogical standard as applied to complex problems. In his words:

> When direct evidence is lacking, but there is contemporary, primary evidence of a number of related facts all pointing in the same direction, and the evidence so accumulated leaves no doubt in the reader's mind that only one reasonable conclusion can be drawn from it, then it is appropriate to say that a fact has been established by a preponderance of the evidence. However, if there is found a single contemporary document that points in a different direction, and it is not possible to show clearly that this document is in error, then the argued case has not been proved acceptably.[6]

Yet genealogy did not completely ignore Stevenson's appreciation of lesser evidence that is still capable of "carrying conviction and satisfying the conscience." In such situations, when the balance scales are just slightly tipped in one direction, careful researchers may still propose conclusions, but clearly qualify them by stating they are only "probable" or "possible" or "subject to further study."

Confusion has resulted from using the term *preponderance of the evidence* (popularly called the *POE* in genealogy) for two different standards of proof—one in law and another higher one in genealogy. That confusion was further compounded by the term's use to describe the evaluation process as well as the standard of proof. Several writers noted the problem in the early 1990s,[7] but the contradiction persisted. In 1997, a number of active genealogists who frequently address the subject in their lectures and writings decided among themselves to drop the term, except in historical discussions of the present type. Concurrently, the Board for Certification of Genealogists revised the wording of its application requirements that treat the handling of complex evidence.[8]

When the balance scales are just slightly tipped in one direction, careful researchers may still propose conclusions but should clearly qualify them by stating they are only "probable" or "possible" or "subject to further study."

Current Principles

Understanding basic terms

Popular genealogy recognizes the need to document sources and evaluate evidence in order to obtain proof, but it frequently treats these three terms—*sources, evidence,* and *proof*—as though they were variant names for the same concept. The confusion reflects genealogy's mixed heritage from history and law. A careful consideration of the differences between these terms can help us analyze the information we obtain and establish the facts about family relationships.

SOURCES

Sources, in the genealogical context, are any means (person, document, book, artifact, or repository) through which we acquire information. The concept comes from the social sciences—particularly history, from which genealogy draws much of its research methodology. Historians traditionally considered only sources in documentary form. More recently they have turned to oral history—recorded or transcribed interviews with participants and witnesses—to fill gaps in the documentary record. Yet modern genealogists apply the term *source* to a significantly broader range of materials than those consulted by the traditional historian—from such memorabilia as samplers and quilts to such artifacts as tombstones, weapons, and home furnishings. All are records capable of yielding evidence.

EVIDENCE

Evidence is the information the source provides—a concept borrowed from law. (While commentators on the methodology of historical research discuss using sources as evidence for proving or disproving hypotheses, the term *evidence* is otherwise rarely encountered in the social sciences.[9]) In the legal setting, a judge makes the selection, and the jury sees or hears only those sources deemed admissible. In genealogy, we personally select our evidence from the mass of available sources and then evaluate it for credibility and relevance to the matter in question.

PROOF

Proof is the thought process by which we reach a convincing *conclusion* based on the *evidence* we gleaned from the *sources* we examined.

Genealogical *proof* is the thought process by which we reach a convincing *conclusion* (assertion of fact) based on the *evidence* (information statements) we gleaned from the *sources* (people, documents, books, artifacts, or repositories) we examined.

Classifying records and information

History, genealogy, and the law tend to divide documentary materials into broad categories that not only overlap but also have somewhat different meanings. Within history, where the term *evidence* is seldom used, both materials and the information therein are usually sorted between *primary sources* and *secondary sources*. Law more commonly applies the terms *original* and *derivative* to source records it handles and uses still other terms for the information within the sources. On the other hand, modern genealogy—which observes the law's clearer distinction between sources and evidence—has developed three sets of criteria by which sources and their information are classed:

- original vs. derivative *sources*.
- primary vs. secondary *information* or *knowledge*.
- direct vs. indirect or circumstantial *evidence*.

ORIGINAL *VS.* DERIVATIVE SOURCES

Originals
In genealogical terms, original sources are those that meet two criteria. They are made at or near the time of the event, and their informants are in a position to know the facts firsthand. Logically, an original is the kind of source preferred.

Historians, on the other hand, frequently apply a broader view of the "best class" of sources. While they usually speak of "primary sources," they define these as the first or earliest documents that record the information—usually manuscripts. But they also extend the term to typescript copies, to such published works as annotated diaries, and to recorded oral interviews that relate tradition or lore.

Derivatives
All records that are not originals are obviously derivatives. In a genealogical sense, this term—borrowed from law—is more practical than the historian's "secondary sources," a term that is then imprecisely extended to include tertiary sources and others even more degrees removed from the original.

Whatever the name by which it is called, this class of record or source varies widely in nature. It may be copied or compiled from original materials, or it may be a synthesis of many sources—original or derivative—that reflect the conclusions of others.[10] We should remember, however, that these distinctions don't automatically determine the reliability of any particular source, although some types are generally more trustworthy than others. The merit of any source must not only consider whether it is an original or a derivative, but also whether the information is *primary* or *secondary* in nature and whether the evidence contained in that information is *direct* or *indirect*.

PRIMARY *VS.* SECONDARY INFORMATION
Any source or record may contain information based on *both* primary and secondary knowledge—one of many reasons that genealogists must distinguish between the source and the information it offers. The factors that differentiate primary from secondary information (or data) may be summarized as follows.

Primary
In modern genealogical usage, primary information is a statement by someone who was a knowledgeable participant in an event or an eyewitness to it. Primary information may be either written or oral. The statement may have been made at the

Any source may contain information based on *both* primary and secondary knowledge—one of many reasons that genealogists must distinguish between the source and the information it offers.

time the event occurred or at a later date. The information contained in that statement may be either correct or incorrect.

Secondary

Statements made by individuals who were not actual participants in an event or did not actually witness an occurrence are classed as secondary information. This category embraces family tradition and local lore, abstracts and unofficial transcripts of original records, and online genealogical databases. It also can include random elements within original or official records—as, for example, birth data found in a death certificate, where the informant who was present at the death was not also present at the birth of the deceased; thus, he or she gave hearsay information regarding that birth.

DIRECT *VS.* INDIRECT EVIDENCE

Direct

Direct evidence is information that provides an answer without the need for additional facts or further explanation. As with primary information, the answer it provides may be true or false.

Indirect

Indirect evidence is information that does not explicitly answer the question at hand, although it relates to it in some other way. In the quest for proof, where direct evidence is lacking or appears to be incorrect, indirect evidence from various sources is often assembled to arrive at a reasonable conclusion or "proof."

Traditionally, genealogists have followed the legal field in using interchangeably the terms *indirect* and *circumstantial* evidence. However, the current consensus among many genealogists is that while *direct* or *indirect* may be used to describe how an individual piece of evidence relates to the matter in question, the term *circumstantial* should be reserved to describe a particular type of proof—the type that reasons from a number of items of indirect evidence to a convincing conclusion on an issue.[11] Most important, we should bear in mind that *direct* and *indirect* are not rigid types of evidence. They are classifications we assign to statements *in relation to a particular issue.* Any piece of information may offer direct evidence on one point and indirect evidence on another.

Screening sources

At law, from which we borrow the term, *evidence* refers to all the information-bearing means that a jury may use to reach a decision or verdict. Before a jury gets that information, it has been carefully screened by the judge (as previously noted), and the jury learns only of those sources deemed admissible—meaning credible and relevant to the matter at hand, and capable of affecting the outcome. As genealogists, we have to perform this screening process ourselves, as our exhaustive and systematic research turns up potentially useful materials. From them we select those that

Direct and *indirect* are not rigid types of evidence; they are classifications we assign to statements in relation to a particular issue.

present the most believable information, so long as it might relate to our problem—regardless of the directions in which it may lead.

Selecting evidence from the mass of available sources is not a linear process. At its simplest, we follow two parallel tracks, as shown in figure 20:

- *Credibility:* whether a source's information is likely to reflect past reality, and
- *Relevance:* whether information relates to the person or question of immediate concern.

CREDIBILITY

In genealogy, the testimony of eyewitnesses is seldom available. Original records, especially those made near the time of the matter at issue, are our first choice for credibility. When they don't exist, we have to use the best available derivatives as evidence, even though they are not generally as reliable as original records. When evaluating for credibility, we should remember that a derivative source *can* be closer to past reality than an erroneous original record. For example, the carefully reasoned conclusion of a competent genealogist, after considering a number of original records, may be more credible than original testimony by someone who falsifies the evidence. (This, of course, is not to say that we should indiscriminately rely on the published conclusions of other genealogists in lieu of examining the original evidence for ourselves.) When we must use a published source and the original records cited are no longer extant, we should assess the general reliability of the work by the quality of its overall documentation and the soundness of its reasoning.

[handwritten margin note: Credibility is an more than an assessment of a source's history of accuracy.]

RELEVANCE

While we screen our materials to determine how reliably they present their information, we also decide whether the content could apply to the person or question we're investigating. At this stage in the process, if it *could* relate we select it as evidence. Later, in the proof process, we'll weigh it further, looking for a sound reason for associating this particular document with a specific individual. If no sound reason emerges, we will likely reject the information as evidence. In the course of our screening, we may go back and forth between these two tracks—credibility and relevance. We may make tentative decisions that a source is useful and then reconsider it as we assess its credibility, its possible relationship to our person or question of interest, and its potential impact. On further evaluation, information originally selected as evidence may turn out to have too little credibility to be considered, or it may prove to be unrelated to the matter at hand.

Weighing evidence

The result of our source screening is *evidence*, but evidence is not *proof*. Proof, as Stevenson made clear,[12] is a process that takes place in the mind—distinct from the information on which it is based or the form in which that information comes to us.

While we prefer original records as evidence, they are not always available for inspection. They may be located at too great a distance from us, or they may be retired

Proof is a process that takes place in the mind and is distinct from the information on which it is based.

EVIDENCE ANALYSIS

**FIG. 20
EVOLUTION OF A
GENEALOGICAL
CONCLUSION**

Fact:
A past reality—an event or relationship.

Information:
An assertion about a fact.

Source:
The person, place, or record from which we obtain information about a fact.

Relevant evidence:
Source items we select from thorough research, as those most likely to give reliable and applicable information (even if negative) to use in reaching a conclusion.

Relative weight:
Significance we give each item of information from each source of evidence.

Validity of argument:
- Are we convinced?
- Can we convince others?
- Have we adequately rebutted all negative evidence?
- Have we met the Genealogical Proof Standard?
- If not, have we added the qualifier "probable" or "possible," as justified by the evidence?

Conclusion:
An assertion of fact based on the evidence we gleaned from the sources we examined.

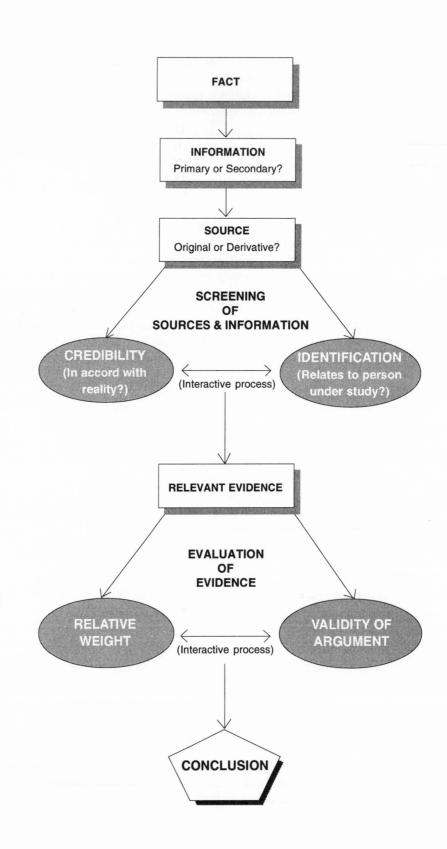

from use to save further wear and tear. We can accept images of the original as satisfactory substitutes if we have reasonable assurance that the image copy reflects the original accurately and without alteration. Copies can include images made from the original by mechanical means (press or carbon paper copies) or photochemical or electronic means (whether stored on paper, film, magnetic media, CD-ROM, or some other medium). However, transcripts, abstracts, and database entries drawn from the originals would not carry the same weight as the original or a valid image copy.

In weighing evidence, we assess two broad areas: the extent to which the information reflects reality, and the strength of the reasons for identifying it with the person or issue under study. Evaluating the individual sources also overlaps another process; simultaneous with weighing the evidence we begin our *reasoning*—the process of reaching a conclusion as to what the entire body of evidence proves.

BASIC FACTORS

In appraising the merits of any piece of information, we pose two broad sets of questions:

Factors that point toward higher reliability of evidence:

- Is the information from an informant in a position to know?
- Was the record made close to the time of the event it discusses?
- Was the record made under oath, or with other formality or ceremony?
- Does the record series show care in its creation and maintenance?

Factors that point toward lesser reliability of evidence:

- Might there be potential bias or self-interest on the part of the informant?
- Is the original (or its image) altered?
- Is the source a transcription or abstract?
- Is there evidence of carelessness in the creation or maintenance of the record?
- Was there a delay in recording the information?

Faced with conflicting evidence from independent sources, we must determine and be able to argue or explain how the quality or weight of one is sufficiently greater than others to permit either a probable or convincing conclusion. Otherwise, the matter remains in doubt.[13]

IDENTIFIERS

A document may discuss an individual of the same name as the individual we seek, but it does not follow that the document relates to our person. If both name and age are given in the document, and they correspond with the name and age of our subject, there is a greater probability that it applies; but, at best, it's only a probability. For a convincing identification, we need a sufficient number of identifiers that correspond with known characteristics of our subject. Frequently, we must build a circumstantial case for identification from indirect evidence, as discussed in chapter 20.

A document may discuss an individual of the same name as the individual we seek, but it does not follow that the document relates to our person.

Identifiers commonly sought in documentary materials include

- name and date of birth.
- names of parents, spouse, children, and collateral relatives.
- occupation.
- location.
- place of birth.
- handwriting, signature, or mark.
- physical characteristics or conditions.

Additional identifiers, some more positive than the usual documentary descriptions, are the result of twentieth-century technology or bureaucracy, but as yet have not found widespread use in genealogy. These include

- appearance (from photographs).
- social security, taxpayer identification, birth registration, military serial, and veterans' claim numbers.
- fingerprints, footprints, palm prints, and eye prints.
- DNA profiles and dental records.

Reasoning and proof

> The evaluation process demands correlative reasoning to convert the individual pieces of evidence into proof.

The evaluation process demands correlative *reasoning* to convert the individual pieces of evidence into proof. There are several formal models that we can use for reaching conclusions upon the basis of the evidence we find and evaluate. Because genealogy is a social science, the "scientific" model used in that discipline is discussed first below. Probably more common, however—due to the heavy influences of legal concepts on genealogical proof—is *deductive reasoning* from evidence to conclusion. Others, briefly touched upon in this section, are occasionally employed.[14]

SCIENTIFIC METHOD

The scientific method calls for a two-step process. First we develop a hypothesis—a theory that appears logical; then we attempt to prove or disprove it through research. That research process may be one of two types: *retrospective*, in which we seek knowledge of past events; and *experimental*, in which we systematically plan and observe a series of future events.

- *Retrospective approach:* the method more commonly used in history, the humanities, business, and the justice system. Here, researchers usually want to understand chains of interrelated events that have led to some particular happening. As one of the social sciences, genealogy can seek knowledge of related events through application of the scientific method.

- *Experimental approach:* the one traditionally used in physical sciences, such as biology, chemistry, and physics. Here, researchers seek to discover general laws of nature that have predictive value. The social sciences, too, may seek to validate general principles that have predictive value; but they depend largely on retrospective research.

There are significant differences in the extent to which genealogy and the other social science disciplines can apply the retrospective approach:

- *Measurements in the social sciences* are more often statistical; a particular value is expressed only in terms of some quantified range of probability. In contrast, genealogy seeks (but cannot always attain) absolute values—yes or no answers—about specific events, with a very high degree of probability.

- *Hypotheses used in genealogy* tend to be quite simple. For example: a relationship did or did not exist; and an event did or did not occur at a particular time and place. Because of this simplicity, we can readily structure our argument in terms of whether or not each piece of evidence supports or negates the hypothesis.

People new to genealogy frequently bring with them research experience in other disciplines, and they may have to make a conscious effort to recognize how the conduct of genealogical research and the interpretation of its results can differ from their previous experiences. For example, a measurement error in the physical sciences may be minimized when averaged with other measurements of the same phenomenon. An erroneous conclusion about a single historical fact may be inconsequential in the account of an entire lifetime, or in the broad sweep of history. The contrast to genealogy is pronounced: an error in one single relationship will be multiplied exponentially with each generation we move backward or forward.

An error in one single relationship will be multiplied exponentially with each generation we move backward or forward.

DEDUCTIVE METHOD

Deductive reasoning is the type that argues *if A is true and B is equivalent to A, then B is also true.* The manner in which we use evidence deductively to prove a point depends upon whether its information—which could be true or false—directly or indirectly addresses the question at hand.

Deduction from direct evidence

As previously noted, direct evidence provides an answer to a question at issue without the need for additional facts or further explanation—although it may not necessarily be in accord with past reality. A birth registration record, for example, states that John Evans, born 14 July 1969, is the child of Nathaniel and Mildred Evans, who are identified by their ages and birthplaces. These facts provide direct evidence of a parent-child relationship and the child's birth date. If there is no reason to suspect the record has been falsified, as in certificates issued for adopted children, the evidence might be judged credible and pass the selection process.

Proof requires more. We must weigh the evidence to determine the degree of confidence we can place in its information. There are no magic formulas and no numeric values we can assign to automate this process of weighing evidence. In each case, the weight we decide to assign will be based on all our knowledge and past experience, what we can learn about the source itself, and whether there's contradictory evidence or corroborating evidence of independent origin.

Deductions from indirect evidence are far more likely to intimidate the geneal-ogist who attempts them or is asked to accept such conclusions of others.

Deduction from indirect evidence

Deductions from indirect evidence are the most complex type. They are also far more likely to intimidate the typical genealogist who attempts them or is asked to accept such conclusions of others. In most cases, the researcher will assemble an assortment of information from various sources—all or most of which will mesh to suggest a reasonable conclusion. The Genealogical Proof Standard, discussed at the start of this chapter, is most often called upon to support deductions from indirect evidence; and chapter 20 discusses the means by which these conclusions ("proof arguments") are developed.

OTHER MODELS

In addition to the scientific and legal models for weighing evidence and arguing from it, two others are sometimes applied by genealogists:

- *Textual criticism*: the method most used by modern biblical scholars to determine the sources of particular manuscripts, the contributions of different authors, and some characteristics of the authors and their environment.

- *Diplomatics:* a method that addresses the authenticity of documents—particularly those evidencing rights, privileges, or wealth—that, by their nature, invite fraud. (These are obviously applicable to genealogy.) Rather than applying abstract principles of evaluation, diplomatics approaches the problems of authenticity and validity by asking what the document itself reveals by its form—external (medium, layout, letter style) and internal (language, vocabulary), by its tradition, by the degree to which it is removed from the original (chain of copies, or mere mention in another document), by its genesis (the events and people that led to its creation), by a critique of the elements that don't ring true when tested against the preceding studies, by the dating system, and by a study of the seals.[15]

Summary Concepts

As genealogists, we make a comprehensive search for all available evidence. We evaluate its quality. We analyze its applicability to a particular person. If all factors align, we arrive at a conclusion of which we are convinced. If we've met the genealogical proof standard, we can be reasonably sure that our conclusion will stand, even while we remain open to the possible discovery of new evidence. If our present evidence is convincing enough, we can state our finding without qualification. Otherwise, we are safer to qualify our conclusion as "probable," "possible," or "open to further study."

NOTES

I especially thank Thomas W. Jones, Ph.D., CG; Helen F. M. Leary, CG, CGL, FASG; Elizabeth Shown Mills, CG, CGL, FASG; and Christine Rose, CG, CGL, FASG, for their perspectives amid drafts of this chapter. But I am also grateful to all colleagues who have debated this issue with me, persuading me to accept some of their perspectives as my own, to the point that I now have difficulty in distinguishing which were originally mine.

1. Donald Lines Jacobus, "On the Nature of Genealogical Evidence," *New England Historical and Genealogical Register* 92 (July 1938): 213–14.

2. The standard was first defined in print by Helen F. M. Leary, "Evidence Revisited—DNA, POE, and GPS," *OnBoard* [newsletter of the Board for Certification of Genealogists] 4 (January 1998): 1–2, 5; and Elizabeth Shown Mills, "Building a Case When No Record 'Proves' A Point," *Ancestry* 16 (April–May 1998): 29.

Among the works that shaped this standard are Donn Devine, "Evidence and Sources— And How They Differ," *Ancestry* 15 (May–June 1997): 26–29; Mills, *Evidence! Citation & Analysis for the Family Historian* (Baltimore: Genealogical Publishing Co., 1997); Christine Rose, *Genealogical Use of 'Preponderance of the Evidence'* (San Jose, California: Rose Family Association, 1995); Val D. Greenwood, J.D., AG, "Evaluating Evidence," *Genealogical Journal* 25 (1997): 51–62; Norman W. Ingham, Ph.D., CG, "Some Thoughts about Evidence and Proof in Genealogy," *The American Genealogist* 72 (July 1997): 380–85; and Thomas W. Jones, "A Conceptual Model of Genealogical Evidence: Linkage between Present-Day Sources and Past Facts," *National Genealogical Society [NGS] Quarterly* 86 (March 1998): 5–18.

Definitions of the major genealogical terms—reflecting a consensus of most of the above writers—appear in Leary, Mills, and Rose, "Evidence Analysis, Definitions, Principles, and Practices," in *Virginia, Where a Nation Began,* 1998 Conference Syllabus, National Genealogical Society (Arlington, Virginia: NGS, 1998), 41–48; and in Board for Certification of Genealogists, *The BCG Genealogical Standards Manual* (Orem, Utah: Ancestry, 2000). See also Mills, "Working with Historical Evidence: Genealogical Principles and Standards," *NGS Quarterly* [issue titled *Evidence: A Special Issue of the National Genealogical Society Quarterly*] 87 (September 1999): 165–84.

3. Mills, *Evidence!*, for example, presents documentation as part and parcel of the analysis process. By contrast, that guide's predecessor by Richard S. Lackey, *Cite Your Sources: A Manual for Documenting Family Histories and Genealogical Records* (1980; reprint, Jackson: University Press of Mississippi, n.d.), presented citation for documentation's sake only. The classic citation manuals used in other fields habitually ignore most record types used for local and family history research—hence the creation of manuals specifically for genealogists. For example, see *The Chicago Manual of Style,* 14th edition (Chicago: University of Chicago Press, 1993); Joseph Gibaldi, *MLA Handbook for Writers of Research Papers,* 4th ed. (New York: Modern Language Association of America, 1995); Kate L. Turabian, *A Manual for Writers of Term Papers, Theses, and Dissertations,* 6th edition, John Grossman and Alice Bennett, eds. (Chicago: University of Chicago Press, 1996); and U.S. Government Printing Office, *A Manual of Style: A Guide to the Basics of Good Writing* (New York: Wings Books, 1986).

4. Mills, "Building a Case When No Record 'Proves' a Point," 29.

5. Noel C. Stevenson, J.D., FASG, *Genealogical Evidence: A Guide to the Standard of Proof Relating to Pedigrees, Ancestry, Heirship, and Family History* (Laguna Hills, California: Aegean Park Press, 1979). A revised edition was published in 1989.

6. Walter Lee Sheppard Jr., CG, FASG, "What Proves a Lineage? Acceptable Standards of Evidence," *NGS Quarterly* 75 (June 1987): 124–30; for the quote, see 125.

7. Paul Drake, J.D., "Some Thoughts Concerning Genealogical Evidence and Proof: Part II: Establishing Proof," *NGS Newsletter* 17 (November–December 1991): 153–55; Donn Devine, "Do We Really Decide Relationships by a Preponderance of the Evidence?" *NGS Newsletter* 18 (September–October 1992): 131–32; Kory L. Meyerink, AG, "Evaluation of Evidence," *Ancestry Newsletter* 10 (November–December 1992): 1–3.

8. "Board for Certification of Genealogists Abandons Term *Preponderance of the Evidence,*" *NGS Quarterly* 85 (September 1997): 227.

9. Jacques Barzun and Henry F. Graff, *The Modern Researcher,* 5th edition (Fort Worth, Texas: Harcourt Brace Jovanovich College Publishers, 1992), 154–59.

10. Mills, *Evidence!*, 49–51, treats the subject of derivatives in greater depth.

11. One prominent genealogist in a recent journal article proposes that we use these two terms more precisely to distinguish between evidence under two different conditions:

Indirect: use for evidence that does not specifically address our question, but from which we can make only one possible inference—and that one does answer the question. For example: a

> The classic citation manuals used in other fields habitually ignore most of the record types used for local and family history research.

EVIDENCE ANALYSIS

Evidence is none the less effective because it is circumstantial, if it be consistent, connected and conclusive.

*—Noel C. Stevenson,
J.D., FASG*[16]

birth date can be derived from a gravestone that records the date of death and the age in years, months, and days; from that, one and only one birth date can be derived.

Circumstantial: use for evidence from which we could make more than one possible inference. In such cases, we would need multiple pieces of such evidence, independently created, to narrow the range of inferences to a single conclusion. See Jones, "A Conceptual Model of Genealogical Evidence," 10.

12. Stevenson, *Genealogical Evidence,* 182.

13. For a more detailed summary of how to evaluate evidence, see the thirteen "Guidelines for Analyzing Evidence," in Mills, *Evidence!,* 44; discussions of each follow at 45–57. Also see Brenda Dougall Merriman, CGRS, CGL, *About Genealogical Standards of Evidence: A Guide for Genealogists* (Toronto: Ontario Genealogical Society, 1997).

14. See, for example, Irving M. Copi and Carl Cohen, *Introduction to Logic* (Upper Saddlebrook, New Jersey: Prentice-Hall, 1998); Gustave Weigel and A. G. Madden, *Knowledge: its Values and Limits* (Westport, Connecticut: Greenwood Press, 1973); and A. S. Woozley, *Theory of Knowledge: An Introduction* (New York: Barnes and Noble, 1966). All three works also appeared in earlier editions.

15. One of the few extensive treatments of diplomatics in English appeared in a special section, "Diplomatics and Modern Records," in *American Archivist* 59 (issue dated Fall 1996, but published Spring 1998): 412–94.

16. Stevenson, *Genealogical Evidence,* 186, quoting from *State* v. *Samuels,* 22 Del. (6 Penn.) 36, 39.

Writing and Compiling

18

RESEARCH
REPORTS

Keynotes

Keynotes (cont.)

Research Reports

by Elizabeth Shown Mills, CG, CGL, FASG

As genealogists, we wear many hats. We may label ourselves *professional genealogists* or *family historians,* or we may work in related fields, but our status matters little to the issue at hand. We may accept client commissions for research and write reports of the search and our findings. We may be librarians or archivists, who respond to mail requests for help at our institution. We may be authors who use research reports to develop our manuscripts. We may be hobbyists, determined to provide our family with the highest quality history possible. Or we may employ professional researchers to assist us with our work. As varied as our positions are, we have a common base: we need to describe and summarize our research in a manner that does justice to the level of work we have done and the reputation we have tried to build.

Genealogy—as a field of social, historical, legal, and medical investigation—is built on a foundation of knowledge, skill, and standards; that is,

- knowledge of subject matter.
- skill at research.
- standards for documentation and analysis.

Practically speaking, the quality and effectiveness of our efforts in all three areas can be judged by one means: the report we make of our research and findings.

- *As librarians* who fill requests for limited searches in our holdings, are we familiar with the standards that have developed in the genealogical world for reporting the results of an investigation? While we may not place our own work in the same category as that of a professional researcher, our correspondents will. Both we and our institution are measured by prevailing standards.

- *As family historians,* are we preparing our research notes and problem analyses in a format that will be clearly understood by those we share with—or by researchers whom we hire? The credibility and acceptance of our work are directly affected by the quality we display. The success of those we employ may hinge upon the skill with which we summarize for them our own prior findings.

- *As writers, attorneys, or geneticists* who entrust our "leg work" to genealogical researchers, what criteria do we use to judge the depth and reliability of their reports? Do we understand the type of groundwork we must provide or the ways in which genealogical criteria differ from—may even be more exacting than—those in our primary field?

- *As professional researchers,* do our reports attest the high level of skill and knowledge, we have attained? Do they protect us in the event that a misunderstanding occurs between us and our clients?

Regardless of the reputation we may have in genealogy or its related fields; regardless of the assertions we make to our clients, correspondents, families, patrons, readers, or students; regardless of the professional or academic degrees that appear after our name—one fact remains. Every time we create a piece of writing that carries our name, our expertise and qualifications will be judged anew by all who see our work.[1]

> We need to describe and summarize our research in a manner that does justice to the level of work we have done and the reputation we have tried to build.

Definition

A research report is an account of research performed—that is,

- the problem to be investigated;
- the resources available—and those used;
- the information found;
- the analysis of that data; and
- the conclusion the research supports or the potential for resolving the problem elsewhere.

A professional-quality research report is not a biography. It is not a summary of what we know to date about a person (which *is* a biography). A research report is not a computer-generated printout with canned wording produced by programming software that converts certain database entries into formulaic phrases. (The term *report,* which some software uses to describe such biographical accounts, is a misnomer.) A research report is a thoughtful, analytical document whose words are uniquely crafted to describe the problem, the mental exercises applied toward the resolution of that problem, and all the findings.

Basic Standards

Every writer of a research report should remember: we'll never have a second chance to make a first impression. Our reports are judged immediately on their appearance. Then they are evaluated on their content. Therefore, this chapter treats style, data selection, and arrangement—including grammar, clarity, and organization—because all have a direct influence upon our credibility. It also presents suggested formats, but these are neither templates nor molds; they are merely blueprints. Some of their features can be adapted to varying situations without undermining the whole; other elements are expected in every sound report. To distinguish between structural foundations and flexible designs, each format is discussed from the standpoint of its advantages, problems, and special concerns.

Appearance

All who view our reports form an immediate impression as to whether we are sloppy and careless clutterbugs or well-organized, logical thinkers. We earn the right impression by close attention to five elements of attractive formatting:

- *No typos.* Modern spell checkers help us avoid most typographical errors; but they do not relieve us of one chore: we must *proofread, proofread, proofread.* Users of our reports who spot a typo will justifiably wonder how many less obvious errors we made—errors on dates and other crucial genealogical detail. For practical help on this point, see chapter 26, Proofreading and Indexing.

- *Standard-sized paper of bond quality.* Cheap paper makes us look cheap and will not last nearly as long as research files should last. Acid-free paper is best.

> A research report is a thoughtful, analytical document whose words are uniquely crafted to describe the problem, the mental exercises applied toward the resolution of that problem, and all the findings.

- *Wide margins*. A generous amount of white space makes a nice "frame" for the document we are preparing. Nothing eliminates the cluttered look more effectively.

- *White space*. Let's spare our readers eyestrain. A professional-looking report is usually single-spaced, because that format is more attractive and conserves paper. However, we should leave extra white space between paragraphs or whenever there is a shift in subject matter. Aside from the visual relief it gives to weary eyes, it also helps separate our presentation into clear sections.

- *Subheads*. The longer the report, the more necessary these become—as illustrated by the samples that accompany this chapter. Subheads provide a road map for readers, helping them follow the direction of our thoughts. Given that most research reports are not indexed (though longer ones need to be), subheads provide markers that help users relocate material when they later come back to our reports.

Grammar

Genealogists represent virtually every walk in life; it naturally follows that most of us are not grammar majors. What's more, the very nature of our work—our daily exposure to massive doses of yesteryear's eccentric prose—can numb us to sins against syntax and grammar. Still, we cannot communicate adequately if we do not use correct punctuation, complete sentences, and appropriately constructed paragraphs. We cannot convey the complexity of a research problem and have our proposed solution understood if we don't use the right words and link them properly. Whatever quirky habits we've fallen victim to are easily slain. Our local bookstores now offer some delightful self-help manuals—pocket- or purse-sized treats we can indulge in while killing time in waiting rooms and elsewhere.[3]

The difference between the right word and the almost right word is the difference between lightning and the lightning bug.

—*Mark Twain*[2]

Clarity and thoroughness

Our reports should be so clear and thorough that no one has to write us for further explanation. Correspondence of that type is a time waster (not to mention a needless sacrifice of bandwidth or tree pulp). A well-written report follows five basic principles:

- We anticipate questions our readers or clients might raise—then answer those questions before they're asked.

- We avoid jargon. In genealogy, there is a continuous influx of newcomers who have not learned those acronyms and specialized terms.

- We avoid regional shorthand—abbreviations and truncated references to books, people, events, and habits that are "old hat" to everyone in our area and a total mystery to folks elsewhere.

- We provide appropriately complete identification of persons, records, and events. For example, the first time we mention a person who is relevant to the record or the problem (e.g., "General Jones"), we provide the full name. If we report that an individual signed the Mecklenburg Declaration, most readers will appreciate a brief comment to identify that document.

- We avoid unprofessional colloquialisms and cliches. A well-done report avoids such banalities as "on a hunch . . . ," "out of curiosity . . . ," "I stumbled upon . . . ," "so I got to thinking . . . , " or "we really mopped up on this!"

When we finish the first draft, we reread it. We seat ourselves in the recipient's chair. We adopt the frame of mind of a hypothetical total stranger. We assume this person to be reasonably intelligent, but we don't make him or her a genealogical expert. (No one knows everything about this diverse field of ours.) Then we critically evaluate what we've said—from the assumed mindset of this other person who did not accompany us while we did the research.

Conciseness

Being concise and thorough at the same time is no easy trick. Most of us learned to write in secondary and undergraduate classrooms, where we inflated our verbiage to fill the assigned page count. As genealogical writers, we now need to put our prose on a diet. Our objective is to say what must be said, but to say it as tightly as possible.

Research Framework

On this foundation, three qualities form the framework of an effective research report:[4]

- appropriate choice of sources.
- care in recording full details.
- judicious photocopying.

Appropriate choice of sources

Most genealogists begin a research project with a review of published literature. Finding compiled genealogies, published abstracts, census indexes, etc., can shortcut our work. Those that offer every-name indexes actually help us do a more thorough search. However, a good research job does not rely solely upon derivative sources; and we are hard-pressed to justify ignoring original materials when they are reasonably accessible. Quality reports often include both; but whenever our source is a derivative, we should make three points clear:

1. The data came from a derivative.

   EXAMPLE:
   If using published deed abstracts for which the compiler identifies the original deed book and page, we cite the publication, with a notation that the compiler references Book X, page x (as illustrated in the sample Formal Report at end of chapter, figure 28). We do not make it appear that we consulted the original deed if we are relying upon someone else's interpretation of it.

   EXAMPLE:
   If using the Soundex or Miracode to certain U.S. censuses, we clearly indicate that the information is from the index, not from the actual schedules.

   EXAMPLE:
   If using New England's early vital records but only the published compendiums

> Our objective is to say what must be said, but to say it as tightly as possible.

are available, we fully cite the published source—not the lazy shorthand, "Plymouth Vital Records" or "Plymouth VR."

2. The derivative is (or is not) appropriately documented.

QUESTIONS TO ADDRESS:
Did the author of the family history reference every fact that is not public knowledge? Did the compiler of the abstracts identify fully the source of each document?

3. The original was not consulted because . . . [lack of access, time, etc.].

Identification of all materials searched

Instinct prompts most researchers to identify, in some fashion, every useful source that's found. But thorough research calls for thorough citations—and not just for findings but for *all* materials searched, even those that produced negative results. Of all the shortcomings frequently seen in reports, these probably head the list:

NEGATIVE RESULTS
"I have searched all possible records and have found nothing." "There is no pension file for John at the National Archives." Such comments litter genealogical accounts. When we read such a report, do we know exactly what was examined? No. Another person's idea of "all possible" is not necessarily the same as ours. Perhaps Reggie Researcher only knew about the M804 microfilm series of Revolutionary War pension files,[6] but we are also aware of relevant material in M853.[7] We need to know that Reggie's "negative" search did *not* include M853. Similarly, our own readers need to know exactly what *we've* combed that was not productive. Even when we find "nothing," we itemize everything we examined; and we provide a full citation of each.

DOCUMENTATION
We document impeccably. We provide a complete and individualized reference for every fact in our report that is not public knowledge. Many of those references warrant explanations, as well. We record a full citation on the margin of every photocopy. We provide individually referenced notes for every name, date, place, relationship, or other fact on a group sheet or ancestor chart. Should we be uncertain as to exactly what pieces of information ought to be recorded for all the myriad types of records, we will likely find guidance in *Evidence! Citation & Analysis for the Family Historian.*[8]

Care in recording full details

The problems that plague genealogical research reports include errors of both omission and commission, with two types of records generating the most shortfalls:

Census abstracts
Regardless of place or time, we need to record the date of enumeration, ward or post office identification (if given), dwelling/family numbers (or line numbers if dwelling and family designations do not appear), and any information on literacy

Documentation is the single most important element of any research effort, for it enables all who follow to evaluate the soundness of one's methodology and conclusions and to plan future avenues of investigation.

—*Marc Erlitz, M.D., family historian, Seattle, Washington*[5]

or property ownership. No detail is too trivial to copy. Moreover—*and this point is absolutely crucial to problems of identity, relationship, and origins*—our census reports on any family or individual should identify several adjacent households (ideally, a "neighborhood" of ten to twenty).

Land abstracts
Regardless of the locale or the type of survey system used, if the document provides a legal description of the land (metes and bounds or rectangular survey, etc.), we should copy that information in full. In years past, some of the best genealogists skipped this labor or deemed it something that could be done later "if needed." Today's genealogists are continually solving problems with these details.

Being precise and thorough in the preparation of abstracts also requires us to ignore a practice often taught in Genealogy 101: the use of abstract forms to extract pertinent details from wills and deeds. In all historical research, one principle is sacred: the original arrangement should be preserved to every extent possible.

Abstract forms serve a purpose in reminding beginners of important elements they should look for in a will, deed, or census; but they force us to violate a sacred historiographical rule: *preserve original order.* As we dissect the original details and scatter them across the designated blanks, we can alter meanings or disassociate connections. Fragmentation of detail is inevitable. (When our ancestors drafted documents, universal consistency of format was not a big concern.) Often, too, the blanks on a form provide inadequate space to record all detail in the document.

As good genealogists, we approach a record with these things in mind:

- We should already know which elements are important in that record type and shouldn't need a form to remind us. (If we are still learning, we can take a form with us and simply use it as a checklist.)

- We abstract the document thoughtfully, maintaining the original order of all detail but condensing each statement to its bare essentials.

- We interject no interpretations, explanations, or "corrections" of our own. Whenever such comments are necessary, we add them in square brackets (if they are extremely short comments) or add an indented editorial notation at the end of the abstract. (Figure 28, at end of chapter, provides illustrations of both ways to handle added comments.)

Judicious photocopying

When we examine a photocopied page from someone's research, we frequently find that needed information is missing. A book of court-session abstracts may offer two dozen pages from a single session, but the compiler may have identified that session on the first page. Consequently, the photocopied page now offers no hint of a date. A collection of newspaper abstracts may cover several different papers but name them only at the chapter heads rather than on each page. When we are the researcher who photocopies from such books, we may have to search several pages backward to find the data—then pen the missing information on our printouts or copy also the page with the needed background.

> In all historical research, one principle is sacred: the original arrangement should be preserved to every extent possible.

If a book uses space-saving codes or abbreviations, we should copy not only the relevant page but also the section that explains the codes. Always, we include a book's title page when we copy other material from it. There, too, we have to pause for a check—to see if all necessary details are on the title page or whether some details (often, publication dates) have to be retrieved from the reverse side.

Report Types

Structurally, an effective research report is governed by three primary factors:

- type of records used,
- type of assignment, and
- time limitations upon the assignment.

In all other forms of writing, we are told that we must consider our audience and tailor our writing toward that audience. In reporting genealogical research, that advice ought to be ignored. No report in our field is a one-on-one document. Its preparation is never a matter between just us and our files or between just us and the person we address. Most reports sail out of file drawers and into the swap-out circuit—or the recipients immediately post them on their websites for all of cyberworld to see. They are read, used, and judged by an endless number of genealogists who come from all backgrounds, have various educational levels, and exhibit widely varying skills. Yet, no matter the hands into which our work falls, we want to be completely understood.

Four formats are commonly used to report results of genealogical research:

- narrative reports,
- genealogy software reports,
- letter reports, and
- formal reports.

One of these formats is better for some occasions, one is less effective in most situations but appropriate in others, and two create so many problems we'd be better off avoiding them. (The problem ones will be addressed first and dispensed with.)

Narrative reports

The narrative format—which reports a block of research as an "interesting account" of a person or family—will sabotage the best of intentions. As writers, we may relish this opportunity to write The Great American Novel. But our recipients—if they have any skill at research themselves—will find it an aggravation and a disappointment.

Writing classes teach the impossibility of presenting a well-crafted story that contains all detail known about the subject. A writer must be *selective*. Thus, drafting a research report as a personal or family narrative means that thoroughness and accuracy suffer. Even if the account is footnoted (and most works cast in this mold are far from adequately referenced), it is difficult to read such a report and decide the

Writing classes teach the impossibility of presenting a well-crafted story that contains *all* detail known about the subject. Drafting a research report as a personal or family narrative means that thoroughness and accuracy suffers.

exact source of each *specific* detail. It is often impossible to determine the extent to which the verbiage of the narrative reflects the opinion or interpretation of the researcher versus the actual detail in the original and its precise wording.

Eventually, most ongoing projects progress to the point that a narrative may be appropriate. A client may want a number of reports summarized into an "interesting story" to give his family for Christmas. Or we decide to turn our own work into an inspiring saga to enthrall our own family. Wonderful! But we don't (or shouldn't!) present our *original* research reports in such a fashion.

Genealogy software reports

Genealogy software "reports" take many forms and serve useful purposes. However, whether they are formatted in table or narrative form, they are not *research reports*. All the problems with using genealogical abstract forms for our on-site research, mentioned by several writers throughout this manual, apply to "reports" that are created from template-based, field-restricted data—and then we must add more. All the caveats just raised for the narrative report apply to the genealogy software report—and more.

The reasons are better understood by defining basic distinctions between research reports and genealogy software printouts:

- *A genealogy software report* is a tabular or otherwise formatted *summary* of selected pieces of data, which we have taken out of their original context and reduced or manipulated to fit the size and nature of certain template fields. While some software permits free-form insertion of analytical or descriptive comments, each comment is attached to a specific document, a specific person, or a specific event. In short, a genealogical program is at heart a database, and the various reports it generates are database summaries, in mechanical prose.

- *A research report* is not a data summary. No matter the length of the report, a good one provides a thoughtful and detailed description of a *research process*. It begins with a definition of the problem or objective, an identification of relevant materials, and an account of the discovery process designed to fulfill that objective. It then moves on to the documentation of the evidence (kept in its original context), an evaluation of the results, and a strategy for building upon those results.

  As figures 21–22 (pages 358–59) illustrate, these objectives can be met in even a one-page report—depending upon the nature of the assignment. But the report is specifically crafted by a human brain and it focuses upon the results of a specific research effort.

It is true: the process of extracting selected data from a stack of relevant documents, entering it appropriately into predesigned templates, properly documenting each "fact" we enter, and adding relevant comments regarding the perceived dependability of that "fact" is a critical process itself. But a basic problem remains: this process requires us to take statements out of their original context and let the template arrange them into whatever order the program prescribes. That loss of context often means inadequate interpretation at each future review of the material.

Genealogy software "reports" take many forms and serve useful purposes. However, they are not *research reports*.

RESEARCH REPORTS

Technology is a marvel, but it has not yet reached the point that it can do our writing for us—much less our thinking.

Technology is a marvel, but it has not yet reached the point that it can do our writing for us—much less our thinking. Most major genealogical software is now programmed to convert its database into narrative sentences, whose content, structure, and order are predetermined by the programmer. Some more sophisticated software allows users to alter the programming to create the style of sentences they prefer. But writing is a *mental* process—not a mechanical one. And our ancestors were not clones. The details of individual lives are often out of kilter with the sentence formula worded to fit "most" cases. Anyone who edits the words of others knows the dangers that lurk within the *nuances* of words. But formulaic sentences are programmed to convert the 0's and 1's of a database into preassigned words and phrases—the nuances of which, in any specific case, escape the software's artificial intelligence.[9]

In an effort to resolve "writing" problems, some users of genealogical software employ various workarounds. For example:

PROBLEM 1:
Computer-generated sentences are stilted.

Commonly suggested workaround:
Move the genealogy software's "report" into a word-processing program and edit it to achieve the fluency we want.

Reality:
This editing for fluency *is* important. But we still lost nuances, perspectives, and clues when we took bits of data from the original documents and inserted them into limited template fields. Those lost elements are not going to materialize, just because we are now using the word-based program we might have used to start with to produce the preciseness, thoroughness, and thoughtful analysis that a research report requires. Either we must retrieve photocopies of the original documents and reevaluate them, to correctly nuance our edited sentences as we reconstruct the whole research problem or family situation, or else crucial aspects and angles will be lost until someone else redoes our work.

PROBLEM 2:
Templates in genealogical software programs (like genealogical abstract forms) often prevent us from recording information precisely. As the simplest of examples: an individual's data template will commonly have fields for recording the facts of a marriage—date, place, and name of spouse. However, the date we have may not be the actual marriage date. We may have only the date of a bond or parental permission slip.

Commonly suggested workaround:
Use the software's "comment" or "freeform note space" to explain the situation.

Reality:
The software's narrative "report" still wants to create a biographical sketch that says "John Smith was born on. . . . John Smith married on. . . . John Smith died on. . . ." It will create those statements from the data we entered into the template; it will not read our appended comments and make the appropriate alterations. After the initial biographical sketch, the program may then print out the contents of those comment fields, in added paragraphs, or it may insert those comments in our

reference notes. There, the facts behind the erroneous marriage date *will* appear. Yet, most readers of our narrative will expect that initial biographical summary to offer the correct, *precise* facts of birth, marriage, and death. Many will hurriedly copy those dates into their own work, without searching for caveats that may be buried several paragraphs or several pages later.

For the family-history explorer with no experience as a writer and no desire or time to acquire writing skills, these automated reports may seem a wondrous thing. If extensively edited, the narratives *can* be readable, bare-bones summaries of all information found to date—just as the narrative report sometimes has a place as a composite summary. But, a quality *research report* cannot be generated by reducing documents to a limited selection of isolated data bits and then relying on preprogrammed sentence structure to "report" the nature of our search and its results.

Few of us would consider abandoning our genealogical software; but maximum success, for us and our clients, calls for a *proper* research report for each segment of research that we conduct. Should the reasons remain unclear at this point, the following discussions of what *appropriate* reports contain should spotlight many other ways that genealogy software reports fall short of professional quality.

Letter reports

Two main characteristics distinguish the letter report. First, it is short. As a rule of thumb: if we can make a thorough report in a page or two, a letter will be more practical; if we have more material than this to cover, a formal report is probably best. Second, its tone is personal. Even if we do not know the individual we are addressing, we would still cast our writing in the first and second persons—that is, *I . . . you . . . my . . . your.* Despite their ease of use, letter reports have their drawbacks as well—including matters of organization, client relations, and standards.

CRUCIAL ELEMENTS OF LETTER REPORTS

The letter report is usually perfect for librarians and society volunteers who conduct very limited searches in response to inquiries directed to their institutions. It's also ideal for record agents who specialize in short-order assignments. It's quick and virtually self-contained. However, its expeditious nature causes its worst problem: writing letters is a thing so ordinary that we can forget this is a *report*—one that must be *planned* before we plunge into it.

Outlining a letter before we sit down to type it is not normal human behavior. But it's necessary if our letter is also our report. A planned organization ensures that all essentials are covered, that all are presented in logical sequence, and that extraneous matter does not obscure the relevant points. Figures 21 and 22 present sample reports prepared in this style—each a tightly organized response to a specific and limited request. Consider the parts of the letter presented in figure 21:

Paragraph 1
In three lines, we state the purpose of the report, repeat the client's instructions, and identify the individuals for whom we conducted our search.

Writing letters is a thing so ordinary that we can forget this is a *report*—one that must be *planned* before we plunge into it.

RESEARCH REPORTS

FIG. 21
LETTER REPORT
SAMPLE A

ELIZABETH SHOWN MILLS, CG, CGL, FASG
MILLS RESEARCH SERVICE
———————————————————————— 1732 RIDGEDALE DRIVE, TUSCALOOSA, AL 35406

10 January 2000

Mrs. A. B. See
123 D Street, NE
Anywhere, US 00000

Dear Mrs. See:

Statement of objective,
repository searched;
identification of subject,
vital data, and kin

As you requested in your letter of 15 December, I have searched the probate files of Tuscaloosa County between 1850 and 1855 for a possible estate record on *Luke Abednigo* (b. 1780, South Carolina; d. ca. 1852, Tuscaloosa County), and his widow *Ruth.*

Summary of results

The search brought mixed results. The probate series in the county courthouse yields no trace of an Abednigo estate file, although one recorded "minute" briefly refers to a guardianship requested on a *minor* named *Ruth Abednigo.* That record is as follows:

Complete extract,
set off from text—
with full documentation

> Estate Minutes C: 111
> Probate Judge's Basement Files
> Tuscaloosa County Courthouse, Tuscaloosa, Alabama
> 23 March 1852
> "James White requests guardianship of Ruth Abednigo, a minor
> under the age of fourteen years. Granted."

Background information
on record collection

In addition to the incomplete series of probate actions that have survived in this county, there also exists an extensive series of "loose" probate files [original, jacketed papers, not yet filmed] that were transferred to the State Archives at Montgomery several decades ago. The collection recently was arranged, cataloged, and indexed by the Tuscaloosa Genealogical Society—Night Group. I have checked its index and find an entry for an unrecorded will (no accompanying papers) under the label *Luke Abednigo, 1852.* It is cataloged as File AAAA.

Helpful advice for
additional research

If you wish to order this file, your inquiry should be addressed to Alabama Department of Archives and History, 624 Washington Street, Montgomery, AL 36130. Please cite the needed record as "Luke Abednigo, unrecorded will, File AAAA, Tuscaloosa County Probate Papers." You should enclose a stamped, self-addressed envelope; but do not include funds until you are notified of the cost.

Closing amenities

Best wishes for success as you continue your work on this and other lines.

Cordially,

Elizabeth Shown Mills

Elizabeth Shown Mills

List of attachments

Attachments: Photocopy of cited book/page
                        Statement of time and charges

FIG. 22
LETTER REPORT
SAMPLE B

Kay Haviland Freilich, Certified Genealogist

395 Kerrwood Drive
Wayne, PA 19087-2136

Phone: 610-293-1221
Fax: 610-293-0999

THE WILL OF JOHN B. KELLY OF PHILADELPHIA
Research Report

8 January 2000

Prepared for: Elizabeth Shown Mills, CG, CGL
1732 Ridgedale Drive
Tuscaloosa, AL 35406-1942

John B. Kelly, the father of Princess Grace of Monaco, died in Philadelphia on 20 June 1960, according to his obituary in the *Philadelphia Inquirer* (21 June 1960, page 1). The will you requested is identified as Will 2118 of 1960 in the Philadelphia Register of Wills Office. Coexecutors were his son John Brendan Kelly and the Provident Tradesmen Bank and Trust Company. The will was proved on 27 June 1960 and the final inventory was dated 2 October 1963.

*Identification of subject
and requested document*

Two copies of the will were located in Philadelphia offices. The first, at the Register of Wills Office in City Hall, is a microform. This version includes several pages of the inventory but is missing pages 1–5 of the will itself. The second copy was found at the Register of Wills Archives. It is a copy certified by Ronald R. Donatucci, Register of Wills, on 24 February 1982, as being a "full and perfect copy" of the original. This copy was located in what is referred to as the "historical file," a file of Philadelphia wills that for various reasons might be of interest to the public. No inventory or account information was attached to this transcript. It was this transcript from which the enclosed photocopy was made.

*Location of search and
discussion of
record anomalies*

According to the clerk in the Archives facility, there was no probate packet for John B. Kelly in the appropriate place in the files. He did locate a note that the packet had been sent to the City Hall Office in 1995. He called the City Hall Office but could get no further information on the whereabouts of the packet.

*Report of further search
with negative findings*

Kay Freilich

Attachments:
        13-page will
        Clerk's invoice
        Freilich's invoice

List of attachments

Genealogical Research in Pennsylvania: Chester, Delaware, Montgomery, and Philadelphia Counties
Friends Historical Library, National Archives–Mid-Atlantic Region, Welcome Society

Certified Genealogist is a service mark of the Board for Certification of Genealogists® and is used under license.

RESEARCH REPORTS

Paragraph 2
Here, we summarize our results—and call attention to missing records. The client deserves to know that a complete search was not possible. She will need to recheck the repository periodically to see if the lost file has surfaced. We need to protect ourselves by recording its absence at the time we visited the premises at the client's request. It may be that someone else has already seen that file and extracted useful material from it. We would not want it to appear that we failed to make a thorough search.

Paragraph 3
The one brief record we found is transcribed fully here and blocked off separately. It's not run into the text of our discussion, where it might leave doubt as to exactly where the abstracted detail begins and ends. Note also the full citation of the source and date, as well as the comment pointing out that the "signature" was not an actual autograph.

Paragraph 4
Here, we offer helpful background on the record collection.

Paragraph 5
Clients also appreciate advice for further research elsewhere.

Paragraph 6
Polite amenities are always in order.

Annotations
Attachments should be noted—not only the photocopied page(s) but also the statement of time and charges that would be inappropriate if posted on this letter to be thereafter disseminated among countless other people.

The letter report in figure 22 presents a slightly different situation. There, the researcher found the record that was sought, but its length (thirteen pages) dictates that the professional would not transcribe the full document into the letter report. In fact, two copies of the record were found, in different repositories. Appropriately, the professional compared the two copies, photocopied the one that was complete, and used the letter report to inform the client of the attending circumstances.

PROS AND CONS OF LETTER REPORTS
Some researchers prefer letter reports under all circumstances, on the premise that they are warmer and friendlier and make more efficient use of the client's time. Others feel they are counterproductive—creating an atmosphere that erodes the limited number of billable hours available outside of continuing education, professional contributions, and such nonbillable essentials as filing and accounting. The negative concerns deserve to be addressed also.

Observing sound business practices
Modern genealogical research is rooted in the concept of hobbyists sharing with hobbyists. That creates a sensitive situation for professionals. Most of us begin as hobbyists ourselves—after which, years of experience and education prompt a career change. As professionals, we value the friendships that often grow out of our client

Some researchers prefer letter reports under all circumstances, on the premise that they are warmer and friendlier and make more efficient use of the client's time.

contacts; but we still must operate by the same principles of time and cost efficiency that other business and professional people observe.

Professional researchers—especially those who receive short assignments from a large number of clients—simply can't afford the luxury of making a pen pal of each. The casual tone of a letter report can easily encourage more time-consuming familiarity than is warranted by the size of a commission. If one hour a day is spent in unnecessary correspondence with one or another client who now becomes chummy, that one hour daily equates to several lost workdays per month. As an end result, the professional can be deprived of thousands of dollars of income over the course of a single year.

Maintaining professionalism

The letter report can create other problems for the less businesslike professional. Its "friendliness" can too easily (and too often) digress into a chattiness that undermines professionalism. Illustrating the point to the extreme is the following passage from one actual report:

> Every time I had a day off, Joe and I packed a picnic lunch (since he's retired and gets bored having nothing to do) and then we'd drive to one of the surrounding county courthouses to see if your Bosephus Bostlethwaite might show up there. Well, he didn't. So I'm only charging you half price for all this travel since we made little excursions out of it. . . .

> Finally, I went over to the university to see what they might have. For no real reason, I decided to look at the census of 1870. I sat there for an hour, cranking away, because the school can't afford to buy those new automatic machines. Then, Lo! and behold! What to my wondering eyes should appear . . . but your Bosephus Bostlethwaite and his wife Bernelia. Oh! I can just imagine how happy you must be right now!![10]

Most professionals who use the letter report do rise above this level of chattiness. More often, their undoing is the litany of excuses they feel obliged to make when they are overextended, timewise. Surely we can subdue the urge to begin our letter reports with such excuses. It is entirely appropriate to thank the recipient for his or her patience in waiting for project results. But do we really want legions of people who read this report, as it circulates worldwide, to know the details of our gallbladder surgery?

Avoiding troublesome shortcuts

A final problem with using the letter report is the temptation to take shortcuts when drafting it. A common scenario would have a friend writing to ask that we check the local courthouse for a probate file on Luke Abednigo. Six days later we write her back. In that short lapse of time, our friend would scarcely have forgotten the nature of her request. Why, then, should we go through the formality (and the time waste) of covering all the points outlined in figure 21? Instead, we dash off our response:

> Hi! Got your letter yesterday and rushed right down to the courthouse. You'll be disappointed. They didn't have what you really need on Luke. The "loose papers" are down at Montgomery. Maybe you can find it there.

If one hour a day is spent in unnecessary correspondence, the professional can be deprived of thousands of dollars of income over the course of a single year.

RESEARCH REPORTS

FIG. 23
FORMAL REPORT:
BASIC ELEMENTS

FIG. 23
FORMAL REPORT:
BASIC ELEMENTS

Formal Report: Basic Elements

Preliminary background
- Identification of client
- Identification of subject
- Summary of problem
- Reiteration of instructions
- Limitations upon assignment
- Identification of repositories/collections

Summary of findings

Detailed account of research and results
(Body of report—see fig. 25)
- Explanation of research process
- Actual notes and documents
- Evaluation of individual records

Closing suggestions
- Resources left to be combed
- Estimation of time and charges
- Recommendation of other researchers (if appropriate)

Appendixes
- Photocopies
- Maps
- Indexes
- Family group sheets or charts
- Etc.

FIG. 24
OUTLINE FOR
BODY OF REPORT:
RECORD SEARCHING

Outline for Body of Report: Record Searching

Assignment:
Gather all Periwinkle records from courthouse

Results:
Limited material found

Research calendar
- Resources searched
- Time frame searched

Actual findings
- Abstracts
- Photocopies

Sources not covered
- Indexed materials
- Unindexed materials

Conclusion
- Further suggestions
- Time and charge estimates
- Recommendation of other researchers (if appropriate)

This quickly answers our friend's query, but a quick-fix response can turn into a long-range problem. When our friend reviews our note five years from now, she'll have a slew of questions: What are we talking about here? Are we referring to Luke Sr. or Luke Jr.? What *exactly* did she ask us to check? Did we look for his probate record or his trial for bigamy? Or did she even know about the other wife at the time she wrote us to check the courthouse? Figure 21 would have answered most of those questions for her, no matter the time lapse. The "Hi" note won't.

The moral: whether we respond to a correspondent who is a close friend or a total stranger, we still should provide thorough details of the problem we investigated.

Formal reports

The characteristics that distinguish formal reports from informal ones are *tone, voice,* and *length*. A formal report is impersonal in voice. If a personal relationship exists between us and our correspondent, it does not inject itself into the report. In short, while a letter report is written from the standpoint of *you . . . I . . . your . . . my,* a formal report does not use these words. This type of presentation is also usually longer, more detailed, and more flexible. Its exact format depends upon the nature of the assignment, although basic elements comprise the points covered in figure 23.

COVER LETTER

Of course, some writers and recipients dislike the impersonal tone of a formal report. It's cold, they argue; but a compromise exists. Our report can be formal, preserving the marks of professionalism and businesslike practices that prevail in society, while our friendliness is conveyed in a cover letter. There, if we wish to discuss our poodle's puppies, the discussion will not be circulated as part of our professional report—and future users of the report will not wonder whether our discussion of "Samantha's little ones" refers to previously unknown offspring of their family.

PRELIMINARY BACKGROUND

Of the five major sections of a formal report (as shown in figure 23), the least flexible is the preliminary background. Here we find several important aspects that are often omitted from research reports. Each of these—when overlooked—can irritate or frustrate readers of the report.

- *Identification of client.* If this is a report we make to ourselves after completing a segment of research, we need only enter "Personal File Copy." Our own identification would appear as a letterhead.

- *Identification of subject.* Here we should enter the name of the individual(s) upon whom we focused—with relevant dates and locations, as well as data on spouse(s).

- *Summary of problem.* If this is our first report for a new correspondent, then we should briefly recap the information provided by the client and any prior researcher(s). If this is a follow-up assignment by us—part of an ongoing project— then we should summarize the data and the problem as it existed when we completed our last report. Thus, each assignment leads systematically into the next.

Whether we respond to a correspondent who is a close friend or a stranger, we still should provide thorough details of the problem we investigated.

RESEARCH REPORTS

- *Reiteration of instructions.* It is important to define the assignment that was given us—or the one we imposed upon ourselves, if this is a personal project.

- *Limitations upon assignment.* The quality and thoroughness of our research is often affected by time or financial restrictions, by displaced records, or client preferences. We state those limitations, tactfully.

- *Identification of repositories or collections used.* Let's be explicit. If we are German genealogists working in Karlsruhe, we'll likely know that the von Gemmingen files are there at the Generallandesarchiv. But someone from Cairo (Illinois or Egypt) who sees our report on the Internet probably won't know that.

Why all this background? It takes a few extra minutes—but only a few—to repeat our understanding of the instructions, to state the limits upon the project, and to review the previously known data. Yes, those few minutes are "taken away from actual research time," but doing so is still in the best interest of both the client and ourselves—in several ways.

Value to client

As we begin the report, this review of objectives serves as a final check, to ensure that we have indeed covered all the requested points. It helps us orient our report toward those objectives, rather than dwelling on something in the project that intrigued *us*. It helps us to accentuate our positive findings and better identify the potential disappointments we will want to explain.

Value to us as professionals

Great disparity often exists between client expectations and their budgets; yet finances are a delicate matter. In subsequent contacts with correspondents and other professionals, clients frequently refer to their hiring of a particular researcher and state that he or she "could not solve the problem." Usually, they circulate the report. Readers who know the subject area may be aghast at an apparent "shallowness" of work or an "irrelevant" search on the part of the professional. Yet, the perceived ineptitude may result from the limitations the client placed on the project or misinformation the client provided as the basis of the investigation. Professionals whose reports do not state the background given or limitations placed by the client set a stage for years of unfair and damaging criticism of their work.

Value to us as researchers

In the months and years ahead, we need a base—a reference point—for evaluating our own notes. At future dates, we will know more about this family than we do now. We will have identified other connections and straightened out some erroneous detail we now believe. When we come back to these notes later, we will have many questions. Exactly what information served as the basis of this research? Exactly what angles did we explore? Did we have time to adequately make this search? Were all the records available to us at the time? Even if we are conducting personal research rather than client work, the larger issue here is simple: as family historians, do we not deserve to give *ourselves* the same quality research report that a good professional would provide a client?

> Do we not deserve to give *ourselves* the same quality research report that a good professional would provide a client?

BODY OF REPORT

The body of a formal report is where the greatest amount of variation occurs. Its scope and structure primarily depend upon the nature of the assignment. Thus, it is germane to examine common types of assignments and suggest fitting approaches.

Assignment: record searching

Figure 25 outlines a typical report structure for a general records search that produced limited results. The length of such a report would usually not exceed several pages. A common concern among preparers of this type of report is whether to provide abstracts or photocopies. While no rigid rule exists, a rule of thumb can be offered:

Make photocopies when
- a vital date or proof of relationship appears in a record.
- a question exists about the reading or interpretation of any passage.
- an actual signature appears in the document.
- a client requests them.

Make abstracts when
- none of the above considerations exists.
- photocopying is not permitted.

If we append photocopies, the body of our report should still offer properly documented abstracts of those records—for three reasons. *First,* documents attached to a typed report frequently are not duplicated when copies of that report are circulated. If abstracts of relevant documents do not appear in the report, then our most crucial findings are overlooked. *Second,* users of our report may not be experienced in reading pre-modern handwriting and would benefit by the guidance of our typed summaries. *Third,* the details of documents are easier to comprehend and reconsult when they are set forth in clear type. Chapter 16, Transcripts and Abstracts, provides more detailed guidance on this subject.

Record agents who provide photocopies and abstracts of legal records should consider one further service in their reports: explaining to clients the meaning of legal terminology used within the documents they uncover. Most serious genealogists own a copy of *Black's Law Dictionary;*[11] but most clients and casual researchers usually don't. When we present an abstract that contains a legal term (for example, a reference to a will *cum testamento annexo*), we would help most users of our work if we add a brief note with the definition from *Black's.*

Assignment: analysis and planning

Many clients prefer to do their own research but seek professional help in the evaluation of their evidence. Figures 25 and 26 outline a typical structure for the body of a report that we prepare when asked to analyze someone's research files and plan their future work. The most difficult section may well be the discussion of strengths and weaknesses. It must be frank, but it must be tactful. As always, a good human-relations strategy is to present the positive points first, before launching into negative ones. Our analysis section might be structured like the sample in figure 27—presenting first an overall analysis and then focusing upon specific concerns.

> Record agents should consider another service in their reports: explaining to clients the meaning of legal terminology used within the documents they uncover.

RESEARCH REPORTS

FIG. 25
OUTLINE FOR
BODY OF REPORT:
ANALYSIS & PLANNING

**Outline for
Body of Report:
Analysis and Planning**

———

Assignment:

**Analyze existing files
and
prepare research plan**

———

Analysis:

Overall evaluation
• Strengths
• Weaknesses

Specific concerns
• Comments
• Questions

Research Plan:

• Materials and repositories to
search—including
    • Location
    • Special advice on usage
• Estimated time and charges for each
• Recommendation of other
researchers (if appropriate)

**Outline for
Body of Report:
Problem Solving**

———

Assignment:

**Identify father
of Peter Periwinkle**

———

Limitations: None

———

Results:
Extensive indirect evidence
suggests a likely identity

———

Summary of findings
• Highlight positive results
• Explain negative results

Actual findings

COUNTY-LEVEL RECORDS
• Research calendar
• Abstracts (with analyses)

CENSUS RECORDS
• Research calendar
• Abstracts

[OTHER RECORD TYPES]
• Research calendar
• Abstracts

Conclusion
• Further suggestions
• Time estimates
• Recommendation of
other researchers
(if appropriate)

Appendixes
• Photocopied documents
• Charts, maps, etc.
• Index (if needed)

FIG. 26
OUTLINE FOR
BODY OF REPORT:
PROBLEM SOLVING

FIG. 27
PRELIMINARY ANALYSIS

MILLS   SMITH REPORT NO. 1   3 MAY 1999

Analysis of Files:

This vast set of materials provides impressive evidence of extensive research performed by the client and his colleagues. In their efforts to track all Smiths of the Southeast, they have covered a far broader geographic area than is typical and have examined a much wider range of resources. They have duly considered variant spellings and have well organized their materials. It is a pleasure to work with such files.

The primary problem seen in these files stems from the breadth of the work attempted. The exceedingly large number of Smiths and their widespread distribution have precluded studying any of these Smith families in the *depth* necessary to resolve thorny problems of relationship.

As a result, so many potentially useful records remain to be covered that it is premature to form any judgment as to the parentage of John Jones Smith. . . . [etc.]

Specific Concerns

FILE: JOHN JONES SMITH

1. COMMENT: By letter of 2 February 1997, Olive Knockwurst informed client that John Jones Smith was an 1815 resident of Washington County, Mississippi. As evidence she cites a petition of Washington County residents photocopied from "Carter, *Territorial Papers,* vol. 5." On that basis she suggests that client should visit Washington County, Mississippi, to search for further records.

However, modern Washington County, Mississippi, did not exist in 1815. Carter's reference is to a site in modern Alabama, which—prior to 1817—was part of Mississippi Territory. Appendix A (a photocopy of the 1818 John Melish Map of Alabama) depicts the area settled by Smith and the neighbors who joined him in the signing of that petition.

2. QUESTION: Client shows that two of John's children married about 1820. In both cases, ministers are identified by name but not by religion. Is a church affiliation known for either? If so, is that church still functioning? Do records survive?

3. ... [etc.]

ASSIGNMENT: PROBLEM SOLVING

Figure 26 reflects a more complex assignment—one that calls for analyzing the client's problem, conducting research, evaluating each new document found, and reappraising the problem on the basis of the new material. In this hypothetical case, extensive indirect evidence emerged to support an answer, while pointing to other highly potential resources.

Organizing the body of a complex and lengthy report such as this can present special difficulties. Genealogists who thereafter use our work will have a dual need. So will we, if we are conducting an ongoing investigation in which the client expects us to maintain order and keep files up to date. In short:

RESEARCH REPORTS

For each family project, there needs to be one place in which we consolidate all relevant materials from a specific place, time, and resource.

• For each family project, there needs to be one place in which we consolidate all relevant material from a specific place, time, and resource—as, for example, all probate files from Timbuctoo County that relate to the Periwinkles. Time and again, it will be necessary to reappraise a specific record in context with the other similar material found on friends, relatives, in-laws, neighbors, and associates.

• For each individual, there needs to be one place in which all relevant material *on that one person* is concisely summarized—i.e., a chronological compendium of abstracts (properly cited) from all documents found to date on this one individual.

A research report for an extensive project is most efficiently prepared with the aid of a word processor (to create the research report) *and* a genealogical software program with precise footnoting capability (to create the individual data summaries). Following the outlines shown in figures 23 and 26, one procedure might be:

Report file

1. Open a report file when the planning stage begins.

2. Import or type our standard format and boilerplate for the preliminary background—i.e., client name and address, details of the problem, client instructions, research limitations (time, money, record loss, etc.), and other necessary background.

3. Based on that data, identify the repositories and collections that we will likely search. For efficiency, we may already have created resource databases, with full citations and background information for those repositories and materials we regularly use in our specialty. If so, we need only select the appropriate items and import the boilerplate into this new report.

4. Add our preliminary analysis of the problem and our research plan, then print the file for use as an on site guide. (Prudence and safety also suggest that we make a backup of this preliminary material—on a removable disk, tape, or CD.)

5. On site, enter research notes directly into this client file, using a laptop computer.

6. When our allotted search time is over, add any untyped notes, an analysis of the individual records, a reappraisal of the problem based on these findings, and a strategy for continuing the search—all within the portion of the assignment that was reserved for the preparation of the research report.

Individual data summaries (genealogy software)

If we use genealogical database software—either for ourselves or for an ongoing client project—another step is needed. Any new information found on an individual who is already in our genealogical database (or who should be added to our database) would be extracted from the research notes and photocopied records. Assuming that our genealogical program allows for attaching lengthy comments to "individual records" (as good ones do), then we need only make an electronic cut-and-paste to transfer, from the research report to the individual records, all abstracts and analytical comments that relate to each individual on whom we maintain an electronic file.

Thus, our family group sheets are updated, with documentation—either for our personal use or for adding to the client report as an appendix.

CONCLUDING RECOMMENDATIONS

Most research reports benefit immensely from a final list of work remaining to be done. This may cover resources in our own area that we did not have time to examine in the present assignment. It may include new prospects suggested by the details of the records we've just found. It may cite potentially useful materials existing in areas that we cannot personally access. If we are preparing a report for our own files, now is the best time to make that work list, while all details of the problem are fresh in our minds. If we are submitting this report to a client, he or she will appreciate these suggestions. Often, they generate a follow-up assignment. At other times, it may be more appropriate for the client to use a researcher in a newly opened area. Some clients will prefer to explore those new possibilities themselves. If so, we have not "lost business" or "given away our expertise for nothing," by suggesting materials elsewhere. When we invest in good service and goodwill, that investment always brings a generous return.

Even the best quality research can disappoint a client. When a particular assignment does not complete a client's objective, it is even more important that we present our quality research in a positive manner. Our analysis of the results should help the reader understand why the findings were negative, how the elimination of certain possibilities has actually advanced the project toward a specific goal, and the fact that the present body of evidence—even though it is inconclusive now—can be the proverbial straws from which solid bricks eventually are made.

OTHER AIDS

A complex report frequently requires special finding aids. An index to names and places is immensely valuable in a long report. Equally helpful can be a table of contents that provides quick access to the various divisions of the research notes. Ancestor charts, family group sheets, individual data summaries, and maps—along with the expected photocopies—could be useful appendixes to help a client better understand the results of our work.

> When we invest in good service and goodwill, that investment always brings a generous return.

Summary Concepts

The purposes of a research report are to record the results of a research segment, to identify the factors and assumptions that influenced the scope of that project, and to lay a sound foundation for future research that will avoid wasted effort. A well-organized report is a powerful aid and a joy to use. A report that is deficient in the areas covered here can be frustrating, confusing, and misleading.

Any instance in which a consumer arranges for genealogical research is a case in which that individual is buying a product sight unseen. Wise consumers will investigate the reputation of the researcher. They will satisfy reasonable doubts that the person they commission has the necessary experience, skill, and judgment to provide a worthwhile service. Nonetheless, they still buy a product sight unseen, because they will not be there to see that service performed or to see the quality of the judgments they receive. The only means by which the consumer can judge the end product is the research report that is produced.

RESEARCH REPORTS

If we are the researcher who has accepted that assignment, we place our reputation at stake with every report we prepare—regardless of how brief or how complex it is. If we are the consumer who has purchased that product, we need to recognize the qualities of sound research and good reporting. If we are avocational genealogists striving for excellence in our personal work, then we will want to create—for ourselves and our progeny—research reports that offer quality evidence and the soundest of foundations upon which future work can be built.

NOTES

1. For a digest of prevailing standards expected of all types of genealogists and for other sample research reports, see Board for Certification of Genealogists, *The BCG Genealogical Standards Manual* (Orem, Utah: Ancestry, 2000).

2. Cern McLellan, *The Complete Book of Practical Proverbs & Wacky Wit* (Wheaton, Illinois: Tyndale House Publishers, 1996), 245.

3. Anyone who suffered through grammar classes in school should be delighted at the latest generation of manuals by mavens who believe learning should be fun, particularly: Patricia T. O'Conner, *Woe Is I: The Grammarphobe's Guide to Better English in Plain English* (New York: G. P. Putnam's Sons, 1996); and Constance Hale, *Sin and Syntax: How to Craft Wickedly Effective Prose* (New York: Random House, 1999).

4. Parts of this discussion are drawn from Elizabeth Shown Mills, "Your Research Report," *OnBoard* [newsletter of the Board for Certification of Genealogists] 2 (May 1996): 9–13. An important auxiliary article that readers are strongly encouraged to consult is Helen F. M. Leary, CG, CGL, FASG, "Reporting Standards: *Client Research* v. *Personal Research*," *OnBoard* 4 (May 1998): 9–10.

5. Marc Erlitz, e-mail message from <mmarc@erlitz.com> to author, 5 January 1999.

6. *Revolutionary War Pension and Bounty Land Warrant Application Files, 1800–1900*, M804 (Washington: National Archives, n.d.), 2,670 rolls.

7. *Numbered Record Books Concerning Military Operations and Service, Pay and Settlement of Accounts, and Supplies in the War Department Collection of Revolutionary War Records*, M853 (Washington: National Archives, n.d.), 41 rolls; and *Special Index to Numbered Records in the War Department Collection of Revolutionary War Records, 1775–1783*, M847 (Washington: National Archives, n.d.), 39 rolls.

8. Elizabeth Shown Mills, *Evidence! Citation & Analysis for the Family Historian* (Baltimore: Genealogical Publishing Co., 1997). An electronic version that can be taken with us on site, to assist in citing any record sources that may be unfamiliar to us, is available from Genealogy.com.

9. This subject has been further addressed in Helen S. Ullmann, CG, "Better Books from Computer Programs," *OnBoard* 5 (September 1999): 21–23; and Elizabeth Shown Mills and Gary B. Mills, "Editors' Corner: Wizardry with Words," *National Genealogical Society Quarterly* 88 (March 2000): 3.

10. Appreciation is due to Anne S. Anderson, formerly of the L. W. Anderson Genealogical Library, Gulfport, Mississippi, for sharing this letter report which she received from a researcher she *once* employed. Names are therein obscured to protect the guilty.

11. Henry Campbell Black, *Black's Law Dictionary: Definitions of the Terms and Phrases of American and English Jurisprudence, Ancient and Modern*. 6th edition (St. Paul, Minnesota: West Publishing Co., 1990).

FIG. 28
FORMAL REPORT

ELIZABETH SHOWN MILLS, CG, CGL, FASG
MILLS RESEARCH SERVICE
————————————————————————1732 RIDGEDALE DRIVE, TUSCALOOSA, AL 35406

DATE: 15 January 2000

REPORT TO: Jane Doe, 123 Anystreet, Middletown, US 00000

SUBJECT: William Preston Hickman of Natchitoches and Rapides Parishes, Louisiana

Born:	1804	Shelbyville, Kentucky	
Died:	1842	Shelbyville, Kentucky	
Married:			
Marianne Baillio	c.1832	Rapides Parish, Louisiana	

Known children:

Nancy Virginia	b. 1835
Mary Felonise	b. ca. 1836
William Paschal	b. 1838
John Webster	b. 1840
George Washington	b. 1842

Alleged kin:
Brothers:

Peter Terry	b. 1810	d. 1853
Thomas Jefferson	b. 1812	d. 1856

Parents:

William Hickman Jr.	"of Kentucky & Virginia"
Mary (Webster) Hickman	" "

Ancestors:

Thomas Hickman	Virginia
wife: Eltonhead (Conway)	Virginia
Daniel Webster	"statesman"

BACKGROUND: Client has supplied the above data, from an undated, typed, 23-page manuscript: "The Hickman Family," by Dr. G. M. G. Stafford, Alexandria, Louisiana

OBJECTIVE: Prove ancestry of William Preston Hickman. If alleged line is correct, client can attach to an approved Colonial Dames lineage.

ASSIGNMENT: Search Natchitoches and Rapides for all possible data on subject and his direct ancestors. Client states she has no interest in pursuing the subject's siblings.

REPOSITORY: My personal library of microfilmed, manuscript, and published Louisiana records.

LIMITATIONS: 8 hours for first research segment.

ANALYSIS OF PROBLEM

Although the Hickman manuscript offers no documentation, it was accepted as "proof" by Colonial Dames in a past era in which research standards were less demanding. Client recognizes weaknesses in the line and hopes to obtain the evidence necessary to prove the alleged relationships.

RESEARCH REPORTS

FIG. 28
FORMAL REPORT
(CONT.)

> E. S. MILLS TO JANE DOE   15 JANUARY 2000   PAGE 2

ANALYSIS (continued):

The primary problem with the lineage, as presented by Dr. Stafford, centers upon Kentucky. According to Stafford, our subject's father and grandfather (William Jr. and Sr.) moved from Virginia to Kentucky, where the 1790 tax lists shows a William Jr. and Sr. in Fayette County and another William Jr. and Sr. in Woodford County. Stafford concludes:

> "Which of these [were our forebears], we are not certain. . . . Be that as it may, the line of descent [to the immigrant ancestor] is as follows. . . ." (p. 3)

Stafford states that no research has been done in Kentucky to better identify any of the four Williams of 1790. Until this is done, it is premature to propose any colonial ancestry for William Preston Hickman.

For the requested Louisiana research, two problems exist:

1.   Rapides's parish-level records were destroyed on 1 May 1864 when Union forces burned the town. Some auxiliary records exist elsewhere, which may be relevant in the Hickman case.

2.   Client has hoped to restrict research to her direct line—ignoring records created by siblings—but that would be a serious mistake. In many cases (including the present one), the records created by collateral relatives offer clues to ancestry that supplement those left by direct ancestors.

CALENDAR OF RECORDS SEARCHED

Natchitoches Parish, Louisiana

OFFICE OF THE CLERK OF COURT
Conveyances (recorded volumes), 1815–80
Successions (recorded volumes and original packets), 1815–80
Marriages (recorded licenses, returns, and contracts), 1815–80
District Court Index, 1815–80*
Parish Court Index, 1815–80*

> *Note by esm:*
> Actual district and parish court files were not checked for want of access. Records can be ordered from parish clerk using citations provided by the indexes.

OTHER ORIGINAL SOURCES
Natchitoches Courier [extant only for 1825–27]

DERIVATIVE SOURCES
American State Papers: Documents Legislative and Executive of the Congress of the United States. 38 vols. Washington, D.C.: Gales & Seaton, 1832–61. Searched only *Public Lands* series, 7 vols.
Mills, Elizabeth Shown. *Natchitoches Church Marriages, 1817–1850: Translated Abstracts from the Registers of St. François des Natchitoches in Louisiana.* Tuscaloosa: Mills Historical Press, 1983.

Federal Census Records

1820, 1830, and 1840: Natchitoches and Rapides Parishes, Louisiana (population schedules only)

**FIG. 28
FORMAL REPORT
(CONT.)**

E. S. MILLS TO JANE DOE   15 JANUARY 2000   PAGE 3

SUMMARY OF FINDINGS

[*See Research Notes for complete details.*]

1. William Preston Hickman was indeed a brother of Peter Terry and Thomas Jefferson Hickman. See attached abstracts from St. François Parish, as translated in my *Natchitoches Church Marriages, 1817–1850* (Tuscaloosa: Mills Historical Press, 1983), 60, 95, 121.

   These three men were indeed the sons of one William Hickman and his wife Mary (née Webster). However, no Kentucky origin has been established for them. To the contrary, William P.'s marriage record states that he was born in North Carolina. Peter T., at marriage, reported that his parents were "of Tennessee." This migration pattern would fit the traditional birth dates given for William (1804, North Carolina); and Peter (1810, Tennessee).

2. William P. Hickman first appeared in Natchitoches Parish records in December 1830, as a resident of Arkansas (Conv. Bk. 10: 82); but he had settled in Louisiana by 1833 (Conv. Bk. 19: 83–84). His brother Peter T., in 1833, still resided in Arkansas, no county stated. (Ibid.) However, prior to 1834, one William Hickman operated salt mines in Hempstead County, apparently in conjunction with the prominent Chester Ashley and John Clark. (*American State Papers: Public Lands* [Washington: Gales & Seaton, 1860], 6:945.)

3. Natchitoches deeds reveal that the three brothers achieved extraordinary wealth from plantations along Louisiana's Red River in the 1830s and 1840s. (See 10:82, 19: 83–84; 23:41–44.)

4. Although William P. and Peter T. each had a young family in 1840, neither appears as a householder that year in Natchitoches or Rapides. There is found one Mary Hickman, a female head-of-household of extraordinary wealth, who is of age to be their mother and lives in the same neighborhood. (1840 U.S. census, Rapides Parish, p. 209, line 6.)

SUGGESTIONS FOR FURTHER RESEARCH

1. **Census research** needs completing, including Arkansas 1820–40, and Rapides/Natchitoches 1850–80. The 1850–80 search should include mortality, slave, agricultural, and manufacturing schedules, as well as the population schedules. (Time estimate: 4–6 hours.)

2. **Hempstead County, Arkansas,** resources should be thoroughly searched for this Hickman family. Here we may find other clues for identifying the specific points of origin in Tennessee and North Carolina. (Time estimate: 1–2 days. For economy, an onsite researcher should be employed.)

3. **U.S. General Land Office Files** at the National Archives should be obtained for each tract mentioned in the attached notes as having been purchased at the Ouachita Land Office, as well as for the salt-lick lands held by William Hickman in Hempstead County. (Time estimate: 1 hour to order; additional time to review.)

4. **Parish and District Court Files of Natchitoches Parish** contain two suits generated by William P. Hickman. These should be ordered from the Clerk of Court, using citations provided in the attached research notes. (Time estimate: ½ hour to order; additional time to review.)

5. **Rapides Parish Newspapers** should be read. For the relevant period, there exist the *Alexandria Gazette & Planter's Intelligence* [1829–34, scattered issues] and the *Red River Republican* [1847–53, relatively complete]. (Time estimate: 6 hours.)

6. **New Orleans Archdiocesan Records,** Archives Department, Notre Dame University, Notre Dame, Indiana, should be searched for marriage dispensations issued to the three Hickman brothers. (Time estimate: uncertain. For economy, an onsite researcher should be employed.)

It has been a pleasure to assist the client with this phase of her research. Should she wish me to proceed with any of the above suggestions, I would be happy to do so.

Elizabeth Shown Mills

RESEARCH REPORTS

FIG. 28
FORMAL REPORT
(CONT.)

E. S. Mills to Jane Doe   15 January 2000   Page 6

RESEARCH NOTES

Natchitoches Parish, Louisiana: Published Sources

Elizabeth Shown Mills
Natchitoches Church Marriages, 1817–1850 . . .
St. François des Natchitoches in Louisiana
Tuscaloosa: Mills Historical Press, 1983

p. 60, no. 236 (citing Register 11, no. 9-1833)
"WILLIAM PRESTON HICKMAN (s)
MARYANNE BAILLOT (x)
19 March 1833
Groom: lawful son of William Hickman and Mary Webster, native of North Carolina and now residing in the parish of Natchitoches. Bride: lawful daughter of Auguste Baillio and of Felonize Lessart [Layssard], residents of the parish of Rapides. Married at the Rapides plantation of Mr. Auguste Baillio. Witnesses: Peter T. Hickman (s); B. Jarreau (s); Joseph Lattier (s); F^s Baillio (s). Priest: Blanc."

Note by esm:
This record contradicts the Kentucky birthplace alleged by Stafford. It supports the contention that William Preston had a brother Peter Terry. The *(s)* and *(x)* used by this publication signify signatures and x-marks. See attached photocopy from cited church register.

p. 95, no. 369 (citing Register 12, no. 24-1837)
"PETER TERRY HICKMAN (s)
LOUISE DÉSIRÉE GAIENNIE (s)
4 October 1837
Groom: major and lawful son of William Hickman and Mary Webster of the state of Tennessee. Bride: minor and lawful daughter of François Gaiennié and Louise Désirée Lalande Ferrier, 'all residing in this parish.' Witnesses: W. P. Hickman (s); F^çois Gaiennié (s); F^çois Metoyer (s); Thomas J. Hickman (s); F. M. Normand (s); L. Desirée Gaiennié née LaLande Ferrière (s); Phanor Prudhomme (s); V. Archinard (s); Valery Gaiennié (s); Benjamin Metoyer (s); C? Duc*otel?* (s). Priest: D'haund."

Note by esm:
Although client stated that she was not interested in records on her ancestor's siblings, this one illustrates the importance of including such data in her study. Note the following:

- While Stafford places the parental family in Kentucky and William P.'s marriage record states a birth in North Carolina, the above document places the parents in Tennessee.

- This marriage record for Peter T. also supports Stafford's contention that he and William had a brother named Thomas Jefferson Hickman.

See attached photocopy from cited church register.

p. 121, no. 490 (citing Register 12: unnumbered entries)
"THOMAS J. HICKMAN (s)
J? EMMA GAIENNIÉ (s)
22 February 1841. 1 ban.
Groom: lawful son of Mr. William Hickman and Mary Webster. Bride: Lawful daughter of François Gaiennié and Louise Désirée Lalande Ferrière. Dispensation from impediment resulting from difference in faiths.

Note that explanations by the researcher are clearly set apart from the transcription.

Also note explanation that the abbreviations (s) and (x) are used in the quoted book.

Underscored portion of "Ducotel," followed by an underscored question mark, flags a questionable interpretation of name.

Scope of research has gone beyond client's expectations. Because the researcher's professional judgment deemed it essential, justification is given to client.

FIG. 28
FORMAL REPORT
(CONT.)

E. S. Mills to Jane Doe   15 January 2000   Page 5

Mills, *Natchitoches Church Marriages* (cont.)
Witnesses: Vve [Widow] F^{çois} Gaiennié (s); B^{min} Metoyer (s); John H. Ransdell (s); P. T. Hickman (s); Valery Gaiennié (s). Priest: Pascual."

Note by esm:
Again, a sibling's record offers new family information and additional possibilities for research. Although all three Hickmans married Catholic girls, Thomas was not Catholic and his brothers were undoubtedly raised in the same faith as Thomas. Dispensation records for this period exist in the New Orleans Archdiocesan Records at the archives of Notre Dame University, Notre Dame, Indiana. See attached photocopy from cited church register.

American State Papers: Documents Legislative and Executive of the Congress of the United States.
38 vols. Washington, D.C.: Gales & Seaton, 1832–61
Public Lands series, 7 vols.

Note by esm:
Numerous index entries appear for relevant names (and for other Hickman names in Natchitoches and Rapides), as follows:

Asa	Natchitoches Parish	4: 108, 135, 144, 146
James	Natchitoches Parish	4: 109, 144
Theophilus	Natchitoches Parish	3: 449; 4: 108, 144
* William:	Natchitoches Ph., La., 1825	4: 109, 135, 144
**William	Arkansas, 1834	6: 945
William:	SW Miss., 1806–15	1: 901, 2: 248; 3: 438–39
	St. Helena Ph., La. 1812	3: 69
	St. Tammany Ph., La., 1811	3: 72
	Missouri, 1812	3: 349

*   This William was an associate of Asa, James, and Theophilus; their land was located on Bayou Santabarb in extreme western Louisiana, dozens of miles from the families into which client's ancestors married.

**   *This William should be pursued.* As subsequently seen, client's family came to Louisiana from Arkansas in stages, beginning about 1830. *American State Papers* cites no county of residence in Arkansas for this William; but *the land description in the abstract below places him in what was then Hempstead County (present Sevier).*

PL 6: 945
Lands sold in District of Little Rock, prior to 26 February 1834:

Cert. no. 164	Jno. Clark & Chest. Ashley	E½ SE¼ S11 T10S R29W	80a	$100
Cert. no. 165	" " " " "			
Cert. no. 166 ‡	William Hickman	W½ SE¼ S11 T11S R29W	80a	$100
Cert. no. 167 ‡	" "	E½ SW¼ " " "	"	"
Cert. no. 173 ‡	" "	E½ NW¼ " " "	"	"

‡ *Note by government clerk:*
"These tracts contain salt licks; purchase money directed to be refunded."

Note 2 items here:

1. *The transcribed record is continued from one page of the report to another. Thus, an identification of the source, in short form, appears on the continuation page.*

2. *The French abbreviation "Vve" is likely unfamiliar to the recipient. Thus, the researcher adds a translation in brackets.*

For the data in the added note marked **, the researcher used a township-range map and converted the book's cryptic detail (shown below the note) into a specific county location for client.

RESEARCH REPORTS

FIG. 28
FORMAL REPORT
(CONT.)

*Note bracketed explana-
tions of uncommon terms
"arpent" and "succession."*

*Note bracketed explanation
of signatures and bracketed alternative spelling of
the hard-to-read "Goedon."*

*Note bracketed correction
of misspelled location,
"Washita."*

*Note underscoring used to
flag an obvious error in land
description.*

*Another bracketed note in-
dicates that the "signature"
is not an autograph. The circumstance warrants flag-
ging in each and every case.*

E. S. Mills to Jane Doe   15 January 2000   Page 6

Natchitoches Parish, Louisiana: Original Sources

Office of the Clerk of Court
Conveyance Book 10: 82
30 December 1830, at Rapides (copied 6 June 1832, Rapides; recorded [no date] at Natchitoches)
John Goodman Young of Rapides to William Preston Hickman "of the Territory of Arkansas," sale of land in Natchitoches Parish, fronting on Rigolet de Bon Dieu, 700 arpents [1 arpent = ca. 2/3 acre]. Young purchased from succession [estate] of Thomas Graham, dec'd. Land is bounded above by "claim of Dubois" and below by John Hudson. $9,087.50 payable by $2,000 due 10 February 1831; $2,362.50 due 15 January 1832; $2,362.50 due 15 January 1833; $2,362.50 due 15 January 1834, with 10% interest. Survey is to be made of the tract; if it measures less than 700 arpents, price will be adjusted $13 per arpent. Young still owes one payment to estate of Graham, due 3 September 1831; if Young fails to pay, Hickman may pay and deduct that, with interest, from his first installment to Young. Signed [actual signatures not in record book]: John G. Young (s); Wm. P. Hickman (s); John M. Jett (s); John A. Amelon (s); J. B. Scott, Notary. 8 Feb. 1831, Young acknowledges receipt before James M. Goedon [Gridon?], Jno. A. Ameling, and J. B. Scott, notary.

Conveyance Book 19: 83–84
27 March 1833 (recorded: no date)
William Preston Hickman of Natchitoches Parish to Thomas Jefferson Hickman of same, sale for $8,620 cash, the following tracts purchased by William at U.S. land office in Washita [Ouachita Parish, present town of Monroe], for which patents are to be issued by the U.S. government:

Lot 1	S6	T6	R3W	51	acres
Lots 5 & 6	S31	T7	R3W	170.36	acres
Lots 2 & 3	S31	T7	R3W	153.72	acres
SE½ SW¼	S30	T7	R3W	79.34	acres
SE½ SE ¼	S30	T7	R3W	79.275	acres

Signed [actual signatures not in record book]: Wm. P. Hickman (s); Thos. J. Hickman (s); R. Finnelly (s); F. C. Tauzin (s); C. E. Greneaux, Parish Judge (s).

Conveyance Book 19: 84
27 March 1833 (recorded n.d.)
William Preston Hickman of Natchitoches Parish to Peter Terry Hickman, "now a resident of the Territory of Arkansas" for $9,583, the following tract purchased by William at Washita Land Office, for which patents have been received:

Lot 2	S10	T6	R3W	88.67	acres
"Fractical"	S9	T6	R3W	39.61	acres
Lot 1	S5	T6	R3W	79.55	acres
SW¼	S4	T6	R3W	163.25	acres
W½ NW¼	S4	T6	R3W	81.63	acres

also land purchased by WPH of John Hinson and Ursula Hinson, his wife, both of the Territory of Arkansas, by deed of 21 December 1832, as follows

Lots 2 & 3	S5	T6	R3W	206.16	acres

Signed [actual signatures not in record book]: Wm. P. Hickman (s); P. T. Hickman (s); F. C. Tauzin (s); A^d Lauve, *fils* (s); C. E. Greneaux, Parish Judge (s).

FIG. 28
FORMAL REPORT
(CONT.)

E. S. Mills to Jane Doe   15 January 2000   Page 7

Natchitoches Parish, Louisiana: Original Sources (cont.)

Office of the Clerk of Court (cont.)
Conveyance Book 21: 398
2 April 1836 (recorded 19 May 1836)
William Hickman of Natchitoches Parish to Joseph Cummings, for $200, sale of 640 acres on Bayou Santabarb, bounded on lower by lands claimed by William Cummings [no legal description]. Signed [actual signatures not in record book]: William Hickman (x); Joseph Cummings (x); John H. Mears (s); Henry S. Roach (s).

> *Note by esm:*
> The above document is surely executed by a different William Hickman—for three reasons: (1) He X'd, while William Preston Hickman signed. (2) He used no middle name or initial, while William Preston consistently did. (3) His Bayou Santabarb land is in an entirely different part of the parish from the region in which William Preston and brothers settled.

Conveyance Book 23: 41–44
14 February 1838 (recorded n.d.)
Marginal notation: "reinscribed 13 Jan. 1848; mortgage canceled [n.d.] Bk M: 313–15"
William Preston Hickman and wife, Mary Ann Baillio, sell to William Smith of Huntsville, Alabama, 1317.58 acres, described as:

1. 908 arpents purchased from John G. Young, "including that portion . . . . adjudged in favor of Hickman at a suit against William Plunket and others"
2. S32 T7 R3—625.58 acres entered by Hickman at Ouachita Land Office
3. S29 T7 R3—except for the SE¼ of SE¼, being 600 acres conveyed

Price: $140,000 to be paid by nine promissory notes, as follows: 2 notes of $10,000 due 1 June 1839; 2 notes of $10,000 due 1 June 1840; 5 notes, each of $20,000, each due 1 June of successive years, payable at counting house of W. M. Lambeth & Thompson, New Orleans at 10% interest. Two mortgages exist on land: $5,000 due to City Bank of New Orleans and $15,000 to Bank of Louisiana. Also Smith buys a tract entered at Ouachita Land Office, which "is to be included in mortgage assumed by Smith in favor of Hickman" — i.e.

E½ SE¼   S30   T7   R32   79.34 acres

Signed [actual signatures not in record book]: W. P. Hickman (s); Marianne Hickman (s); Wm. Smith (s); J. V. Bossier (s); T. E. Tauzin (s); C. E. Greneaux, Parish Judge (s).

> *Note by esm:* This document offers three possibilities for further research:
> 1. *Hickman* v. *Plunket et al.* suit
> 2. Business papers of the two New Orleans banks
> 3. Business papers of the factor, W. M. Lambeth & Thompson

Parish Court Index
Wm. P. Hickman vs. *Collier Graham* — microcopy PC.25 (1830)

> *Note by esm:*
> This document should be ordered from the Clerk of Court, Natchitoches.

Succession (Probate) Index
Marriage Index

> *Note by esm:*
> No relevant entry appears in either volume.

Note inclusion of "negative findings," so client will know the source has been searched.

RESEARCH REPORTS

FIG. 28
FORMAL REPORT
(CONT.)

Federal Censuses

1820 U.S. census, population schedule, National Archives microfilm M33, roll 31
1830 U.S. census, National Archives microfilm M19, roll 44

Note by esm:
No entry found in Natchitoches or Rapides for this Hickman family.

1840 U.S. census, population schedule, National Archives microfilm M704, rolls 127–28

Note by esm:
No entry found in Natchitoches or Rapides for William P. Hickman.
A possible sibling and mother appear, as follows:

Rapides Parish, Louisiana (M704, roll 128)
p. 209, line 6

Hickman, George W.	1 male	30–40	1 female	30–40	3 total
			1 female slave	24–36	

Note by esm:
William Preston Hickman named a son George W. The George W. above, the only other Hickman in the parish, is of the same age bracket as William P.'s brothers. However, this George's wealth is not comparable to that of client's family.

p. 216, line 24

Hickman, Mary	1 male	30–40	1 female	40–50	
	2 males	30–40	2 females	20–30	
	3 males	20–30	1 female	0–5	
	1 male	0– 5			
	5 male slaves	36–55	1 female slaves	36–55	58 in ag.
	10 male slaves	24–36	12 female slaves	24–36	
	25 male slaves	10–24	22 female slaves	10–24	
			3 female slaves	0–10	

neighborhood:

Nicolas & L. Gracia   HICKMAN
S. & Louis Wright   J. H. Hyrison?
Narcisse Laforee   Tim? Driscole
J. R. Meade   N. B. Gill
J. M. Moore   F. Wootten
[*cont. at right*]

Note by esm:

Two of the three known Hickman brothers were married by this time. If Stafford is correct, William P. (aged 30–40) and wife should have had 2 daughters and 2 sons by the date of this census. Peter T. should have had 2 daughters. The children's information in the above household does not suggest the presence of either young family.

This neighborhood is well known to the researcher from much prior work. It lies along the Rapides-Natchitoches parish border, near that of the Gaiennié family into which Peter T. and Thomas J. Hickman married.

Could this Mary Hickman be Mary, mother of William P., Peter T., and Thomas J.?

[*End of research notes for this assignment*]

Identification of neighbors is useful for identifying Mary Hickman's neighborhood and for linking her to William P.

(Actual report also included neighbors for George W. Hickman, but they are omitted from this condensed example to save space)

19

GENEALOGY
COLUMNS

Keynotes

Genealogy Columns

by Regina Hines Ellison, CGRS

Writers who promote family history through newspaper or magazine columns often feel a kinship to Ann Landers—or even Heloise. Most of these professionals give research tips, inform the public on new sources of information, and help readers solve their problems. Some have been known to reunite long-lost kin. Gradually, a bond develops; some readers even feel as if the writers are part of their own families. Being a columnist is a rewarding pursuit for the genealogist who enjoys writing, as well as teaching and helping others.

Surveys show that millions of people are interested in their forebears. Obviously, only a small percentage are seriously digging into the past. Comparatively few belong to genealogy or history societies, attend conferences or workshops, or subscribe to advanced-level journals. Through the popular media, genealogy columnists can not only reach active researchers but touch countless others who have a latent curiosity.

Genealogy column-writing is not a modern idea. Pioneering columns appeared in scattered papers of the late-nineteenth and early-twentieth centuries. The *Boston Transcript* carried a genealogy feature from 1872 until 1940—starting a question-and-answer format in 1896. The *Baltimore Sun* also ran a column from 1905 until 1908;[1] another in the *Hartford Times* predated World War One.[2] Of 175 or so columns published today in more than 200 newspapers, many were introduced in the late 1970s, when the Bicentennial and the novel *Roots* fueled an already spiraling interest in family history.[3] New columns continue to emerge, and many magazines that are not specifically genealogical in nature now include family-history features.

Many of today's columnists belong to the International Society of Family History Writers and Editors (ISFHWE).[4] Formed in 1987 as the Council of Genealogy Columnists, the society has grown steadily in membership. Its April 1997 publication, *Be a Genealogy Columnist,*[5] presents essays on myriad topics about genealogical writing—giving varied points of view and addressing many of the questions that budding column writers ask.

> Through the popular media, genealogy columnists can not only reach active researchers but also touch countless others who have a latent curiosity.

Breaking into the Field

Designing the column

As prospective columnists, the first decision we need to make is the format and composition of our offering. Most fall within one of the following types:

- *Ethnic columns.* Those that concentrate on specific ethnic groups are usually found in magazines or newspapers also marketed to those groups, although some popular magazines (such as *Heritage Quest*) have ethnic sections also.

- *General-interest columns.* Commonly seen in newspapers, these offer a potpourri of genealogical information—combining how-to articles, queries, news of genealogical happenings, and brief discussions of sources or new publications.

- *How-to columns.* Commonly, these are short essays on specific aspects of research—resources, methodology, or record interpretations. Most are found in popular print magazines and e-zines, or as special features at commercial genealogical websites.

- *Local-history columns.* Features on people, places, and happenings of the past are often popular with newspaper readers and subscribers to regional magazines—stimulating an interest in area history.

- *Query columns.* Of dwindling popularity today, but still seen, this traditional type of column presents questions from researchers who need help, seek correspondents working on mutual lines, or inquire about local places or events. The Internet is rapidly replacing the need for query columns in national-level publications, but they are still a staple of many local newspapers and genealogy society magazines.

- *Question-and-answer columns.* This genre is mushrooming everywhere, as new genealogists turn to the popular magazines and websites for advice. The columnist, who is expected to have considerable expertise in a specialized area, answers reader questions—selecting those that would be of most help to other researchers.

Attracting an editor

Depending upon the forum we target, our first hurdle may be to convince an editor that genealogy *is* a subject of wide interest to readers. Newspapers and magazines rarely seek out someone to be a genealogy columnist. Whether our idea is accepted or rejected often depends on the editor's personal interests, the policies of the publication, and the ability we show in the initial contact. If a first attempt is not successful, let's not be discouraged. We can simply try again later, or consider another forum.

Preparation improves our chances. Marketing surveys are as important here as they are in any business. If we have targeted our local newspaper or city magazine, we might rally the support of our area libraries and genealogy or history societies. With their help, we could gather approximate figures on how many people in our area might be interested in such a column. Most history society libraries and family history sections of public libraries keep track of the number of patrons who use their facilities. As prospective columnists, we might approach an editor with a letter outlining the need. If we have no response, we could follow the letter with a phone call. Persistence often pays off, but so does patience. Being pushy or obnoxious could be more harmful than helpful.

Preparation improves our chances. Marketing surveys are as important to commercial writing as they are to any business.

Making a persuasive presentation

THE PROPOSAL

When an editor shows interest and requests samples, we should have five to ten varied examples ready to submit. As we prepare these, we bear in mind several considerations:

- *Writing skill.* Editors look for the ability to present a subject in a clear, concise, and appealing manner. Submissions that need major editing don't sell themselves or us. Even if we are brilliant researchers, a manuscript filled with typographical errors, misspelled words, or poor grammar will sabotage our chances.

- *Length.* The amount of space devoted to special-interest columns varies with each publication, but articles of 450 to 600 words stand a better chance of acceptance than wordier submissions.

- *Flexibility.* The editor may recommend a format or have an idea that would make the column more appealing to readers. If we're novices, it's best to heed this advice.

- *Reliability.* As columnists, we must meet deadlines with no excuses—and demonstrate stick-to-it-iveness. "Popular" publications are reluctant to promote a special-focus column, only to have the writer lose interest after a few months.

We anticipate all these concerns and plan a convincing presentation. Our proposal should include not only the sample columns, but a resume listing previous work experiences and accomplishments—in genealogy or other pursuits—as well as personal references. Credentials increase our credibility in the view of both the editor and readers. If we are not certified in genealogy, we should consider taking this step.

THE INTERVIEW

When we secure an interview—in person or by telephone—we will want to discuss and take notes on several critical points:

- *Publication details.* We'll need an agreement as to the frequency of the column, the day of the week or month our material is due and (if for a newspaper) the day of the week it will appear, and the section of the publication in which it will be featured. Length restrictions must be clearly understood.

- *Style.* We need to know the publication's writing style and then buy a copy of the preferred style manual. Most newspapers use the *Associated Press Stylebook and Libel Manual*,[6] which sets forth professional standards for newswriting. Arranged alphabetically according to topic, the AP manual gives rules for abbreviation, punctuation, spelling, and word usage. Magazines often prefer other manuals. Whatever style the publication follows, the editor will expect us to follow also.

- *Mode of submission.* Many editors today prefer that writers prepare and submit their material electronically.

- *Copyrights.* We may wish to hold the copyright ourselves, offering the publisher first serial rights. This is greatly to our advantage should we ever decide to compile past columns into a book.

- *Compensation.* Informal surveys taken during the past ten years among ISFHWE members show that about one-third receive no remuneration or just a nominal sum. A few are already on the staff of the publication that sponsors their column. Occasionally, payment is by the inch; but most genealogy columnists report a standard per-column amount. A few write for more generous publishers

Editors look for the ability to present a subject in a clear, concise, and appealing manner.

who underwrite column-related expenses—perhaps business cards, books, subscriptions, or seminars. (Genealogy columnists also consider it a valuable perk to have first glimpse at new publications received for review. But many donate these works to local libraries or genealogy societies, after telling their readers about them.)

Writing the Column

Observing standards

A genealogy column is written for general appeal—not in the same style we use for scholarly journals. Not everyone who sees our work will be interested in genealogy, so our column needs to pique the public curiosity and motivate readers to begin their own searches. At the same time, we have to inform active researchers of wide-ranging expertise. The following tips help to ensure the appeal of our offering:

- *Avoid or explain words and terms special to research.* If, for example, we discuss the Soundex, then we define or describe what the Soundex is and how it is used. Several years ago at a meeting of one local genealogy society, a member of several years' standing whispered in this writer's ear during a program: "They keep talking about microfilm. What is microfilm?" Clearly, we cannot take for granted that even those who are involved in genealogy are familiar with every aspect of research.

- *Develop a unique voice.* This helps us relate to our readers. Styles of writing and methods of conveying a message to the reader differ between individual columnists. Analyzing the writing of others, taking classes, or reading books on writing technique can help; but the key to good style is practice at polishing our own prose. Let's not just write but *rewrite* and *rewrite*.

- *State the message simply.* To achieve clear writing, we can imagine ourselves telling a story to a friend. We will want to avoid cliches, "too cute" phrases, or remarks that could offend our readers.

- *Write tight.* As we review our draft, let's think how the same thoughts could be conveyed as clearly in fewer words. Style is not necessarily strict in column writing, but editors appreciate less fluff and more substance.

- *Prepare columns in advance of deadline.* It's wise to reread them after they have gone cold, then self-edit. Another day and a fresh mind can make a wondrous difference. Wisdom also suggests asking someone else to read the column before our editor does. Other eyes often pick out errors that we writers overlook in our own drafts.

- *Keep a copy of each column, as submitted.* After each is published, we should study the changes made by our editor and ask questions about the revisions—not to challenge, but to learn.

- *Follow the inverted pyramid principle.* Busy editors often trim too-long columns from the bottom, in the event of space problems. Therefore, we place the most-

We should study the changes made by our editor and ask questions about the revisions—not to challenge, but to learn.

important details as close to the top of the column as possible, to ensure that they won't be lopped off when space is tight.

- *Add human interest.* Articles with the most readership in a newspaper or magazine are those about "real" people and true-life situations. So we try to inject these stories into our column to add interest. Instead of a standard article about a particularly good source of information at the local library, we might lead into the topic by relating the experience of a researcher who made an exciting breakthrough in this material.

- *Avoid "I" disease.* Mentioning our own experiences occasionally can foster a relationship between us and our readers, but we should refrain from too many personal references.

- *Check facts.* Always, we need to ensure that the information we present is current—even if verification requires long-distance calls or a delay in using the item. Facts gathered from secondhand sources should also be verified. We double-check phone numbers and addresses.

- *Recognize responsibilities.* Once we are established and respected in the community, whatever we write may be taken as gospel. It is a heavy responsibility to guide readers in the right direction. So we consider carefully before recommending any book, software, library, or genealogical service to our readers. A good reputation and friendships with other genealogy enthusiasts may suffer if we make an unwise decision.

Maintaining momentum

The life of a column depends upon three factors: the writer's commitment, the loyalty and interest of the readers, and the extent to which the newspaper or magazine is pleased with the results. Writing an interesting column is a challenge, but probably the most difficult task for the columnist is planning new material and selecting topics that make readers eagerly turn the pages to that section, issue after issue. One key to success is to involve the readers, but thought-provoking feedback and ideas can be gleaned in a myriad of ways. For example, we can

- Listen to the people who read the column. A reader's query about the first steps in finding an unknown birth parent can be the topic for an entire column.

- Ask local librarians and genealogical society members about the type of information they want to read.

- Solicit information from readers on their research projects or books that are in progress locally. Mention these, or use their personal stories and experiences as a basis for your articles.

- Invite readers to describe how they solved perplexing research problems, or query them about "amazing coincidences" of the type recently popularized by genealogist Hank Jones.[7]

- Occasionally pen a personal, nostalgic piece that may evoke memories in others and bring out good column material.

It is a heavy responsibility to guide readers in the right direction. So we consider carefully before recommending any book, software, library, or service to our readers.

- Build upon seasonal events. Guy Fawkes Day is a perfect occasion to discuss early English criminal records—or the American columnist could use it to write about the Pilgrims and their counterpart celebration, Pope's Day. Military research is a timely topic on the anniversary of a local battle.

- Offer practical, unusual information applicable to our readers' own work—such as lists of ancient medical terms or definitions of unusual words appearing in old documents. Give tips for cemetery research or tracking down unknown maiden names of ancestors.

- Take note of columns that are well received and repeat their theme or type.

- Find out what topics work well for other writers.

Good columnists, like teachers of any subject, continue to learn and keep abreast of current events, resources, and technology. They do this by reading genealogy publications from throughout the country, attending conferences and seminars, and networking with others in the family-history field. Members of the ISFHWE regularly use all these approaches and exchange ideas as well through their newsletter, *The Column*s.

> Good columnists, like teachers of any subject, continue to learn and keep abreast of current events, resources, and technology.

Spreading the word

Publicizing a column is particularly important to writers who thrive on reader participation or need a constant supply of queries to survive. Contests, puzzles, and offers of free items useful to genealogists can also boost readership. We might offer a sheet that gives beginning tips, addresses of nearby libraries, and recommendations for good how-to books. Charts that show relationships are also popular and inexpensive giveaways.

ISFHWE members employ other ideas as well. Kenneth Thomas Jr., longtime writer of a genealogical feature for the *Atlanta Constitution,* devotes one column a year to beginners. This special item is often clipped by readers and librarians, to share with those who need help getting started. Their distribution of his column has proved to be a good public-relations move, Thomas says. Retired columnist George Miller of Tampa, Florida, always had good ideas about promoting a column. Miller, who started "Family Trees, Twigs, and Chips" in the *Madison (Indiana) Courier* in 1971 and was one of the founders of the early Council of Genealogy Columnists, once offered these suggestions for keeping a column's name before the public:[8]

- Liberally distribute attractive business cards printed with our full credentials.

- Use an informative letterhead.

- Design a query form that will simplify submissions; prominently identify our column and include our ground rules for publication.

- Print calendars that include the name of the column, the publication in which it appears, and our own name and address. Send these to courthouse offices, libraries, chambers of commerce, and other places that attract people seeking genealogical help.

- Send a folder of business cards to these same outlets. Include a copy of our query form—though we may want to glue or otherwise attach it to the folder in a way that will prevent its removal while permitting its duplication.

Encouraging readership is also important to the life of the column. Publishers frequently reassess their special-interest features, making cuts and adjustments to better serve the community. A strong, loyal readership can make the difference whether your column is cut or kept as a regular feature.

Expanding markets

Most genealogy columns are written for one newspaper or magazine, or perhaps two or three in a certain region. Today's technology—particularly the Internet—has broadened the vista for all genealogy writers, opening new markets and opportunities. Online journals and newsmagazines need writers. Commercial publishers and software firms employ online columnists. And family organizations are setting up their own web pages.

ISFHWE member Myra Vanderpool Gormley, a Certified Genealogist who lives near Seattle, Washington, personally illustrates the growth potential. Myra's newspaper column, "Shaking Your Family Tree," has been syndicated nationwide since 1985 by the Los Angeles Times Syndicate. As online services began to court the genealogical public, Myra branched out in 1990—answering genealogy questions for Prodigy® subscribers, writing a weekly online column for it, and creating its genealogy-related web pages. Now, she and Julia M. Case, a Virginia-based professional genealogist, author, and former genealogy bulletin-board leader for Prodigy, are coeditors of the electronic publications, *RootsWeb Review* and *Missing Links*. These weekly newsletters are distributed worldwide via e-mail, each with a current circulation of about 400,000. They, along with their fellow ISFHWE member, Rhonda R. McClure, author the Web-based interactive genealogy lessons at RootsWeb.com.

> Technology has broadened the vista for all genealogy writers, opening new markets and opportunities.

Summary Concepts

Advances in technology continue to have an impact on the field of genealogical writing and research. The computer has replaced the typewritten column of the 1970s and 1980s. Fax machines and modems now allow writers to transmit columns to their publishers in an instant and to receive information just as quickly. But the function of the genealogy columnist has changed little over the years. The emphasis is still on people helping people, as we explore our individual and collective heritage.

NOTES

1. Anita Cheek Milner, *Newspaper Genealogical Column Directory,* 6th edition (Bowie, Maryland: Heritage Books, 1996), 54–55.

GENEALOGY COLUMNS

2. Frederick C. Hart Jr., CG, "The *Hartford Times* Genealogical Column," *Connecticut Ancestry* 35 (February 1993): 111–12.

3. Alex Haley, *Roots* (New York: Doubleday, 1976). Although the genealogical community decries misrepresentations and unreliability, Haley's fictional ancestry did much to arouse interest and persuade the masses that family-history research is both exciting and doable. For the invalidity of the Kinte-Waller-Lee "line" that *Roots* asserts, see the following scholarly and journalistic investigations: Donald R. Wright, "Uprooting Kunta Kinte: On the Perils of Relying on Encyclopedic Informants," *History of Africa* 8 (1981): 205–17 (which analyzes the African generations); Gary B. Mills and Elizabeth Shown Mills, "Roots and the New 'Faction': A Legitimate Tool for Clio?" *Virginia Magazine of History and Biography* 89 (January 1981): 3–26 (which analyzes the American generations in *Roots*); Mark Ottoway, "Tangled Roots," (London) *Sunday Times,* 10 April 1977 (which analyzes Haley's research in England as well as Africa); and Philip Nobile, "Uncovering Roots," (New York) *Village Voice,* February 23, 1993, 31–38 (for a chronicle of how the book was commercially manufactured from Haley's failed search for ancestry—including material from Haley's personal papers at the University of Tennessee, Knoxville). In "My Search for Roots," *Tuesday Magazine* (October 1965), 4–7, Haley reveals the actual tradition passed to him by his elders—an account that treated no one earlier than his great-grandfather, George Lee.

4. See website for membership and subscription information.

5. Council of Genealogy Columnists, *Be a Genealogy Columnist* (N.p.: The Council, 1997).

6. Norm Goldstein, ed., *Associated Press Stylebook and Libel Manual,* rev. edition (Reading, Massachusetts: Perseus Books, 1998).

7. Henry Z "Hank" Jones, FASG, *Psychic Roots* (Baltimore: Genealogical Publishing Co., 1994); and *More Psychic Roots* (Baltimore: Genealogical Publishing Co., 1996).

8. George H. Miller, "Business Cards?" *Council of Genealogy Columnists Newsletter* 1 (Summer 1988), 2.

9. Quoted in Alex Ayres, *The Wit and Wisdom of Mark Twain* (New York and Middlesex, England: Penguin Books, 1989), 252.

Advice for the aspiring columnist:

"Write without pay until somebody offers pay. If nobody offers within three years, . . . look upon this circumstance . . . as the sign that sawing wood is what [you're] intended for.

—*Mark Twain*[9]

FURTHER STUDY

Collins, Walton R. "Are You in Touch with Your Readers?" *National Capital Area Tenth Anniversary Conference: Syllabus.* Arlington, Virginia: National Genealogical Society, 1990. Vol. 1: 151–55.

Ellison, Regina Hines, CGRS. "Share Your Knowledge: Write a Genealogical Column." *Association of Professional Genealogists Quarterly* 5 (Summer 1990): 35–36.

Gale Directory of Publications and Broadcast Media. Detroit: Gale Group, current edition). Long known as the *Ayers Directory of Publications,* this huge work is usually found in larger libraries.

International Society of Family History Writers and Editors. *The Column.* Quarterly newsletter, 1988—, previously known as the *Council of Genealogy Columnists Newsletter* and *Genealogy Columns.*

Moulton, Joy Wade, CG. "Writing a Genealogical Column: Tips and Suggestions." *National Genealogical Society, 1991 Conference in the States: Syllabus.* Arlington: The Society, 1991. Pages 357–59.

20

PROOF ARGUMENTS
AND
CASE STUDIES

Keynotes

Proof Arguments <u>and</u> Case Studies

by Elizabeth Shown Mills, CG, CGL, FASG

The problem was a thorny one. Our research has been exhaustive. The evidence points overwhelmingly toward one conclusion. All contradictory evidence is reasonably rebutted. All that remains is the essay we must write to set forth our findings. *How is that done?* How does one distill months or years of intensive research into a handful of pages—and do so convincingly?

Genealogical literature is filled with examples we can follow, reflecting all levels of skill. As serious genealogists we are undoubtedly analyzing these already, seeking to define the qualities that render a work effective or unconvincing, memorable or dull. This chapter tries to help in several ways:

- by defining our options and public expectations for each.

- by providing organizational guidelines we can adapt to each specific case.

- by defining stylistic qualities that best attract and hold the genealogical reader.

- by examining—within a genealogical framework—the structural principles expected of well-written essays.

How to write so we'll be *read*, how to write so we'll be *understood*, how to write so we'll be *believed*—all these are major concerns for us as genealogists.

> How to write so we'll be *read*, how to write so we'll be *understood*, how to write so we'll be *believed*—all these are major concerns for us as genealogists.

Defining Our Approach

Basic formats

Most essays in our field fall into one of four categories: compiled genealogies, source discussions, proof arguments, or methodological case studies. Here, we'll focus on the last two, closely related types. Their differences, subtle but significant, deal largely with our purpose and our intended market. At the core of each is a successful and difficult piece of research that needs to be detailed on paper so that our solution will be understood and accepted.

PROOF ARGUMENTS

The purpose of this type of paper is simple: a genealogical point needs "proving." Typically, no one can find a record that makes an acceptable statement of identity, origins, or parentage for a certain person—but extensive research has produced an argument that seems solid. In other cases, a published book or article may set forth claims we think are wrong and should be corrected in print. Argument writing is the vehicle by which we accomplish both goals.[1]

CASE STUDIES

Case studies are dual-purpose essays whose core is a genealogical argument. A sound piece of research has been performed. It is of obvious value to everyone

**PROOF ARGUMENTS
AND CASE STUDIES**

working on that line. However, because it resolves a thorny problem, the *methodology* or the *unique resources* used in this case could benefit a wider range of researchers with similar problems in their own lines. So, the thrust of our argument is different. We develop a case study, in which our methodology becomes the prime offering and the actual piece of research becomes the example by which that methodology is explained.[2]

Publishing concerns

Should we publish this piece of work? Most of us do end up publishing, although we may not think of it that way. Given that *publishing* is the act of distributing copies, it's really a matter of what venue we choose. We may aspire to have our work appear in a major journal—after all, the very fact of acceptance and publication there will enhance our credibility and circulation, spare us the costs of printing and distribution, and probably build our reputation and client base. We may prefer to post it on our website, which is now a common and relatively cheap way to self-publish—although it may be harder to earn acceptance for our hypothesis if our argument is not subjected to the peer-review process of a good journal. Or we may just send out copies when someone inquires. All are forms of publishing, and most of the issues discussed in this chapter apply to all these forms. Even if we just "send out copies to whoever's interested," those individuals will judge our manuscript by the qualities they see in conventionally published material.

If we want to have our proof argument or case study published by others, at their expense, then we must objectively appraise our potential outlets. Obviously, public expectations and demands will influence the acceptability of our work. They also shape the manner in which we should craft our written paper. In general, three types of genealogical periodicals—in print and electronic forms—accept the types of arguments or case studies under discussion.

SURNAME PERIODICALS

Publications that specialize in material relating to one surname offer the best chance for articles that focus upon a person or a family. But if the problem is a complex one, the acceptance of our conclusion may hinge upon the reputation our outlet has for discriminating standards. Some surname periodicals have standards for thorough research, documentation, and evidence analysis that rival the best journals in our field; others will print anything sent to them.

If we prefer to publish in a surname periodical, odds are we'll have few to choose among—there are likely not a lot of them dealing solely with people named Humpersnickle. If *Humpersnickle Happenings* does not measure up to our standards, we'll probably opt for something other than the surname periodical. Even if *Humpersnickle Happenings* will gratefully print our writings word for word, in whatever fashion we choose, with none of that painful "constructive criticism" we know we'll get from discriminating journals, we still might be swayed by another thought: the purpose of that prepublication critique is to help ensure

Even if we just "send out copies to whoever's interested," those individuals will still judge our manuscript by the qualities they see in conventionally published material.

that our argument is as good as it can be—*before* it goes into print. That way, it stands a better chance of surviving years or generations of further research by countless others.

GEOGRAPHIC OR ETHNIC MAGAZINES
Periodicals of this type are usually interested in all families and all types of problems within their focus area. Their distribution may be widespread or scant—a point we'll want to check ahead of time if circulation is a major concern to us. Within their geographic or ethnic parameters, these magazines usually offer the most freedom of structure or type, although they may have other criteria that affect their selection process. Here again, quality varies widely.

SCHOLARLY JOURNALS
Scholarly journals in most learned fields—and genealogy is no exception—are usually published by major societies. Some few focus on a particular state.[3] Most are national or international in scope.[4] All have several common qualities:

- They publish advanced-level research on wide-ranging subjects, areas, and people.
- They have exacting standards for research, documentation, and evidence analysis.
- They are peer-reviewed, meaning that manuscripts are not accepted for publication until and unless they pass an evaluation by well-known authorities in their specific subject area.
- Their accepted manuscripts are still likely to undergo revision by the author—commonly with the editor's help—based upon the counsel of both the peer-reviewers and the editor.
- The proof arguments and case studies they offer the public enjoy the highest degree of acceptance in the field. (This is not to say that the details and conclusions presented in all scholarly journal articles are infallible, only that they have a noteworthy degree of accuracy and are more likely to withstand the tests of time and further discoveries on the subject.)

Among scholarly journals, those at the national level usually enjoy the widest possible circulation; but their obligation to aid the greatest number of people results in selection criteria that are generally the most demanding.

Meeting standards

In the best of worlds, the issue of *thoroughness* would not arise. Regardless of whether we write this paper for our own files, our family, a popular magazine, or a scholarly journal, we would still hold ourselves to the same standards for completeness. Realistically speaking, differences do exist. Our own files are a work in progress; and writing proof arguments while we still consider our work to be "preliminary" is a valuable approach. As James L. Hansen, FASG, of the State Historical Society of Wisconsin Library points out:

In the best of worlds, regardless of whether we write for our own files, our family, a popular magazine, or a scholarly journal, we would hold ourselves to the same standards.

Argument writing is worth doing even if we are not looking to publish. It's an excellent way to see the results of our research and to recognize holes, in both the research and the defense of our hypothesis.[5]

"Holes" are to be expected. We all have them in our research and they are tolerable to various degrees. If we are genealogical hobbyists writing our own family history, we can leave all sorts of holes and be forgiven (so long as the information we provide is correct). If we're writing for family or local-society periodicals, few readers in those circles will be critical. If we are professional genealogists, the public's expectations from us rise considerably. If we plan to submit our work to a scholarly journal, whether we are professionals or hobbyists, we are expected to fill the obvious holes.

If the problem is one we investigated for a client and the client is willing for it to be published but unwilling to fund thorough research, then we are obligated to finish the project on our own rather than put our half-done "solution" into print. If our investigation is based upon a set of "facts" provided by the client and we have not verified their accuracy, then we do so before going to press. This publication will be our showpiece, one of the model works in our portfolio, and a permanent advertisement of our skill. We would ill serve ourselves to send to press a proposed solution while the investigation is obviously incomplete.

> If the problem is one we investigated for a client and the client is willing for it to be published but unwilling to fund thorough research, then we are obligated to finish the project on our own before we put our "solution" into print.

Maximizing odds of acceptance

After we decide the type of article and periodical that seem most suitable, we will want to target one or more specific publication(s). Common sense dictates that we stand a better chance of acceptance by any periodical if we understand the material it publishes and then craft our paper to match its style and standards. This means that we study a number of recent issues—analyzing the content (both subject matter and style of presentation) and the length of its articles. When we have a short list of likely outlets, we might write the editors and inquire whether they offer an author's stylesheet. Or we can check their websites, where guidelines are typically posted.

All these efforts can spare us needless rejections. Even though major scholarly journals may have similar reputations—and may even appeal to the same audience or the same level of scholarship—their thrusts may be quite different. Consider, for example, the *New England Genealogical and Historical Register* and the *National Genealogical Society Quarterly*. Both enjoy comparable circulation and hold similar standards. The *Register,* however, adheres more closely to the traditional concept of a genealogical journal as a "journal of record" and sees its primary mission as the identification and reconstruction of New England's early settler families. Compiled genealogies and proof arguments are its meat and potatoes. On the other hand, the *Quarterly*—which must serve all regions of the country and far more diverse ethnicities—has developed a reputation for instruction in problem-solving methodology. It publishes few compiled genealogies; instead, its emphasis is on case studies that demonstrate techniques and resources for resolving thorny research dilemmas.

One other "rule of submission" should be understood from the start: we should not plan to submit our paper to several periodicals simultaneously. Despite media stories of newly discovered authors, whose agents sent their manuscripts out to a gaggle of publishers to get the best deal, journals do not bid and they do not rush to gobble up untested articles. Quality periodicals invest considerable labor in critical analysis and fact checking prior to any decision to accept or reject. Once editing begins, they invest much more. Their subscribers expect them to present original material that is not available elsewhere. No journal expects to be told, after much work has been done, that the object of its labor is about to be—or has just been—published elsewhere.

Crafting the Article

Stylistic concerns

Frankly speaking, genealogy has a terrible reputation as literature. The Biblical begats are not read for enrichment, guidance, or pleasure; and modern begats are often just as boring. One lesson is clear: *if we want our work to be read, we have to write to be read*. Our brilliant conclusions and exemplary research will simply be ignored unless ours is an ancient family from whom an unusually large number of people descend or some special quality piques a reader's interest.

Modern readers are conditioned by a web-surfing, channel-hopping, page-flipping, distraction-riddled world. Interesting stimuli constantly battle for attention. Gone are the halcyon days in which "genies" devoured everything in print that bore the word *genealogy*. Today's researchers graze their way through more "food for thought" than any person could ever digest. So, both writers and journals must actually *tempt* readers to pause and sample their offerings. It's the natural tendency of researchers in our field to look first for the surname of interest. That means any piece of writing that appears to offer nothing but data on one family or person will have limited appeal. We attract wider readership by

- convincing readers that our Muckelfuss work offers advice or approaches they can apply to their own search for Garfunckles.
- crafting a manuscript that is as readable as possible.
- *instantly* convincing potential readers that we have succeeded with 1 and 2!

In short, we have to grab their attention, and studies show we have only a few seconds to do that. Style is important.

Organizational guidelines

Whatever writing classes we have taken probably taught us three basics: we say what we are going to say, we say it, and then we say what we've said. Beyond the classroom, every field of inquiry develops its own patterns—realizing that certain formats enhance and clarify its particular type of information. Genealogy is no

> Modern readers are conditioned by a web-surfing, channel-hopping, page-flipping, distraction-riddled world. Both writers and journals must actually *tempt* readers to pause and sample their offerings.

exception. A convincingly written proof argument or case study in our field typically follows a pattern:

- Introduction
- Body of essay
  - Description of research problem
  - Explanation of hypothesis
  - Discussion of resources
  - Presentation of findings
  - Rebuttal of contradictory evidence
- Summation
- Notes

This sequence is common but not rigid. The hypothesis may be the basis of the introduction. The discussions of resources, findings, and contradictory factors may overlap. Studying other essays that treat problems similar to ours can help us decide whether modifications might clarify our particular case.

INTRODUCTION

When our work falls into the hands of page flippers, we have—perhaps—thirty seconds to persuade them that reading all our words will not waste their time. Our first paragraph or two must introduce our subject in a fashion that shouts, "Read me! I can teach you! I won't bore you! I've got something you should know!"

That first paragraph is the toughest one we have to write. One workable process is this: we first jot down what we want to cover. Then we complete the rest of the paper. Once done (though, of course, it really isn't *done* yet), we go back to the start and revise the introduction, making certain that its stated purpose is still on target. Then we revise it yet again, to make it as interesting as possible. We put it aside and let the whole work grow cold. Finally, we come back to it and reread our opening as though we're totally new to the subject. Did it make us want to read on? Or did we cringe at the thought of going back through that paper for the thirty-ninth time? If that first paragraph did not make *us* want to continue, then it won't hook readers.

The exact nature and length of our lead will depend upon the type of essay we're crafting. If we decide to write a proof argument, then our introduction should identify the focus of our problem and the nature of our hypothesis. If we're writing a case study, our opening paragraphs will focus upon the *principle* we're teaching, while pointing out the use of a specific family as our example.

DESCRIPTION OF RESEARCH PROBLEM

Thoroughly but *concisely*, we summarize the problem we have resolved or the situation we're illustrating. If this instruction sounds contradictory, it isn't! Our readers must be told every detail relevant to the problem, but we must carefully cull everything that is not absolutely essential. Newspaper journalists have an apocryphal tale that the genealogist might remember here. A cub reporter was berated by his editor for turning in stories sadly lacking in detail. So, the next day he tried to do better: "Two of Cal Cooper's cows died of clover bloat last night. Their names were Daisy and Old Red." Yes, *detail* is essential—but we have to use good judgment in deciding *which* details are vital to the story and what information will benefit our readers.

If we've done a thorough research job, odds are we have a whole passel of material that seems to fit this forebear. All that may be perfect in the family history we eventually write. But *this* paper must focus on the detail that's basic to (*a*) understanding the problem we define and (*b*) developing our case. Including all that peripheral detail won't impress our readers, it will just overwhelm them. If the monickers of those cows are intrinsic to the problem, then it's appropriate to name them. If not, that's just clutter. From the start to the finish of our paper, every word, every fact, every sentence that is not absolutely indispensable to our argument or methodology must be ruthlessly slashed—or else we lose readers.

EXPLANATION OF HYPOTHESIS

Whether we explicitly state our hypothesis at the start of our paper usually depends upon the type of article we're crafting. In proof arguments, the hypothesis is usually stated early on—often in the first paragraph. In case studies, the hypothesis is often *not* stated in advance. Instead, the author presents a problem and describes the available resources, then unfolds the search and the evidence, step by step. Aside from injecting a suspense factor that genealogists appreciate (don't we all view ourselves as Mr. Holmes's reincarnation?), there is an instructional advantage to not giving away the solution in advance: readers can analyze each piece of evidence as it unfolds and test their own ability to see where the evidence is headed.

DISCUSSION OF RESOURCES

To ensure the credibility of our argument or example, we might pause at this point and discuss the resources upon which our work is built. Here, we identify the records that exist and their locations. We tell our readers about any inherent flaws or shortcomings within this material. We inform them about any documents that *should* exist but haven't been found. Our readers need assurance that we do know the resources and that we have used them all (or at least tried to find them all). There's a side benefit, too: readers may know of other materials we've missed or the whereabouts of those we looked for in vain. Sometimes, we may feel that this kind of discussion interrupts the flow of the text we're developing. If so, then we simply relegate it to our notes. But we do have to be careful not to make readers feel they are following two separate threads—one in the text, one in the notes. Discursive notes are useful, but they shouldn't compete with the text for attention.

PRESENTATION OF FINDINGS

The discussion of our research is the most difficult part of our paper to craft, and our toughest task may be removing the chaff. Whether our research produced one file or several drawers of material, we must still cull, cull, cull. Usually, we can distill this mass into an effective argument through a three-step process:

In case studies, the hypothesis is often *not* stated in advance. Instead, the author presents a problem and describes the available resources, then unfolds the search and the evidence, step by step.

**PROOF ARGUMENTS
AND CASE STUDIES**

- Briefly list the pieces of evidence that most strongly make our case.

- Outline the reasons that each point deserves to be on our "most valuable" list.

- Plan the approach by which those pieces of evidence can best unfold themselves to the reader.

The step-by-step "unfolding" will usually not be the actual step-by-step process in which we uncovered the information itself. Our research seldom follows the straightest path to the solution. Yet the direct path is the one most proof arguments and case studies need to take.

As we lead our readers through the research process by which we arrived at our solution, we explain our reasoning at each point. We explain our interpretation of ambiguously worded materials. We explain the clues we drew from those crucial records. We explain why we presume one person of a surname is related to another of the same. We explain why we think someone of a certain name in one locale is identical to the individual of that name elsewhere. *We explain, explain, explain!* In presenting our evidence, we clearly separate the documented fact from opinion. We plainly distinguish the wording used within record sources from our own rephrasing of that data. Above all, each and every statement of fact we make—if it is not public knowledge—needs its own, individual, citation of source. Any statement based upon the correlation of several pieces of indirect evidence should specifically identify the source of each of the pieces.

In presenting facts, we diligently avoid those vague but common generalities, "we know that" or "records show." For credibility, we must explain *how* we know this information. We should explicitly state *which* records show the point we're making—and exactly what they say. "We know that . . ." and "records show . . ." are the breeding grounds of speculation and misinformation. Readers interpret such generalities in one of two ways: *(a)* we are too lazy or careless to properly identify our material; or *(b)* we don't really know where the information came from. Whether either assumption is true or not, we lose credibility.

Writers of proof arguments should also heed the sage advice of Mark Twain: "Only presidents, editors, and people with tapeworm have the right to use the editorial 'we'."[6] Yes, it is used throughout the present volume; but different types of writing call for differences in voice, tone, and mood; and writers should select the right ones for each presentation. Proof arguments and professional manuals are two drastically different breeds. In brief:

- This manual represents a group of people who are "all in this boat together." Dozens of writers, editors, and contributors have collaborated to shape this material, and all of you readers are daily involved in the conduct of the activities discussed here. *We* are all part of these issues.

- However, when *I* labor to resolve a problem with *my* Simon Snucklefuss, when I develop a proof argument or a case study to set forth *my* work and *my* reasoning, I'm hoping to convince *you*—but *you* are not part of *my* project. If I were to say that *we* know Simon was born in 1752, odds are *you* don't know that at all. The *we* to whom I would refer would be some nebulous, undefined

"We know that . . ." and "records show . . ." are the breeding grounds of speculation and misinformation.

Writers of proof arguments should also heed the sage advice of Mark Twain: "Only presidents, editors, and people with tapeworm have the right to use the editorial 'we'."

entity who would remain unidentified in my argument. No argument is made more convincing by invoking the knowledge of unidentified people.

Other issues also determine the voice we choose for proof arguments and are later discussed under the section "I" Disease.

REBUTTAL OF CONTRADICTORY EVIDENCE
Rare is the well-done research project that produces no contradictions. Presenting them frankly will strengthen—not weaken—our argument. If our conclusions are valid, then we'll have already disproved or discounted each contradictory piece of evidence we found. If our written work ignores the presence of claims or implications to the contrary, then others will assume our research is not complete. So we discuss those flaws. We explain exactly why we disbelieve records that seem to be credible. Doing so will head off needless challenges to our work.

SUMMATION
We have one final chance to convince readers of all the points we have labored to make. Even those who skimmed through much of our important detail may give us this last shot. So let's aim well. We briefly summarize the main points we want them to remember long after our words have become dust-collectors on their shelves. The summary is no place for new detail; but as we restate our hypothesis or our technique, we try to do so in a different and memorable way.

> The summary is no place for new detail; but as we restate our hypothesis or our technique, we try to do so in a different and memorable way.

NOTES
Whether this section appears on each page (as footnotes) or at the end of the article (as endnotes), its purpose is

• to precisely cite the sources of our information.

• to inform the reader of anomalies or shortcomings within those records—discussions we may not be able to work smoothly into the text.

The current trend in genealogical journals is toward footnotes. The *readability factor* is again at work, of course, but two other forces fuel the trend. The convenience of footnotes encourages readers to match each assertion in the text to its source—making them more critical thinkers. Footnotes also allow for discussions of quirks within our sources—something usually glossed over in articles that embed stripped-down citations within parentheses in the text. Even journals whose house styles still require parenthetical source citations will usually accommodate necessary discussions of resources in an appended section of notes. Use that option. All sources are not created equal. The fact that we, the writers, have made our best effort to use that material judiciously does not relieve our readers of the responsibility of making their own evaluations. Nor does it relieve us of the necessity of informing readers of any information they need in order to make accurate value judgments. So, along with the expected publication details, a well-crafted genealogical article includes such statements as

The cited family history seems to cover most branches of the family, but it offers no evidence to support any of its statements.

or

Deed Book 1, dated 1647–53, is not an *original* record book. The inside cover carries an 1857 affidavit of the county clerk, attesting this to be a transcription made from fragments of the original.

Enhancing Our Writing

Effective guidelines for writing usually fall into two types—theoretical rules and practical examples. Until now, this chapter has focused upon theory. It should also address several problems that genealogical writers commonly experience in trying to implement the pattern. The guidelines that follow are not unique. They reflect the standards of quality that exist for *all* types of writing—outside of genealogy as well as within. But they specifically consider the difficulty our particular field has in applying widespread standards to genealogical detail. Attention to these points will enhance our potential for getting published and being *read*.

Paragraph development

All papers must be organized logically. The point at which organization commonly breaks down—and the point at which readers are usually lost—is the most basic units of writing: (*a*) the paragraph, and (*b*) the sentences that comprise it. Probably more than any other factor, this one determines whether we keep or lose those readers we've struggled to hook. Discouraging though the thought may be, readers *skim*. They jump from paragraph to paragraph, looking for something interesting or trying to grab the *essence* of what we have to offer. If several paragraphs catch their attention, they may return to the start and read our work more closely—convinced now that we are worth the time. If that skimming process dazes them with droning detail, we lose them.

What are the spots that catch their eye in that skimming process? *The opening paragraph and the first sentence of each paragraph.* Page formatting ensures this in virtually every printed work. So, we give special thought to those opening sentences throughout our text.

The world of literature and communication has a basic formula for this aspect of writing—*a paragraph contains two parts:*

- a controlling idea (or topic sentence), and

- a series of sentences that develops the idea.

This concept battles mightily with traditional genealogical writing—and right here is a major reason researchers ignore articles that don't treat their own families. Sane people tend not to subject themselves to unnecessary mental torture.

Discouraging though the thought may be, readers *skim*. What are the spots that catch their eye in that skimming process?

So let's lift a section from a tiresome gaggle of detail often seen in genealogy and try to identify the cause of the stupor it induces:

> Two years later, in January 1697, Saml. Snodgrass sold to John Jones the Meeting House land on Crooked Neck, reserving the one acre set aside for the cemetery, though it wasn't until 13 March 1701 that mention of his wife, Ruanna, first appeared on record when she released her dower rights to 23 acres on Spindletop Hill "which said land Sam had previously sold to Thos. Thomas," for 7 shillings, as "a part of the tract on which Will. Walker operates a blacksmith shop for me." In 1703 when Roberta Roe made her will, she referred to Saml. Snodgrass as her son-in-law, but named her own sons John and James as executors. Ruanna Snodgrass is twice named again in this period, first on 3 March 1706 when she and Saml. Snodgrass each received a mourning ring from the estate of Samuel's brother Sylvester Snodgrass, then again on 6 September 1706 when the estate of Will. Walker paid Ruanna Snodgrass and Samuel Snodgrass 4 pounds and 9 shillings for board and care of "my son Weyhauser Walker."
>
> Also of significance, Saml. Snodgrass "of Spindletop" and his wife (unidentified in that document), appeared again on record on 14 August 1706 when they were mentioned in Ralph Rogers's suit against David Doe regarding 23 acres on New River that Rogers had inherited from his parents, but Saml. was called yeoman of Charlesburg that November when he sold (without mention of wife) the last five acres of his Spindletop land and bought from Obadiah Oak's heirs a house on Market Street at the south end of town (now lying on Enterprise Thoroughfare at its juncture with River Road) but which had at that time a "peach orchid," several outbuildings, and "other appurtenances" that Samuel apparently occupied until at least July 1708 when he executed his last known document at Charlesburg, a deed in which he . . . .

Did you read all the way through this passage? Probably not! Any genealogist dedicated enough to stick with such prose ought to be frustrated at this point and left wondering: *What is the writer getting at?* Somewhere, amid this litany of notecard abstracts, there must be a *point* the writer is trying to make. *What is it that we're supposed to remember or conclude?*

This is why every paragraph is expected to have a *theme*, one that is planned and clearly stated. This is why writers are expected to construct their paragraphs along five principles:

- The purpose of a paragraph is to make a point.

- The topic sentence tells the reader what that point is.

- The remainder of the paragraph develops that point, breaking detail into digestible chunks called *sentences*—each of which expresses a separate aspect of that paragraph's theme.

- When that point is finished, a new paragraph begins.

- That new paragraph is thematically linked to the old one, to keep thought and action flowing smoothly.

How, then, might poor Samuel Snodgrass's life of drudgery be more tolerably cast? First, we ask one question of each paragraph: *What is the theme?* If these

> Every paragraph is expected to have a *theme*, one that is planned and clearly stated.

documents are sensibly grouped, they must make a common point. Beyond that, the purpose of each paragraph should be to present a set of facts that advances the overall goal of the essay. From this vantage point, the question becomes: *What point needs to be made here in order to strengthen our theme and advance the action or argument?* We can't expect our readers to muddle through endless detail and analyze our purpose for themselves. Why should they? We're the ones who want them to read our work. So it's up to *us* to clear away the brambles and lay out a clear path.

In poor Samuel's case, by thoughtfully analyzing the stack of note cards strung together by his careless chronicler, we *can* define the controlling thought of each paragraph:

> *Para. 1.* His wife is identified during 1701–06 (but only for that period) and a clue exists to her birth family.

> *Para. 2.* During fall 1706, apparently, she died; then Samuel left Spindletop and moved into town.

Defining the common elements in each paragraph lets us plan a more digestible narrative. It helps us distinguish between details that support our theme and those that bog it down. We might now rewrite text that's a tad more tolerable.

> Samuel's wife is named, and her family hinted at, in records from 1701 to 1706. The couple seem to have married after the 1697 sale of Samuel's Meeting House tract on Crooked Neck, in which no wife participated.[101] On 13 March 1701, one Ruanna Snodgrass visited the county justice to relinquish her dower rights in 23 acres on Spindletop Hill, saying that her husband Samuel had sold it the prior month to Thomas Thomas.[102] In 1706, she is named twice again: on 3 March, when Samuel and Ruanna both received mourning rings from the estate of his brother Sylvester,[103] and on 6 November when the estate of William Walker paid Ruanna 4 pounds and 9 shillings for the board and care of Walker's son Weyhauser.[104] Unfortunately, the document that suggests a possible maiden identity for Ruanna does not actually name her—that is, the 1706 will of Roberta Roe who referred to Saml. Snodgrass of Spindletop by the ambiguous term *son-in-law*.[105]

> Ruanna appears to have died in the fall of 1706, after which Samuel moved into Charlesburg. On 14 August of that year, both were said to be "of Spindletop" when they were cited as neighbors in a lawsuit between Ralph Rogers and David Doe.[106] In November, without mention of a wife, Samuel sold his last five acres of Spindletop and purchased a lot with several outbuildings and a peach orchard in nearby Charlesburg.[107] (Situated on Market Street at the south end of that village, its modern site should be the juncture of Enterprise Thoroughfare with River Road.[108]) The last known record of Samuel is dated there at Charlesburg in July 1709, when he acknowledged a deed by which he . . . .[109]

The writer who wishes to be *read* cannot ignore the basic principles of good writing.

Genealogy is sometimes labeled *technical* writing. In one sense, it is. Certain technical formats are best followed—numbering systems and reference styles being the most obvious examples. The writer who wishes to be *read* cannot ignore the basic principles of good writing or the differences that distinguish between various types of compilations. If it is our intent to present a collection of abstracts, then we should do so in proper form for abstracted material—not in amalgamated text. If it is our intent to *author* a case study or other form of genealogical essay, then we cannot fulfill that intent by merely typing a string of note cards. By common definition, authors are people who take raw pieces of data, analyze them, correlate them, and then paint an interpretive picture in their own words and thoughts— following common rules of grammar, syntax, and sentence and paragraph construction. If we fulfill this last set of technicalities, then our writing will be far more meaningful—and far more often *read*.

Syntactical sins

The Snodgrass passage also introduces another infelicity genealogists have difficulty avoiding: quotations that sin against the canons of grammar. Among cautions we should observe, when weaving quotes into text, are the following two.

DIRECT QUOTES

Syntax is easily violated when extracts from documents are combined with our own prose. A very typical infraction is the pair of phrases in the first paragraph of the "bad writing" example: "Will Walker operates a blacksmith shop for me" and "my son Weyhauser Walker." In both cases, the voice of the paragraph shifts from the impersonal *third* person to the possessive of the *first* person. Adolescent boys undergo voice changes. Good writing does not.

PARAPHRASING

Lifting phrases from *public records* that we identify, without punctuation to set off the quoted words, does not constitute a copyright infringement or plagiarism—just bad research habits. Writing standards also require the clear identification of material that is quoted verbatim. Failure to do so can create ill-worded text that reflects poorly upon our abilities as a writer. The following illustrates a typical example in which "lifted" text (in italics) should have been rephrased in more grammatical terms:

> On 25 December 1772, Collier MacMillan purchased a tract of land *situated between the New and York Rivers on a branch of Company Creek, the waters of Liberty River bounded on the Southeast by Wm. Strunk land and Northwest part by Ed. B. White and partly by vacant land, originally surveyed on 5 November 1771.*[7]

Plagiarism

As genealogical writers we probably understand the legal restrictions placed upon copyrighted work (see chapter 7) and would scrupulously avoid reproducing any copyrighted books, articles, or lecture materials. The one type of infringement that many writers naively commit is the borrowing of random sections of data from someone else's writings under conditions that do qualify for the label *plagiarism*— that is, the reuse of someone else's material without permission or explicit credit.

Adolescent boys undergo voice changes. Good writing does not.

The taint of plagiarism can be avoided by observing three practices:

- Put quotation marks around any string of three or more words copied precisely from any other source—manuscript or printed, public or private, antiquated or modern. Then properly acknowledge the original author.

- Get written permission from authors and publishers before reproducing "long" portions of their work. A generally safe rule of thumb for "long" quotations from an article or book would be anything in excess of one or two paragraphs.

- Never "borrow footnotes." If someone's references cite an apparently relevant item we have not used, then we find and study that item. Otherwise, we imperil our reputation. The fact or opinion attributed to that source by the author we're reading might contain error—or that author's note may cite a wrong book, page, or other publishing detail.

The perils of plagiarism—with explicit examples—are treated in far more detail in a September 1998 lead article in the Board for Certification of Genealogists' educational newsletter, *OnBoard*.[8]

"I" disease

Excellent advice here has been given by Margaret Costello and Jane Fiske of the *New England Historical and Genealogical Register*. It deserves repeating:

> The author should remain unobtrusive, letting [the] story seem to tell itself. . . . Direct personal observations and intrusions in the text, very popular in books written a century ago, are best avoided. Behind the scenes, however, the author must always be in control, carefully selecting and arranging the material, and guiding the narrative along with a minimum of clutter and confusion.[9]

Two issues are involved:

- *Vanity*. We all like to talk about ourselves, but few readers are interested in *us* at all. They're interested in the help or the information our paper promises to give them. Our focus should stay on that help or that information.

- *Time and setting*. By its very nature, most genealogical problems center upon a past era and forebears long removed. In a proof argument whose purpose is to establish that Mordacai Michaux fought in the French Revolution, our narrative is set in the eighteenth century. That's where it ought to stay. We took no part in storming the Bastille and have no business injecting ourselves into that scene. We live in the cyberworld. As authors, we should stay here, discreetly— "behind the scenes . . . in control, carefully selecting and arranging the material, and guiding the narrative along with a minimum of clutter and confusion."

Tight writing

In every recipe for writing, the main ingredient is the shortening. Gunning's famed "Fog Index" calls for an average sentence length of twenty words. Flesch's older readability formula tolerates an average of thirty.[10] But all experts agree:

The author should remain unobtrusive, letting the story seem to tell itself.

words kill—if we string too many of them together without giving our readers a chance to catch a breath. The preceding Snodgrass saga illustrates the point (to the extreme). Using many words, or big words, won't make us seem smarter—just windy. To readers, rambling writers are a bore and a waste of time. To those who pay the printing costs for our work, verbosity is a gross expense.

When we find ourselves suffering from what James Thurber dubbed "inflammation of the sentence structure,"[11] then we should reread each sentence for ways to say that thought in fewer words. We can trim prepositional phrases; several in the same sentence virtually guarantee convoluted writing. We should use adjectives and adverbs sparingly; we are not writing a romance novel. We particularly watch for passive verbs—those that limp along using two or three helpers (forms of *to be*) as crutches. While passive constructions have their place, excess or unnecessary use slows the flow of whatever we're trying to say. Chapter 25, Editing Periodicals, treats this issue in greater detail.

House styles

Every journal, magazine, or newspaper (of quality) has a house style. It follows a consistent format. Its material projects a certain tone. It has built a following of readers comfortable with that style. As writers, if we seek publication we should observe the house style of the journal to which we will submit our work. We note the length of the articles it customarily publishes—*then aim for less*. The bane of most genealogical editors seems to be overlong manuscripts. We note the layout of material on the printed page: are there one, two, or three columns? We note the typical length of paragraphs. Journals that use a wide-column format require paragraphs of longer length; magazines with two or three narrow columns need very short paragraphs. If we do not trouble ourselves to write appropriately, the editor must rewrite our work—or reject it.

Certain requirements for writers are virtually universal, regardless of other stylistic variances. We should always submit "clean copy." No penciled corrections. We double-space everything (yes, even quotations and reference notes). We leave ample margins for editorial ink to bleed: at least one inch on all sides. Editors will not be the least bit impressed by our fancy typography, but they will appreciate a manuscript that eliminates eyestrain and makes it easier for them to spot problems. Finally, whatever manuscript we submit, we should *finish* it before we mail it. Our work will not long be welcome if we send revisions and yet more revisions after our editor has expended hours or days evaluating and even editing the draft we first submitted.

Should our editor *ask* for revisions, we should not be surprised; but we should limit our alterations to the points the editor has flagged. And we should clearly mark the changed portions on the new draft. Providing another disk with the complete text of our revised manuscript is no service at this point. Once our editors have labored to finesse the original submission, it's too late for them to begin again with a new electronic version—and few have the time or staff to read the whole new manuscript against the old one, line for line, word for word, to spot our infusions

Why Write Tight?

*Consider
these word counts:*

The Lord's Prayer	56
23rd Psalm	118
Gettysburg Address	226
Ten Commandments	297
U.S. Department of Agriculture order on the price of cabbage	15,629[12]

and juggleries. They will address their attention to the portions they flagged for us, and our other unmarked changes will likely go unnoticed.

Summary Concepts

The most frequent mistake made by genealogists who solve difficult problems is a failure to detail their argument, on paper, in a convincing form. As discriminating researchers, we would scoff if told, "Oh, take my word for it; I have looked at all the records, and the evidence shows Benijah is the son of Polycarp." *What evidence?* we would ask. *Exactly what records did you examine? What did each of them say? Why do you interpret those documents as you do?*

Nor will any discriminating genealogist accept an unsupported generalization of *ours*. No matter how superior our research may have been, we still have to convince others of that point. When our exhaustive search seems done, when a logical conclusion takes shape and withstands every possible test, then we owe it to ourselves and others to draft a thorough, *written* essay in which we set forth all points bearing upon our problem and our conclusion. And we must craft that paper skillfully to entice a readership already suffering from information overload.

An old saw holds that writing is one percent inspiration and ninety-nine percent perspiration. We can ease the chore by following guidelines that create success for others. We define our purpose, our intended mode of distribution, and our desired audience. Then we craft our work accordingly. We identify those points that best advance our argument, then vigorously excise the rest. We treat this piece of genealogical writing as we would any work of serious or pleasurable literature. It should be both. We observe the same standards of writing that characterize good writing everywhere. The result will be a family account that justifies all the labor we have invested—one that demonstrates our research in a manner that is understood, believed, and enjoyed.

Once our argument has been prepared (unless our family or client requests otherwise), we best serve our cause by submitting our work for publication—to the best-quality journal possible. At least two benefits accrue:

- First, the written word has *power!* We would never take undue advantage of that fact, but we should put it to legitimate use. To be candid: many researchers who discount our hypotheses on the basis that no written evidence exists are the very individuals who readily embrace anything in print. Having our proof argument published will enhance our credibility. The more discriminating the journal that presents it, the greater the weight our conclusion will likely carry.

- Second, publication will more broadly circulate our findings. Our work will be seen by a greater number of capable genealogists, some of whom may have other information or viewpoints to strengthen our argument—or to correct it, if need be. If we are research professionals, publication in a major journal is a valuable form of advertising. Our proof argument or case study can attract significant new clients.

We've become scanners for information, picking and choosing from the media salad bar like finicky children.

—*David A. Fryxell*[13]

Yet the most important benefit is one we'll derive even if our work never goes to press. As put by Alfred Kazin, one of twentieth-century America's most respected educators and editors, "The writer writes in order to teach himself, to understand himself, to satisfy himself; the publishing of his ideas, though it brings gratification, is a curious anticlimax."[14] It's the Kazin spirit, in the end, that prompts so many genealogists to feel like Edward Strother: "Now I'll have to write *another* paper. I've learned so much from this process that I shouldn't let all this knowledge go to waste!"[15]

NOTES

1. Excellent models for proof arguments appear in *The American Genealogist* (an independent journal founded by Donald Lines Jacobus, FASG, in 1922) and the *New England Historical and Genealogical Register*, published by the New England Historic Genealogical Society, Boston.

2. Case-study models appear in every issue of the *National Genealogical Society [NGS] Quarterly* (produced at the University of Alabama since 1987), whose articles usually couch proof arguments as "instructional lessons" that are broadly adaptable, regardless of family.

3. The best known American examples of state-level journals with exacting standards are the *Record*, published by the New York Genealogical and Biographical Society; the *Virginia Genealogist*, privately produced by John Frederick Dorman, CG, FASG, of Fredericksburg; and the *Maine Genealogist* under the editorship of Joseph C. Anderson III, CG, FASG.

4. In addition to the periodicals cited in notes 1 and 2, well-known examples of scholarly journals include the *Genealogists' Magazine*, published by the Society of Genealogists (London); and *The Genealogist*, an international journal founded by Neil D. Thompson, Ph. D., CG, FASG, and now published by the American Society of Genealogists through Picton Press.

5. James L. Hansen, FASG, State Historical Society of Wisconsin Library, to author, in his 7 February 1997 critique of an early draft of the present chapter.

6. For the Twain quote, see Edmund Fuller, ed., *6200 Wise Cracks, Witty Remarks, & Epigrams for All Occasions* (New York: Wings Books, 1971), 321.

7. Attention is hereby called to William Strunk Jr. and E. B. White, *The Elements of Style*, 4th ed. (Boston: Allyn and Bacon, ca. 1999), whose classic discussion of grammar and syntax should be familiar to every writer.

8. Elizabeth Shown Mills, "That Awful P-Word: Plagiarism," *OnBoard* 4 (September 1998): 17–20.

9. Margaret F. Costello and Jane Fletcher Fiske, FASG, *Guidelines for Genealogical Writing: Style Guide for* The New England Historical and Genealogical Register *with Suggestions for Genealogical Books* (Boston: New England Historic Genealogical Society, 1990), 17.

10. Robert Gunning, *The Technique of Clear Writing* (New York: McGraw-Hill, 1968); Rudolph Flesch, *The Art of Readable Writing, with the Flesch Readability Formula,* 25th anniversary edition, rev. and enlarged (New York: Harper & Row, 1974).

11. Gerald F. Lieberman, *3,500 Good Quotes for Speakers* (Garden City: Doubleday, 1983), 282.

12. Borrowed from "The Editor's Desk," *Editor's Workshop* (December 1991): 4.

13. David A. Fryxell, *Writer's Digest,* quoted in "Quotable Quotes," *Reader's Digest* (August 1999): 61.

14. Eugene E. Brussell, *Webster's New World Dictionary of Quotable Definitions* (New York: Webster's New World, 1988), 618.

15. Edward L. Strother, Steilacom, Washington, to editor, *National Genealogical Society Quarterly*, 15 August 1998.

16. Extracted from Twain's 1895 essay, "Fenimore Cooper's Literary Offenses." For eleven more rules, see the full extract in Alex Ayres, *The Wit and Wisdom of Mark Twain* (New York and Harmondsworth, Middlesex, England: Penguin Books, 1989), 253–54.

17. (Sidebar, p. 408) Truman Capote (1904–84), American author, quoted in Rhoda Thomas Tripp, comp., *The International Thesaurus of Quotations* (New York: Thomas Y. Crowell, 1970), 1062.

Mark Twain's rules of good writing—that apply to genealogy as well:

- A tale shall accomplish something and arrive at somewhere.

- The episodes of a tale shall be necessary parts of the tale and shall help to develop it.

- The personages in a tale shall be alive, except in the case of corpses, and . . . . the reader [should] be able to tell the corpses from the others.

- The personages in a tale, both dead and alive, shall exhibit a sufficient excuse for being there.

- The personages in the tale shall confine themselves to possibilities and let miracles alone; or, if they venture a miracle, the author must so plausibly set it forth as to make it . . . reasonable.

- The author shall make the reader feel a deep interest in the personages of his tale and in their fate.

- The author shall use the right word, not its second cousin.[16]

**PROOF ARGUMENTS
AND CASE STUDIES**

Writing has laws of perspective, of light and shade, just as painting does, or music. If you are born knowing them, fine. If not, learn them. Then rearrange the rules to suit yourself.

—*Truman Capote*[17]

FURTHER STUDY

REFERENCE MANUALS

Department of the Secretary of State of Canada. *The Canadian Style: A Guide to Writing and Editing.* Toronto: Dundurn Press, 1985.

The Chicago Manual of Style: The Essential Guide for Writers, Editors, and Publishers. 14th edition. Chicago: University of Chicago Press, 1993. A one-volume encyclopedia to answer almost every style question that begins "how should I . . . ?" But no one reads this in one sitting.

O'Connor, Patricia T. *Woe is I: The Grammarphobe's Guide to Better English in Plain English.* New York: G. P. Putnam's Sons, 1996. O'Connor is about as lively as a grammarian can get. Even if we don't read her for pleasure, if we heed her common sense, we up the odds that others may read *us*.

Ross-Larson, Bruce. *Edit Yourself: A Manual for Everyone Who Works with Words.* Rev. edition. New York: W. W. Norton, 1996. Nitty-gritty advice for whipping our writing into shape.

Taylor, Priscilla S., and Mary T. Stoughton. *The Great Grammar Challenge: Test Yourself on Punctuation, Usage, Grammar—and More.* Alexandria, Virginia: EEI Press, 1997. An excellent self-help manual.

Venolia, Jan. *Write Right! A Desktop Digest of Punctuation, Grammar, and Style.* Revised ed. Berkeley, California: Ten Speed Press, 1995. The approach is similar to O'Connor's, but each little book includes material the other omitted.

SAMPLE ARGUMENTS AND CASE STUDIES

Brasfield, Curtis, CGRS. " 'To My Daughter and the Heirs of Her Body': Slave Passages as Illustrated by the Latham-Smithwick Family." *NGS Quarterly* 81 (December 1993): 270–83. Case study.

Evidence: A Special Issue of the National Genealogical Society Quarterly. Vol. 87 (September 1999). In addition to an overview of the latest principles of evidence analysis, this volume offers an example of case-building in each of the four evidence situations that require genealogists to present proof arguments.

Harris, Gale Ion, FASG. "John[2] and Mehitable (Danks) Harris of Northampton and Springfield, Massachusetts: Probable Parents of Mary Harris, the Deerfield 'Indian Captive'." *TAG* 72 (July/October 1997): 333–43. Proof argument.

Johnson, Linda Bennett. "Name Changes within the Melting Pot: The Search for 'Frances Vera Gilmore' of Detroit." *NGS Quarterly* 85 (June 1997): 85–93. Case study.

Jones, Thomas W., Ph.D., CG. "Howerton to Overton: Documenting a Name Change." *NGS Quarterly* 78 (September 1990): 169–81. Case study.

Mills, Donna Rachal, CGRS. "Rachael 'Fanny' Devereaux/Martin of Alabama and Florida—A Free Woman of Color: Discovering a Name Change through the Federal Census." *TAG* 70 (January 1995): 37–41. Case study.

Mills, Elizabeth Shown, CG, CGL, FASG. "A Husband for Phoebe Jefferson." *The Virginia Genealogist,* 29 (April–June 1985), 83–104. Proof argument.

———. Identifying Jean Baptiste Derbanne of Louisiana's Natchitoches Militia, 1780–82: Participant in the Gálvez Campaigns of the American Revolutionary War Era." *TAG* 68 (January 1993): 33–44. Case study.

———. "The Search for Margaret Ball: Building Steps over a Brick-wall Research Problem." *NGS Quarterly* 77 (March 1989): 43–65. Case study.

——— and Sharon Sholars Brown, "In Search of Mr. Ball: An Exercise in Finding Fathers." *NGS Quarterly* 80 (June 1992): 115–34. Case study.

Remington, Gordon L., FASG. "Mary Doggett, Wife of George[1] Lewis of Brenchley, Kent, and Scituate, Massachusetts." *TAG* 72 (July/October 1997): 321–28. Proof argument.

Rising, Marsha Hoffman, CG, CGL, FASG. "Trousers for Elijah: The Probable Identity of Elijah Robinson of Conewango Twp., Cattaraugus Co., NY." *TAG* 63 (April 1988): 82–90. Proof argument.

Saxbe, William B. Jr., CG, FASG. "Thomas[2] Walling and His Way with Women: Seventeenth-Century Misconduct as an Aid to Identification." *TAG* 73 (April 1998): 91–100. Proof argument.

21

BOOK AND MEDIA
REVIEWS

**BOOK AND MEDIA
REVIEWS**

Keynotes

Book and Media Reviews

by Elizabeth Shown Mills, CG, CGL, FASG

Publishing houses submit their print, film, and electronic publications for review, hoping for sales. Writers subject themselves to reviews, hoping for praise. Readers seek out reviews, hoping for skilled and impartial guidance. Reviewers exist to serve those readers. Ideally they do it with sensitivity, scholarship, and style—though not necessarily in that order.

Modern genealogy has become incredibly broad and increasingly specialized. Professionals and laypeople alike are victims of information overload. Within this environment, the need for—and the role of—the discerning reviewer has grown in both respect and responsibility. As skilled professionals, we admit an obligation to contribute to the intellectual growth of family history. Appraising the wares of the marketplace, within our particular specialties, is a vital social service that each of us can perform. But let's face reality: doing so with the verve and polish expected by a world accustomed to glossy magazines and erudite journals can be an intimidating thought. It doesn't have to be.[1]

> Reviewers exist to serve readers. Ideally they do it with sensitivity, scholarship, and style—though not necessarily in that order.

Basic Qualifications

A well-done review in genealogy springs from a knowledge of the

- role of the reviewer.
- mechanics of review writing.
- criteria for appraising different classes of materials.
- subject matter treated by the publication under review.

A *scintillating* review might boast other qualities that range from wit to brilliance. Fortunately for the reviewer, most readers of genealogical literature do place more emphasis upon information than entertainment—though that balance sometimes threatens to shift.

Of the four basic qualifications cited above, this manual presumes that we possess the last of them: expertise within our own subject areas. Therefore, our discussion can limit itself to the *role* of the reviewer, the *mechanics* for presenting a critique, and *criteria* for judging the research and writing of others.

Role of the Reviewer

A patron of a genealogical library is said to have complained to the staff: "It's a sin and a crime the way a piece of paper just lays there and lets *anybody* print *anything* on it!" He's right—and our field must share the guilt for contributing to such intellectual vice. Enthusiastic family writers have printed, still print, and will continue to print absolutely anything and everything without supporting evidence—not to mention things that fly in the face of all known evidence. Unfortunately, other searchers will continue to believe these things simply because they have been published.

As reviewers, we face an uncomfortable question: *What role should we play in the reporting of genealogical publications to the public?*

Is it our function to

- simply report the existence of a certain book, microform collection, or CD-ROM so that those who are interested can acquire a copy?

- set ourselves up as the proverbial one-person judge and jury, issuing a verdict that might damage the writer's psyche or the publisher's purse?

- thoughtfully analyze the product and courteously describe both its pros and cons?

As active reviewers, we can be well rewarded by a multitude of good materials that will enrich our own library. But realism demands that we anticipate a measure of mediocrity as well. From the start we need to establish a personal policy that we'll consistently follow in dealing with the disappointments. Which of our field's three "typical" kinds of reviewers should we be: the Charitable Reviewer, the Overworked Reviewer, or the Conscientious Reviewer?

The Charitable Reviewer

The Charitable Reviewer who hates to mention a publication's problems is being very *uncharitable* to countless readers who may be misled into wasting their money.

Authors and publishing firms give their products to reviewers. Their generosity is fueled by economics. The response of the reviewer is far more complex. One who places diplomacy above all else is likely to agree with Aldous Huxley: "A bad book is as much of a labour to write as a good one; it comes as sincerely from the author's soul."[2] Thus, the kindhearted reviewer (or the acquisitive one who never looks a gift horse in the mouth) produces a noncommittal review—a mere book *report*. Typically, a quote is pulled from the author's preface or cover letter, to tell what the publication supposedly provides. But the Charitable Reviewer would never produce so frank a critique as that of Ambrose Bierce, who is credited with the world's shortest review: "The covers of this book are too far apart."[3]

As well intentioned as Charitable Reviewers may be, they do not fulfill the objectives of a review. To borrow a quote from a classic manual on the subject: "A wishy-washy review is *useless*. A review that's [merely] a book report is a *waste of space*."[4] The Charitable Reviewer who hates to mention problems within a book is, most assuredly, being very *uncharitable* to countless readers who may be misled into wasting their money.

The Overworked Reviewer

Closely akin to the Charitable Reviewer is the overworked one, whose society journal or commercial magazine regularly features more books than any single human could adequately absorb. The customary response of the Overworked Reviewer to this mass-processing dilemma is the same as that of the Charitable Reviewer. A blurb is pulled from the publicity flyer that came in with the product. What, exactly, is the service that is being provided here—and to whom?

The purpose of a review is not to promote a product. That is the domain of the publisher's catalog or the flyer of the self-publishing author. The function of a review is to provide a thorough and reliable critique of the author's material—its usefulness and its shortcomings.

The Conscientious Reviewer

Our path as a Conscientious Reviewer is clearly the most difficult. A good and honest review is a *time-consuming* one. We are expected to make a thorough study and evaluation of the material in that publication. We often find it necessary to check the author's information or conclusions against some of the original materials he or she used. It is our knowledge of those sources that justifies our byline on the review. It is our responsibility to our readership to apply our expertise to the evaluation of that book. It is our obligation to ourselves to protect the integrity of our reputation.

Two decades ago, the book-review manual in the famed Writer's Guide series put the matter bluntly: "[We] must work to achieve fairness, objectivity, accuracy, and sensitivity . . . to make [our] opinions respected by readers. Aiming for this kind of credibility is an absolute necessity if [we] are to grow and develop as . . . reviewer[s] whose judgement will serve as an informal reader's guide."[5] Yet, mixed opinions (and mixed emotions) still exist in the genealogical field over the appropriateness of candid reviews—no matter how tactfully the constructive criticism must be expressed. Two anecdotes are worth considering.

> We often find it necessary to check the author's information or conclusions against some of the original materials he or she used.

- In 1962, the eminent Milton Rubincam, FASG, became book review editor of the *National Genealogical Society Quarterly*. He swiftly announced that the journal would thereafter publish *real* reviews—critical analyses—rather than "sweetheart reviews" that just parrot praise from the publisher's flyer. The society's librarian was aghast: "Nobody will donate books to the library any more!" Rubincam rapidly proved her wrong. Not only did his reviews become the most read feature in the *Quarterly,* but the stream of writers eager to have their work reviewed by such a discriminating editor soon became a flood. At the present time, the society receives ten times more books than it has space to review.[6]

- In 1998, George Handran, J.D., CG, wrote for this same journal a review essay analyzing a highly promoted CD-ROM edition of an essential source for Irish genealogy. Being knowledgeable about the research area and experienced in the use of both printed and manuscript versions of that particular source, Handran invested numerous additional hours in testing the CD-ROM before drafting his review. He produced an incisive, authoritative essay that courteously discussed a number of previously undiscovered omissions, confusions, and misconceptions. The result was exactly what the best reviews achieve in such cases: a reevaluation of the product by the publisher and a commitment to correct the shortcomings in the next edition.[7]

Mechanics of Writing

The artistic side of any writing can never be reduced to a formula, although certain guidelines govern good writing in every field. Book reviewing is no exception. Figures 29 and 30 define basic terms that should be understood by all reviewers. Beyond this, we also need to consider the audience, the format, and appropriate criteria to apply.

BOOK AND MEDIA
REVIEWS

FIG. 29

BASIC TERMS:

TYPES OF "REVIEWS"

Basic Terms:
Types of "Reviews"

———

Notice
A short and quickly prepared blurb, usually pulled directly from the advertising copy. Tells what the book purports to include, but does not assist readers in evaluating the merits of the work.

Review
A critical analysis of a publication that evaluates and discusses its strengths, its weaknesses, and the degree to which it succeeds in fulfilling the writer's purpose. Time consuming to prepare. Needs a complete study of the book as well as familiarity with other works by the same creator and books on the same subject by other authors.

Basic Terms:
Types of "Writers"

———

Abstractor
One who reads a document, evaluates it, and writes a concise summary that contains all important detail.

Author (nonfiction)
One who accumulates a body of knowledge through research and/or practical experience, analyzes that knowledge, evaluates the comparable usefulness of each and every part, determines how to link the most relevant information, and presents a smooth and meaningful narrative that reflects considerable skill in the development of original ideas and the use of words.

Compiler
One who assembles a collection of abstracts, transcriptions, etc.

Editor
One who selects and prepares material for publication—making corrections, additions, deletions, reorganizations, and explanatory comments as necessary and according to accepted practices.

Transcriber
One who copies records verbatim—without corrections, alterations, or deletions.

Translator
One who transcribes documents from one language into another, making limited stylistic substitutions to retain the sense of the original.

FIG. 30

BASIC TERMS:

TYPES OF "WRITERS"

Audience

Our first consideration as a reviewer must be our audience. We are asking readers to give up a block of their time—two minutes, five, or even more—that they can never regain. The magazine or journal that publishes our review has built a following by presenting information in the manner its subscribers prefer. As reviewers, we earn our claim to their time by writing to the style of that forum and that audience. Both our tone and the focus of our content should be influenced by the nature of those particular readers. Are they budding family searchers or advanced genealogists? Do they seek down-home inspiration or intellectual challenge? We study the reviews currently printed in the publication for which we are preparing our critique; then we craft our work accordingly.

Format

Regardless of the audience, five distinctive elements make up a good review: the publication data, the grabber, the discussion of the content and the writer, the evaluation of the work, and the conclusion.

PUBLICATION DATA

The core elements here are the simple basics of citation that genealogists use in all notetaking and writing:

- author, editor, compiler, translator, etc. (We should be precise. See figure 30.)
- title of publication
- place of publication
- name of publisher
- date of publication

Additionally, other data will help our readers judge the suitability of a book to their needs:

- listing of auxiliary material (prefaces, indexes, illustrations, maps, etc.)
- number of volumes and number of pages in each
- construction of book (hardback or softback, special paper, etc.)
- price and shipping charges

Two other items often appear in review headers within the genealogical field, where so many books are privately released or issued by relatively obscure presses.

- full address of the publisher
- ISBN number

GRABBER

The opening sentence should always hook the reader's attention. In simpler years, so little was published on genealogy that family historians devoured every word. Those days are gone. Modern researchers have much to choose from and a dearth of time to cover it all. Their attention has to be *grabbed!*[8]

Modern researchers have much to choose from and a dearth of time to cover it all. Their attention has to be *grabbed!*

**BOOK AND MEDIA
REVIEWS**

A fair review informs
readers of the extent to
which the work meets the
creator's purposes. . . . A
good review also appraises the work by the standards of the field.

*—Thomas W. Jones,
Ph.D., CG[9]*

DISCUSSION

One-half to two-thirds of a review should present a precis of the publication and its creator's qualifications. Typically, this section reports whatever purpose or goals are set forth in the compiler's preface and then discusses the content of the publication—avoiding a dreary chapter-by-chapter recital of the table of contents. This main body of the review may compare the quality or scope of the material to that of other publications by the same writer, or—where appropriate—contrast the present work against publications on the same subject by others. In discussing the author's personal qualifications, of course, we're careful to limit ourselves to matters relevant to that particular publication. Both the author's private life and personal characteristics are beyond comment, although qualifications are relevant. *Ad hominem* remarks are beyond the pale—as are sarcasm and self-promotion.

EVALUATION

This second major section customarily covers a third to a half of the review. Key issues considered at this point usually include

- the extent to which the product fulfilled the stated purpose.
- the existence of any serious flaws.
- the quality of the writing or composition.
- the range of resources or depth of analysis.

CONCLUSION

The purpose of the closing is simple. From the standpoint of researchers and librarians who expect quality in exchange for their investment, the issue is this: *Is the product worth buying?* We do need to express our opinion in terms more imaginative than the clichéd "This book belongs on every library shelf," and we should be certain that our concluding recommendation is compatible with the positive-negative balance of our remarks overall.

Criteria for Appraisal

A fair examination of any publication begins with the question: *What is its purpose?* By the time we have finished our evaluation, we should be able to answer another question: *How well is that purpose fulfilled?* Between the answers to these two questions, we consider countless points. Some general principles of reviewing are outlined in figure 31. From a genealogical standpoint, the criteria for evaluation of a published work is influenced by two basic questions:

- Does it offer information in an original or derivative form?
- Can the information be considered primary or secondary in nature?

Chapter 17 provides a refresher course in the distinctions between these types of materials.

**FIG. 31
ALWAYS AND NEVERS
FOR
REVIEW WRITING**

Always

- *Always make every word count.* Most publications have a limit on the number of words a review can contain. As reviewers, we never think it's enough. So, every word we use must do double duty. We ruthlessly trim unnecessary verbiage. If we don't, our editor will.

- *Always present material in a professional manner.* That means: standard-sized paper, generous margins, double-spacing, clean pages, and copy prepared in the house style of the publication that will print the review.

- *Always provide full and correct information.* We provide our editor with all publication data for the header. We double-check all names, figures, dates, and facts. We triple-check all points on which we criticize the author, to be certain that we have made no error or misreading. We cite exact page(s) for all material we quote.

Never

- *Never review a book by a friend, enemy, or competitor.* No matter how subjective we try to be, personal feelings can still creep into our evaluation.

- *Never use our position as a soapbox.* A review should focus upon *what the author has tried to do* and *what the author thinks,* as well as *how well the author succeeded.* It should address standards but not treat our pet peeves or favorite causes.

- *Never inject our own person into a review.* Frankly, our readers aren't interested in our experiences; and we can't offer them any without appearing egotistical. We delete any references to ourselves, so the focus remains on the publication and its creator.

- *Never climb on a bandwagon.* Media hype is persuasive. Mass reactions are contagious. Recognizing this, many reviewers who value a reputation for objectivity will refuse to critique a book if they have already read someone else's review of it.

- *Never impale a writer upon his minor mistakes.* Every author makes some. Serious errors or a high margin of error should be called to a reader's attention, but we don't nitpick over a few gremlins.

- *Never submit the first draft.* Good reviews are the product of painful rewrites and bloody cuts. (If we don't do it, the editor will.) Review-writing can be harder than many other types because of the need to say so much in so few words, while maintaining reader interest.

- *Never review a given book for more than one publication.* There exists a relatively small number of influential outlets for reviews in genealogy. We should not try to dominate them with our opinion. Besides, most major journals take pride in presenting their readers with exclusive material; let's keep ours exclusive if we wish to be published by them again.

Original form

For the most part, publications that offer material in original form will be electronic or microform releases. Occasionally, we see a book that offers a facsimile copy of original records, but those occasions are rare. Among the considerations we commonly weigh when we appraise publications that offer image copies are these six:

- *Content.* Are the facsimile pages legible?

- *Completeness.* Does the publication include all material available in the reproduced volume or collection—or just selected data. (A pair of National Archives microfilm series, M804 and 805, conveniently illustrate this point. Both represent the pension files of Revolutionary War veterans, their widows, and their orphans. However, one offers the full contents of each file; the other series offers only selected contents of each.[10])

- *Informational background.* Has the publisher or editor added a foreword that describes the material to whatever extent necessary for us to be knowledgeable users? If the publication is not comprehensive, does the foreword or the instruction manual warn us on this point?

- *Organization.* Does the publication maintain the order of materials in the original collection? If not, is the digression explained? Does the explanation validly justify the publisher's decision to override the original sequence?

- *Transcription.* Does a typescript accompany the facsimile, to benefit those who may have trouble with the original handwriting?

- *Index.* Has the publisher or editor added an index? If so, is it an every-name index or surnames only? Does it include topical and geographic entries?

Derivative form

Publications that represent derivative works can usually be divided into two groups: those whose information is of primary origin and those of secondary origin.

PRIMARY INFORMATION

Derivative works based on material created by informants who were participants in the recorded events are a cornerstone of genealogical research. Thoughtfully prepared reviews of these materials can do much to educate beginning genealogists as to the standards and criteria they should apply to their own work (as the examples illustrate in figures 32–36). Typical points for the reviewer to consider would be these:

Abstracted source material

- *Documentary standards.* Is there a proper source citation for each abstracted or transcribed record? Is there a thorough preface, in which the compiler discusses the nature of this group of records and any inherent problems? Does each page carry a header that identifies the file or the collection or the name of the newspaper being abstracted or the court session whose minutes are transcribed?

- *Clarity.* If abbreviations or source codes are used, are these prominently identified? Are the abstracts sensible—or are they so cryptic that the meanings of many

> Thoughtfully prepared reviews can do much to educate beginning genealogists as to the standards and criteria they should apply to their own work.

passages are unclear? (Chapters 16 and 22 provide excellent guidance on the criteria that distinguish good abstracts and transcriptions.)

- *Accuracy.* How dependable a job did the copyist do? Arriving at this answer usually requires spot-checking the work. Sample documents may have to be ordered if the originals are not at our disposal. It can be embarrassing to give a glowing review to a publication, only to have more thorough users point out careless readings or even more egregious errors.

Diaries

- *Relativity.* How much value does this memoir's content have to genealogy?

- *Content.* Did the diarist gossip daily about kith, kin, neighbors, and enemies— recording a wealth of personal detail? Or is the diary a mere daily weather report? The latter can be useful to creative family historians, but prospective buyers of this material want to know whether they will receive dry seeds or juicy plums.

- *Editorial contribution.* Did the editor conduct research on the individuals mentioned by the diarist, to ensure accuracy in transcribing names? Did he or she add identifications (in proper editorial form) at the first mention of each person? Did the editor point out contradictions in things the diarist had to say—errors of fact or similar problems?

All types

- *Enhancements.* Is there an index? Has the compiler added photographs, maps, or other illuminating material? Is the binding of special quality or the paper of acid-free stock? Is the image quality fine or fuzzy?

SECONDARY INFORMATION

Genealogies and histories

Compiled histories and genealogies—authored by individuals who were not witnesses to or participants in the events about which they write—represent information of a secondary nature. They must be judged by even more complex standards than primary materials, the most important of which are generally considered to be these:[11]

- *Arrangement of data.* If the work is a compiled genealogy, the numbering system and the text format should conform to recognized standards. Did the author use the *NGSQ* System or the *Register* System? Did he or she concoct an idiosyncratic one that took us four hours and fifty-seven minutes to decipher? Our readers deserve to know.

- *Explanation of mechanics.* Does the preface explain the method used in compiling or organizing materials? Does it forewarn the reader of deficiencies that the author recognizes in his or her own work?

- *Documentation.* Is there a specific reference citation for each statement of fact that is not public knowledge? Are references even cited at all? Is there a mere list of sources at the end of each section (or at the end of the whole) with no guidance as to which specific pieces of information came from which source? Today's discriminating genealogists want to know.

> It can be embarrassing to give a glowing review to a publication, only to have more thorough users point out careless readings or even more egregious errors.

- *Interpretation.* Did the author accurately interpret and represent the facts appearing in the records he or she cited? Biographer Leon Edel offers sage advice on this point: "Imagination *must* be used [by an author] in putting the materials together, but [the author] must not *imagine the materials!*"[13]

- *Completeness.* Does the author systematically give full names, dates, and places? Are *all* lines of descent traced or just the narrow line that produced the author? Are female branches ignored because they do not carry the family surname? Such matters affect the usefulness of the work.

- *Chronology.* Are lines of descent validly reconstructed? We should spot-check several. We specifically look for (*a*) number of years between generations, (*b*) ages of men and women at time of marriage, and (*c*) ages of mothers at childbirth. "Generation skipping" and "generation merging" are common problems in published family histories. Authors who present marriages at uncommonly young ages or first marriages uncommonly late in life do bear an extra burden of proof. Has this particular author supplied the evidence or a satisfactory proof argument to validate the claim? (Chapter 20 discusses the points that constitute a valid proof argument.)

- *Pre-American ancestry.* Is the link adequately proved between the immigrant ancestor and the individual abroad who is alleged to be the same person? Does the publication boast a "family coat of arms" for a line that cannot be traced out of an American colony or state—or heraldic devices when descent has not been proved from a specific person who legally possessed them?

- *Perspective.* Has the author portrayed individuals with realism as well as sensitivity? Or are we led to believe that every member of the family was rich, beautiful, pious, industrious, and of noble ancestry? Has the author put the raw genealogical data into relevant and reliable historical perspective? (Are we merely told that someone's great-grandfather appeared on the 1880 census with $850 in property—or did the writer take the trouble to determine and report how that level of property owning fit the community pattern?)

- *Readability.* Does the text read like a collection of strung-together note cards—or the robotic writing of a computer-genealogy program ungraced by editing? Or has the writer consciously followed the principles of good writing that the world seems to expect from everything except government publications? Genealogy inherently possesses many factors that work against readability—not the least of which is the necessity of presenting so many names, dates, and source citations, as well as all the *ifs, ands,* and *buts* regarding the author's conclusions. Financial limitations may require an author to severely cut the narrative in order to produce a less-expensive manuscript. Nonetheless, a good family history does strive for readability and does follow all customary rules of grammar and essay construction.

Databases

Electronic publishing is so new a form that any attempt to describe its products will quickly be dated. However, many of the materials being released now in electronic form are databases—a genre that needs to be evaluated by criteria both similar to and different from the preceding list for other materials of a secondary nature. As a beginning point, we would consider the following elements:

> The superior genealogical compilation is not limited to names, dates, and places, but includes . . . family history, biography, interpretation and explanation of the facts.
>
> —*Noel C. Stevenson,*
> *J.D., FASG*[12]

- *Completeness.* Does the publication include all material available in the larger realm from which this data set was extracted?

- *Explanations.* Does the publisher provide a discussion that satisfies all our basic questions about the origin of this material? If the data set does not comprehensively treat its subject matter, are we explicitly told what has been omitted and why?

- *Documentation.* Does each entry in the database carry an adequate citation of its source? (Here, of course, the term *documentation* refers to source citation; it is not used in the tech-industry manner, as a synonym for *instruction manual.*)

- *Reliability.* Is the data set based upon material we would consider reasonably reliable? Has the information been reliably keyboarded? Random spot-checking of the data is essential to a trustworthy review.

Electronic anthologies

A second popular feature of genealogical CD-ROMs is the electronic anthology. Most major journals now exist in a compact disc edition that offers all back issues—for example, the *National Genealogical Society Quarterly* and the *New England Historical and Genealogical Register.* In the case of some publications, the CD-ROM editions are far from comprehensive. Occasionally, the selective nature of the publication is clear from its title—as with the electronic edition of the four-volume printed anthology *Genealogies of Virginia Families from Tyler's Quarterly Historical and Genealogical Magazine.*[14] At other times, the electronic title provides no inkling of the fact that the collection is incomplete—a notable case being *The Mayflower Descendant on CD-ROM,* which omits some ten years of that journal, then includes other publications not named at all in the title.[15]

For all anthologies of this type, the quagmire of possibilities is so murky that we can expect to spend considerable time analyzing not only the content and quality of the original material but also the thoroughness of the electronic compilation (as well as its user-friendliness).

Special considerations for electronic products

Electronic publications of all types make extraordinary demands upon the reviewer, who must evaluate them from at least four different angles:[16]

- Quality of the original material from which this electronic version was created—for which we will apply all the standards of evaluation that the particular type of material requires.

- Quality of the editorial decisions and care that governed the assembly of the electronic edition.

- Quality of the features added by the electronic version—appraised by the scholarly criteria that govern genealogical research, analysis, and compilation.

- Quality of the features added by the electronic version—appraised by the technological criteria that the computer industry sets.

The bottom line is a basic one: an electronic edition can be no better than the quality of the material it digitizes. Readers who are technologically savvy will expect our

Databases are still relatively new to historical research. Infelicities and shortcomings are to be expected as publishers experiment. However, it is not remiss to hope—nay, to expect—that producers will learn from user responses to their products.
—George Handran, J.D., CG[17]

Your review essay mentions some omissions of data on our . . . CD. We now realise . . . some omissions did occur, mainly due to the various stages of computerisation, and we are trying to update our data.
*—Publisher to Handran
in response to review*[18]

Thorough reviews *do* help publishers, authors, and consumers!

reviews to evaluate its interface and take note of its bells and whistles; but as genealogists, our primary responsibility is to critique the value of the *content*.

Summary Concepts

Reviewing is a service and a skill as old as the publishing process itself. Academic journals were actually born of reviews, when quarto news books were created in the mid-1600s "to acquaint the learned with each other's work."[19] Now that learning is the domain (and the right) of all classes of people, the function of the reviewer has not changed. It has been magnified. And the challenge continues to grow, as new types of material are put into print. Figures 32–36, at the end of this chapter, provide examples for several of these types.

Evaluating the work of others thrusts one into a powerful role, in genealogy as in all other fields. A reviewer's judgment and the manner in which it is expressed can significantly influence a publication's acceptance, even the future success of the author and publishing house. It can strongly shape the expectations of readers and the direction of scholarship. It can introduce countless people to the rewards of genealogy, and it can positively or disastrously effect the standards those people adopt. To test, to teach, to stimulate—this is our challenge as well as our purpose.

To test, to teach, to stimulate—this is our challenge as well as our purpose.

NOTES

1. All genealogical reviewers are urged to read Katherine Scott Sturdevant, "Writing Analytical Book Reviews," *Association of Professional Genealogists Quarterly* 4 (Fall 1989): 59–60; and Thomas W. Jones, Ph.D., CG, "Guidelines for Book and Media Reviews," *National Genealogical Society [NGS] Quarterly* 86 (June 1998): 138–39. Jones's guidelines also appear in appendix B of this manual, amid the several statements of standards set forth by the National Genealogical Society.

2. Aldous Huxley, *Point Counter Point* (New York: The Modern Library, 1928), 194.

3. As reported by Gerald F. Lieberman, *3,500 Good Quotes for Speakers: A Treasury of Pointed Observations, Epigrams, and Witticisms to Add Spice to Your Speeches* (Garden City, New York: Doubleday, 1983), 65.

4. Sylvia E. Kamerman, ed., *Book Reviewing: A Guide to Writing Book Reviews for Newspapers, Magazines, Radio, and Television, by Leading Book Editors, Critics, and Reviewers* (Boston: The Writer, 1978), 20.

5. Kamerman, *Book Reviewing*, ix–x.

6. Elizabeth Shown Mills, CG, CGL, FASG, and Gary B. Mills, Ph.D., CG, "Responsible Book Reviewing," *NGS Quarterly* 83 (September 1995): 163.

7. George B. Handran, J.D., CG, "Griffith's Valuation—An Essential Irish Source Now Indexed on CD-ROM: A Review Essay," *NGS Quarterly* 86 (June 1998): 140–47. Feargal O'Donnell, Manager, Heritage World, to Handran, excerpted in "Feedback: The Readers' Page," *NGS Quarterly* 86 (December 1998): 245.

8. Professional writers well know the merit of the grabber. Writing for the e-zine *Slate,* Lucianne Goldberg opened her review of *Newsweek's* Michael Isikoff's presidential exposé with the following grabber: "One of the many amazing things about 'Spikey' Isikoff's new book, *Uncovering Clinton,* is the dexterity of its execution. It must be difficult to type and cover one's butt at the same time." Who would not read on after being socked by that line?

Goldberg's grabber is also instructive in other ways. The popular media often takes a more personal tack than scholarly objectivity permits, and hers is clearly an *ad hominem* attack. Readers familiar with the principals will recognize that Goldberg and *Slate* violated another credo of scholarly reviewing: one should not review a publication by an adversary. For the review, see Goldberg, "Spikey's Hypocrisy," at the website *Slate—Miscellaneous Articles* <www.slate.com/features/spikey/spikey.asp> posted 30 March 1999.

9. Jones, "Guidelines for Book and Media Reviews," 138.

10. *Revolutionary War Pension and Bounty Land Warrant Application Files, 1800–1900,* microfilm publication M804 (Washington: National Archives), 2670 rolls. *Selected Records from Revolutionary War Pension and Bounty-Land Warrant Application Files,* M805 (Washington: National Archives), 898 rolls.

11. Noel C. Stevenson, J.D., FASG, *Genealogical Evidence: A Guide to the Standard of Proof Relating to Pedigrees, Ancestry, Heirship and Family History* (Laguna Hills, California: Aegean Park Press, 1979), 146.

12. Stevenson, *Genealogical Evidence,* 155–56, provides an excellent, concise list of qualities to look for in a well-crafted family history. For more explicit guidance on these criteria, see Patricia Law Hatcher, CG, *Producing a Quality Family History* (Salt Lake City: Ancestry, 1996).

13. Quoted by Kamerman, *Book Reviewing,* xxvi.

14. *Genealogies of Virginia Families from Tyler's Quarterly Historical and Genealogical Magazine,* 4 vols. (Baltimore: Genealogical Publishing Co., 1981). The electronic edition is issued by Brøderbund Software, Novato, California.

15. *The Mayflower Descendant on CD-ROM* (Wheat Ridge, Colorado: Search & ReSearch Publishing Corp. and Massachusetts Society of Mayflower Descendants, 1996). An exemplary review of this publication, by Patricia Law Hatcher, appears in the *NGS Quarterly* 86 (March 1998): 72–73.

16. For other considerations that are essential to the evaluation and description of electronic publications, see Elizabeth Shown Mills, *Evidence! Citation & Analysis for the Family Historian* (Baltimore: Genealogical Publishing Co., 1997), 31–33.

17. Handran, "Griffith's Valuation," 146.

18. O'Donnell, "Feedback," *NGS Quarterly,* 86: 245.

19. A. J. Walford, ed., *Reviews and Reviewing: A Guide* (London: Mansell Publishing Limited, 1986), 34, quoting from Virginia Woolf, ed., *Reviewing* (London: Hogarth Press, 1939), 29.

20. Walford, *Reviews and Reviewing,* 9.

FURTHER STUDY

Curtis, Anthony. *Lit Ed: On Reviewing and Reviewers.* Manchester, England: Carcanet, 1998.
Lindholm-Romantschuk, Ylva. *Scholarly Book Reviewing in the Social Sciences and Humanities.* Westport, Connecticut: Greenwood Press, 1998.
Steiner, Dale R., and Casey R. Phillips. *Historical Journals: A Handbook for Writers and Reviewers.* 2d edition. Jefferson, North Carolina: McFarland and Co., ca. 1993.

With ever-tightening budgets, librarians look for critical reviews as a guide to what is really worthwhile purchasing.

—*A. J. Walford*[20]

**BOOK AND MEDIA
REVIEWS**

FIG. 32

SAMPLE REVIEW:

TRANSCRIBED

CEMETERIES

Lay Down Body: Living History in African American Cemeteries. By Roberta Hughes Wright and Wilbur B. Hughes III. Published by Visible Ink Press; 835 Penobscot Building; Detroit, MI 48226-4094; 1996. xxvii, 339 pp. Index, photographs. Softback. $17.95 (shipping: $1.75).

Publication data.

Grabber

Lay Down Body is an important work, featuring three hundred African American cemeteries in the United States and Canada. Included are burial places of famous blacks, as well as unheralded slaves. Descriptions of smaller graveyards include several complete lists of interments and headstone inscriptions. Fascinating rituals of funeral and burial practices are discussed, many of which originated in Africa. Also chronicled are deplorable destructions, such as that occurring to early slave cemeteries of the Sea Islands, now being lost to developers of luxurious golf courses.

Discussion

The scope of the project is enormous. Criteria for inclusion, stated in the introduction, center upon conflict and struggle—although brief descriptions of several sites mention neither. For example: the Chicago-area Burr Oak Cemetery is listed, because of the tragic death of Emmitt Till, who is buried therein; but absent is any mention of the struggle against racism to open Burr Oak, which required armed guards and a court order.

Evaluation

Despite its valuable information, the volume appears disjointed, its organization confused. The first chapter deals with superstitions; the second with cemeteries in the Southeast. All other cemeteries are lumped together, followed by a chapter on genealogy for beginners. The title of the subsequent chapter, "Preserving Historic Cemeteries," is not indicated in the table of contents. The book concludes with chapters on burial societies and funeral and burial customs, a bibliography, and an index.

A future edition could serve researchers better if several needs are addressed. The index should include the personal names from the complete lists of interments and headstone inscriptions. Also beneficial would be a separate list of the three hundred cemeteries covered in the book—and footnotes to document the wealth of information offered.

Evaluation continued

Similarly, the chapter on genealogical instruction could make several useful points. Beginners should be told that cemetery records exist not only in libraries but also in nearby churches, funeral homes, and private possession. The authors state incorrectly that gravestones are "primary, original sources of raw material." To the contrary, gravestone detail, by its very nature, is often secondary and may not even be contemporary; the gravestone could have been purchased long after the interment.

Hughes and Wright are to be applauded for increasing awareness of black cemeteries, burial practices, and preservation needs for burial grounds representing all ethnicities.

Conclusion

Tony Burroughs

From: *NGS Quarterly* 84 (December 1996): 307

FIG. 33
SAMPLE REVIEW:
TRANSCRIBED RECORDS

Publication data

Upstate New York in the 1760s: Tax Lists and Selected Militia Rolls of Old Albany County, 1760–1768. Compiled by Florence Christoph. Published by Picton Press; Post Office Box 1111; Camden, ME 04843-1111; 1992. viii, 312 pp. Index, maps, photographs. Hardback. $43.00.

Grabber

"If you are not having difficulty with your New York research, you are doing something wrong," one frustrated genealogist is supposed to have quipped. While research difficulties generally know no state boundaries, pinpointing individuals and families in Upstate New York prior to the 1790 federal census is, with few exceptions, a challenge. Some published help is found through probate abstracts and military-service lists, as well as in sundry church records. The task is now much easier, thanks to the efforts of Florence Christoph and the publication of mid-eighteenth-century tax records for Albany County.

Discussion

Prior to the American Revolution, most of Upstate New York was Albany County. Its southern border was Dutchess and Ulster counties; on the east were the colonies of Connecticut and Massachusetts; and northern settlements stretched to Lake George. Essentially, the western line was undetermined. . . . The settled area of Albany County, as it existed in the 1760s, now encompasses fourteen counties.

Except for one tax list made in 1763, all the levies in this work date from 1766 and 1767, transcribed by Christoph from the original lists housed in the New York Public Library. To these are added Albany County's 1760–68 militia rolls that were first published in the 1890s. The combined tax and militia records provide a virtual census for Upstate New York a generation before the first federal count.

Evaluation

Christoph—a Certified Genealogist known for her Schuyler-family genealogy and for coediting the papers of New York's colonial governor, Sir Edmund Andros—adds helpful explanations to the transcribed material. Each list carries its own introduction. Discrepancies, Dutch terms, and interpretive readings are clarified through numerous footnotes. Material is presented in its entirety and its original form; and individuals are quickly found through the every-name index. Period maps and photographs of sample tax lists enhance the work, as does the fascinating 1760s map of "the Western Country" used for the endpapers.

Conclusion

As with all its publications, Picton Press has produced a handsome and durable book that complements the valuable historical and genealogical material contained therein.

Roger D. Joslyn, CG, FASG

From: *NGS Quarterly* 82 (September 1994): 229.

COMMENTS

Note particularly in the discussion:

- Readers are told exactly what records are included in the compilation, but they are not numbed by an item-for-item recital of the table of contents.

- Readers are informed that part of the records are already in print—a point of interest to anyone who has already used the earlier publication and may contemplate purchasing this one.

- The compiler has identified the location of the records used for this book and the review helpfully points out that fact.

- Readers are assured that the proffered collection is complete and precisely rendered. Dates of coverage are clarified.

Note particularly in the evaluation:

- The compiler is personally discussed but only to the extent that bears upon her qualifications for preparing this book.

- The compiler's enhancements are described and appraised.

- The reviewer includes no constructive criticism of the type commonly expected from a critical review. Most publications do have room for improvement, but occasional exceptions occur. A good review will tactfully address shortcomings; but if criticism is not warranted, a reviewer should not feel obliged to create any.

- The physical quality of the book is also addressed.

BOOK AND MEDIA REVIEWS

FIG. 34

SAMPLE REVIEW:

FAMILY HISTORY

Grabber

Discussion

Family. By Ian Frazier. Published by Farrar, Straus, and Giroux; New York; 1994. 386 pp. Charts, drawings, maps, photographs. Hardback. $23.00.

Stunned by the deaths of his parents (David Frazier and Margaret Kathryn Hursh) in 1987 and 1988, Ian Frazier literally took stock of his heritage. They had left an immense quantity of family papers and heirlooms, and he was intrigued by the clues they provided about ten generations of ancestors. Surely a family that had made and kept so many records had something to say. "I believed bigger meanings hid behind little ones," Frazier mused. "I wanted to pursue them. I hoped I could find a meaning that would defeat death" (p. 39).

As a journalist, he asked the reporter's questions: *who, what, where, when, how,* and—most of all—*why!* After six years of research, he produced an unconventional family history. Transcending the confines of begats, personal but neither parochial nor pedestrian, *Family* is an attempt to illuminate American history by recounting the lives of individual Americans who happened to be the author's forebears. For the most part, his effort succeeds. It is true that his ancestry is not a model for every American's background. Few families will have had so many ancestors who sent, received, and saved thousands of letters— or who kept and identified hundreds of family photographs. Fewer still will be those with forebears so uniformly Protestant or so thoroughly associated with small-town middle America.

Frazier strives for a broad view— analyzing ancestors by generation and placing them firmly in their time and place. Whether they came from New England, Pennsylvania, Virginia, or North Carolina, they all moved to the frontier—settling mostly in Ohio. The roles they and their contemporaries played in this vast migration and in the developing drama of the nineteenth century are reasonable

Publication data.

(Publisher's address omitted. The book was issued by a major and easily identifiable publishing house.)

facsimiles of the history of many Americans. Frazier follows their lives throughout the nineteenth and twentieth centuries, telling a narrower and more individualized tale with each passing generation.

Religion was central to the lives of his forebears, many of whom were ministers. Their letters and diaries are replete with religious thoughts, feelings, and experiences. Frazier imagines an encounter with them and guesses they would disdainfully dismiss him and his contemporaries as nothingarians. To bridge the gap between his philosophies and theirs, he read widely in American religious history. Ultimately, he concluded that to know our ancestors and ourselves, it is essential to know both what *they* believed and what *we* believe.

Frazier provides informative endnotes about his sources; but he made a critical error in omitting personal-name, place-name, and subject indexes for a book that explores broad sweeps of the country and introduces a wide range of individuals within and outside his family. A good editor would also have pruned the book by about one-quarter.

Helen Hinchliff, Ph.D., CG

Extended discussion

Limited but pointed analysis. Conclusion is implicit rather than explicit.

From: *NGS Quarterly* 83 (June 1995): 143

FIG. 35
SAMPLE REVIEW:
GENEALOGICAL HISTORY

The Cottons of Catahoula and Related Families. By William Davis Cotton with Carole Cotton-Winn. (Rayville, La.: Privately published, 1987). xvi, 273 pp. Acknowledgments, preface, indices of photographs, documents, charts, family names, appendices, notes. Cloth. $33.00.

Publication data.

(Private publisher's address omitted—as per journal's house style)

Grabber

The Cottons is a tribute to stalwart ancestors and the printer's art. Few privately published books offer the quality of type, paper, or graphics that this family history displays. Illustrations are not merely ample, they are often exquisitely poignant reflections—in portrait and pen—of the generations that comprise the nineteenth- and twentieth-century Cottons and their kin.

Discussion

The social, economic, and political roles played by the ancestors of William Davis Cotton and his daughter Carole Cotton-Winn are herein replayed on the frontier stages of primarily Cabarrus and Rowan counties in North Carolina and Catahoula Parish, Louisiana. The cast ranges from English knights to German farmers, from bound orphans to judges, from Revolutionary privates to steamboat captains. The Cottons offer indisputable proof that begats need not be boring.

Evaluation

It is regrettable that the discrimination shown in the physical assembly of the book is not reflected in the genealogical research upon which the book is built. Once that cast of characters moves out of those generations of recent memory, the strength of the characters—and the evidence that supports their roles—pales drastically. While most of the central lines begin somewhere in the Middle Ages, pre-1580 documentation is rare (and even more rarely acceptable). Medical marvels are wrought, as for example (p. 15) when the obviously hardy Anna Maria (Fischer) Faggart bore her son George at the age of fifty-eight. Late-life fecundity apparently was a family trait, since Anna Maria herself was born to a seventy-three-year-old father—or so the reader is told (sans proof).

If the student of the family believes that all sources are of equal reliability; that every person's date and place of birth, marriage, and death are carved in granite atop Mount Sinai; and that the genealogist need only look up an ancestor's name in a book somewhere in order to learn these dates and names of parents, then he will be enchanted by the present volume. But if the reader permits herself to wonder what proof there is (p. 6) for the alleged identities, parentages, and places of the first three generations of Cottons in Jamaica, Virginia, and North Carolina, she will be sorely frustrated. (She need not worry about proof of dates since blanks appear instead of dates for fourteen of the fifteen births, marriages, and deaths which one can expect to occur in the lives of any three couples who comprise a single line of descent.)

Evaluation continued

The idealist who lurks inside the present reviewer cannot recommend this work as a model for other genealogists to follow. The realist within her recognizes, still, that most of the family members for whom this history was prepared will find much pleasure and pride in the Cottons. Most, in fact, will be grateful that the compilers have "traced their family for them," and not for a moment will they quibble, as this reviewer has done, over documentation. But many of those same family members will eventually be surprised and disappointed—when they attempt to join one or another lineage society on the basis of this publication, only to receive a letter saying "I am sorry, but the assertions of a family history which offers no proof are no longer acceptable."

Conclusion

Elizabeth Shown Mills, CG, CGL, FASG

From: *Louisiana History* 31
      (Summer 1990): 224–25

**BOOK AND MEDIA
REVIEWS**

FIG. 36

SAMPLE REVIEW:

HOW-TO BOOK

*Publication
data*

Grabber

Discussion

Italian Genealogical Records: How to Use Italian Civil, Ecclesiastical, & Other Records in Family History Research. By Trafford R. Cole. Published by Ancestry; Post Office Box 476; Salt Lake City, UT 84110–0476; 1995. xiii, 251 pp. Appendixes, glossary, illustrations, index, maps, photographs. Hardback. $34.95 (shipping: $4.50).

Some books should come with a label like washing instructions for a garment. If this one did, it would say: *Read from cover to cover. Do not skim. Then rest. Repeat.*

The need for clear, concise, user-friendly how-to books remains a staple in the ever-changing field of genealogy, especially because of the specific needs that the ethnic genres have. For Italian-Americans, there is now hope—and help—in *Italian Genealogical Records,* although the book is not meant for novices. It will assist genealogists in using record sources in Italy and can be applied to the limited resources available on microfilm via the Family History Library in Salt Lake City. However, researchers of Italian ancestry must do their homework with U.S. records before using this book to find Italian materials.

In a logical progression, this guide builds upon the groundwork already laid in earlier articles by Cole (an American living in Italy, who draws upon years of research experience in that country), as well as by the work of John Philip Colletta, Priscilla DeAngelis, and others. After brief discussions on beginning research, Italian history, surname meaning and origin, and nobility, Cole dives into the records. Civil, parish, and diocesan resources are treated—including Waldesian, Jewish, and Greek Orthodox sources. Such auxiliary materials as census, emigration, military, notarial, passport, tax, and university records (all elusive to most Italian researchers) are also covered. Cole illustrates his discussions with transcribed and translated documents; he explains them in detail—including variations based on type, time period, and location—and points out the genealogical importance contained within each type. The section on research procedure is extremely important to the reader who might travel to Italy. . . . It offers much insight on accessibility, problems and problem-solving techniques, the hiring of a professional researcher, and correspondence. Sample letters appear in both Italian and English.

Unfortunately, over-generalizations occur in the book regarding the availability and location of various record types. The general censuses for the province of Lucca from at least 1861 through 1881 are not held at the state archives (Archivio di Stato) in that province, but rather at the local (comune) archives. However, the tax and census records through 1851 are at Lucca's Archivio di Stato—not at Florence in Tuscany (as the reader has been told). Lucca was not considered a part of Tuscany until 1851. Contrary to Cole's opinion, these censuses are indeed useful in documenting and constructing several generations of families. Also, not all state archives hold notarial records; there are several notarial archives separate from the state archives. Readers should write to each repository to ascertain its holdings for specific record types and the dates encompassed. A future edition of this guide should adjust these oversights and include more in-depth discussions of comune archives and court records.

Cole provides superb enhancements. The documents he discusses are illustrated by manuscripts, photocopies, photographs, relationship charts, and maps that highlight important political and geographic changes affecting research procedure and methodology. All are especially well presented for the later period, 1812–70. Tables of essential terminology include numbers and ordinals, months, days of the week, occupations, and common names—as well as address lists for the various state archives and the Catholic diocesan seats. The tables of common male and female names provide the Italian spelling and abbreviation, the Latin spelling and Latin abbreviation, the English equivalent, and a dialect or nickname for each. While the whole is excellent, many common names are missing; and abbreviations would have been better indicated by using the customary superscript letters and elongated superscript dash to indicate abbreviations as they appear in original records. The section on the explanation of names found in documents should be carefully noted, especially the discussion of the various grammatical cases used in Latin.

All in all, *Italian Genealogical Records* is almost one-stop shopping for the Italian genealogist. Readers who comb it cover to cover, with close attention to details and explanations, will glean a much better understanding of this country's resources and their regional variances.

Jonathan Galli, CGRS

Evaluation

Conclusion

From: *NGS Quarterly* 84 (March 1996): 53–54

22

RECORD COMPILATIONS

Keynotes

Record Compilations

by Bettie Cummings Cook, CG

What motivates genealogists to become compilers? Most who choose this endeavor have a unique fondness for records—even when their own ancestors are not in them—and a desire to make sources available to others. They are excited by the discovery of previously unknown materials. They worry over collections that are deteriorating to the point that their information will soon be lost. Many are "local historians," as well as genealogists, and realize the rich knowledge they can glean about their region from the process of studying every word of every record and creating finding aids that foster the reassembly of lives and events.

Compiling records is a service of value to many related disciplines. Historians need these raw materials but often lack the access, time, or training necessary to glean the specifics they need. Biographers, demographers, and cultural geographers need conveniently published records for their own synthetic studies. Geneticists, historic-preservation officers, and legal researchers routinely comb library shelves for "processed records" that will expedite their research projects.

Records suitable for abstracting—records that virtually *beg* for publishing—are legion. They exist at every level of government, from town halls to county courthouses to state, provincial, and national archives: censuses; court cases involving crime, debts, divorces, and other disputes; land deeds, grants, and surveys; military rosters, pension papers, and service files; registrations of births, deaths, and marriages; and wills and probated estate records. In the private domain, we find diaries and letters at libraries and elsewhere; church minutes, ministerial journals, and sacramental registers; account books of doctors, lawyers, merchants, tradespeople, and others active in our community. In their original state, the sheer volume of records available can overwhelm many people who need them. Skillfully abstracted, indexed, and published, the mass becomes manageable as well as accessible.

Expertise

Enthusiasm is no substitute for skill. Done well, record compilations are invaluable. Ineptly done, they can harm more than they help. The public tends to give all printed matter more credence than it may deserve. Those trained in other disciplines are usually unfamiliar with the exacting standards of genealogy; they tend to trust whatever record compilations they find in print, rather than reinvent the wheel by seeking out the originals of crucial documents to verify details in the publication. At best, errors on our part will add to the proliferation of inaccurate genealogies. At worst, mistakes we make in identity or interpretation could undermine genetic research, cause justice to go awry in legal cases, or lead to warped historical or social theories.

Skill in the compilation of records requires a sound knowledge base and significant experience in at least three areas: editorial practices, paleography, and terminology. We should not consider preparing abstracts or transcripts for publication until we

Skill in the compilation of records requires a sound knowledge base and significant experience in at least three areas: editorial practices, paleography, and terminology.

Preparing records for press
is a responsibility, not a
training exercise.

have acquired that knowledge base and experience—but this piece of logic often gets lost amid another circular argument. Individuals who realize early in their genealogical pursuits that they want to make the field a career are frequently advised to gain experience and name recognition by abstracting local records—for publication in local-society magazines or for posting online at sites such as WorldGenWeb, if not for self-publication. Yet, *reliable* abstracts and transcripts require a sound foundation in editorial principles, an understanding of the records being used, and considerable experience in the reading of handwriting. Enthusiasm, a willingness to volunteer, or a desire to learn are praiseworthy but not sufficient. Learning is a lifelong process, but preparing records for press is a responsibility, not a training exercise.

Editorial practices

Most record compilations consist of abstracted materials; less commonly, they are transcripts, translations, or translated abstracts. Regardless of their specific nature, the work we do to prepare them is a form of editing. That means we need to know and apply editing conventions—not just copyediting rules but also the fundamentals of *documentary editing*. Chapters 16 and 25 provide a beginning point. Beyond that, other useful manuals are cited in the FURTHER STUDY section of the present chapter.

Sharp-eyed readers will notice a few differences between the counsel given in chapter 16's guidelines and examples and the advice appearing in the present chapter. No disagreement exists between the authors; the issue is simply this: one must know the rules before one can know when, why, and how to break them. Chapter 16 approaches the subject from the standpoint of handling individual documents as a function of notetaking. Editing and consolidating an entire body of records follows most conventions for abstracting individual records. However, the compilation process also introduces other necessities that create minor variances in the conventions we apply.

INDIVIDUAL ABSTRACTS

A genealogical abstract is a summary of the facts. A two-page document shrinks to a paragraph. An 800-page court-record book becomes a 300-page volume of abstracts. This reduction is accomplished by eliminating superfluous words. Knowing *which* words are superfluous and *which* pieces of "legal rigmarole" contain valuable clues requires a knowledge of the subject matter and experience in working with that particular type of record. Chapter 16 treats many of the distinctions. It also introduces (among others) five principles that need to be further addressed now.

- *Editorial annotations,* when inserted amid the material being abstracted, are set off by square brackets.

- *Ellipses* (three or four dots, depending upon the circumstances) are used amid quoted matter to indicate omitted words.

- *Names (personal and place)* should be rendered exactly as they appear in the document—not spelled out. Names fully written in the original should not be abbreviated.

- *Sequences* of items should be the same in the abstract as they are in the record.

- *Misspellings* amid quoted matter are typically flagged by the use of *sic,* placed in square brackets.

COMPILED ABSTRACTS

All five guidelines for individual abstracts are sound, but they may require adjustments when we prepare large collections of abstracts for publication. A well-done compilation requires consistency, despite the quirks that vary from document to document in the original collection—hence the adage: we must know the rules before we can ignore them. When adjustments are made for the sake of consistency, they should be slight, infrequent, and cautious.

For a compilation, those five rules might be amplified or modified as follows:

Editorial annotations

Use judiciously. When words are dim, illegible, or smeared in the original record, we should make note of that defect in our abstract—adding the appropriate explanation in square brackets at the troublesome spot. For example, a will abstract might read:

> I leave all my wearing apparel to my granddaughter Alice Smith, daughter of my deceased son [*torn page*] Smith.

Bracketed annotations of this type are called for in a few other situations. When a will spells a testator's name one way, but the signature in his or her own hand spells it differently, an annotation would flag the discrepancy. *However, the use of such editorial additions should be kept to a minimum.* In creating a set of compiled records, our purpose is to record the information in the originals, not to explain or interpret it as we would do in a research report.

Ellipses

Use sparingly. This convention is invoked whenever material is copied verbatim and quotation marks are placed around the whole string of copied words. If some words are omitted in the quote, the omission is indicated by the ellipsis. However, abstracts are, by nature, a highly condensed version of a document, rather than an exact quote with only random words omitted. Readers know that compiled abstracts omit many unimportant words. If ellipses replace each omission, the number of dots on a page would be distracting, even overwhelming.

Careful rephrasing is the key to a good abstract. On occasion an exact quotation may be necessary—for example, when the meaning of a phrase is unclear; but direct quotes are more the exception than the rule. Rephrasing to avoid having to use quotation marks and ellipses can require the addition of judiciously applied commas, periods, and semicolons. (A period shows the end of a thought, a comma represents a small interruption of thought, and the semicolon marks a more important division than the comma.[1]) As a simple example, consider the following from Posey County, Indiana, Minute Book, 1832–46: first, a transcription of the original; and then the abstract that our publication would actually use.

> When words are dim, illegible, or smeared in the original record, we should make note of the defect in our abstract.

Original court minute (complete transcription)
(p. 127) 4 August 1848. "On Motion it is ordered that Henry Williams be hereby appointed Guardian of the personal estate of John Acuff Heir at law of Francis Acuff deceased The said Henry Williams having first posted Bond conditioned according to law in the sum of eight hundred Dollars with Nathaniel Miller as Security such is duly Sworn into office."

Abstract for a compiled volume
(p. 127) 4 August 1848. Order. Henry Williams appointed guardian of personal estate of John Acuff, heir-at-law of Francis Acuff, deceased. Williams posted required bond for $800, with Nathaniel Miller as security.

Names (personal and place)
Abbreviate consistently and minimally. Most sets of compiled records use abbreviations to conserve space, but our abbreviation policy should be thought through carefully in advance. If we are abstracting a large body of records from Switzerland County, Indiana, it is likely that we will have to include that place name many times. It is logical to abbreviate it, but we should do so consistently each time—*Switzerland Co., Ind.,* being the form recommended by most style manuals. We would not want to waffle between that and Switz. Co., Ind.; Switzerland CO, IN; and Switz. Co. Ia. (an old abbreviation for Indiana, which is now the standard abbreviation for Iowa). Such abbreviations as *dec'd.* for *deceased* are well-known, but any abbreviation whose meaning might be unclear should be spelled out. (Would *D.S.* mean *Deputy Sheriff* or *Deputy Surveyor*? Would *Aus.* mean *Ausberg, Austria,* or *Australia*?)

Most readers are frustrated by abstracts that force them to constantly turn to a key to determine the meaning of yet another abbreviation or acronym. It would be even worse, however, to follow the old footnoting habit of citing a phrase in full at first usage and saying "hereinafter cited as." Combing hundreds of prior abstracts to find the embedded first usage of an abbreviation is too much to demand of any reader. A prominently featured key is a logical solution, but those abbreviations should still be kept to such a minimum that the user of our work seldom has to consult it.

Sequence of abstracts
Stay faithful to original record order. Almost without exception, sound documentary editing calls for faithful adherence to the sequence in which materials were created. Completed abstracts should not be rearranged—alphabetically, chronologically, or otherwise. If (let us say) space, time, or financial constraints require us to limit our compilation of parish abstracts to just baptismal entries, fine. But we would still maintain the sequence in which entries are arranged.

Sequence of details
Be consistent, but stay faithful to the facts. In a compilation, we strive for a uniform format that maintains consistency without changing facts. Documents in a set, for the most part, have a pattern of wording that is similar from record to record. Once we understand the pattern of wording, we should be able to design an abstract pattern that precisely follows most documents in that set. However, an occasional adjustment

> In a compilation, we strive for a uniform format that maintains consistency without changing facts.

may be needed. For example, most American court records begin with a case heading that cites the date the record is written, followed by the names of the plaintiffs and defendants. Occasionally, though, the date the document was penned may not appear until the last paragraph. If the record volume we are abstracting follows this pattern, then that should be the order of our abstracts. When a random document "misplaces" the date, we may move that date to the beginning of the abstract for consistency—a slight adjustment that did not change facts or obscure any embedded clues.

Misspellings

Use *sic* sparingly. The types of records we commonly abstract are rife with misspellings. If *sic* is used in all such cases, it will be overworked. For example, consider the following deed abstract:

> 4 May 1812. Robbard [*sic*] Jones of Kwebeck [*sic*], to friend Jeemes [*sic*] Brady of Saint John, New Brunswick, power of attorney to collect all monies due from estate of Jones's bruther [*sic*]. Recorded 4 May 1812, Saint John.

Misspellings appear in both given names (Robbard/Robert and Jeemes/James), as well as the first place name and the reference to "brother." When abstracting many records for publication, the compiler usually exercises discretion as to how frequently *sic* is repeated. Most researchers know that personal names are likely to be spelled phonetically; as abstractors, we need not bother flagging each creative variation. The word *bruther* might be placed in quotation marks, to prevent our being suspected of making a typo. The most serious misspelling is that of the place name, but users of our abstract would be better served by putting the correct identification in brackets rather than just the word *sic*. All points considered, a better form for the published abstract would be:

> 4 May 1812. Robbard Jones of Kwebeck [Quebec], to friend Jeemes Brady of Saint John, New Brunswick, power of attorney to collect all monies due from estate of Jones's "bruther." Recorded 4 May 1812, Saint John.

EDITORIAL SELECTION

One of the most crucial decisions facing an editor who compiles record abstracts is the selection of material to process. Genealogists of yesteryear, when very little material was in print, could expect kudos for offering "Some Wills of Nowheresville." Anything was better than nothing. Not so today. When we send a set of abstracts to press, our publication is expected to *completely* cover the universe of records it represents. If we abstract from Generic Will Book 1, 1831–1850, then we should abstract *every* will from that volume; otherwise, we do not present a true picture of who created wills in that time and place. Similarly, a compilation of unrecorded documents should include every document in that collection of loose papers. For example:

- A file drawer of manuscripts bears the label "Certificates of Military Services Performed in 1787." We would abstract every document in that file: depositions, pay vouchers, rosters, and lists of invalid absences. Every paper down to the smallest fragment should be abstracted.

When we send a set of abstracts to press, our publication is expected to *completely* cover the universe of records it represents.

- An archival file is labeled "Fergus McDougald Trade Records, 1792–1837." The file contains material from a weavers' guild, with licensing records, membership lists, miscellaneous accounts and complaints, poor rolls, and varied correspondences. We would not limit ourselves to just the lists or accounts; completeness requires abstracting all documents in the collection. Some of the lists appear to be repetitive over a several year period, but we still copy them all. The very fact that any particular name is repeated from year to year in a particular order is an important consideration to researchers.

- Province-level pension files are arranged in alphabetical order. If we launch an abstracting project in these files, starting with applicants whose surnames begin with *A,* then the project is not complete until we have abstracted all files through *Z.* If the whole body is unmanageable, we could reasonably delimit our project to all files for service in a particular war; even so, all individuals in that universe would have to be covered.

Paleography

Before we attempt to compile any record abstracts, we should be knowledgeable and experienced in the handwriting of the place and time. When American genealogists see a published will abstract that states an heir "had moved south to Mipipipi," we groan but deduce that the abstractor was inexperienced. We can be fairly confident the place name should be *Mississippi,* although we are likely to have little confidence in the rest of that abstractor's offerings. But when the errors are less blatant, as most are, we can easily be misled. If that location clue to misinterpreted penmanship did not exist and the compiler who was inexperienced with the long *double-s* had rendered the heir's name as *Jep,* would that be a short form for *Jeptha*—or might it be *Jess,* the nickname of the *Jesse* we seek?

If *we* are the abstractors who need more experience, there are countless ways in which we could mislead others. If we read yesteryear's "open e" as the *o* it looks like to most people today, then the name *Heard* becomes *Hoard;* and the corresponding index entry could be misplaced by many pages. When we encounter the letterform called *thorn* that several Western languages of past centuries used for *Th,* and we mistake it for a *Y,* the error is even more grave. The initial-capital *F* that is frequently misread as a *double-F* and even as an *H,* the uppercase *L* that is misread as an *S,* and a few dozen similar tricksters can render worthless hundreds of hours by a well-intentioned compiler. In fact, compiled records with misreadings are not simply worthless—that is, something neutral that simply has no value. Rather, they are actively harmful, because their errors will confuse and thwart legions of future researchers.

Skill in reading the handwriting of a time and place is achieved in two ways: training and experience. Training can be a matter of self-education; good guidebooks and practice books exist.[2] Experience should mean hundreds of hours of research in records with comparable penmanship—including that of the scribe(s) whose records we want to publish. Once we are confident we have obtained the minimal level of skill and experience necessary to produce trustworthy material, wisdom suggests that we put ourselves to a test. If we seek certification or accreditation, our ability to

> Compiled records with misreadings are not simply worthless. Their errors will confuse and thwart legions of future researchers.

decipher and abstract old records of our area will be part of the examination. If not, we'd be wise to transcribe and abstract a sample block of records, then employ a credentialed genealogist of considerable experience in that area to compare our sample to the photocopied originals and critique our performance.

Terminology

Almost every type of record involves a vocabulary that is more or less distinctive to it. Courthouse and town hall records are laced with legal phrases. Vital records (particularly death registrations) and the daybooks and journals of physicians, druggists, and even midwives demand familiarity with medical and pharmacological terms. Church minutes and sacramental registers use everyday words in ways special to particular denominations. Ordinary probate and mortgage records of the past tax our knowledge of antiquated clothing, fabric, farm implements, and household furnishings. Military records are replete with references to obsolete armaments, ranks, and tasks. Diaries and letters can offer a sampler of any and all of these, along with quaint names for social activities and relationships.

Whatever body of records we choose to abstract, we should be certain we correctly interpret the language. If we have not already built a library of specialized dictionaries, we may need to invest in a few reference works we can handily consult when strange words confront us. *Black's Law Dictionary,*[3] Chapman's *Weights, Money and Other Measures Used by Our Ancestors,*[4] Christensen's *What Did They Do?,*[5] the Harrises' *Concise Genealogical Dictionary,*[6] Jerger's *Medical Miscellany for Genealogists,*[7] and Picken's *Dictionary of Costume and Fashion*[8] represent a smattering of the technical references that can help us correctly interpret obsolete and legal terms.

Miscellaneous qualities

When we publish compiled records on a particular area or subject, we will win (or hope to win) a reputation as a specialist in those materials. To *earn* that reputation, we should truly *be* a specialist. We need local expertise, genealogical expertise, and certain personal traits to meet public expectations of a records specialist.

LOCAL EXPERTISE
We need to know the major figures involved in our subject matter and members of the more active families of the region whose records we are abstracting. We'll call upon that knowledge many times as we attempt to decipher a particular scribe's unique set of quirks. We need to be thoroughly familiar with area topography; we would lose credibility if we incorrectly render the names of waterways and landmarks in our specialty.

GENEALOGICAL EXPERTISE
We should well know the nature of the records we are using. Those documents we choose to abstract and compile may have other materials directly related to them. Marriage records are a basic example. Depending upon the time and place, the law

We need local expertise, genealogical expertise, and certain personal traits to meet public expectations of a records specialist.

may have required the maintenance of marriage bonds and license applications, as well as a marriage register. Where they exist—usually as unbound original slips in a file box—these applications may identify parents or have parental letters of consent attached. The application forms may call for the male and female applicants to state their occupations, exact ages, and street addresses, or to cite (at least by number) any prior marriages.

Similarly, if we are abstracting probate records, we should know the steps and timetables involved in the probate process and the type of records that state and local law required in that time and place. Before launching a project to abstract legal records of *any* type—probate or marriage files, tax rolls, or court suits—we will want to visit an area law library to research the statutes that applied to the records we are using during the period covered by our project. (A summary of all this information would make a preface very useful to our users.)

PERSONAL TRAITS

Inquisitiveness, meticulousness, and persistence help us achieve excellence. We should be willing to do auxiliary research in atlases and gazetteers to correctly decipher any referenced places that are outside our area. We should read the histories and printed newspapers of the same era, if they exist, and auxiliary records—to ensure that we properly interpret the references to people, places, and events involved in our particular set of records. Accuracy is absolutely essential. We compulsively check and recheck the names and dates we transcribe; we proof and reproof our typed abstracts against the original documents. When all abstracts are completed, we compare the whole against the original, item by item, to be certain that no electronic cut-and-paste procedure garbled an entry or duplicated a section and that no document has been omitted. We may rest assured that dedicated searchers will compare our work to the originals and publicize their opinions of our competence.

Preparation

Choice of project

The materials we choose to work with should be ones that hold our interest—a boring job is soon abandoned. The records should be easily accessible. Nothing is more discouraging than to be denied access to records we need to complete a project already under way. We need to consider whether the records are private (as many church and business records are), restricted (as with some library and archival collections), or public (in which case they may or may not have restrictions also). If our compilation is to be offered for sale, we may prefer to select records with broad appeal. Interest in specific church registers, cemeteries, and other highly localized materials is confined to a far smaller audience than, say, petitions to the governor.

Wisdom suggests discussing the planned project with the custodians of those records. Even if we don't need their permission, we often need their cooperation and goodwill. They may be able to tell us whether someone else has a similar project

We may rest assured that dedicated searchers will compare our work to the originals and publicize their opinions of our competence.

under way in that same collection. If we are lucky, they may be willing to grant us special access or workspace.

If the custodians give a green light and report no knowledge of other projects involving those records, then we need to do sleuthing of our own. The Library of Congress holds copies of most (but not all) works that have been copyrighted. We may check its website online. A check of the LDS Family History Library's catalog, available at a nearby Family History Center as well as online, may turn up other books and manuscripts not at the Library of Congress; and the several online project registries may alert us to something already in progress.[9] We should consult local libraries and genealogical and historical societies; they may know of projects that have not come to the attention of the actual custodians of those records. If we find that the records have already been abstracted and published, we should check their thoroughness and accuracy. In a few cases, the quality may be so poor that it would be merciful of us to do a fresh compilation.[10]

We may also want to consider whether the work is copyrightable. As chapter 7 makes clear, many records popular among genealogical compilers are types for which the Library of Congress rigidly restricts the issuance of copyrights. In general, its Copyright Office expects books to display *creativity* of content or arrangement. The very qualities that produce an excellent set of record abstracts—faithful adherence to original order, consistent coverage of all items in the series, preciseness in recording details, and resistance to the temptation to "add in" information from other sources— are all factors that prompt the Copyright Office to rule *against* us. Even so, we may be able to protect our investment by copyrighting the distinctive format of our publication as well as the content of any preface we may write, illustrations or maps we may draw, and similar enhancements. A creative index that goes beyond mere personal and place names to include topical entries could earn a copyright for our index.

The very qualities that produce an excellent set of record abstracts are all factors that prompt the Copyright Office to rule *against* us.

Choice of work site

The ideal situation would be a project site where we can work on the records at our convenience and our own pace. If the material has been microfilmed, we might purchase the film or try to borrow it through an interlibrary loan arrangement that permits us to work at home. Investing in a microfilm reader is worthwhile, if several compilations are intended. Institutions, court clerks, or private sources may be willing to photocopy original records for our use in return for a typed, bound copy. When we work in a library, courthouse, or other repository, we should investigate the best hours to ensure an empty chair and access to the records. If our site is a public facility, we may have to learn to concentrate and ignore distracting surroundings and situations. We are much more likely to make copying errors amid those interruptions.

If we must conduct our work in a public facility, wisdom suggests consulting with the record custodians. We are likely to spend hundreds of hours on the scene; we will want a work spot that is comfortable for us but will not inconvenience the facility or its other patrons. If we wish to use a laptop, a scanner, or other appliances, we should get permission before we plug in our equipment; if the record custodians are unenthusiastic about paying our power bill, then we should plan to work off our own

RECORD COMPILATIONS

Planning the scope and
size of our project requires
careful estimations and
projections.

batteries. If actions planned by us might adversely affect the records—tracing or scanning documents, using pens at the work station, or even the mere handling of records that crumble when unfolded—then we should seek advance approval.

Setting parameters

PROJECT LIMITS

Planning the scope and size of our project requires careful estimations and projections. To ensure that we can include all the records within the limits we have defined for our project (type of record; particular collection, volume, or file; and specific time period) without the project becoming unwieldy, we will need a fairly accurate count of the number of documents involved. If, for example, we are abstracting a set of marriage-return volumes, then we would count the original entries, prepare a dozen or two sample abstracts, and format our notes in the style we plan to use. From this, we should be able to project how many published pages would be required for the planned project. On the other hand, if we are abstracting probate files, filled with all types of loose papers of varying length, we may need to abstract several complete files of "average" size in order to make a fairly accurate projection of the amount of material we can cover within the page count we have decided upon for our publication.

ORGANIZATION

Often, the chosen records are complex enough to present organizational dilemmas. A county's marriage records, for example, might include bonds, certificates, licenses, permissions, and recorded returns by ministers and justices of the peace. There may be auxiliary materials elsewhere—perhaps registers of vital statistics at the state level or extant marriage records kept by local churches. In genealogical literature, we find several ways in which such situations are handled, most commonly these:

- limiting each project to one type of marriage record. The first project, let us say, might cover *bonds* from the time the county was created through the year that the state revoked its marriage-bond requirement. The second project, then, might cover *licenses* from the earliest year in which they are extant through some appropriate cutoff point (perhaps, the same year at which the licenses stop, or the year at which our bonds project stopped, or the end of that particular century).

- limiting each project to a smaller time period—perhaps a decade—and including all extant marriage records of that time frame. If we choose this option, there are both appropriate and inappropriate organizations that are seen in the literature:

Appropriate
We preserve the integrity of the original record divisions by treating each type of record in a separate division within our compilation. We abstract all marriage bonds, in their original sequence. All licenses, in their original sequence. Etc. Each record group becomes a separate section in our compilation.

Inappropriate
It might seem "helpful" to create a consolidated entry for each couple, bringing

together every piece of information found in sundry record collections, and then arranging the couples in alphabetical order by either the bride or groom. However, that kind of "helpfulness" violates the integrity of the original records and destroys clues inherent in the original arrangement. We should let our future readers create their own summaries in their own project management systems. Our role as abstractors is to preserve all data in the original, and that includes indirect implications inherent in the arrangement as well as direct statements of fact.

RECORDING PROCEDURES

The fewer times a record is copied, the less chance there is for error. This basic principle suggests the wisdom of typing our abstracts directly into a word-processing program, rather than making handwritten notes for transcribing later. For whichever procedure we decide upon, a few special considerations would apply.

Direct keyboarding

- *Macros* can be created to save time in typing certain words and phrases that are continually repeated. If, for example, we're abstracting convict records of New South Wales, 1788–1800, then a macro that permits us to type just *NSW* and have the whole place name appear would save a significant amount of time over the life of the project. We might also make the macros *AR, CI,* and *CSC* (for Alphabetical Register, Convict Indents, and Colonial Secretary's Correspondence)—all timesaving substitutions that would not set the stage for misunderstanding at transcription time. However, such "working abbreviations" (and this is all they ought to be) should be limited to basic words we'll have no trouble remembering.

- *Continuous-speech dictation programs* are new and highly controversial (especially for genealogy) although they hold promise. Some have a reasonably good accuracy rate; others do not. When using any dictation equipment, all names need to be spelled out to ensure accuracy; words whose misspellings we want to preserve would call for spelling out also. When we directly quote a passage, we'll want to verbally indicate ellipses, open and closed quotation marks, and other punctuation. There will, in fact, be many times in which we'll want to dictate the precise punctuation used in the original to ensure correct interpretations. For example, when we abstract a list of heirs named in a will—such as Mary Susan, John Franklin, and William (which suggests three heirs, rather than Mary Susan John Franklin and William (which could just as easily be four or five heirs). Also to be considered: the use of dictation equipment may not be courteous in a public facility.

- *Signatures and marks* present both an opportunity and extra labor. If the record custodians do not object, we might use a hand-held scanner to embed in our abstract an exact image of the original signature or mark. If the custodians ban scanning but permit tracing, we can maintain a supplemental notebook or pad of tracing paper, on which we identify each signature or mark by the appropriate citation of the original file and document numbers. We may later scan or paste the tracings into our text.

Handwritten notes

- *A legal pad or spiral notebook* is more convenient than loose sheets, and both prevent accidental shuffling.

> Our role, as abstractors, is to preserve all information in the original, and that includes indirect implications inherent in the arrangement as well as direct statements of fact.

- *Index cards* do not have enough writing surface and are also easy to spill and shuffle.

- *Notes* should be taken on just one side of the paper to save time and ensure legibility later.

- *Transcriptions* should be made promptly, before our recollection of those particular notes grows cold.

- *Abbreviations of names* is a highly controversial matter. A fundamental rule for abstracts and transcripts is that names abbreviated in the original record should not be spelled out, lest our abstracts present a wrong guess as to what the abbreviation represents. However, there are a handful of given names so common that we might be justified in using personal shorthand for them in the *working notes* we will later transcribe. For example: James, John, Mary, Sarah, Thomas, and William represent a significant percentage of the given names we copy from most English-language records prior to the twentieth century.

If we choose to use shorthand for these few names, then cautionary procedures should be applied:

(a) We do not use just the initial. At transcription time, an entry for *T J. Tucker* may leave us wondering whether "T J." is our shorthand for "Thomas J." or whether just the initials were used in the original and we forgot to punctuate the first one. One safe, quick method is to use the first initial plus a short line to represent the dropped letters: J— (for John), J—s (for James), M—, S—, T—, and W—.

(b) We use this shorthand only when the original record spells the name out in full. If the original abbreviates a name, then we copy the abbreviation exactly as it appears in the record.

(c) Whatever shorthand we choose, we should use it consistently in our notes.

Presentation

Certain basic conventions apply whether we plan to compile volumes for publication by a commercial press, to self-publish, to donate our materials to a magazine for installment printing, or to post it online. Chapter 27, Preparing Books for Press, has much valuable advice on assembling a whole volume. Material contributed to periodicals should conform to their fomat, standards, and style. (If their standards should fall short of ours, we might reconsider the wisdom of contributing to that publication!) Beyond this, several other considerations deserve serious thought.

Enhancements

INTRODUCTIONS

Users of our abstracts need background material. Our introduction or preface or foreword should identify the type of records we are presenting, the time period covered by the series, and the whereabouts of the originals from which we worked—as well as any peculiarities concerning the collection. The length of the background

Material contributed to periodicals should conform to their format, standards, and style. (If their standards fall short of ours, we might reconsider the wisdom of contributing to that publication!)

discussion will depend upon the particular situation, although the introduction to a volume of records usually would be longer than the introduction to a short set of abstracts published by a journal. By way of example, the introduction to Bockstruck's *Revolutionary War Bounty Land Grants Awarded by State Governments,* a 608-page volume, offers a 22-page introduction that covers the following:[11]

- definition of land bounties.

- colonial roots of bounty grants in British America.

- importance of land bounties to the Revolutionary War effort.

- quirks in the awarding of bounty grants by the various states.

- identification of previous publications on this subject.

- explanation of military ranks found in the records.

- tips for using these records to extend family lines and determine places of origin.

- state-by-state discussions of the specific process, the underlying laws, and quirks within the individual states.

- location of the original records represented in this book and whether the abstracts were made from microfilm of those originals.

Compilers who provide this kind of background essay understand that it is not enough to provide just names and details to their buyers and users. Nor is it enough to just tell readers where to go to find the original records. Researchers also need to *understand* the materials and the circumstances under which these were created—to know why a particular ancestor did or did not appear in that set of records, what personal facts about the ancestor can be deduced from the regulations set forth in the law, and what quirks in the records might further enlighten or stymie their investigation.

In the simplest of cases, we should take care to note whether the source record is a file of loose papers, a book in a courthouse or other repository, or a microfilmed copy of those materials. When microfilm is the source of the abstracts, we should cite any identifying labels or call numbers that appear on that film—not just the number itself, but the library, archive, or film producer who assigned that number. Some materials have been filmed several times by different parties, with considerable variation in image quality and thoroughness of content. The reader needs to know not just where to find one of them, but *which specific one* we used.

> It is not enough to just tell readers where to go to find the original records. They also need to *understand* the materials and the circumstances under which these were created.

INDEXES

Our work deserves an index. This appendix is a major strength of compiled record abstracts—the means by which researchers can quickly determine whether a particular person appears in a given set of records. Despite all the time, labor, and cost we invest in the abstracting, few people will bother to examine our work if that index is omitted. From the beginning of the project, we should adopt the mindset that when abstracting is done, indexing will take more time and effort that is just as important to the final work. Major word processors can streamline that chore for us. At the least, if the idea of creating an index is too intimidating, then we should think

RECORD COMPILATIONS

seriously about donating our compilation to a periodical that indexes the material it publishes.

Our index should not be limited to surnames; researchers today expect *every-name* indexes. Because this is a finding aid, it need not—*should* not—be confined to *just* names. Indexing towns, counties, states, provinces, and countries will enable researchers to reconstruct migration patterns applicable to their ancestors. Indexing watercourses and local landmarks will enable researchers to identify their ancestor's neighbors—an important step toward establishing identities correctly.

Before creating the index, wisdom suggests that we print a final draft of our compilation and carefully study each page. We should run our software's spellchecking function and look for misplaced headings or single lines that may shift to the top of a subsequent page or the bottom of a preceding page. Any name, place, or term that appears on those lines will assume a new page number.

Appearance

Page layouts need to be eyepleasing and promote ease of use. The human eye unconsciously skims a page of print, grasping phrases and pausing at periods and paragraph breaks. Extra white space between entries prevents confusion as to where one record ends and another starts. This point is more important than it may superficially seem, because many types of records are a consolidation of individual items. (For example: petitions have attachments; court minutes may summarize a proceeding in the current session and then add a summary of an earlier proceeding.) Well-arranged pages provide a contrast of light and dark that fosters comfortable reading.

Beyond these basics, we should consider

- *Justification*. In printers' language, this means blocking the right margin evenly. A ragged margin distracts the eye when researchers skim for names.

- *Headers*. At the top of each page there needs to be specific identification of the material that appears on that page. Typically, a book's title appears as a header on the left-hand pages and the chapter titles appear on the right-hand pages. (Other acceptable variations include the one followed by the present manual, on which both the volume title and chapter title appear on every page.) Each page may also need a running head. For example:

> Book title: *Court Minutes of Timbuctoo, Wherever, 1800–1900*
> Chapter title: "Minute Book 3, 1818–1827"
> Running head: "March 1821 Court Term," "November 1822 Court Term," etc.

The running head is necessary because each individual minute may not (and commonly *does not*) individually cite a specific date. If a new term begins in the middle of page 133 and the minutes carry over through page 157, the only subdivisions that we would otherwise add would be page numbers. Thus, without that running head to identify the court term, the researcher who finds a name of interest on page 155 would have no idea of the date of the record without scanning every prior page back to 133 to identify the court session.

At the top of each page there needs to be specific identification of the material that appears on that page.

Similar situations are common with newspaper compilations, in which abstractors cover several different papers in the same volume but forget to add page headings that identify the specific journal for the abstracts on that page.

In short, we should thoughtfully consider the nature of the material we are abstracting to ensure that whenever a single page is photocopied, the user has full information as to dates, page or file numbers, and specific volume or collection names. Users are not happy with us when they photocopy a page of interest, diligently photocopy the title page also, and then—after returning home—discover that the photocopied text is missing crucial identification.

- *Capitalization.* Some compilers prefer full capitalization (capitalizing all letters within names or surnames) on the premise that it helps readers skim for names of interest. Feelings are mixed on the subject. Chapter 16 discusses it in fuller detail.

- *Design elements.* Some individuals who compile abstracts as a source of livelihood add watermarks (faint images of initials, etc.) or other designs to each page as a means of identification, should their material be duplicated for inappropriate use.

- *Final copy.* Ink jet and dot matrix printers provide inexpensive drafts. They do not provide clear copy for reproduction. Laser printers are the standard today, with the final copy being run on bright-white paper that has a slick (calendared) surface. The cost of laser printers has plummeted to the point that they are quite affordable. In exceptional circumstances, we could save our material to a portable disk and take it to a quick-print shop that can run a laser master for us. Material contracted to a publisher may have other requirements for submission.

Hatcher's *Producing a Quality Family History* offers a wealth of other suggestions that are just as appropriate for record compilers.[12]

Advertising

After all the work we put into our compilation, we should not fail to advertise it well. Many good compilers become discouraged and give up when they see their stock of books languishing on the storeroom shelf. Often, the fault does not lie with the compilation but with poor publicity. If we contract our book to a publishing house, that publisher provides advertising. If we donate our work to a periodical, it reaches a targeted membership. But self-publishers are on their own. At the least we should

> Many good compilers become discouraged and give up when they see their stock of books languishing on the storeroom shelf. Often, the fault does not lie with the compilation but with poor publicity.

- donate one or more copies of the completed work to the person or facility that gave access to the records.

- prepare flyers that can be left with the record keepers; many prefer to send these to inquirers rather than specifically answer research requests.

- distribute other copies of the flyer at appropriately related facilities and the area's genealogical or historical conferences.

- ask area societies if they will include the flyer with their next periodical mailing. Some will; some won't.

- donate copies of the book to libraries and archives in areas to which the work relates.

- send copies to appropriate genealogical periodicals for review.

- build a mailing list, starting with our incoming orders. Colleagues may be willing to share names and addresses from their own mailing lists or their personal correspondence.

Many would-be compilers ask the question: can we make a living by self-publishing abstracted records? The answer is both yes and no. Some people do, but they have usually built a significant book list of publications. Before reaching that point of eminence as compilers, we should view record compilation as just one facet of a well-rounded professional enterprise. We should not expect to factor into the sale price of our books all the time spent on abstracting; to do so would produce an exorbitantly priced product. Most genealogists conduct their record abstracting during lulls between client commissions or lecture appearances. Or they abstract in their personal time, while they are employed elsewhere. Or they are retired and pursue record compilation as a stimulating supplement to their retirement income.

> We should view record compilation as just one facet of a well-rounded professional enterprise.

Setting a price on any compiled work is as much an art as a science. We typically calculate the costs of printing, binding, freight, advertising, postage and bagging to ship the orders, and sales taxes on the income. We should also consider the costs of long-term storage and the amount of interest we could earn elsewhere if our capital had not been invested in the publication. A reasonable percentage above the base cost is a fair price. We should also study our market and the prices other publishers set for books of comparable type, size, and quality. If our books are overpriced, we defeat ourselves and become discouraged by the lack of sales. Worse yet, unethical people will do a bit of quick math and figure out that photocopying our work is less expensive than buying it.

Summary Concepts

We want our completed work to make a contribution to both the hobby and profession of genealogy. It can—if we meet the field's standards for quality. We need to develop our skills and thoughtfully plan our project. We should carefully and truthfully summarize all the facts in each document and abstract every record in the set we have chosen. We should avoid rearranging facts within the records or rearranging records within the set. We preserve original spellings. We properly cite each individual record that we abstract.[13] We supply an introduction with a clear, concise description of the originals we are using, inform our readers of their location, and provide them with any necessary background to understand the nature and use of those records. We add a comprehensive index. We give the finished product an eye-pleasing appearance. And then we advertise, never forgetting the old adage: *He who whispers down a well, about the goods he has to sell, will never reap the golden dollars until he climbs a tree and hollers!*

NOTES

1. For much more explicit guidance on punctuation, see chapter 5 of *The Chicago Manual of Style: The Essential Guide for Writers, Editors, and Publishers,* 14th edition (Chicago: University of Chicago Press, 1993).

2. For example, Kip Sperry, AG, CG, CGI, FASG, *Reading Early American Handwriting* (Baltimore: Genealogical Publishing Co., 1998). Paleography aids for a number of languages and countries are listed in chapter 4, The Essential Library.

3. Henry Campbell Black, *Black's Law Dictionary: Definitions of the Terms and Phrases of American and English Jurisprudence, Ancient and Modern,* 6th ed. (St. Paul, Minnesota: West Publishing Co., 1990). The 4th ed. (1957) has more obsolete terms.

4. Colin R. Chapman, *Weights, Money and Other Measures Used by Our Ancestors* (Baltimore: Genealogical Publishing Co., 1996); also published as *How Heavy, How Much and How Long? Weights, Money and Other Measures Used by Our Ancestors* (Gloucestershire, England: Lochin Publishing Society, 1995).

5. Penelope Christensen, *What Did They Do? Was Your Ancestor a Doddle Doo Man? Or a Gentleman of the Horn Thumb? Or Was He a Rag and Bone Man?* (Toronto: Heritage Productions, 1997).

6. Maurine and Glen Harris, *Ancestry's Concise Genealogical Dictionary* (Salt Lake City: Ancestry Publishing, 1989).

7. Dr. Jeanette L. Jerger, *A Medical Miscellany for Genealogists* (Bowie, Maryland: Heritage Books, 1995). Researchers may also want to consult, where available, classic works such as James Copland, *Dr. Copland's Medical Dictionary* (Boston: Lilly, Wait and Co., 1833).

8. Mary Brooks Picken, *A Dictionary of Costume and Fashion: Historic and Modern* (1957; reprinted, Mineola, New York: Dover Publications, 1998).

9. For example, see the project registries at the websites for the USGenWeb, WorldGenWeb, and the National Genealogical Society.

10. A well-known example is provided by Lyman Chalkley's popular three-volume set, *Chronicles of the Scotch-Irish Settlement in Virginia, Extracted from the Original Court Records of Augusta County, 1745–1800* (Rosslyn, Virginia: privately printed, 1912–13). Despite the fact that it was rejected for publication by the National Society, Daughters of the American Revolution, who issued a "substantial pamphlet" detailing its rampant omissions, transcription errors, misrepresentation of the contents of many records, and its general "condens[ation] to the point of mutilation," Chalkley's *Chronicles* have been trusted by perhaps millions of unsuspecting genealogists in the near century since its release. A new compilation from the same set of originals would be merciful indeed.

For much more specific details on Chalkley's problems, see Twenty-first Congress, National Society, Daughters of the American Revolution, *Report on the Chalkley Manuscripts* (Washington: The Society, 1912), and Daphne Gentry, "VA-Notes, Chalkley's Chronicles," Library of Virginia website, from which the above quotes are drawn.

11. Lloyd D. Bockstruck, *Revolutionary War Bounty Land Grants Awarded by State Governments* (Baltimore: Genealogical Publishing Co., 1996).

12. Patricia Law Hatcher, CG, *Producing a Quality Family History* (Salt Lake City: Ancestry, 1996).

13. To ensure that we properly document our abstracts, we should keep at hand a citation guide such as Elizabeth Shown Mills, CG, CGL, FASG, *Evidence! Citation & Analysis for the Family Historian* (Baltimore: Genealogical Publishing Co., 1997).

14. W. John Murray (1851–1928), English author, quoted in Tryon Edwards et al., *The New Dictionary of Thoughts: A Cyclopedia of Quotations,* rev. edition (N.p.: Standard Book Co., 1961), 63.

A dose of poison can do its work only once, but a bad book can go on poisoning people's minds for any length of time.

—*W. John Murray*[14]

FURTHER STUDY

Anderson, Dorothy. *A Guide to Information Sources for the Preparation, Editing, and Production of Documents.* Aldershot, England, and Brookfield, Vermont: Gower, ca. 1989.

Board for Certification of Genealogists. *The BCG Genealogical Standards Manual.* Orem, Utah: Ancestry, 2000.

Documentary Editing. Quarterly journal of the Association for Documentary Editing <etext.lib.virginia.edu/ade>.

RECORD COMPILATIONS

Every job is a self-portrait
of the person who did it.
—*Anonymous*

Leary, Helen F. M., CG, CGL, FASG. "Skillbuilding: Converting Records into Reliable Copies." *OnBoard* [educational newsletter of the Board for Certification of Genealogists]. Vol. 5 (May 1999): 20.

Luey, Beth. *Editing Documents and Texts: An Annotated Bibliography*. Madison, Wisconsin: Madison House for the Association for Documentary Editing, 1990.

Stevens, Michael E. *Editing Historical Documents: A Handbook of Practice*. Walnut Creek, California: AltaMira Press, ca. 1997.

23

FAMILY
HISTORIES

FAMILY HISTORIES

Keynotes

Keynotes (cont.)

Family Histories

by Christine Rose, CG, CGL, FASG

A family history is an exciting goal, a daunting prospect, and an excruciating labor—all of which leads to a considerable amount of dread, once our work is done. How will others respond to all our efforts? Will our book reflect the pride we feel? Will it vividly and accurately convey the dimensions of the lives we studied? Will it be a worthy contribution to genealogical literature? Whether we invest our labor in a client project or our own family's past, the tasks we do, the standards we fill, and the problems we have to overcome are much the same.

- *Our clients* may spend years amassing boxes and files of family notes. Frustrated in their attempts to correlate the mass of it, they turn to us for help and there is much we can do. The time, effort, and expense that go into the commission will depend upon the genealogical practices those clients followed. If they did not know and apply certain basic research principles, we may spend hundreds of hours organizing the collection, finding missing citations, and broadening the search.

- *Our own project* likely evolved over many years, as we progressed from rank beginner to skilled professional. Our family has waited patiently, and our elders are aging fast. We feel the prod of time; if they are to know and enjoy their ancestral history, we need to put our findings into print. So we pull out our many folders, critically appraise them, and groan. (Is this *our* work? Yes!) Standards were more lax when we started. Our files, like those of our clients, have serious holes—even missing citations, unproved statements, and weak evaluations. Obviously much needs redoing. "I wish I knew then what I know now," we lament, because we know how stringently others scrutinize the work of professionals. At this point, many of us feel we should start all over again.

The Objective

Creating a family history

When traditions have led to a body of proven facts, when we know enough to weave names and vital dates and personal data into the fabric of historical events that unfolded around each ancestor, when we proceed to assemble individual lives with skilled insight and analysis, we create a family history—a legacy the family will treasure for generations.

As authors, we help families preserve the stories their elders told. We illustrate their chronicles with photographs that capture the old farms before the last remnants disappear—or the sober likenesses of forebears who sat stiffly before unforgiving cameras in elegant studios or their own bare yards. Well done, our accounts will make older family members weep or laugh, as they relive treasured memories. We'll thrill young ones with sagas of ancestors in the Civil War or wagon trains going west. When we compile our own genealogies or when clients ask for direction in the research stage, we are in a unique position to shape a final product that will be everything a family history should be.

When we compile our own genealogies or when clients ask for direction in the research stage, we are in a unique position to shape a product that will be everything a family history should be.

The Preparation

Establishing standards

As professionals, we know what standards to follow. Our own family histories will reflect them. But what do we say to the clients who contend, "I'm just doing this for fun," and resist such basics as documentation, indexes, and standard numbering systems? We explain that documentation of detail, at research stage, is not just "extra work." It's essential to the process of understanding and evaluating the evidence. After all, recording sources and finding the *best possible sources* is the only way to ensure accuracy of fact and conclusion. We explain that family histories without indexes go unread, because busy people look first for their names of interest; only after finding those names do they consider spending time on the whole book. We explain that easily understood numbering systems are a hallmark of quality and a consideration readers appreciate. We explain the importance of studying genealogy's scholarly journals for style and technique: their articles illustrate family narratives, genealogical formats, and the handling of complex problems, while their reviews point us to other family histories we can use as models. In the end, our clients will derive immense satisfaction from knowing they have properly presented their work and preserved their family's story in a durable, creditable manner. And *we* will have the satisfaction of knowing that our guidance has shaped and preserved a piece of Americana.

Sound practices from the beginning save hundreds of hours in the writing process. Ideally, the compilation starts the day we or our clients begin research on a family. If we—or they—know how to properly investigate, analyze, and assemble findings, our work will help others whether or not a book materializes. If we do publish, putting that research into proper form as we collect data means we'll have much of our work done before formal compilation begins. Computer software, both database and word-processing programs, can help us organize our findings in the style in which we'll publish it, while allowing us to easily update our files as we collect more records. In the research process, we should think of each family as an eventual book or article. When we focus on the *possibility* of publishing, we are much more attentive to details.

Planning scope and structure

Family histories take various forms that reflect the preferences, as well as the research and writing skills of their authors. Bare-bone begats, commonplace in the past, are yielding to narratives that combine history and genealogy. Within this context we can choose from a rich array of compilation types within three traditional groups:[1]

Lineages   (or lineage histories, if the treatment qualifies)
Pedigrees   (or pedigree histories)
Genealogies   (or genealogical histories)

LINEAGE HISTORIES

The simplest of all structures, this one holds to a single line. It may represent either an ascending or descending lineage:

When we focus on the *possibility* of publishing, we are much more attentive to detail.

453

- *Ascending,* which begins with one individual and traces his or her direct line to a remote ancestor. (Example: Our client has validly traced her ancestry to Charlemagne and wants a book that begins with her grandchildren and traces through her to the legendary emperor.)

- *Descending*, which starts with a remote ancestor and comes down to a recent individual. (In a descending lineage for this same family, the book would start with Charlemagne and follow the direct line down to the client's grandchildren.)

Even though the emphasis in each generation is upon the ancestor from whom the client descends, known brothers and sisters would be identified in each case—and even discussed in detail, if we choose to do so. Each ancestor in the direct line (but not the spouse) is numbered, beginning with *1* and assigning numbers consecutively. The children's list for each direct ancestor is usually numbered in lowercase roman numerals, starting with *i* in each family unit.

As the name implies, when we produce a lineage history our account not only provides the known vital statistics of each ancestor in that one direct line but also puts each ancestral generation into historical context.

PEDIGREE HISTORIES

A pedigree, in its purest sense, is a chart of all known ancestors for an individual—not just a direct line. Thus a pedigree history is a narrative that focuses on direct ancestors, covers all of them (or all within specified limits), and provides both genealogical data and historical context for each (with identification but limited treatment of siblings in each generation). This, too, may be presented in an ascending or descending arrangement.

A pedigree history is a narrative that focuses on direct ancestors, covers all of them (or all within specified limits), and provides both genealogical data and historical context for each.

- *Ascending (Ahnentafel or Sosa-Stradonitz)* compilations are familiar to all genealogists, and follow a numbering system used by virtually every ancestor chart in paper or electronic form. (The most recent individual is numbered *1*, his or her father is *2*, mother is *3*, grandparents are *4–5* and *6–7*, etc.) Among narratives that focus upon the pedigree, this format has not been as popular as the descending pedigree, discussed below. However, it is a type far easier to compile, much easier for families to comprehend, and equally appropriate for articles or books.[2]

- *Descending ("All-My-Ancestors")* compilations have been a quite popular form for more than a century. Clients often request them because they have seen many models, but it is a more complex type to craft. Commonly, it emphasizes one particular family that often represents the author's or the client's surname. Chosen usually for books, this form opens with the featured family and traces its lineage from the earliest known ancestor. Full treatment is given each direct forebear in that line. The list of children in each generation may provide biographies of each child and even identification of their own children, but the only child carried forward for a full treatment is the one who is a direct ancestor. Separate chapters focus on other ancestral lines, each tracing a line in similar fashion until it reaches a female direct ancestor who married into one of the other lines. Within each family, the numbering scheme usually follows one of two standard systems: the *NGS Quarterly* System (aka *NGSQ* System) or the *Register* System.[3]

GENEALOGICAL HISTORIES

Full-scale genealogies are typically descending accounts that begin with a single forebear or couple (usually the earliest one known for a particular family) and include collateral as well as direct lines. To qualify as a genealogical history, an account should endeavor to place all individuals or family units into appropriate historical context. Within this framework, two types of genealogies or genealogical histories are commonly seen: the single-surname study and the full-family study.

- *Single-surname* studies focus upon biological descendants who carry the featured family name. Typically, each family account lists all children; for daughters, it discusses their marriages and immediate offspring. As a rule, however, females are not carried forward into full-blown discussions unless they lived well-documented lives as single mothers or married a kinsman of the featured name.[4]

- *Full-family* studies—genealogies or genealogical histories that treat all lines of descent, by whatever surname—have become the common choice today. Typically this genre begins with the earliest identified generation of the family or with the individual who first settled a particular country or region. Both male and female descending lines are equally treated, so far as each individual life can be reconstructed.[5]

Both types are commonly arranged by one of two standard numbering schemes: the *NGSQ* System or the *Register* System.

MISCELLANEOUS TYPES

Depending upon the nature of the information that research yields—and upon personal interests as well—genealogists also adapt the foregoing types in various ways. For example:

- *Hourglass genealogies* typically center upon a not-too-distant forebear: a favored great-grandparent, for example. The author commonly includes all (or most) known ancestors for that person and all descendants as well. The result is a hybrid, with the first section of the study being an Ahnentafel or all-my-ancestors lineage (or lineage history) and the last section being a full-family genealogy (or genealogical history).[6]

- *Multivolume series* usually treat several interrelated families or all descendants of one large family. Multivolume sets are also common when exhaustive research yields great detail on the earlier generations but later ones need more study. If this is our situation, rather than delay publication we might cover the first four or five generations in volume one and hold subsequent generations for later books in the series. In fact, this approach has an added advantage. More recent generations are far more likely to require an update, as research uncovers new lines of descent. Reissuing only the part with significant revisions is far more practical.

Assigning responsibilities

Most published genealogies have a single author—or a pair at most. For a large undertaking, however, families sometime split the effort among several descendants, with each assigned a different branch to research. In cooperative efforts, as editor or

> To qualify as a genealogical history, an account should endeavor to place all individuals or family units into appropriate historical context.

FAMILY HISTORIES

project manager, we establish the basic research principles—and teach them if necessary. We oversee the project to ensure consistency in fact and style. We examine every segment of the research and results for discrepancies, beginning with the basics covered in figure 37. We arrange for further documentation or analysis when questions or problems arise. We are the catalyst. Others expect us to furnish the ideas and the expertise that will make the family proud of their efforts. (And, of course, we remember to give proper credit to everyone who assisted.)

Reviewing research basics

Experienced genealogists know the value of constantly reexamining basics. As professionals, when clients ask for our help in preparing a family history we need to review with them several fundamentals critical to the research process.

DATES

For many events that lack recorded dates, we can estimate time frames to guide our research and reconstruct the family's chronology. Correlating census data lets us approximate birth years for family members. The dates on which a will first was signed and then probated provide a time bracket for the testator's death. Children's births in pre-modern families commonly occurred two years apart—a pattern that helps us estimate births—and the marriage date of the parent typically (but not always) occurred at least nine months before the birth of the first child. When age at death is stated, we can calculate a birth date. If a minor chooses a guardian, we know that he or she was likely to be over the age of fourteen years. When grantors deeded land without the assistance of guardians or court officers, they were at least twenty-one (although they could own land before that age). All such estimations based upon legalities, of course, require us to allow for variances in statute law across gender, place, and time—and this allowance means that our research must include legal *statutes* of each time and place, as well as legal *records*.

DOCUMENTATION

We learn at the onset how to cite sources, and we record full citations for every source we use—even when we are not sure of the source's relevance.[7] Otherwise, we can lose an enormous amount of time relocating these materials at a later date.

NAMES

While abstracting, extracting, or transcribing, we copy names exactly as they appear in the record. When we read a name as *Ben,* we are tempted to convert it to *Benjamin;* but we must resist. Ben may prove to be *Bennet, Benajah,* or *Benedict.* Later in the writing stage, after we evaluate all the records and knowledgeably assign documents to specific people, our *narrative* can use a standardized form of the name for each person; but the name still remains unchanged in our notes from that record.

RESEARCH LOGS

As we conduct our investigation, we keep a list of references and sources examined—

FIG. 37
COMMON
GENEALOGICAL
GREMLINS

The project manager or editor should watch for:

- Births stated for women above or below normal childbearing age.

- Births dated after the death of the mother or more than nine months after the death of the father.

- Births of siblings less than nine months apart.

- Marriages of couples at exceptionally young ages for the place and time.

- First marriages at ages considerably above the norm of that society.

---

whether the results were positive or negative. Commonly in tabular form, this log includes the date we consulted the source; the book, document, series, or person consulted; the library or other location; and citation details. Even if the search was not fruitful, we still record full details about the source and the effort. In months and years to come, our recollection of that day's work will have faded. We'll wonder if we checked that census or visited that cemetery. In the case of negative searches, we help ourselves and others if we include a comment stating *exactly what* we examined. If we used only the census index and did not have access to the manuscript returns, then a note such as *"Sylvio Spadini and family do not appear in an 1861 census index of Toscano, as published by . . . "* will continue to remind us of work that needs doing. Or, if we personally examine the manuscript returns for Pofi, a note such as *"A page-by-page search of this census reveals no Sylvio Spadini family"* will prevent later repetition of that task.

> Even if the search was not fruitful, we still record full details about the source and the effort.

RESOURCE LIST

Early researchers did not have our easy access to vast resources and excellent finding aids. Authors frequently went to press without having performed searches we consider basic today. Given modern advantages, readers will not be forgiving if we (or our clients) fail to use available materials to fill obvious gaps in the reconstruction of a human life.

In a biographical sketch of an ancestor, let us say, if we state that Dougald MacFarland was born in the United States in 1842 and we make no reference to Civil War service or to any effort to find military or civilian wartime records for him, we fall short of modern expectations for thorough research. Using every available census over the course of a specific lifetime and consulting the standard public records that exist for the place and era (e.g., court records, deeds and patents, and tax rolls—not just newspapers and birth, death, marriage, and will registers) are essential tasks.

To better ensure that all available resources are used, we might prepare a list of common materials for us, the client, or all team members to follow. A typical guide would include at least the following:

- Bibles
- Biographical dictionaries
- Birth and death registrations
- Cemetery inscriptions and cemetery office records
- Censuses
- Church minutes
- County histories
- Court records—civil, criminal, and local administrative courts
- Deeds, homesteads, mortgages, patents, and other land records
- Family papers
- Funeral home files
- Immigration records
- Legislative petitions
- Manuscript collections
- Marriage bonds, contracts, licenses, permissions, and returns
- Military benefit and service file
- Naturalization petitions and oaths
- Newspaper advertisements, articles, and obituaries (commercial and denominational presses)
- Probate files and wills
- Sacramental registers
- School records
- Tax rolls
- Voter registrations
- Wartime damage claims

Setting up a style sheet

Before any writing begins—even before data entry into any genealogical software—we set up a style sheet. We will refer to it often as the work progresses. At the least, we will want to specify styles in four technical areas:

ABBREVIATIONS

Most professionals prefer to write out place names, rather than abbreviate them; and style manuals routinely frown on abbreviations amid text—with the exceptions of *Dr., Mr., Mrs., Jr., Sr.,* and *St.* (for *Saint,* not *street*). Because genealogists work across national and linguistic bounds, avoiding abbreviations ensures greater comprehension and fewer errors of interpretation. If and when we do decide to use abbreviations (as, perhaps, in footnotes or endnotes), we should make a list of those to be used, apply them consistently under the specified circumstances, and publish that list in the book. If we abbreviate names of states and provinces, we should use the standard abbreviations—not the two- or three-letter postal codes rendered in full capitals.

DATES

Careful researchers do not use all numbers for recording dates unless quoting specifically from a record, in which case quotation marks go around the quote. Genealogy follows the international convention of recording day first, then month, then year—e.g., 17 June 1850. Adhering to both of these practices eliminates many possible misunderstandings. (See also chapter 1, Defining Professionalism, for DATE AND CALENDAR USAGE.)

NUMBERING SYSTEMS

Genealogical convention calls also for using standard numbering systems that are long-standing, clearly defined, and widely understood. For descending genealogies (as previously mentioned), the conventional choices are the *NGS Quarterly* System and the *Register* System. For ascending genealogies, the Ahnentafel (aka Sosa-Stradonitz) is the one universally recognized. All three systems, together with modernizations that embrace more complex families and immigration patterns, are well discussed in Curran, Crane, and Wray's *Numbering Your Genealogy;* but they will not be illustrated here, to avoid oversimplification that ill serves the professional.[8]

STANDARDIZED SPELLINGS

Historically, spelling has been anything but standardized; we find many variances in names of both people and places. In the note-taking process, we preserve those variances. When we compile a narrative, we are expected to use standard spellings. For geographic places, we consult atlases to determine what the standard is or was. For individuals who were literate, we use the manner in which each person signed. For those who could not sign, we are left to our own best judgment. When the spelling of an individual's name varied widely, we commonly address those variances in his or her narrative. When research conclusions hinge upon spelling variances, we will definitely want to note the particulars. When we quote from documents, our quotation always retains the original spelling.

Genealogical convention calls for using standard numbering systems that are long-standing, clearly defined, and widely understood.

The Compilation

Planning the structure

A recent book review points out the basic question faced by genealogical writers: *How do we structure the contents?* "Genealogies and family narratives are different species and cannot be mated," William Thorndale writes, "but a good published family history should contain both animals."[9] Thorndale advises separating the historical narrative from the genealogical summary—a practice suggested by the National Genealogical Society for its annual family history writing contest and demonstrated each December in the *NGS Quarterly's* presentation of that year's winning entry. This approach is particularly useful in family histories that treat each generation or family unit in a separate chapter. Other writers prefer to use a strictly genealogical format with historical context woven into each biographical sketch. Regardless of approach, however, good genealogists follow several principles:

- Make it readable, and make it interesting.

- Present the information in some logically organized order.

- Add *relevant* historical context.

- Include documents—and transcriptions, if space permits—or at least abstracts and quotations to add the "flavor" of each place and time.

- Elaborate in the narrative upon clues and other revealing details that the documents offer.

- Add visual interest throughout.

- Index every personal name—ideally, place names and subject references as well.

FORMATS
Genealogical accounts, whether or not they are prefaced by a historical overview of the family, traditionally do two basic things: *(a)* they assign a unique number to each family member; and *(b)* they provide a separate biographical account for each traceable individual who survived childhood and married. That biographical account follows a common pattern:

Paragraph 1: Genealogical Summary
The initial paragraph identifies the person, states the line of descent from the earliest ancestor, and summarizes that person's vital statistics: birth date and place, death date and place, marriage date and place, similar data on the spouse, and parental data for the spouse (if known). While some genealogists argue (validly) that this creates a "dry" introduction to a human life, readers still need these basics—and they need them consolidated in one single place. Otherwise, they may have to comb many pages to dig out enough of the basic vital statistics to determine if this is the particular John Smith they seek.

Paragraph 2 (and ff.): Biography
After the vital details are summarized, we are free to develop a life story in any

Separating the historical narrative from the genealogical summary is an approach particularly useful in family histories that treat each generation or family unit in a separate chapter.

FAMILY HISTORIES

logical fashion—chronological or topical. Historical context, quotations, documented facts, traditions, illustrations, and virtually every other type of relevant material are appropriate in the biographical section.

Final paragraph: List of children
Here, we cite all known children born of this person, following birth order or probable order. If the person had more than one union, we group his or her children by spouse, preceding each list with an introductory statement naming the father and mother. Modern practice calls for the list of children to specifically state each one's surname (as well as given name) and then summarize the child's vital data. If a child is not carried forward to his or her own individual sketch—as common when the child died young or did not marry—we also include at this point of the parental sketch whatever is known on that child.

This basic format applies regardless of the numbering system we choose. Careful writers and editors also strive for consistency in presenting the genealogical elements within the opening and closing paragraphs. When reciting the vital events in the genealogical summary or the children's list, for example, we should use a consistent sequence for date and place. If we report that John Smith was "born 2 February 1851 at the Mormon mission in Lanai, Hawaii," we should not then cite his brother James as "born on the island of Lanai, Hawaii, 13 July 1853, at the Mormon mission"—at least not without overriding justification. (This caveat is appropriate because sometimes we have additional detail about the event that would create a grammatically incorrect sentence if we do not modify the sentence structure.) As a rule, consistency aids both comprehension and data comparison within a family unit, and it renders a more professional appearance; but neither comprehension nor professionalism requires a rigid sequence of words in a manner that violates syntax or principles of smooth writing.

CITATIONS

Readers have nothing by which to judge our credibility if we do not cite our sources. This fact holds true, even if we include transcriptions of original documents and excellent evaluations. Modern standards require an individual citation of source for each and every fact that is not public knowledge. (A statement that President John F. Kennedy was assassinated in November 1963 is public knowledge. A statement that Uncle Caesar died in November 1963 is not.) A generic list of references at the end of a section of narrative does not suffice. We need to let our readers know exactly which fact came from which source.

Where do we place those references? All the major scholarly journals in American genealogy have eliminated in-text citations. Abbreviated parenthetical references do work well in scientific and other fields where they are limited to a few published works. However, in genealogy—where complex citations to unpublished works are typical—parenthetical citations amid the text greatly reduce readability. Most major journals in our field also use footnotes for the convenience of readers, although the more easily formatted endnotes are also acceptable so long as two criteria are met: we must *cite a source for every fact* and we should *use one form consistently*.

Modern standards require an individual citation of source for each and every fact that is not public knowledge. A generic list of references at the end of a section of narrative does not suffice.

FIG. 38
APPROPRIATE
DOCUMENTATION

Unacceptable

John Murphy was born 5 July 1825, in Lancaster County, Pennsylvania. He died 18 August 1891 and is buried in the family cemetery at Murphy Corners, Lancaster County. On 8 August 1843, in Lancaster County, John wed Mary Jordan, who had been born about 1828–29 in Pennsylvania as the daughter of John and Matilda (Smith) Jordan.[101]

> 101. Murphy research by Willie Nilly.

Appropriate

John Murphy was born 5 July 1825,[101] in Lancaster County, Pennsylvania.[102] He died 18 August 1891 and is buried in the family cemetery at Murphy Corners, Lancaster County.[103] On 8 August 1843, also in Lancaster County, John wed Mary Jordan,[104] who had been born about 1828–29 in Pennsylvania[105] as the daughter of John and Matilda (Smith) Jordan.[106]

> 101. John Doe, *Lancaster and Its Leaders* (New York: Vanity Press, 1890), 222.
> 102. Obituary, *Murphy Corners Gazette*, 20 August 1891, p. 3, col. 1.
> 103. Gravestone, Murphy Family Cemetery, situated just north of Murphy Corners, along River Road.
> 104. Lancaster Co. Miscellaneous Marriage Book, 5th page, unnumbered.
> 105. Doe, *Lancaster and Its Leaders,* 222.
> 106. John Jordan Family Bible in possession of John Jordan IV, Hershey, Pa. The cover and title page are missing; family entries are recorded in the margins of the foreword.

The fictitious examples in figure 38 illustrate the point. The passage in the first example falls short of standards because it puts forth many names and dates without offering proof of any point. Readers need specific references, as the second example illustrates. Clarity and preciseness also require us to be careful in the placement of our reference notes. The sentence covered by note 103 in the second example illustrates a technicality that can be handled in two different ways.

- If consecutive facts come from the same source and there is no opinion interjected or other data added from other sources, then a single reference note can cover the reported detail from that source. However, if so many consecutive facts come from a single source that the information must be broken into multiple paragraphs, then we should place a reference note at the point of the paragraph break as well as at the end of the data.

- Alternatively, if a large block of material (say, a long paragraph's worth) comes from a single source, it would suffice to cite the source just once, along with a statement that clearly indicates all facts came from this source. As an example: if an ancestor's widow filed for a pension and recited facts of his birth, death, service, marriage, and children—all in that one document—we might preface the discussion with: *The widow's petition speaks poignantly of the war's impact as she relates a wealth of detail about their family and friends. John had gone to war, she said, with Paddy O'Duill—a cousin who had been raised with John in the family cottage back in Carrickfergus . . . [etc.].*

Executing the details

ASSERTIONS

We should not state as fact anything we cannot substantiate. Even though we cite the source upon which our conclusion is based, we must be careful that our conclusion does not exceed the evidence. Fulfilling this standard requires careful reporting of detail and the use of appropriate qualifiers.

Careful reporting

In countless ways, genealogists can easily overstate or misstate the evidence they find. A fictional census entry (partial extract) makes the point:

> *1851 York County, Ontario*
> Jordan Johns   48
> Martha Johns   46   [no relationship stated]
> George Johns   15   "   "   "

For this household, let us say, we have found no other records that cite ages or relationships. We cannot make a simple subtraction of figures and assert that Jordan was born in 1803, Martha in 1805, and George in 1836—even if we assume that the ages are correct (a risky assumption in using census records). Because the 1851 Ontario census was actually taken in January 1852 and the age question was *Age at next birthday?,* all the facts actually support is a statement that Jordan was born between mid-January 1804 and mid-January 1805, that Martha was born in the same time frame of 1806–07, and George in 1837–38.[10]

Nor can we state from this record that Martha was the wife of Jordan or that George was their child. Odds may favor this; but it is also possible that John's wife had died and his unmarried sister had taken over the care of the family, or that Martha was a second wife. Jordan and Martha may indeed be the parents of George; but Martha may be his stepmother, or Jordan may be raising his deceased brother's child, or George may have been born to Martha before her marriage to Jordan—or any one of other possibilities as well. Unless we have other supporting evidence, we have to reserve our judgments about relationships or else add qualifiers.

Appropriate qualifiers

Assumptions, hypotheses, and conclusions are permissible so long as we clearly identify them as such. Let us say that we are tracing John Gordon, whom we find on the 1841 census of Stepney District, London; we cannot find him in 1851, but a Stepney tombstone dated 1856 carries his name. To state that John Gordon died in Stepney District would overstate the evidence. He may have died in another district of London—or even abroad—after which his body was returned to Stepney. Unless the tombstone or some other evidence actually states that he died there, then we have to *qualify the statement.* We can state that John *may have died in Stepney District, where he was enumerated in 1841 and was buried in 1856.* Or we may build a case for the death from indirect evidence when additional records warrant it. For example, if deeds, affidavits in military files or court cases, birth records of children, and so forth, clearly suggest a continuous presence *and no credible evidence to the*

Even though we cite the source upon which our conclusion is based, we must be careful that our conclusion does not exceed the evidence.

contrary surfaces, then we may omit the qualifier or upgrade it to *probably,* depending upon the strength of our indirect evidence. Qualifiers are honest and emphasize points that need further research.

Two other cautions apply to the use of qualifiers: First, we should take care to insert qualifiers in the right place. (Consider this statement: "Wong Lee probably died at San Francisco in 1897." Did he *probably die* or did he die in 1897, *probably at San Francisco*?) Second, we give due attention to the weight of the words we use. The following demonstrates the range of choices we have:

Possibly	There is a remote possibility	He could have
Probably	There is a slight chance	He must have
Certainly	There is a chance	He certainly must have

In the prior case of John Gordon of 1841–56, for example, for us to say *there is a remote possibility* that he died in Stepney would be too weak; and *he certainly must have died there* is too strong. We should use the right qualifier for the situation— bearing in mind the differences already established in genealogical usage for the basic *possibility* (a speculation), *probability* (an hypothesis based upon suggestive evidence), and *reasonable certainty* (used at "proof" stage when a hypothesis passes all tests).[11]

DATA CONFLICTS

Our readers deserve to know when data conflicts exist. Credibility and trust depend upon it. If we have resolved the conflict to our satisfaction, we explain the particulars. If we have not, we alert readers to a possible problem. What issues do we consider (or discuss) in that process? Using the common problem of conflicting dates, let us analyze a situation constructed for a fictional Conrad Weiss, for whom four different records cite three different death dates:

Civil War pension file:	25 February 1885
Family Bible:	23 February 1885
Gravestone:	23 February 1885
Obituary:	26 February 1885

Should we pick 23 February as the date because two sources agree on that one? Or would the pension file carry more weight because it is a government record? What of the obituary, which is more contemporaneous than the pension file and may be more so than the gravestone or Bible record? Let us assess the information.

Civil War pension file. We evaluate the date and the informant's identity. If the date appears in an affidavit made some years later, it may not be as accurate as a date recorded contemporaneously with the death. If the informant was the postmaster, let us say, the error rate is likely to be higher than if she were the daughter (although daughters certainly can and do make errors).

Family Bible. We evaluate the date and the penmanship. If the Bible was published after the earliest entry or if all entries appear to be in the same hand and ink, the record may be a transcription from an earlier Bible or a reconstruction made at a later time. The data may not be as credible as if created at the time of the event. However, if the hand appears to be the same but varies in ink and steadiness, it is more likely that the scribe made the entries contemporaneously with each event.

FAMILY HISTORIES

Gravestone. We evaluate the nature of the source, the clarity of the carving, and the style of the stone. If the source of the data is a published transcription, we would consider the possibility of a transcription error. If we viewed the original stone at some point in the past, we should reconsider whether the condition of the stone may have caused us to misread the date. If we are reconsulting the stone, we appraise whether its material and the nature of its inscription are compatible with other markers in that cemetery for the same time period.

Obituary. We evaluate the time differential between the death and the publication of the notice, as well as the publishing habits of the journal in which it appeared. If the issue of 25 February carried the obituary, the death date of 26 February seems an obvious error. On the other hand, it may be that the newspaper was a weekly that was often late in going to press. Perhaps the death made the issue before press time, in spite of the printed date.

Every facet of all the evidence needs to be appraised, and chapter 17 adds other useful insight. After careful analysis, we state our conclusion and explain our reasoning.

DATE ESTIMATES

The dates we have estimated for research purposes are just as essential in the writing stage, when we must place ancestors into a specific time frame. However, all estimated dates have to be clearly identified as such. Within family history, two established conventions help us describe more precisely the basis for our estimations:[12]

> Within family history, two established conventions help us describe more precisely the basis for our estimations.

About, circa, or ca. These terms are appropriate when the estimation is based on a record that states at least two figures from which we may approximate a third. For example:

- If Matthias von Damen's military file states that he enlisted in the American army in 1812, at age 17, we can say he was born "about 1795." (That seemingly straight calculation could be a year or so off. If he enlisted on 5 June 1812, let us say, and his unknown birthday was 4 September, he was actually born in 1794.)

- If the 1840 census (official date: 1 June) states that Matthias von Damen was over age 40 but under age 50, then we may say that he was born "about 1789–1800."

- If both these records apply to the same person, we can narrow it to "born about 1794–1800."

Say. This term is conventionally used by genealogists when an estimate is extrapolated from less explicit evidence. For example:

- If we know nothing about José Gonzalez except that he volunteered for service in the Mexican War (1846–48), we might state, "José was born, say, 1814–26," assuming that he was in the likely age bracket of 18–30 at the time he enlisted. (If he had been an officer, we might reconsider and show his age as "born, say, 1806–26," on the premise that he may have served in an earlier conflict and enjoyed officer status in the later war on the basis of experience.)

- If we know nothing about José Gonzalez except that a school census in 1853 reported five children for him, aged 5 to 12, we might state that "José was born, say, 1815–20," assuming that he married at age 20–25 and that the first child's birth followed within a year.

However, in all cases of *about* or *say* dates, we are obliged to explain our reasoning and cite the sources of the information we used in our reasoning process. Depending upon the complexity of the deduction and the ease with which it flows into the narrative, we may make the explanation in the text or in a footnote or endnote.

EDITORIAL ADDITIONS

The myriad details of editing oneself, clients, or team members are beyond the scope of this chapter, but two particular issues deserve comment: the handling of errors found in documents and the treatment of maiden names and nicknames. Beyond these basics, several chapters in this book address essentials of writing and editing.

Document flaws

We should alert our readers when a name, date, or word is uncertain. Some conscientious genealogists flag such points with a question mark, but an unexplained question mark adds to the confusion. Let us say that the will of one Guiseppi Martini names several children and that one of the names is partly unreadable. The first letters are clearly *Juli*, but there are additional letters. If we transcribe this as *Juli?*, our readers will assume there are four letters but that we aren't sure we have read the four correctly. A better way is to show it as *Juli—?* or, even better, *Juli---[?]*, with hyphens indicating the exact number of unclear letters. Beyond this, there are still other methods we can use to convey to readers exactly where a problem exists:

Julian [?] Martini   10 February [?] 1856
[Julian?] Martini   10 February 1856 [?]
Julian ___tini [?]
Julian [Martini?]

Chapter 16 offers much other valuable advice on this subject.

Maiden names and nicknames

Family histories that are not professionally produced often exhibit some unfortunate confusion in the handling of maiden names and nicknames. We can avoid similar problems if we keep three rules in mind:

- *Maiden names* (when following the English tradition of coupling maiden names and married names) are shown in parentheses—e.g., *Mary (Gordon) Smith.* If Mary was a widow, with a subsequent marriage to a Martin, we write her name as *Mary (Gordon) Smith Martin.* Alternately, we may refer to married women as *Mary Smith née Gordon.*

- *Unknown maiden names* may be indicated by substituting editorial brackets (square brackets) for the parentheses and filling those brackets with a single dash or (more clearly) a question mark amid dashes—e.g., *Mary [—] Smith* or *Mary [–?–] Smith.*

- Nicknames are enclosed within quotation marks—not parentheses—e.g., *Mary "Polly" Gordon* or *Mary "Polly" (Gordon) Smith.* Once nicknames have been introduced as part of the full name (as just shown), quotation marks are dropped in subsequent usages that do not include the formal given name—e.g., *At eighteen, Polly married John Smith.*

> In all cases of *about* or *say* dates, we are obliged to explain our reasoning and cite the sources of the information we used in our reasoning process.

If we progress far enough
. . . pride is bound to suffer
one of more jolts when we
discover we had ances-
tors with whom . . . we
ourselves would not care
to associate intimately.

—*Donald Lines Jacobus,*
FASG[13]

FAMILY SECRETS

Every family has skeletons. Handling them forces difficult decisions upon us. Should we relate that great-uncle John was whipped for stealing a horse or that great-aunt Matilda was too fond of her alcoholic "medicine"? It is true that our ancestors were humans and had weaknesses as well as strengths, and family histories cannot present reliable perspectives if their authors do not treat their subjects with objectivity. (This point is especially important in today's interdisciplinary environment, where social historians, geographers, and other scholars base conclusions upon details that family histories present.) On the other hand, there might be times when an incident is best left alone. Whether a family secret warrants publication is a matter we have to decide case by case—and with wisdom. Indeed, families may come to us as professionals specifically to assist them in handling such delicate matters.

Adoptions and illegitimacies

Few subjects evoke as much emotional response as the publication of details relating to adoptions and illegitimacies. Modern genealogies now frequently trace branches that are adoptive as well as biological, and the *NGS Quarterly* System has been modernized to accommodate this trend.[14] Regarding adoptions that have been hidden, we need to consider whether a living person might be hurt by this knowledge. Adoptions in the more distant past trigger fewer problems. Illegitimacies deserve the same careful consideration. When writing for a client, we should thoroughly discuss the issue; then the client, who has intimate knowledge of the family, should judge what to reveal. We assist by offering wise counsel based on our broader perspective.

Divorces and similar "scandals"

Contrary to popular belief, separations and divorces were not uncommon in many past societies; but sensitivities over marital problems remain a common reason for tight-lipped relatives. The manner in which we handle such cases will usually rest upon common sense and time proximity—recognizing that explanations may be helpful or necessary to explain incongruities or contradictions in the records. (Fictitious example: Why is Bruno Wysinski listed in the 1900 census of Union County, Iowa, with a woman called his "wife," while the wife named in the family Bible is reported in Dallas County, Missouri, that year?) When an event took place a hundred years or more ago, full explanations can enrich our understanding of a family. For more recent scandal, we may want to give abbreviated facts, with a citation to the source of more data that interested readers can consult.

Insanity and sexual aberrations

Cases of ancestral insanity, incest, or sexual aberrations can be even touchier subjects. Present-day descendants may become unduly alarmed by reports of "insanity" in the family and fear their children will inherit the tendency—although other family members may value any and all types of medical information. We should consider and perhaps discuss the reliability of the information. For example:

- Did the 1850 census show "insane" by the elderly wife's name? If so, by whose judgment was she insane? Might she have been senile instead? Although we should not withhold information (a statement such as this, after all, could point to other valuable records), we need to remember that medical terms used in the past were seldom as accurate as modern diagnoses and that conditions were known by different terms in different eras.[15] Considering that family members who are not well versed in the subject might not understand the situation, we might add a qualifying note based upon our careful study of medical history—and perhaps cite relevant medical sources for that era.

- On the other hand, if we discover a family letter describing incest or a court case trying an ancestor for "deviant sexual conduct"—incidences the family has no current knowledge of—we are likely to weigh even more thoughtfully the value of publishing the details. If a case of incest affects the paternity or maternity of an ancestor, whether ours or someone else's, the genealogical significance of remaining silent about the situation is obviously much greater than if no offspring had resulted from the affair.

FAMILY TRADITIONS

Family traditions and anecdotal accounts present us with dilemmas and opportunities. We know how easily facts become confused and details embroidered when passed through the generations; our clients and our families may not have that perspective yet. We can help others understand that family stories have value but must be tempered with caution and researched until evidence justifies accepting or discarding them. By way of examples:

- *The Three Brothers Tale.* Descendants may believe their ancestor immigrated as one of "three brothers, of whom one went north, one went south, and one went west." We know such traditions are common and often unfounded. How do we treat this one? Disregard it? Include it as fact? Publish it but dismiss it as just common lore? None of these is appropriate. The tradition deserves an attempt to verify it. If we cannot confirm or disprove it, we still present it but clearly identify it as a tradition. Doing so preserves the story but warns others that it is unsubstantiated. Leaving it out would leave readers to assume we are unaware of it.

- *Illustrious ancestors.* More difficult to handle, perhaps, is the issue of including "research" by earlier members that set forth illustrious ancestors with no valid documentation. We need tact to help our families realize the inappropriateness of including unsubstantiated lineages. An otherwise credible book can be vastly diminished by flimsy or disproved claims.

- *Anecdotes.* Handed-down stories about proved ancestors do have a place in the family history—so long as we do not confuse them with unsupported traditions. For example, one California family often told the story of Marsena Parmilee Stone, their pioneer ancestor who kept bees. On many a cold morning, he'd bring two or three half-frozen bees into the house and put them in a slightly heated oven to "warm up"—despite his wife's scolding when she would open the oven and they would fly out.[16] What better way to show the nature of this man than through this anecdote?

HISTORICAL PERSPECTIVE

Statistics are dry. It is important to know dates and places for births, marriages, and

> We need tact to help our families realize the inappropriateness of including unsubstantiated lineages. An otherwise credible book can be vastly diminished by flimsy or disproved claims.

deaths; but statistics don't impart to readers a sense of who the ancestors were or what they endured. Historical context can—but it has to be *relevant*. For example:

- If the family moved to Tasmania or South Africa during the "Great Sailing Era," we can go to history books for background and let our readers know what the family might have experienced.

- If a couple lived in Texas and their only son was killed at the Alamo, a historical aside about the contemporary king of Siam would be incongruous. Relevant perspective might include insight into (*a*) why families moved to Texas at that early date; (*b*) what conditions led to the siege at the Alamo; (*c*) how area families felt about those conditions; and (*d*) what effect the death of an only son had on the life of a family that operated a small ranch.

- If American ancestors went west by overland wagon train, excerpts from the diaries and journals of those who shared the experience and penned their recollections can make the ancestral journey come alive. We give our readers a sense of the planning it took and the dangers our ancestors faced. We help readers experience, through our words, what daily life on the plains was like. Recollections of the wagon-train children, written years later, can enthrall our young readers as they try to imagine "great-great-great-grandpa's" adventure at the age of seven.

As good writers we will find out what was happening in the ancestral place and time, and share these details with our readers. We will want to weave historical perspective into material drawn from actual ancestral records. We can illuminate details from dry records with relevant quotations from others who witnessed these events, followed the same occupations, or lived similar lives. In the research phase, we will have explored a wealth of materials such as those outlined in figures 39 and 40—calling upon agricultural censuses, as well as population schedules (for example), to describe the family's livestock and identify their crops. We'll look for deeper meaning in records—as when a will assigns each child (or the widow!) a specific room with careful instructions on kitchen privileges. We'll closely scrutinize inventories, mortgages, and wills for such personal items as dictionaries, religious tracts, or tools that offer clues to education, faith, and occupation. We'll have interviewed elderly and distant kin for personal recollections and details of the physical appearance of the forebears we recall.[17] Diligently pursued, all this wide-ranging research and penetrating analysis will have created a substantial lode of personal details we can mine to portray richly textured ancestors.

Sharpening ancestral images

Conventional libraries and digital ones offer many resources for sharpening the ancestral images we verbally sketch. Local histories reveal the factors that motivated emigration and the cultural differences that greeted ancestors upon arrival in their adopted homeland. Social histories of each country and specific ethnic groups offer broader perspective on national and religious groups. Published historical time-lines, in which significant happenings are listed on a daily or weekly basis, suggest events that might bear upon the ancestor's life. Reference works in the textile field depict clothing worn in almost all times and places. Similar publications that focus on specific trades—glassblowing, weaving, or cigar manufacturing, for example—depict

Published historical time-lines, in which significant happenings are listed on a daily or weekly basis, suggest events that might bear upon the ancestor's life.

Known facts

If ancestor was . . . then check . . .

- Church goer: Local church and denominational minutes, histories, and newspapers can provide background and may mention ancestor.
- Farmer: Use tax lists and agricultural censuses that enumerate livestock and crops; check for existence of farm directories in that community.
- Officeholder: Check contemporary law codes for requirements of office in that time and place; also newspapers at election time and during tenure.
- Tradesperson: Use tax lists and manufacturing censuses; look for ads in city and farm directories and newspapers.
- Veteran: Check for bounty land and pension applications by men who served in same unit; the ancestor may have filed an affidavit for the friend, and any affidavit could shed light on the unit's activities. Fellow soldiers and officers may have written unit histories. Medical files provide physical details, as well as health data.

Known records

If these exist, take a broader view of the evidence.

- State/local censuses: Many record unexpected detail, such as cloth and similar commodities owned.
- Tax rolls: Compare holdings and valuations with those recorded for contemporaries, to generate statistics and clues to ancestor's economic and social standing.
- Probate inventories and wills: Compare with those for contemporaries, for clues to economic and social status. Irregular provisions, such as admonitions to children or assignment of specific rooms or kitchen privileges to children and widows, hint at family interaction and relationships.

Other possibilities

- Descendants: Collateral branches of the family may have preserved mementos, memoirs, portraits, and skilled handiwork such as carvings, furniture, quilts, or samplers.
- Local professionals and tradespeople: Doctors, lawyers, and merchants regularly kept account books on clients; and many of those journals have survived.
- Neighbors and fellow church members: Their records may include affidavits by or details on our elusive ancestors.

**FIG. 39
IDEA LISTS
FOR ADDING
FACTUAL INTEREST**

Photographs

- Family homesite for photographs of the home or its ruins, barns, or other outbuildings.
- Family churches and cemeteries for images of extant family stones or contemporary markers of associates to depict the "flavor" and "tone" of their society.
- Family Bible—external as well as internal views.
- Memorabilia of all types—owned by family or other items contemporaneous with time and place:
  - Buckboards, coaches, wagons
  - Branding irons for cattle or crops
  - Clocks, medallions, watches
  - Dental or medical equipment
  - Furniture
  - Kilns/forms used to make brick
  - Samplers, quilts, other handiwork
  - Surveying instruments
  - Tools of other trades

Other illustrations

- Calling cards
- Charts
- Deeds, inventories, wills, and other legal records
- Funeral notices
- Letters
- Maps
- Military enlistments
- Newspaper advertisements
- Pen sketches or woodcuts from copyright-free sources
- Signatures
- Wedding announcements

**FIG. 40
IDEA LISTS
FOR ADDING
VISUAL INTEREST**

tools and work environments. Specialized dictionaries define quaint and obsolete terms for occupations and household items. Some other broader reference works cover countless facets of everyday life, century by century.[18] Legal codes and legislative reports detail for us the laws that existed at the time ancestral events took place. In the research phase, we will have tried to learn all we can about community and religious life; legal and linguistic problems; and medical, military, and political conditions. Now, in the writing phase, we sift this data judiciously, choosing the accounts most relevant and most true to the documented character and experiences of the ancestor under discussion.

Separating fact from fiction

When putting family into historical context, we must remain factual. We cannot manufacture conversations, no matter how much that "technique" might "enliven" our narrative. We may be delighted by sensational events and aberrations of our ancestors' time, but we cannot put our forebears on those stages and make active characters of them if they left no evidence of such performances. The following examples illustrate other points at which we might cross the line between fact and fiction:

- *Dialog.* If our family's community was a battlefront in one or another war, we would have read newspapers, local histories and diaries, and memoirs of soldiers who saw action there. We would have noted hardships that area families endured— scarce food, marauding soldiers, widespread hunger. So how do we relate those circumstances?

    FACTUAL APPROACH
    The opposing army came down the river, pillaging a broad swath through the valley in which wartime maps place John and Annie's farm. The wholesale slaughter of livestock reported in the area surely included their hogs and cattle as well as those of their neighbors. That invasion left the Valley View families desperate and in despair, scavenging for food the hordes of soldiers may have overlooked. Hunger was rampant. Farms did not recover for years after the end of the war—and many never did, according to stories the children later told.

Such facts about the ancestral community, reliably documented, make our readers acutely aware of the very difficult time that the family endured. But consider another treatment—typically produced by writers who have a bit of family lore and feel compelled to invent a scene to add "interest" or "color."

    FICTIONAL APPROACH
    John was in despair. He expressed his fears to his wife Annie, telling her they would have little food with which to feed the children in a few days. She cried when realizing that the efforts of their hard labors had been taken away. She tried to make the children understand that they would have little to eat; but Tommy, the youngest, could not understand what she was telling him. Lucy, aged twelve, tried to comfort her little brother: "Tommy, we'll be okay."

Conversational accounts, moods, and thoughts are valid elements of a family history *only* when ancestors left affidavits, diaries, letters, or memoirs that

Conversational accounts, moods, and thoughts are valid elements of a family history *only* when ancestors left affidavits, diaries, letters, or memoirs that specifically relate these.

specifically relate these. Without such evidence, we weaken our narrative by inventing dialog, feelings, and thoughts. Readers immediately go on guard when they sense that information has departed from facts. We may write a historical *novel,* if we label it as such, but we cannot fictionalize the evidence in a *family history.* What we do is use actual events to place our family in the proper setting.

• *Characterization.* We also take care not to force ancestral characters into the mold of statistics that may not fit. If a local newspaper from 1921 reports that Prohibition had lured half the state's youth into speak-easies, we cannot depict Grandma as a bobbed and beaded flapper swilling Cherry Dynamites at the local Do Drop Inn— not without evidence that she followed that lifestyle. She may have been among those who preferred cakewalks at the local church. What we *can* do is introduce the Eighteenth Amendment and tell the effects it had on her generation. As background, we can quote the newspaper and relate the statistics (with documentation), then perhaps point out that Grandma and her friends likely faced these same temptations, although the records yield no evidence that she indulged. To *assume* that she succumbed—or to present any general statistics as the *likely behavior* of any one person—would be unjust to ancestors who may, with great difficulty, have held themselves to a higher code.

HUMAN INTEREST

Suggesting scandalous behavior for a forebear who left no such records is not the way to add interest to family history. The only valid way to make ancestors "human" is to *thoroughly research their lives.* Despite courthouse fires, ancestral illiteracy or poverty, and other situations commonly cited as reasons that "no records exist" for an ancestor, the skilled genealogist with an extensive knowledge of sources, a commitment to thorough research, and the habit of studying not only the elusive ancestor but also friends, neighbors, and kissing kin can usually find enough civil, military, occupational, or religious detail to "put feathers on the ancestral hat."

There are many ways in which we can expand even meager details to heighten human interest. While we can't fabricate facts, an active imagination can lead us to many resources, textual and visual, that we might otherwise overlook—as the idea lists in figures 39 and 40 suggest. A good camera, a good photo studio to help with restoring damaged or faded images, or good software for photo enhancement are all valuable tools for the family historian.

Overcoming the final block

Untold numbers of family histories progress to this point and then languish in the author's files—victim of a malady that James L. Hansen of the State Historical Society of Wisconsin, home of the famed Lyman C. Draper Manuscripts, calls the Draper Syndrome. Like Draper, many genealogists are fascinated by research. They spend a lifetime gathering information and writing segments toward the day their investigation will be *finished* and the whole will at last be worthy of publication. In the meanwhile, there are still questions to be answered, still records to be consulted. Given the labor that has already gone into the study, surely nothing short of perfection is enough. And so, the work never actually gets done.

Suggesting scandalous behavior for a forebear who left no such records is not the way to add interest to family history. The only valid way to make ancestors "human" is to *thoroughly research their lives.*

Perfection is impossible. Sooner or later, every research project reaches the point of seriously diminishing returns. Eventually, we face the reality that mother is now ninety and will not last forever. Nor will we. Once our work meets general standards of the field for *reasonable* research—so long as we thoroughly document each finding we report—it is time for us to write *finis* to our first edition. Future discoveries can always be addressed in revisions or further volumes.

Summary Concepts

The benefits we reap from a well-done family history—whether it be our own or one we have helped a client's family prepare—will exceed anything we anticipated. As professionals, the rewards are much more than monetary. By the time we finish, we'll feel part of the family. Aunt Maude and Uncle Harry will be as real to us as they are to our client. We will have favorites: the adventuresome fourteen-year-old lad who ran away from home and became an Indian scout; or the spunky fifteen-year-old lass who shepherded her younger brother and sister around the Horn to join their widowed father in California. If the undertaking was for our own family, we have the immense satisfaction of sharing a rich ancestral heritage with our loved ones.

Even if we are never able to see our book to fruition, following the guidelines in this chapter can ease fears that our massive files will be discarded by our survivors. We will have conducted our search thoroughly, supported our findings with documentation to ensure their reliability and credibility, and compiled them in a form that will be understood by others. We will have shared a glimpse of our ancestors' personalities, adventures, triumphs, and pain. Great-great-grandchildren, long after we are gone, will be excited when they discover our work. They will know and understand at least this much of their roots, because we took the time to preserve it.

> Even if we never see our book to fruition, following the guidelines in this chapter can ease fears that our massive collection will be discarded by our survivors or those of our clients.

NOTES

1. Examples of all types of genealogical compilations can be identified from the scholarly journals that publish critical reviews—e.g., *National Genealogical Society [NGS] Quarterly, New England Historical and Genealogical Register,* and *The American Genealogist.* The annual winners of the Donald Lines Jacobus Award, chosen by the American Society of Genealogists, are also excellent examples; and the annual winners of the NGS Family History Writing Contest, published in the December issues of the *NGS Quarterly,* are well-crafted short models.

2. A model of the Ahnentafel or Sosa-Stradonitz type that is commonly cited in lectures on genealogical writing is Elizabeth Shown Mills, CG, CGL, FASG, "(de) Mézières-Trichel-Grappe: A Study of a Tri-caste Lineage in the Old South," *The Genealogist* 6 (Spring 1985): 4–84.

3. Both the *NGS Quarterly* (aka *NGSQ*) System and the *Register* System are well explained in Joan Ferris Curran, CG; Madilyn Coen Crane; and John H. Wray, Ph.D., CG, *Numbering Your Genealogy: Basic Systems, Complex Families, and International Kin* (Arlington, Virginia: National Genealogical Society, 2000). The *Register* System alone is detailed in Thomas Kozachek, *Guidelines for Authors of Compiled Genealogies* (Boston: Newbury Street Press, 1998). Both systems and the various types of genealogies discussed here are further covered in Board for Certification of Genealogists, *The BCG Genealogical Standards Manual* (Orem, Utah: Ancestry, 2000).

The classic examples for the "all-my-ancestors" pedigree approach are the numerous volumes produced by Walter Goodwin Davis, FASG, on his sixteen great-grandparents.

4. Numerous examples of this type could be cited, published before modern genealogy developed more stringent standards. Readers are encouraged to study recent family histories in their libraries and to emulate those that embody current standards of scholarship.

5. For samples of full-family studies that use various numbering systems, see Joan Ferris Curran, CG, *Descendants of Salomon Bloch of Janowitz, Bohemia, and Baruch Wollman of Kempen-in-Posen, Prussia* (Baltimore: Gateway Press for Henry Wollman Bloch, 1996); Margaret Swett Henson and Deolece Parmelee, *The Cartwrights of San Augustine: Three Generations of Agrarian Entrepreneurs in Nineteenth-Century Texas* (Austin: Texas State Historical Association, 1993); and Lewis Bunker Rohrbach, CG, *Höffelbauer Genealogy: 1585–1993* (Camden, Maine: Picton Press, 1993).

6. For an hourglass type of genealogical history cited by critics as a model for placing ancestors into rich historical context, even in "burned county" areas, see Donna Rachal Mills, CGRS, *Some Southern Balls: From Valentine to Ferdinand and Beyond* (Orlando, Florida: Mills Historical Press, 1993). In this case, the client's great-grandfather, Ferdinand, was used as the center of the hourglass into which ancestors flowed and from whom descendants dispersed.

7. Elizabeth Shown Mills, CG, CGL, FASG, *Evidence! Citation & Analysis for the Family Historian* (Baltimore: Genealogical Publishing Co., 1997).

8. Curran, Crane, and Wray, *Numbering Your Genealogy*, previously cited.

9. William Thorndale, review of J. Roderick Heller III, *An Upcountry Chronicle: The Heller Family of South Carolina* (Washington, D.C.: Carnton Press for the author, 1998), reviewed in *NGS Quarterly* 87 (December 1999): 306–7.

10. For more on the 1851 Canadian census, see Brenda Dougall Merriman, CGRS, CGL, *Genealogy in Ontario: Searching the Records*, 3d edition (Toronto: Ontario Genealogical Society, 1996), 77–78, 86.

11. For more on the subject of words that properly qualify genealogical statements, see Norman Ingham, CG, "Some Thoughts about Evidence and Proof in Genealogy," *The American Genealogist* 72 (July–October 1997): 381; and Elizabeth Shown Mills, "Working with Historical Evidence: Genealogical Principles and Standards," *NGS Quarterly* 87 (September 1999): 181–82.

12. Various other authors have recently published explanations of *about* and *say* dates that differ slightly from the explanation in the text—and from each other as well. To summarize:

• THOMAS KOZACHEK writes: "If you have calculated a given date from a later record or other circumstantial evidence, include that information in your presentation of the facts, using the appropriate qualifying phrase—'ca.' or 'about' for approximate dates reckoned from fixed dates [and] 'say' for dates assigned to make the available evidence (e.g., a known birth order) internally consistent." Kozachek, *Guidelines for Authors of Compiled Genealogies* (Boston: Newbury Street Press, 1998), 7. Kozachek refers readers to Anderson, below, for further explanation.

• ROBERT CHARLES ANDERSON, FASG, proposes: "If an age at death, or an age at the time of a deposition is available, then a year of birth may be estimated, and in such a case the entry will read 'b. about 1634,' indicating a date that is reliable with a relatively narrow span of years, *perhaps just two years above or below the estimated date*. More frequently the evidence for estimating an age will be less precise, and we will have to state an age in a different way: saying that someone was 'b. say 1634,' meaning that this is our best estimate, but that it may be *some years off* in either direction." Anderson, *The Great Migration Begins: Immigrants to New England, 1620–1733*, 3 vols. (Boston: New England Historic Genealogical Society, 1995), 1: xx. Emphasis added.

• PATRICIA LAW HATCHER, CG, advises: "Use *about* or *circa* . . . when you can place an event *within a year or so*, as when you find an age on a census, deposition, or tombstone. . . . Use *say* . . . when *roughly estimating a date* (estimating the year of birth from a deed or marriage, for example). Usually the year is *divisible by 5*. 'John Jones was born in, say, 1815.'" Hatcher, *Producing a Quality Family History* (Salt Lake City: Ancestry, 1996), 39. Emphasis added.

13. Donald Lines Jacobus, FASG, *Genealogy as Pastime and Profession*, 2d edition, rev. (Baltimore: Genealogical Publishing Co., 1968), 18.

14. Curran, Crane, and Wray, "Numbering Your Genealogy." See particularly the chapter by Crane.

What is written without effort is in general read without pleasure.

—*Samuel Johnson*[19]

FAMILY HISTORIES

15. For a useful overview, see William B. Saxbe Jr., M.D., M.P.H., CG, FASG, "Nineteenth-Century Death Records: How Dependable Are They?" *NGS Quarterly* 87 (March 1999): 43–54.

16. Related by Seymour Webster Stone, late resident of Oakland, California, to the author; previously recited in Christine Rose, *Ancestors and Descendants of Anson Parmilee Stone, Descended from John Stone of Guilford, Connecticut* (San Jose, California: Privately printed, 1963), 30.

17. For helpful advice, see Roseann R. Hogan, Ph.D., "Using Oral Histories for the Rest of the Story," *Association of Professional Genealogists Quarterly* 10 (September 1995): 72–76.

18. For example, see Paul Drake, J.D., *What Did They Mean by That? A Dictionary of Historical Terms for Genealogists* (Bowie, Maryland: Heritage Books, 1994); Barbara Jean Evans, *A to Zax: A Comprehensive Dictionary for Genealogists & Historians,* 3d edition (Alexandria, Virginia: Hearthside Press, 1995); Dale Taylor, *The Writer's Guide to Everyday Life in Colonial America: From 1607–1783* (Cincinnati, Ohio: Writer's Guide Books, 1997); and Marc McCutcheon, *The Writer's Guide to Everyday Life in the 1800s; For Writers of Historical Fiction, Westerns, Romance, Action/Adventure, Thrillers, and Mysteries* (Cincinnati, Ohio: Writer's Digest Books, 1993). *The Oxford English Dictionary* is also very useful.

19. Dr. Samuel Johnson (1709–84), English lexicographer, essayist, and poet, quoted in Rhoda Thomas Tripp, comp., *The International Thesaurus of Quotations* (New York: Thomas Y. Crowell, 1970), 1062.

20. Quoted in Tryon Edwards, comp., *The New Dictionary of Thoughts: A Cyclopedia of Quotations,* Ralph Emerson Browns, ed. (1891; rev. edition, n.p.: Standard Book Company, 1961), 270–71.

An historian ought to be exact, sincere, and impartial; free from passion, unbiased by interest, fear, resentment or affection; and faithful to the truth.

—*Anonymous*[20]

FURTHER STUDY

Two special issues of the *National Genealogical Society Quarterly* offer much additional advice for writers of family history:

Putting Family History into Context . . . NGS Quarterly 88 (December 2000), which includes
Clunies, Sandra MacLean, CG. "Writing the Family History: Creative Concepts for a Lasting Legacy," 246–65.
Colletta, John Philip. "Building Context around Biographical Facts: A Process Illustrated by the Backcountry Birth of George F. Ring," 293–98.
Kyle, Noeline J. "Rethinking the Writing of Family History: Memory, Interpretation, and Thematic Frameworks," 299–308.
Zublic, June Riedrich, CG. "Biblical Namesakes: The North Country's Enoch Phillips and His Tribe," 266–92. (The NGS 2000 Family Writing Contest winner.)

Reassembling Female Lives. . . NGS Quarterly 88 (September 2000), which includes
Freilich, Kay Haviland, CG. "Was She Really Alice Fling? Righting a Wrong Identity," 225–28.
Ingalls, Kay Germain, CGRS. "*Cherchez la Femme!* Looking for Female Ancestors," 166–78.
Lennon, Rachal Mills, CGRS, and Elizabeth Shown Mills, CG, CGL, FASG. "Mother, Thy Name is *Mystery!* Finding the Slave Who Bore Philomene Dorat," 201–24.
Little, Barbara Vines, CG. "Teasing the Silent Woman from the Shadow of History: Mary Fitzhugh (Stuart) Fitzhugh of Virginia," 179–200.

Other useful materials for study include
Finley, Carmen J., CG. *Write Your Family History.* Rev. edition. Arlington, Virginia: National Genealogical Society, ca. 1997.
Greenwood, Val D., J.D., AG. "Family History: Going Beyond Genealogy." *The Researcher's Guide to American Genealogy.* 3d edition. Baltimore: Genealogical Publishing Co., 2000.
Hatcher, Patricia Law, and John V. Wylie. *Indexing Family Histories: Simple Steps for a Quality Product.* Arlington: National Genealogical Society, 1994.
Jacobus, Donald Lines. "Genealogy and Chronology." *Genealogical Research: Methods and Sources.* Vol. 1. Milton Rubincam, ed. Washington, D.C.: American Society of Genealogists, 1980.

24

**LINEAGE
PAPERS**

Keynotes

Lineage Papers

by **Mary McCampbell Bell**, CLS, CGL
Elisabeth Whitman Schmidt, CLS

Lineages have always been the thread from which genealogy is woven. From the Biblical begats through the Medieval Visitations—until the modern era in fact—the words *lineage* and *genealogy* have been virtually synonymous. Yet in the current century's professionalization of genealogy, lineage work is given short shrift. True, a lineage is basically a series of relationships, each individually proven. To identify each individual and each kinship that link to form a lineage, one must know resources, methodology, and principles of evidence analysis; so, an emphasis upon those components is justified in professional literature. But the role of lineage-society applications, their value to the preservation of genealogies, and the standards by which quality is judged are too-seldom addressed.

Realistically speaking, much of the genealogical research conducted in the past century has never been published and probably won't be. Most people pursue genealogy out of curiosity with no interest in publication. Cases are legion in which years of research are abandoned by those who conducted it or discarded by their heirs. Yet much of that work has been preserved for posterity simply because the researcher or some relative used part of it to apply for membership in a lineage society.

On the surface, we might even dismiss this traditional value of the hereditary society application as irrelevant in our post-modern world of cyber-genealogy. When lineages posted on the Web are replicated, disseminated, and propagated endlessly, the concept of societies as a preservation agency is obsolete, no? No! Cyber-posting of work in progress—with no checks and balances, no standards applied or expected in many cases, and no safeguards against fraudulent or misguided alterations—does not constitute "proof" of a lineage or preservation of research.

A lineage-society application, well prepared and well verified, is a singular contribution to genealogy as a field and to society's efforts to know and understand itself. *How to prepare a quality application that can be efficiently verified* is the point of this chapter.

The Responsibility

Research is intoxicating, although challenging. Reporting that research borders on drudgery, although the construction of a client report can be a challenge of its own. By comparison, preparing a lineage paper on the basis of all that has been found and reported is a virtual postscript to an occasional project. An anticlimax. Paperwork. Small wonder it is that so many applications are prepared with obvious haste and too little attention to detail.

As professionals, it is our responsibility to prepare lineage papers that reflect well upon ourselves, our clients, and our field. Our most basic obligations center in three areas: knowledge of sources, knowledge of standards, and knowledge of society rules.

As professionals, it is our responsibility to prepare lineage papers that reflect well upon ourselves, our clients, and our field.

Knowledge of resources

Familiarity with genealogical bibliography is one of the most critical skills needed by a lineage genealogist. We should know not only what exists for the area in which we work but also the strengths and weaknesses of each specific resource. Our clients and the prospective members we volunteer to help are likely to have used these and may need help in evaluating and interpreting them. We must know which materials are published and which of those are trustworthy. We must know which compiled genealogies are reliable and which seemingly documented ones harbor serious flaws.[1] Just as important, we must know the original resources that go beyond published works in every locale and every time frame involved in the papers we prepare.

> Familiarity with genealogical bibliography is one of the most critical skills needed by a lineage genealogist.

Knowledge of standards

Most lineage papers rely heavily upon published, derivative works. Odds are, our clients will expect us to; and many will not understand when and why it is necessary to examine original records by primary informants. Still, part of our responsibility as creditable genealogists is the education of the public as to what constitutes reliability in source materials and acceptable standards of documentation. Chapter 21, Book and Media Reviews, covers guidelines for appraising derivative sources that may be usefully shared with clients. The *BCG Genealogical Standards Manual* offers other perspectives for original materials, as do guides to the evaluation of evidence such as those by Mills and Stevenson.[2] Should we be overruled by a client in the application of standards that we have tactfully explained, we will probably weigh the value of that commission against the seriousness of producing work under our own names that compromises our standards.

We may also encounter verifying genealogists in some societies who prefer the ease of working with published materials as opposed to original records. Not infrequently, we find that the fulfillment of professional standards requires us to do a better job of research and documentation than the society expects. As we become more involved with particular groups, we may need to encourage their policymakers to apply more discriminating standards—particularly in the acceptance of such popular but controversial works as Virkus's *Compendium,*[3] DAR *Lineage Books*, and databases of the Family History Library or commercial concerns.[4] Such sources often provide convenient clues but should never be used as an authority.

On the other hand and in many respects, lineage applications require much more stringent standards of proof than the usual genealogical project. Verifying genealogists at most societies are reluctant to accept circumstantial cases for connecting generations (proof of parentage). They are more likely to do so, however, when a well-written, well-documented proof argument has been published in a respected journal with discriminating standards—particularly a peer-reviewed journal.

Applicants often have difficulty understanding the criteria that underlie the two most critical elements in the paper: proof of parentage at each generation and documentation of service. Many, unfortunately, suffer The-Name's-the-Same Syndrome. If the applicant descends from Mesopotamia Jones (or even just plain Martha Jones) and a contemporary will by one Jedediah Jones names a daughter

Mesopotamia (or Martha), then *the name's the same—it must be my ancestor* is a tempting conclusion. If a contemporary military roster lists Jedediah, then *the name's the same—it must be my man.*

Again, it is the responsibility of the professional genealogist to teach the client or the protégé a different game: Devil's Advocate. (To quote a colleague: we "challenge our own theory. We go back to the evidence—seek out more material if possible—and try to find flaws in our own logic."[5]) Genealogical literature is rife with examples in which well-meaning researchers have been deceived by a *same-name, same-man* conclusion. Lineage societies and standards of the field both require that we attempt to disprove any such conclusion or theory.

Knowledge of society rules

Every lineage society has its individual regulations that must be observed by candidates and anyone else who prepares applications. Before investing any effort or expense toward membership in a particular society, one should obtain a current copy of the society's instruction sheet. Addresses appear in numerous reference works; Szucs and Luebking's *The Source,* which is conveniently accessible to most genealogists, offers addresses and descriptions for more than a hundred hereditary groups.[6] Some societies do not respond to unsolicited inquiries, their membership being a closed matter. Others prefer to supply the regulations only to an applicant who has been officially proposed for membership. Thus, if a client approaches us seeking help with an application we should first ask the client to obtain a copy of the instructions. In the case of more open societies, particularly those that hold workshops at major conferences, well-prepared genealogists will contact the societies on their own initiative and obtain instructions for their own reference files.

With an invitation and instructions in hand, we obviously familiarize ourselves with those regulations and follow them explicitly, even when they go counter-grain to our own concept of "how things should be done." (This is not to say, of course, that we cannot seek a way to fulfill both expectations—about which more will be said shortly.) Some societies provide not only written instructions but also style sheets as an explicit pattern. Others require that a "preliminary worksheet" be filled out and submitted for approval to their national headquarters before the "final worksheet" and application form are submitted. Some groups ask for multiple "copies" of the application, and specify that each "copy" be a typed original. Other organizations accept one original and a specified number of photocopies. Some require acid-free paper, and some insist that signatures be affixed in black ink only. In a few national organizations, each individual state has its separate rules. Some societies require that applications be notarized; others allow the applicant to swear before the chapter regent or registrar as to the correctness of all information on the application. Never should we expect any society to accept a crossover application from another organization, although in rare situations that policy may exist.

In sum, the only thing we may assume is that the preparation of lineage applications is a minefield—one no professional should venture into without explicit and up-to-date directions from the society that seeds the field.

The preparation of lineage applications is a minefield—one no professional should venture into without explicit and up-to-date directions from the society that seeds the field.

> We are expected to prepare and present applications that look neat, contain accurate content, and are organized so efficiently that they sail through the society's verifying process.

The Preparation

As professional genealogists, we are expected to prepare and present applications that look neat, contain accurate content, and are organized so efficiently that they sail through the society's verifying process. That effort requires no specialized training—only great attention to detail and a clear sense of organization.

Documentation

GENERAL GUIDELINES

Preparing the documentation before typing the application minimizes the likelihood of errors or discrepancies. Despite the variances that exist between societies, almost all agree on the following general guidelines:

- Documentation must be complete. Every fact and every relationship must be accompanied by reliable "proof."

- Handlettering applications is not acceptable, no matter how neatly or artistically the lettering is done.

- Highlighter should never be used across the text of anything that needs marking. When microfilmed, microfiched, or photocopied, the highlighted portion is usually rendered gray or black. (Red ink or lead is acceptable for underlining text we want the genealogist to read.)

- Photocopies of documents are best. We should never send an original document or an original certified copy unless specifically asked to do so.

- Photocopied pages from books are acceptable, so long as the source itself is valid.

- Photographs of tombstones are admissible evidence, provided (a) they are submitted in photocopied form; (b) the cemetery name and location are typed on the photocopy; and (c) a complete transcription of the tombstone data is added to the photocopy as well. (When papers are microfilmed or fiched and tombstone data is in actual photograph form, the inscriptions are often rendered unreadable.) Some societies require that cemetery records be validated by a cemetery official or submitted on official stationery of the cemetery—and preferably notarized.

- Staples should not be used.

Every society urges that we choose our documentation wisely. Quantity is no substitute for quality. Verifying genealogists quickly spot the padding and snow jobs that exist when preparers attempt to cover up a lack of proof in one area by sending a heap of redundant "proofs" for other points.

IDENTIFICATION

The front side of each piece of documentation must identify two things: applicant and source.

Applicant identification
A typed note or label should identify (a) name of applicant, (b) name of chapter, (c)

name of ancestor, *(d)* generation to which this piece of evidence applies (e.g., "Generation 4"), and *(e)* the information it supports (e.g., "Birth date of John Smith").

Source Identification
A typed note should identify the book or record source fully, following an appropriate style manual for genealogical sources.[7]

ORGANIZATION

Following these guidelines, we prepare each individual piece of documentation and arrange the whole by generation, starting with Generation 1 (which may be the applicant or the qualifying ancestor, depending upon the society). Within each generation, materials should be arranged according to the point each documents—parentage, birth, marriage, or death. During the work stage, many genealogists attach gummed notes to the stack for each generation—listing the four areas in which proof is needed. As each piece of "proof" is added to the stack, the corresponding item is then checked off on the note. This kind of systematic organization not only prevents oversights on our part but also facilitates checking by the society genealogist. Figure 41 offers a list of items commonly used as "proof records" for each of the four critical areas.

Application

Societies *want* to approve our applications, but we must take pains to ensure that all their requirements are met and all stated facts are accurate. The preparation of the form itself should be at least a six- or seven-step process:

1. Photocopy the form.

2. Prepare a rough draft. Using the photocopy, we fill in every appropriate blank and every request for name, date, and place. In the space between generations, we insert an identification of whatever record proves the parentage or connection between generations.

3. Verify accuracy. Once the draft is finished, we check every detail against our documentation for accuracy—making checkoffs on the draft just as though we were the verifying genealogist.

4. Prepare "original" form. Not until and unless we are satisfied that the rough draft is complete and every fact is correct do we transfer the information to the form that will actually be submitted.

5. Photocopy the completed original.

6. Verify accuracy. Using the photocopy this time, check every detail against the documentation again—making checkoffs on the copy.

7. (If necessary) make corrections to the original.

Completing the application form may present a special challenge in one particular area: the identification of references. Many forms still provide inadequate space to fully cite sources by modern standards. In such cases, the Board for Certification of

TIPS

If a previously approved lineage paper offers a list of children for the qualified ancestor, do *not* assume that the society has verified and approved the accuracy of all detail on the list. In many organizations, verifiers check parentage and dates *only* for the one child that is the applicant's ancestor.

If the applicant's line has already been approved by that society, still run a literature search to be certain no article has been published since then in which the asserted line has been disproved.

Contributed by Barbara J. Brown, CGRS, CLS

LINEAGE PAPERS

FIG. 41
RECORDS
COMMONLY USED
FOR LINEAGE "PROOFS"

Record type . . .	*What it may support . . .*
Affidavits by adult relatives	Birth data and/or parentage
Baby books	Birth data and/or parentage
Baptismal certificates	Birth date (or approximation) and/or parentage
Bible records	Birth, marriage, and/or death dates; parentage and/or spousal identities
Birth announcements (card/newspaper)	Birth data and/or parentage
Burial certificates	Death date (or approximation), spousal data
Censuses, 1850 and later	Birth year (approximated)
Censuses, 1880 and later	Birth date (approximated) and/or parentage
City directories	Death year (when male household listing is replaced by that of widow)
Deeds (e.g., heirs selling land)	Death data, parentage
Funeral cards	Death data
Funeral home records	Burial data (possibly death date, family or spousal data)
Homestead applications	Birth year (approximated); marital data; death of spouses
Hospital registrations	Birth data and/or parentage
Letters (contemporary with lifetime of individual for whom they are used as proof)	Birth data, parentage; marital data; death data (Enough data about the writer must be supplied to show that the statements are credible.)
Mortician records	Death/burial date; possibly places, parentage, and/or birth data
Military pension records	Birth year (approximated from age at enlistment or application); marital data; identity of heirs
Military service records	Ancestral eligibility; birth year (approximated from age at enlistment)
Orphan's court records	Parentage, death data for parents; ages of minors
Passports	Birth data
Probate files	Parentage for heirs; death data for the deceased
School records	Birth data and/or parentage
Social Security applications	Birth data and/or parentage
Social Security Death Index entries	Death date, possibly residence and birth date
Tax rolls	Birth year (approximated) from first and/or last appearance on poll rolls; death year or last known year to be living
Wills	Death date
World War I draft registration cards	Birth date and place

Genealogists advises its Certified Lineage Specialists to add one further attachment—a cover sheet for the documentation on which, generation by generation, the supporting evidence is cited in full form. Few societies find this addition objectionable. Even if they do, the client deserves this full bibliography.

Finally, before packaging our application, we make one last quality-control review, following the Summary Checklist in figure 42.

The Submission

If the papers we have prepared are not our own, then we will not submit them directly to the society but to the client or the candidate we have assisted. As the package leaves our control and we become dependent upon the client or candidate to preserve the quality of our work, it is important that we make clear three points:

- No papers should be removed or added to the package.

- All papers should be kept in the precise order in which we have prepared them.

- The client should not submit to the society any invoices we have issued (some clients do so in a mistaken assumption that this will impress the society with the quality of the work done) or other miscellaneous correspondence that has taken place between us and the client.

As professional preparers, we also submit the applications with three ethical guidelines in mind. First, we should have prepared the application with such care that the client or candidate will undergo no embarrassment. Second, we should inform the client that we stand behind our presentation; if the society should find it lacking in any regard and need additional information, we will provide that without charge. Third, if we are also a society officer, we should bear in mind one stricture recently codified by

---

Before submitting the package, recheck the following points:

- Has each generation been checked to assure that the husband lived long enough to be father of the child and that the mother was neither too young nor too old to have borne a child then?
- Has the application been checked for typographical errors?
- Has the documentation been checked against the application for discrepancies in detail?
- Does each piece of documentation have an identification label on its front?
- Has pertinent information on the document been underlined with either a red pencil or pen?
- Have all pictures of tombstones been photocopied, identified by location, and transcribed?
- Have file copies been made of the completed application form *and* the full set of proofs?
- Has all superfluous documentation been removed?

FIG. 42
SUMMARY
CHECKLIST

the American Society of Genealogists: "It is unprofessional and unethical to serve as the verifying officer on one's own lineage papers or on papers that one has personally prepared for a prospective member of the society."[8]

Summary Concepts

Lineage society applications are based on a broad spectrum of qualifications. Some simply will establish an ancestor in a particular location and time frame. Others seek to connect living generations to ancient and noble houses in foreign lands. No matter how few or how many generations are involved, the goal of the professional genealogist is to prepare an application that will withstand the test of time and further scholarship.

NOTES

1. Kory L. Meyerink, AG, "Family Histories and Genealogies," in Meyerink, ed., *Printed Sources: A Guide to Published Genealogical Records* (Salt Lake City: Ancestry, 1998), 573–624, provides an indispensable overview.
2. Elizabeth Shown Mills, CG, CGL, FASG, *Evidence! Citation & Analysis for the Family Historian* (Baltimore: Genealogical Publishing Co., 1997); Noel C. Stevenson, J.D., FASG, *Genealogical Evidence: A Guide to the Standard of Proof Relating to Pedigrees, Ancestry, Heirship, and Family History,* rev. edition (Laguna Hills, California: Aegean Park Press, 1989).
3. Frederick A. Virkus, *The Compendium of American Genealogy,* 7 vols. (1925–42; reprint; Baltimore: Genealogical Publishing Co., 1987).
4. The Family History Library's International Genealogical Index™ and FamilySearch™ databases are indispensable finding aids, but they are not sources per se.
5. Elizabeth Shown Mills, "Building a Case When No Record Proves a Point," *Ancestry* 16 (March–April 1998): 29–30.
6. Grahame Thomas Smallwood Jr., CALS, "Tracking through Hereditary and Lineage Organizations," in Loretto Dennis Szucs and Sandra Hargreaves Luebking, *The Source: A Guidebook of American Genealogy,* rev. edition (Salt Lake City: Ancestry, 1997), 684–708.
7. The commonly used guides in genealogy are Mills, *Evidence!* and the now somewhat outdated Richard S. Lackey, CG, FASG, *Cite Your Sources: A Manual for Documenting Family Histories and Genealogical Records* (Jackson: University Press of Mississippi, 1980).
8. "Standards: The American Society of Genealogists on the Preparation of Lineage Papers," *National Genealogical Society [NGS] Quarterly* 86 (December 1998): 270.

FURTHER STUDY

Board for Certification of Genealogists. *BCG Application Guide.* Washington: The Board, 2000.
———. *The BCG Genealogical Standards Manual.* Orem, Utah: Ancestry, 2000.
Brown, Barbara J., CGRS, CALS. "Tips for Preparing Professional Lineage Society Applications." *Association of Professional Genealogists Quarterly* 8 (March 1993): 7–10.
Grundset, Eric G., and Steven B. Rhodes. *American Genealogical Research at the DAR, Washington, D.C.* Washington: National Society, Daughters of the American Revolution, 1997.
Sheppard, Walter Lee Jr., CG, FASG. "Documentation for Lineage Papers: Two Perspectives— What Proves a Lineage? Acceptable Standards of Evidence." *NGS Quarterly* 75 (June 1987): 124–30.
White, Elizabeth Pearson, CG, FASG. "Documentation for Lineage Papers: Two Perspectives— Survey of Requirements, Procedures, and Pitfalls." *NGS Quarterly* 75 (June 1987): 131–40.

Editing and Publishing

25

EDITING
PERIODICALS

Keynotes

Editing Periodicals

by Elizabeth Shown Mills, CG, CGL, FASG

A major manual for editors describes our labor as "an excruciating act of self-discipline, mind-reading, and stable-cleaning. If it seems like a pleasure, something is probably wrong."[1]

Pungent advice, indeed! And mostly apt. *Self-discipline* is vital for the editor. It keeps deadlines met and standards enforced. *Mind reading* is essential. We must understand what our readers want, even the ones who never write us. We must comprehend what authors are trying to say, even when their prose is fuzzy. *Stable-cleaning?* Perhaps that could be expressed more daintily. Yet even editors surrounded by Derby stars recognize that both delicate and drastic cleanup is a daily fact of life. *No pleasure?* On that score, the manual errs. When Michelangelo confronted a ton of marble, he did not see just the drudgery that lay ahead; he appraised the strength and nuances of the Creator's handiwork, and he saw *la Pietà.* So it is—or should be—with genealogical editing. It is indeed a pleasure to take an author's beautiful research, apply the tools that editors are supposed to wield facilely, and see a work of verbal art materialize for posterity to enjoy.

Defining the Role

What, exactly, is an editor? What does the job entail? These questions are major ones in a field of scholarly inquiry that tends to pick editors on the basis of their reputations as genealogists rather than their training in the editorial world. To the uninitiated, the term *editor* may be no more than a fancy word for *typist*—one who takes incoming manuscripts, retypes them so pages match, collates the whole, and trots a master copy down to the print shop. To the wag, an editor is somebody whose job it is to argue with writers. Neither stereotype does justice to the breadth or complexity of our challenge. In a sense, editors are *information brokers.* It is our job to find information among those who have it and to pass it on to those who need it—making certain that, somewhere in the process, the information is put into a form others will want to read.

Genealogical editing is an eclectic job. Other literary outlets offer specialties to those who sit behind an editorial desk: they may choose to be a managing editor, an acquisitions editor, a production editor, a copy editor, a line editor, a style editor, or an art editor. In genealogy, we usually find that our job entails all these positions and more—from advertising manager to mail clerk, from secretary to typesetter, graphics designer, and even indexer. But the diversity of these tasks cannot overshadow our primary purpose. Between beating the bushes for exciting material and meeting our press deadlines, our primary job as a genealogical editor is to *edit*—to take an author's superb research or valuable information and shape it into a manuscript that a targeted group of readers will *read,* enjoy, and learn from.[2] As explained by Bruce Boston of the educational consulting and publishing firm Editorial Experts:

> What most editors mostly do . . . is to read manuscripts with pencil in hand, correcting the errors of organization and presentation that may confuse a reader, offend the

> Our primary job as a genealogical editor is to *edit*—to take an author's superb research or valuable information and shape it into a manuscript that a targeted group of readers will *read,* enjoy, and learn from.

canons of standard English usage and grammar, or aggravate the ulcer of a printer . . . [thereby] . . . creating that arrangement of the author's words that best expresses the author's intention.[3]

For new editors who might need a guide—as well as current editors who seek a yardstick by which to measure their own roles—we will examine the range of functions typically assigned to the genealogical editor. Because virtually all editors in our field are engaged in the production of periodicals, our discussion is slanted to that market. Four primary concerns are targeted:

- how to define our editorial needs,
- how to find the raw material that fills those needs,
- how to put that material into proper form, and
- how to deal with writers who don't understand the last point above.

Identifying Editorial Needs

Managerial functions aside, our first task as an editor is to define our publication. We must have a clear statement of purpose, an understanding of our audience, guidelines for our journal's scope, a policy for its style, and a set of standards. These definitions and policy statements then govern all editorial decisions. They ensure the consistency our readers expect, the fairness our authors deserve, and the respect we hope to earn from our society and our colleagues.

Defining our purpose

A statement of purpose may exist already for our publication. If it does not, then we prepare one. If we inherited one, then we reappraise it in light of current circumstances within our society and the genealogical world at large. The start of a new editorial era is always an appropriate time for reevaluation of the direction in which a publication is headed. Why does our journal or magazine exist? What does our society or corporation want to provide? Abstracted records? Essays on resources and methodology? Case studies? Compiled genealogies? Book reviews? We must clearly define our reason for existing and the service we can supply before we can embark upon effective work.

Understanding our readership

The material we publish must be governed by a clear concept of what our constituency needs and wants. What type of readership do we currently have? Is this the type we want to keep, or do we feel that a different market would better serve our goals? Why do current readers subscribe? Are they happy with the product they are receiving? What is their experience level? Are they avocational genealogists or professionals in the field? Different classes of readers demand different types of material, different styles, and different viewpoints.

We must have a clear statement of purpose, an understanding of our audience, guidelines for our journal's scope, a policy for its style, and a set of standards.

Defining our scope

The devoted followings enjoyed by major journals such as *The American Genealogist* and the *National Genealogical Society Quarterly* (on the one hand) and the immensely popular commercial magazines such as *Ancestry* and *Heritage Quest* (on the other hand) plainly illustrate the diverse interests and tastes of family searchers. Just as plainly, these examples emphasize the degree to which success hinges upon a clear concept of *who* our readers are and *what* those readers value.

So, what type of material should we publish to satisfy the purpose and audience we have defined for our periodical? It may be that the very title of our publication defines its scope—the *Mennonite Review* or the *Northumberland Genealogist* being obvious examples. If our title is less specific, we should provide our readership with a regularly published policy statement that defines the range of material we offer them. Then we adhere to that policy.

Setting our style

Every quality magazine and journal has its *style*—a tone, look, and feel that distinctively identifies it. Readers expect this consistency. As editors, we set that style. As editors, we enforce that style. But, as genealogical editors, we find this to be a particular challenge. By its very nature, our field attracts practitioners from widely varying backgrounds—many of whom have had extensive education in other research fields. Writers of history are trained differently from those in law, and the investigative reports of genetic researchers are not constructed in the same manner as those in anthropology. Our development of a "house style," consistently used, provides a pattern for our diverse contributors. Some will follow it. Others won't. Most will fall somewhere in between. We, as editors, must see that the submissions are revamped to whatever extent necessary to produce consistency from cover to cover. The first step toward a house style is drafting a style sheet that covers

- the type of material our publication seeks,

- the style manual that we follow (genealogists commonly use the historical writing section of *The Chicago Manual of Style*),[4]

- any specific points on which our house style varies from this style manual, and

- other guidelines for submitting manuscripts—i.e., page formatting, number of copies to be submitted, whether electronic disks are desired, arrangements for return of unaccepted manuscripts, etc.

Setting our standards

The concept of standards goes considerably beyond the technical listings of a style sheet. Standards reflect *quality,* a subjective matter that we must decide for ourselves and one that our readers will perceive for themselves from the product we send to press. As editors of genealogical publications, we have far more impact than we may realize upon the value of research produced in our field. We have the potential to

As editors of genealogical publications, we have far more impact than we may realize upon the value of research produced in our field. We have the potential to advance quality or to degrade it.

advance quality or to degrade it. If ours is a local publication, then we provide the training ground for tomorrow's leaders. If ours is a nationally oriented journal or magazine, then we set the mark to which new writers aspire.

The standards we set must be applied universally. Consistency tells our prospective writers what is expected of them if they want to appear on our pages. Consistency tells our readers what they can expect for the investment they make in our publication. Consistency helps us deal with authors whose submissions may fall short of their professional rank, or the size of their donations, or the number of their academic degrees, or the prominence they enjoy in the world at large. There can be no double standards in our presentation of material—or else we will have no standards at all.

> There can be no double standards in our presentation of material—or else we will have no standards at all.

Attracting Submissions

Editors of genealogical periodicals invariably have to solicit manuscripts, and we have to do so actively. The competition for good material is keen. If we merely use filler space to invite submissions we'll soon find ourselves with little to publish. Solicitation means personalized contact with researchers known to be doing superb work in specific areas. How do we find those people?

- *We attend meetings, seminars, and conferences.* We identify outstanding lecturers and invite them to submit *formal* drafts of their papers. Some will be reluctant to have a presentation published, for a variety of reasons, but they may offer us something else. Some may be pressed for time and offer us the draft from which they spoke. We usually decline politely. There is a drastic difference between the spoken word and the written word. If that lecturer had prepared a properly constructed written paper and then read it, we would not have considered it outstanding. If we publish a transcript of a fascinating oral presentation, odds are that our readers won't consider it outstanding either—unless we rewrite it entirely.

- *We editorially monitor our genealogical conversations.* We keep our mental meter running, constantly measuring the potential within research problems or newly discovered sources that our contacts mention to us.

- *We read other publications.* We identify good writers there—those whose work seems compatible with our own style and focus. Then we invite submissions from them.

- *We appraise our contacts who have recently become certified.* What did they submit? If they applied for Certified Genealogist status, they researched and wrote a quality genealogy. For that same category or that of Certified Lineage Specialist, they presented a complex-evidence case study. Regardless of category, they submitted client reports. These often contain good samples of problems solved, and most clients are delighted to see their family accounts published at no extra cost to them.

- *We connect hot ideas with good writers!* We are genealogists in our private lives. We find ourselves wishing that *we* had advice or guidance on certain subjects and yet nothing can be found in print. So we mentally comb our network of contacts. Someone among them probably does have the expertise to address the subject, but has never been tempted with the idea. We tempt them!

Three cautions are also in order:

- *We always work a year or two (or more) in advance of needs.* Most writers fulfill their promises eventually, but greater urgencies intervene. (Making a living, for example.) As genealogical editors, we usually have nothing to offer but our appreciation, the "honor" of appearing on our pages, and quite often an IOU for a similarly sizable favor.

- *We never promise publication, sight unseen.* Of course we solicit carefully. We approach potential contributors whose reputation is sound. Still, we have no guarantee that the final product will be the one we envision or that it will meet the needs or standards of our publication. Therefore, we make it clear to prospective writers that all incoming manuscripts must pass editorial review, whether that be a peer-review process or the approval of our editorial board.

- *We don't even think of copying from other publications!* Doing so without permission from the writer and other editor is plagiarism. Asking for permission to reprint articles *in toto* is seldom a welcome flattery. Editors who labor to find good manuscripts and invest days or weeks in editing that material are not ecstatic when less industrious colleagues fill space by copying their work. Editors who routinely reprint material someone else has already published will find their own subscriptions waning. Too often, the end product of such editorial laziness is the perpetuation of misinformation that should never have been put in print in the first place.

Evaluating Submissions

No editor could claim, or qualify, to be an expert on all aspects of genealogy. In the interest of quality control, as well as fairness to writers, most quality journals use some type of peer-review process, sending potentially good manuscripts out for expert evaluations before the editor decides upon acceptance or rejection. A typical system of evaluating submissions might involve three steps.

Initial appraisal

Does the manuscript comply with the guidelines we've set for our journal? If not, does it have potential that can be developed? If both answers are *no,* the author should receive an immediate letter thanking him or her for the submission, while reporting that it does not meet our current needs. When a manuscript appears usable, then we notify the author that the review process has begun. Either at this point or the point of acceptance, we need the writer's signature on a contract that provides us with

- a guarantee that the manuscript has not been submitted or published elsewhere,

- an agreement that the manuscript can be edited in accordance with house style,

- an assignment of license or copyright to the work (a legal point on which our society should seek expert guidance),

- a warranty that the material contains nothing libelous or otherwise actionable, and

- an assurance that the manuscript represents the writer's own work.

Figure 43 offers one sample contract—that used by the *National Genealogical Society*

A major challenge of periodical publishing is to match the article the author wants to write with the article the editor wants to publish, which is (hopefully) the article the reader wants to read.

*—James L. Hansen, FASG
Reference Librarian
State Historical Society
of Wisconsin*

EDITING PERIODICALS

FIG. 43
PUBLISHING CONTRACT
  —*NGS Quarterly*

1 November 2000

Dr. Jefferson D. Jones
1000 Ivy Street
University City, US 00000

Dear Dr. Jones:

LETTER OF AGREEMENT

Thank you for your submission, "Resources and Methodology for Medieval Research." Upon receipt of your signed copy of this agreement, the manuscript will be forwarded to a panel of peer reviewers. Should it be accepted and published, you will receive two complimentary copies of the issue in which it appears.

Please confirm to us, via this letter, that

1. You have not submitted and will not submit your manuscript to any other person or entity for publishing, unless and until we notify you that it is no longer under consideration by this journal.
2. The compilation is your own work.
3. You are the sole compiler of the article.
4. The article was not created pursuant to your employment or, if resulting from commissioned client work, you have obtained the permission of the client to use the results of that work in this manuscript.
5. The material does not violate any copyright, proprietary, or personal rights of others.
6. The material is factually accurate to the best of your knowledge.
7. The article contains no libelous or otherwise unlawful matter.

We also request that you formally grant NGS the following rights:

1. To edit the article as to style and content so as to conform to the standards of the *Quarterly*.
2. To publish the article in the *Quarterly*.
3. To distribute copies of the article in the *Quarterly*, separate reprints, and/or future collections of *Quarterly* articles.
4. To hold exclusive publishing rights to the manuscript for one year following its publication in the *Quarterly*, after which you, as the holder of the copyright, will be free to use the article (or portions thereof) in your other writings or to grant reprinting rights to others, provided that such reuse of the material carry an acknowledgment of its first publication in the *NGS Quarterly*.

FIG. 43 (CONT.)
PUBLISHING CONTRACT
—NGS Quarterly

Mills to Jones
NGS Quarterly Letter of Agreement
1 November 2000
Page 2

We also request that you affirm your willingness to promptly review the galleys and/or page proofs, when they are provided to you, and to return corrected proofs within the designated time.

If the foregoing arrangement is acceptable to you, please sign the enclosed copy of this letter of agreement and return it to us at your earliest convenience. We very much appreciate your interest in contributing to the advancement of family history through publication in the *Quarterly*.

Sincerely,

Elizabeth Shown Mills, Editor

AGREED TO AND ACCEPTED:

_____
Author's signature

_____
Date of signature

_____
Author's phone number

_____
Author's fax number

_____
Author's e-mail address

Quarterly. Another appears in the previously cited *Chicago Manual of Style.* We may adapt either model, with permission, but our adaptation should be approved by our society's attorney. Or we might have legal counsel draft a new version that covers these points and other considerations of importance to us.

Peer review

If a manuscript seems to meet our basic guidelines, then serious evaluation begins. We seek help from authorities in that subject area before we attempt to make a decision. Ideally, we use a double-blind process in which the identities of the writer and the readers are unknown to each other. If authors place their names on the manuscript itself, we remove it. (Our style sheet might eliminate this problem by requesting the author's name on the cover sheet only.) Then we ask reviewers not to identify themselves on their critiques. This double-blind process prevents the outside possibility that a reader might pan a manuscript because of a prior disagreement with its author—or that an offended writer might harbor a grudge against the volunteer who critiqued the manuscript for us.

Editorial decision

The final decision on a manuscript is *always* our responsibility. We are the editors. Of course, we consider the opinions of the experts we called upon, and we might reasonably delay our decision pending the response of the writer to whatever suggestions those readers have made. But the ultimate editorial decision will consider matters other than the accuracy of fact and interpretation that our reviewers should address. Basic among these are the following issues:

- Does the manuscript fall within the topical or geographic coverage of our periodical?
- Is it of proper length?
- Have begats been put into social and historical context?
- Is documentation thorough? Are conclusions justified? Is evidence correctly analyzed?
- Have uncommon or faulty resources been adequately explained?

Answers to these questions are not always clear-cut. Some manuscripts may fail on one or more points and yet offer possibilities. Arthur Plotnik, former editorial supervisor for the Library of Congress and author of a standard manual in the field, tells us: "Truth is, an editor doesn't always think a raw manuscript is worth very much. What attracts an editor to it in the selection process often is its *potential for being shaped* into a successful product."[5] How do we decide if a paper has potential? With experience, editors tend to develop a sixth sense about the matter. Until we reach that point, there are basic guidelines to help us nurture our intuition.

Is this what our readers want or expect from us?
As editors, we walk a tightrope. Being human, we possess a definite set of ideas as to what constitutes *interesting* and *valuable*. We have undoubtedly decided upon certain

Truth is, an editor doesn't always think a raw manuscript is worth very much. What attracts an editor to it in the selection process often is its *potential for being shaped* into a successful product.

—*Arthur Plotnik*

issues and qualities that we think should be conveyed to our constituency. But we must also consider a final point: *what will our readership tolerate?* Good editors do try to challenge their readers, to gently nudge their interests and capabilities beyond their present limits. Intellectual stimulation is good for genealogists, but the editor must wield the prod carefully. When conflict arises between what an editor personally likes and what the readers value, the editor almost always should yield.

Will it grab the reader's attention?
Our readers are just like us—busy. Editors have only moments to sell readers on the value of an article. When readers pick up our journal and skim the title page, will this subject catch their attention? If readers are motivated to turn to the article itself, will it be possible to hook their interest in the first paragraph or two? If we see no hope for tempting our typical subscriber to read the paper, then what is our justification for publishing it? The National Endowment for the Humanities exists to underwrite the costs of presenting scholarship that public enterprise will not financially support. Few genealogical societies can afford to be miniature versions of NEH. If members of our society don't read what we publish, they won't renew. As in all fields, authors who believe their work to be good, although it does not meet the criteria of targeted journals or publishers, can always self-publish their writings or post them on the Internet.

Will it edify our readers?
There are generally two types of articles that satisfy genealogists: those that carry their ancestors' names and those that teach them something to help them find their ancestors. If we edit a local publication, odds are much better that any given issue will have some name of interest to individual subscribers. If we edit a periodical that covers a wide geographic area, then the odds are slim that any given reader will actually find an ancestor in any given issue or year. Obviously, wide-ranging periodicals have to rely far more heavily upon the teaching aspect.

If we edit a more general publication, we will find ourselves looking for articles that offer exemplary techniques or unusual resources. More often than not, a good manuscript will have this inherent teaching value, although the author may not have emphasized it. Many writers will not have even recognized it, wrapped up as they are in the fascination of their own family. As editors, we have to discern the *angle* that will make this manuscript attractive to *our readers* and then see that its potential gets developed before the manuscript goes into print.

Working with Writers

Once we have considered the advice of our advisors and applied these other guidelines, we should be able to make our editorial decision. We might reject the paper; accept it as is; or promise publication, pending certain revisions. In any case, we would customarily send the writer a copy of the critiques. If we are accepting the article, then we undoubtedly have questions of our own and may wish to add other comments regarding points raised by the critics. Now is the time to let our writers know our thoughts and our expectations. Most writers are cooperative. Most will respond politely

> Good editors try to challenge readers, to gently nudge their interests and capabilities beyond their present limits.

EDITING PERIODICALS

to the critiques, which they may or may not agree with. They will make whatever revision they feel is necessary. Then we settle down to the *real* task that editing is all about—*editing*.

Editor-writer relationship

Before we ever sully an author's lily-white manuscript with red ink, we must acquire a good, basic library of editing manuals—and learn what they have to say. The notes for this chapter name several that are worth their space on our editorial shelves. Some, such as Boston's *Stet! Tricks of the Trade for Writers and Editors,* do more than guide us through the rules and regulations that are the editor's stock in trade. They also give new editors the backbone needed to work with writers whose egos are more dynamic than their writing style—as well as those dedicated to the task of convincing new editors that they aren't supposed to edit at all. Most new editors are either dismayed or reassured by the advice such manuals offer. To quote Boston:

> What we mostly do is *rewrite*. It falls to us to keep the paragraphs, sentences, and clauses from tripping over one another in the author's headlong rush to make the point. The author relies on us to sort out the rats' nests of usage, administer the trivia of capitalization and punctuation, and make the written word look good on the page. . . . We write—and rewrite—because the most significant difference in the world is the one between "good" and "better."[6]

Our greatest challenge in trying to sort out the words and phrases our authors trip over is the avoidance of one editorial sin: *violating the author's meaning.* All manuals acknowledge this is an easy transgression to commit—Murphy's Law being such as it is. Those writers who are most in need of editing are those whose meanings are fuzzy in the first place. In trying to clarify whatever we *think* they mean to say, we can easily misconstrue a point. For this reason (among others) it is important to provide our writers with revised drafts—after which another round of editing might ensue. There do have to be reasonable limits placed upon such games of verbal ping-pong, however. We not only have to put out a periodical, we should do it on time. In this respect, one dean of genealogical editing, John Frederick Dorman, has counseled:

> Changes in a submitted manuscript are often necessary for a variety of reasons, and authors should not be upset when an editor suggests them. Alterations may be needed to make the text fit the page format of the periodical, to eliminate extraneous material that does not relate directly to the thrust of the article, or to expand portions so that readers can more fully understand the reasoning behind conclusions based upon circumstantial evidence. . . .
>
>   An editor has the right to make additions of this sort and to make alterations in a manuscript without asking the author's approval, as long as the editor can back up his additions and alterations with good proof. If I were continually sending revisions back for approval, issues of *The Virginia Genealogist* might never come out. The writer who objects need not submit any more articles.[7]

Neither editor nor author (assuming both are sane) enjoys a duel of words at this point. Both should have a common objective: to work together toward a manuscript that is as clear, smooth, and energetic as possible. As editors, we can forestall

We write—and rewrite—because the most significant difference in the world is the one between "good" and "better."

—Bruce Boston

some protests by developing a boilerplate statement to accompany the edited galleys we send out for approval. Writers do appear to be less wounded when they realize that all manuscripts go through the same editing process. Figure 45 presents the generic statement currently in use by the *NGS Quarterly*, "The Editorial Process: What Your Editors Look for—and Why."[8]

It is also wise to create and preserve a careful paper trail throughout our chain of contact with the reviewers and contributor of each manuscript. Ours is a field in which writers report *facts*—theoretically. Yet an author's interpretation of those facts does involve *opinions*. The reviewers' appraisals of a writer's ability to collect and report those facts are judgment calls. The editor's decision regarding acceptance or rejection can impact the professional career of the contributor. In a culture as litigious as ours, editors must protect themselves. Contracts with writers help. A published policy statement also helps. But it is also prudent that thorough and exact documentation of our own work on a manuscript—and the author's responses—be kept at every step.

Copyediting and substantive editing

Most genealogical editors expect to apply the quick-checks itemized in the sidebar at right; but effective copyediting goes far beyond this point. In pursuit of the clarity, smoothness, and vitality that make a good article, editing manuals typically cite five levels of surgery most manuscripts endure:

- correcting errors in punctuation, grammar, and spelling;

- making sentences more effective;

- correcting improper word usage;

- making formatting changes; and

- reorganizing content, if necessary. (Many editors place this as level 1.)

Linda B. Jorgensen, author of *Real-World Newsletters,* elaborates in a piece titled "What's Substantive Editing? It's What You Do":

> To arrive at publishable copy, some articles need no more than the rearranging of a few paragraphs and a spell-checking pass for the whole thing to click. But *in most cases, newsletter editors must substantively edit the drafts they receive.* . . . What's that? Simply defined, substantive editing is the editing of meaning. It happens at the word, sentence, and paragraph levels, but at any level it's *based primarily on analysis, separating the components of something to discover what's essential about it and looking for the logical relationships that make up the whole.* As a result of a good substantive edit, important material won't have to fight for attention or require much mulling.
>
> Substantive editing involves reorganizing sentences within paragraphs, moving paragraphs around till they feel at home, deleting irrelevant or redundant material, recommending changes in terminology or wording to authors, supplying missing words, and rewriting where necessary to clarify meaning and condense copy for the space where it must fit. Here are the basic substantive editing tasks newsletter editors perform: Analyzing, filling gaps in thought, reducing, reorganizing, rewording, rewriting.[9]

FIG. 44
EDITORIAL QUICK-CHECK:
COMMON GENEALOGICAL
PROBLEMS

- Are all genealogical dates and time frames reasonable?

- If the date of an event is given in more than one place, do the instances agree?

- Is each name spelled consistently throughout—unless used in a quote?

- Are all quotes copied precisely? (Authors should furnish copies of documents or published materials not available at the editor's library.)

- Are all quotes integrated smoothly into the text, so that syntax is not violated?

- Are all reference numbers consecutive? Are they all there? Does each reference number in the text match the content of the corresponding note?

EDITING PERIODICALS

FIG. 45
THE EDITORIAL PROCESS:
WHAT YOUR EDITORS
LOOK FOR—AND WHY
    —NGS Quarterly

1. *Accuracy of facts.* Are the details within the text, explanatory notes, and reference citations free of obvious problems? To every extent possible, facts, quotations, and citations are checked by your editors. The most common problems are found within the citations.

2. *Elimination of ambiguities and completeness of facts.* Do all impersonal pronouns (this, that, etc.) have clear antecedents? Is the situation under discussion self-explanatory to the uninformed reader? This is a major problem for most writers (including editors when they do their own writing). The fact that an author is thoroughly familiar with his or her subject makes it difficult to recognize how much detail the unfamiliar reader will need.

3. *Relevancy of detail.* How necessary is each piece of information? In the composition of every essay there are many interesting facts that could be included; but these are often dispensable. The criteria here must be: does the reader *have* to know this fact in order to understand the problem or use these records? Among genealogists, *names* present the greatest temptation. Since names are fundamental to genealogy, writers hate not to include the identity of anyone involved with each event under discussion. Yet, too many names confuse readers. How are they to know which persons are so important to the subject that they must be remembered? Writers must do this judicious culling of names and facts, or their editors must do it for them.

4. *Organization.* Are related facts treated together? Do all subjects within a paragraph correspond to the subjects covered within the topic sentence? *Is* there a topic sentence? (A lack of the latter is a common problem.) Are all paragraphs of reasonably the same length? Exceptions exist; but one-sentence paragraphs and those that will typeset at only two to four lines ordinarily should be combined with the paragraph immediately preceding or following—adding a new topic sentence, if necessary, to link the material that appeared in both of the shorter paragraphs.

5. *Consistency.* Are there facts stated in one place that later seem to be contradicted? Are all subject headings presented in parallel form? Do subheadings at the same level treat the same type of subjects? When a single sentence presents items in a series, do all elements of the series actually parallel each other—in grammatical form and subject matter? Are words and terms spelled in the same manner each time they are used? Do reference citations follow the same format throughout the essay?

6. *Repetition or redundancy.* Are the same subjects treated in more than one place? Are the same statements made more than once? Is the same word used over and again (especially in close proximity) when a synonym would make the sentence or paragraph less monotonous? Are words or statements within a sentence redundant? Example: "a *census listing* of Kalamazoo" (when, obviously, a census *is* a listing).

7. *Voice.* Is the essay presented in a chatty first-person voice or in the third-person that is usually expected of objective analyses and formal discussions? Most readers don't care to hear about the *writer;* they want to know about the *subject.* (Some writers admirably handle the first-person voice; far more often, those who write "I did . . ." and "I think . . ." wander onto many personal digressions that are more interesting to them than to their readers.)

8. *Passive and remote verb structure.* Both of these are appropriate at times. However, the use of active verbs and present tense keeps writing concise and readers moving on to the next piece of action.

9. *Quotations.* Are these woven into the text in a manner that does not violate grammar and syntax? Special care is needed to be certain that the words selected for quotation are in the same voice and verb tense as the remainder of the sentence and paragraph. (This is a special problem for genealogists who quote from old documents.) Is the quotation absolutely necessary in the first place, or would the sentence be more direct if the writer put it into his/her own words?

10. *Miscellaneous points of grammar.* Are there clichés? Unnecessary capitalizations? Subject-verb disagreements? Incompatible pronouns and antecedents? Punctuation problems? Nouns used improperly as adjectives (e.g., *genealogy libraries* instead of *genealogical libraries*)? Distracting or inexplicable abbreviations? A need for a smoother transition from each paragraph to the next?

11. *Writing tight.* Is there unnecessary verbiage? The biggest problem an editor has is *space*. A lazy editor or a journal in need of material is grateful for long articles. More words help fill space. If a journal is in good health, the amount of material being submitted is greater than that which can be accepted; and readers expect as much and as varied content as possible. Space, then, is at a premium. *NGSQ* is a journal that must use space judiciously. Therefore, after all else is considered, your editors must read and reread each manuscript from the standpoint of the maxim *write tight*. If something can be said in one word instead of four, or three words instead of a sentence, then excess verbiage must be deleted. At this stage, manuscripts are likely to go through several rounds of "tightening." A typical example of the results is:

> Archivists are *now in the process of* indexing . . .
> Archivists are *now* indexing . . .

This small alteration saves roughly one-third of the space. Without this attention to detail, *NGSQ* would pay for 120 pages of printing each quarter instead of 80 and membership dues would have to be increased proportionately.

12. *Final thought.* No writer's work escapes the editing process at any legitimate press in any field, no matter "how big a name" that writer has. It is impossible for authors to have the same detachment and objectivity that outside readers of their manuscripts will have. Obviously, if writers could perceive all problems within their work, they would remove these problems themselves; and editors could be dispensed with entirely. For whatever consolation it is worth, when editors change desks and pen their own works, even *they* get edited!

As your editors (as well as writers in our private lives), we view the production of an article as a cooperative effort between author and editor—with two interrelated objectives: to make both parties and the society look as good in print as possible; and to present an article that will have permanent value. We are pleased that your paper exemplifies these goals.

—*Elizabeth Shown Mills*

These are universal basics. Most literary fields adapt and expand them to meet the needs of their specific discipline. Figures 45 and 46 offer more explicit guidance for genealogical editors, based upon the policies of the *National Genealogical Society Quarterly*.

FACT CHECKING

The one serious responsibility not covered by those who drafted the five levels of manuscript surgery is *fact checking*. Few areas of responsibility weigh as heavily as this one or are as loaded with potential problems. Genealogical editors bear a particularly acute burden since the presentation of facts—accurate facts—is the raison d'être for almost every genealogical article. Every manuscript must be read and reread for inconsistencies and discrepancies. Cited references should be checked to every extent possible. Citations to virtually all printed sources are available via OCLC, the Library of Congress Catalog, and other online book lists from libraries globally. We may also ask writers to provide photocopies of crucial material they used or quoted.

FIG. 46
FROM MANUSCRIPT TO PAGE PROOFS:
15 STEPS
—NGS Quarterly

1. Verify correctness of quotations and citations, via library resources.
2. Correct problems with organization and clarity of argument, querying writer as needed.
   - Move text blocks or notes if necessary.
   - Delete less crucial sections if manuscript is overlong.
3. Prepare a corrected draft.
4. Proofread revised text and notes.
   - Use two-person process, reading aloud for comparisons.
   - Highlight all reference numbers in text and notes to be certain all are there.
5. Edit revised text against notes.
   - Read each statement in text, then analyze corresponding note.
   - Be certain the note matches text, is complete, and has no extraneous data.
6. Edit the text for smoothness, tightness, and fine points of grammar; then proof again.
7. Repeat step 6!
8. Typeset revised draft (if we are "desktopping")—otherwise reverse steps 8–9 with steps 10–11.
9. Finish with a repeat of step 4.
10. Send to writer.
11. Correct draft in response to author's returned manuscript; consult with author on any points of disagreement but retain final authority.
12. Send out for first round of proofreading.
13. Make corrections.
14. Send out for second and third rounds of proofreading, correcting after each.
15. Pray.

However, common sense dictates that we cannot redo the entire research of every writer; no editor has the necessary time, funds, or access. For this reason, our published policy should include a standard disclaimer, such as "Unless otherwise indicated, the facts, interpretations, and opinions printed herein are those of the author; however, proved errors will be corrected." Then we should promptly, and without prejudice to any party, correct any problems that might arise.

LINE EDITING

It is beyond the scope of this chapter to cover the skills required for the line-editing process. Some are outlined in figure 44, The Editorial Process: What Your Editors Look for—and Why. All are treated abundantly in the manuals referenced at the end of this paper. We must learn those principles. We cannot earn the respect of knowledgeable writers (much less fellow editors) if we are unacquainted with such esoteric things as the difference between *imply* and *infer* or if we do not know when to use an em-dash or an en-dash. Should we be fortunate enough to edit a manuscript that will go to a typesetter, then we must know how to mark up manuscripts and encode typesetting instructions. Whether we send our work out for page preparation or whether we "desktop" it, we must understand such things as fonts, point sizes, leading, and procedures for calculating the number of pages that any typed manuscript will produce. As editors, we would find it helpful to study most of the other chapters within the present manual—particularly those relating to writing, abstracting, documenting, proofreading, and indexing.

Summary Concepts

Editing is an exacting pursuit, but a rewarding one. Few areas of genealogy offer a comparable opportunity to influence the breadth of knowledge available to our field— or the standards that guard this knowledge against damage by the careless, the inept, and the deceptive. An editor's post is not one to accept quickly or lightly. It is not a position to seek if we aspire to high office or public popularity; conscientious editors cannot help but leave behind them a trail of rejected writers and wounded egos. Nor is it a venture to embark upon if we are awed or intimidated by the fame, fortune, or degrees possessed by others. As guardians of standards within our field, we make certain that all writings we publish do adhere to current guidelines for literature, scholarship, and good taste. And we apply those standards equitably, with no privilege for the prominent and no disdain for the novice. The work we put into print will survive long after us. Knowing that it will aid our progeny—and that we will be proud to have them see our name attached to it—should be our ultimate reward.

NOTES

1. Arthur Plotnik, *The Elements of Editing: A Modern Guide for Editors and Journalists* (New York: Collier Books, 1982), 34.

2. Everyone knows, of course, that sentences "should not" end in prepositions; but Winston Churchill put that maxim in its proper place: "This is the kind of nonsense up with which I will not put." For advice on all those occasions in which common sense dictates breaking entrenched

> We apply standards equitably, with no privilege for the prominent and no disdain for the novice.

EDITING PERIODICALS

Even editors, when they are writing, need editors. We get as close to our work—and need as much support—as the authors we work with.

—*Renni Browne and Dave King*[10]

grammatical rules, see Theodore M. Bernstein's classic *Miss Thistlebottom's Hobgoblins: The Careful Writer's Guide to the Taboos, Bugbears, and Outmoded Rules of English Usage* (New York: Farrar, Straus, and Giroux, 1971); and Patricia T. O'Conner, *Woe Is I: The Grammarphobe's Guide to Better English in Plain English* (New York: Grosset/Putnam Books, 1996).

3. Bruce O. Boston, ed., *Stet! Tricks of the Trade for Writers and Editors* (Alexandria, Virginia: Editorial Experts, 1986), 3. Also see that volume's sequel, *Stet Again! More Tricks of the Trade for Publications People* (Alexandria: EEI Books, 1996).

4. *The Chicago Manual of Style: The Essential Guide for Writers, Editors, and Publishers*, 14th edition (Chicago: University of Chicago Press, 1993).

5. Plotnic, *Elements of Editing*, 30.

6. Boston, *Stet! Tricks of the Trade*, 99. Emphasis added.

7. John Frederick Dorman, CG, FASG, "The Editor's Responsibility to Edit," Part II of "How to Have Your Article Accepted or Rejected by the Editor," *Association of Professional Genealogists Quarterly* 4 (Fall 1989): 62–63.

8. This first appeared as an appendix to "Editing a Society Journal: A Summary of Obligations and Limitations," under the byline of the present writer, in *National Genealogical Society Newsletter* 15 (March–April 1989), 39–44; portions of the present paper have been adapted from that briefer work.

9. Linda B. Jorgensen, *Real-World Newsletters to Meet Your Unreal Demands* (Alexandria, Virginia: EEI Press, 1999), 5. Emphasis added.

10. Renni Browne and Dave King, *Self-Editing for Fiction Writers: How to Edit Yourself into Print* (New York: Harper Perennial, 1994), ix.

FURTHER STUDY

EDITING

Beach, Mark. *Editing Your Newsletter: How to Produce an Effective Publication Using Traditional Tools and Computers*. Portland, Oregon: Coast to Coast Books, 1988.

Getting it Printed: How to Work with Printers and Graphic Imaging Services to Assure Quality, Stay on Schedule, and Control Costs. 3d edition. Cincinnati, Ohio: North Light Books, 1999.

Bunnin, Brad. *The Writer's Legal Companion*. 3d edition. Cambridge, Massachusetts: Perseus Books, 1998.

Merriam-Webster's Manual for Writers & Editors. Rev. edition. Springfield, Massachusetts: Merriam-Webster, 1998.

Craig, Ruth Parlé, and Vincent F. Hopper. *Barron's 1001 Pitfalls in English Grammar*. Hauppauge, New York: Barron's Educational Series, 1986.

Goldstein, Norm, ed. *The Associated Press Stylebook and Libel Manual*. Rev. edition. New York: Associated Press, 1998.

O'Conner, Patricia T. *Words Fail Me: What Everyone Who Writes Should Know about Writing*. New York: Harcourt, Brace & Co., 1999.

Rees, Nigel. *Cassell Dictionary of Clichés*. London: Cassell Wellington House, 1996.

Shaw, Harry. *Errors in English and Ways to Correct Them*. 4th edition. New York: Harper Perennial, 1993.

Stoughton, Mary T. *Substance & Style: Instruction and Practice in Copyediting*. Rev. edition. Alexandria: EEI Books, 1996.

Williams, Joseph M., and Gregory G. Colomb. *Style: Toward Clarity and Grace*. Chicago: University of Chicago Press, 1990.

LAYOUT AND TYPESETTING

Siebert, Lori, and Mary Cropper. *Working with Words & Pictures*. Cincinnati: North Light Books, 1993.

Stopke, Judy, and Chip Staley. *An Eye for Type*. 3d expanded edition. Ann Arbor, Michigan: Promotional Perspectives, 1992.

Williams, Robin. *The PC [Mac] Is Not a Typewriter: A Style-Manual for Creating Professional-Level Type on Your Personal Computer*. Berkeley, California: Peachpit Press, 1992.

26

PROOFREADING
AND INDEXING

**PROOFREADING
AND INDEXING**

Keynotes

Keynotes　(cont.)

Proofreading <u>and</u> Indexing

by Birdie Monk Holsclaw

Finishing touches make a difference in any endeavor. With genealogical writing, two finishing touches—good proofreading and indexing—can make *all* the difference. When these are ignored or given inadequate attention, the reader or potential user misses valuable information and the publisher loses sales. Proofreading not only makes a work easier to understand by removing distractions; but, more important, it ensures the accuracy of the content. Indexing makes this wealth of genealogical material accessible. No genealogical publication should go to print without these two finishing touches, and the services of skilled professionals in both areas are keenly needed by organizations and individuals who prepare material for our field. Although much proofreading and indexing are performed on a volunteer basis for colleagues and societies, there are growing opportunities for contractors. Whether working for a fee or donating a service, conscientious proofreaders and indexers conduct their assignments in a professional manner. Even if we do not engage in either activity professionally, we must be able to handle or supervise the proofing and indexing of our own material.

Proofreading

Everyone needs a proofreader. Even the best writers can and do make errors of grammar, spelling, syntax, and typography. All authors must proof their own work, and most catch many of their own mistakes; but none of us can be completely objective with our own material. We are too familiar with it. As genealogical writers—and as lecturers preparing visual and written material to accompany our presentations—no matter how meticulous we are, we need the "outside" eye of someone else to scrutinize our finished products. As editors, we should ensure that our publication is a top-quality one by engaging the services of an outside proofer.

The task

Proofreading is difficult to separate from copyediting. Technically, the terms refer to actions performed at different stages of the publishing process: copyediting involves changes to a manuscript before it has been typeset; proofreading entails corrections to typeset material. Copyediting typically produces considerably more substantial changes to content, whereas the explicit purpose of proofreading is to ensure that the final copy is accurate. However, the good proofreader is also a skilled copyeditor and reads the proof copy with an editorial eye.

The skills

Good writers are not necessarily good proofreaders. The latter are a special breed, whose instincts are particularly suited to the task in three particular ways:

ATTENTIVENESS

Proofreaders need a critical eye—meaning a gift for finicky attention to detail, a flair for spotting what to others might be trivial inconsistencies, a wariness for *possible* error (should this name be *Newcastle* or *New Castle?*), and a willingness to resolve questions. Also useful is an eye for good layout design and good spatial perception.

KNOWLEDGE

To be successful proofreaders, we need a solid understanding of grammar and punctuation principles, good spelling habits, and broad skills in finding answers to questions. In our field, it also requires a general knowledge of genealogical formats, procedures, resources, and terms, as well as standard genealogical reference books.

OBJECTIVITY

Proofreaders have to cultivate detachment. We must focus on the readability and accuracy of the material, divorcing ourselves from any opinions about the subject or feelings toward the author. We also need considerable skill in conveying suggestions (particularly criticism) clearly and pleasantly.

The tools

To gain a general knowledge of the proofreader's role and job requirements, we should study a range of manuals treating this craft in particular and writing style in general. Several of the best appear in the FURTHER STUDY section of this chapter. Beyond these basics, the manner in which we conduct our proofreading will differ with each assignment and it should be guided by the wishes of our client (the author or editor). Therefore, before we begin, we need three specific sets of guidelines: a clearly stated assignment, a general style sheet, and a notational style sheet.

ASSIGNMENT

What level of proofreading or copyediting does this client expect? Should we watch for improper grammar and punctuation or just obvious typographic errors? Should we check transcribed records for accuracy or evaluate the readability of narrative material?

GENERAL STYLE SHEET

What guidelines should we follow? As pointed out in earlier chapters on writing family histories and editing periodicals, every project should have a style sheet. The author or editor should provide us with one that describes such matters as preferred abbreviations, date formats, layout conventions, and spelling. If not, we may wish to encourage the client to prepare one and assist with its development if necessary. As supplements to (or substitutes for) a specific style sheet, we should also use basic style guides such as *The Chicago Manual of Style*, for text;[1] *Evidence! Citation & Analysis for the Family Historian,* for reference notes and bibliography;[2] and *Numbering Your Genealogy*, for the technicalities of formatting genealogical data.[3]

> To be successful proofreaders, we need a solid understanding of grammar and punctuation principles, good spelling habits, and broad skills in finding answers to questions.

PROOFREADING

AND INDEXING

FIG. 47
STANDARD
PROOFREADING MARKS

MARK / MEANING		EXAMPLE
✗	Delete	*Research: Methods and and Sources*
◡	Delete space	the wife of John Smith
∧∨	Insert here	*The Source: A Guidebook of American Genealogy*
ℙ	Begin new paragraph	thus the lineage is disproven. Thomas Jones
[	Move left	[Jacob's birthplace appears in each census.
]	Move right	I give to each of my children, to wit:]John Jernigan Jenkins Susan Jenkins Jones Mary Jenkins Schwartzfelt
‖	Align vertically	George Jamison, 25 Mary Jamison, 24 Susan Jamison, 1
∿	Transpose	hte village in Cork
lc	Use lowercase	*lc* the Affidavit was signed
cap	Use capital letter	*cap* the Revolutionary war erupted
bf	Use boldface	*bf* He married Helen Hun on 25 May 1777
ital	Use italics	*ital* He wrote, "I maryed [sic] her last month."
∧	Insert colon, comma	His sons were as follows John James, Sam and
⊙	Insert period	along the Susquehanna Sylvester bought
∨	Insert apostrophe	a welcome addition to anyones library is the
stet	Stet (Latin for *let it stand as is*)	*stet* the careless handwriting of the enumerator

NOTATION STYLE SHEET

How should proofreaders mark their copy? A knowledgeable client will expect us to be familiar with standard proofreading notations. Some are shown in figure 47. More complete tables can be found in most dictionaries and style manuals, including the above-referenced *Chicago Manual*. If the author or editor is unacquainted with these traditional forms, we might include a copy of the marks when we complete our labor and return the material. Some clients may prefer that we verbally annotate the problems we spot. However, the standard marks—because of their precise meanings and uncluttered appearance—are the common preference of editors.

The process

As we work with the client's proof copy, we bear in mind that we are only making suggestions. The author or editor makes the final decision about revising the material. It might help to explain our suggestions, such as "Sentence needs a subject" or "Inconsistent date format." If we have been asked to watch for problems that slipped through the copyediting process, our suggestions may involve restructuring—even rewriting—sentences; but we should not change the intent or style of the writer. We would not, for example, use vocabulary this author probably would not use.

GENERAL PRINCIPLES

The length of time needed for a proofreading or copyediting assignment depends on the material and the guidelines we have been given. Generally, we can read and mark narrative much more quickly than abstracted records, genealogical "begats," and reference notes—all of which have a high density of dates and names. Detailed material requires a stronger level of concentration. Some clients may give us only a finished copy to work from—a common practice when the editing has been extensive or the client is an author who has compiled a narrative from many sources. On the other hand, when we are expected to proof lists and highly technical material, we need access to the original to do adequate proofing.

The more exacting the client's requirements for readability (good grammar, punctuation, and sentence structure), the more time we need for proofreading. Far more so than with writing or editing, we can break up proofreading jobs to fit in with other activities—although interrupting the work may cause us to inadvertently bypass some material or overlook inconsistencies. To ensure that we resume reading at the same place, we might flag the spot with a gummed sticker. Some proofreading is portable, because material can be read while riding the bus or waiting for an appointment. However, we should save detailed copy for times when we have access to our reference materials. Figure 48 summarizes the basic principles to be applied.

SPECIAL GENEALOGICAL CONCERNS

Beyond these basics, our field calls for particular attention to several areas in which genealogists are particularly vulnerable:

- *Dates.* For the genealogist, dates are of vital importance; identities and relationships hinge upon their correctness. Therefore we should be particularly scrupulous in

The more exacting the client's requirements for readability (good grammar, punctuation, and sentence structure), the more time we need for proofreading.

our examination of dates, bearing in mind that there is a far greater likelihood of inadvertent error in typewritten numbers than in handwritten numbers.

- *Names.* Spelling variants are commonplace in genealogical research; some should be preserved and some should be considered errors or inconsistencies. For the most part, family historians tend to identify families by the spelling that their own branches use or by the variant that was the most common across the generations. Once they adopt a spelling for a book or article, then convention calls for using that spelling consistently for all *general* references to the family and for all family members who left no evidence of having used a different spelling. Writers are expected to state their policy in a preface to their writing, where they will also identify the other variants found. When they treat an individual who left samples of his or her signature and used one spelling consistently, then genealogical authors usually identify that individual according to his or her self-identity. However, when the author quotes from a particular source, placing quotation marks around the extracted words, the author is expected to spell the name exactly as it was rendered in the original record. As proofreaders, we respect these policies; and we flag any incidences that appear to vary from accepted practice.

- *Numbers.* In several regards, genealogical writing is technical writing. We offer numbered lists of individuals and children, numbered superscript references that correspond to reference notes, and other numbered superscript references that

FIG. 48
BASIC PROOFREADING
PRINCIPLES

1. A solid reference library is necessary for professional proofreading. It should include general works on grammar, spelling, and style; and specialized works on genealogical principles.

2. Responsibilities should be clearly understood. Some clients may expect only a reading for offenses against typography and page layout; others may expect the proofer to check behind them on copyediting detail (consistency, grammar, spelling, etc.).

3. General style sheets used by the client should guide the proofreader's decisions for abbreviations, dates, and other conventions. If the client provides none, the proofer should develop one with the client or adapt one from a proofreading manual.

4. "Mini" style sheets help when proofing highly technical matter such as genealogical data. Focusing on individual chapters or sections, these sheets serve as a place to jot the spelling used at first reference for each place or person and the dates assigned to events that are likely to be mentioned again.

5. For lists with heavy concentrations of names and numbers, careful proofing requires two people. One reads from the original sheets, vocalizing spelling and punctuation, while the other reads the proofs to ensure a precise copy.

6. Proofreading marks should be the conventional proofreading notations, unless the client directs otherwise.

7. Preliminary markings may be in pencil; final markings should be in bold color— preferably red.

8. All proofreader marks are suggestions only; the author or editor makes the final decision as to content of the pages.

denote generations (commonly italicized, today, to distinguish them from reference numbers). Our endnotes or footnotes are numbered, as are chapters and figures and appendixes. As proofreaders, we should recheck the sequence of numbers in every group we encounter.

- *References.* Genealogical proofreaders pay special attention to citations of source information. Following the guidelines set by the writer or editor, we watch for completeness and consistency in format, as well as correct spelling and punctuation of the names of authors, publishers, and places. Inconsistencies in citing abbreviated or subsequent references are a common error. For example, after the first full citation of *Guide to Genealogical Research in the National Archives,* if the author chose *Genealogical Research in the National Archives* as the shortened title, then the work should not alternately appear as *Guide to Genealogical Research* or as *Guide to the National Archives.*

Several standard and specialized techniques help us avoid oversights with all the above problems.

BASIC TECHNIQUES

Proofreaders commonly use one of the following procedures—and often more than one—for a given task:

- *Multiple reading*s. The most common procedure is to make multiple passes through the manuscript to assure attention to varied items. For example, the first reading may be for an overview of content and style, at which time the most obvious typos are flagged. Subsequent readings would then focus individually on common problem areas. Figure 49 outlines the multiple-reading process used by one national-level journal in our field.

- *Oral reading.* For highly technical material, two proofreaders work together. One reads aloud from the original copy, while the other follows along in the typeset draft watching for discrepancies. The reader vocalizes such things as punctuation ("Smith comma John"), spacing ("new paragraph"), and unusual spellings ("B-e-r-t-r-u-m-b").

- *Single-line comparison.* Here, we lay flat our working copy (or the original page and the typeset page side by side, if we have both drafts) and we use a straight edge, such as a ruler, to help focus our attention on one line at a time.

- *Backward reading.* The most tedious of all, but the best for catching misspelled words, is to read the text in reverse order. This removes our attention from what is being *said* and refocuses it upon the characters actually typed.

SPECIALIZED TECHNIQUES

Because genealogists work so intensely with detail, some of our colleagues apply other techniques to help ensure accuracy. For example, in addition to the general style sheet that covers policy issues for abbreviations, etc., a project might call for us to create "mini" style sheets for chapters or subsections of the manuscript. On a legal pad, with one sheet for each letter of the alphabet, we would list all places and persons as we come to them in the manuscript, recording the spelling used at first reference to each. On a separate pad and pages, we would record events and the dates attributed to each.

TIP

To ensure accuracy in numeric text, we read for consistency in context. In a series of birth dates, for instance, we would watch for such implausible sequences as *1814, 1816, 1813, 1819*—in which case *1813* is likely to be a misreading of *1818.*

PROOFREADING
AND INDEXING

FIG. 49
EDITORIAL PROCESS
FOR PROOFING
TYPESET COPY
—*NGS Quarterly*

Editor

First pass
Skim galleys for reference numbers amid text. Mark each with highlighter, checking that no numbers are missing or duplicated. Repeat for corresponding notes.

Second pass
Read closely for content, flagging obvious typos and spacing problems. (If the initial skim for reference numbers left a duplicated number unflagged, the unmarked number should be obvious in this reading.)

Third pass
Read for conformity with general style sheet (abbreviations, date conventions, placement of citation elements and punctuation in footnotes, etc.)

Fourth pass
Read for consistency between detail (e.g., if a cited date is later repeated, check to see that each reference uses the exact date; if an individual name is repeated, check to see that each spelling is consistent; if a spousal or parental identity is repeated, check to see that the identity is the same in each case).

Fifth pass
(*For genealogies*) Skim "individual" numbers to ensure none is missing or duplicated. Repeat for roman numerals in each family unit and generation numbers in each parenthetical citation of ancestry. In lists of children, check sequence of birth dates, then check those birth dates against maternal age and father's date of death.

*Proofreader 1**

First pass
Read for content—focusing upon clarity. (Is "final" content clear to outside reader who has not been involved with writing, fact checking, or editing?)

Second pass
Read closely for inconsistencies, misspellings, etc.

*Proofreader 2**

First pass
Read for conformity with general style sheet and for offenses against grammatical or typographical principles. Check spellings of all locations, all foreign words, etc.

Second pass
Read for consistency between detail, preciseness in number sequences, etc.

*Proofreader 3**

Single pass
Read closely to ensure no remaining typos.

---

* Each proofreading stage is followed by the necessary editorial corrections, before fresh proofs are passed to the next proofreader.

Or, if we set up a sheet for each person, we might jot down any dates attributed to him or her, along with nicknames or names of spouses or children. As we proceed through the relevant section of the manuscript and we encounter those individuals and events again, we check each against the guide sheet to ensure consistency. The labor can be time-consuming in genealogy; but there is no better way to ensure that *Michael Arundson* on page 31 does not become *Michel Arondson* on page 39—or that his firstborn child did not die in 1827, according to page 40, and 1829, as per page 43.

COMPUTERIZED ASSISTANCE

Modern writers and editors have additional assistance in the form of spelling and grammar checkers that are built into most word-processing, page layout, and graphic programs. However, most names and many words—particularly words in the specialized vocabulary of genealogy—will not be included in a spell-checking dictionary; and there are other times (as when quoting from documents) that spell-checkers should not be relied upon (or allowed) to alter text. Even the best of the programs cannot decide whether *liable* or *libel* should be used. There are hundreds of correctly spelled words that are incorrect when used in the wrong context, and there is no substitute yet for the human eye and brain.

So, too, can a computerized grammar-checker assist writers and editors—if used appropriately. These programs "read" a narrative, looking for problems in grammar, punctuation, structure, style, and syntax. When one program was used on the poem in the sidebar, it offered only two suggestions: a comma might be missing after the word *mistakes,* and the last four lines could be broken into two sentences!

When we produce our own work, we are wise to use both spelling and grammar checkers. When we proofread for a client, we hope the client has done so. Then we apply human attention and intelligence to catch what "artificial intelligence" cannot. Every review adds to the excellence of a publication.

The proofreader's goal

Simply put, our goal is to achieve a publication that is completely error free. While this may seem a lofty but impractical ideal, for us to aim toward any lesser mark would be unworthy of our professional standards. Multiple readings by several proofers will ensure excellence, if not perfection. The process is worth it. The result of all our proofreading efforts will be superior genealogical publications—a service to our readers and a tribute to our field.

Indexing

The task

Indexes are prized by genealogists, arguably even more so than by any other type of researcher. Speaking out emphatically on the subject, *The Chicago Manual of Style* tells us, "Every serious book of nonfiction should have an index if it is to achieve its maximum usefulness."[5] Yet genealogists complain that scholarly works (even those

Put to the test, the spell checker in one major word-processing program found no errors in the contemporary ditty *Spellbound:*

I have a spelling checker,
It came with my PC;
It plainly marks four my revue
Mistakes I cannot sea.
I've run this poem threw it,
I'm sure your please to no,
Its letter perfect in it's weigh;
My checker tolled me sew.[4]

that follow *Chicago Manual*) provide incomplete indexes. Our publications are judged in great part by the indexes we provide. The lack of one—or a poorly prepared one—is likely to be cited negatively in reviews. Although indexes are now the norm for family histories, the quality still varies widely. What constitutes high quality? According to the above-cited arbiter of style:

> A good index records every pertinent statement made within the body of the text. The subject matter and purpose of the book determine which statements are pertinent and which peripheral. An index should be considerably more than an expanded, alphabetical table of contents. It should also be something other than a concordance of words and phrases.[6]

Naturally, "pertinence" is a matter of opinion and our readers are the final judges. In the pages of a community history, architects might seek information about historical buildings, while genealogists are more likely to be interested in personal names. Even family historians show considerable diversity in focus. A major challenge for us as genealogical indexers is to envision all possible uses for the material we are indexing—including the needs of researchers in related disciplines.

The skills

Many genealogists are attracted to this specialty because they recognize the absolute essentialness of indexes to a field that specializes in identifying and linking people. In addition to our strong motivation, we should make good indexers if we possess three other qualities: an ability to conceptualize, a knowledge of indexing principles, and a considerable degree of patience.

CONCEPTUAL ABILITY
A good indexer sees the "big picture" as well as the smallest detail. According to *Chicago Manual*, "The ideal indexer sees the book as a whole, both in scope and in arbitrary limits; understands the emphasis of the various parts and their relation to the whole; and, perhaps most important of all, clearly pictures potential readers and anticipates their special needs."[7]

KNOWLEDGE OF PRINCIPLES
Indexers should have an understanding of selection practices, alphabetizing rules, and format standards—and not just for our native language. Increasingly, genealogists and their publications transcend ethnic and national bounds. Naming conventions and alphabetizing rules vary according to the nature of the material we handle and the names and terms therein. The FURTHER STUDY section of this chapter identifies manuals for self-study, and the website of the international Society of Indexers offers helpful courses and links to other professional groups.

PATIENCE AND SELF-DISCIPLINE
Not all indexing work is tedious, but the precision and attention to detail that are necessary to achieve a quality index do require a considerable degree of patience.

TIPS

When we begin to index a new publication, wisdom suggests allowing more time than we anticipate.

If a production deadline seems unreasonable, we negotiate! Once we agree upon a deadline, we consider it a commitment.

Because most of our indexes must be fitted into a tight production schedule—after the manuscript revision is completed and before the work can be sent to press—we must be able to work quickly without sacrificing accuracy and thoroughness.

The tools

A familiarity with modern indexing tools is essential. Some top-notch professional indexers still use manual methods, and *Chicago Manual*'s indexing chapter well describes the process. However, convention has shifted to the use of computers; and efficient indexers should be able to select the best tool for each job, based on an awareness of the standards discussed in this chapter. If we produce annual indexes with the possibility of combining them at a future date, the right software can turn a massive undertaking into a workable project.

INDEXING PROGRAMS

Software designed solely for the purpose of preparing indexes offers a wide range of features and corresponding variations in price. Most are designed for interdisciplinary use; the present writer knows of only one full-featured program that targets the genealogical community. Practically speaking, we should not expect any program to meet every need and standard of our field, as well as those of the publishing industry and scholarship in general. There are no magic shortcuts to good indexes, although there is some common-sense counsel that often gets short shrift:

- *Have realistic expectations.* We should not use a computer program for indexing with an exaggerated expectation of how much time it will save. We still have to do all the thinking and make the same accurate entries—the most time-consuming parts of the job. (Computer programs that automatically select index entries invariably produce inferior results.)

- *Choose software carefully.* If we index names and words with diacritical letters, we should make certain that the program we choose will allow us to type those letters and that it will alphabetize or sort them properly. If our index needs to include cross-references (and the best ones usually do), the software should accommodate that. We should never sacrifice scope or quality (accuracy, clarity, completeness, or readability) because of a software's built-in limitations.

- *Don't reinvent the wheel.* Odds are, adequate software is available for whatever type of project we launch—and at reasonable costs. We may be tempted to accept the services of computer enthusiasts who offer to write us an indexing program or to adapt application software for our indexing project. We should keep in mind, however, that writing, debugging, and supporting software is an ongoing and time-consuming process, and that the programming requirements of indexing are much more demanding than meet the eye.

SORT UTILITIES AND DATABASE SOFTWARE

Both database software and sort utilities will rearrange data into alphabetical order. As subsequently discussed in detail, however, an alphabetical arrangement is not an index. In the first place, most sort utilities and database programs do not properly

We should not expect any program to meet every need and standard of our field, as well as those of the publishing industry and scholarship in general.

alphabetize mixed capitalization and letters with diacritical marks. Even if our database has "programmable" report-printing capabilities, the effort of producing a proper index through programming approaches the complexity of writing an indexing program from scratch. Second, using a database program can tempt us to include more data than necessary, because we have the ability to include several fields (columns) of information; thus our focus shifts away from the index's proper role as a finding aid to textual material. Finally, the most readable and compact indexes use a standard format, such as those described in figure 50—with major and minor headings, indentations, lists of page numbers with commas between them, and cross-references. By contrast, most database programs simply print reports in tabular format that wastes space, while offering none of the embellishments that make indexes most useful.

WORD-PROCESSING UTILITIES

Word-processing and high-end page-layout programs usually include some indexing capabilities. These produce attractive results, and the process seems almost automatic. There are limitations, however. Such programs generally work by embedding "hidden" entries directly into the text being indexed. The program then collects all the index entries together, including their page references, and prints an alphabetical index in its interpretation of "standard style."

Although built-in indexing features can produce fairly good results, they make the index a by-product of the writing process, rather than something we create separately. Editing the index or revising it when we alter the text can be both tedious and complicated. To quote one voice of experience, we are "polishing and shaping . . . the index at one remove from it, by playing with the embedded entries themselves. This is hard going, a little like using a mirror to tie a necktie."[9] However, if we plan to spend a goodly part of our professional life creating indexes for colleagues and clients who routinely use these programs, then we would be wise to invest in—and learn to use—the leading programs. Proficiency with them means we can accept the author or editor's material in electronic form (by disk or modem) and apply our conceptual skills to the formatted data even if we forego the indexing automaton built into it.

The process

An index is *not* an alphabetical arrangement of data, although the two are still often confused by self-publishers. To save publishing costs, many genealogists and agencies whose goal is to extract and preserve records will present their material in alphabetical order—for instance, published tombstone transcriptions are frequently grouped by name, rather than by gravesite order. *But an alphabetical arrangement is not an index.* Conscientious authors and publishers preserve the precious clues inherent in original groupings and give additional time and space for the preparation of an actual index, which Webster defines as follows:

> *Index.* A usu[ally] alphabetical list that includes all or nearly all items (as topics, names of people and places) considered of special pertinence and fully or partially

An index is *not* an alphabetical arrangement of data, although the two are still often confused by self-publishers.

covered or merely mentioned in a printed or written work, gives with each item the place (as by page number) where it may be found in the work, and is usu[ally] put at or near the end of the work.[10]

GENERAL PRINCIPLES

Good indexes have appropriate scope, and decisions about scope prescribe the extent to which we index the different items found in the text. Should we index all names in a family history or just some of them? If we are processing county-level marriage registers, will we index them one volume at a time or as a consolidation of several volumes? In a periodical, will we index subjects and localities, or just people?

As genealogical indexers, we have a wide and varied audience. Beginning genealogists may concentrate on references to direct ancestors. Intermediate researchers have widened their focus to include collateral relatives. Advanced genealogists will use the records of neighbors and associates. Non-genealogists also use our publications for their studies in demography, genetics, history, law, medicine, sociology, and other fields. The scope of our index should be broad enough to serve all constituencies. *Therefore, a general guideline is to index anything that might be of value to anyone.* The compilers of the National Genealogical Society's special guide to indexing elaborate a bit more on "subject" indexes, suggesting that family historians consider including all events; family stories; locations; and such nontextual items as artifacts, buildings, documents, maps, and photographs—even pets—when these are given notable treatment in the text and references.[11]

SPECIAL GENEALOGICAL CONCERNS

Special considerations apply to each of the four major types of genealogical publications: families histories, periodicals, previously published (but unindexed) materials, and record extractions.

- *Family histories.* Theoretically, the full names of all people and places should be included—exceptions are few. *Chicago Manual* recommends one that many genealogists do not care to observe: scene-setting material. By way of example, if the text states that our ancestor served in the Continental Army under the command of General George Washington, *Chicago Manual* considers Washington a "scene-setter." Genealogists, however, are likely to want to flag this kind of contextual reference. Place names deserve to be indexed far more frequently in family histories, given that sophisticated researchers commonly track ancestors and ancestral associates by locations as well as by family names.

- *Periodicals.* Newsletters, magazines, and journals offer a range of material from local record extractions and queries to articles on resources and methodology. If our periodical focuses on a single town or church parish, then we might justify including only personal names. More likely, even a location-based periodical treats a county, province, state, or other jurisdiction that embraces a number of locales, thus calling for a place-name index—including, ideally, historic buildings, land forms, public institutions, and watercourses, as well as the expected names of towns. If the journal publishes instructional articles and resource information, we serve our users well by including topics as well.

As genealogical indexers, we have a wide and varied audience. Non-genealogists also use our publications for their studies in demography, genetics, history, law, medicine, sociology, and other fields. The scope of our index should be broad enough to serve all constituencies.

PROOFREADING
AND INDEXING

FIG. 50
BASIC INDEXING
PRINCIPLES

1. A good index flags each and every piece of information that users are likely to need. For genealogists, that means:

- PERSONAL NAMES—given names, patronyms, and surnames; farm names, military names, and slavemaster names; aliases, *dits,* and nicknames.

- PLACE NAMES—cities, towns, townships, villages, and lesser jurisdictions; provinces and states; countries; geographic landmarks such as named hills, mountains, valleys, and watercourses; institutions such as churches and schools.

- SUBJECT MATTER—ethnicity and religion; memorabilia of special note; methods and resources; objects and eras of historical note, such as ships and wars.

2. All named individuals should appear in the index—including those from the text; the notes (with possible exception of those merely *cited* in notes as opposed to *discussed* in the notes); and any appendixes, charts, illustrations, lists, and tables.

3. Cross-references should appear for married females and any males or females who used varying names for whatever reason. For example, a text reference to Mary Elizabeth "Betsy" (Jelks) Lutz should generate the following entries:

> Jelks
>   Betsy. *See* Mary Elizabeth Jelks
>   Jehosaphat . . . .
>   Mary Elizabeth "Betsy" (m. Lutz), 2, 37, 59, 172, 238, 431
> Lutz
>   Betsy. *See* Mary Elizabeth "Betsy" (Jelks) Lutz
>   Lawrence . . . .
>   Mary Elizabeth "Betsy" (Jelks), 2, 37, 59, 172, 238, 431

Similarly, for Abraham Derr whose name is variously spelled as *Abraham Terr,* a cross-reference should alert readers to the variants. For example:

> Derr (*var.* Terr)   Terr. *See* Derr
>   Abraham
>   Caleb . . . .

4. For multiple individuals of the same name, when separate identifies are clear, a qualifier can usefully clarify the distinction between them. For example:

> DeJeune   Whitefeather
>   Pierre (Canada)   Dawn (b. 1880)
>   Pierre (France)   Dawn (b. 1905)

5. One consolidated index—as opposed to separate indexes in which entries are divided by type—is preferred by most users and is more space-efficient.

6. Basic elements of an entry are the *heading, subheading,* and *locator.* In a simple name entry, this would be *surname, given name, page number.* In a simple place entry, this would be *major jurisdiction, minor jurisdiction, page number.* In a subject entry, only heading and locator may be needed. For example:

> Sammarco, Sebastian, 37   [*if there is only one entry for the surname*]
> Sorensen   [*if there are multiple entries for the surname*]
>   Jens, 110, 120
>   Nils, 111, 127
> Spain, Madrid, 238
> Spanish-American War, 239

FIG. 50
BASIC INDEXING
PRINCIPLES
(CONT.)

7. Headings, subheadings, and multiple columns conserve space and boost readability. For example, consider these alternatives for indexing a family of four:

No major headings, one column only (database or sort-program style)

TER HUNE, Annetje, 5, 10, 15–18, 23   [*rest of line space is left blank* . . . .]
TER HUNE, Jan, 3, 20–25, 31, 179
TER HUNE, Jorge, 1–3, 5, 8–15, 132
TER HUNE, Pietra (Rapalje), 4, 7, 9

No major headings, double columns

ter Hune, Annetje, 5,
   10, 15–18, 23
ter Hune, Jan, 3, 20–25
ter Hune, Jorge, 1–3, 5, 8–15,
   132
ter Hune, Pietra (Rapalje), 4,
   7, 9

With major headings, double columns

ter Hune
   Annetje, 5, 10, 15–18, 23
   Jan, 3, 20–25, 31, 179
   Jorge, 1–3, 5, 8–15, 132
   Pietra (Rapalji), 4, 7, 9

8. Subject entries with many page references should be broken down into subentries. For example:

North American Indian tribes: *or*
   Apache, 78–91; Caddo, 22;
   Chitimachas, 23, 31, 43–44;
   Huron, 53, 59; Piute, 104–5;
   Seminole, 331; Washita, 23

  or
North American Indian tribes:
   See specific tribal name

North American Indian tribes
   Apache, 78–91
   Caddo, 22
   Chitimachas, 23, 31, 43–44
   Huron, 53, 59
   Piute, 104–5
   Seminole, 331
   Washita, 23

9. Readability dictates that entries be set in *flush and hang style,* meaning that main headings are flush with the margin, while the rest of the entry is indented under it. When subheads are used, they may follow *run-in style* (as with the first example in first column of point 8) or *indented style* (as with the second column of points 7 and 8). Run-in style conserves space. Indented style is more readable.

10. En-dashes (not hyphens) should signify a range of pages, when the discussion of the subject continues across consecutive pages. (See points 7 and 8 for examples.)

11. *See* is used when readers might be expected to search for a subject under any of several keywords (as in points 3 and 8) or when indexing conventions call for names to be indexed under an element readers might not expect. For example:

De Soto, Hernando. *See* Soto,
   Hernando de

12. *See also* is used when additional information can be found in a related entry. For example:

Tax rolls, methodology for, 14.
   See also Censuses and census
   substitutes

13. An introduction should state the conventions followed within the text.

PROOFREADING
AND INDEXING

- *Previously published works.* Many individuals and societies today see a valuable contribution that can be made by reprinting and augmenting works issued in the past without an index. To illustrate the scope of the issue, consider Colorado's Statewide Marriage Index, 1900–39, an undertaking of that state's Depression-era Work Projects Administration. Those who conducted the original project indexed all grooms for this forty-year period, but no brides. Might it have been better to index only half as many records, for a twenty-year period, and include all named individuals? Genealogists with differing needs may give different answers to that question. In this case, a half-century later, the records are being re-indexed to include the female partners.

- *Record extracts.* The foregoing example also illustrates the added value that compilers and indexers can contribute with more thorough coverage. Marriage records typically name not only the brides and grooms but also witnesses, officials, and sometimes parents. By current standards, a well-prepared index should include all of these as well—with the possible exception of the officials. (If the official is a county clerk who is named in virtually every record, indexing his entries would add little value. When the officials are neighborhood ministers or justices of the peace, then users are likely to value their inclusion in the index—since this will isolate for researchers all other couples who attended that church or lived in that neighborhood, a winnowing process that often leads to breakthroughs in genealogical identifications.)

SPECIALIZED STANDARDS

We strive for excellence in all our genealogical work, but common measures of quality have their own definitions when viewed in the context of genealogical indexes—primarily accuracy, clarity, completeness, and readability.

- *Accuracy.* Each entry for the index should match the text entry exactly. We preserve diacritical marks found on the pages we work from, as with such letters as ç, é, or ñ. These variations in letterform affect the meaning and pronunciations of words, as well as the order in which they should be indexed—meaning that we should consult indexing guides for the rules of alphabetizing these special characters. By way of example, we might consider the difference when the tilde is omitted from the Spanish surname *Peña:*

  | Peña | pronounced *pain-yuh* | means *rock* |
  | Pena | pronounced *pain-uh* | means *sadness, shame* |

The pursuit of accuracy calls for special care when moving to a new page, lest we forget to advance the page number. It also calls for *proofreading* the index—something we should do and something we should have someone else do behind us. As professional indexers, who read the client's work closely, we may discover typographical errors or unintended inconsistencies in the spelling of names or localities. We should takes notes and pass them to the client, who may be able to correct the text before it goes to press.

The pursuit of accuracy calls for special care when moving to a new page, lest we forget to advance the page number.

- *Clarity.* We can greatly help our readers understand the information they need with one simple addition. On the first page of our index, we should define its scope, explain the conventions we applied, and list the abbreviations we used. If we are indexing a multivolume work, our introduction should note which pages appear in each volume. By way of example, the well-prepared annual indexes to the *National Genealogical Society Quarterly* typically state

> Entries for persons with no surnames or with unknown surnames are found at the beginning of this index. Royal or noble individuals without commonly used surnames are listed under *Royalty and nobility*. The modifier *cited* indicates a reference or source of information, whether mentioned in the text or in a note. Authors, contributors, and reviewers are identified as such, to distinguish them from individuals treated historically. Known maiden names appear in parentheses, as do dates that distinguish between individuals of the same name.
>
> Subject entries appear under the following broader headings . . . [*a list follows*]. Abbreviations are limited to states, titles, and the following identifiers . . . [*a list follows*].[12]

- *Completeness.* Standards call for indexing each person under all names that person used, as illustrated in figure 50 (point 3). Cross-references enable us to be complete without duplicating entries fully; they are particularly useful with variant spellings—entries can be grouped under one spelling with an added cross-reference to alert readers to the variants. Standards of completeness in genealogy also ask us to index distinct individuals separately, adding whatever qualifier necessary to clarify the distinction between them (figure 50, point 4). However, if the material we are indexing does not make conclusions about identity—for instance, if we are indexing extracted marriage records—then it may be misleading for us to create distinctions in the index.

- *Readability.* The most common factor cited for omitting indexes or preparing skeletal ones is the issue of cost. Our insistence upon thoroughness will intensify the cost factor, and it is natural to seek ways to minimize the number of pages needed. Still, usability should not be victimized by economy. Arranging indexes in columns is an effective cost cutter, and narrower columns let us reduce the point size—typically to two points less than the text. However, we (and our possible client) should weigh the value of the savings against the problems faced by older readers with impaired vision; a one-point reduction might be an effective compromise. Standard indexing formats include the use of major and minor headings, which not only make the index more readable but can also reduce its size.

Summary Concepts

The qualities that make us good genealogists—meticulousness, patience, and a probing mind—make us good proofreaders and indexers. But in both cases we are likely to do a far better job of finessing the work of others than we can do with our own material. Both processes require us to look more closely at textual matter than we might otherwise—to step outside the bounds of our concerns as authors and editors and view the information with fresh objectivity. To some, proofreading and indexing the work of others may seem like mundane labor, devoid of the excitement of the chase and thrill of discovery that lures us into research. On the other hand, proofreading and indexing the work of others, because these tasks require such close attention, are superb ways to expand our education.

Proofreading and indexing, because these tasks require such close attention, are superb ways to expand our education.

**PROOFREADING
AND INDEXING**

Producing clean text and a good index is gratifying. It leaves us with the feeling of having wrapped up a package and tied the bow. We also have the satisfaction of making a worthwhile contribution to the field of genealogy. Our special challenge is to meet the standards in three fields—genealogy, indexing, and publishing. We must keep pace with high standards in all of these, while learning to exploit the technology that is changing each of them.

Producing clean text and a good index is gratifying. It leaves us with the feeling of having wrapped up a package and tied the bow.

NOTES

1. *The Chicago Manual of Style: The Essential Guide for Writers, Editors, and Publishers,* 14th edition (Chicago: University of Chicago Press, 1993).
2. Elizabeth Shown Mills, CG, CGL, FASG, *Evidence! Citation & Analysis for the Family Historian* (Baltimore: Genealogical Publishing Co., 1997).
3. Joan Ferris Curran, CG; Madilyn Coen Crane; and John H. Wray, Ph.D., CG, *Numbering Your Genealogy: Basic Systems, Complex Families, and International Kin* (Arlington, Virginia: National Genealogical Society, 2000).
4. Quoted by Pennye Harper in "Toward More Picturesque Speech," *Readers Digest* (March 1992): 175.
5. *Chicago Manual of Style,* 703. Also excellent is the indexing chapter of *Merriam-Webster's Manual for Writers & Editors,* rev. edition (Springfield, Massachusetts: Merriam-Webster, 1998).
6. *Chicago Manual of Style,* 703.
7. Ibid., 710.
8. Among the industry leaders in indexing software designed for a widespread market are Cindex and Macrex; Sky Index is particularly aimed at the genealogical market.
9. John Taylor, "Index of Progress: Embedded Entries," *American Society of Indexers Newsletter* 102 (January/February 1991): 1, 20.
10. *Webster's Third New International Dictionary of the English Language* (Springfield, Massachusetts: Merriam-Webster, 1986).
11. Patricia Law Hatcher, CG, and John V. Wylie, *Indexing Family Histories: Simple Steps for a Quality Product* (Arlington, Virginia: National Genealogical Society, 1994).
12. Patricia Law Hatcher, indexer, *National Genealogical Society Quarterly* 86 (December 1998): 328.

FURTHER STUDY

Beare, Geraldine. *Indexing Newspapers, Magazines, and Other Periodicals.* Sheffield, England: Society of Indexers, 1999.

Bell, Hazel K. *Indexing Biographies and Other Stories of Human Lives.* 2d edition. Sheffield: Society of Indexers, 1998.

Corbett, Maryann, ed. *Directory of Indexing and Abstracting Courses and Seminars.* Phoenix, Arizona: American Society of Indexers. 1998.

Fetters, Linda K. *Handbook of Indexing Techniques: A Guide for Beginning Indexers.* 2d edition. N.p.: Fetters Infomanagement Co., 1998.

Judd, Karen. *Copyediting: A Practical Guide.* Rev. edition. Los Altos, California: Crisp, 1990.

Leach, Anne. *Marketing Your Indexing Services.* 2d edition. Phoenix: American Society of Indexers, 1998.

Mulvany, Nancy C. *Indexing Books.* Chicago: University of Chicago Press, 1994.

Smith, Peggy. *Letter Perfect: A Guide to Practical Proofreading.* Alexandria, Virginia: EEI Books, 1995.

———. *Mark My Words: Instruction and Practice in Proofreading.* Alexandria: EEI Books, 1997.

Wellisch, Hans. *Indexing from A to Z.* 2d rev. edition. Bronx, New York: H. W. Wilson, 1996.

Zaffran, Enid L., ed. *Starting an Indexing Business.* 3d edition. Phoenix: American Society of Indexers, 1998.

27

PREPARING BOOKS
FOR PRESS

Keynotes

PREPARING BOOKS
FOR PRESS

Keynotes (cont.)

Preparing Books for Press

by Joan Ferris Curran, CG

Our manuscript has taken months or even years to complete. Now comes the task of getting it into print. If ours is a work of wide genealogical interest (an instructional manual, for example) we may be successful in having it published commercially. On the other hand, if our book will have a relatively limited market (as with a family history or abstracted records of a parish, town, or province), then self-publishing may be our only choice. A difficult undertaking? Not really—not if we understand the process, plan our work carefully, know where to seek guidance when needed, and pay meticulous attention to copy preparation. Our goal is to produce the most eye-appealing (as well as readable) book possible within our budget, and most criteria will apply whether or not we are our own publisher.

Planning the Book

Models

Long before our manuscript nears completion, we should be able to envision the finished product. For many of us, the process begins at a genealogical library. Our eyes are drawn to the most attractive and professional-looking books. We pull those from the shelves and study them in detail for factors that make each one appealing—overall size, cover style and color, font choice and point size, and page format. We consider the quality of the photographs and the manner in which the author presents maps and other illustrative materials. We also note what we *don't* like—narrow margins, poorly formatted indexes, and nondescriptive titles, for example. As we build our lists of elements we'd like to adopt, adapt, and avoid, we'll create both a mental image and written guidelines for producing an attractive volume of our own.

Terminology

The more we know about printing and binding, the better equipped we are to discuss our project with the printing house that will produce the book according to our specifications. *The Chicago Manual of Style,* a bible for serious writers, has an extensive section on production and printing.[1] More specialized guides—such as Beach, Shepro, and Rosson's *Getting it Printed*[2] or Carl Boyer's *How to Publish and Market Your Family History*[3] are helpful introductions. Hatcher's *Producing a Quality Family History* has outstanding chapters on almost every aspect of book compilation and self-publishing.[4]

The so-called vanity presses (printing companies and book manufacturers that specialize in working with self-publishers) often have instructional booklets or videos on book preparation.[5] Although valuable, they are seldom a substitute for the personal attention and guidance that many reputable companies offer self-publishing authors.

> The more we know about printing and binding, the better equipped we are to discuss our project with the printing house.

If we are first-time publishers, the peace of mind these firms provide may be well worth the added cost. Their guidance through every step of the process can make the difference between a mediocre book and an outstanding one.

Specifications

The specifications we eventually use will be determined by many factors—the first of which will be whether we self-publish or use a publishing house. Often, a commercial press will have its own specifications, dictated by its equipment and its experience in curtailing costs. If we self-publish, we have (for better or worse) more freedom of choice in content, design, and size. Regardless of the ultimate decision, before we approach any printing house or publisher, we should draw up a set of *preliminary* specifications based on the best possible estimate of our needs and desires. Prime considerations include design of pages and cover; finish (or trim) size; page count; print run; and quality of cover and binding, paper stock, photographs, and typography.

DESIGN

The visual image we have already formed of our finished product likely includes many of its design elements. The final appearance of our text and pages must also consider several of the other specifications discussed in this section—particularly the finish size, the cover and binding, the paper stock, and our choice of printer. If we are new to book production, we may find it necessary to revise our planned design after talking with potential publishers or printers. Still we should *have* a design—not just in mind but also described on paper—as a starting point for discussions. Among the main design elements to consider are the following six. (Figure 51 provides others.)

Text block

The size of the block in which we type will be determined by the finish size we choose for the book. For example, if we choose a 6-by-9-inch trim size and allow ¾-inch margins, the block in which all of our type appears on any given page will be limited to 4½ by 7½ inches. If we choose an 8½-by-11-inch finish size, with 1-inch margins, then our text block is limited to 6½ by 9 inches.

Margins

Three general rules apply: (*a*) margins should be the same width throughout the book; (*b*) larger pages require wider margins to maintain a pleasing balance between "color" and "white space"; and (*c*) with any size book, margins should be generous, to improve appearance and readability.

Columns

Ideally, text columns should be no more than 5 inches wide—the distance a human eye can scan without strain. Columns narrower than 3 inches (the scholar's margin in this volume, being a case in point) tend to create spacing problems for the typesetter and demand paragraph structures that are much too short for historical narratives. These basic guidelines have both typographic and genealogical implications.

Before we approach any printing house or publisher, we should draw up a set of *preliminary* specifications based on the best possible estimate of our needs and desires.

**PREPARING BOOKS
FOR PRESS**

FIG. 51

GUIDELINES FOR

LAYOUT AND TYPOGRAPHY

Layout

- Margins should be generous and the same margins should be maintained throughout.
- Running heads should identify the name of the book and the name of the chapter (on left- and right-hand pages, respectively—or on both as in the style of this manual).
- Maps, newspaper clippings, photographs, and other illustrative materials should all be oriented in the same direction. Readers should not have to twist their necks to read a single page (or facing pages).

Typography

- Serif fonts produce more legible text. Sans-serif fonts make attractive headers.
- Multiple fonts on the same page generally work only when limited to one serif and one sans serif.
- Periods and colons are followed by just one space. The "two spaces follow a period" rule that applied when using monospaced typewriters does *not* apply to fine typography or today's word processors that use proportional spacing.
- Use "real" quotation marks and apostrophes (') not ditto or inch marks (") and not foot or minute marks (').
- Use dashes correctly. A proper em-dash is —, not --. A proper en-dash, not a hyphen, should be used to indicate a range of numbers or time (e.g.: 22–23, not 22-23; October–December, not October-December). All word-processing programs offer em/en dashes.
- When letters have accents, don't omit the accent. We may not understand umlauts (as in *ä*) or tildes (~) in languages that are not native to us; but accent marks can make a serious difference in meaning, identity, and data sorting.
- Underlining is passé—another relic of the typewriter era. Book titles and passages that deserve emphasis should be italicized.
- Italics and boldface should be used sparingly. A narrative full of emphasized passages is annoying; mature writers achieve emphasis through thoughtfully structured sentences. Genealogical situations which generally call for italics and boldface include:
  - KEY WORDS—in manuals such as the present volume.
  - KEY NAMES—in formal genealogies that follow the *NGSQ*, *Register*, or Sosa-Stradonitz numbering systems, for example. (See chapter 23.)
- Uppercase letters for surnames are unnecessary, confusing, and an affront to fine typography. (The habit began in a past era when indexes were rare and surnames were capitalized in genealogical publications so they could be easily spotted.) Not only are words harder to read when rendered in all capitals but their use obliterates proper distinctions between uppercase and lowercase letters in surnames (should DELAVERGNE be DeLaVergne, DelaVergne, delaVergne, or deLaVergne?) and causes surnames to be sorted differently in databases and indexes.
- Small capitals should be used for postnomials, most acronyms, headers placed in uppercase, and the abbreviations *A.M.* and *P.M.*
- Widows and orphans are pitied in typography as well as in real life. Learn the terms and avoid them.[6]
- Postal codes should not be used amid text as abbreviations for provinces and states.

- Typographically, if we choose 8½-by-11-inch paper, we are virtually obligated to use double columns—or one column and a scholar's margin, as in the present manual. Wide lines of text strung across typing-paper-sized pages are derided by many typographers as "Kitchen Table Press Style."

- Genealogically, if our book is a family history that uses the common numbering systems, the standard indentations would create an awkward appearance if double columns were used. For this reason, most attractive genealogies use the smaller trim sizes that are common at quality presses.

Fonts

The term *font* refers to the names of individually designed type styles. Along with the size of the print, it has more to do with readability than virtually any other factor in our design. The marketplace offers us thousands of styles and hundreds of manuals to guide our choices,[7] but a few basic rules are worth noting here.

- *Serif fonts* (those with crossbars, called *extenders,* on the feet of such letters as *h, i,* and *l* and either crossbars or nubs on the side and top ends of such letters as *c, s,* and *y*) are the easiest to read in large blocks of text. (This manual uses the serif Century Schoolbook as its text font.) Serif fonts may also be used as headlines and subheads; but if we are not trained in graphic design, we should not try to mix multiple styles of serif fonts on the same page.

- *Sans-serif fonts* (those without the embellishments) are more difficult to read in text blocks, but often make an attractive counterpoint to serif type when used for headlines, headers, and pull-quotes. (This manual uses Helvetica as a sans-serif font for accent.) Again, the above caution applies: we should not mix two or more sans-serif fonts in the same layout, unless we are trained in far more technical principles of graphic design.

- *Full capitals*—whole words rendered in full-sized capital letters—are deplored by typographers. This habit, left over from days when the typewriter offered no means of emphasis except capitalization and underscoring, creates crowded type and a "busy" page. The practice is obsolete in today's typesetting environment, which lets us choose between boldface, italics, small capitals, subscript, and superscript, as well as such specialty styles as condensed, extended, narrow, and poster within the same font family.

- *Small capitals*—letterforms that appear to be capitals but are chiseled to be clear at smaller sizes—are used when we have a justifiable need for "all capitals." Common usages include subheadings, as with the words FINISH (OR TRIM) SIZE and PAGE COUNT on the next page; and acronyms (as with professional postnomials, academic degrees, or "abbreviations" of agencies—e.g., NARA and FHL in genealogical usage or UPS and BBC in commercial usage). Most quality font packages offer special sets of "small caps." If our chosen font does not, then we can simulate small caps by manually reducing the size of "all caps" by one to three point sizes.

- *"True" italics and boldface* are special editions within a font family. While cheaper fonts often permit us to slant or darken the basic font to simulate italics or boldface,

If we are not trained in graphic design, we should not try to mix multiple styles of serif fonts (or multiple styles of sans-serif fonts) on the same page.

typographers consider these to be bastardized versions. If we prepare camera-ready masters for our printing house, it matters little whether we choose the "true" or simulated versions; odds are, only professional typographers will see the difference. However, if we plan to submit our text to the printing house digitally, for typesetting on a machine that produces the highest quality print, then we should be aware that most printing houses expect us to use "true" italics and boldface.

- *Book fonts.* Our wealth of choices today also includes fonts that are specifically designed to enhance readability within the usage to which we put them. One of the most common fonts built into word-processing programs, Times Roman (aka Times, New Times Roman, etc.) was actually crafted for use in newspapers, where narrow columns require a font with tightly fitted letters. By contrast, book designers, who work with wider columns, typically use a wider font such as Bookman or the present Century Schoolbook.

Point size

Modern word processors require us to choose a type size that is measured in *points*. One rule of thumb—the larger the page, the larger the point size; the smaller the page, the smaller the point size—enables us to maintain an attractive ratio of type size to surface area. For 8½-by-11-inch pages (one column), 11- to 13-point type is the optimum range. For double columns on this size page—and for the smaller pages used by most publishing houses—9- to 11-point type is optimum. Within those ranges, the point size we actually choose should be determined by the x-height of the font we have selected. (The body of the present manual is 9.5 points, with lines set slightly wider apart than normal—at 12.5 *leading*—to improve readability.)

Other design elements

Headers, footers, and similar elements that involve content as well as design should also be planned before any text is typeset or page count is projected. The running heads that readers expect across the top of book pages, naming the book and the chapter titles (sometimes on alternating pages), should be fitted within the planned text block. When such items are forgotten and added later, they encroach upon the margin and cramp the appearance of the page; or else their addition will require us to reformat the entire manuscript.

FINISH (OR TRIM) SIZE

Standard-sized books cost less to produce, because they eliminate trim loss when printers cut commercial-sized sheets. Americans who are new to publishing usually think of 8½-by-11-inch paper as "standard"; and, indeed, it is when we choose a quick-copy shop that buys pre-cut paper. However, within more professional printing houses, 6 by 9 inches or 5½ by 8½ inches are the conventional finish sizes. If our heart is set on another size, then we must absorb the costs for the paper that ends up on the cutting-room floor.

PAGE COUNT

Professional printers (as opposed to quick-copy shops) usually price books by the

---

One rule of thumb—the larger the page, the larger the point size; the smaller the page, the smaller the point size—enables us to maintain an attractive ratio of type size to surface area.

---

signature—a printer's term for a large sheet of paper that, when repeatedly folded, becomes one unit of pages. Signatures are calculated in multiples of four. Eight, sixteen, thirty-two, or sixty-four book pages are commonly created from each sheet. When printed on both sides and folded to page size, the signature is then trimmed to book dimensions. Because charges for books printed in this manner are based on the number of signatures used and extra charges are common for partial signatures that require pages to be cut out, we should plan carefully to achieve the most economical use of the signature size common at the press we choose. Printing houses typically divide our projected number of pages by its standard signature size and quote us an estimate accordingly. If we choose a quick-copy shop, for reproduction of pre-cut sheets, we might project a round number of pages—say 150 or 200—and then ask for estimates based on that projection and additional blocks of ten.

PRINT RUN

Probably no question in the whole publication process is as problematic as the question, *how many copies should we print?* The more copies we order, the lower our per-copy price. Three hundred copies of a book may cost very little more than one hundred, because the company's setup cost is usually covered in that first hundred. Opting for five hundred or a thousand copies often generates significant price breaks— enabling us to move from more costly "short-run" presses to more economical "long-run" ones. On the other hand, to order more than we can reasonably dispose of would be false economy. Assuming "every library will want one" is a common mistake— unless we are prepared to *donate* those copies. Rare is the library that purchases family histories; and the number willing to purchase abstracted records will depend upon such intangibles as (*a*) the importance of the subject matter or geographic area to national history, (*b*) the reputation of the compiler, and (*c*) the library's commitment to building a comprehensive or concentrated genealogical collection. Wisdom suggests consulting with associates who have published books on similar subjects. Experienced colleagues often suggest that we tally the number of individuals who have expressed an interest in the book and add the number of libraries known to carry its type (as well as those to which we want to donate a copy), then consider ordering 150 to 200 percent of that number. Both reviews and word of mouth generate a significant number of sales we don't anticipate.

> Assuming "every library will want one" is a common mistake—unless we are prepared to *donate* those copies.

COVER AND BINDING

Casebound books

Called hardcover by the layperson, this kind is the most durable; thus, they are the first choice of libraries and the preference of most individuals who purchase family histories. They are also a common choice for reference works and other publications, when durability is more important than cost. The best casebound covers, made with high-quality book cloth stretched over a heavy binding board, are foil-stamped on the spine and the front. They are expensive; but the price is worth considering, in view of their durability and reader appeal. For casebound productions, we have two other options that affect our book's ability to withstand use:

Smyth-sewn binding, which is ideal for books printed in signatures. This procedure calls for each signature to be stitched with heavy thread through its inside gutter and then to its adjoining signatures. Because the stitching makes the bound side thicker than the opposite side, a good casebound book will be mechanically *rounded* before the spine is applied.

Side-sewn binding (aka *saddle-sewn* or *oversewn*), which is common for hardcover books printed by the single page, calls for stitching the assembly as close to the gutter edge as possible. Although side-sewn books are sturdier and more durable than Smyth-sewn ones, they will not open as flat or remain open as easily.

Well-done casebound books use one further precaution we may want to discuss with the printer: the addition of *headbands* and *footbands*. In this process, a stout cord or a thin leather or vellum strip is added across the top and bottom of the spine to strengthen it against damage done when fingers pull the book off the shelf.

Paperback books

Soft covers are an attractive choice for both genealogical publishers and buyers because of their lower selling price. If we choose this option, we should select a cover stock of sufficient weight and quality to stand up to heavy use, and we might seriously consider asking the printer to laminate the cover for added durability and appeal. Three binding procedures are common for softcover works:

Perfect binding, which is the most lasting, calls for the gutter side of the gathered signatures or pages to be shaved away. Then the binding apparatus applies a thin layer of flexible glue to the new edge, which has been roughened or notched so that the glue will adhere better. Finally, the machine forces the glued surface against the inside spine of the cover until a secure bond is made.

Saddle-wired or side-wired binding (sometimes called *saddle stitching*, although no thread is used) is a stapling process. Used for relatively thin booklets printed on paper large enough to accommodate two side-by-side pages, saddle wiring places staples through the center fold. Side wiring usually consists of three heavy-duty staples placed parallel and close to the gutter edge of a stack of pages.

Mechanical bindings are common for books produced at quick-copy shops but are sometimes chosen for works produced in signatures. Of the various processes available, spiral binding (with either plastic or wire spirals) is preferred for books that need to lie flat. Post binding is seldom used for genealogical works, and books held together with small plastic posts cannot withstand much use. These mechanical bindings are not a good choice if we hope to market our books to societies and libraries—libraries deplore them because pages tear out more easily and cataloging data seldom can be added to the spine.

Artistic covers

These are not yet common in the genealogical marketplace, but some authors and publishers choose them for special cases. The two basic options are book jackets and laminated boards.

Mechanical bindings are not a good choice if we hope to market our books to societies and libraries— libraries deplore them.

Book jackets—paper wrappers added to cloth-covered, casebound books—lend themselves to photos and other highly graphic designs and add a touch of "class" to family histories. The cost is often lower than expected.

Laminated boards is a process that combines the durability of casebound books with the enhanced graphics made possible by choosing a paper cover rather than cloth. This process, which is increasingly seen on manuals and textbooks (including the present volume), calls for an attractively designed paper cover to be wrapped over sturdy binding boards, and then laminated for durability.

PAPER STOCK

Our choice of paper will require decisions in three areas: acidity, opacity, and weight. To ensure that our books last for generations, we should have them printed on *acid-free* paper, which will not become yellow or brittle with age. The cost is now only slightly more than that of standard book paper, with a wide range of types available. We will want the paper stock to be *opaque* enough that photographs and line art will not visually "bleed through" to the reverse side of a sheet. The printing houses with whom we deal will also ask us to choose our paper by *weight*. Here, options are commonly stated in terms that confuse the novice. To greatly simplify:

> To ensure that our books last for generations, we should have them printed on acid-free paper, which will not become yellow or brittle with age.

- *Bond weight* (United States), a term used for bond and photocopying paper, is based on standard-sized sheets of 17 by 22 inches, which are then cut into four 8½-by-11-inch sheets. The common labels of 20-pound (relatively thin) to 28-pound (relatively substantial) refer to the weight of a ream (500) of the 17-by-22-inch sheets.

- *Book weight* (United States) describes the larger-sized book papers used by publishing houses. Here, the common measure for text pages is based upon 25-by-38-inch sheets (thus, a 50-pound book-weight paper—which is the equivalent of a 20-pound bond-weight paper—is one in which 500 sheets of 25 by 38 inches weigh 50 pounds). The common size for cover stock, which is necessarily heavier, is just 20 by 26 inches. Most genealogical books use 50-pound to 70-pound book-weight paper for the text, depending upon the thickness and durability desired, and a cover stock that's 40-to-50-pound.

- *Grammage* (common international usage) is a far simpler system in which all types of paper are measured by grams per square meter and stated in terms of g/m^2 or *gsm*. Common book weight, under this system is 74 to 104 g/m^2, while cover weight is commonly 118 to 148.[8]

In addition to the measurement terms used by the paper industry, we need to consider two other options—thickness and finish.

- *Thickness* of paper, although it seems illogical at first, does not necessarily depend upon its weight. A 60-pound paper stock designed for opacity may be significantly thinner than (but just as durable as) a 60-pound "ordinary" paper. Thus, a slim book can be made to seem larger by choosing a thicker paper; an overlarge book that might otherwise strain its binding can be reduced in size by choosing a thinner but more opaque stock. (Similarly, journal publishers—to conserve shelf space in home and institutional libraries—may choose a thinner, more opaque paper.)

When we print camera-ready pages for press, our stock should have a high "brightness" measure and a calendared finish that does not absorb ink.

- *Finish* traditionally refers to glossy, semi-glossy, and matte surfaces, although today's paper designs offer a wide range of choices within these options. At press time, our printing house will help us choose a finish appropriate to the end use. Those choices commonly range from *antique* (soft and dull) through *vellum* to *english finish* (hard and shiny, but with no added treatment). Papers that undergo further processes to be made glossy, enameled, or supercalendared (exceedingly smooth and hard) are common for pages dedicated to photographs or for books in which photographs dominate text. Matte stock is preferred over glossy for text pages of better quality because it produces less glare and is more comfortable to read.

When we print camera-ready pages for press, we have one other paper choice to make: the stock on which we run the masters from our desktop printers. Our stock should have a high "brightness" measure (at least 94) and a calendared finish that does not absorb ink. Brightness enhances the contrast between type and paper, making print seem sharper. On the other hand, when we use uncalendared stock, ink tends to "bleed" into the paper, creating fuzzy print.

PHOTOGRAPHS

Today's software options provide many tools for artistically enhancing photographs. Even if we forego these electronic tools, we must still make choices that greatly influence both our costs and the finished appearance of our book. Our most basic decisions are whether to use halftoned photographs and whether to consolidate pictures into one central location.

- *Halftoning* or *screening* is a process in which an original photograph is reshot or electronically scanned through a screen that breaks the image into tiny dots. When reproduced in print, these dots form an impression of continuous shading. The finer the screen (that is, the greater the *dpi* or number of dots per square inch), the better the resolution of the printed picture. Printing houses assess a one-time charge for producing a halftone of each photograph, and that charge is unaffected by the number of books we order. Although we can produce halftones on home scanners, their reproductive quality is not (at this writing) equal to those of most commercial processes. Obviously, too, the genealogist who cares about quality will avoid using photocopied pictures in lieu of actual black-and-white, glossy photographs.

- *Placement* affects costs as well as appearance. It is true that scattering photographs across many pages will add interest throughout the book, but centralizing photographs into a single and well-laid-out section will enable us to present them on better-quality photo stock and reduce costs as well.

PRINT QUALITY

Print quality is determined at two stages of preparation—first, as mentioned earlier, when we prepare camera-ready masters; and second, when we choose the printing house and the process by which those masters are reproduced. As an overview:

- *Masters*. Two cardinal rules exist for today's technology: (*a*) use a *laser* (not ink-jet) printer, with the highest dpi available; and (*b*) use a bright-white paper, with a rating of 94 or higher and a calendared finish. Even laser printers offering the same resolution will vary in the clarity of their print output. We can test the quality by printing a 30- or 40-point capital *O* or *C* and examining its curved edges under a magnifying glass for crispness and smoothness. There should be no hint of fuzzy or jagged edges. If our current printer does not measure up and the purchase of a new one is not feasible, we might consider renting one from a local supplier or copy shop. Figure 51 offers a convenient list of typographical guidelines for preparing masters that meet standards of quality in the publishing industry.

- *Printing process.* The most obvious quality-control issue, in regard to printing, is also one commonly disregarded: professional printers that use lithographic offset or web presses can produce substantially better quality than copy shops using xerographic machines. Given the complexity of issues involved in choosing a publisher or printing house, this topic warrants a much more extensive discussion.

Choosing a Company

While selecting role models for our book, we will have formed opinions about the work of many publishers and printing houses. Advertisements in genealogical literature offer us other options; and several of the companies who place these ads have booths at major genealogical conferences, where they are available for consultation. Our colleagues who have published can offer valuable "insider" views, from their own experience with particular firms. From all these choices, we should carefully select three or four for serious consideration and price quotes; more than that would be a waste of time and energy—both ours and theirs.

For very limited print runs (100 copies or less), a quick-copy shop may be the most economical option; but even here we should bear in mind that the fewer copies we print, the higher the per-copy cost. While first-time self-publishers are frequently tempted to choose quick-copy shops on the premise that they can "run off copies as orders are received," they eventually realize they have been the victim of false economy; that practice is invariably the most expensive form of printing and binding. As a rule of thumb, for more than 100 copies a printer who uses an offset or a web press will offer the most economy and the best bindings.

Preliminary contact

Our initial discussion should take place before we begin final copy preparation. Face-to-face dialog is ideal, but time and travel costs seldom make this possible. Communication by telephone is an adequate opener, but mail or fax correspondence is ultimately necessary, when personal meetings are not possible. The firm should have a written copy of our specifications and sample pages of our proposed format. If we are not familiar with books published by the companies we contact, we should ask for inspection copies of comparable works. For the most part, our discussions with printing houses will center upon costs, form of submission, material samples, optional services, overruns and underruns, and schedules for delivery and payment.

> Professional printers that use lithographic offset or web presses can produce substantially better quality than copy shops using xerographic machines.

**PREPARING BOOKS
FOR PRESS**

**FIG. 52
REQUEST FOR BID**

GENE A. OLOGY

111 Any Street, Centerville, US 00000

DATE:	1 January 2000
MEMO TO:	Millennium Publishing
SUBJECT:	Request for bid

SPECIFICATIONS:

TITLE:	*From Lloyd to Gene: The Welsh ap Ology Family*
COPY:	Option A: Camera-ready masters, without bleeds Option B: Digital copy, produced in PageMaker 6.5, PhotoShop 5.0
QUANTITY:	300; 500; additional 100s
TRIM SIZE:	6" x 9"
PAGES:	320
STOCK:	Text: 60# acid-free Endpapers: 80# acid-free
TEXT INK:	Black
PHOTOS:	20, halftones required; printed amid text (quote price per photo)
INSERTS:	1 fold-out chart, 11" x 17"; 80# acid-free stock
COVER:	A-grade cloth, black, over .088" binder boards. Foil stamped, spine & front cover, 1 impression, imitation gold foil
BINDING:	Casebound, rounded & backed, headbands & footbands Smythe sewn, first & last signatures reinforced
PRESS:	Offset lithography; one set of bluelines
PACKING:	Shrink-wrap individual items Bulk pack in banded, single-wall cartons on pallets
SHIPPING:	FOB, point of manufacturing; curb delivery

MISCELLANEOUS ISSUES:

- Other services available? (Graphics layout? Storage and order fulfillment?)
- Taxes added as surcharge?
- Company policy for overruns and underruns?
- Payment terms?

COSTS

It is important to supply each company with exactly the same specifications and to inquire about the same extras. Only then can we accurately compare the prices and services offered. We should not be surprised by a wide range between the highest and lowest prices quoted. Cost will certainly be a factor in our final decision, but it should not be the overriding consideration. Far more important are the quality of the company's past work and our own sense of the firm's willingness to redo work that inadvertently falls short of its standards. The level and quality of its guidance are also major considerations. Figure 52 offers a sample bid request that covers the most common issues.

> It is important to supply each company with exactly the same specifications and inquire about the same extras. Only then can we accurately compare the prices and services offered.

FORMS OF SUBMISSION

Modern printing houses usually offer two options for preparing our copy: we may supply camera-ready masters or we may submit electronically. Publishers generally offer a third option: they will typeset professionally from our manuscript. Different considerations apply in each case:

- *Camera-ready masters.* We should supply the firm with a sample of our intended product to ensure its acceptability; that sample should include whatever "printer's marks" our desktop publishing software produces. (See figure 53.) Some companies may prefer that we print our masters on or according to templates they supply.

- *Electronic copy.* The key issue is compatibility. We need to use desktop publishing and graphics software, as well as fonts, that our chosen printing house supports. Many presses, for example, specify the use of Postscript® fonts, or a firm might ask that we convert our electronic data into Portable Document Format® or another that works across platforms. We also need to discuss whether the material should be submitted on disk or via modem and, in the case of the latter, whether a special communications program will be needed. Again, samples should be submitted to ensure that both the book's layout and our electronic medium are acceptable.

- *Manuscript for professional typesetting.* This option, although costly, is one we might consider if we or our clients want premium quality in all respects.

MATERIAL SAMPLES

Typically, when we approach a printing house, we have a general idea of the type of paper and cover stock we'd like. Within that general description, companies can provide samples of the materials they regularly use. In most cases, they offer an acceptable variety of color and quality. Ordering from their stock, which they purchase in bulk, can be more economical than special-ordering a particular paper or cloth we have admired elsewhere.

OPTIONAL SERVICES

Most printing houses offer an array of optional services. Graphic artists may be available to design artwork, covers, text layouts, and other features. Some companies offer storage and order-fulfillment services, as well. Costs are extra but often within reason.

PREPARING BOOKS
FOR PRESS

FIG. 53

CAMERA-READY MASTER

WITH PRINTER'S MARKS

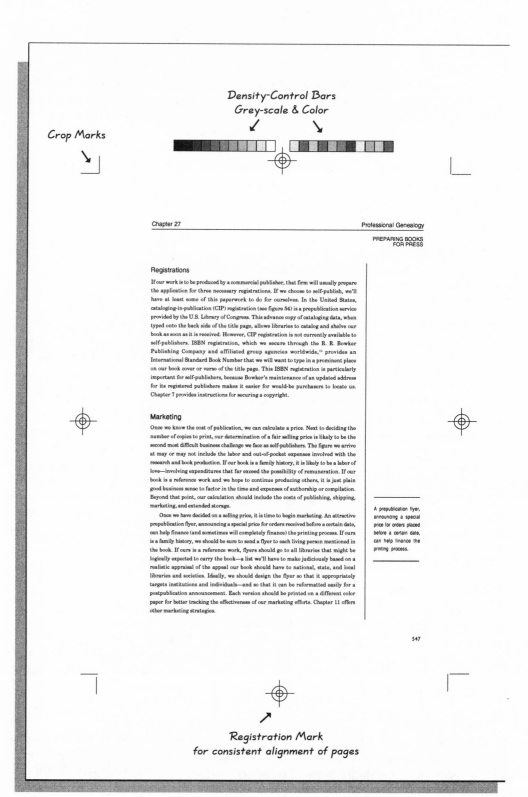

OVERRUNS AND UNDERRUNS

Because of the difficulty in printing an exact number of perfect copies, we may expect to receive more or fewer books than the number we order. Trade policy allows companies to charge for up to 10 percent more copies delivered and to deliver (and give credit for) up to 10 percent fewer. They should *not* charge us for copies produced and delivered over that percentage. Because printers make generous allowances for spoilage, overruns are far more likely than underruns. (Of the seven books I've sent to press, there has never been an underrun; and overruns have varied from 15 to 30 percent. With the overruns, three clients were billed for the first 10 percent and the others for the first 5 percent.) Because company practices vary, we should clearly understand in advance the policy that will govern our job.

SCHEDULES

Three schedules need discussing: (1) delivery date for copy, (2) turnaround time for production, and (3) payment dates. Most printing houses schedule our jobs when the masters or the electronic data arrive, although some may suggest certain periods in which work can be produced more quickly or at a special rate. After our materials are received, two to three months is considered the average turnaround, although some companies offer faster service. Payment policies vary. Some require complete payment in advance; others ask for a deposit when the contract is signed, a second installment at a specified point in the production schedule, and final payment before delivery or within thirty days thereafter. (Shipping charges are seldom part of the quoted price, but the press can usually estimate them. We pay shipping fees directly to the freight company upon its curb delivery of the cartons.)

Contract stage

Because final costs depend upon the precise number of pages and other items that may vary from the original proposal, our contract to print will usually be drawn up and signed after the final manuscript has been delivered. A good contract will itemize every specification we and the company have agreed upon. A contract should at least cover costs, the payment schedule, the company's policy on underruns and overruns, shipping information, and estimated delivery date. We may also expect the company to clearly state the limits of its liability in the event of unforeseen problems, as well as possible penalties for any payment delays on our part.

Preparing Final Copy

Basics of assembly

If we self-publish, we have considerable freedom in the design of our book and its content; but we should not confuse freedom with license. Well-produced books follow certain rules of assembly; our failure to observe them would brand our work as an amateur effort. The previously cited *Chicago Manual of Style* and Hatcher's *Producing*

> A contract should at least cover costs, the payment schedule, the company's policy on underruns and overruns, shipping information, and the estimated delivery date.

a Quality Family History both offer explicit, step-by-step guidance for the assembly process, with details that go considerably beyond the following basics.

BOOK PARTS

Aside from the body of the text and illustrations, a book is expected to contain certain front matter and back matter. Front matter typically consists of a half-title page, a title page, a copyright page, a table of contents, and a preface. It can also include acknowledgments, a dedication, a foreword, a frontispiece, and lists of appendixes and illustrations. (*Note:* a preface is written by the author or compiler; a foreword is written by another individual.) Back matter commonly consists of appendixes (as necessary), an index, and a bibliography or reference notes (if the latter does not appear as footnotes or endnotes after each chapter). The main body of the text, beginning with the first chapter, is assembled and numbered first, followed by the front and back matter.

PAGINATION

Every sheet, whether printed or blank, is considered a page and must be assigned a number—even when the number is not actually printed there. Numbers do not usually appear on illustration and divider pages and never on blank pages. Traditionally, front matter is assigned lowercase roman numerals and the main body of the text and the back matter are assigned consecutive arabic numerals; however, some publishers today request that arabic numerals begin with the very first sheet. The title page, the table of contents, the first page of each new chapter, the appendix, and the index should all start on right (recto) pages. In a two-page spread (left page, right page), even-numbered pages appear on the left (verso) and odd-numbered pages on the right.

> Every sheet, whether printed or blank, is considered a page and must be assigned a number—even when the number is not actually printed there.

Exhibits

Charts, documents, line art, maps, and photographs—all bring life to a book. Like other content, they should be chosen for balance, interest, quality, and relevance. A few special considerations apply in each case.

CHARTS

Charts that outline the family (or sections of it) help our readers visually identify each individual's position within the family as a whole. The best of these charts contain only brief information—usually the individual's year of birth and death and sometimes the year of marriage. (Assuming that the charts only cover individuals treated more fully in the text, documentation is not necessary on the charts. However, if our charts cover auxiliary lines that are not documented in the narrative, genealogical standards of quality require that we individually cite an acceptable source for each piece of data provided on any chart we print.) Five-generation ancestor charts and drop charts that begin with the ancestor are both frequent features of surname genealogies and multifamily studies.

DOCUMENTS

Historic records—for example, an unusual will, an early deed written in a distinctive hand, or a family sampler or Bible page that is especially artistic—add authenticity as well as interest to the text. Ancestral signatures are favored items, not only for "interest" but also because they help identify people correctly. Photocopies of key documents that may have questionable wording can also enhance and support cases we build for identification or relationships. When used as a substitute for the lack or shortage of ancestral photographs, historic documents should be chosen for variety, eye appeal, and legibility. If retouching is needed, that work should not alter the content or character of the document.

MAPS

Maps provide valuable geographic orientation and a priceless sense of place. Old maps have particular appeal when matched to particular events or life spans. When contemporary maps are not available, we can produce attractive substitutes by tracing the bounds of a state or region and then locating key towns or counties referred to in the text. In either case, we should avoid maps so blurred or so minute that their detail will be unreadable when our pages are reproduced. Larger maps (and family charts) can be placed on the endpapers or facing pages, or they can be incorporated into the cover design or used as a foldout. The latter is the costliest option, because the printer must insert them by hand.

PHOTOGRAPHS

Ancestral daguerreotypes, pen sketches, photos, reproduced paintings, silhouettes, and watercolors are valuable enhancements to all types of genealogical books, not just family histories. As with all graphics, their effectiveness depends upon their quality. Photocopied pictures do not do justice to the effort and expense we invest in our publication. Black-and-white glossy copies have the best reproductive quality, although commercial photographers and presses usually can process sepia-tone and color photographs satisfactorily if the prints are not too dark and have sufficient contrast between light and dark elements. Where any doubt exists, wisdom suggests having a colored or brown-toned photograph reproduced in black-and-white glossy by a professional printer before allotting space for that photograph within finished pages.

> Photocopied pictures do not do justice to the effort and expense we invest in our publication.

Tools and supplies

Modern page production calls for both technological products and staple supplies. Among the common materials are these.

TECHNOLOGICAL TOOLS

- *Drawing software.* If we plan to include charts, maps, or other line art of our own creation, odds are we will produce far more professional quality by executing these in a drawing program rather than by freehand.

- *Page-layout or word-processing software.* Most modern genealogists are experienced with word processing, and today's word-processing software offers powerful features. For true polish and the most precise control, however, we may wish to consider a page-layout program. (The present manual, by way of example, has been edited and formatted in PageMaker from manuscripts submitted in a variety of word-processing formats.)

- *Photographic retouching software.* Ancestral photographs and documents are notorious for the damage they've suffered—particularly scratches, tears, fading, and spotting. Acceptable retouching is within the capability of most patient people, given adequate practice with the electronic tools offered by software producers. The printing houses we consult can advise us as to which programs are currently the industry standards. If we have only one or two photographs that need retouching, it will likely be more economical to have the work professionally done. If our needs are greater than this, we may considerably reduce our costs by acquiring a program and learning to use it. Additionally, most such software offers an array of artistic effects that can enhance the design of photo pages.

- *Scanner.* With either a flatbed or sheet-fed scanner, we can embed documents, line art, maps, photographs, and even three-dimensional scans of some family mementos into all page-layout and most word-processing programs. Thus, we can place the illustrations exactly where we want them and add appropriate captions and artistic embellishments. The quality of any scan, however, depends not only upon the equipment used but also the expertise with which we choose our settings. If we venture into this area, we should allow time to study professional-quality scanning manuals aside from the basic booklet that comes with our equipment.[9]

TRADITIONAL TOOLS

- *Color-swatch books.* If our work is to have any color elements that we digitally produce, we cannot trust the colors rendered by our monitor—even when calibrated. Our drawing program, page-layout or word-processing software, or photographic retouching tools will typically offer several color systems from which we can choose. Their literature usually specifies which systems should be used for commercial printing as opposed to color processes designed for slide or photographic reproduction. To ensure that we achieve exactly the tints and shades we envision, we should purchase a corresponding color-swatch book from a graphic arts or paper supply shop; some software catalogs carry these also.

- *Light box.* This traditional basic for graphic artists is indispensable for fine tracings and precise positioning of paste-ups. The larger the better.

- *Mounting supplies.* To do a quality job of mounting illustrations, we need to use either a heated waxer (available at art-supply stores) or a plastic tape that is especially designed to be removable. Each allows us to easily reposition material we may mount incorrectly. Regular tape and rubber cement perform poorly. The former will likely lift print off the page when we have to reposition a paste-up, and the latter makes removal practically impossible without damaging the object. While an electronic waxer costs considerably more than plastic tape, it is a sound investment if we have many illustrations and captions to mount or if we plan to produce additional books.

If our work is to have any color elements that we digitally produce, we cannot trust the colors shown on our monitor.

- *Nonreproducing blue pencils.* These are used for making notations on the final copy that we do not want picked up by the camera. For example, to guide the printer, we will blue-pencil pagination on sheets that do not have printed numbers. Or we may have graphic elements to be printed in spot colors, in which case we'll need to flag each element with an identification of the exact color number we have chosen.

- *T-square or transparent ruler.* One or the other is essential for paste-ups to ensure that we properly position our exhibits.

Final preparation

Our preliminary page layout and design elements may need tweaking after we discuss them with our chosen printer. Whether we decide to supply camera-ready masters or digital copy, there are several steps to further ensure that the finished product will live up to our vision.

THE MOCKUP

Once we have designed a template in our page-layout or word-processing program—setting our headings, margins, and right-margin style; our choice of font, point size, and line spacing; and the page-number position—we should print a test copy of the first chapter. Then we trim it to the planned book size and arrange the pages so that left and right pages can be seen together as a two-page spread. Turning the pages with a critical eye, we ask ourselves

> Once we have designed a template in our page-layout or word-processing program, we should print a test copy of the first chapter.

- Is the format as attractive and readable as we have envisioned it?

- Is the print large enough that it can be easily read, but not so large that it seems to jump off the trimmed page?

- Is there sufficient white space in the margins, so that the text block does not overwhelm the page, and enough white space between sections of text to provide "rest spots" for our readers' eyes?

- Is there a pleasing proportion among the various sizes and styles of print—particularly at chapter and section headings, reference notes, and points emphasized in bold or italicized type?

If the answer to any of these questions is no, we should modify the format before proceeding. An editor or manuscript reader can be particularly helpful at this stage (as well as at the final check before we submit our copy to the printer).

After we are completely satisfied with the appearance of the text in this first chapter, then we proceed to a stage that is likely to be even more time consuming: the selection, arrangement, and insertion of the chapter's illustrations. We should test photocopies or scans of these exhibits amid the text—placing them on pages facing the related text. Repeating this process with each chapter, our arrangement and pagination of the text will be complete when the final chapter comes off our laser printer.

BACK AND FRONT MATTER

When the body of our manuscript is completed, we focus on the supporting back and

**PREPARING BOOKS
FOR PRESS**

front matter. Appendixes and bibliography may or may not be needed. An index will be. Before proceeding to the index, we should complete the front matter, making sure that all chapters, appendixes, and the index are included in the table of contents and that all documents, maps, and photographs are itemized on the table of illustrations. Because the material covered in our acknowledgments and introductions will have to be indexed, that index will necessarily be the last section created. An every-name and every-place index is obligatory; a subject or topical index will enhance most volumes. We prepare the entries with care, following a good manual such as Hatcher and Wylie's *Indexing Family Histories*[10] or the guidelines in chapter 26 of the present volume.

Miscellaneous Concerns

Our labors have been intense, but they are not yet over. Three important tasks remain: our quality control checks, our registrations, and our marketing.

Quality-control checks

Alterations to copy after it has been submitted to the printer can be expensive; the discovery of errors after the book has been printed can be humiliating. Thus, it hardly seems necessary to say that quality-control checks are in order; yet the number of production errors that make their way to press justifies a reminder. First, we should go back over the whole assembly ourselves, checking for correct order, pagination, and consistency of elements. We need to pay particular attention to the recently added front matter, exhibit captions, and the index. Then we should have the entire book proofread by a copyeditor and one or more proofreaders, correcting the manuscript after each reading—with the cleaner copy going to the next reader.

**FIG. 54
CIP CATALOGING DATA**

Library of Congress Cataloging-in-Publication Data

Curran, Joan F. (Joan Ferris)
     Numbering your genealogy : sound and simple systems / Joan Ferris
Curran.
     p. cm. -- (Special publication / National Genealogical
Society ; no. 59)
    Includes bibliographical references.
     ISBN 0-915156-59-8
     1. Genealogy--Methodology. I. Title. II. Series : Special
publications of the National Genealogical Society ; no. 59.
CS42.N43 no. 59
[CS21]
929'.1'06073--dc20
[929'.1'01]   91-47672
                                       CIP

Registrations

If our work is to be produced by a commercial publisher, that firm will usually prepare the application for three necessary registrations. If we choose to self-publish, we'll have at least some of this paperwork to do for ourselves. In the United States, cataloging-in-publication (CIP) registration is a prepublication service provided by the Library of Congress. This advance copy of cataloging data, when typed onto the back side of the title page prior to printing, allows libraries to catalog and shelve our book as soon as it is received. (See figure 54.) However, CIP registration is not currently available to self-publishers. ISBN registration, which we secure through the R. R. Bowker Publishing Company and affiliated group agencies worldwide,[11] provides an International Standard Book Number that we will want to type in a prominent place on our book cover or verso of the title page. This ISBN registration is particularly important for self-publishers, because Bowker's maintenance of an updated address for registered publishers makes it easier for would-be purchasers to locate us. Chapter 7 provides instructions for securing a copyright.

Marketing

Once we know the cost of publication, we can calculate a price. Next to deciding the number of copies to print, our determination of a fair selling price is likely to be the second most difficult business challenge we face as self-publishers. The figure we arrive at may or may not include the labor and out-of-pocket expenses involved with the research and book production. If our book is a family history, it is likely to be a labor of love—involving expenditures that far exceed the possibility of remuneration. If our book is a reference work and we hope to continue producing others, it is just plain good business sense to factor in the time and expenses of authorship or compilation. Beyond that point, our calculation should include the costs of publishing, shipping, marketing, and extended storage.

Once we have decided on a selling price, it is time to begin marketing. An attractive prepublication flyer, announcing a special price for orders placed before a certain date, can help finance (and sometimes will completely finance) the printing process. If ours is a family history, we should be sure to send a flyer to each living person mentioned in the book. If ours is a reference work, flyers should go to all libraries that might logically be expected to carry the book—a list we'll have to make judiciously based on a realistic appraisal of the appeal our work should have to national, state, and local libraries and societies. Ideally, we should design the flyer so that it appropriately targets institutions and individuals—and so that it can be reformatted easily for a postpublication announcement. Each version should be printed on a different color paper to better track the effectiveness of our marketing efforts. Chapter 11 offers other marketing strategies.

> A prepublication flyer, announcing a special price for orders placed before a certain date, can help finance the printing process.

Summary Concepts

When we send our manuscript to press, we will do so with trepidation but we should

**PREPARING BOOKS
FOR PRESS**

A book on cheap paper
does not convince. It is not
prized, it is like a wheezy
doctor with pigtail tobacco
breath, who needs a man-
icure.

—*Elbert Hubbard*[12]

also send it out with pride. The careful attention we have given it should ensure
satisfaction that we have done our job to the best of our ability and that we have put
it in the hands of a company that will do an equally superior job of printing and
binding it. Considering our major investment of research and writing time, the care
we take in getting a handsome final product will pay for itself many times over.

NOTES

1. *The Chicago Manual of Style: The Essential Guide for Writers, Editors, and Publishers,*
14th edition (Chicago: University of Chicago Press, 1993).
2. Mark Beach, Steve Shepro, and Ken Rosson, *Getting It Printed: How to Work with Printers
and Graphic Arts Services to Assure Quality, Stay on Schedule, and Control Costs,* rev. edition
(Cincinnati, Ohio: North Light Books, 1998).
3. Carl Boyer 3d, *How to Publish and Market Your Family History,* 4th edition (Newhall,
California: C. Boyer, 1993).
4. Patricia Law Hatcher, CG, *Producing a Quality Family History* (Salt Lake City: Ancestry,
1996).
5. One such video is *Prepare to Publish* (Baltimore: Gateway Press, current edition).
6. These and much else are explained in Robin Williams, *The PC is Not a Typewriter: A
Style Manual for Creating Professional-Level Type on Your Personal Computer* (Berkeley, California: Peachpit Press, 1992). Also available in a Mac version.
7. For example, see Judy Stopke and Chip Staley, *An Eye for Type,* 3d expanded edition.
(Ann Arbor, Michigan: Promotional Perspectives, 1992).
8. *Chicago Manual of Style* has a convenient comparative chart on page 827.
9. Wayne Fulton, *A Few Scanning Tips* (Plano, Texas: Scantips.com, 1999), in 200 pages,
offers considerably more than the "few" tips the title promises.
10. Patricia Law Hatcher, CG, and John V. Wylie, *Indexing Family Histories: Simple Steps for
a Quality Product* (Arlington, Virginia: National Genealogical Society, 1994).
11. In the U.S., contact R.R. Bowker—ISBN Division. A list of ISBN Group Agencies for many
countries internationally is available from Bowker's website.
12. Elbert Hubbard (1856–1915), American writer and printer, quoted in Rhoda Thomas
Tripp, comp., *The International Thesaurus of Quotations* (New York: Thomas Y. Crowell, 1970),
59.

FURTHER STUDY

Carroll, David L. *How to Prepare Your Manuscript for a Publisher.* 2d edition. New York: Marlowe,
1995.
Cook, Claire Kehrwald. *Line by Line: How to Improve Your Own Writing.* Boston: Houghton
Mifflin for the Modern Language Association, 1985.
Copyrighted Content: The Cautious Editor's Guide to Using Printed Material. Ann Arbor:
Promotional Perspectives, 1991.
Goldstein, Norm, ed. *The Associated Press Stylebook and Libel Manual.* Rev. edition. Reading,
Massachusetts: Perseus Books, 1998.
Hamilton, John R. *Things Your Printer Might Tell You (or Not).* Ann Arbor: Promotional
Perspectives, 1990.
Mills, Elizabeth Shown, CG, CGL, FASG. *Evidence! Citation & Analysis for the Family Historian.*
Baltimore: Genealogical Publishing Co., 1997.
Poynter, Dan. *The Self-Publishing Manual: How to Write, Print, and Sell Your Own Books.* 6th
edition. Santa Barbara, California: Para Publishing, 2000.
Siebert, Lori, and Mary Cropper. *Working with Words & Pictures.* Cincinnati, Ohio: North Light
Books, 1993.
Williams, Joseph M., and Gregory G. Colomb. *Style: Toward Clarity and Grace.* Chicago:
University of Chicago, 1990.

Educational Services

28

**CLASSROOM
TEACHING**

CLASSROOM TEACHING

Keynotes

Keynotes (cont.)

Classroom Teaching

by Sandra Hargreaves Luebking

Teaching well involves more than good ideas. It requires a mastery of both subject matter and application techniques, as well as the ability to communicate that knowledge and those skills to others. But it also requires a third component, one that all good teachers recognize intuitively and one to which all poor teachers remain pathetically oblivious: an awareness of the attitudes that are created during each and every instructional session. Although the teaching process appears simple—we just tell them what we know—good teachers find the communication channel to be exquisitely complex.[1]

Attitudes

Attitudes are prescriptions for behavior, perspective, and demeanor. In genealogy, attitudes manifest themselves in numerous ways: the manner in which researchers approach a county clerk, the attention they give to detail when searching or evaluating, and the extent of their awareness that no researcher is an island and that the performance of one searcher directly or indirectly affects all others.

> In teaching, attitudes can be transmitted without the conscious awareness of either the teacher or the student.

In teaching, attitudes are not always so obvious. They can be transmitted without the conscious awareness of either the teacher or the student. Yet attitude is the most lasting of the three components. Students who leave the genealogy classroom will refine or lose skills and knowledge, depending upon the degree and timing of application. According to psychologists, however, those students retain the attitudes they have acquired. Of course, not every graduate of a genealogical class actually pursues genealogy. But among even those who don't, positive attitudes generate support from taxpayers, voters, and designers of open-records legislation and public record-maintenance policy.

Among those who continue in genealogy, positive attitudes determine the level at which each of them works. Economist and editor Robert B. Reich could have written these words for genealogists:

> The intellectual equipment needed for the job of the future is an ability to define problems, quickly assimilate relevant data, conceptualize and reorganize the information, make deductive and inductive leaps within, ask hard questions about it, discuss findings with colleagues, work collaboratively to find solutions and then convince others.[2]

Does one teach this high plane of intellectualization through knowledge and skills? Or is it transmitted through the attitudes teachers create by the care and sensitivity with which they approach the classroom? When a teacher understands the complexity of transmitting attitudes, knowledge, and skills and then applies this understanding to every lesson plan, every visual aid, and every student contact, genealogy gains the most benefit from education.

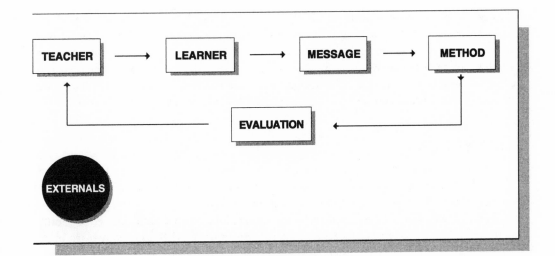

FIG. 55
THE EDUCATIONAL
PROCESS

The Process

The transmittal of attitude, knowledge, and skills can be diagrammed as a circuit of instruction comprised of six components. Five of them are intrinsically related (teacher, learner, message, method, and evaluation). Externals, the sixth, are separate but inevitable influences. Figure 55 illustrates this educational process.

The teacher

Our talents, our abilities and liabilities, and our willingness to plan and organize, update and share knowledge, and manage a classroom—all are part of this essential component. In most parts of the country, lamentably, one can teach genealogy without being interviewed, tested, or credentialed. Why? Because many administrators classify genealogy as a noncredit course to be packaged somewhere between square dancing and assertiveness training. The genealogical community takes a far less liberal view of genealogical education. The Board for Certification of Genealogists, which offers the only recognized genealogical teaching credential, requires a Certified Genealogical Instructor (CGI) to demonstrate

- thorough understanding of the subject matter and relevant historical background;
- familiarity with the subject bibliography;
- knowledge of the various types of records for genealogy in general and one's specialty, in particular;
- expertise in making genealogical investigations, reporting the findings, and citing all sources;
- experience in compiling family histories that track (and reconstruct the lives of) all descendants, of whatever surname; and
- understanding of the techniques of genealogical education, so that knowledge can be imparted in a manner understood by and useful to other genealogists.[3]

These criteria make a good model for all teachers. In addition, as genealogy instructors we must be willing to monitor our own performance, because we set our own pace in the classroom, deciding what to teach and how to teach it. Even though credentials may not be required by our employer, we will be expected to possess the skills necessary to transmit information in a precise and effective manner. To do so, we must understand the second person in the educational process: the learner.

The learner

Exactly who do we teach? How do we define the learner in terms of age? Physical and mental capacities? Enthusiasm? Ability to retain instruction? Willingness to concentrate? All these dimensions determine how well our students will learn.

Genealogy classrooms, as a rule, are composed of adults—not children.[4] Every adult who attends a class wants to learn and can be taught. Although educators once believed learning ability declines with age, numerous studies for the past quarter-century have disproved this.[5] However, the teacher of adults needs to know how mature students differ in expectations, life experiences, and power and speed of learning. These differences should be considered in lesson preparation and presentation. Different approaches are required, particularly for those accustomed to teaching children.

EXPECTATIONS

Adults attend genealogy classes because they want to. They come with a high degree of enthusiasm and do not need to be motivated. They bring high expectations as well. They expect a professional approach, with well-prepared lessons and delivery. Time is important to them; they want to make the most of it, and they want instruction to start on time and proceed systematically.

LIFE EXPERIENCES

Adults bring a wide variety of experiences to a learning situation. These may result from formal education, occupational background, travel, or wide reading in a variety of subjects. Their intellectual backpack may include a knowledge of research techniques or skills transferrable from related fields—as with history professors, title searchers, and engineers trained to be analytical thinkers, for example. These life experiences and skills provide a schema, a vast frame of reference that adults draw upon or scan in learning new material. Understanding the presence of schemata is critical to knowing how to present new material to mature learners.

POWER VS. SPEED

Power is the ability to organize and process new information and merge it with what is already known. Speed is the rate at which one absorbs new information. The power aspect of learning does not diminish with age—in fact, for particular subjects, power may increase. However, the speed of learning may decrease due to physiological and emotional changes that accompany the aging process. Sensitive and creative teachers who understand these differences can easily compensate for them.

Although educators once believed learning ability declines with age, numerous studies for the past quarter-century have disproved this.

Physiological changes

Visual and hearing alterations are the most obvious ones that affect learning. Gradual deterioration in vision begins soon after age eighteen, and the years from forty to fifty-five mark the most rapid decline. Hearing loss begins even earlier—at age fifteen or so—and continues at a consistent rate until one reaches sixty-five or seventy, when impairment increases sharply. Eyeglasses and hearing aids improve performance substantially, but an alert instructor can go one step further and insist on adequate lighting and good acoustics in the classroom.

Emotional changes

Equally manageable are the emotional changes that affect learning. Fearing one is "too slow" or "has been away from school too long" can reduce a student's self-confidence and hinder performance. Encouragement, delivery at a moderate pace, and willingness to repeat material can empower our students to overcome their emotional inhibitors. The message we deliver through our overall course structure and our individual lessons can also compensate for emotional and physiological changes.

The message

Message is content. No single person can teach everything that needs to be taught. The reasoning by which we set instructional goals, plan our course structure, and select specific bits of information will determine the message we deliver.

> The reasoning by which we set instructional goals, plan our course structure, and select specific bits of information will determine the message we deliver.

COURSE STRUCTURE

Our message begins with the design and description of our course. Adults who bring high expectations to the genealogy classroom may believe that a six-week course will result in a six-generation lineage. Or they may assume that a week of intense instruction, such as Samford University's Institute of Genealogy and Historical Research, will make them a professional. These expectations need to be addressed when planning begins, as part of our description, design, and instructional content.

Design and description

Even before we select curriculum, we should think about how we can influence the expectations of our students. How can we let them know in advance what we will teach? The best way is through our course description—the brief paragraph that follows the title in catalogs of course offerings. Never should we let someone else write that description. It is the cornerstone of our goals and the summary of our efforts. Most important, the wording of the description will determine the expectations of our students. A good description hinges upon a goal. That goal, for a beginning genealogy class, should not be overly ambitious—just well formulated and written in clear, concise English. For example:

INSTRUCTOR'S GOAL

Upon completion of this course, students will have a working knowledge of eight types of post-1880 American records [*itemized here*]. They will be able to perform certain basic research steps—including writing a research plan, creating a pedigree and family chart, properly citing and organizing sources, and writing effective queries. They will have learned to use microform readers and card catalogs and will know the basics of distinguishing between good and bad genealogical information on the Internet.

From this we can extract a specific and unambiguous course description:

COURSE DESCRIPTION
This course will examine the most often used late 19th-century and 20th-century American research sources and methods for the new family historian. Basic hands-on library work and an introduction to Internet materials are included.

After publishing this clear but concise description, there need be no first-session explanations as to why we are not teaching German script or Slavic sources or British archival techniques. We will not need to apologize to a student who expected advanced instruction. In contrast, let's consider a pair of more typical course descriptions:

Interested in finding your roots? Join us as we climb the family tree!
(What expectations does that create in the daughter of a 1978 Russian immigrant?)

Do you know who your great-grandfather was? Come and find out!
(How does a teacher defend that description to an adoptee?)

While the prescribed description may sound dull by comparison, it is accurate and removes unpleasant surprises for registrants. If we feel the need to be creative or humorous, we might do so with the title, keeping the description precise.

Content selection
Once we have a goal and a working description, we need to broadly plan our content. Among the parameters we consider are logistics, outcome, and student need.

- *Logistics* refer to the number of actual classroom hours available for instruction, the research facilities in our area, the anticipated experience level of our students, and our own areas of expertise.

CLASSROOM HOURS
We determine this by multiplying the *number of meetings* by the *allotted time* and subtracting minutes for nonteaching activities. We should be realistic. Housekeeping chores (roll call, announcements, etc.) and breaks can absorb a half-hour per meeting—or 25 percent of a sixteen-hour course. If we teach in fifty-minute segments, we will reduce our course content by four lessons.

EXPERTISE
None of us can be proficient in every aspect of research and record knowledge. We build on our strengths and recognize our limitations. Honesty is the best policy here, as everywhere: if we are not well-versed in a particular area, we should carefully consider its importance to the curriculum. If it's critical, we'll need to concentrate on improving our knowledge. If it is not essential, we might just cite a source for the students' future exploration.

RESEARCH FACILITIES
The proximity of research facilities determines what to teach. If we live near a

Housekeeping chores and breaks can absorb a half-hour per meeting—or 25 percent of a sixteen-hour course.

state or national archives, we should expect to spend classroom time on the holdings found there. We may even want to include a conducted tour. If our students must travel a considerable distance to use those facilities, they will have less immediate need to know those holdings.

STUDENT PERFORMANCE

Less easily defined is the performance level we may expect from our students. As we acquire teaching experience, this becomes easier for us to predict. As new teachers, we are better served by *underestimating* the knowledge of our students. Never should we assume they will know things. For a beginning class, we prepare as if they will know nothing. We can more easily raise the level of teaching during a session than reduce it. (Too, the effects of various experience levels are modified by our explicit course description. If that description clearly targets beginners, then we choose subject matter accordingly. An advanced researcher would enroll knowing what to expect.)

> For a beginning class, we prepare as if students will know nothing. We can far more easily raise the level of teaching during the sessions than reduce it.

- *Outcome*—knowing what we want our students to be able to do when they leave our class—is even more critical than logistics. In what country and time period do we want them to work during this course? What basic skills do we want them to acquire? Our course content must reinforce our outcome aims. Do we follow the genealogical principle of "working from what one knows to what one doesn't know?" If so, we'll want beginners to first identify *themselves* through public and private records and then work backwards, generation by generation, carefully documenting each. This scenario would, necessarily, rule out teaching them to use seventeenth-century land grants or eighteenth-century military pensions. This is not to say that these are not important subjects for genealogical research; rather, they do not belong in a class teaching beginners to start with themselves and proceed slowly and methodically into the past.

- *Student need*—the number of times a new researcher will have to use the information or skill—should decide whether we include a subject and the amount of emphasis we give it. Obviously, if we expect our students to work backward generation by generation, we need to teach the census. However, the emphasis would logically be on the twentieth and late-nineteenth centuries, while earlier returns would get only slight treatment.

Frequency of use is one area in which our expertise can work against us. A teacher whose personal research or client work centers around the late-eighteenth century is tempted to draw upon this period for examples and visual aids, but we must block any such inclination or else teach advanced researchers rather than beginners.

Not only do new researchers need to work back carefully and systematically, they need to master research techniques before attempting earlier time periods. Just as a new driver should not access the expressway during rush hour, the new researcher should be discouraged from launching searches that require advanced knowledge and techniques—and it is our responsibility, as teachers, to guide this.

Both outcome and immediate need might best be explored by asking ourselves how far back can a beginner work and still function successfully—*success* meaning the discovery of people with the right names and accuracy in identification and relationships.

LESSONS

Writing in *Mastery Teaching,* Madeline Hunter proposes three basic principles by which we can impart information more effectively.[6]

- *Determine basic information and organize it.* This "bull's-eye approach" requires us to sort essential information from details that are useful but supplemental and can be acquired later. After selecting our basic information, we should organize it so students can absorb the more complex details and see the relationships between parts. For example, in explaining census records, our essential information might include why the census was taken, how it was taken, and how researchers can access it. This basic information needs to be organized, then enhanced with only those details essential to the students' ability to use that source.

- *Present basic information in simplest and clearest forms.* We should use language that is unambiguous to the listener and examples that highlight the essence of our material. To continue the census example: what would be the simplest format in which to teach the subject? While many textbooks and lessons begin with a country's earliest extant returns and work forward, family historians who have just been counseled to work from the present to the past would expect to have the last-released census presented first. We should draw our examples from that year as well, since that will be the starting point from which our students will make research decisions.

- *Model the information or process.* Modeling means to show a product or demonstrate a process that elicits understanding from the student. If our students can visualize (or have experienced) the concept being taught, a tangible model may not be necessary. But when the process is new—as a pedigree chart is to most beginners—we will help our students by presenting an example of the process or completed chart as a visual aid. Remembering Hunter's second point above, we would not use a chart of five or more generations, as that would not be presenting information in its simplest and clearest form.

Scripts

The importance of preparation cannot be overemphasized. Planning takes time and effort. We do not walk into a classroom and "wing it." Students know the difference and don't appreciate a cavalier approach. Without structure, lesson time can evaporate before all our essential points are covered. Or, the time can mysteriously expand until we find ourselves talking nonsense or going off on tangents to fill it.

Careful preparation requires scripting. Drafting a script allows us to check our message for accuracy, currency, and preciseness. Updating or substituting examples is far easier with a typed lecture. Accuracy is ensured when we can compare our script to reliable sources of information. As researchers, we learned the value of writing down a problem and a plan of action. As teachers, we find this scripting and

Drafting a script allows us to check our message for accuracy, currency, and preciseness.

analyzing just as critical to our success. Reading and rereading our lesson material enables us to be more precise—a quality and an attitude worthy of transmission to students interested in family research. We would not want to say "the 1890 U.S. census burned" and forget to note that all was not lost. Scripting and rehearsal ensure that we remember to identify and provide access information for the remaining portions.

Using a script does not mean that we deliver our message by *reading*. Instead, a thoughtful and repetitive review of context permits us to lecture from memory, to focus on our students and change pace or review certain points as needed. If we work from notes or (worse) from memory and improvisation, we risk leaving out critical elements due to poor timing or forgetfulness. On the other hand, knowing that we won't fall prey to these common errors—or digress at inopportune times—actually frees us for a better delivery.

Having a script, even though we present the material as if we were working from an outline, also enables us to monitor and control the class. At genealogical institutes, year after year, as critiques roll in, any new lecturer who has been careless can count on one overwhelming complaint, loud and angry: "The instructor failed to control the class and allowed student questions and interruptions to absorb time or change the lecture direction." Scripts keep us on target. They empower us to be in control. When students sense they are in capable hands, they feel free to learn, knowing that our message will have been carefully considered and devised.

Visual aids

Studies conducted by the Applied Research Center at the Wharton School in Pennsylvania show that visual aids increase learning while shortening the presentation time.[7] Good visuals range from handouts to props, slides, transparencies, and video-tapes. Few (except for the latter) are produced commercially. Most instructors are left to their own devices in the design and creation of their material; and their time and financial limitations often result in inadequate reproductions of documents or maps, as well as poorly typed handouts.

The three principles proposed for lecture construction by Madeline Hunter also apply to the preparation of visual materials:

- Determine and organize the basic information.

- Present that basic information in the clearest and simplest form.

- Model that information or process only when necessary.

We need not bring an elephant to class to teach the color gray. Nor do we need a page from every census to teach the basics of that source type. In fact, students can be overwhelmed and frustrated by too much gray or too much material, whether it is too many pages in a handout or a slide whose text is so crowded students cannot read or understand it in the time allotted.

Keeping material concise and legible may require us to manipulate the original document. For example, maps can be powerful visuals if we let their message-carrying elements dominate and dispense with secondary elements. On a transparency depicting early transportation routes, it is better to delete all those names of small towns. In

> We need not bring an elephant to class to teach the color gray. Nor do we need a page from every census to teach the basics of that source type.

showing a deed, we might cut it in thirds, magnify each within a neat border, and show three legible visuals instead of one inscrutable shot. Props can be valuable. Old newspapers, a surveyor's compass, even attire for cemetery searching can be a key element in a lecture. However, ill-chosen props can be distracting and can divert attention from what we are trying to teach, rather than reinforce it.

The method

To be dull is a sin, Kierkegaard once said.[8] To be dull in teaching is a double sin, because we have a captive audience that fervently wants to know the information we possess. Dullness results from poor lecturing skills or a dependence on the lecture, excluding other and more viable methods.

LECTURES

This classic approach is the best way to get across a large body of knowledge in a short time—if the lecturer is well-rehearsed, maintains good voice and pace control, and projects well. On the other hand, we reduce our effectiveness if we drop our voice at the end of sentences, speak to the screen when showing visuals, look down at our notes too often, or simply talk so fast or so softly that we lose our listener. Wisdom suggests recording or videotaping ourselves during class, then critically analyzing our delivery as though we were a student. We should also experiment with other means of relaying information. Alternatives abound.

ALTERNATIVES

> As innovative teachers, we will not only seek out models but also develop creative ideas of our own.

As innovative teachers, we will not only seek out models but also develop creative ideas of our own. Among the most common approaches that effective teachers adapt are case studies, delegation, demonstration, discussion, programmed instruction, role play, and simulation.

- *Case studies.* Either as individuals or small groups, students can analyze "typical" research problems and devise solutions. If we require written answers to case studies, we will help the students channel and clarify their thinking while simultaneously reinforcing a lesson on, say, the interpretation of a deed or will.

- *Delegation.* Appointing someone else, usually an expert from within or outside the classroom, to present a topic can add welcome variety and perspective to our classes. In these cases, we should set a time limit and reach an agreement on the material we want covered. As examples, we might introduce an archivist to teach document preservation, a geography professor to teach migration patterns, or a librarian to describe local holdings.

- *Demonstration.* Students more easily learn by doing than by listening, and some skills especially lend themselves to genealogy classrooms—for example, abstracting, preparing pedigree forms, or using microform readers. Demonstration is more effective when promptly followed by an opportunity for supervised practice.

- *Discussion.* Almost any lecture can be adapted to discussion, where students cluster in small groups to share their findings on an assignment. In problem-solving situations, discussion works best after students have received basic information and instruction.

- *Programmed instruction.* Textbooks or outside reading assignments from genealogical journals can provide the extra help needed by students whose experience or skill level makes it difficult for them to keep up with the class.

- *Role play.* Lessons on oral interviews and effective personal contact with record keepers also set a stage on which role playing can be an effective learning tool. After we assign students their "identities" and lay out their performance guidelines, the active participants would elicit information, respond to questions, or deny access. The rest of the class would observe the skit, examine the rationale behind each portrayal, and appraise the effectiveness of the methods the role players used to achieve the needed goal.

- *Simulation.* Some concepts—for example, the evaluation of sources—lend themselves to exercises that allow students to make decisions and perform skills required in actual research situations. As instructors, we would "set up" the situations in advance and facilitate the simulation by giving directions and some coaching.

We should be creative and daring in the classroom—preparing diligently and evaluating each use of a different method of lesson presentation. We'll be far more effective and neither we nor our students need ever fear dullness from us again.

The evaluation

Evaluation is the teacher's passport to becoming the very best instructor possible. Viewing a videotape of our lecture is helpful, as previously suggested, but asking a mentor or someone whose teaching we admire to evaluate the tape at the same time adds priceless objectivity and broader perspective. A far better evaluation will come from our students. It is a truism that nothing has been taught until it is learned. Therefore, what our students learn is a good benchmark for appraising our own success as a teacher. The most popular method of measuring student learning is student testing. However, a more effective means for us may be to ask our students to evaluate us. For example:

- *Student committees.* Wilbert McKeachie, in his now-classic *Teaching Tips: A Guidebook for the Beginning College Teacher,* describes an ideal method for encouraging evaluation while stimulating student participation. He chose a student lecture committee from volunteers, asking them to read the coming week's assignments and lecture scripts. Committee members also interviewed other class members for reactions to past lectures. The committee then met with McKeachie to suggest revisions of the forthcoming lectures. Their evaluations, McKeachie reports, were quite frank because each member could cloak criticism by saying, "Some of the students I interviewed said. . . ."[9]

We should be creative and daring in the classroom—preparing diligently and evaluating each use of a different method of lesson presentation.

- *Student critiques.* At the Samford University Institute of Genealogy and Historical Research students submit detailed critiques at the end of their week. Most class coordinators ask the students to jot down a few notes after each lecture—very specific remarks on the effectiveness of that presentation—rather than wait until the end of the week to pen a general overview. These lesson-by-lesson evaluations are of critical value to the instructors as they modify lecture content and reorganize the sequence of certain lessons from year to year.

The externals

We seldom have control over outside noise; the comfort of student desks; or the configuration, lighting, or size of the room—or control over whether the pop machine is working in the lounge. But such externals do have both positive and negative effects on the learning process. Some negative influences can be improved by attentive instructors who voice concerns to the administration. If our classroom is next to the lounge where other students gather to talk, we might be able to arrange for a different site. If lighting is a problem, we might have students bring high-density portable lamps and extension cords to class on nights when desk work is required. External distractions can also be avoided or modified by, for example, testing projectors before use and bringing spare bulbs or extension cords in our briefcase for emergencies.

The Practice

Getting started

The theories behind effective classroom teaching are easy to acquire, given the wealth of literature available on the subject. Gaining the actual experience is often a more problematic matter. If we are just at the point of trying to break into genealogical teaching, we might begin by learning what educational courses are being offered in our area and what potential might be available. Then we create our own niche. Let us suppose, for example, that we are newcomers in an area where one teacher has dominated classroom activities for a decade.

- We might talk to that teacher. Perhaps it will be a relief to him or her to know that someone else is interested in assuming part of the educational responsibilities. Or the instructor might be interested in team teaching, dividing particular topics between us.

- If the established teacher is not receptive, then we might tell the local genealogical or historical societies about our interests. We might create our own following by offering to speak to alumni associations, business groups, and professional organizations. The "chicken dinner circuit" is a great training ground. After we become known as a good lecturer, we will be accepted as a teacher.

- Once we have speaking skills and confidence in our material, we might consider offering a course under the name of our genealogical business—renting meeting

Once we have speaking skills and confidence in our material, we might consider offering a course under the name of our genealogical business.

space at a church, hotel, restaurant, or YMCA. Advertising in the local newspaper or through area societies will attract some students. Word of mouth, as we gain experience, should attract even more.

- We might call local schools and offer our services as outside resource persons whom teachers can call upon to develop or assist with secondary-classroom units on family history.

- We might contact our local newspaper's editorial office, offering ourselves as a resource person or outside consultant for matters relating to family history. A copy of our resume, showcasing our genealogical expertise and especially our teaching interest, should accompany our written contact or immediately follow our telephone contact.

- We might create a web page—either for ourselves or for a local genealogical or historical society—at which we offer a series of "mini-lessons" on research and resources.

In short, if we are willing to lecture and teach anywhere and everywhere, if we make ourselves known in the community for our expertise, we'll gain both the experience and the reputation we need to find a sponsor—which may be an adult-education program, a church, a genealogical or historical society, or a library. In our contacts with potential sponsors, we further our chances by offering to do individual tutoring or mass lecturing—and by making these approaches with a concrete proposal for hours, dates, and contract terms. We should include our resume, course description and goals, and a curriculum and sample lesson plan—with complete handouts and teaching aids. We should not be reluctant to negotiate salary. In the beginning, we may want to accept requests for free lectures. But as our skill and professionalism mature, we'll have to be more selective in agreeing to pro bono presentations. Wisdom suggests that we establish a firm policy *before* gratis requests become a problem. Too many teachers burn out financially or psychologically from demands made on their energy, pocketbook, and time.

Improving skills

"Nothing is more dangerous than an idea when it is the only one you have," the essayist Émile Chartier once quipped.[10] And nothing is more dangerous than a teacher who chooses not to keep current, expand knowledge, and explore other teaching options. Most of us, when we begin to teach, draw heavily upon our own formal education, perspectives, and research experiences. This is entirely understandable and forgivable in a novice. But, as we continue to instruct, specific personal experience and anecdotes have to be augmented by much more general knowledge and examples. The best teacher is cosmopolitan in approach—and better equipped to meet the needs of students, better able to precisely describe and comprehensively discuss content and methodology—than is the new teacher.

Attendance at national conferences or large workshops enables us to observe alternate methods, styles, and views while learning the latest in resource availability

Wisdom suggests that we establish a firm policy *before* gratis requests become a problem. Too many teachers burn out financially or psychologically from demands made on their energy, pocketbook, and time.

and interpretation. While the finer points brought out at these conferences are not always suitable for presentation to beginners, teachers who attend these specialized lectures acquire a depth and understanding that adds considerably to their base of knowledge. Attending sessions geared for beginners can be equally helpful. Here, we can observe content as well as techniques that might be adaptable for our own classroom. We can observe the students in those classes and note their expectations. We can talk to the attendees afterward and ask if they acquired confidence from the session. We can approach the instructor, inquiring about the philosophy behind the selection of material or the method of presentation. And, as we appraise this class, we should evaluate our own by comparison.

As our skills grow and our gifts blossom, we should identify other researchers who show potential as teachers. Let's mentor one, encouraging the development of all the skills discussed in this chapter. Then, we might provide our protégée an opportunity to teach an occasional class in our course—or even team-teach with us. And we can make our societies aware of the roles they can play in educating future researchers. Let's not hesitate to seek their help and not forget to recommend them, as organizations, to our students.

The Sponsors

Although this chapter focuses upon effective classroom teaching, the role of societies in genealogical education is intrinsically entwined. As experienced professionals, we can give back to our field by helping societies better understand their opportunities and responsibilities.

A society needs to identify those who are teaching in its region. It should get to know them, their credentials, and their strengths and needs. It should provide encouragement to up-and-coming instructors and offer its library as a resource or the services of members who can provide invaluable teacher support. Societies can start educational groups, composed either of practicing or potential teachers, as well as society members who support teaching effort. And they can devise formal educational programs to fill the void of genealogical training that exists within traditional academic programs. As part of a society, we can encourage it to recognize the efforts of good, local teachers and promote their courses in our newsletter. We might establish special awards for their efforts. Just as societies honor officers, editors, and project chairmen, so too should good teachers be recognized. The award of a trip to a national conference, for example, would subsequently benefit a society as much as the teacher it sent.

Genealogical organizations must insist on excellence from local teachers and be willing to adequately compensate them. They should discourage "free" teaching, because it blocks others who may want to teach but cannot afford to subsidize classes or lectures, year after year. If our organization's teacher insists on no pay, we should encourage the group to transfer student fees to the society's library, or finance a special educational project, or establish a support fund for new teachers in the name of the generous instructor who volunteers his or her services.

> As part of a society, we can encourage it to recognize the efforts of good, local teachers and promote their courses in our newsletter.

Summary Concepts

The genealogy classroom is the future of our field. As individual professionals, we have a responsibility to help shape that future wisely. As teachers, we are expected to develop exceptional expertise—we should be known for the reliability of our information as well as the depth and breadth of our knowledge. As society members, we need to instill the message that educational administrators must be informed, so as to select teachers on experience and proficiency, not just availability. Genealogy needs the best and the brightest of its professionals as teachers, and the entire genealogical community must support the efforts of educators and encourage the best of them to continue.

> Who dares to teach must never cease to learn.
>
> —*John Cotton Dana*[11]

NOTES

1. This chapter incorporates material from Dr. James R. Johnson, Dixon Barr, and Robert C. Anderson, FASG, with whom I worked the earliest "Seminars on Education" for the Instructor Development Committee (IDC) of the National Genealogical Society. Credit is also due to the late Richard S. Lackey, CG, FASG, and F. Wilbur Helmbold, head of the Samford University Library, who, prior to their deaths, encouraged quality education in general and me in particular. Finally, sincere thanks to Anne D. Budd and Marsha H. Rising, CG, CGL, FASG, who successively served as my cochairs of the IDC. Their ideas and examples both inspired and humbled me.

2. *Quotes to Inspire You: Robert B. Reich* website <www.cyber-nation.com/victory/quotations/authors/quotes_reich_robertb.html>.

3. Adapted from *BCG Application Guide* (Washington: Board for Certification of Genealogists, 2000).

4. Literature and teaching aids for use in the secondary-school system are identified in Sandra Hargreaves Luebking, "Instructional Materials," being chapter 2 of Kory L. Meyerink, AG, ed., *Printed Sources: A Guide to Published Genealogical Records* (Salt Lake City: Ancestry, 1998). The list appears under "How-To Guides and Manuals for Young People," 87–88.

5. For example, see Patricia K. Cross, *Adults as Learners* (San Francisco: Jossey-Bass Publishers, 1981).

6. Madeline Hunter, *Mastery Teaching* (El Segundo, California: TIP Publications, 1982), 31.

7. Audio Visual Division, 3M Business Products, *How to Present More Effectively and Win More Favorable Responses from More People in Less Time*, Pamphlet 78-1751-9635-7.

8. Søren Kierkegaard (1813–55), Danish philosopher, quoted by Robert Sarkissian, *The Kierkegaarden* website <www.island-of-freedom.com/gaarden/gaarden.htm>.

9. Wilbert J. McKeachie, *Teaching Tips: A Guidebook for the Beginning College Teacher* (Lexington, Massachusetts: D. C. Heath, 1962). An amplified edition of this classic has been issued recently as *McKeachie's Teaching Tips: Strategies, Research, and Theory for College and University Teachers, with Chapters by Graham Gibbs et al.* (Boston: Houghton Mifflin, 1999).

10. Émile August Chartier (1868–1951), French-Canadian philosopher and essayist writing under the simple nom de plume *Alain*, quoted in Bob Phillips, *Phillips' Book of Great Thoughts, Funny Sayings* (Wheaton, Illinois: Tyndale House Publishers, 1993), 166.

11. John Cotton Dana, nineteenth-century American librarian, quoted at *TPCN Quotation Center* <www.cybernation.com/victory/quotations>, downloaded 8 January 2000.

12. (Sidebar, p. 568) Lucius Annaeus Seneca (c. 4 B.C.–A.D. 65), Roman philosopher and playright, quoted in Rhoda Thomas Tripp, comp., *The International Thesaurus of Quotations* (New York: Thomas Y. Crowell, 1970), 629.

CLASSROOM TEACHING

My joy in learning is partly
that it enables me to teach.

—*Seneca*[12]

FURTHER STUDY

Benedict, Sheila, CGRS. "Teaching Genealogy." *Association of Professional Genealogists [APG] Quarterly* 14 (September 1999): 121.

Hunter, Madeline C. *Teach More—Faster!* Thousand Oaks, California: Corwin Press, 1995.

Kellow, Brenda, CG, CGI. "Are You Ready to Teach?" *APG Quarterly* 14 (September 1999): 127–28.

McCarthy, Michael J. *Mastering the Information Age: A Course in Working Smarter, Thinking Better, and Learning Faster.* Los Angeles: Jeremy P. Tarcher, 1991.

Timpson, William M., and David N. Tobin. *Teaching as Performing: A Guide to Energizing Your Public Presentation.* Englewood Cliffs, New Jersey: Prentice-Hall, 1982.

Warren, Paula Stuart, CGRS. "The Nuts and Bolts of Genealogical Teaching and Lecturing." *APG Quarterly* 14 (September 1999): 117–20, 122–25.

29

LECTURING

Keynotes

Keynotes (cont.)

Lecturing

by Helen F. M. Leary, CG, CGL, FASG

There's no getting around it—lecturing is a performing art. Like an actor's dramatic readings, a speaker's lectures are delivered alone; there is no supporting cast to mitigate an audience's judgment of the performance. Unlike dramatic readings, genealogical lecturing is primarily an educational medium. Its purpose is to teach, not to entertain. To fulfill its purpose a worthwhile presentation will be based on independent thought, careful research, and meticulous preparation. A good lecture cannot be copied from another's material or delivery style; it must arise from our own enthusiasm for the subject and our joy of teaching.

A professional lecturer must reduce to manageable proportions the stark terror that the thought of public speaking triggers in most people. True, some speakers do seem to have more natural talent for it than others; but anyone who can overcome stage fright can learn to deliver accurate, competent, well-received lectures. Even the most talented speaker, however, cannot deliver quality, consistently, without a hidden investment of considerable time. Whether we are at the point of contemplating our first or our hundred-and-first lecture, the way we use those hidden hours will directly affect our audience and ultimately determine our success or failure as speakers. Our degree of background preparation will be obvious from our content, our delivery style, and our visual aids, as well as from the written material we prepare for the sponsoring organization's syllabus or for the audience to take home as "handouts."

Written Preparation

The design of a lecture is crucial. Our goal is a coherent presentation, accurately titled, that tells the audience what it wants (and needs) to know about our subject. Communication must be immediate and direct—an oral presentation is not designed for prolonged study. Our delivery should be clear enough for our audiences to understand at the time and dramatic enough for them to remember later.

Preliminary analysis

Every topic has endless ways in which it can be developed. Deciding how to approach the assigned subject is our first challenge. Our best guide will be one we write ourselves: a brief plan of attack that answers the following questions:

- What is my point of view? What do I think is most important about this topic?

  SAMPLE ANSWERS: "I think we genealogists are not using this [*source/repository/technique*] the way we should." Or: "I made so many beginner mistakes myself that I think I can help others avoid them."

- What is the audience's point of view? How much do they already know? How receptive will they be to new data or novel techniques?

SAMPLE ANSWERS: "The program chair describes them as absolute beginners, for whom everything will be new." Or: "These are advanced researchers who want to learn more sophisticated methodology." Or: "This is a mixed-experience group who will need a multilevel lecture."

- What should they do or learn as a result of my lecture?

SAMPLE ANSWERS: "They should understand the importance of citing sources." Or: "They should be able to more accurately interpret the legal language within property conveyances."

- What do they have to gain by doing this? How will they benefit?

SAMPLE ANSWERS: "They will be able to better judge the reliability of their data." Or: "They will avoid overlooking important clues."

- What do I consider the most essential aspects of the topic? What order of priority should I assign to these? Should I limit the topic to a particular time frame or geographic area?

SAMPLE ANSWERS: "The five most common types of property conveyances found in British colonial records are [*arrange in order of commonness*]." Or: "The ten most often misunderstood terms are [*arrange in order of perceived need*]."

This preliminary analysis gives us a clearer concept of our subject, our audience, and our role as the link between them. It gives us control of the topic, narrowing it to a practical framework for a lecture full of pertinent advice and encouragement.

Title

This preliminary analysis is also a saving grace that enables us to avoid one sin at the podium audiences rarely forgive: a lecture that bears little resemblance to the announced topic. Program planners commonly ask for precisely worded titles long before we have time to actually write the lecture. Taking an hour (or several) to analyze the topic, before we word the clever title, will ensure that our topic does not take on a different incarnation during the writing process.

Many speakers pride themselves on their tempting titles—but temptation, unfulfilled, doesn't win a following. The title does have to accurately describe the lecture's content, but it doesn't have to begin with the words "How to. . . ." Often, a catchy lead followed by a descriptive subtitle will accomplish our need to be expressive and descriptive at the same time—for example: "What Now, Coach? How to Manage Large Quantities of Information for Genealogical Analysis." Yet a straightforward title such as "Effective Cash Flow Management by a Genealogist Who Actually Makes a Living at It" can draw crowds just as well. The bottom line in writing titles is that genealogical audiences want to know what they are getting and they want to get what they paid for.

Research

Sound research is the cornerstone of a good lecture. As genealogists we accept the fact

The bottom line in writing titles is that genealogical audiences want to know what they are getting and they want to get what they paid for.

that no written work can be better than the research upon which it is based. That same principle applies to lectures, which are—or should be—written works designed to be delivered orally. The research needed for oral presentations takes many forms. Even if we have studied the subject for years, we will need to verify stated facts and update our bibliography. Our lecture plan will spotlight areas in which we need additional data or more in-depth understanding of certain aspects of the topic—not only for our planned remarks but also to prepare ourselves for audience questions. Attendees may want to know, for example, if the phenomenon we describe just gradually disappeared by 1800 or did it end abruptly after a particular incident in 1784. They will want us to tell them if some aspect applies generally enough to cover a certain situation in their own research; if not, why not? Because we are billed as the "expert" on our subject, we must be able to state with confidence (not arrogance, *confidence*) whatever is intrinsic to our subject.

Lecture research is similar to client research. We prepare a plan that outlines the information needed and the sources most likely to supply it. It should be an efficient plan that produces the data quickly; few professionals have time to wander along unnecessary byways. As we execute the plan, we'll need to take adequate notes and cite sources properly. The most helpful of these may end up in our lecture handout; even if they don't, we'll still need to know our sources to answer audience questions.

Outline

If we truly know the subject, we'll have far more to say than time constraints allow. Talking really, really fast is not the solution.

Our preliminary analysis will have narrowed our subject to a workable topic. If we truly know the subject, however, we'll have far more to say than time constraints allow. Talking really, really fast is not the solution. (That, itself, is a problem.) The only approach that works is a well-planned outline that carefully culls the possibilities— followed by practice and precise timing. In this outline stage, we should

- select the major points we want audiences to remember.

- arrange them in logical sequence (perhaps chronological, step by step, or in order of importance).

- support each with subsidiary points.

- select anecdotes, case studies, examples, etc., to illustrate each important point. (These, we keep as simple, short, and relevant as possible—culling all side issues and matters of minor consequence.)

Effective speakers use many types of outlining techniques—from computer programs that collapse and expand outline points; to index cards, perhaps color-coded by outline level; to gummed notes that can be arranged and rearranged on the page. The method we choose is not nearly so important as the fact that *somehow* we create an outline.

Draft

The classic advice to writers, "Tell them what you're going to say, say it, then tell them what you said," also applies to speakers. In the opening section of our lecture, we state in a sentence or two what we will cover, together with some indication of the order in which we will treat it. Then we work our way through the points and supporting details on our outline. As we finish each major issue, we should summarize it briefly, then make a clear transition to the next item. The close of our lecture should bring our presentation full circle. We might recapitulate our major concerns, offer an encouraging restatement of the benefits of the sources or techniques discussed, or return to the opening statement and cast it in variant words. Whatever we do, however, in our summary we *refrain absolutely* from introducing new material.

Within this structure, three techniques warrant our special attention: the grabber, the transition, and the parting shot.

GRABBER
We never get a second chance to make a first impression: that old adage applies to speaking as well as meeting people. As speakers, we should "grab" the audience's attention in some manner that is brief, dramatic, and relevant. It need not be humorous, although a laugh does relax the audience and prepare them to listen more attentively. Grabbers are highly personal to the speaker and can be almost anything: a quip that relates the topic to common research problems; a mysterious quotation that will be explained in the lecture; a series of questions to determine the audience's experience level; or a good-natured remark about the size of the room, the seats, or the temperature. But we avoid the artificial joke and anything that smacks of school. (We don't tap the lectern impatiently or bark, "All right! Settle down now!")

TRANSITION
Effective lecturers have many ways of making (and marking) a smooth transition from one major point to another. Some are masters of the pause—the silent break in lecture rhythm. A plain but common approach is to say, "The next important point to consider is. . . ." If we are using slides or overhead transparencies on which we list key concepts, then we may plan our visual aids so that a certain design denotes a major break. Or we may use a recurring list of major ideas that we flash on the screen at transition spots, using an arrow or highlighting to show our shift to the next point.

PARTING SHOT
Memorable lectures often end with a vivid comment that lodges in the audience's memory and reminds them later of the lecture content. This "parting shot" can be almost anything: a restatement of the grabber, with a new twist derived from the lecture; a dramatic, one-sentence endorsement of the sources or methods we have mentioned; or a "just-between-you-and-me" plea to save and study the lecture handout. However, our grabbers and parting shots must be memorized; they lose all effect if we read them or, worse yet, garble their delivery.

Final form

When we make cookies, we decide on the recipe, then gather the ingredients and blend them—but we still don't have cookies at that point. The dough has to be cut out and baked, and the baking has to be timed. When we write a speech, we decide on the

> Our grabbers and parting shots should be memorized; they lose all effect if we read them or, worse yet, garble their delivery.

topic, gather the information, and blend the details. That leaves us with a rough draft—raw dough—not a speech that's ready to be served. We still have to shape our dough, cut away the excess, and bake it at exactly the right time and temperature to produce the crisp, savory treat our audiences expect. Speaking manuals offer an endless array of techniques for the shaping and baking, from memory maps to storyboards. In genealogy, where lecturers must *teach* as well as speak, two approaches are common: the script and the detailed outline.

- *Script.* Nothing is more reassuring than a script—properly prepared and used. Writing the text word for word and polishing it allows us to phrase our thoughts precisely, time our lecture repeatedly, and trim or expand our revision until it is exactly the right length. To be effective, though, our script must be written to *sound* natural. This means no stiff, overly formal language and no tightly packed sentences. The rhythms and speech patterns of our written words have to match that of ordinary conversation. On the other hand, as reassuring as a script can be, it has a drawback: it encourages reading—another sin for which audiences don't forgive the "speaker." Any temptation to read can and must be overcome by repeated rehearsals until the text is comfortably committed to memory. On the script itself, we can highlight keywords or phrases that will stimulate our recall of the next block of text. Whatever techniques we use, the key consideration is to prepare the pages in a way that lets us maintain eye contact with the audience without losing our place in the script.

- *Detailed outline.* Condensing our polished and well-timed draft into a detailed outline we can speak from means *flexibility.* We can alter the lecture, mid-delivery, in response to audience reaction or responses to our questions. However, speaking from an outline has its disadvantage, too: it makes our presentation difficult to time accurately. As a safeguard, we might insert flags throughout the outline, marking 10- or 15-minute intervals, so that during the lecture we are aware of how we are progressing timewise. Whatever controls we use, speaking from an outline requires us to exercise stern discipline in our practice sessions and at the podium.

Speaking from an outline requires us to exercise stern discipline in our practice sessions and at the podium.

Whether we opt for a script or a detailed outline, our lecture language must be straightforward and understandable. We have to use correct terminology for our subject but be certain to define unfamiliar words in the lecture and the handout. We should avoid technical jargon (not everyone knows that GRO means the General Register Office at Edinburgh), as well as clichés, obscure euphemisms, excessive slang, long words, and convoluted sentences. We should prepare our presentation in the active voice ("he did it") rather than the passive ("it was done"); but above all, what we say should be expressed in *our* voice. If city-slicker is our style, we shouldn't try country-boy—or try to assume the accent of the region in which we speak.

Enhancements

Lecture enhancements commonly include two types of materials: what the audience members see while they are in the room (visual aids) and what they take with them when they leave (the handout or the society's syllabus with our complimentary material included). Both are essential parts of a quality lecture.

VISUAL AIDS

Audiences learn in basically three ways: hearing, seeing, and doing. Visual aids depict graphically the main points we make orally, so that two of the three learning processes are involved. To be effective, visuals should be so directly relevant to the lecture topic and so well integrated into the presentation that the oral and visual components merge into a single learning experience. To get that effect, we should be sure that our visual aids are legible and we must carefully gauge their possible impact. If the audience is confused, entranced, or upset by what is on the screen, it cannot listen well. If attendees are racing to copy data from the screen before it blinks off, they are probably not listening at all—and *listening* is what an oral presentation is all about. Visual aids are best used to

- illustrate information (examples: a migration-route map, or sample documents).

- emphasize a point (examples: a brief list of lecture points that highlights the one being discussed, or a cartoon that makes the point humorously).

- demonstrate a technique (examples: genealogical charts showing documentation; or a series of overlays showing development of a tract map).

Options

The visual aids most commonly used for genealogical lecturing are overhead transparencies and slides (traditional or computer-driven).

Slides are often preferred because of their portability. However, they require advance preparation, because they take time to produce commercially, and they cannot be altered at the last minute. When we properly prepare them, we can rely on our slides being legible in a large room. Although they usually require a lower-than-normal level of lighting, we should design them so that a *dark* room is not necessary. Photographs, maps, and detailed line drawings are generally more suited for slides than for overhead transparencies.

Transparencies are relatively inexpensive and can be changed at the last minute by the speaker. They are handy when we want to draw on the visual or turn its orientation to demonstrate a point. To do this, however, the overhead projector must be within arm's length and at the right height relative to the microphone. Although transparencies are generally less legible than slides in a large room, they can be effective if the projector is far enough away from a bright, large screen and the overheads themselves are prepared in larger print. The major negative factor to consider, where transparencies are concerned, is their sheer weight. Speakers who use thirty to fifty visuals per hour are far less likely to choose transparencies—especially when traveling out of town to deliver multiple lectures.

Using visual aids effectively requires careful planning and attention to detail. Figure 56 addresses several areas in which the details make a drastic difference in the effectiveness of our presentations.

> Visuals should be so well integrated into the presentation that oral and visual components merge into a single learning experience.

LECTURING

FIG. 56
TIPS FOR
MASTERING VISUAL AIDS

Preparation

- Text should follow one basic rule: the fewer the words the greater the comprehension. Strip all text down to keywords.

- Font size, applied to standard-sized slide or transparency templates, should be 20 to 24 points for projection in a small room and 36 to 40 points for a large room.

- Sans-serif fonts are more legible on screen than serif fonts. (See discussion of font types in chapter 27.)

- Text typed in mixed upper and lower cases is more legible than text typed in all upper-case.

- Slide text, to be readable when projected, should be readable to the naked eye when the slide is held to the light.

- Slide masters, if prepared on paper for a photographer, should be run on bright-white, calendared paper. (See discussion of paper stock in chapter 27.)

- Negative slides (white text on intense black background) provide better visibility than positive slides (black text on white background).

- Color slides lose visibility in large rooms with standard lighting; to avoid plunging audiences into blackness, choose colors wisely—using dark or vivid background and white or very light letters.

- Plastic frames for slides are more durable than cardboard frames and are less likely to bend and jam the projector.

- Glass slides are more durable than those on plastic film, which can warp if subjected to hot or moist temperatures in vehicles or airplane luggage compartments.

- Orientation (vertical *vs.* horizontal layout) should not be mixed within a single presentation, if possible to avoid. Horizontal orientation is better; a vertical layout often means that bottom lines of text are visible only to people in the front rows.

- Transparency overlays—when used to build a list, plat, or migration route, for example—require careful calibration to ensure each overlay matches precisely.

- Transparencies may need to be mounted in cardboard frames or easel notebooks designed for lecturing, to prevent static electricity that can cause them to cling together.

- Masked portions of a transparency (commonly accomplished with gummed sheets) create a black block on the screen that tells the audience something more will be revealed; we should never use masking unless we intend to eventually reveal the hidden material.

- Copyrighted maps or artwork should not be used without permission of the copyright holder, and credit should appear on the slide or transparency.

- Dual production of slides *and* transparencies, for each lecture, is a useful safeguard. No matter how explicit we are in specifying the equipment we need, we may still discover that the only projector available in the lecture room is the "wrong" type.

Preparation

Most word-processing and drawing programs offer templates for slides and transparencies. Let's use them. They are preconfigured to provide a correctly sized text block—thereby eliminating the possibility that part of a slide may end up masked by its frame or that a transparency may be too large for a projector. (The standard size for slide preparation is $7\frac{1}{3}$ by 11 inches. For overhead transparencies, the maximum feasible limit is 8 by 10 inches, given that transparency film is commonly sold in $8\frac{1}{2}$-by-11-inch sheets and that most overhead projectors have a 10-by-10-inch glass stage.) Drawing programs, which also include the ability to handle small amounts of text, offer more flexibility for alterations and resizing than do word-processing programs— an important consideration if we prepare our material for both types of projections or later decide to convert from one to the other. Using a drawing program, for example, we can select or *marquee* all material on the slide master and shrink it slightly to resize it for the transparency—although we should do no more than *slight* stretching or shrinking, lest the letterforms and graphics end up visibly distorted. By comparison, a word-processing program generally requires us to resize each line of text and other elements individually. Figure 57, which focuses on the preparation of handouts, has useful advice for selecting typefaces and sizes that applies to slides as well.

- *Slides* are commonly produced by one of three processes: paper masters that we send to a photographer; digital files that we send to a service bureau; or digital data that we show directly from our computer using presentation software and an LCD [liquid crystal display] projector. Each has its special considerations:

PAPER MASTERS

For the crispest images, we should print the masters on bright-white, hard-surfaced paper, with a good-quality laser printer. Color masters are possible if we have color printers; or we may be able to add spot color manually. For black and white slides, we can improve our projection quality by asking our photographer to produce negative slides—white print on a black background—rather than the standard black print on a white field. If the map or artwork that we want to use is too small for the recommended $7\frac{1}{3}$-by-11-inch template, we can avoid the loss of quality caused by photocopy enlargements if we simply mount the artwork on standard paper and ask the photographer to shoot the artwork at maximum magnification. Our choice of photographer is a prime consideration. We are usually far better served by taking our masters to one who specializes in presentation slides. Shops that offer quick service and mass processing of film rolls do not usually produce the strong black-white contrast needed for high-quality visuals.

DIGITAL FILES

When we produce all slide material in a software program, we have the option of sending our digital files to a service bureau for direct production. This elimination of the paper-master stage almost always results in a higher quality slide. Service bureaus typically accept data on disk or by modem, so long as we use software that they support and so long as we prepare our files according to their particular specifications. As a rule, most service bureaus accept recent versions of the most commonly used graphic and word-processing software, and the preparation they ask for is seldom difficult. The company

Drawing programs, which also include the ability to handle small amounts of text, offer more flexibility for alterations and resizing than do word-processing programs.

FIG. 57
TIPS FOR PREPARING
HANDOUT MASTERS

Design

- "Color" makes a page more attractive. On handouts, color is achieved through contrasts between white space and various intensities of black type and other design elements. Headlines (title, author's name and affiliation, etc.) that are significantly larger in type than the body of the text provide color contrast. Subheads that are moderately larger than the text body or in a complementary font add variation in color, while helping to direct the eye to breaks in subject matter.

- Layout (margins, type size, etc.) should adhere to the requirements of the sponsor, if our material is to be part of a published syllabus.

- Point size should be proportional to the layout. If we use one column on standard 8½-by-11-inch sheets, then a larger size (11 or 12 points) is appropriate. If we format two or three columns on the page, then a smaller size (9, 10, or 11 points, depending upon the x-height of the font) renders better balance.

- Proportionally spaced fonts (for example, Garamond, Goudy, Palatino, Times Roman) create a more professional appearance than monospace fonts (e.g., Courier), which appear to come from a typewriter.

- Serif fonts (e.g., the present Century Schoolbook) are more legible for large blocks of type. Sans-serif (e.g., the Helvetica font used for marginal headings on this page) are less legible when used for text blocks, but provide attractive contrast and color.

  (More than one serif font should not be used in the same layout—nor more than one sans-serif font—without graphic-design training to guide us in the mix.)

Content

- Addresses referred to in the lecture should be included in the handout.

- Artwork, maps, or textual material from any other source—anything more than a brief quote—should be accompanied by permission to reuse that material.

- Bibliographies should be numbered for easy reference and location during the lecture.

- Bibliographies should include every published source mentioned in the lecture. Annotated bibliographies are especially appreciated by audiences, who value our assessments of the works we recommend.

- Citations should be complete, by the standards of modern genealogical scholarship.

- Clip art is effective if it makes a pertinent point—otherwise, it looks gimmicky.

- Content should be updated if this handout has been used before.

- Copyright notices should also appear on each page that meet national and international copyright-registration guidelines. If we wish to grant partial reproduction rights, conditions should be explicitly stated.

- Handwritten notations diminish quality, unless we are skilled calligraphers.

- Lecture titles and speaker names are essential items on every page.

- Maps and other graphics of diminished quality should be redrawn.

- Outlines, if presented, should be in standard academic format.

- Proofreading—for consistency, grammar, spacing, spelling, and typography—is never complete until we ask someone else to carefully read what we think is already perfect.

we choose will fax or e-mail its instructions for our particular software, or we may download instructions from its website. Most providers also request that we download (or they will mail us on disk) their preferred print driver. Once we design our slides to our satisfaction, we need only save the file to the specified driver, "zip" the file to reduce its size, and then revisit the website for modeming. Or, we may mail the saved file on disk. Service can be as quick as overnight—or just hours if we live in the city in which the provider is located—although we pay a premium for this level of service.

LCD PROJECTION

Using presentation software, a laptop computer, and an LCD projector, we can deliver presentations that are technologically impressive as well as factually accurate and personally dynamic. Animation, fade-outs, freezes, zooms, and other cinematic effects are commonplace; and—as with transparencies—we can make last-minute changes. Again, there are trade-offs. While the costlier projectors keep images legible under ordinary lighting, they can still lose effectiveness in large rooms. Their cost may be a significant concern for us—as it is for program chairs whom we may expect to rent projectors for us. Traveling with our computer (and possibly the projector) involves both economic risk and inconvenience that we do not have with slides or transparencies. And, technology being as it is, we can face a greater risk of unforeseen glitches during our presentation.

- *Transparencies* can be entirely produced from our desktop if we have a laser or quality ink-jet printer. Using plain paper, we experiment with layout and content, saving our costly transparency film for the final product. Color is easy to add, given the relatively low price of color, ink-jet printers; or we can purchase transparencies with colored or decorative frames. The most important consideration, where transparency film is concerned, is that we carefully match it to the type of printer on which we plan to use it. Laser and ink-jet printers require different finishes for the ink to adhere, and photocopiers require transparencies of still another type. Improper film can also jam or melt, causing serious equipment damage. If we use a photocopier to enlarge maps, diagrams, or documents, we should take special care to ensure that the magnification does not diminish the readability of the material. We may need to skillfully draw over any faint or broken lines on the final copy.

HANDOUTS

Even the most attentive audiences will have trouble remembering all our important points once they leave the lecture hall. Note taking is often difficult or impossible for them, given that theater-style seating is common and lighting is often reduced for better showing of the visual aids. We help our audiences overcome these handicaps by providing written material that summarizes our main points, reproduces certain key graphics, provides technical data to supplement the lecture, or suggests further reading. Effective handouts are neither word-for-word drafts of our lecture nor skeletal outlines (although many audiences do appreciate *detailed* outlines), and they should not include our opening grabber or our parting shot.

Whether we distribute our material as independent handouts, or whether we submit them to the sponsoring agency for publication in a syllabus with material from other speakers or the agency itself, the same basic parameters apply. We produce the masters;

Effective handouts are neither word-for-word drafts of our lecture nor skeletal outlines.

LECTURING

Within the genealogical field, four pages per lecture hour is the "industry standard" for handouts and syllabus material.

the sponsor typically reproduces them in sufficient quantity for the audience. Within the genealogical field, four pages per lecture hour is the "industry standard" for handouts and syllabus material. If we proffer less than that, our audience may feel shortchanged or conclude that we put minimal time and effort into the preparation. Most genealogical speakers find it a challenge to reduce the universe of possibilities to "just" four pages. Doing so is a test of our judgment as to what materials are the most essential, as well as our ability to organize and lay out the material attractively and concisely. The effort is worth it. Well-designed and accurate handouts help us as much as they do our audiences.

Our layout usually represents a balancing act between the standards of typography, guidelines of the society, and the customs and needs of our field. For example:

- *Bibliographic citations* should be in good academic format. Genealogical convention, however, calls for one modification: style manuals in the academic and publishing arenas specify that bibliographies be alphabetized but not numbered. Genealogical lecturers number them. We do so because, amid our lectures, we often refer to certain items in the bibliography; and our audiences prefer numbers that we can quickly cite and they can instantly spot.

- *Layout and presentation* should conform to the specifications of the sponsoring agency. Occasionally, a society or program chair may request that we format our pages in a manner that is inappropriate for the material we need to deliver. The instructions, perhaps, may specify that everything be typed in a single column of a certain point size, when we have tables or forms that are essential but cannot be formatted in that manner. In such cases, a tactful discussion of the problem with the sponsor—illustrated by samples of the attractively formatted material we propose to include—will usually effect a compromise.

If we are new lecturers or experienced ones who would like to improve the graphic quality of our handouts, we can find a variety of models (both positive and negative) by studying the syllabi for the annual conferences of the Federation of Genealogical Societies and the National Genealogical Society.

Like visual aids, handout masters should be prepared on a calendared, bright-white paper, using a laser printer. While some ink-jets produce almost equal quality, their ink is more likely to smear if the masters suffer moist conditions in the mail or during assembly or reproduction. Each page needs a number for accurate assembly. If we are distributing our own handouts directly to the audience, we may type the numbers onto the pages in a customary location. If we are submitting the masters to the sponsor for inclusion in a syllabus, we should *not* type our number on any page. Instead, using a nonreproducing light-blue, soft-lead pencil, we lightly note the numbers—preferably on the back. We mail the masters flat—never fold them—in a sturdy envelope reinforced with cardboard. Most sponsors prefer two copies of each master as a safeguard in case of mishap. As a general rule (the national conferences and their large, published syllabi are a common exception), the sponsors also need from us a statement explicitly granting them the right to reproduce our copyrighted material. Otherwise, their local print shop may not permit the reproduction of our pages.

Delivery

Rehearsal

At this point, our entire oral presentation is still on paper. It cannot stay there. Having prepared what we are going to say, it's time to prepare how we are going to say it. Responsible preparation means *practice, practice, practice*—with our family, friends, mirrors, and tape recorders. The object of these rehearsals is to fine-tune all elements of delivery: the text, timing, and visual aids, as well as our poise at the lectern.

TEXT

In the first few practices, we edit the text at every spot where the written words do not come naturally when spoken. As we continue, we shift our focus from the words to the *expression* with which we voice them. A monotone will not do. A singsong rhythm will not do. Let's experiment with changes in voice level, speaking speed, and even body posture to emphasize our major points and subjugate the minor ones. One helpful technique is the "empty chair routine"—we put a real chair before us and envision a beloved relative sitting there as we speak, then we see a friend, next a neutral stranger, and finally an enemy. The relative will spur us to avoid boring our audience, the friend will help us correct faults, the stranger will prod us to greater energy in our delivery, and the enemy will remind us to be accurate and precise.

TIMING

We should time our lecture in each practice session. We allow a few minutes for our introducer's remarks and any necessary announcements about the use of handout material or tape recordings. (If we must do that housekeeping detail ourselves, we should practice it, too.) We include pauses for emphasis and to change visuals, then add five minutes or so for miscellaneous interruptions. When the presentation turns out to be too long, we do not plan to talk faster; we omit something. Finally, we mark our lecture notes with timed reference points (e.g., "10 minutes to here").

VISUAL AIDS

Not only must our visual aids be relevant, but their relevance must be immediately clear to the audience. Thus, as we practice, we adjust the timing of a visual's appearance on screen to suit its purpose. A map, for example, might appear early in its discussion so our audience sees it as we speak; but a pedigree chart might wait until after its use is explained. We should mark our lecture notes for the beginning *and end* of each visual's time on the screen—and we should practice the technical side of handling visuals, also. If someone else will operate the projector, we need to practice together on timing and signals. If we will run the machine ourselves, we must learn to do it smoothly. Overheads should be placed accurately the first time, not on the second or third attempt; and they must not be twitched about as we speak. The location of "advance" and "reverse" buttons on our slide projectors should be memorized, not punched haphazardly. After our last practice before giving the lecture, we should make certain that all visuals are in their correct sequence, oriented right side up.

Responsible preparation means *practice, practice, practice*—with our family, friends, mirrors, and tape recorders.

POISE

It is not necessary to eliminate all our ingrained habits, but it is necessary to control the annoying ones (verbal and physical); and many disasters that test our poise can be avoided with thoughtful anticipation and preparation.

- *Verbal mannerisms* are usually the easiest to manage—voice volume can be adjusted to avoid mumbling into the lectern or swallowing the ends of sentences. Regionalisms should be kept to a reasonable minimum: what we think is cute, our audience might not. Mispronunciations and malapropisms are not mannerisms; they are mistakes that must be corrected. Nervous verbal tics ("uh," "ah," "ya know," and all their kith and kin) must be eliminated.

- *Physical mannerisms* can be somewhat harder to control. If we really must use our hands to speak naturally, then we should change those frequent, awkward movements into occasional full-fledged gestures that coincide with the discussion (for example, making a large circle as we speak of "the whole family"). We should severely limit our eyeglass-adjusting, tie-tugging, hair-patting activities to an occasional or humorous punctuation. Clutching the lectern, leaning on it for support, or swaying back and forth are mannerisms of the nervous beginner and should be excised for poised delivery.

- *Disasters* will strike. Equipment will fail, explode, or crash to the floor; or we'll fall up the steps to the platform. Caustic (or embarrassed) remarks about whose fault it is are pointless; it is better to find a quick, imaginative solution and carry on with good grace. Advance preparation can often minimize the effects of a disaster. We can prepare a few humorous, all-purpose ad-libs so they pop into our mind when needed. We can bring both transparencies and slides with us, in case our projector request has been misunderstood. We might bring both small-room and large-room transparencies with us—in case the attendance proves to be more or less than we anticipated. We might rehearse an alternate, nonvisual lecture as a backup should there be irreparable equipment failure. We can mark lecture notes with passages to omit, should there be a lengthy interruption. And we should always carry a spare set of lecture notes, one in our luggage that will be checked and one on our person, as a safeguard against lost baggage or mislaid briefcases.

Presentation

Preparedness is our watchword, on site as well as in rehearsal. Figure 58 offers helpful tips in that regard. If possible, we visit the lecture room the day before our presentation to plan for any adaptations necessary in the management of our delivery, lighting, or visuals. In any case, we should arrive at least one hour ahead of time—ideally before the room fills with attendees eager to introduce themselves and share their problems. We test the microphone and learn to adjust its height and volume; we test the visual equipment and adjust its placement if necessary and possible. We decide which lights need to be dimmed or doused, who will do it, and on what signals. If we move about as we speak, we should notice the placement of steps, drop-offs, and electrical cords. We survey the room for other sources of possible distraction and devise

Clutching the lectern, leaning on it for support, or swaying back and forth are mannerisms of the nervous beginner and should be excised for poised delivery.

FIG. 58
TIPS FOR
POLISHED LECTURES

- Equipment needs and instructions should be clearly conveyed to the program chair—in advance and in writing—to ensure that correct types of microphones, projectors, and screens are set up prior to the session.

- Early arrival on our part ensures that we have time to check the equipment and have problems resolved.

- Planting the script on the lectern before we are introduced is dangerous. A nervous introducer may walk off with it.

- Professionally packaging the script we carry to the podium adds polish. A sheaf of papers is intimidating. A briefcase is too cumbersome. An attractive folder with open sides, one that is thin and will lie flat, is just right.

- Lapel or lavaliere microphones are needed when we must move from lectern to projector or from lectern to screen.

- Masked portions of a transparency (commonly done with gummed sheets) create a black block on the screen that tells the audience something more will be revealed; we should never remove the transparency without revealing that masked portion.

- Noisy overhead projectors should be turned off during periods that a transparency is not actually being shown and discussed.

- Screens should always be beside us, rather than behind us, so we do not have to turn away from the audience to point out items on the screen or to ensure that the remote projector has indeed advanced to the next slide.

- Hawking products from an educational forum is unseemly—this applies not only to our own books or tapes but also those of others. Works of scholarship and genealogical tools may be recommended, as appropriate. Presumably works of scholarship are cited for their *unique* content or value. With products, if they must be named, we try to recommend more than one that offers the helpful feature, to avoid the appearance of marketing a particular product.

- "I don't know" is okay to admit, when we truly don't know the answer to a question; we can then ask if someone in the audience has a suggestion. (If we have to say "I don't know" too often, we'd better study our subject more deeply!)

- Lists, addresses, and bibliographic citations should not be read during the lecture. We include them on the handout, as a numbered item amid the bibliography or resource list, so we can quickly reference them during our presentation.

- Quotes can add authority or "punch" but they should be short and used sparingly.

- "Thank you" is not an effective parting shot.

- Writing the program chair a "thank you" after we return home is sound business as well as courtesy. It may generate return engagements or a reply with positive remarks about our performance, which we can add to our presentation portfolio for use when subsequent groups inquire about our offerings.

strategies to minimize or ignore them. Finally, we stand at the lectern and memorize the room thoroughly enough to see it in our mind when we close our eyes.

Then we leave—and find a quiet, private place somewhere. Reading our preliminary plan will switch our focus from our apprehensive self back to the audience. Again, we close our eyes, visualize the room, and say aloud our opener and the first few paragraphs, while we listen to ourselves speak in the context of *that* place. Well-psyched now, we can return to the lecture room—with at least ten minutes to spare and with full cognizance that *the instant we step into the lecture hall* we are officially "on." Everyone in the room knows who we are and why we are there, and they expect us to be serenely confident. Let's not disappoint them.

At the lectern, after we have adjusted the microphone, thanked the introducer, and made any necessary (and unavoidable) announcements, we *pause*. We look out at the audience and choose several "eye-contact" points—individuals we will look at again and again as we speak. We'll need at least five, spread out across the room so our eyes travel and our head moves naturally from side to side. During this pause, we look at each eye contact in turn, smile warmly, and consciously relax our body posture. Then, *without looking at our notes,* we launch into our grabber. The lecture has begun.

We have rehearsed well. We are confident. We know exactly what we plan to say. We are prepared to fill the needs of our audience and to field, with grace, any mishaps or miscreants. *We are professional lecturers.*

> The instant we step into the lecture hall we are officially "on." Everyone knows who we are and why we are there, and they expect us to be serenely confident.

Evaluation

We finish our lecture. The crowds throng and they praise us profusely, as a prelude to asking their burning question about their toughest research problem. We leave with a heady sense of having weathered another challenge and delivered exactly what our audience came to learn. But are we sure? Was the praise truly sincere or pleasantly courteous? How do we know? Something more is needed.

We have prepared for our audiences something they could take home and study—and we need them to do the same for us. We need their feedback, anonymously and frankly. If we lecture at a major institute, odds are that the administration has developed a critique it regularly uses for all presenters. Elsewhere, that may not be the rule. If and when critiques are not customarily supplied by the sponsoring society or agency, we have two options. We might (indeed, should) encourage the organization to adopt a critique form and offer to help in its development. Or, for those occasions when we are the sole presenter, we may provide the society with our own form, thoughtfully constructed to allow our audiences to provide useful feedback, with reasonable ease. Figure 59 offers one sample.

Business Management

Booking agents are as rare as five-figure honorariums in the field of genealogical lecturing. As professionals, we attend to all business details. Bookings, contracts, and financial negotiations are our own responsibility—travel arrangements usually are.

FIG. 59
CRITIQUE FORM

[Society • Date • Speaker]

Evaluator's background:

Number of prior seminars/conferences *of this type* I have attended: _____.

Genealogy for me is a hobby _____; a profession _____; part-time profession_____.

Years engaged in genealogical research (select current status and note years):
    New researcher _____; intermediate researcher _____; advanced researcher _____.

Areas of particular interest: Ethnic _____.

              Geographic _____.

              Other _____.

Evaluation of program:
(Please rate each item 1–5, with 5 being the highest possible score.)

SESSION NO.	A	B	C	D
Speaker's presentation style				
Usefulness of subject matter				
Value of visual aids				
Quality of visual aids				
Value of handout material				
Quality of handout material				

Helpful comments:

_____

_____

_____

_____

_____

_____

* Permission to reproduce and use or adapt this form is hereby granted, so long as this manual is cited as its source.

By the time we consider a lecturing career, we should have attended national conferences and institutes as well as regional ones.

Bookings

Few genealogical lecturers are engaged on the basis of their advertising. They normally speak by invitations, which are based on their reputation for (*a*) speaking with authority on subjects that fit a program theme or prospective audience; and (*b*) delivering well-prepared presentations that draw crowds. Earning a reputation takes time, but designing a suitable and honorable strategy for getting on the program can speed up the process.

STRATEGY

By the time we consider a lecturing career, we should be advanced genealogists with accurate and broad understanding of sources and extensive, hands-on background in sound methodology. Presumably, we have considerable experience with genealogical education from the audience side—having attended national conferences and institutes as well as regional ones—and are thoroughly familiar with local, state, and national lecture-sponsoring societies. We should also familiarize ourselves with the requirements for certification as a genealogical lecturer and chart a path that will qualify us to attain that credential. If we are not already members of the Genealogical Speakers Guild and the Association of Professional Genealogists, now is the time to join—for both education and networking.

To begin lecturing, we examine our own community. Local program planners are normally the ones most hard-pressed to find new speakers and topics. We identify significant subjects that are not being addressed—those that suit our areas of enthusiasm, experience, and knowledge. After we develop and practice two or three lectures, so that we can deliver them instantly, it is time to approach local planners and offer to speak for the "going rate" (which, even today, can be just a handshake and a thank-you). When our offers are accepted, we should resolve never to give less than our very best, even if ours is the last lecture on a long day and just ten people remain. Taping our presentation, for our own post-performance dissection, will help us adjust the contents and delivery appropriately. Gradually, then, we expand the number and scope of our topics to establish a reputation for versatility as well as competence.

PRESENTATION PACKET

As our reputation grows and we are approached more often for lectures, we will need an easily duplicated portfolio of materials to send in response to inquiries. A typical presentation packet includes

- a list of our lecture titles.
- an enticing one-paragraph summary of each, suitable for publicity flyers, with a notation of the experience level for which each is designed.
- a resumé of our genealogical qualifications and lecturing experience.
- a fee schedule, covering honorarium and expenses.
- a brief personal biography, with a genealogical focus, for newspaper publicity (reporters often prefer a "popular angle" rather than a technical one).
- a recent and reasonably flattering photograph.

- newspaper publicity from prior engagements—especially ones that reflect our special spark and pizazz.
- thank-you letters or testimonials from societies we have already addressed—assuming these convey obvious enthusiasm or good results that our appearance generated.

Needless to say, all items should be of good quality and reflect our personal and professional approach to lecturing.

LECTURE PROPOSALS

When we have enough experience and confidence to hazard a national audience, it is time to watch the major newsletters for "calls for papers" issued by conference sponsors. For those that appear suitable to our expertise, we respond promptly, offering at least one lecture proposal—perhaps up to four, but more are seldom welcomed. (Figures 60 and 61 offer two samples.) Canned proposals rarely work. We need to tailor our descriptions to the planned program and adhere precisely to the announced guidelines. To give each lecture a better chance of being chosen, we may need to redesign it, re-research it, and retitle it to reflect the program theme. If, for example, the conference slogan is "Migrations through the Middle West," we might revise our lecture on the federal census to emphasize its use in migration studies and alter the title accordingly. However, two pieces of counsel are worth applying here:

- We should keep the title descriptive of the whole lecture. Misleading the planner or the audience will ensure that our first national lecture is our last.
- We never retitle a lecture whose content has not been substantially altered. Anyone who has heard the presentation under the old title and is attracted by a different title will go away feeling gypped—and they tend to say so every time they hear that speaker's name thereafter.

Correspondence and contracts

As with any business writing, correspondence with a sponsoring society should be prompt, clear, direct, and "business-friendly." Although details of scheduling and fees may have been worked out in personal contact, we must confirm every detail in writing. Contractual agreements tend to vary, depending upon the scope of the event and the formality of the sponsoring agency. For national conferences, the sponsoring society (rather than the individual speaker) provides the contract. Some limited options are built into those agreements (for example, a speaker may choose to allow or deny audio-taping), but most terms (finances, travel arrangements, room accommodations, etc.) are set by society policy and are not open for negotiation. Sponsors of local and regional conferences and seminars are generally more flexible; as a rule, speakers present their own contracts (and terms) for these engagements—which may or may not be accepted, of course.

Legally, a contract can be as simple as a letter or an exchange of letters between the society and the speaker, so long as they spell out the performance terms and are countersigned or acknowledged in writing by the recipient. A better practice is to devise

Sponsors of local and regional conferences and seminars are generally more flexible; as a rule, speakers present their own contracts (and terms) for these engagements.

FIG. 60

LECTURE PROPOSAL:

SAMPLE A

LECTURE PROPOSAL
2000 NGS Conference In the States

───────

"Grand Army of the Republic"
By Kathleen W. Hinckley, CGRS

PROGRAM SUMMARY:
The Grand Army of the Republic [GAR] was a fraternal organization for Union veterans of the Civil War that reached its largest membership in 1890: nearly one-half million veterans representing slightly over 50 percent of all surviving Union veterans of the Civil War. The records created by the GAR can reveal birth, death, burial and service data.

LECTURE OUTLINE:

    I. Introduction to G.A.R.
       A. Origin and History
       B. Purpose
       C. Membership Requirements
       D. Auxiliary Organizations

    II. Types of Records
       A. Post Descriptive Books
       B. Post Record and Minute Books
       C. Rosters
       D. Transfer Cards
       E. Other

    III. Location of Records
       A. Family History Library
       B. Internet
       C. Other Libraries and Archives

    IV. Case Study: Elias H. Webb

AUDIENCE:
Beginning/Intermediate/Advanced

ABOUT THE SPEAKER:
Kathleen Hinckley, CGRS, is a professional genealogist and private investigator specializing in locating living persons. She is Executive Secretary of the Association of Professional Genealogists and the author of *Locating Lost Family Members & Friends* (Cincinnati: Betterway, 1999) and "Tracking Twentieth-Century Ancestors" in *The Source: A Guidebook of American Genealogy*, rev. ed. (Salt Lake City: Ancestry, 1997). She has lectured at national conferences since 1985, is a columnist for *FamilyTreeMaker Online*, and has articles published in *APGQ, NGSQ, BCG OnBoard, GSG SPEAK!* and *Heritage Quest*.

Kathleen W. Hinckley • Family Detective
P.O. Box 740637• Arvada, CO 80006-0637 • 303-422-9371
hinckleyk@mindspring.com
www.familydetective.com

FIG. 61
LECTURE PROPOSAL:
SAMPLE B

Elizabeth Shown Mills

DATE: 17 March 1999

SUBJECT: **2000 NGS Conference Program Proposal**

CONTACT INFO:
Phone: 205-752-4031
Fax: 205-752-5979
E-mail: eshown@msn.com
Address: 1732 Ridgedale Drive, Tuscaloosa, AL 35406-1942

LECTURE TITLE: **"Finding Females: Wives, Mothers, Daughters, Sisters, and Paramours!"**

SYNOPSIS: One of the toughest challenges faced by researchers, among all ethnic groups, is the difficulty of identifying and tracking females. Wives and mothers traditionally have been "supporting characters" to the roles played by their husbands and sons—bearing no known name other than that of the males whom they married or bore. Historically, social mores and law codes made them "second class citizens," without a legal identity of their own and few rights or opportunities to create the range of records that genealogists customarily use to track males. This discussion presents an array of resources—and, more importantly, methodological techniques—by which the identities of elusive females can be established. Actual case studies illustrate the suggested methodology.

(Detailed outline attached)

PROGRAM SUMMARY: Wives and mothers are history's "supporting characters"—bearing no known name other than that of the males whom they married or bore. This discussion presents an array of resources and methodological techniques by which elusive females can be identified.

LEVEL: Mixed: Beginner to Advanced

AUDIO-VISUALS: 43 color slides covering methodological principles & case studies

LECTURING EXPERIENCE: NGS and FGS national conference lecturer, 1983—
Samford University IGHR lecturer/course coordinator, 1979—
NIGR lecturer, 1985–1997
State, regional, other national, & international conferences, 1974—

Certified Genealogist
Certified Genealogical Lecturer
President & Fellow, American Society of Genealogists
Editor, *National Genealogical Society Quarterly*
Trustee & former president, Board for Certification of Genealogists

a specific contract that contains all necessary detail in one document. Figure 4 (see chapter 6, Executing Contracts) provides one sample contract for a lecture engagement. Others have appeared randomly in *Speak!* (the newsletter of the Genealogical Speakers Guild). In general, any such contract should cover the following items:

- *Identification:* names of the contracting parties; date, time, and place of the lecture(s).

- *Travel and accommodation:* mode of transportation; type of sleeping room needed; responsibilities of society and speaker for making reservations.

- *Fees and expenses:* amount of honorarium, date payment is due; specific expenses to be reimbursed.

- *Contingencies:* conditions under which lecture can be canceled, with or without penalty to one party or another (with specifics).

- *Audiovisual requirements:* microphone type (if nonstandard), projector type, other specific equipment, special room-arrangement (if applicable).

- *Handout materials:* submission date, format (if applicable), financial responsibility for duplicating, physical responsibility for distribution, permission (either given or withheld) to sell or distribute excess copies or reprints and financial considerations surrounding such cases (royalties, etc.).

- *Lecture taping:* permission to tape (given or withheld); if given, then to whom (audience, company, society), what type (audio, video), and financial considerations.

- *Approval rights:* arrangements and deadlines for submitting planned publicity, program flyers, etc., to lecturer for approval (common for local seminars with limited speakers, but not for major conferences).

Our correspondence with the society will also include noncontractual information: when and by what means we will arrive, whether we will be met at the airport; when we should mail the handout master (if no deadline is stated in the contract); and, usually, miscellaneous questions and suggestions about program timing and room setup. Typically, there may be proffers of hospitality or social events, as well as communications with a publicity chairperson or local newspaper reporter. All such correspondence should be kept in the separate file we have set up for that event. Wisdom also suggests that we carry with us all correspondence relating to equipment, facilities, finances, and schedules.

Wisdom suggests that we carry with us all correspondence relating to equipment, facilities, finances, and schedules.

Financial negotiations

No matter how eager we may be to get on a program, it is unwise to speak without reasonable payment. We will work harder, the society will plan better, and the audience will be more appreciative if the engagement is put on a business footing. Because professionalism in genealogical lecturing is a relatively new phenomenon, defining "reasonable payment" can be a thorny problem. Historically we have received thanks in the form of a strange gewgaw, a good book, or a *token* check. (The term used today for a speaker's payment—*honorarium,* meaning no fee set or legally obtainable—reflects this history.) Nevertheless, in recent years the concept of fair payment for professional work has generated a few basic guidelines for expenses, fees, and royalties.

EXPENSES
Speakers should not expect to expend their own funds to deliver lectures. At a minimum, they should be reimbursed for all reasonable expenses relating to accommodations, meals, transportation, and registration for the event.

FEES
Speakers should expect to be paid for making their presentations. There are several ways to establish lecture fees: (*a*) We might find out what others are charging and set comparable fees—not an unreasonable technique, if we keep in mind our experience level; (*b*) we might judge how much in demand we are and charge what the market will bear—also not unreasonable, although we could price ourselves out of the market; and (*c*) we might develop a formula for arriving at an average per-lecture or per-day fee. One set of formulas, based on an eight-hour business day, is this:

1. Determine an hourly rate, based on our *lecturing* expertise;

2. Figure that a one-hour lecture is equal to one business day—i.e.,
    8 HOURS X 1 DAY X $___/HOUR = PER-LECTURE FEE

3. Figure that an all-day series or seminar equals four business days—i.e.,
    8 HOURS X 4 DAYS X $___/HOUR = PER-SEMINAR FEE

The above formulas represent the *minimal* amount of time that a speaker typically invests in a lecture or a seminar, *outside of actual lecture research, writing, and preparation of handouts and visual aids.* It includes (but certainly is not limited to) the time given to

- communicating with the society;
- making the necessary travel arrangements;
- assembling and packing materials to take with us;
- traveling to and from;
- actual time spent on site;
- unpacking and refiling lecture materials on our return; and
- post-event correspondence with the sponsors and with attendees who write follow-up letters for one reason or another.

Because the time needed for some of these activities (particularly travel and communication) varies, our compensation for one engagement will be slightly more advantageous than our hourly rate, while payment for another could be significantly less than that.

Whatever our approach, we should review our fee schedule at least annually. If it does not produce the hourly rate we need (or the one we feel is justified), then it

We should review our fee schedule at least annually. If it does not produce the hourly rate we need, then it warrants revision.

If our contract calls for payment the day of the event, we should bring with us an invoice that itemizes our fees and expenses. That provides the documentation from which the society pays us for our services.

warrants revision. Central to the concept of *honorarium* is the idea that payment is established by the sponsor. In today's world of professional lecturing, however, we should expect to establish our own payment goals and enter into normal business negotiations with the sponsors to meet these goals. When a lecture invitation includes a proffer markedly lower than our norm and negotiations have not produced a higher one, we must decide whether the honor and possible benefits of sponsorship by that organization justify the financial loss. If not, we are under no obligation to accept the invitation.

ROYALTIES

As a rule in genealogical lecturing (and a recent one, at that), royalties are paid only when lectures are *taped* for resale by the sponsoring society or a professional company whose services it engages. The standard has been 15 to 20 percent of the sale price, with payments made semiannually so long as a minimum has been earned. Royalties are not paid by major conference sponsors for *syllabus material* that is distributed to registrants or subsequently sold. (By accepted custom, they continue to sell only until they have depleted the stock that was printed for the estimated number of registrants.) However, some individual speakers do negotiate with local and regional sponsors for royalties on copies of the syllabus that are sold to nonregistrants.

DEVELOPMENT COSTS

Until per-lecture and per-seminar fees can be raised high enough to include gradual recovery of developmental costs, we cannot expect financial compensation for the hours needed to design, research, write, and rehearse a lecture. Nor can we expect reimbursement for the costs of producing visual aids. At the present time and for the foreseeable future, we can only view these costs as volunteer contributions to our audiences and the societies that sponsor educational forums. If we are also vendors, another consideration exists. While we are expected *not* to advertise our products amid an educational presentation (as opposed to a specifically labeled product demonstration for which the sponsor does not pay us), the exhibit hall can still offer an opportunity to augment our income. At best, if we belong to the vast majority of speakers who do not vend, we may simply "write off" our heavy investment in lecture development as a form of advertising—an opportunity to showcase our research expertise and our writing talents before audiences that may include potential clients.

Summary Concepts

Designing the lecture, delivering it, and managing the business are the three major elements of a professional career in lecturing. Good design requires a reasonably narrow definition of the topic, sufficient research and experience to address it with authority, coherent organization and discussion, and suitable visual aids and handouts. Effective delivery requires considerable practice of the text, timing, and visual-aid manipulation to permit a seamless presentation by a poised speaker. Competent business management requires a sound strategy for launching oneself as a speaker and a clear-sighted approach to lecture contracts. The primary focus of all this activity is genealogical education. Ideally, everyone connected with it benefits. The audience receives accurate and practical guidance, speakers receive payment for their time and expertise, and sponsors receive a financial profit on their expenditure.

FURTHER STUDY

BUSINESS MANAGEMENT:

Mills, Elizabeth Shown, CG, CGL, FASG. "Economics of Genealogical Lecturing." *Federation of Genealogical Societies [FGS] Forum* 3 (Summer 1991): 4–7. Although compensation has risen somewhat since this article's appearance, so has inflation. The basic issues remain.

———. "How to Market Yourself as a Lecturer." *Association of Professional Genealogists [APG] Quarterly* 9 (December 1994): 98–101.

———, Helen F. M. Leary, CG; Joy Reisinger, CGRS; and Marsha Hoffman Rising, CG. "Lecturing, Taping, and Lecture Materials: A Discussion of Copyrights and Other Considerations." *FGS Forum* 2 (Winter 1990): 11–13.

ENHANCEMENTS:

Able, Charles L. "Preparing the Message, Projecting the Image: Slide Preparation." *APG Quarterly* 6 (Summer 1991): 34–38.

Freilich, Kay Haviland, CGRS. "Some Thoughts on Lecture Handouts." *APG Quarterly* 11 (December 1996): 107–8.

Gosney, Michael, John Odam, and Jim Schmal. *The Gray Book: Designing in Black & White on Your Computer.* Chapel Hill, North Carolina: Ventana Press, 1990.

Hatcher, Patricia Law, CG. "Will They Use Them After They Go Home? Preparing Effective Handouts." *In Your Ancestors' Image: A Conference for the Nation's Genealogists.* Syllabus, National Conference of the Federation of Genealogical Societies and the Rochester Genealogical Society. Rochester, New York: FGS, 1996. Pages 108–10.

Mills, Elizabeth Shown. "Creating Masterful 'Masters'." *APG Quarterly* 11 (December 1996): 102–6.

Stopke, Judy and Chip Staley. *An Eye for Type.* 3d expanded edition. Ann Arbor, Michigan: Promotional Perspectives, 1992.

PRESENTATIONS:

Davis, Julie Bawden. "'And Our Speaker Is...': Introductions Prepare the Audience and Speaker for Each Other." *APG Quarterly* 5 (Spring 1990): 11–12.

Finkel, Coleman. "How to Introduce Speakers." *APG Quarterly* 4 (Spring 1989): 11.

Hoff, Ron. *I Can See You Naked.* Rev. edition. Kansas City, Missouri: Andrews and McMeel, 1992. A classic best-seller, whose focus is on presentation style.

Lucas, Stephen E. *The Art of Public Speaking.* 4th edition. New York: McGraw Hill, 1992. Aimed at public-speaking students and professionals in other fields, this needs to be adapted sensibly by genealogical lecturers who do not teach in classrooms, have a semester to make their points, read papers at conferences, or sell products. Caveats aside, its advice is valuable.

Parker, Roger C. "Presentation Planning." *APG Quarterly* 11 (December 1996): 108–9. Reprinted, with permission, from *Technique,* January 1996.

Warren, Paula Stuart, CGRS. "The Nuts and Bolts of Genealogical Teaching and Lecturing." *APG Quarterly* 14 (September 1999): 117–20, 122–25.

MISCELLANEOUS:

Figures 62–64 (pp. 596–98) offer advice on all aspects of speaking, in three sets of "commandments" that program chairs frequently share with their speakers.

Speak! Newsletter of the Genealogical Speakers Guild, 1992—.

SpeakersVoice, website of the SpeakersVoice Association. The online offerings of this trade group include useful articles on dynamic lecturing.

If your mind goes blank, be sure to turn off the sound.

—*Anonymous*

LECTURING

FIG. 62

**TEN COMMANDMENTS FOR
GENEALOGICAL SPEAKERS***

1. Thou shalt not read thy lecture.
   No. 1 audience complaint: I can read for myself at home a whole lot cheaper.

2. Thou shalt not forget to prepare handouts.
   Fact: The most popular lecturers, year after year, are those who put their important points on paper for audiences to take home and study.

3. Thou shalt not forget to prepare a lecture.
   Tip: Audiences do know the difference between a well-planned lecture, given with ease, and an unplanned hour of "shooting the breeze."

4. Thou shalt not present a "canned" lecture.
   General consensus: An appearance on a national conference program merits a fresh paper with innovative ideas.†

5. Thou shalt plan thy lecture with the audience in mind.
   Tough self-exam: Will each point I make help the audience do better research or better analyze evidence—or am I showcasing my own pet project or beating the drum for my favorite bandwagon?

6. Thou shalt make sure that thy visual aids are visible.
   Yes, even to the back of the room. But not to yourself! Include your projected data in your text at the lectern. Audiences don't want to stare at the back of your head while you read off the screen.

7. Thou shalt keep a sense of humor.
   Especially when the projector light blows or the sound system goes out.

8. Thou shalt not forget to arrive a few minutes early to double-check facilities and equipment.
   As someone once put it: The best-laid schemes of mice and men gang aft agley. Conference planners do goof sometimes and systems break down.

9. Thou shalt show thy enthusiasm for thy subject.
   If it's ho-hum to you, how do you think the audience is going to feel?

10. Thou shalt not forget to pick up thy honorarium.
    After all: You earned it!

---

* Elizabeth Shown Mills, CG, CGL, FASG, *Association of Professional Genealogists Quarterly* 4 (Fall 1989): 72. Reprinted with permission. Annotated here by the author.

† As a rule, this principle remains the ideal. In reality, another viewpoint has been regularly practiced in the intervening decade by both speakers and program chairs. Given that conferences, institutes, and seminars are virtually the only forums for advanced genealogical education and that most national conferences draw almost an entirely different audience each year, many lecturers *are* asked to repeat their particularly successful presentations from prior conferences. While these are seldom retitled, they and their accompanying handouts and audio-visuals will be updated as a matter of course.

FIG. 63
TEN MORE COMMANDMENTS
FOR GENEALOGICAL
SPEAKERS*

1. Thou shalt carry a dual set of notes and AVs—one with thy person and one with thy luggage—in the event one set is mislaid or misrouted.

2. Thou shalt not use any other speaker's examples, case studies, or outlines. If thou are worthy of lecturing on that subject, thou should have developed thy own material.

3. Thou shalt not borrow a colleague's jokes, laugh lines, or pithy sayings. The other speaker won't think it's funny.[†]

4. Thou shalt tell no jokes that might be offensive to portions of thy audience.[‡]

5. Thou shalt interject no politics or other provocative nongenealogical subject matter.

6. Thou shalt not use thy podium to sell a product. Thy appearance is educational, not commercial.

7. Thou shalt not use thy podium to criticize or demean a colleague, agency, or institution.[§]

8. Thou shalt not lose your cool before the audience or fault others if things go wrong.

9. Thou shalt not criticize the organization that invited thee. Miss Manners frowns upon scolding a host, privately or publicly.

10. Thou shalt not neglect to thank thy host society when thou returns home.

---

[*] Elizabeth Shown Mills, CG, CGL, FASG, *Speak! Newsletter of the Genealogical Speakers Guild* 2 (March 1993): 5. Reprinted with permission. Annotated here by the author.

[†] Wisdom suggests adding *lecture titles* to this list as well. While some titles are so straightforward that it can be difficult to avoid similarity, the diversity of human speech suggests it is more than coincidental when titles of ten or fifteen words manage to duplicate themselves.

[‡] The speechmaster Ron Hoff catalogs these as jokes that make fun of the audience, those with "four-letter" words and off-color themes, and satire. (See Hoff, *I Can See You Naked,* 114–15). Other writers on the subject advise against jokes that relate to ethnicity, religion, and physical appearance.

[§] Educational forums do call for forthright discussions of scholarship. If and when it is necessary to disagree with a colleague over such matters, the disagreement should be directed toward the issue rather than the person.

FIG. 64
ANOTHER TEN
COMMANDMENTS FOR
SPEAKERS WHO WANT
CONFERENCE INVITATIONS*

1. Thou shalt read all communications from the conference committee.
   Don't assume that unexpected letters are just junk mailings from the society.

2. Thou shalt return all acceptances, contracts, and bios on deadline.
   Program money wasted on phone calls to nag a hundred forgetful speakers means less money available for speaker honorariums.

3. Thou shalt not lose thy instructions and call for replacements.
   Have mercy on the program chairs. They're busy professionals too—and they receive no honorarium for the time they give to the conference effort.

4. Thou shalt provide the program chair with a home address and phone number at which thou can be reached—and then return thy calls.†
   Remember: volunteer program chairs have jobs like you do; their conference planning is an after-hours task. Please allow them to call you at home.

5. Thou shalt prepare attractive syllabus pages, according to specifications.
   Audiences expect professional quality material from all presenters today. Outdated typing and haphazard formats don't measure up. Nor is it the responsibility of program planners to cut, shrink, and paste your work for a makeshift fix.

6. Thou shalt not hide old lectures under new titles.
   Conference-goers give you an hour of their lives; they don't like to be duped.

7. Thou shalt not give lectures that do not match thy proposal or the agreed-upon title.
   Lectures, like products, should live up to their advertising.

8. Thou shalt not be condescending to thy audiences.
   Audiences look up to speakers who don't look down at them.

9. Thou shalt help to introduce other speakers, if thou wishes to be introduced thyself.
   There are never enough volunteers to run a conference. Help out.

10. Thou shalt not bad-mouth the organization and the program if thou aren't invited.
    Proposals outnumber slots five or ten to one. Not everyone can be invited every year. Planners must provide well-balanced programs with fresh topics and new faces, as well as dependable pros with drawing power. Developing innovative material and building a reputation for delivering what audiences want are the surest ways to earn the slots you seek.

---

* Elizabeth Shown Mills, CG, CGL, FASG, *Speak! Newsletter of the Genealogical Speakers Guild* 4 (March 1995): 72. Reprinted with permission. Annotated here by the author.

† Given the technological advances since this was written, we should now add fax numbers and e-mail addresses as well.

Appendix A

ABBREVIATIONS
AND ACRONYMS

Abbreviations <u>and</u> Acronyms

AAGRA .... Australasian Association of Genealogists and Record Agents, Australia and New Zealand

AG .... Accredited Genealogist. Credential of the International Commission for the Accreditation of Professional Genealogists, Salt Lake City, Utah; formerly the credential used by the Accreditation Program of the Family History Department of The Church of Jesus Christ of Latter-day Saints

AGRA .... Association of Genealogists and Record Agents, England

APG .... Association of Professional Genealogists. Based in the United States, with international membership

APGI .... Association of Professional Genealogists in Ireland

ASG .... American Society of Genealogists

ASGRA .... Association of Scottish Genealogists and Record Agents

BCG^{SM} .... Board for Certification of Genealogists®. Based in the United States, with international coverage

BQACG .... Bureau Québécois d'Attestation de Compétence en Généalogie

BYU .... Brigham Young University, Provo, Utah

CAILS^{SM} .... Certified American Indian Lineage Specialist^{SM}. Credential and service mark of the Board for Certification of Genealogists

CALS^{SM} .... Certified American Lineage Specialist^{SM}. Credential and service mark of the Board for Certification of Genealogists

CG^{SM} .... Certified Genealogist^{SM}. Credential and service mark of the Board for Certification of Genealogists

CGI^{SM} .... Certified Genealogical Instructor^{SM}. Credential and service mark of the Board for Certification of Genealogists

CGL^{SM} .... Certified Genealogical Lecturer^{SM}. Credential and service mark of the Board for Certification of Genealogists

CGRS^{SM} .... Certified Genealogical Record Specialist^{SM}. Credential and service mark of the Board for Certification of Genealogists

CG^{SM} .... Certified Genealogist^{SM}. Credential and service mark of the Board for Certification of Genealogists

CGC .... Council of Genealogy Columnists (now the International Society of Family History Writers and Editors)

CG(C) .... Certified Genealogist (Canada). Credential of the Genealogical Institute of the Maritimes

CLS^{SM} .... Certified Lineage Specialist^{SM}. Credential and service mark of the Board for Certification of Genealogists

DipFHS .... Diploma in Family Historical Studies. Credential of the Society of Australian Genealogists

FASG .... Fellow, American Society of Genealogists. Credential based on quality and quantity of published genealogical scholarship

FHC .... Family History Center(s), located worldwide under administration of the Family History Library, Salt Lake City

FHL .... Family History Library, Salt Lake City, Utah

FNGS .... Fellow, National Genealogical Society. Honorific based on service to society and the field of genealogy

FUGA .... Fellow, Utah Genealogical Association. Honorific based on service to society and the field of genealogy

(G) .... Genealogist. Credential of the Australasian Association of Genealogists and Record Agents

G.F.A. .... Généalogiste Filiation Agréé. Credential of the Bureau Québécois d'Attestation de Compétence en Généalogie

Abbreviations <u>and</u> Acronyms

GIM .... Genealogical Institute of the Maritimes, Halifax, Nova Scotia

GIMA .... Genealogical Institute of Mid-America, Springfield, Illinois

G.R.A. .... Généalogiste Recherchiste Agréé. Credential of the Bureau Québécois d'Attestation de Compétence en Généalogie

GRINZ .... Genealogical Research Institute of New Zealand. The acronym is also used as a credential by graduates of the institute

GRS(C) .... Genealogical Record Searcher (Canada). Credential of the Genealogical Institute of the Maritimes

GRO .... General Register Office, Scotland

GSG .... Genealogical Speakers Guild. Based in the United States, with international membership

GSU .... Genealogical Society of Utah

ICAPGEN .... International Commission for the Accreditation of Professional Genealogists, Salt Lake City, Utah; an arm of the Utah Genealogical Association

IGHR .... Institute of Genealogy and Historical Research, Samford University, Birmingham, Alabama, and London, England

IHGS .... Institute of Heraldic and Genealogical Studies, Canterbury, England

ISBG&FH .... International Society for British Genealogy and Family History

ISFHWE .... International Society of Family History Writers and Editors (formerly the Council of Genealogy Columnists)

LDS .... The Church of Jesus Christ of Latter-day Saints

L.H.G. .... Licentiateship in Heraldry and Genealogy. Credential of the Institute of Heraldic and Genealogical Studies

M.G.A. .... Maître Généalogiste Agréé. Credential of the Bureau Québécois d'Attestation de Compétence en Généalogie

NARA .... National Archives and Records Administration (U.S.)

NEHGS .... New England Historic Genealogical Society, Boston, Massachusetts

NGS .... National Genealogical Society. Based in the United States, with international membership

NGSQ .... *National Genealogical Society Quarterly*. Scholarly journal published by NGS

NIGR .... National Institute on Genealogical Research, Washington, D.C.

PRO .... Public Record Office, England

QFGS .... Quebec Federation of Genealogical Societies

RA .... Record Agent. Credential of the Australasian Association of Genealogists and Record Agents

SAG .... Society of Australian Genealogists

SLIG .... Salt Lake Institute of Genealogy, Salt Lake City, Utah

TAG .... *The American Genealogist*. An independent, scholarly journal

TG .... *The Genealogist*. Scholarly journal of the American Society of Genealogists

Appendix B

Keynotes

NOTE:

A comprehensive list of all useful agencies, associations, and credentialing bodies worldwide is beyond the scope of this publication. This appendix treats only the more longstanding programs discussed by the various chapter authors. For most other organizations of value to the professional genealogist, information is readily available through the Internet and a myriad of printed directories.

Association of Professional Genealogists

AS A MEMBER OF THE ASSOCIATION OF PROFESSIONAL GENEALOGISTS, I agree that professionalism in genealogy requires ethical conduct in all relationships with the present or potential genealogical community. I therefore agree to abide by the following standards:

THE PROFESSIONAL GENEALOGIST PROMOTES A COHERENT, TRUTHFUL APPROACH TO GENEALOGY, FAMILY HISTORY, AND LOCAL HISTORY. The professional presents research results and opinions in a clear, well-organized manner; fully and accurately cites sources; and does not withhold, suppress, or knowingly misquote or misinterpret sources or data.

THE PROFESSIONAL GENEALOGIST PROMOTES THE TRUST AND SECURITY OF GENEALOGICAL CONSUMERS. The professional honestly advertises services and credentials, avoiding the use of misleading or exaggerated representations; explains without concealment or misrepresentation all fees, charges, and payment structures; abides by agreements regarding project scope, number of hours, and deadlines or reporting schedules; keeps adequate, accessible records of financial and project-specific contacts with the consumer; and does not knowingly violate or encourage others to violate laws and regulations concerning copyright, right to privacy, business finances, or other pertinent subjects.

THE PROFESSIONAL GENEALOGIST SUPPORTS RECORDS ACCESS AND PRESERVATION. The professional is courteous to research facility personnel and treats records with care and respect; supports efforts to locate, collect, and preserve the records by compiling, cataloging, reproducing, and indexing documents; and does not mutilate, rearrange, or remove from its proper custodian any printed, original, microform, or electronic record.

THE PROFESSIONAL GENEALOGIST PROMOTES THE WELFARE OF THE GENEALOGICAL COMMUNITY. The professional gives proper credit to those who supply information and provide assistance; does not knowingly supplant another researcher; encourages applicable education, accreditation, and certification; and refrains from public behavior, oral remarks, or written communications that defame the profession, individual genealogists, or the Association of Professional Genealogists.

(REV. 1997)

CODES, GUIDELINES

AND STANDARDS

Association of Professional Genealogists

GUIDELINES

FOR USE OF

CREDENTIALS

AND POSTNOMIALS

CREDENTIALS ARE A WORTHY ACHIEVEMENT FOR ANYONE ENGAGED IN THE CONDUCT OR PRACTICE OF GENEALOGY. Properly used, they attest knowledge, skill, and ethics. They enhance the professional's credibility as a researcher, writer, consultant, lecturer, or court witness. They can facilitate access to limited-access records and repositories.

The Association of Professional Genealogists also recognizes that genealogical credentials are not widely known or understood in the public sector. Thus the public can be easily misled by an inappropriate use of postnomials implying special qualifications. To avoid misunderstandings and misinterpretations of the credentials held by APG members, the association sets forth the following guidelines:

EDUCATIONAL CREDENTIALS

Earned degrees are appropriate descriptors of a professional's educational background, within the following framework:
- if the degree is earned in a field other than genealogy, the professional should identify, in parentheses following the degree, the field in which the credential was earned.
- the degree should be granted by an accredited institution.
- honorary degrees, as opposed to earned degrees, should not be presented as credentials.

PROFESSIONAL CREDENTIALS

Postnomials of a professional nature, earned outside the field of genealogy, may or may not be relevant, depending upon the circumstances of use:
- postnomials earned in an adjunct field would be appropriate if the nature of one's genealogical work combines both fields (example: a genealogist with genetic-research credentials who lectures on the applicability of genealogy to genetics or seeks research assignments that focus on family-health issues).
- outside this limited context, the genealogical use of non-genealogical credentials is commonly considered inappropriate.

Professional postnomials that imply genealogical expertise should be awarded by an accrediting or certifying body that
- conducts a rigorous examination program separate from membership in its own or another society; and
- publishes in professional genealogical literature, and provides in response to public requests, a clear and detailed explication of its examination policies and procedures—setting forth the specific standards that successful applicants must meet; and
- administers its tests on a nonexclusionary basis, without regard for race, creed, or color, and without need for personal recommendation by a current member of that agency; and
- makes public, upon request, its pass-fail ratio for applications in order to substantiate the group's high testing standards; and
- provides its applicants with an appraisal of the strengths and weaknesses of their applications, in support of its ruling for acceptance or rejection; and
- publishes, and makes available upon request, a roster of its approved genealogists; and
- does not usurp the preexisting credentials of any other testing agency.

Association of Professional Genealogists

HONORARY CREDENTIALS

Honorary postnomials, to have meaning, must denote exceptional expertise or service. As in other professional and scholarly fields, meaningful honorary postnomials are those

- awarded without application for the honor and without assessment of fees; and
- awarded by open-membership organizations to a very limited number of members, in recognition of noteworthy service (example: fellows of the National Genealogical Society, Utah Genealogical Association, or Genealogical Society of Pennsylvania); or
- awarded by scholastically oriented societies on the basis of published scholarship that has withstood peer review and public criticism—provided that such a society makes public the specific criteria upon which its honorees are chosen and makes available, upon request, its list of honorees.

Used within this framework, genealogical credentials will accurately reflect the high standards of expertise and ethics that underlie all legitimate professions.

Policy 13
APG POLICY MANUAL (REV. 1995)

CODES, GUIDELINES
AND STANDARDS

Board for Certification of Genealogists

CODE*

TO PROTECT THE PUBLIC

- I will not publish or publicize as fact anything I know to be false, doubtful, or unproven; nor will I be a party, directly or indirectly, to such action by others.
- I will identify my sources for all information and cite only those documents I have personally used.
- I will quote documents precisely, avoiding any alterations that I do not clearly identify as editorial interpretations.
- I will present the purpose, practice, scope, and possibilities of genealogical research within a realistic framework.
- I will delineate my abilities, publications, and/or fees in a true and realistic fashion.

TO PROTECT THE CONSUMER (CLIENT OR COLLEAGUE)

- I will keep confidential any personal or genealogical information given to me, unless I receive written consent to the contrary.
- I will reveal to the consumer any personal or financial interests that might compromise my professional obligations.
- I will undertake paid research commissions only after a clear agreement as to scope and fee.
- I will, to the best of my abilities, address my research to the issue raised by the consumer and report to that question.
- I will seek from the consumer all prior information and documentation related to the research and will not knowingly repeat the work, as billable hours, without explanation as to good cause.
- I will furnish only facts I can substantiate with adequate documentation; and I will not withhold any data necessary for the consumer's purpose.
- If the research question involves analysis of data to determine a genealogical relationship or identity, I will report that the conclusions are based on the weight of the available evidence and that absolute proof of genealogical relationships is usuallly not possible.
- If I cannot resolve a research problem within the limitations of time or budget established by contract, I will explain the reasons why.
- If other feasible avenues are available, I will suggest them; but I will not misrepresent the possibilities of additional research.
- I will return any advance payment that exceeds the hours and expenses incurred.
- I will not publish or circulate research or reports to which the consumer has a proprietary right, without prior written consent of the consumer; I will observe these rights, whether my report was made directly to the consumer or to an employer or agent.

TO PROTECT THE PROFESSION

- I will act, speak, and write in a manner I believe to be in the best interests of the profession and scholarship of genealogy.
- I will participate in exposing genealogical fraud; but I will not otherwise knowingly injure or attempt to injure, the reputation, prospects, or practice of another genealogist.
- I will not attempt to supplant another genealogist already employed by a client or agency. I will substitute for another researcher only with specific written consent of and instructions provided by the client or agency.

Board for Certification of Genealogists

- I will not represent as my own the work of another. This includes works that are copyrighted, in the public domain, or unpublished. This pledge includes reports, lecture materials, audio/visual tapes, compiled records, and authored essays.
- I will not reproduce for public dissemination, in an oral or written fashion, the work of another genealogist, writer, or lecturer, without that person's written consent. In citing another's work, I will give proper credit.

---

* The BCG Code was also ascribed to by genealogists accredited by the Family History Department of The Church of Jesus Christ of Latter-day Saints and continues to be used by that program's successor, the International Committee for the Accreditation of Professional Genealogists (ICapGen).

CODES, GUIDELINES
AND STANDARDS

National Genealogical Society

STANDARDS
FOR SHARING
INFORMATION
WITH OTHERS

CONSCIOUS OF THE FACT THAT THE SHARING OF INFORMATION OR DATA WITH OTHERS, WHETHER THROUGH SPEECH, DOCUMENTS, ELECTRONIC MEDIA, OR DATA FILES, IS ESSENTIAL TO FAMILY HISTORY RESEARCH AND THAT IT NEEDS CONTINUING SUPPORT AND ENCOURAGEMENT, RESPONSIBLE FAMILY HISTORIANS CONSISTENTLY—

- respect the restrictions on sharing information that arise from the rights of another as an author, originator or compiler; as a living private person; or as a party to a mutual agreement.
- observe meticulously the legal rights of copyright owners, copying or distributing any part of their works only with their permission or to the limited extent specifically allowed under the law's "fair use" exceptions.
- identify the sources for all ideas, information and data from others, and the form in which they were received, recognizing that the unattributed use of another's intellectual work is plagiarism.
- respect the authorship rights of senders of letters and electronic mail, forwarding or disseminating them further only with the sender's permission.
- inform people who provide information about their families as to the ways it may be used, observing any conditions they impose and respecting any reservations they may express regarding the use of particular items.
- require some evidence of consent before assuming that living people are agreeable to further sharing of information about themselves.
- convey personal identifying information about living people—like age, home address, occupation or activities—only in ways that those concerned have expressly agreed to.
- recognize that legal rights of privacy may limit the extent to which information from publicly available sources may be further used, disseminated, or published.
- communicate no information to others that is known to be false, or without making reasonable efforts to determine its truth, particularly information that may be derogatory.
- are sensitive to the hurt that revelations of criminal, immoral, bizarre, or irresponsible behavior may bring to family members.

National Genealogical Society

REMEMBERING ALWAYS THAT THEY ARE ENGAGED IN A QUEST FOR TRUTH, FAMILY HISTORY RESEARCHERS CONSISTENTLY—

- record the source for each item of information they collect.
- test every hypothesis or theory against credible evidence, and reject those that are not supported by the evidence.
- seek original records, or reproduced images of them when there is reasonable assurance they have not been altered, as the basis for their research conclusions.
- use compilations, communications, and published works, whether paper or electronic, primarily for their value as guides to locating the original records.
- state something as a fact only when it is supported by convincing evidence, and identify the evidence when communicating the fact to others.
- limit with words like "probable" or "possible" any statement that is based on less than convincing evidence, and state the reasons for concluding that it is probable or possible.
- avoid misleading other researchers by either intentionally or carelessly distributing or publishing inaccurate information
- state carefully and honestly the results of their own research, and acknowledge all use of other researchers' work.
- recognize the collegial nature of genealogical research by making their work available to others through publication, or by placing copies in appropriate libraries or repositories, and by welcoming critical comment.
- consider with open minds new evidence or the comments of others on their work and the conclusions they have reached.

CODES, GUIDELINES
AND STANDARDS

National Genealogical Society

STANDARDS
FOR USE OF
RECORDS,
REPOSITORIES,
AND LIBRARIES

RECOGNIZING THAT HOW THEY USE UNIQUE ORIGINAL RECORDS AND FRAGILE PUBLICATIONS WILL AFFECT OTHER USERS, BOTH CURRENT AND FUTURE, FAMILY HISTORY RESEARCHERS HABITUALLY—

- are courteous to research facility personnel and other researchers, and respect the staff's other daily tasks, not expecting the records custodian to listen to their family histories nor provide constant or immediate attention.
- dress appropriately, converse with others in a low voice, and supervise children appropriately.
- do their homework in advance, know what is available and what they need, and avoid ever asking for "everything" on their ancestors.
- use only designated work space areas, respect off-limits areas, and request permission before using photocopy or microform equipment, asking for assistance if needed.
- treat original records at all times with great respect and work with only a few records at a time, recognizing that they are irreplaceable and that each user must help preserve them for future use.
- treat books with care, never forcing their spines, and handle photographs properly, preferably wearing archival gloves.
- never mark, mutilate, rearrange, relocate, or remove from the repository any original, printed, microform, or electronic document or artifact.
- use only procedures prescribed by the repository for noting corrections to any errors or omissions found in published works, never marking the work itself.
- keep note-taking paper or other objects from covering records or books, and avoid placing any pressure upon them, particularly with a pencil or pen.
- use only the method specifically designated for identifying records for duplication, avoiding use of paper clips, adhesive notes, or other means not approved by the facility.
- unless instructed otherwise, replace volumes and files in their proper locations.
- before departure, thank the records custodians for their courtesy in making the materials available.
- follow the rules of the records repository without protest, even if they have changed since a previous visit or differ from those of another facility.

National Genealogical Society

MINDFUL THAT COMPUTERS ARE TOOLS, GENEALOGISTS TAKE FULL RESPONSIBILITY FOR THE RESULTS OF THEIR WORK, AND THEREFORE THEY—

STANDARDS
FOR USE OF
TECHNOLOGY IN
GENEALOGICAL
RESEARCH

- learn the capabilities and limits of their equipment and software, and use them only when they are the most appropriate tools for a purpose.
- refuse to let computer software automatically embellish their work.
- treat compiled information from online sources or digital databases like that from other published sources, useful primarily as a guide to locating original records, but not as evidence for a conclusion or assertion.
- accept digital images or enhancements of an original record as a satisfactory substitute for the original only when there is reasonable assurance that the image accurately reproduces the unaltered original.
- cite sources for data obtained online or from digital media with the same care that is appropriate for sources on paper and other traditional media and enter data into a digital database only when its source can remain associated with it.
- always cite the sources for information or data posted online or sent to others, naming the author of a digital file as its immediate source, while crediting original sources cited within the file.
- preserve the integrity of their own databases by evaluating the reliability of downloaded data before incorporating it into their own files.
- provide, whenever they alter data received in digital form, a description of the change that will accompany the altered data whenever it is shared with others.
- actively oppose the proliferation of error, rumor, and fraud by personally verifying or correcting information, or noting it as unverified, before passing it on to others.
- treat people online as courteously and civilly as they would treat them face-to-face, not separated by networks and anonymity.
- accept that technology has not changed the principles of genealogical research, only some of the procedures.

CODES, GUIDELINES
AND STANDARDS

National Genealogical Society

NGS QUARTERLY
GUIDELINES
FOR BOOK AND
MEDIA REVIEWS

BOOK AND MEDIA REVIEWS, like journal articles, exist to educate readers—almost all of whom are writers, publishers, or consumers of publications. This objective goes far beyond informing readers of the availability of particular works—a purpose more appropriately accomplished by advertising. A review, by comparison, should provide an objective analysis of a publication in a way that explains its value, reveals any shortcomings, and teaches a lesson that benefits readers.

BASIC ELEMENTS OF A REVIEW

Good book and media reviews are built upon three elements—description, evaluation, and education.

- *Description:* A review should note the primary purposes of the publication and explain its main ideas. The description should be sufficient for consumers to discern the applicability of the work to their own interests. Description, however, does not mean a recitation of the names of all sections of a work or item-by-item summaries.

- *Evaluation and education:* The most important function of a review is analysis. Performed properly, the evaluation is inseparable from the review's educational role. A fair review informs readers of the extent to which the work meets the creator's purposes—as just defined. A good review also appraises the work by the standards of the field. If it is a compiled genealogy, readers should be informed whether it is appropriately documented and follows one of the standard numbering systems (i.e., the *NGSQ* or *Register* Systems). The review may compare the publication to others on the same topic or relate the work to earlier products by the same author.

  This analytical function requires a balanced explanation of strengths and weaknesses. Authors and publishers particularly appreciate reviews that point out the strengths of their efforts—and these observations can be quite valuable to readers who seek role models for their own writing or publishing efforts. An identification of significant problems can be just as helpful—not only to readers of the review and potential consumers of the product, but also to the authors and publishers of the work under review.

  Unfavorable comments, to have full value, need to be constructive. Reviewers should specify how weaknesses could have been prevented or can be corrected. Any discussion of errors should be courteous and avoid words that might be inflammatory. Readers seldom appreciate criticisms that appear petty, derogatory, or personal—or those that seem designed to showcase the reviewer's expertise. Even if a work is seriously substandard, a review can be constructive and helpful, although it may require extra tact to write.

QUALIFICATIONS OF THE REVIEWER

Expertise, objectivity, and a reasonable ability to write clear and readable prose are the three essential qualifications for reviewers.

- *Expertise:* Readers expect reviewers to address the accuracy of published works. For this reason, a reviewer should be someone who thoroughly knows the subject covered by the publication. Obviously, genealogical materials produced in electronic form call for dual expertise. The reviewer needs not only specialized knowledge of the subject matter but also skill in the use of the medium by which the material was produced.

- *Objectivity:* To earn trust and confidence in their analyses, reviewers should not have

National Genealogical Society

conflicts of interest. They should be neither a competitor nor a close ally of the producer of the work they agree to appraise. To better ensure objectivity, some journals do not accept unsolicited reviews.

- *Writing skills:* Reviewers, like other authors, should write in a style that is clear and concise. This includes organizing the review carefully and avoiding the passive voice, clichés, redundancy, and wordiness. When quoting from the book, they should identify the page number on which the quoted material appears. If they reference any outside sources, they should cite those fully. Experienced writers also analyze the reviews in the journal to which they are contributing—for examples of format, style, tone, and length. They should also consider submitting their critiques on diskettes or by e-mail, with backup paper copies.

SELECTION OF MATERIALS FOR REVIEW

Genealogists want and need to know about many different types of published works—not only family histories but also guides and indexes, methodological manuals, and record extracts. Their interests include general history—economic, local, political, religious, and social—as well as anthropology, biography, genetics, law, and sociology. Faced with a vast quantity of books and electronic media, most review editors set parameters. If their journal focuses upon a specific locale or ethnic group, some of their delimiters are obvious. Even so, the most effective selections are those with potential for yielding good reviews. Many books or CD-ROMs may be of interest to the readers, but far fewer are likely to generate critiques that are educational and interesting in their own right.

Readers of genealogical journals frequently view the book and product review sections as "must-read" material. With such an intent audience, reviewers find satisfaction in knowing that their efforts will be carefully read. When those reviews are descriptive, analytical, and educational—as well as unbiased and well-grounded in a solid knowledge of the subject—the reviews will both interest readers and benefit the field.

Thomas W. Jones, Ph.D., CG (and *NGS Quarterly* Review Editor), "Guidelines for Responsible Editing in Genealogy," *National Genealogical Society Quarterly* 86 (June 1998): 138–39.

CODES, GUIDELINES
AND STANDARDS

National Genealogical Society

MOST GENEALOGICAL EDITORS are dedicated volunteers, learning—through trial and error—the duties of their post. Some are blessed to have a journalism or publishing background. Others are trained in writing, but according to the canons of their primary vocation. Some have limited experience in formal communication methods but, because of their genealogical expertise, have been chosen for the position of editor.

Editing manuals abound. Yet few offer concise discussions of the main concerns of genealogical editors—the obligation to present only the most reliable publication possible, by appropriately choosing material, by editing manuscripts for clarity and consistency, and by properly citing all sources.

The present guidelines are offered to help new colleagues identify the policies and procedures they should establish for a stable and trustworthy publication.

NOTIFICATION

Contributions should be immediately acknowledged. Beyond that, authors should be informed in writing whether their manuscripts are accepted, rejected, or accepted pending a satisfactory revision. Journals that conduct a peer review of manuscripts commonly notify writers of a decision within two to five months.

NONDUPLICATION

The most respected genealogical publications seek fresh and original material their readers cannot find in other magazines and newsletters. To avoid an embarrassing duplication of articles, most editors request that contributors submit only manuscripts not under consideration elsewhere.

VERIFICATION

Responsible editors take reasonable steps to ensure the accuracy of their content. Fundamental checks include the verification of

- material "borrowed" from other publications. The better policy is not to borrow; but, when a reuse of material is appropriate, the editor's responsibility to verify its accuracy is not relieved by merely citing the publication from which it is reproduced. Tips, addresses, and controversies should be verified through authoritative sources or major guidebooks before presenting them to trusting readers.
- manuscript content. Each seemingly usable contribution should be submitted to at least one authority in its subject area, who can suggest corrections or amplifications, if necessary. Journals commonly use more reviewers than do newsletters.
- quotations—when attributed to active genealogists, public officials, or other individuals who are locatable without undue difficulty. Not only courtesy but also prudence is at stake.
- source citations (or quotations from published sources). Authors, titles, and publication details can be checked through library or online catalogs. If the cited archival material is accessible, a cautious editor will at least spot-check it to appraise the contributor's accuracy. When archival materials are unavailable, contributors can be asked to supply photocopied documents—or sample photocopies, if a large record group is being abstracted.

AUTHORIZATION

If justification exists to reprint the work of another editor—or to quote extensively (perhaps more than three paragraphs) from another publication—advance permission

National Genealogical Society

must be sought in writing from both the original editor and the author or compiler of the material. Either or both may wish to add to or correct their information before it is reprinted. Additionally, many archives expect that permission be sought before their manuscript material is published.

The issues of copyright, plagiarism, and fair use are all involved. While *facts, opinions, and historical discoveries* are not copyrightable, ethics demand that prior developers of this material be acknowledged and their contribution clearly defined. The *arrangement of words* used by an author is copyrightable, and permission must always be obtained before using lengthy quotations from material under copyright.

STANDARDIZATION

The widely varying backgrounds of genealogists guarantee that manuscripts submitted to any editor will form a mosaic of style and format. Yet readers expect consistency. Editors are the conduit through which manuscripts progress from raw material to a well-finished product. Much editing can be avoided by preparing a writers' style sheet that defines the type and length of manuscripts desired and the manner in which the writers should prepare them. Useful contributions that do not meet these guidelines can be returned to writers for revision, or they must be revamped editorially to achieve the consistency that readers expect.

DOCUMENTATION

All genealogical compilations today are expected to be documented. That is, each and every statement of fact that is not public knowledge must carry its own individual and complete citation of source. Undocumented compilations—or those that merely cite a generic list of sources in which information of interest supposedly appears somewhere—do not meet current standards of acceptability.

CORRECTION

No publication can be error free; but, when misstatements are brought to the attention of editors, they should be corrected in print, with reasonable promptness.

Editing is a delightful challenge, but it carries considerable responsibility. Geneticists, historians, social scientists, courts of law, and untold future generations—as well as current genealogists—depend upon the reliability of the material we put into print. Conscientious attention to these several points will help ensure that our contribution to genealogy will advance the state of research in this field and enhance the quality of our journals and newsletters.

These guidelines were developed and endorsed in 1996 by the editors of five of America's major genealogical periodicals. See Elizabeth Shown Mills and Gary B. Mills (*National Genealogical Society Quarterly*), Jane Fletcher Fiske (*New England Historical and Genealogical Register*), David L. Greene and Robert C. Anderson (*The American Genealogist*), Henry B. Hoff and Harry Macy Jr. (*New York Genealogical and Biographical Record*), Sandra Hargreaves Luebking (*Federation of Genealogical Societies FORUM*), "Guidelines for Responsible Editing in Genealogy," *National Genealogical Society Quarterly* 84 (March 1996): 48–49.

**CODES, GUIDELINES
AND STANDARDS**

Australasian Association of Genealogists & Record Agents

CODE

ARTICLE I

The profession of genealogy calls for scholarly and personal accuracy and integrity: thus, the genealogist is obliged to be honest in research, adhere strictly to the highest standards and methods, and be discreet in relations with clients and the public.

ARTICLE II

The genealogist, whether employed in independent research or acting in a paid, consultative, advisory or assistant capacity, must not engage in exaggerated, misleading or false publicity, or knowingly publish as fact anything known to be false or unproven, nor to be a party to such actions by others.

ARTICLE III

The genealogist must respect the confidential nature of the relationship with his or her client; shall not, without the prior consent of the client, divulge any information concerning the client or the client's affairs, nor publish the results of research for which clients have paid.

ARTICLE IV

In undertaking research, the genealogist must try at all times to examine the original, rather than printed, sources and avoid, so far as possible, the misquotation of documents or the citing as authoritative of any questionable source.

ARTICLE V

The genealogist, in dealing with a client, must make reports as clear and definite as the facts allow, offer candid advice concerning the possible and probable results of lines of research, and avoid unnecessary duplication of effort and research.

ARTICLE VI

The genealogist shall not knowingly injure or attempt to injure the professional reputation, prospects, or practice of any other bona fide genealogist or record agent.

ARTICLE VII

The genealogist must strive to uphold at all times the integrity and reputation of the profession and not to act in a manner detrimental to its best interests.

Genealogical Institute of the Maritimes

CODE

1. I will treat with the greatest care and respect all public and private records and other source materials of whatever kind that I may consult in the course of my research.

2. I will not tear, erase, or remove any public record or library book, nor in any way mutilate, deface, or otherwise destroy any part of such public record or library book.

3. I will refrain from marking, annotating, or otherwise attempting to alter or correct any record or other source materials, even if I am convinced that such record or source material is erroneous.

4. I will abide by all the rules and regulations of the various record repositories and libraries in which I do research, and be courteous to their employees, reserving my right to suggest to the proper authorities possible improvements in the services rendered or the work relations between archivists or librarians and genealogists. In accordance with this promise, I will take particular care to return, to its proper or designated place, every record, book, or other item that I consult in my research.

5. I will work conscientiously on behalf of any and all of my clients, reporting within reasonable time the results of my work.

6. In undertaking genealogical research for hire, I will:
   (a) Fix and agree upon in advance, with my client, the rate and approximate total payment that I will require;
   (b) Explain carefully to my client any potential difficulties involved in the projected research.

7. In presenting my findings to a client, I will:
   (a) Report accurately all information that I have uncovered;
   (b) Indicate clearly all gaps or deficiencies in the materials that I have consulted;
   (c) Indicate clearly any other sources which, to the best of my knowledge, would or might yield additional information.

8. Upon publication, or in reporting my findings to a client, I will:
   (a) Give full and clear references to all sources of information that I have consulted;
   (b) Refrain from stating as fact anything I know to be of a speculative or interpretative nature, and, instead, indicate carefully any degree of speculation or interpretation involved in such information;
   (c) Refrain from deliberately disseminating information that may embarrass or defame a third party.

9. I will respect the rights of all other researchers and authors in the records, books, or other materials with which I work, claiming as my own no part of the work of another.

10. After completing any work which may substantially advance genealogical knowledge, I promise:
   (a) To publish it, or cause it to be published, or
   (b) To deposit a copy in a repository where it may be made available to other researchers.

I understand, in signing this document, that I pledge not only my own honour, but also the honour of the Genealogical Institute of the Maritimes, of which I am hereby becoming a member. Consequently, I recognize the right of the Institute to penalize me, according to its rules and regulations, for any breach of the foregoing promises.

CODES, GUIDELINES
AND STANDARDS

Quebec Bureau for Attestation of Competence in Genealogy...

CODE

1. MUTUAL ASSISTANCE

1.1 The genealogist will collaborate in different ways with peers, with the genealogical society of which he or she is a member, and with other organizations working in the field of genealogy or in related fields.

1.2 The genealogist will share research findings by publishing, or by depositing his work at the library of the society to which he belongs.

1.3 The genealogist will let others know about his area of research to avoid unwitting duplication of work by several individuals.

2. INTELLECTUAL HONESTY

2.1 The genealogist will not knowingly change, disguise, minimize or exaggerate information collected in the course of his work, nor publish unverified material, or any known to be false.

2.2 The genealogist is careful to avoid spreading erroneous genealogical information by verifying data in advance and using primary sources (vital statistics, notarial acts, etc.); or, when that is not possible, by stating that the primary sources are not accessible; or, at the very least, by identifying the sources of his information.

2.3 The genealogist will respect copyright and intellectual property laws applicable to manuscripts, published or otherwise produced by others, and not appropriate their content without the author's permission, except as allowed by law.

2.4 The genealogist will not plagiarize; he will indicate sources consulted in the course of his work, being careful to identify clearly extracts of other authors, and to give recognition, as needed, to the collaboration of colleagues or groups.

3. RESPECT FOR PLACES OF RESEARCH AND FOR DOCUMENTS

3.1 The genealogist will respect instructions of the authorities and the rules established in the various research centers or facilities that he uses.

3.2 The genealogist will conduct research with an attitude of respect for researchers around him.

3.3 The genealogist will treat with the greatest care the finding aids and documents accessible to him, whether they be books, registers, cards, manuscripts, maps, photos, microfilms, microfiches, or electronic information; when dealing with original works, he will be particularly careful not to damage them.

3.4 The genealogist will not annotate or write on finding aids or documents, even in order to correct them; but he is encouraged to notify the person responsible of any corrections that he feels are needed.

3.5 The genealogist will not appropriate, deface, damage, or mutilate finding aids or documents accessible to him.

4. RESPECT FOR PRIVACY

4.1 The genealogist will respect the confidential nature of certain information gathered about the private life of individuals, using discretion and judgment regarding the communication, publication, and distribution of such information, and obtaining permission of the concerned persons if necessary.

4.2 The genealogist will under no circumstances distribute genealogical information that might prejudice a third party.

4.3 Unless the persons concerned consent, or unless what he asserts is a well-known fact, the genealogist will not divulge the biological line of an adopted person.

4.4 The genealogist will promise discretion upon receiving confidential information, and he will answer for any eventual violation of such a pledge.

Bureau Québécois d'Attestation de Compétence en Généalogie

**CODE (CONT.)
(TRANSLATION*)**

5. INTEGRITY AND COMPENSATED RESEARCH

5.1 The genealogist who conducts research for another in return for remuneration will agree in advance upon the basis for payment, preferably in writing.

5.2 If the work cannot be completed as agreed, the genealogist will inform the client, request authorization in advance to continue the research, and agree in advance upon the supplementary costs.

5.3 The genealogist must clearly indicate to the client any instances where there might be doubts about his findings and furnish, upon request, the evidence from which he has drawn his conclusions.

5.4 Acting with integrity, the genealogist will present the facts in an objective manner, respecting the above-mentioned rules regarding discretion and confidentiality.

6. SANCTIONS

6.1 Any infringement of the ethics code brought to the society's attention can cause sanction to be brought, but only after an inquiry during which the member concerned has had the chance to defend himself against the allegations.

6.2 For sanctions to be brought against a member, the code of ethics must have been signed.

Article 4.16
GENERAL RULES (1995)

* Translation by
Claire Mire Bettag, CGRS

Association of Genealogists & Record Agents (England)

CODE

A REGISTERED GENEALOGIST AGREES

- to apply his knowledge, experience, scholarship, accuracy, and integrity to his research work;
- to maintain the highest professional standards;
- to be discreet in his relations with clients, the public, and the profession;
- to establish a proper professional relationship with his clients.

THE GENEALOGIST MUST NOT

- engage in exaggerated, misleading, or false publicity, or knowingly publish as fact anything known to be false or unproven, nor be a party to such action by others.

THE GENEALOGIST MUST ENDEAVOR

- continually to update his knowledge and improve his abilities in the interests of his clients;
- to work always as economically and efficiently as he can in the client's best interests;
- to avoid unnecessary duplication of effort and research;
- to offer sincere advice concerning the possible or probable results of any projected research and, if possible, suggest alternative avenues of research;
- to avoid, as far as possible, the misquotation to any documents or the citing as authoritative of any questionable source;
- at all times to try to examine the original rather than secondary sources;
- not to conceal or withhold data relevant to a client's case;
- to respect the confidential nature of a client's work when specifically asked to do so;
- not to divulge any information concerning a client's family, business, or personal affairs without prior consent;
- not to publish the results of research for which clients have paid, without prior consent;
- to act entirely impartially towards a client.

A REGISTERED GENEALOGIST WILL

- not knowingly injure or attempt to injure the professional reputation, prospects, or practice of any other bona fide genealogist;
- strive at all times to uphold the integrity and reputation of the profession;
- not present as his own work that of another;
- not act in any manner detrimental to the best interests of the profession.

CODE (1961)

Chambre Syndicale des Généalogistes et Héraldistes de France

1. GENEALOGIST: MEMBER OF CSGHF

1.1 Members admitted at the annual general assembly can use the title "Genealogist, Member of CSGHF."

1.2 Members who interrupt their professional practice after having worked at least two years as members of CSGHF can be readmitted without going through the probationary period.

2. MISSION OF THE GENEALOGIST

2.1 CSGHF members may practice in France as well as abroad.

2.2 Members must be qualified to conduct research and to publish works in the fields of history, genealogy, or related disciplines.

3. RESPONSIBILITY OF THE GENEALOGIST TO THE CLIENT

3.1 Members are bound by professional confidentiality; they cannot, without authorization, divulge information from their research that is not in the public domain, nor the names or addresses of their clients.

3.2 Members will refuse or stop all research that exposes the client or a third party to serious moral prejudice.

3.3 Members will honor the contract with the client, abiding by the terms therein.

3.4 Members will use all means at their disposal to successfully achieve the research goals communicated to them.

3.5 Members will inform the client of the possibility of gaps in the archives that may impede their research.

3.6 In the event of unfruitful research, members will provide the client with a detailed list and description of all documents consulted.

3.7 Members will not conduct research without advance authorization of the client.

3.8 Members will provide the client with reports of a quality compatible with the reputation of the CSGHF and its members.

3.9 Members, whose obligation is to undertake responsible research rather than to produce specific results, will invoice all research conducted as a result of a contractual agreement.

4. RESPONSIBILITIES OF THE GENEALOGIST TO ARCHIVES AND PUBLIC AGENCIES

4.1 Members agree to respect law 79-18 of 3-1-1979 and related laws regulating the archives.

4.2 Members agree to respect reading room regulations.

4.3 Members agree to respect scrupulously the laws regulating the restrictions on the accessibility of archival records.

4.4 Members agree not to report marginal notations of a judicial nature and less than one hundred years old, written into civil registration records.

4.5 Members will be careful not to damage records that they consult.

4.6 Members will not photocopy bound documents, even if allowed; they will opt to photograph such documents instead.

5. MEMBER RELATIONSHIPS WITH ASSOCIATIONS

5.1 Members will not belong to another French association of professional genealogists.

5.2 Members agree to respect the rules and regulations of the amateur genealogical associations of which they may be members.

5.3 Members agree not to post queries about client research in genealogical society bulletins or journals.

6. RESPONSIBILITIES OF THE GENEALOGIST TOWARD COLLEAGUES

6.1 Members needing assistance in their research will give priority to the services of fellow members of CSGHF. It there is no member in the region in question, they can call upon a non-member professional genealogist, but not an amateur genealogist.

6.2 Members will give priority to members of the CSGHF when referring researchers.

6.3 When seeking assistance in another country, members will do all possible to enlist the help of those known to respect the laws in effect in their countries relative to genealogical research.

6.4 When advertising, members will make clear their professional status in any case where there may be confusion.

* Translation by
Claire Mire Bettag, CGRS

Association of Professional Genealogists in Ireland

CODE

A MEMBER OF THE ASSOCIATION, HEREAFTER REFERRED TO AS THE "GENEALOGIST," WILL ADHERE TO THE FOLLOWING GUIDELINES:

1. The Genealogist must at all times uphold the integrity and reputation of the Association and not act in a manner in any way contrary to its interest.

2. In advertising or dealing with the public, the Genealogist should not
   - issue exaggerated, misleading, or false information regarding the prospects of successful research;
   - knowingly publish, as fact, any false information or unproven statement, nor be party to such an action by others.

3. When engaged by a client, the Genealogist should not
   - offer misleading or false advice concerning projected research;
   - divulge any information concerning the client or the client's affairs, without prior consent;
   - publish the results of research for which a client has paid, without prior consent.

4. While engaged in research, the Genealogist should not
   - unnecessarily duplicate work already carried out by the Genealogist or the client;
   - misquote any document;
   - cite questionable sources as being authoritative;
   - examine a secondary source when it is possible and practical to examine the original.

5. In reporting to the client, the Genealogist should
   - compile a report as coherent and lucid as the material allows;
   - distinguish clearly between what is proven and what the Genealogist believes to be possible or probable;
   - explain, if unable to resolve the client's research requests, the reason why;
   - offer candid advice concerning further research possibilities;
   - give a full list of sources consulted, indicating the relevant repositories;
   - not withhold or conceal material or information relevant to the client's request.

6. With regard to other members and bona fide genealogists outside the Association, the Genealogist should not knowingly injure or attempt to injure the professional reputation, prospects, or practice of another.

7. The Genealogist must not claim by statement or implication the work of another.

8. The Genealogist should declare any personal or financial interest which might compromise impartiality towards a client.

Association of Scottish Genealogists & Record Agents

IT IS EXPECTED OF PROFESSIONAL GENEALOGISTS that they will adhere strictly to recognised research procedures, always seeking to maintain the highest standards of accuracy. Both in their research work and in their dealings, they will seek to uphold the integrity of the profession and to enhance its best interests.

The professional genealogist has obligations to his clients, to other professional genealogists, and to the public:

DUTIES TO CLIENTS
In dealings with clients, the genealogist must:
• endeavour to answer all inquiries from clients or prospective clients promptly;
• offer candid advice when appropriate concerning the possible or probable results of any projected research;
• present his reports clearly, accurately, and logically with such information as is necessary to justify the genealogical conclusions;
• if unable to resolve a client's problems, clearly explain why and, if possible, suggest alternative avenues of research;
• take care to present as fact only such information as has been proved from adequate documentation, drawing a clear distinction between what is proven and what is probably or possibly correct;
• take care to cite only authoritative sources;
• take care to quote relevantly as well as accurately from any documents;
• always include reference to any data which do not support the conclusions of the research;
• respect the confidential nature of the client's work and not publish the results of the research without the client's consent;
• keep an accurate record of financial transactions relating to the client's account.

DUTIES TO PROFESSIONAL COLLEAGUES
The genealogist must
• respect the professional reputation of other genealogists, never consciously injuring or attempting to injure the prospects or practice of colleagues;
• be prompt in remitting payments for services rendered.

DUTY TO THE PUBLIC
The genealogist should
• seek to promote greater public interest in genealogy and a fuller understanding of the subject;
• be careful to refrain from exaggerated, misleading, or false publicity, especially when advertising for commissions.

COMPLAINTS
If a researcher is unable to complete his current workload due to unforeseen circumstances, the Chairperson or a member of Council should be advised of this to enable assistance to be arranged. On a complaint being received by the Association in relation to the work of a member, concerning
• the quality of the work;
• the failure to complete a search in a reasonable time; or
• any activity of the researcher which, in the opinion of the Council, is likely to bring the Association into disrepute:

Association of Scottish Genealogists & Record Agents

**CODE
OF PRACTICE
(CONT.)**

The Chairperson or nominee will contact the member to ascertain the substance of the complaint and thereafter may decide whether the matter should be brought before the council or not.

The Council, on receiving a complaint, will decide whether the complaint is valid and sufficiently serious to merit a written warning to the member concerned.

The Chairperson will arrange for the required work to be completed either by the original researcher or by another member of the Association within an agreed time limit.

If, after three written warnings, a further valid complaint is received, all within a period of three years, the member will be removed from the list of researchers.

On receiving a complaint, the Chairperson will write to inform the complainant that the matter is being investigated.

A further letter will be sent following the delivery of the report to enquire whether the complainant is satisfied with the outcome.

The Council has the right to order the researcher to return all or a proportion of any pre-paid amount to the complainant.

Index

Index

Index

Index

Index

Index

Index

Index

Index

Index

Index

Index

Index

Index

Index

Index

Index

Index

Index

Index

Index

Index

Index

Index

Index